INTERVIEWING

Principles and Practices

TWELFTH EDITION

Charles J. Stewart
Purdue University

William B. Cash, Jr.
National Louis University

Boston Burr Ridge, IL Dubuque, IA Madison, WI New York San Francisco St. Louis
Bangkok Bogotá Caracas Kuala Lumpur Lisbon London Madrid Mexico City
Milan Montreal New Delhi Santiago Seoul Singapore Sydney Taipei Toronto

INTERVIEWING: PRINCIPLES AND PRACTICES
Published by McGraw-Hill, an imprint of The McGraw-Hill Companies, Inc., 1221 Avenue of the Americas, New York, NY 10020.

This book is printed on acid-free paper.

3 4 5 6 7 8 9 0 DOC/DOC 0 9

ISBN: 978-0-07-340671-8
MHID: 0-07-340671-6

Editor in Chief: *Mike Ryan*
Publisher: *Frank Mortimer*
Sponsoring Editor: *Suzanne Earth*
Marketing Manager: *Leslie Oberhuber*
Development Editor: *Larry Goldberg*
Production Editors: *Melissa Williams/Aaron Downey, Matrix Productions*
Manuscript Editor: *Yonie Overton*
Cover Design: *Cassandra Chu*
Interior Design: *Laurie Entringer*
Senior Production Supervisor: *Tandra Jorgensen*
Composition: *10/12 Times Roman by ITC, Inc.*
Printing: *45# New Era Matte by R. R. Donnelley & Sons*

Library of Congress Cataloging-in-Publication Data

Stewart, Charles J.
Interviewing : principles and practices / Charles J. Stewart, William B. Cash, Jr.—12th ed.
p. cm.
Includes bibliographical references.
ISBN: 978-0-07-340671-8; ISBN: 0-07-340671-6 (alk. Paper)
1. Interviewing—Textbooks. 2. Employment interviewing—Textbooks. 3. Counseling—Textbooks.
I. Cash, William B. II. Title.
BF637.I5S75 2007
158′.39—dc22 2008048996

www.mhhe.com

To Jane F. Stewart and the memory of Christine M. Cash for their patience and inspiration during the many editions of this book

To our children—Gregory, David, Melissa and Jason, Whitney, Nathan—for their love and support

ABOUT THE AUTHORS

Charles J. Stewart

Charles J. Stewart is the Margaret Church Distinguished Professor of Communication at Purdue University where he has taught since 1961. He teaches undergraduate courses in interviewing and persuasion and graduate courses in such areas as persuasion and social protest, apologetic rhetoric, and extremist rhetoric on the Internet. He is the recipient of the Charles B. Murphy Award for Outstanding Undergraduate Teaching from Purdue University and the Donald H. Ecroyd Award for Outstanding Teaching in Higher Education from the National Communication Association. He has written a number of articles, chapters, and books on interviewing, persuasion, and social movements.

Each year Charles Stewart makes presentations on interviewing to classes, student organizations, and conferences on and off the Purdue campus. He has served as a consultant to such organizations as the Internal Revenue Service, the American Electric Power Company, Libby Foods, and the United Association of Plumbers and Pipefitters.

William B. Cash, Jr.

William "Bill" Cash began his work life in his father's shoe and clothing store in northern Ohio. While still in high school, he began to work in broadcasting and advertising, and this led to bachelor's and master's degrees in broadcasting and speech communication at Kent State University. After completing his academic work at Kent State, he joined the speech communication faculty at Eastern Illinois University and began to consult with dozens of companies such as Blaw-Knox, IBM, and Hewitt Associates. Bill took a leave from Eastern Illinois and pursued a Ph.D. in organizational communication under W. Charles Redding. He returned to the faculty at Eastern Illinois and created and taught a course in interviewing.

Within a few years Bill Cash left college teaching and held positions with Ralston Purina, Detroit Edison, Baxter, and Curtis Mathis, often at the vice president level. After several years in industry, he decided to return to teaching and took a faculty position at National-Louis University in Chicago. He became the first Chair of the College of Management and Business and developed courses in human resources, management, and marketing.

BRIEF CONTENTS

CONTENTS

3 Questions and Their Uses 51

4 Structuring the Interview 77

5 The Probing Interview 105

PREFACE

This twelfth edition of *Interviewing: Principles and Practices* continues to reflect the growing sophistication with which interviewing is being approached, the ever-expanding body of research in all types of interview settings, the recent interpersonal communication theory, and the importance of equal opportunity laws on interviewing practices. We have made a concerted effort to include the latest research findings and developments throughout the text while continuing to maintain the emphasis on building interviewing skills for both interviewers and interviewees. The increasing diversification of the American workforce and the influences of the global village receive special treatment in several chapters.

We have attempted to make this edition student-friendly with precise explanations, additional sub-headings, fewer lists, and boldface print that calls attention to important words and phrases. Important guidelines, observations, principles, and cautions appear in the margins. A list of key terms is provided at the end of each chapter, and there is a glossary of important terms and theories at the end of the text.

Changes in the Twelfth Edition

Each chapter includes new or revised examples and illustrations, student activities, suggested readings, updated research findings, and an interview that challenges students to apply theory and principles to a realistic interview. In each interview, the parties do some things well and others poorly. We want students to be able to identify strengths and weaknesses and to offer alternatives that would have made the interview more effective for each party. We have restructured some chapters and developed separate chapters for each party in employment and persuasive interviews.

Major changes include:

- Chapter 1 includes a new quiz on what is and is not an interview, an expanded treatment of the interview as relational, and the use of videoconferencing, cell phones, and the Internet to conduct interviews.
- Chapter 3 includes new materials on question types and pitfalls.
- Chapter 4 includes two additional question sequences, the diamond and hourglass, and drawings to aid in explaining types of question sequences.
- Chapter 5 includes expanded suggestions for respondents and a discussion of the videoconference interview.
- Chapter 6 includes discussions of quantitative and qualitative surveys and using the Internet to conduct survey interviews.
- Chapter 8 includes materials on posting resumes online, the dangers of including inappropriate materials on personal Web sites and blogs, and handling rejection.

- Chapter 9 includes new material and increased emphasis on a coaching approach to performance review interviews.
- Chapter 10 includes expanded treatment of ethics and credibility and new material on developing reasons or arguments.
- Chapter 11 includes an expanded treatment of the interviewee as consumer.
- Chapter 12 includes expanded discussions of culture, relationships, and the telephone interview.
- Chapter 13 includes expanded discussions of sex, age, and culture, including language barriers and the use of interpreters and the inappropriate use of baby talk and elderspeak with older patients. Updated research includes discussions of general inquiry and confirmation questions and seeker vs. nonseeker patients.

Chapter-By-Chapter Overview

Chapter 1 develops a definition of interviewing in detail. It contains a theoretical treatment of relationships in interviews, and discusses how perceptions affect relationships, the nature and development of relationships in other cultures and countries, and how women and men differ in their relationships. The interview as a relational form of communication sets the stage for Chapter 2. Students are introduced to the growing use of electronic interviews over the telephone and through Internet interviews.

Chapter 2 takes students through a step-by-step development of the Cash–Stewart model of interviewing as it treats the interview as a complex interpersonal communication process. This chapter emphasizes the importance of self-concept in interviews and shows how concepts such as self-image, self-esteem, and self-reliance differ in non-Western cultures that are collectivist rather than individualist. The discussion of the importance of self-disclosure in interviews incorporates politeness theory and notes how self-disclosure differs between sexes and among cultures. The nature and uses of verbal and nonverbal communication are highlighted and so are language use and space according to age, sex, culture, and ethnicity. John Stewart's notion of dialogic listening is developed as listening for resolution, and presented with the traditional treatments of listening for comprehension, empathy, and evaluation. And students are introduced to the potential influences of "outside forces" on each interview party.

Chapter 3 introduces students to the many types and uses of questions in interviews, literally the tools of the trade. It contains an identification and illustration of common question pitfalls that plague both parties in interviews. This chapter discusses the apparent relevance of questions to interviewers and interviewees from other cultures. It also addresses responses to questions that require personal disclosure and discusses how men and women and those of differing cultures may disclose information differently.

Chapter 4 focuses on the structure of interviews, including openings, bodies, and closings. It emphasizes how verbal and nonverbal communication in openings and closings differs between males and females and how cultures other than Western ones regard handshaking, touching, and eye contact. This chapter contains a discussion of question sequences as well as outline sequences in discussions of interview guides and schedules to help students develop the bodies of interviews.

Chapter 5, on the probing interview, focuses on ways to enhance the effectiveness of probing interviews in a wide variety of situations, including journalistic ones. It applies probing principles to interviews conducted by attorneys, police officers, recruiters, health care professionals, insurance claims investigators, and teachers, as well as journalists. There is strong emphasis on preparation, relationship, and motivation.

Chapter 6, on the survey interview, stresses the importance of meticulous preparation, structure, question development, and conducting of interviews when replicability and reliability are essential to successful outcomes. Special attention is given to question strategies and scales and to methods of sampling the target population.

Chapter 7, on the recruiting interview, reflects the employer's roles of attracting and selecting new employees. It contains discussions of recruiting in a rapidly changing world, assessing what applicants want in positions and careers, use of computers and the Internet to attract and inform applicants, and job fairs. This chapter continues to refine its discussion of electronic systems for scanning resumes, quantitative tests to assess applicants, videotaping and videoconferencing, the behavior-based interview, nontraditional interviewing approaches, and on-the-job questions.

Chapter 8 addresses the selection interview from the applicant's perspective. It contains discussions of the changing world of work, the reality of cultural diversity, the universal skills and attitudes essential for work in the twenty-first century, databases and Internet resources for searching for positions and learning about organizations, positions, and careers or job fairs. There are guidelines for preparing resumes and cover letters and sample resumes, including one designed for electronic scanning. Although this chapter places strong emphasis on responding to questions effectively, including those that violate EEO laws, there is corresponding emphasis on asking questions effectively.

Chapter 9, on performance review interviews, contains discussions of visions for organizations in the twenty-first century, the balanced scoreboard approach, preparing for the review, and the force choice review model. This chapter continues to introduce students to a variety of models for conducting performance reviews, while emphasizing the interview as a coaching rather than judgmental opportunity and process. It also introduces students to the "performance problem interview," which avoids the negative connotation and implication of guilt associated with the old "discipline interview."

Chapter 10, which focuses on the *persuader* in the persuasive interview, emphasizes the ethical responsibilities of the persuader. It incorporates discussions of several persuasion theories, including identification, balance or consistency, inoculation, forced or induced compliance, and psychological reactance. Its focus is on persuasion in everyday life, not merely in sales situations. This chapter also addresses values differences in cultures and how cultures view time, bargaining, and relationship building. There is strong emphasis on structuring the persuasive interview.

Chapter 11 focuses on the *persuadee* in the persuasive interview. It emphasizes the ethical responsibilities of the persuadee and the need to be an informed participant. Students are introduced to a variety of common psychological and language strategies persuaders employ. The chapter focuses on the persuadee as an active and critical participant who understands how to identify and assess logical strategies and the evidence that supports them.

Chapter 12 focuses on preparing, structuring, and conducting counseling interviews by lay counselors who have minimal training in counseling. It emphasizes the need for self-analysis as well as analysis of the interviewee, selection of appropriate interviewing approaches, listening, observing, and responding in appropriate and effective ways. The interviewer must be people-oriented rather than task-oriented. Students are introduced to a sequential phase model and a client-centered approach to counseling.

Chapter 13 focuses on the health care interview as a collaborative effort between provider and patient and addresses the relationships and interactions of the two parties. It discusses the effect of gender, age, ethnic group, and culture on the provider–patient relationship and treats information getting, information giving, counseling, and persuading as joint efforts of patient and provider. This chapter notes differences in information seeking, nonverbal interactions, and preference for verbal communication among differing cultures.

Some of the principles and guidelines presented in these thirteen chapters may seem simple or obvious. However, in our experiences as professors, managers, practitioners, and consultants of interviewing in academic, professional, industrial, business, and social settings, we have found again and again that overlooking the simple and the obvious creates problems in real-life interviews.

Chapter Pedagogy

We have included a **sample interview at the end of each chapter,** *not* as a perfect example of interviewing but to illustrate interviewing types, situations, approaches, and *mistakes* and to challenge students to distinguish between effective and ineffective interviewing practices. We believe that students learn by applying the research and principles discussed in each chapter to a realistic interview that allows them to detect when interview parties are right on target as well as when they miss the target completely. The **role-playing cases** at the ends of Chapters 5 through 13 provide students with opportunities to design and conduct practice interviews and to observe others' efforts to employ the principles discussed. **Student activities** at the end of each chapter provide ideas for in- and out-of-class exercises, experiences, and information gathering. We have made many of these less complex and time-consuming. The **up-to-date readings** at the end of each chapter will help students and instructors who are interested in delving more deeply into specific topics, theories, and types of interviews. The **glossary** provides students with definitions of key words and concepts introduced throughout the text.

Intended Courses

This book is designed for courses in such departments as speech, communication, journalism, business, supervision, education, political science, nursing, criminology, and social work. It is also useful in workshops in various fields. We believe this book is of value to beginning students as well as to seasoned veterans because the principles, research, and techniques are changing rapidly in many fields. We have treated theory and research findings where applicable, but our primary concern is with principles and techniques that can be translated into immediate practice in and out of the classroom.

Ancillary Materials

For the Student

Student's Online Learning Center (OLC)

The Student's Online Learning Center Web site that accompanies this text offers a variety of resources for students, including—for each chapter—a chapter summary; an interactive quiz with multiple-choice, fill-in, and/or true/false questions; flashcards of key terms; and a crossword puzzle of key terms. Please visit the *Interviewing* OLC at www.mhhe.com/Stewart11.

For the Instructor

The Instructor's Manual, written by Charles Stewart, Test Bank, and PowerPoint slides are available to instructors on the **Instructor's Resource CD-Rom (IRCD).** The Instructor's Manual and PowerPoints are also available on the **Instructor's section of the Online Learning Center Web site.**

Acknowledgments

We wish to express our gratitude to students at Purdue University and National Louis University-College of Management, and to past and present colleagues and clients for their inspiration, suggestions, exercises, theories, criticism and encouragement. We thank Suzanne Collins, Ellen Phelps, Rebecca Parker, Mary Alice Baker, Kasie Roberson, Emily Stine, Kathleen Powell, Garold Markle, and Patrice Buzzanell for their resources, interest, and suggestions.

We are very grateful to the following reviewers for the many helpful comments and suggestions they provided us:

Mary Alice Baker, Lamar University

Christina Beck, Ohio University

Richard Edwards, Baylor University

Julie Ehrhardt, Des Moines Area Community College West Campus

Angela Celeste Farr, North Carolina State University

Hank Flick, Mississippi State University

Dirk Gibson, University of New Mexico

Kathleen Golden, Edinboro University of Pennsylvania

Louis Harris, Faulkner University

Michael Hilt, University of Nebraska at Omaha

Kathleen B. Hom, University of Utah

Virginia M. McDermott, University of New Mexico

Rick Soller, College of Lake County

Esin C. Turk, Mississippi Valley State University

Stacey Young, California State University, Long Beach

CHAPTER 1 An Introduction to Interviewing

When did you last take part in an interview? Don't be surprised if you try to recall the last time you interviewed for a job or internship. Most people, not just students, think of interviewing as synonymous with employment interviews. A few years ago one of the authors was talking with the administrator of a local hospital. He commented that he had several nursing students in his interviewing course, to which the administrator replied: "Nurses don't need a course in interviewing; there are plenty of nursing positions available all over the country." It did not occur to the administrator that interviewing courses cover a variety of interviews other than employment and that nurses are involved in information giving and getting, counseling, and persuasive interviews every single day, most of them involving the health and safety of patients. When we give or get information, counsel or are counseled, interview for a position or recruit for a position, persuade or are persuaded, we are taking part in interviews, the most common form of purposeful, planned communication. Interviews may be formal or informal, unstructured or structured, simplistic or sophisticated, supportive or threatening. They may last for a few minutes to hours and be intimate or highly functional.

Interviews are daily occurrences.

Interviews share characteristics with intimate interactions, social conversations, small groups, and presentations, but they are significantly different. This chapter identifies the essential elements of interviewing, distinguishes interviewing from other forms of interpersonal communication, focuses on the interview as a relational form of communication, and discusses the uses and challenges of participating in electronic interviews.

The Essential Elements of Interviews

Interactional

Interviews involve exchanging and sharing.

Roles may switch from moment to moment.

An interview is **interactional** because there is an **exchanging,** or sharing, of roles, responsibilities, feelings, beliefs, motives, and information. If one person does all of the talking and the other all of the listening, a speech to an audience of one, not an interview, is taking place. Although we traditionally identify the interviewer and interviewee in interviews, we often interchange these roles as interviews progress. For instance, if as an interviewee we ask questions about Internet security with one of our school's Web specialists, make a counteroffer for a hybrid automobile, quiz a recruiter about a summer position at a dude ranch in Colorado, or request a nurse practitioner to explain the possible side effects of a prescribed drug, we assume the role of interviewer for the moment and the interviewer takes on the role of interviewee. As the other person responds, makes a counteroffer, answers questions, or gives explanations, the roles switch back to traditional ones.

Interactional does not mean equal. In some interviews, such as journalistic, counseling, and recruiting, an ideal division of speaking time might be 70 percent to 30 percent, with the interviewee doing most of the talking. In others, such as information giving and sales, the ratio might be reversed with the interviewer doing most of the talking and questioning. Both parties must determine an appropriate ratio.

Interactional also means a sharing of responsibilities. When thinking of common interviews such as recruiting, journalistic, health care, and persuasive, we tend to focus on the responsibilities of one party—the applicant in the recruiting interview, the investigator in the journalistic or police interview, the health care professional in the medical interview, and the persuader in the persuasive interview. Both parties are responsible for the success or failure of each interview. The interview is truly a mutual activity and will not work if either party fails to appreciate the collaborative nature of the effort. For example, the recruiter is responsible for studying the applicant's credentials, preparing insightful and challenging questions, being up-to-date on information about the organization, and replying honestly and fully to the applicant's questions. On the other hand, the applicant is responsible for doing a careful self-analysis, preparing thorough and honest credentials, researching the organization and position, replying honestly and fully to questions, and asking carefully phrased questions about the position and organization. It takes two parties to make an interview a success. That is why we will address the roles of both interviewer and interviewee throughout this book.

It takes two to make an interview a success.

Few interviews are successful if either party is unwilling to share feelings, beliefs, motives, and information. Before an interview begins, be aware of your **feelings** (pride, fear, anger, sympathy), **motives** (security, belonging, freedom, ambition), **beliefs** (social, political, historic, economic, religious), and **information** (facts, data, opinions) and those of the other party. John Stewart writes that communication "is a collaborative process of verbal and nonverbal meaning-making through which we construct the worlds of meaning we inhabit."[1] Our creating and sharing comes from words and nonverbal signals—touches, hugs, handshakes, and facial looks—that express interest, concerns, and reactions. Close interpersonal interchanges such as interviews involve risk that can be minimized but never eliminated, and if either party "plays it safe," the interview is likely to fail.

All interviews involve risk.

Process

A **process** is a dynamic, continuing, ever-changing interaction of variables with a degree of **system** or **structure.** The parties in each interaction generate energy through their desires to achieve specific goals. Communication interactions are not static. Role changes, exchanges of information, and revelations of feelings and motives produce reactions and insights that lead to new and unexpected areas of insight and exploration. John Stewart claims that "Human communicators are always sending and receiving simultaneously. As a result each communicator has the opportunity to change how things are going at any time in the process."[2] Although each interview is unique in some respects, all involve an interaction of communication ingredients such as perceptions, verbal and nonverbal messages, levels of disclosure, feedback, listening, motivation, expectations, and assumptions. Each party brings knowledge, experiences, expectations,

An interview is a complex, ever-changing process.

No interview occurs in a vacuum.

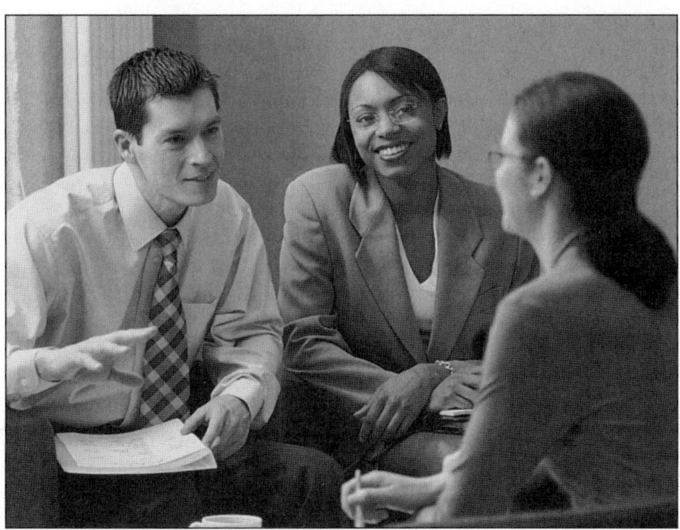
photo by Digital Vision/Getty Images

More than two people may be involved in an interview, but never more than two parties—an interviewer party and an interviewee party.

pressures, and personal limitations to the interaction. An interview occurs at a specific time and on a specific date; takes place at a specific location surrounded by objects, persons, and sounds; and is preceded or followed by events that may impact it for good or ill. Sarah Trenholm and Arthur Jensen, for instance, note that "Communication always takes place in a cultural context."[3]

Once initiated, the interview is an ongoing process.

Like other processes, once an interview begins, we "cannot not communicate."[4] We may communicate effectively or poorly, but we will communicate something as long as we are within sight or sound of one another. The result may be success or failure. Chapter 2 develops a general summary model that introduces, discusses, and illustrates the many communication variables that interact in the interviewing process.

Parties

A dyadic process involves two parties.

Interviews may involve two or more **people** (two recruiters interviewing a graduating senior, two police officers interviewing a crime victim, three friends interviewing an apartment owner), but never more than two **parties.** If more than two parties are involved (for example, three accountants discussing a financial report or four unrelated buyers making different offers to the owner of a fishing boat), a small group interaction is taking place, not an interview. There is one party in the first setting and five parties in the second. The interview is a **dyadic** process, and adding parties transforms it into a distinctly different interaction.

Purpose

All interviews have a degree of structure.

At least one of the two parties must come to an interview with an important goal—other than mere enjoyment—and intention to focus on specific subject matter. This **predetermined** and **serious** purpose distinguishes the interview from social **conversation** or informal, unplanned interactions such as meeting a friend on the street. While conversations are rarely organized in advance, interviews must have a degree of advanced planning and structure, even if we have little more than a purpose and topics in mind. In most effective interviews, the interviewer will plan the opening, select topics, prepare questions, gather information, and determine how to close the interview. Chapter 4 deals with the principles and techniques of opening, developing, and closing interviews.

Although good conversations and interviews share many characteristics such as exchanging speaking and listening, mutual concern that each party finds the interaction

An interview is a conversation and much more.

pleasant and rewarding, and effective verbal and nonverbal messages, they are very different. Imagine going to an employer to ask for a raise or time off or to a recruiter for a summer internship without giving thought to how you will begin, the case you will present, information you might provide, questions you will ask, answers you will give, or what you will say if your request or application is rejected. On the other hand, imagine visiting a friend or coworker who always plans conversations ahead of time. Most of us would send an e-mail instead or avoid contact.

Questions

All interviews involve questions and answers.

Asking and answering **questions** are important in all interviews. Some interviews, such as market surveys and journalistic interviews, consist entirely of questions and answers. Others, such as recruiting, counseling, and health care, include a mixture of questions and information sharing. And still others, such as sales, training, and performance review involve strategic questions from both parties designed to obtain or clarify information and to change another person's ways of thinking, feeling, or acting.

Questions play multiple roles in interviews.

Without either party asking and answering questions, how could we discuss a grade with a professor, counsel a roommate who is skipping too many lectures, interview for an internship, take part in a performance review, or explain a difficult psychological theory? Questions are the tools interviewers and interviewees employ to obtain information, check the accuracy of messages sent and received, verify impressions and assumptions, and provoke feeling or thought. Chapter 3 introduces you to a variety of question types and their uses and misuses.

An interview, then, is an interactional communication process between two parties, at least one of whom has a predetermined and serious purpose, that involves the asking and answering of questions.

This definition of interviewing encompasses a wide variety of interviews, many of which require specialized training and specific abilities. W. Charles Redding developed a "situational schema" that arranged interviews according to functions. Figure 1.1 is an elaboration of this schema.

Quiz #1—What Is and Is Not an Interview?

With our definition of interviewing in mind, determine which of the following interactions constitutes an interview and which does not.

1. An Air Force recruiter is meeting with a potential recruit and her parents at her home a few weeks after her graduation from a community college. The purpose is to get the recruit to sign up for basic training.
2. A representative from a large construction management firm is meeting with a student during an engineering job fair on campus.
3. A person is meeting with his doctor and her nurse practitioner to determine whether he will be able to play on the soccer team this spring.
4. A supervisor is conducting a quarterly performance review meeting with an associate in his division.

Figure 1.1 *Types of interviews*

1. Information giving
   a. Orientation
   b. Training, instruction, coaching
   c. Job-related instructions
   d. Briefings
2. Information gathering
   a. Surveys and polls
   b. Exit interviews
   c. Research interviews
   d. Investigations: insurance, police, etc.
   e. Medical, psychological, diagnostic, caseworker, etc.
   f. Journalistic
3. Selection
   a. Screening
   b. Determinate
   c. Placement
4. Problems of interviewee's behavior
   a. Appraisal, evaluative, review
   b. Separation, firing
   c. Correction, discipline, reprimand
   d. Counseling
5. Problems of interviewer's behavior
   a. Receiving complaints
   b. Grievances
   c. Receiving suggestions
6. Problem solving
   a. Discussing mutually shared problems
   b. Receiving suggestions for solutions
7. Persuasion
   a. Selling products and services
   b. Recruiting members
   c. Fund-raising and development
   d. Changing the way a party feels, thinks, or acts

5. A professor is asking questions in her class concerning assigned readings and their practical applications to public relations.

6. Three members of a consulting firm are discussing a draft of their recommendations over lunch prior to presenting the proposal later in the day.

7. An academic counselor is discussing next semester's classes with a counselee.

8. A sales representative is attempting to sell a rolltop desk to a couple who are creating an office in their home.
9. A television reporter is meeting with the mayor and police chief to discuss a recent crime wave on the north side of the city. The result will be a 10-minute special on the evening news.
10. A telemarketer is talking to a person on the phone about investing in a new alternative fuel, start-up company.

A Relational Form of Communication

Each interview contributes to a relational history.

The notion of **relationship** is inherent in our definition of interviewing because interviews are reciprocal interactions between two parties and something two parties do together, not something they do to each other.[5] Both parties in interviews are connected interpersonally and have varying degrees of interest in the relationship and the outcome of the interview. This relationship may commence with the start of the interview or have a history that began days, months, or years before. For example, you may encounter a recruiter or counselor for the first time, or you may interact with a sales representative or supervisor with whom you have a long-standing and long-lasting relationship. Anxiety may be high because one or both parties may have "negative expectations based on a previous interaction."[6] Interviews with no prior history may be difficult "precisely because we don't know the rules and so we don't know exactly how to coordinate our conversational moves."[7] Stereotypes often play significant negative roles in interactions between strangers, particularly during the first few minutes when parties have exchanged little personal information.[8]

Our relationships may be **intimate** with close family members, friends, and long-time acquaintances. They may be **casual** with co-workers, neighbors, fellow professionals, or persons we have known for some time: physicians, restaurant owners, clothiers, and teachers. Or they may be **distant** or **formal** and purely functional, such as sales associates, plumbers, consulting physicians, attorneys. Trenholm and Jensen warn that "once a label is firm in our mind, it tends to limit our perception of what we can do together."[9]

Relationships change over time and during interactions. John Stewart and Carole Logan claim that "each time they communicate, relational partners construct and modify patterns that define who they are for and with each other."[10] And Stephen Littlejohn writes that "people in a relationship are always creating a set of expectations, reinforcing old ones, or changing an existing pattern of interaction."[11] Trenholm and Jensen caution that "relationships are not something we create once; they are something we recreate and refine every time we communicate."[12]

The situation may alter a relationship.

Relationships change because situations change. For instance, we may have a pleasant, supportive relationship with a fellow employee until we become this person's department head or we begin to compete for a promotion. Many of us are adept at dealing with routine and simple situations but encounter difficulty adapting to new situations and unexpected demands. Trenholm and Jensen claim interactions take "experience and flexibility. A person who knows only one way to do things will have trouble confronting new approaches; the more we learn about alternative ways of organizing relationships, the more flexible we can become."[13] Above all, both parties in a relationship must strive to be skillful communicators and to assume new roles while understanding what are acceptable and fitting behaviors in these roles.

Relational Dimensions

There are many relational dimensions, but five are particularly relevant to interviews.

Similarity

Relationships are cultivated when both parties share cultural norms and values, training, experiences, personality traits, attitudes, and expectations. We may come from the same neighborhood, share ethnic heritage, be career-oriented, attend the same college, or want to exchange information and ideas. In fact, we tend to form relationships most often with those in close proximity to us at work, church, social and religious activities, and professional associations. We may find it easier to interact with a person of the same sex, age, or race. Awareness of similarities enables interview parties to understand one another, establish common ground, and adapt to perceptions.

A few similarities do not equal relational peers.

Be careful of noting a few surface similarities—dress, age, ethnicity—and assuming you have a great deal in common. These obvious similarities may be all that you have in common. Judith Martin and Thomas Nakayama write that "similarity is based not on whether people actually are similar but on the perception of a similar trait."[14] The authors have discovered during their long careers that people they came to know primarily through contacts and experiences at professional conferences were not nearly as similar as they assumed from these contacts. They thought that since they were competent, friendly, thoughtful, and caring at professional meetings, they were the same when they got back home and dealt day-to-day with departmental colleagues, staff, and students. These assumptions often proved to be untrue. The similarities exhibited at professional conferences were superficial at best.

Inclusion/Involvement

Wanting to be involved leads to meaningful interchanges.

Relationships are cultivated when both parties want to take part and become actively involved as speakers and listeners. The more we get involved and share, the more satisfying we are likely to find the relationship and to anticipate future interactions. We show this satisfaction through words and actions.

Unfortunately, an applicant may be interviewing merely for the experience rather than interest in the organization, and the recruiter may want to end a long day of endless interviews. Sometimes we are "talked to" and "talked down to" rather than communicated with, and we don't like it. Effective relationships develop when the parties literally become interdependent, when "Each becomes aware that what" they do and not do "will have an impact on the other" and "each begins to act with the" other party "in mind."[15] Their actions become joint actions and neither takes part with expectations that are either too high, and thus unattainable, or or too low, and thus unrewarding or unfulfilling.

Affection

Relationships are cultivated when parties like and respect one another, when there is warmth or friendship. Affection or liking occurs in an interview when there is a "we"

We communicate more freely with people we like.

instead of a "me–you" or "we–they" feeling. We are unlikely to establish a lasting friendship in a 5- to 10-minute interview, but we can communicate in a way the other party finds pleasant, productive, and fair.

Some of us find showing affection difficult, particularly in formal settings. We may fear "closeness" and prefer to keep others, acquaintances as well as strangers, at a comfortable distance. Professors often fear getting too close to students they evaluate and reward, and students often fear closeness with professors because of the effect this may have on evaluations and how the professor and others may perceive it. We may come to an interview with an ambivalent, negative, or hostile attitude toward the other party. James Honeycutt writes that "even though relationships are in constant motion, relationship memory structures provide a perceptual anchor [so] individuals can determine where they are in a relationship."[16] Relational memory is a double-edged sword, however. Negative memories may doom an interview before it starts while positive memories may assure that it will be a pleasant and productive interaction.

Control

Because each party in interpersonal interactions, such as interviews, is "a participant in an ongoing process," neither can control the process completely.[17] John Stewart claims that "nexting" is the most important communication tool because "Whenever you face a communication challenge or problem, the most helpful question you can ask yourself is, 'What can I help to happen next, and how?' "[18] The intent is to keep the interaction progressing toward a productive end for both parties. Thus, relationships are cultivated when both parties share control and neither seeks a dominant role. Either party may have considerable control over the interaction; the decision is how to use it. A respondent may say no to a political pollster or hang up the telephone during a call from a charity. An interviewer may do most of the talking in a sales interview or withhold information during a crime scene investigation. Chapter 2 discusses **directive** and **nondirective approaches** to interviewing, in which the interviewer controls the process or enables the interviewee to have considerable control over the process.

Upward and downward communication is often a challenge in interviews.

Control often poses problems during interviews because they involve organizational hierarchies or chains of command: president over vice president, manager over associate, professor over student, supervisor over an intern. This **upward** and **downward communication** may handicap both parties. One may have the power and authority to determine when, where, or if an interview takes place; who the other party will be; and the results of the interview. As John Stewart points out, however, "No one person can completely control a communication event, and no single person or action causes—or can be blamed for—a communication outcome."[19]

Trust

Trust alone may determine the outcome of an interview.

Fisher and Brown claim that trust is the "single most important element of a good working relationship" and that we must be trustworthy but not necessarily "wholly trusting."[20] It is healthy to be skeptical at times. Unfortunately, some people trust few people, are inherently suspicious, and may border on paranoia. This leads some to claim that trust is a mind-set, an attitude that influences our interactions.

Trust is essential in interviews because how they are conducted, with whom, the climate encountered, and their potential outcomes typically affect us directly—our incomes, careers, purchases, colleagues, profits, health, understanding, safety. Relationships are cultivated when the parties trust one another to be honest, sincere, reliable, truthful, fair, even-tempered, and of high ethical and moral standards, in other words **safe.** Gudykunst and Kim write that "When we trust others, we expect positive outcomes from our interactions with them; when we have anxiety about interacting with others, we fear negative outcomes from our interactions with them."[21] Martin, Nakayama, and Flores warn that "in intercultural conflict situations, when we are experiencing high anxieties with unfamiliar behavior (for example, accents, gestures, facial expressions), we may automatically withhold trust."[22]

We will not open up to persons we cannot trust to keep their word or fear will be negative or hostile. Unpredictable persons and outcomes lead to caution in questions and answers and the sharing of information. Risk may be too high. One of the authors dealt frequently with an administrator on his campus who was often understanding, helpful, and kind but was notorious for losing his temper and shouting at faculty and staff during interactions. There was no way to determine which person would appear at any moment, so interviewees tended to be cautious, measured their words carefully, and prepared themselves for the worst. The climate of the interview clearly affects trust. A supportive, friendly, positive, helpful, or constructive climate enhances trust and the quality of communication between the interview parties. On the other hand, a critical, hostile, negative, obstructive, or hurtful climate severely limits trust and inevitably affects the disclosure that takes place and the sharing of ideas, attitudes, and feelings.

Global Relationships

We must understand cultures to live and work in the twenty-first century.

Our social and work worlds have become global, so it's important to understand how relationships are shaped and cultivated in different countries and cultures. In the United States, we tend to have numerous friendly, informal relationships and to place considerable importance on how a person looks, particularly early in relationships.[23] While Americans create and discard relationships frequently, Australians make deeper and longer-lasting commitments. Arabs, like Americans, develop relationships quickly but, unlike Americans who dislike taking advantage of relationships by asking for favors, Arabs believe friends have a duty to help one another. Chinese develop very strong, long-term relationships and, like Arabs, see them as "filled with obligations."[24] Germans develop relationships slowly because they believe relationships are very important. Using first names before a relationship is firmly established is rude behavior. Japanese prefer not to interact with strangers or foreigners, want background information on parties before establishing relationships, prefer doing business with people they have known for years, and take a great deal of time establishing relationships.

Men and Women in Relationships

Men and women communicate differently.

Sex of participants is critical in establishing and refining relationships because they are influenced by what we say and how we say it. Women use communication as a primary way of establishing relationships, while men communicate "to exert control, preserve independence, and enhance status."[25] Men's talk tends to be directive and goal-oriented, with statements that "tend to press compliance, agreement, or belief." Women's talk, in contrast, tends to be more polite and expressive, containing less intense words, qualifiers (perhaps, maybe), and disclaimers ("Maybe I'm wrong, but . . ." "I may not fully understand the situation, but . . .").[26]

Electronic Interviews

The Telephone

When we hear the word *interview,* we tend to think of a face-to-face meeting of two parties involved in information getting or giving, recruiting, selling, counseling, performance reviews, and other familiar settings. With the invention of the telephone, however, interviews no longer had to be face-to-face encounters; they could be ear-to-ear. Telephone interviews became so commonplace and irritating that many states and the federal government created "Don't Call" lists to protect our privacy and sanity.

Organizations have turned to the telephone to conduct initial employment screening interviews, fund-raising campaigns, and opinion polls to save time, reduce monetary expenses, and eliminate the time necessary to send staff to numerous locations. They use conference calls to enable several members of an organization to ask questions and hear replies from staff and clients in multiple locations scattered over a wide geographical area. Interviewers and interviewees can talk to several people at one time, answer or clarify questions directly, be heard while responding, and receive immediate feedback.

The telephone interview is convenient and inexpensive.

A major problem with telephone interviews is the lack of "presence" of parties. Hearing a voice is not the same as being able to observe an interviewer's or interviewee's appearance, dress, manner, eye contact, face, gestures, and posture. Some studies comparing telephone and face-to-face interviews suggest that the two methods produce similar communicative results, with respondents giving fewer socially acceptable answers over the telephone and preferring the anonymity it provides.[27] Other studies urge caution in turning too quickly to the telephone. One study found that interviewers do not like telephone interviews, and this attitude may affect how interviewees reply. Another study discovered that fewer interviewees (particularly older ones) prefer the telephone, and this may lower degree of cooperation.[28] People may feel uneasy about discussing sensitive issues with strangers they cannot see, and it is difficult to make convincing confidentiality guarantees when not face-to-face.

The Cell Phone

The introduction of the cell phone just a few years ago has created a whole new world of "talking," and we assume some listening, that seemingly takes place everywhere, from dorm rooms, kitchens, and backyards to restrooms, parks, and classrooms. When we walk through our campuses at 7:00 in the morning and see, and hear, students on their cell phones, we wonder who they are talking to that early in the morning.

A new concern for the **privacy** of professional, business, and personal cell phone interviews results from users, apparently feeling they must talk loud enough for all of us within 75 feet to hear, shouting to the person on the other end. We could go to any restaurant, lounge area, or airport boarding area today and hear complete conversations that otherwise would be held behind closed doors to assure confidentiality. If these were just social conversations, the problem would be merely annoying. However, we have heard executives discussing mergers, profit margins, and personnel changes; patients discussing their diagnoses and prescriptions with medical practitioners; and students requesting help with assignments, grade adjustments, and personal problems.

The growing sophistication of two-way video technology may reduce the problems and concerns caused by critical nonverbal cues missing from the telephone. Cell phone technology that allows parties to send visual images of one another while they are talking is a recent development. Tiny headshots, of course, are far from the presence of face-to-face interviews, but they are a critical step forward in the interview process.

The Videoconference

By the late 1990s, surveys indicated that 82 percent of companies were using or planning to use **videoconference** technology to conduct recruiting interviews because it was less expensive, enabled parties to see one another, and could be conducted globally.[29] Some ten years later, videoconferencing has expanded well beyond this figure and to include many types of interviews. Although this technology would seem to be as good as "being there in person," there are significant differences from face-to-face interviews.

Since visual cues are limited to the top half or faces of participants, or group shots in the case of multiple-person interview parties, there are fewer nonverbal cues. One result is fewer interruptions that lead to longer and fewer turns by participants. It is more difficult to interact freely and naturally with people on a screen. Perhaps this is why participants provide more negative evaluations of others in the interview who may appear to dominate the process. One study showed that interviewers liked the videoconference because they could "unobtrusively take more notes, check their watches, or refer to resumes without disrupting the flow of the interview" or, perhaps, being noticed by the other party. On the other hand, they had trouble "reading nonverbal behaviours such as facial expression, eye contact, and fidgeting" and telling "whether a pause was due to the technology, or the applicant being stumped." Although a significant majority of interviewers (88%) indicated that they would be willing to use videoconferencing for interviews, a significant majority (76%) said they preferred face-to-face interviews.[30]

Interviewees in teleconference interviews should be aware of the length of their answers to enhance turn-taking and avoid the appearance of trying to dominate the interview. They, too, can check their lists of questions, take notes, and watch their time without being noticed. Above all, interviewees should be aware of the importance of upper-body movement, gestures, eye contact, and facial expressions that will attract favorable and unfavorable attention. With technology, there is no traditional handshake and the interviewee is alone in a room with the interviewer, and these factors

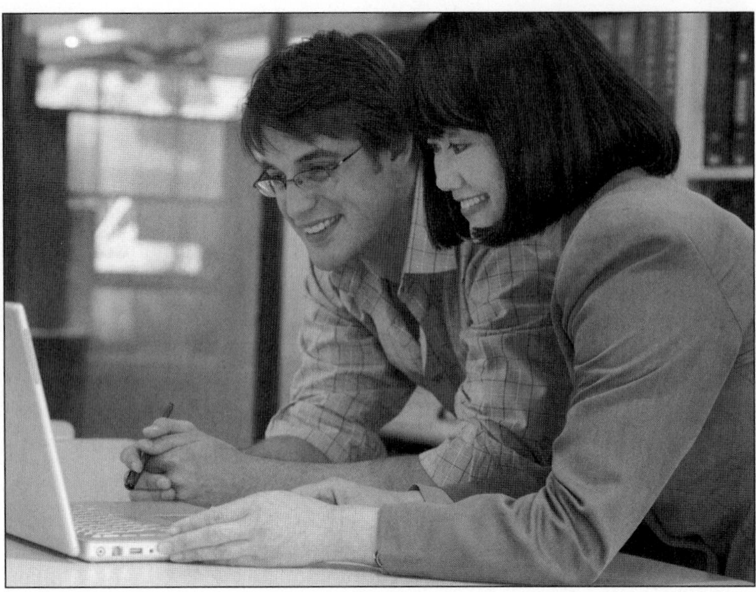
photo by Lucido Studio Inc./Corbis

The Internet can provide important information on positions and organizations and background on interviewers and interviewees.

may generate tension for some. Follow these suggestions for a more effective and enjoyable interview: speak up so you can be heard easily, dress conservatively in solid colors, look at the camera full-face, limit movements, try to forget about the camera, expect some lag time between questions and responses.[31] One study indicated that applicants in recruiting interviews were more satisfied with their performance in face-to-face interviews when the interviews were less structured and more satisfied with their performance in videoconference interviews when the interviews were highly structured.[32] Since questions in highly structured interviews tend to require shorter answers, interviewees may have felt less pressured to determine length and content of answers and turn-taking.

The Internet

The Internet lacks the nonverbal cues critical in interviews.

With the introduction of the Internet, many interviews went from face-to-face and ear-to-ear to finger-to-finger. It has enabled large numbers of people to make inquiries, send and receive information, and discuss problems at any time of the day or night and nearly anywhere in the world. But are these multiple-party interactions electronic mail rather than interviews? If two parties use the Internet to interact in real time, it meets our definition of an interview. Small video cameras mounted on the computer that

ON THE WEB

Learn more about the growing uses of electronic interviews in a variety of settings. Search at least two databases under headings such as telephone interviews, conference calls, and video talk-back. Try search engines such as ComAbstracts (http://www.cios.org), Yahoo (http://www.yahoo.com), Infoseek(http://www.infoseek.com), and ERIC (http://www.indiana.edu/~eric_rec). In which interview settings are electronic interviews most common? What are the advantages and disadvantages of electronic interviews? How will new developments affect electronic interviews in the future? How will the growing use of electronic interviews affect the ways we conduct traditional face-to-face interviews?

sends live pictures and sound between interview parties may make electronic interactions superior to the telephone and ever closer to the face-to-face interview. One obstacle to overcome is the reluctance of parties to type lengthy answers to questions that they can provide easily in person or over the telephone. The Internet's potential seems unlimited and, as it becomes more visually interactive, it will take on more of the properties of the traditional interview in which both parties not only ask and answer questions but communicate nonverbally through appearance, face, voice, and gesture. Unfortunately, the small screen will continue to limit the visibility and effectiveness of nonverbal communication.

Summary

Interviewing is an interactional communication process between two parties, at least one of whom has a predetermined and serious purpose, that involves the asking and answering of questions. This definition encompasses a wide variety of interview settings that require training, preparation, interpersonal skills, flexibility, and a willingness to face risks involved in intimate, person-to-person interactions. Interviewing is a learned, not an inherited, skill and art, and perhaps the first hurdle to overcome is the assumption that we do it well because we do it so often. The increasing flexibility of the telephone and the Internet is resulting in significant numbers of interviews no longer occurring face-to-face, and this is posing new challenges and concerns.

Because we are involved in interviews every day, we assume the process is simple and requires little, if any, formal training. What is so difficult about asking a few questions, providing a few answers, or exchanging a bit of information or advice? But if you think interviewing is simple and basic skills come naturally, recall some of your recent experiences. Most of us learn how to interview by observing others or taking part in interviews, thus perpetuating many poor interviewing practices handed down from one generation to another. We assume that practice makes perfect, but 20 years of experience may be one year of flawed experience repeated 20 times, sort of like our golf swing, driving, or cooking.

There is a vast difference between skilled and unskilled interviewers and interviewees, and the skilled ones know that practice makes perfect only if you know what you are practicing. Studies in health care, for example, have revealed that medical students, physicians, and nurses who do not receive formal training in interviewing patients actually become less effective interviewers over time, not more effective.

The first essential step in developing and improving interviewing skills is to understand the deceptively complex interviewing process and its many interacting variables. Successful interviewing requires you to understand both parties, the exchanging of roles, perceptions of self and other, communication interactions, feedback, situation, and the influence of outside forces. Chapter 2 explains and illustrates the interviewing process by developing a model step-by-step that contains all of the fundamental elements that interact in each interview.

Our purposes in writing this book are twofold. First, we want to introduce you to the basic skills applicable for all interviews (Chapters 2, 3, and 4) and specific skills needed in specialized settings (Chapters 5 to 13). And, second, we want to help you improve your interviewing skills for a lifetime, not merely while you are a student or a recent graduate looking for your first position.

Key Terms and Concepts

The online learning center for this text features FLASHCARDS and CROSSWORD PUZZLES for studying based on these terms and concepts.

Affection
Beliefs
Casual
Control
Conversation
Culture
Directive approach
Distant
Downward communication
Dyadic
Electronic interviews
Exchanging
Feelings
Formal
Global relationships
Information
Interactional
Internet
Interpersonal
Interview
Intimate
Involvement
Motivate
Motives
Nondirective approach
Parties
People
Predetermined purpose
Privacy
Problem solving
Process
Purpose
Questions
Relational
Relational dimensions
Relational distance
Relational history
Relationships
Safe
Sex
Similarity
Structure
System
Telephone
Trust
Upward communication
Videoconference

An Interview for Review and Analysis

Luis Martinez and Mary O'Reilly are neighbors in a historic neighborhood called Jefferson Hill near a large university campus. As an increasing number of students have chosen to live off campus and enrollments have far exceeded available residence hall capacity, developers have purchased large homes and either turned them into multiple apartments or demolished them to build apartment complexes. Noise, parking, traffic, trash, and vandalism have become problems. Luis and Mary are attempting to create a Jefferson Hill Neighborhood Association to maintain the historic, single-family nature of their area. They are talking to neighbors, and Sarah Hershberger, their contact this evening, is a single mother of two grade-school-age children who moved into the neighborhood approximately one year ago. Although the homes of Luis and Mary are only a block from Sarah, they have never met her. Their children do not play with one another. The interview is taking place at 6:00 p.m.

As you read this interview, think about answers to the following questions: Why is this an interview and not a small group discussion? How is this interaction fundamentally different from a speech or conversation? What is the approximate ratio of listening and speaking, and how appropriate is it? What is the predetermined purpose of this interview? When is it revealed? What roles do questions play? Assess the relationship between the parties by considering similarity, inclusion/involvement, affection, control, and trust. Is the relationship enhanced or lessened as the interview proceeds? How does lack of a "relational history" affect this interview?

1. **Luis:** Hi Sarah.
2. **Sarah:** Uh, hi.

3. **Luis:** We live around the corner on Hill Top Drive.
4. **Sarah:** Uh huh?
5. **Mary:** I'm Mary O'Reilly and this is Luis Martinez.
6. **Sarah:** Hi. I'm Sarah Hershberger. I don't think we've met.
7. **Mary:** No I don't think we have, though we've been wanting to meet our new neighbors.
8. **Luis:** How long have you lived in the neighborhood Sarah?
9. **Sarah:** Nearly a year, but I'm still trying to get unpacked. We're just about to sit down for dinner. What can I do for you?
10. **Luis:** It's really something we hope to be able to do together.
11. **Sarah:** Oh?
12. **Luis:** Since you've lived here only a short time and not during football season, you may not be aware of the problems we're having with large numbers of university students moving into the neighborhood. Apartment buildings pop up like mushrooms each June.
13. **Mary:** The neighborhood has changed a lot in the past few years.
14. **Sarah:** Well, it's been fairly quiet. I was concerned at first about traffic because of my two children, but there have been no major problems.
15. **Mary:** Wait until August and nearly 75,000 fans show up for the first football game. It can be a madhouse around here with a lot of drinking.
16. **Luis:** Mary and I are trying to organize a Jefferson Hill Neighborhood Association that would fight to maintain the historic, single-family nature of the area. We are afraid both are rapidly disappearing.
17. **Sarah:** Is a formal association necessary? I've actually enjoyed many of the students, and they've helped me with the yard and babysitting.
18. **Mary:** We feel very strongly that it is way past due.
19. **Luis:** It certainly is. If we don't organize now, it will soon be too late.
20. **Sarah:** What's this association supposed to do? I don't want to be seen as antistudent and, frankly, some of my neighbors are less neighborly than the students.
21. **Luis:** Well, for starters, we would like to have Jefferson Hill rezoned for single-family dwellings only. This would stop developers from turning homes into apartments or tearing them down for apartments.
22. **Sarah:** I see. (pause) I must admit that I've thought about renting a room or two to college students. I'm a single mother and need the income.
23. **Mary:** That's how it started! A few residents rented rooms, then apartments, and finally whole homes. It was a slippery slope that started with one room.
24. **Sarah:** I don't think I'm going to run down the neighborhood by renting a room, and some of us do not have the income of well-established faculty and staff.

25. **Luis:** We understand that and want young families to move into the neighborhood. We're not as concerned about live-in owners as we are about landlords who live miles away, many in big cities.
26. **Mary:** Could we count on you to come to a neighborhood meeting to discuss the association and its concerns?
27. **Sarah:** Maybe, but you may not like to hear what I have to say, and I'm not a joiner of causes.
28. **Mary:** None of us are joiners; that's been part of the problem. Our homes and lifestyle are at stake.
29. **Luis:** We would really value your input.
30. **Sarah:** Well, I'll think about it. My children are waiting for dinner.
31. **Mary:** Don't think too long.
32. **Luis:** If you have any questions, you can call me at 235-2000.
33. **Mary:** And you can reach me at 235-4555. It was good to meet you and welcome to Jefferson Hill.
34. **Sarah:** Thanks.

Student Activities

1. Keep a journal of interviews you take part in during a week. Note their length, size of the parties involved, the roles you played, and the purpose of each interview. What surprised you about your participation in interviews during a single week?
2. Select another person (roommate, friend, classmate, family member, co-worker) who is willing to interview you and be interviewed by you. Take part in two five-minute interviews to discover everything you can about one another. What did you learn that was new? What assumptions proved faulty? What proportion of time did you spend speaking and listening? How were the interviews like and unlike social conversations? What roles did your relationship play?
3. Make a list of what you consider to be the essential characteristics of good interviews, and then observe two interviews on television. How well did each interview meet your criteria? What should each party have done differently to improve the interviews? What influences did these interviews have on what you consider to be essential criteria? What influences did relationships between interviewers (Oprah Winfrey, Larry King, Barbara Walters) and interviewees (George W. Bush, Julia Roberts, Bill Gates) have on your assessment?
4. Take part in three 10-minute interviews: one face-to-face, one over the telephone, and one over the Internet. Make note of their characteristics. What were the similarities and differences? Which similarities and differences were due to interview type: face-to-face, ear-to-ear, and finger-to-finger? How did interactions vary? What problems resulted from lack of presence, eye contact, appearance, facial expression, gestures, voice? How did you and the other party compensate for these?

Notes

1. John Stewart, ed., *Bridges Not Walls,* 7th ed. (New York: McGraw-Hill, 1999), p. 21.
2. Stewart, p. 20.
3. Sarah Trenholm and Arthur Jensen, *Interpersonal Communication* (New York: Oxford, 2004), p. 9.
4. Michael T. Motley, "Communication as Interaction: A Reply to Beach and Bavelas," *Western Journal of Speech Communication* 54 (Fall 1990), pp. 613–623.
5. Trenholm and Jensen (2004), p. 16.
6. Judith H. Martin and Thomas K. Nakayama, *Intercultural Communication in Contexts* (New York: McGraw-Hill, 2004), p. 336.
7. Trenholm and Jensen, p. 104.
8. Martin and Nakayama, p. 335.
9. Stewart, p. 161.
10. John Stewart and Carole Logan, *Together: Communicating Interpersonally* (New York: McGraw-Hill, 1998), p. 277.
11. Stephen W. Littlejohn, *Theories of Human Communication* (Belmont, CA: Wadsworth, 1996), p. 251.
12. Trenholm and Jensen (2004), p. 33.
13. Trenholm and Jensen, *Interpersonal Communication* (Belmont, CA: Wadsworth, 1996), p. 44.
14. Martin and Nakayama, p. 345.
15. Trenholm and Jensen (2004), p. 29.
16. James Honeycutt in Trenholm and Jensen (2004), p. 30.
17. Stewart, p. 17.
18. Stewart, p. 18.
19. John Stewart, *Bridges Not Walls: A Book about Interpersonal Communication,* 8th ed. (New York: McGraw-Hill, 2002), p. 18.
20. R. Fisher and S. Brown in Judith N. Martin, Thomas K. Nakayama, and Lisa A. Flores, *Intercultural Communication: Experiences and Contexts* (New York: McGraw-Hill, 2002), p. 334.
21. William B. Gudykunst and Young Yun Kim, *Communication with Strangers* (New York: McGraw-Hill, 2003), p. 339.
22. Martin, Nakayama, and Flores, p. 334.
23. Donald W. Klopf, *Intercultural Encounters* (Englewood, CO: Morton, 1998), pp. 176–193; Carley H. Dodd, *Dynamics of Intercultural Communication* (New York: McGraw-Hill, 1995), pp. 21–24; Martin and Nakayama, p. 343.
24. Martin and Nakayama, p. 340.
25. Stewart and Logan, p. 84.

26. Trenholm and Jensen (2000), pp. 100–101.

27. Theresa F. Rogers, "Interviews by Telephone and in Person: Quality of Responses and Field Performance," *Public Opinion Quarterly* 39 (1976), pp. 51–65; Stephen Kegeles, Clifton F. Frank, and John P. Kirscht, "Interviewing a National Sample by Long-Distance Telephone," *Public Opinion Quarterly* 33 (1969–1970), pp. 412–419.

28. Lawrence A. Jordan, Alfred C. Marcus, and Leo G. Reeder, "Response Style in Telephone and Household Interviewing," *Public Opinion Quarterly* 44 (1980), pp. 210–222; Peter V. Miller and Charles F. Cannell, "A Study of Experimental Techniques in Telephone Interviewing," *Public Opinion Quarterly* 46 (1982), pp. 250–269.

29. Derek S. Chapman and Patricia M. Rowe, "The Impact of Videoconference Technology, Interview Structure, and Interviewer Gender on Interviewer Evaluations in the Employment Interview: A Field Experiment," *Journal of Occupational and Organizational Psychology* (2001), p. 279.

30. Chapman and Rowe, pp. 279–298.

31. Carole Martin, "Smile, You're on Camera," Interview Center, http://www.interview.monster.com/articles/video, accessed 30 September 2006.

32. Derek S. Chapman and Patricia M. Rowe, "The Influence of Video Conference Technology and Interview Structure on the Recruiting Function of the Employment Interview: A Field Experiment," *International Journal of Selection and Assessment* (September 2002), p. 185.

Resources

Guerro, Laura K., Peter A. Andersen, and Walid A. Afifi. *Close Encounters: Communicating in Relationships.* New York: McGraw-Hill, 2001.

Lancaster, Lynne C., and David Stillman. *When Generations Collide*. New York: HarperBusiness, 2002.

Martin, Judith N., Thomas K. Nakayama, and Lisa A. Flores. *Intercultural Communication Experiences and Contexts.* New York: McGraw-Hill, 2004.

Monsour, Michael. *Women and Men as Friends: Relationships across the Life Span in the 21st Century.* Mahwah, NJ: Lawrence Erlbaum, 2002.

Stewart, John. *Bridges Not Walls: A Book about Interpersonal Communication.* New York: McGraw-Hill, 2006.

Trenholm, Sarah, and Arthur Jensen. *Interpersonal Communication.* New York: Oxford, 2004.

CHAPTER 2 An Interpersonal Communication Process

Interviewing is more than asking and answering questions.

Every interview is a **deceptively complex communication process.** If you are to be a successful interviewer or interviewee, you must understand and appreciate the entire process, not merely the questions and answers that are its most obvious characteristics. This chapter delves into this complex and often puzzling process by developing part-by-part a model that portrays its many elements and interactive nature.

Two Parties in the Interview

Each party consists of unique and complex individuals.

The two circles in Figure 2.1, represent the two parties that are the heart and soul of the interviewing process. Each is a unique product of culture, environment, education, training, and experiences. Each is an interesting mixture of personality traits. For instance, a person may be optimistic or pessimistic, trusting or suspicious, flexible or inflexible, sociable or unsociable. And each adheres to specific beliefs, attitudes, and values and is motivated by an ever-changing variety of expectations, desires, needs, and interests. In a very real sense, the whole person speaks and the whole person listens in interactions we call interviews.[1]

Although each party consists of unique individuals, both must act together to produce a successful interview because, as John Stewart writes, Communication is a continuous, complex, collaborative process.[2] Neither party can **go it alone** in an interview.

Interchanging Roles during Interviews

A single party cannot make an interview a success but can ensure its failure.

Interview climate affects the exchanging of roles.

Both parties speak and listen from time to time, are likely to ask and answer questions, and take on the roles and responsibilities of interviewer and interviewee. Neither party can sit back and expect the other to make the interview a success single-handedly. Some claim that "human communicators are always sending and receiving simultaneously. As a result, each communicator has the opportunity to change how things are going at any time in the process."[3] The small circles within the party circles in Figure 2.2 portray the interchange of roles in interviews. John Stewart's "nexting" consists of the verbal and nonverbal signals parties send to "keep conversations going, responding to what's just happened, taking an additional step in the communication process."[4]

The degree to which roles are exchanged and control is shared is often affected by the status or expertise of the parties who initiated the interview, type of interview, and atmosphere of the interaction—supportive or defensive, friendly or hostile,

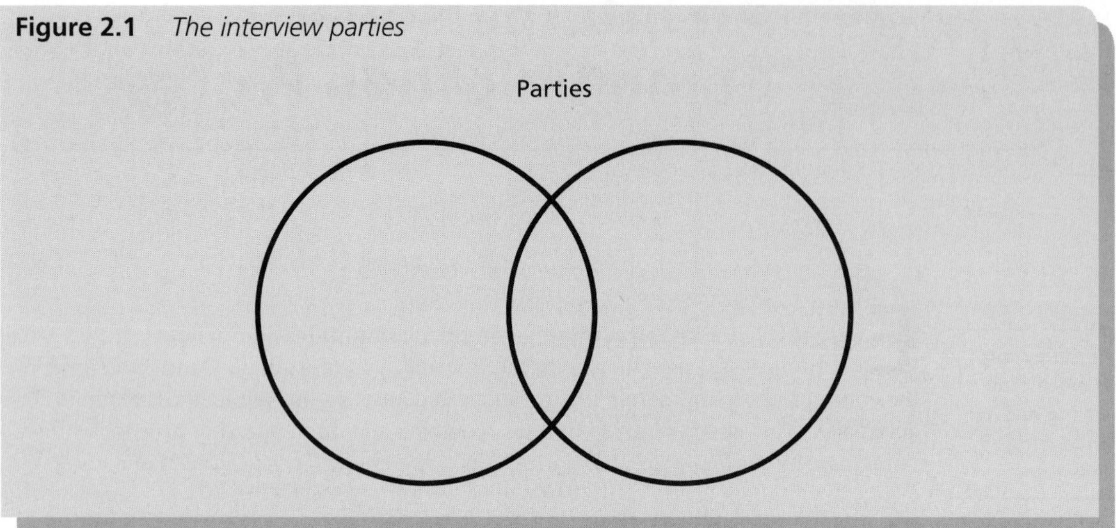

Figure 2.1 *The interview parties*

A directive approach allows the interviewer to maintain control.

warm or cool, formal or informal. These factors determine which of two fundamental approaches an interviewer selects—**directive** or **nondirective**—and this choice affects the exchanging of interviewer and interviewee roles.

Directive Approach

When selecting a directive approach, an **interviewer** establishes the purpose of the interview and attempts to control the pacing, climate, formality, and drift of the interview. Questions are likely to be closed with brief, direct answers. Although an aggressive

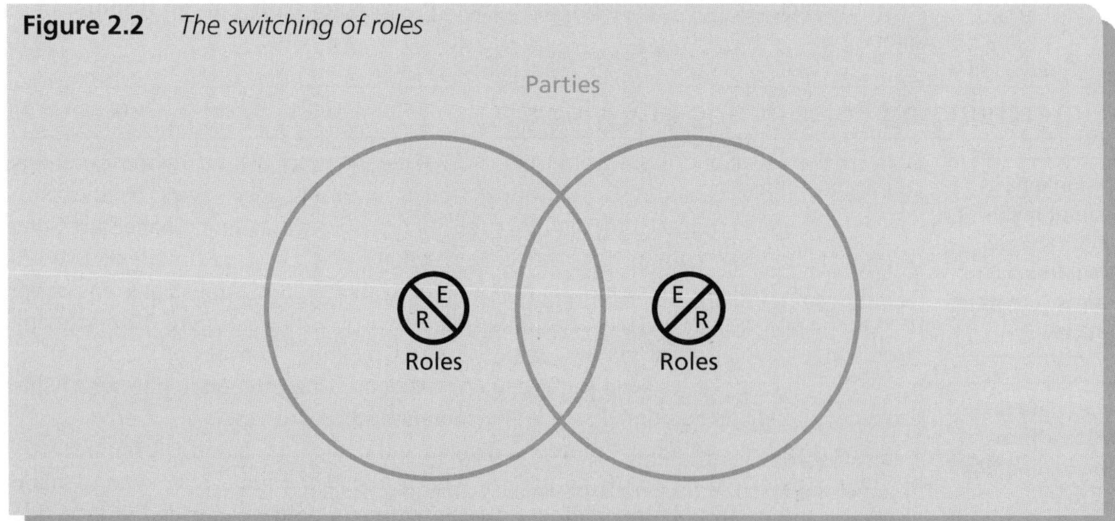

Figure 2.2 *The switching of roles*

interviewee may assume some control as the interview progresses, the interviewer intends to control the interview. Typical directive interviews include information giving, information gathering (surveys and opinion polls), employee recruiting, and disciplinary and persuasive interviews (particularly sales). The directive approach is easy to learn, takes less time, enables you to maintain control, and is easy to replicate from one interview to the next.

The following exchange illustrates a directive interviewing approach:

1. **Interviewer:** Were you at the Vice President's briefing yesterday?
2. **Interviewee:** Yes, I was. It was well attended.
3. **Interviewer:** What was her primary focus?
4. **Interviewee:** Diversity issues.
5. **Interviewer:** Good. I want you to summarize these and forward them to our campus recruiters.

Nondirective Approach

A nondirective approach enables the interviewee to share control.

In a nondirective approach, **interviewees** have significant control over subject matter, length of answers, interview climate, and formality. Questions are likely to be open-ended and neutral to give the interviewee maximum opportunity and freedom to respond. Typical nondirective interviews are information getting (journalistic, oral history, investigations), counseling, performance review, and problem solving. The nondirective approach allows for greater flexibility and adaptability, encourages probing questions, and invites the interviewee to volunteer information.

The following is a nondirective interview exchange:

1. **Interviewer:** Why are you interested in studying medicine?
2. **Interviewee:** I've always been interested in medicine and spent the last few summers working at clinics in my hometown. These experiences made me certain that I want to pursue a medical career.
3. **Interviewer:** I see.
4. **Interviewee:** My grandfather was a medic during World War II, and my aunt Ruth was an Army nurse during the Vietnam War. I've really enjoyed talking to them about their experiences.

Combination of Approaches

Interviewers may select a combination of directive and nondirective approaches. For instance, an academic counselor might use a nondirective approach to get a student talking about recurring academic issues and then change to a directive approach when referring to university regulations pertaining to incompletes or dropping courses. A recruiter may use a nondirective approach at the start of an interview to relax an applicant, then switch to a directive approach when giving information about the organization and position, and return to a nondirective approach when answering the applicant's questions.

Be flexible and adaptable when selecting approaches.

The roles we play should guide but not dictate approaches.

Be flexible in determining when an approach is most appropriate and when to switch from one approach to another or use a combination. Too often the choice of an interviewing approach is governed by societal roles and expectations. We tend to behave as prescribed by the roles we play in life. For instance, an employee, applicant, client, or patient "enters an interview expecting that the interviewer will direct and influence one's conversational behaviors much more extensively than one will influence the interviewer's behavior. We both make it happen that way."[5] Unfortunately, adherence to societal roles and expectations may not produce a productive interview.

Perceptions of Interviewer and Interviewee

Each party comes to an interview with perceptions of self and of the other party, and these perceptions may change positively or negatively as the interview progresses. Theorists claim that our relationships are largely due to these perceptions and determine how we communicate. Be aware of four critical perceptions portrayed by the double-ended arrows in Figure 2.3.

Four perceptions drive most of our interactions.

- Self-perceptions.
- Perceptions of the other party.
- How the other party perceives us.
- How the other party perceives self.

Perceptions of Self

Your self-perceptions, or **self-concept,** come from your physical, social, and psychological perceptions derived from your experiences, activities, attitudes, accomplishments, possessions, and interactions with others, particularly your superior and subordinate

Figure 2.3 *Perceptions of self and others*

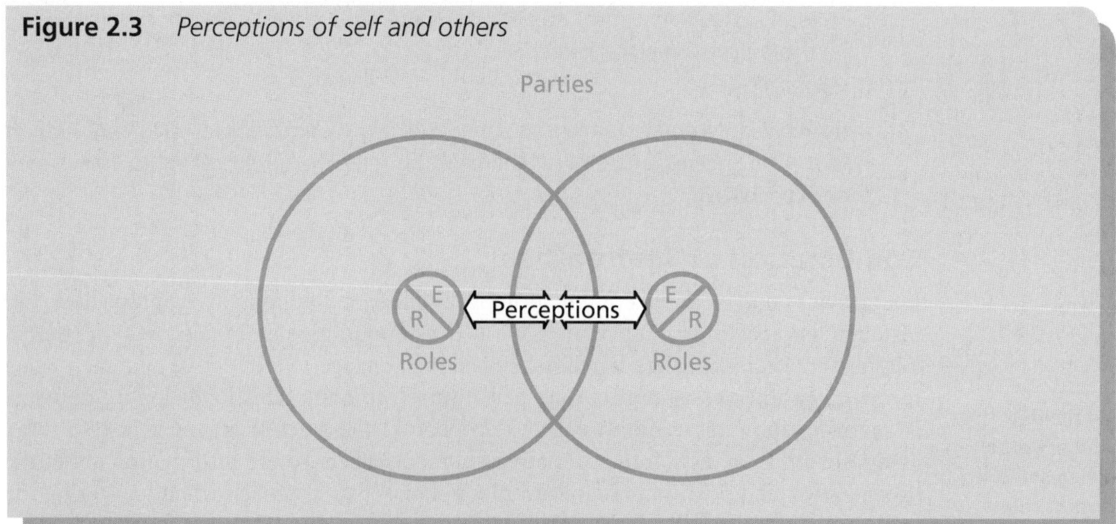

What we perceive ourselves to be may be more important than what we are.

roles and relationships. Self-concept is a dual creation of interpretations and how you perceive others to have interpreted who you have been, are, and will be—**self-identity.** These others include groups to which you belong or desire to belong and so-called significant others.

Your self-concept and self-identity are affected by the expectations family, society, professions, and organizations place upon you. You may experience different self-concepts as you move from one situation or role to another, from a situation in which you feel comfortable and in charge to one in which you feel inexperienced, inept, or fearful.

We see ourselves differently under different circumstances.

Self-esteem, the "positive or negative feelings we associate with our self-images," is an important element of self-concept. Trenholm and Jensen claim that a person with high self-esteem is more perceptive, confident, and likely to express attitudes that are popular or unpopular. Persons with low self-esteem may want the approval of others but are so self-critical that they cannot interpret accurately the behavior and communication of others.[6] You must understand how you perceive yourself and how other parties perceive themselves, because self-concept (particularly self-esteem) may determine whether an interview takes place and its ultimate success or failure. You may succeed or fail in an interview because you are convinced you will—a **self-fulfilling prophecy.** Self-perceptions influence messages sent and received, risks taken, confidence, and degree of self-disclosure.

Self-esteem is closely related to self-worth.

Cultural Differences

Many citizens of the global village are less concerned with self than with group.

Concepts such as self-image, self-identity, self-esteem, self-reliance, and self-awareness are central in American and Western cultures because we emphasize the individual. They are not central in Eastern cultures and South American countries. Japanese, Chinese, and Indians, for example, are collectivist rather than individualist cultures and are more concerned with the image, esteem, and achievement of the group. Attributing successful negotiations to an individual in China would be considered egotistical, self-advancing, and disrespectful. Success is attributed to the group or team. Failure to appreciate cultural differences causes many communication problems for American interviewers and interviewees.

Perceptions of the Other Party

Perceptions are a two-way process.

How each party perceives the other also affects how they approach the interview and how they react during the interview. For instance, you may be in awe of the other's reputation or position—a leading biochemist, the CEO of your company, the college president. Previous encounters with a party may lead you to look forward to or dread an interview. Your **perceptions** may be influenced by the other's age, sex, race, ethnic group, size, and physical attractiveness—particularly if they differ significantly from you. A positive endorsement of a third party may alter the way you perceive a person. If you are flexible and adaptable, perceptions of the other party may change as an interview progresses by:

Allow interactions to alter or reinforce perceptions.

- The way an interview begins or ends.
- The other party's manner and attitudes.
- The other party's dress and appearance.

- The other party's listening and feedback.
- Verbal and nonverbal interactions.
- Questions asked and answers given.

The nature of interview exchanges may enhance perceptions. For instance, perceptions become positive when questions are followed by information requested rather than refusals or evasions, when requests are followed by discussion or agreement rather than demands followed by compliance, and when constructive criticism is followed by understanding rather than by fear or resentment.

Communication Interactions

The curved arrows in Figure 2.4 that link the two parties symbolize the communication levels of verbal and nonverbal interactions that occur during interviews. The three numbered levels differ in degree of self-disclosure, risk encountered, perceived meanings, and amount and type of content exchanged.

Level 1 interactions avoid judgments, attitudes, and feelings.

Levels of Interactions

Level 1 interactions are relatively safe, nonthreatening interchanges about such topics as hometowns, professions, sporting events, college courses, and families. They

Figure 2.4 *Communication interactions*

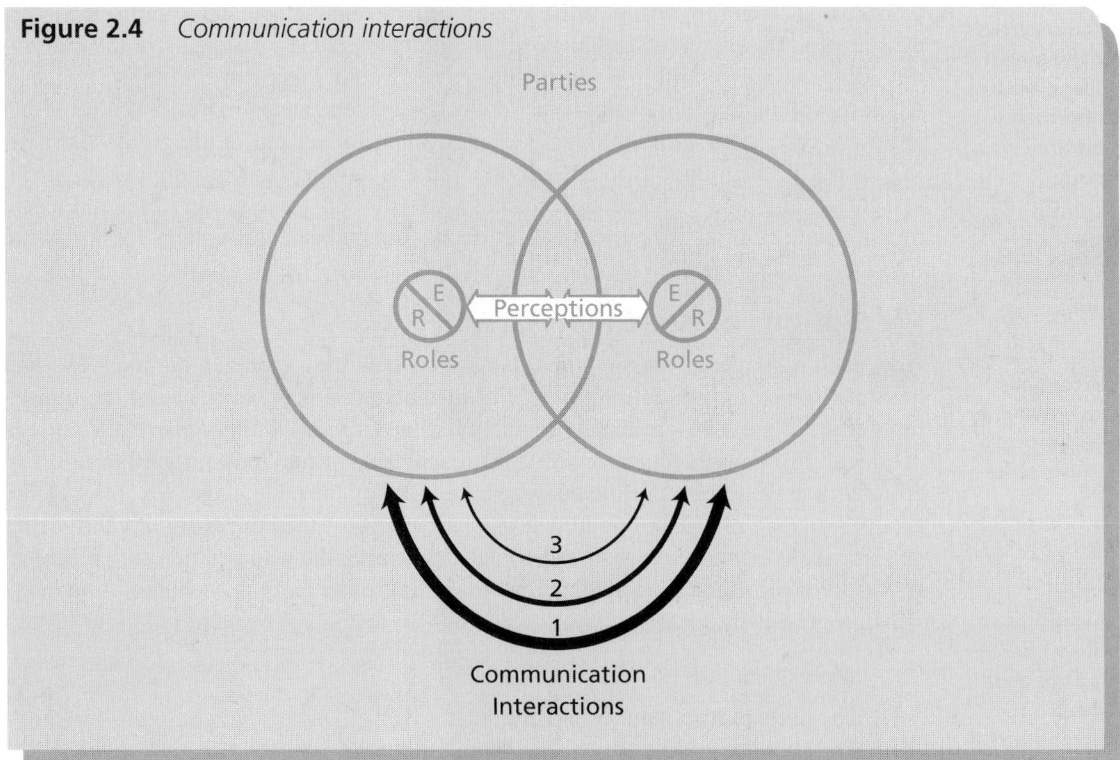

generate answers that are safe, socially acceptable, comfortable, and ambiguous. When we respond with phrases such as "Pretty good," "Not bad," and "Can't complain," they are indicative of Level 1 interactions that do not reveal judgments, attitudes, or feelings.

Level 1 interactions are safe and superficial.

Each level is a metaphorical door, with the door being slightly open in Level 1 interactions. General ideas, surface feelings, and basic information pass through, but either party may close the door quickly and safely if necessary. The thickness of the arrow indicates that Level 1 communication interchanges are most frequent in interviews, and the length of the arrow symbolizes **relational distance.** Level 1 interactions dominate interactions when there is little relational history, trust has yet to be established, and the role relationship is between a superior and a subordinate. This interview segment illustrates Level 1 interactions.

1. **Interviewer:** How is your advertising class coming along?
2. **Interviewee:** Pretty good.
3. **Interviewer:** And the advertising campaign project?
4. **Interviewee:** It's coming along.

Notice how parties play it safe during these interchanges. The topics are not threatening, and neither party reveals feelings or attitudes.

Level 2 interactions require trust and risk-taking.

Level 2 interactions deal with personal, controversial, or threatening topics and probe into beliefs, attitudes, values, and positions. Responses tend to be half-safe, half-revealing as parties seek to cooperate without revealing too much. The metaphorical door is half open (the optimist's view) or half closed (the pessimist's view) as more specific and revealing ideas, feelings, and information pass through. Though willing to take more risk, parties retain the opportunity to close the door quickly. The thickness of the arrow signifies that Level 2 interactions are less frequent than Level 1, and the length of the arrow indicates that a closer relationship between parties is necessary to move from the superficial to the more revealing exchanges. This interview segment illustrates Level 2 interactions.

1. **Interviewer:** What are you doing for the campaign project?
2. **Interviewee:** I'm thinking about a campaign for ethanol as an alternative fuel.
3. **Interviewer:** That sounds interesting. Have you decided on a brand name?
4. **Interviewee:** No, not really. I'm still researching some Web sites.

The interviewee, though cautious, is more specific and revealing.

Level 3 interactions involve full disclosure.

Level 3 interactions deal with intimate and controversial areas of inquiry. Respondents fully disclose their feelings, beliefs, attitudes, and perceptions. Little is withheld, and sometimes questioners get more than they bargained for. The metaphorical door is wide open. The risk is great to both parties, but so are the benefits. The arrow is thin to indicate that Level 3 interactions are infrequent in interviews and may be unattainable during first contacts. The arrow is short because the relationship between parties must be due to perceived similarities, desire to be included and involved, feelings of warmth or friendship, sharing of control, and a high level of trust. This interview segment illustrates Level 3 interactions.

A positive relationship is essential for Level 3 interactions.

1. **Interviewer:** Your brother tells me that you are not excited about this advertising campaign project.
2. **Interviewee:** That's true. I feel that, on top of the group projects, exams, and campaign case studies, this is too much to expect in a three-hour course.
3. **Interviewer:** I can understand your concern, but isn't an advertising campaign project critical to your future career in advertising?
4. **Interviewee:** Yeah, I guess so, but it's the amount of time involved, and it only counts for 20 percent of our final grade. I'm not sure how the professor is going to grade the projects or give us meaningful feedback. It just seems like a lot of busy work.

We are on the line in many interview settings.

Relationships, perceptions, responses, and the **situation** make communication levels unpredictable and difficult to change. It is essential in most interviews, however, to get beyond Level 1 to Level 2 or Level 3 to obtain information, detect feelings, attain self-disclosure, discover insights, and achieve necessary commitments. Unlike small groups or audiences into which we can blend or hide, the intimate, interpersonal nature of the interview is often threatening because it places our egos and sometimes our social, financial, professional, psychological, or physical welfare on the line. Interviews deal with *our* behavior, *our* performance, *our* reputation, *our* decisions, *our* weaknesses, *our* feelings, *our* money, or *our* future. Stewart and Logan address the risks of self-disclosing:

> When you choose to make some of your personal self available to someone else, you give that person some options or choices that you cannot completely control. The person may dislike the you that he or she comes to know. You may be ridiculed for your thoughts and feelings. Or the other person may tell someone else something you don't want known. You may feel embarrassed, hurt, angry, or something even worse.[7]

Sex, Culture, and Interactions

Women disclose more freely than men.

Sex and **culture** of interview participants may influence the levels of **communication interactions** and the **self-disclosure** that takes place during an interview.

Sex

Women tend to disclose more than men and, except for anger, are allowed to express emotions (fear, sadness, sympathy) more than men. Because women are perceived to be better listeners and more responsive than men, disclosure is highest between woman-to-woman parties, next highest between woman-to-man parties, and lowest among man-to-man parties.[8]

Culture

The culture of interview parties may determine what is disclosed to whom and how. For example, Americans of European descent may disclose about a wider range of topics than Japanese and Chinese, disclose more about their careers and less about their families than Ghanians, and disclose to more different types of people than Asians. Asians tend to disclose more to those with expertise and ability to exhibit honest and

Culture may dictate what we disclose and to whom.

positive attitudes than to those who like to talk and show more emotional feelings. Research suggests that people in high-context, collectivist cultures, such as Japan and China, in which they are expected to work for the good of the group and to know and follow cultural norms, disclose less than those in low-context, individualist cultures, such as the United States and Great Britain, in which they strive to succeed as individuals and cultural norms are less well known and more flexible. Conflict may result if we overdisclose, underdisclose, or disclose to the wrong person in differing cultures.

While cultures vary in how, when, and to whom self-disclosure is appropriate, some theorists claim that the notion of politeness—maintaining positive rather than negative face—is universal. According to **"politeness theory,"** all humans want to be appreciated and protected. Littlejohn writes:

Positive and negative face are universal motives.

> *Positive face* is the desire to be appreciated and approved, to be liked and honored, and *positive politeness* is designed to meet these desires. Showing concern, complimenting, and using respectful forms of address are examples. *Negative face* is the desire to be free from imposition or intrusion, and *negative politeness* is designed to protect the other person when negative face needs are threatened. Acknowledging the imposition when making a request is a common example.[9]

We encounter situations in which politeness is essential not only when dealing with persons from other cultures but whenever we are involved in challenging, complaining, evaluating, disciplining, advising, and counseling. Guerrero, Andersen, and Afifi write that "people face a constant struggle between wanting to do whatever they want (which satisfies their negative face needs) and wanting to do what makes them look good to others (which satisfies their positive face needs)."[10] They identify several severe "face threatening acts," such as behavior that violates an important cultural, social, or professional rule (missing an anniversary date or failure to follow the chain-of-command); behavior that produces significant harm (damaged relationship or lost income); behavior for which the party is directly responsible (an accident or poor hiring decision); and the more power or authority the other party has over the offending party (professor, supervisor, or military officer).

Verbal Interactions

Communication interactions in interviews are intricate and inseparable combinations of verbal and nonverbal symbols, some intentional and some not. Although inseparable on many occasions, we will separate them in this chapter for instructional purposes only.

Never assume communication is taking place.

Verbal interactions, words, are merely arbitrary connections of letters that serve as symbols for people, animals, things, places, events, ideas, beliefs, and feelings. Their imperfect nature is brought home to us nearly every day in misunderstandings, confusions, embarrassments, antagonisms, and hurt feelings over what we assume to be perfectly clear, common, and neutral words. Perhaps *the greatest single problem with human communication is the assumption of it.* Journalism professor Michael Skube has written about the lack of familiarity many college students have with what he has *assumed* to be commonly understood words. These include impetus, lucid, advocate, derelict, and brevity.[11]

I'm sure we've all thought that if others would use words properly, we would have few communication breakdowns. In fact, the arbitrary nature of language, not improper use, causes most problems.

Multiple Meanings

A word rarely has a single meaning.

Simple words have many meanings. Those for *argue* range from giving reasons or evidence to disagreeing in words and persuading. *Game* may refer to a basketball game, a wild animal, or a person willing to try new things. To *reveal* may mean to tell, disclose, make known through divine inspiration, or violate a confidence.

Ambiguities

Words may be so ambiguous that any two parties may assign very different meanings to them. What are a "nice" apartment, an "affordable" education, a "simple" set of instructions, a "small" college, and a "living wage"? When is a person "young," "middle-aged," or "old"? How do we know that something is "one of the best" or "one of the rarest"? Have you ever met a U.S. citizen who was not "middle class" regardless of income?

Sound Alikes

Beware of words that sound alike.

Similar sounding words may lead to confusion in interviews because we usually only hear, not see, words. Examples include see and sea, do and due, sail and sale, and to, too, and two. We have been startled by words only to realize later that we had misinterpreted what was meant. Pronunciation or enunciation may add to this problem. A banker in Los Angeles related an incident in which she was talking to a banking associate in Chicago and thought she heard the other say, "We're axing John." The associate had meant "asking John."

Connotations

Words are rarely neutral.

Many words have positive and negative connotations. We can describe an interview suit as "expensive" or "cheap," an older car as "used" or "preowned," or the purchase of a painting as a "cost" or an "investment." Chapters 10 and 11 address the persuasive interview, but the word *persuasion* has many negative and positive meanings:

Negative Meanings	Positive Meanings
incite	inspire
contrive	lead
pressure	motivate
sway	convince
cajole	assure
induce	sell

Not many years ago a professor in a large communication department attempted to *persuade* his colleagues that it was unethical to teach a course in *persuasion* without apparently seeing the incongruity of his impassioned persuasive appeal.

Jargon

You may create communication problems by altering or creating words. For instance, every profession has its own specialized jargon. "Vehicular control devices" are stoplights. "Spin doctoring" is explaining or defending issues. "Dyads" are interviews. An "invasive procedure" is surgery. A hammer, according to the military, is a "manually powered fastener-driving impact device." Try to use the simplest, clearest, most appropriate words in each situation and for each interview party. Be aware of your own personal, cultural, or professional jargon. A few days before the huge gathering in Times Square on New Year's Eve, an organizer was demonstrating to a reporter how to throw confetti most effectively from a window high above the Square. He remarked that the 150 staff members who would toss confetti from several buildings at midnight were "confetti dispersal engineers."

Slang

Slang comes and goes and often determines who's in and who's out.

Each generation has a kind of unofficial jargon we call *slang.* Fast, powerful cars went from "keen" and "neat" in the 1940s and 1950s, to "hot," "cool," "groovy," and "far out" in the 1960s and 1970s, to "decent," "tough," and "mean" in the 1980s, to "awesome," "way cool," "outrageous," and "white hot" in the 1990s. In the twenty-first century, these cars are "rockin'," "slammin'," "jammin'," "poppin'," and "kickin'." Using slang properly places us in the in-group, and we may ridicule those who do not understand us or use the slang incorrectly.

Euphemisms

We substitute better sounding words for common ones. We're likely to see a lifelike Christmas tree advertised rather than an artificial one. A person may inquire about the location of the "powder room" or facility rather than the toilet. We purchase appliances from "sales associates" rather than clerks, and we don't experience "pain" from an "invasive procedure," only "discomfort."

Naming

Naming is an effort to alter social reality.

We label people, places, and things not merely to make them sound better but to alter reality. We rarely experience recessions, only "downturns" and "market adjustments." We purchase diet soft drinks, but would we order a round of "diet beers" rather than "lite beers"? McDonald's and other hamburger makers know we are more likely to order a "quarter-pounder" than a "four-ouncer." Names are important. When we substitute woman for girl, flight attendant for stewardess, or firefighter for fireman, we are not being "politically correct" but are attempting to affect perceptions of reality. "Girls" and "boys" do not work as engineers, physicians, teachers, firefighters, and managers; women and men do. Clearly words matter to us and to others and they may alter or reinforce our visions of reality.

Hear what you are about to say before saying it.

Ordering Words

How we order words in a sentence can communicate different messages, lead to confusion, or provoke laughter. Strange headlines or statements may embarrass one party and provide humor for another. Here are a few examples:

For anyone who has children and doesn't know it, there is a day care on the first floor.
Study: Dead patients usually not saved.

Sign in a safari park: Elephants please stay in your cars.

Toilet out of order. Please use floor below.

Think before selecting words and placing them in sentences. Order matters.

Power Words

Words may be powerful or not.

There are power and powerless speech forms.[12] Power word forms include certainty, challenges, orders, verbal aggression, leading questions, metaphors, and memorable phrases such as "Read my lips!" "Make my day!" "Take your best shot!" "Live with it!" "Let's roll!" and "Get a life!" Powerless forms include apologies, disclaimers, excuses, indirect questions, and nonfluencies such as "Uh," and "Umm." "Know what I mean" and "You know" have become all too common in our everyday and professional communications and seem to dominate many broadcast interviews. They are powerless, meaningless distractions that communicate the inability of a party to articulate thoughts and sentences. Few people are impressed with opening phrases such as "I didn't mean to . . . ," "It's not my fault that . . . ," and "Do you think maybe . . . ?"

Regional and Role Differences

We assume all Americans speak "English," but there are regional and role differences. People in New Jersey go to the "shore," while those in California go to the "beach." A person in New England is likely to ask for a "soda," a person in New York may order "pop," while a person in the Midwest is likely to ask for a "coke." A government "entitlement" program such as Social Security has different meanings for 24-year-old and 64-year-old interview parties. Employees and management view "downsizing" and "outsourcing" very differently.

Gender Differences

Gender differences may lead to power differences.

Studies of gender and communication have noted a variety of differences in language use among men and women. For example, men tend to be socialized into developing and using power speech forms and to dominate interactions, while women tend to be socialized into developing powerless speech forms and to foster relationships and exchanges during interactions. Research indicates that women's talk is more polite and expressive, contains more qualifiers and disclaimers, makes more color distinctions, includes fewer mechanical and technical terms, and is more tentative than men's talk.[13] Men not only can use more intense language than women, but they are often expected to do so because it is considered masculine. If a woman uses the same language, she may be termed bitchy, pushy, or opinionated or accused of trying to be a man. Speaking styles, ingrained in us since childhood, explain why many women find it difficult to operate equally and effectively in a male-dominated society.

Stereotypes are dangerous assumptions.

Be cautious when stereotyping language and interaction differences among genders. Julia Wood writes that "despite jokes about women's talkativeness, research indicates that in most contexts, men not only hold their own but dominate the conversation."[14] In addition, men tend to interrupt women more than other men and do so to state opinions; women tend to interrupt to ask questions. Recent studies also indicate, however, that both men and women use tentative forms of speech in specific contexts and with a variety of people to facilitate communication.

Global Differences

Global use of words may be more significant than foreign words.

Language differences are magnified in the global village, even when parties are speaking the same language. North Americans tend to value precision, directness, explicit words, power speech forms, and use of "I" to begin sentences. We value tough or straight talk.[15] Other cultures value the group or collective rather than the individual and rarely begin with "I" or call attention to themselves. Chinese children are taught to downplay self-expression. Japanese tend to be implicit rather than explicit and employ ambiguous words and qualifiers. Koreans prefer not to give negative or "no" responses but to imply disagreements to maintain group harmony. And Arab-speaking peoples tend to employ what is referred to as "sweet talk" or accommodating language with elaborate metaphors and similes.

Guidelines for Reducing Language Problems

Famous linguist Irving Lee wrote years ago that we often "talk past" one another instead of with one another.[16] There are guidelines for enhancing effective use of language during interviews.

Language problems are avoidable.

- Choose words and phrases carefully.
- Expand your vocabulary.
- Be aware that slight changes in words can alter meanings.
- Order words carefully in sentences and thoughts.
- Listen to the context in which words are used.
- Learn the jargon of professions and groups.
- Keep up to date with changing uses of language.
- Know how the meaning of words may be affected by sex, age, race, culture, ethnic group, and situation.

Nonverbal Interactions

Nonverbal signals send many different messages.

The oral, face-to-face nature of the interview means that successful communication relies heavily upon nonverbal signals such as physical appearance, dress, eye contact, voice, touches, head nods, pauses, handshakes, winks, glances, silence, posture, and proximity of the two parties. Nonverbal communication is important because both parties are likely to detect what the other does and does not do. Our facial expressions may be our most effective nonverbal channel.

The interactive nature of the interview depends upon nonverbal signals to regulate the flow of communication and turn taking. Research shows that we rely on nonverbal cues to express ourselves and interpret the expressions of others. Facial expressions and eye contact, for example, are primary means "to indicate whose turn it is to talk."[17] Research also indicates that nonverbal cues are often misread.

A single behavioral act may convey a message. Poor eye contact may tell the other party that we have something to hide, a limp handshake that we are timid, a serious facial expression that we are sincere, touching a hand or arm that we are sympathetic or understanding, or a puzzled expression that we are confused. Our speaking rate may communicate urgency (fast speed), the gravity of the situation (slow speed), lack of interest (fast speed), lack of preparation (slow speed), nervousness (fast speed and breathless voice), or indecision (halting voice). **Silence** may encourage the other to talk, signal that we are not in a hurry, express agreement with what is being said, and keep the other party talking, but it can also signal apathy, boredom, fear, or intimidation.[18]

Usually we send and receive messages with a combination of nonverbal acts that enhances the impact of the message. For instance, we may show interest by leaning forward, maintaining good eye contact, nodding our head, and having a serious facial expression. On the other hand, when we fidget, cross and uncross our arms and legs, sit rigid, look down, furrow our brows, and speak in a high-pitched voice, we may reveal a high level of anxiety, fear, or agitation. A drooping body, frowning, and slow speaking rate may reveal sadness or resignation to anticipated failure or discipline. Leaning backward, staring at the other party, raising an eyebrow, and shaking our head may signal disagreement, anger, or disgust. The way we shake hands and look the other in the eye may signal a degree of trust and trustworthiness. Body movements, gestures, and posture may show dynamism or lack of it. We indicate positions of power through physical appearance, spatial behavior, eye behavior, body movements, and touch.[19] Any behavioral act may be interpreted in a meaningful way by the other party. The message may be intentional or unintentional, accurate or inaccurate, but it will be interpreted.

Any behavioral act, or its absence, can convey a message.

Physical appearance and dress are particularly important during the first few minutes of interviews as the parties get to know and respect one another. This critical first impression often begins before words are exchanged. We respond more favorably to attractive persons who are neither too fat nor too thin, tall rather than short, shapely rather than unshapely, pretty and handsome rather than plain or ugly. Parties see attractive persons to be more poised, outgoing, interesting, and sociable. How we dress and prepare ourselves physically for an interview reveals how we view ourselves, the other party, the situation, and the nature and importance of the interview.

Nonverbal communication may be more important than words. Some research indicates that nonverbal actions exchange feelings and emotions more accurately; convey meanings and intentions relatively free of deception, distortion, and confusion; are more efficient; and are more suitable for suggesting or imparting ideas and emotions indirectly. Nonverbal behaviors are assumed to be more truthful than words and, if verbal and nonverbal messages conflict—sending mixed messages, we are likely to believe the nonverbal. *How* tends to dominate the *what.*

In mixed messages, the *how* may overcome the *what*.

Some theorists argue, however, that it is nearly impossible to isolate the verbal from the nonverbal because they are so intertwined during interviews. For example, the nonverbal may **complement** the verbal. Vocal stress may call attention to an important word (like underlining or italicizing in print):"I'm planning to change programs in *May*," "My *net* income last year was *slightly* over $52,000," or "I'm *not* thinking of leaving." We may complement words with a sincere tone of voice and deliberate speaking rate. A serious facial expression and direct eye contact may help words

Verbal and nonverbal messages are intricately intertwined.

communicate sympathy and understanding. The nonverbal accentuates and verifies our words. Nonverbal actions may **reinforce** verbal messages: a head nod while saying yes, a head shake while saying no. A nonverbal action may act as a **substitute** for words. We may point to a chair without saying, "Sit here," or smile to express recognition or friendship. Nonverbal substitutes, a kind of everyday sign language, may be more effective and less disruptive than words. Silence, for instance, can signal agreement or disagreement.

Sex

Women are more adept at nonverbal communication.

Gender differences often affect interviews because women seem to be more skilled at and rely more on nonverbal communication than do men. Research indicates, for instance, that facial expressions, pauses, and bodily gestures are more important in women's interactions than men's, perhaps because women are more expressive than men. Women tend to gaze more and are less uncomfortable when eye contact is broken. Men's lower-pitched voices are viewed as more credible and dynamic than women's higher-pitched voices. Female parties stand or sit closer than opposite-sex parties, and males maintain more distance than opposite-sex or female parties.

photo © Bob Daemmrich/The Image Works

Be aware of cultural differences in nonverbal communication.

Culture

Differing cultures share many nonverbal signals. For instance, around the world people nod their heads in agreement, shake their heads in disagreement, give thumbs down for disapproval, shake fists in anger, and clap hands to show approval. On the other hand, nonverbal communication differs significantly among cultures.

In the United States, black participants tend to maintain eye contact more when speaking than when listening. They give more nonverbal feedback when listening than whites. In general, black Americans are more animated and personal, while white Americans are more subdued. Black Americans tend to avoid eye contact with superiors out of respect, a trait that is often misinterpreted by white superiors who see lack of eye contact as a sign of disinterest, lack of confidence, or dishonesty. And black Americans tend to touch more and stand closer together when communicating than do white Americans.[20] John Stewart writes that silence is important in Apache culture and that Apache "ridicule 'the whiteman' because they talk so often, so loudly, and so much."[21]

On the global scene, Americans are taught to look others in the eye when speaking, while

Black and white Americans use different non-verbal signals.

Africans are taught to avoid eye contact when listening to others. An honest "look me in the eye" for a Westerner may express a lack of respect to an Asian. An American widens his or her eyes to show wonder or surprise, while the Chinese do so to express anger, the French to express disbelief, and Hispanics to show lack of understanding. Americans are taught to smile in response to a smile, but this is not so in Israel. Japanese are taught to mask negative feelings with smiles and laughter. Americans are taught to have little direct physical contact with others while communicating, but Mediterranean and Latin countries encourage direct contact. On a loudness scale of 1 to 10, with 10 being high, Arabs would be near 10, Americans would be near the middle, and Europeans would be near 1. Arabs perceive loudness as signs of strength nd sincerity and softness as signs of weakness and deviousness. Not surprisingly, many Americans and Europeans see Arabs as pushy and rude. A firm handshake is important in American society but signals nothing in Japan. Common gestures have a wide variety of meanings. A circular motion of a finger around an ear means crazy in many countries, while it signals "You have a telephone call" in the Netherlands. Fingers in a circle means okay in the United States but is an obscene gesture in Brazil. Thumbs up is a rude gesture in Australia and a simple okay or all's well in other countries. As intercultural contacts become increasingly common, it will become ever more critical to understand the interconnections between words and nonverbal actions and how these are interpreted by diverse people and cultures.

Be aware of the diversity of nonverbal messages in different parts of the world.

Feedback

Feedback is more immediate and pervasive in interviews, and meaningful feedback, sent and received, is essential to verify what is being communicated and how well it is being communicated. The large, double-ended arrow that links the top of the party circles in Figure 2.5 symbolizes the heavy stream of feedback between interview parties. Feedback is both verbal (questions and answers, arguments and counterarguments, agreements and disagreements, challenges and compliances) and nonverbal (facial expressions, gestures, raised eyebrows, eye contact, vocal utterances, and posture).

Be perceptive, sensitive, and receptive.

We detect feedback through **observing** and **listening.** Observe everything that does and does not take place during an interview, including the tone of the interaction, seating arrangement, and proximity of the parties.

- Does the other party move closer or farther away?
- Does the other person select a power position (seated behind a desk, standing over you) from which to conduct the interview?
- Does the opening conversational tone become more or less formal as the interview progresses?
- Does eye contact diminish?
- Does the other party seem more or less willing to disclose information, feelings, and attitudes?

Be particularly observant of changes in eye contact, posture, attentiveness, voice, and manner. Be careful of reading too much into small nonverbal actions and changes.

Figure 2.5 *Feedback*

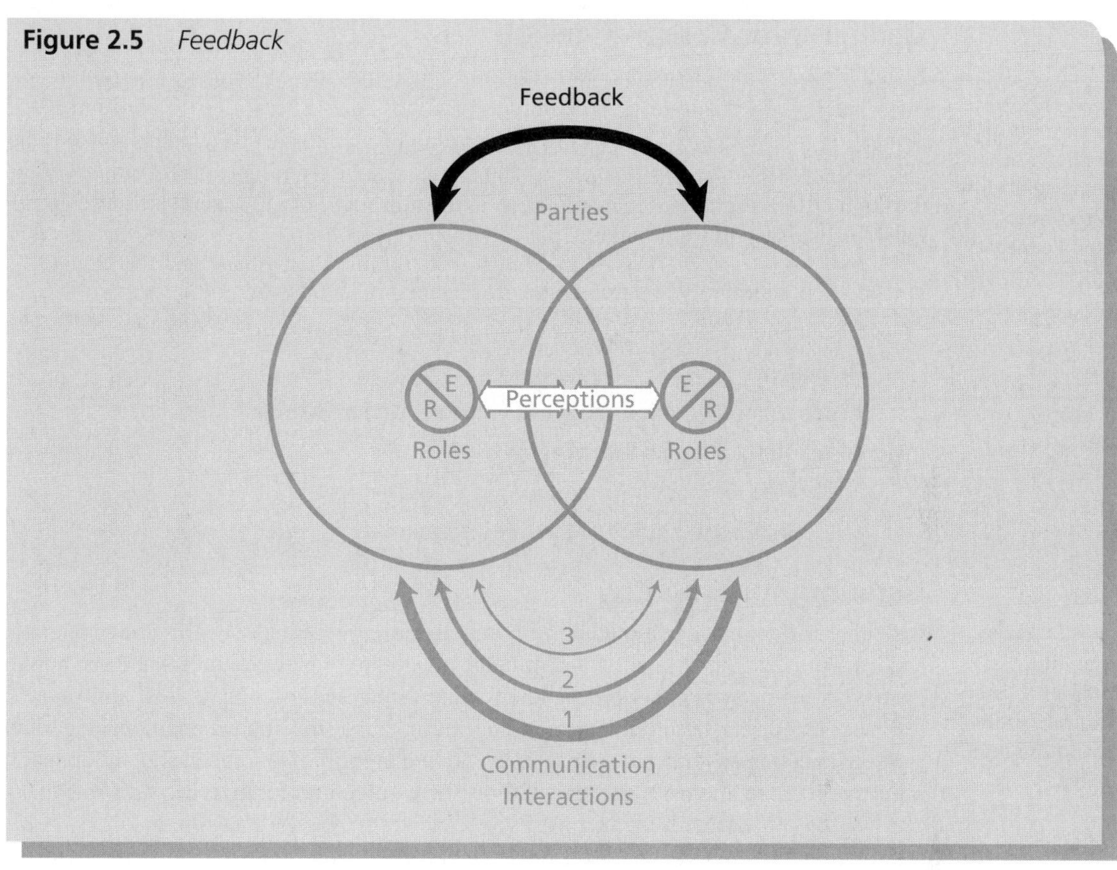

A person may be fidgeting because a chair is hard, not because of questions or answers. A person may be paying less attention because of noise and interruptions, not disinterest. A person may speak loudly because of habit, not because of a hearing impairment. Poor eye contact may indicate shyness or culture, not deceptiveness or mistrust.

It is difficult to listen with your mouth open and your ears closed.

Listening skills are essential to obtaining information, detecting cues, and generating Level 2 and Level 3 responses. Few of us listen well. Surveys of hundreds of corporations in the United States reveal that poor listening skills create barriers in all positions from entry level to CEO.

An interviewer may not listen carefully to answers received, while an interviewee may not listen carefully to questions asked. Both may lead a friendly critic to remark, "Did you hear what you just asked?" or "Did you hear what you just said?" Often we are so concerned about our primary role as questioner or respondent that we do not listen. Most of our training has prepared us for talking, not listening.

Be flexible in selecting listening approaches.

There are four approaches to listening: for comprehension, for empathy, for evaluation, and for resolution. Each approach is designed to play a specific role in giving, receiving, and processing information during interviews; and any one of the approaches may dominate an interview.

Listening for Comprehension

The intent of listening for comprehension is to understand content.

Listening for comprehension is a method of receiving, understanding, and remembering a message as accurately and completely as possible. The goal is to concentrate on a question, answer, or reaction to understand and remain objective, not to make judgments. This listening approach is essential when giving and getting information and during the first minutes of interviews when determining how to react. Use these guidelines for listening for comprehension:

- Listen attentively to a question before phrasing an answer.
- Listen attentively to an answer before phrasing a question.
- Be patient.
- Listen to tone of voice and vocal emphasis on key words.
- Listen for content and ideas.
- Take notes to retain information.
- Use questions to clarify and verify information.

Listening for Empathy

The intent of empathic listening is to understand the other party.

Listening for empathy is a method of communicating genuine concern, understanding, and involvement. Strive to put yourself in the other party's place to understand and appreciate what the party is experiencing and feeling. Empathic listening is total and genuine response: reassuring, comforting, expressing warmth, and showing unconditional regard. It is not synonymous with expressing sympathy or feeling sorry for someone but the ability to place one's self in another's situation. Follow these guidelines for listening with empathy:

- Show your interest and concern verbally and nonverbally.
- Do not interrupt.
- Be comfortable with strong displays of emotion: anger, fear, sadness.
- Remain nonevaluative or nonjudgmental until there is no choice.
- Listen with an eye toward giving options and guidelines.
- Reply with tact and understanding.

Listening for Evaluation

The intent of evaluative listening is to judge content and actions.

Listening for evaluation, or *critical listening,* is a means of judging what you hear and observe. Evaluative listening often follows comprehension and empathy because you are not ready to judge until you comprehend the verbal and nonverbal elements of interactions. It is essential in many interviews, but openly expressing criticism may diminish cooperation and levels of disclosure. Follow these guidelines for evaluative listening:

- Listen carefully to entire questions and answers before judging.
- Listen to content (reasoning, evidence, words).
- Observe nonverbal cues such as facial expressions or change in eye contact, tone of voice, gestures, and mannerisms.

- Ask for clarification.
- Avoid defensive reactions.

Listening for Resolution

John Stewart has developed a fourth type of listening called **dialogic listening.**[22] Dialogic listening focuses on *ours* rather than *mine* or *yours* and believes the agenda for resolving a problem or task supersedes the individual. Dialogic listening is most appropriate for problem-solving interviews when the goal is the joint resolution of a problem or task. Stewart likens dialogic listening to adding clay to a mold together, to see how the other person will react, what the person will add, and how this will affect the shape and content of the product. Follow these guidelines when listening for resolution:

The intent of dialogic listening is to resolve problems.

- Encourage interchanges between parties.
- Trust the other party to make significant contributions.
- Focus on the communication, not the psychology, of the interview.
- Focus on the present rather than past or future.
- Paraphrase and add to the other party's responses and ideas.

Although active and insightful listening is critical to both parties, listening is difficult. It is an invisible skill, so it is difficult to learn by observing. We learn to be passive listeners as children, students, employees, and subordinates. We've had experiences with persons who would not listen to us, regardless of what we had to say. A few months ago, a charity called the home of one of the authors. He was interested in giving to the charity but wanted written information on the charity and the opportunity to send a donation through the mail. The fund-raiser was determined to get an immediate commitment of a specific dollar donation over the telephone that evening and commented that it cost money to send out information. When the author commented that he would add a donation to defray this expense, the caller commented sarcastically, "Sure you will!" That ended the interview.

You can become an effective listener. First, strive to be as satisfied when listening as you are when talking. Second, overcome the "entertainment syndrome," the expectation that you must be entertained at all times and the attitude that anything "boring" is to be ignored. Third, be an active listener by attending carefully and critically to content and nonverbal signals. Fourth, concentrate on listening despite distractions such as physical surroundings, interruptions, mannerisms, appearance, and dress. Fifth, use the most appropriate listening approaches during each interview.

Listening, like speaking, is a learned skill.

The Interview Situation

No interview takes place in a vacuum. Each interview occurs at a given *time,* in a given *place,* with given *surroundings.* Either party may initiate the process and each comes with perceptions of what is about to take place in this setting and why. The many situational variables that influence interviews are symbolized by the imploding arrows in Figure 2.6.

Figure 2.6 *Situational variables*

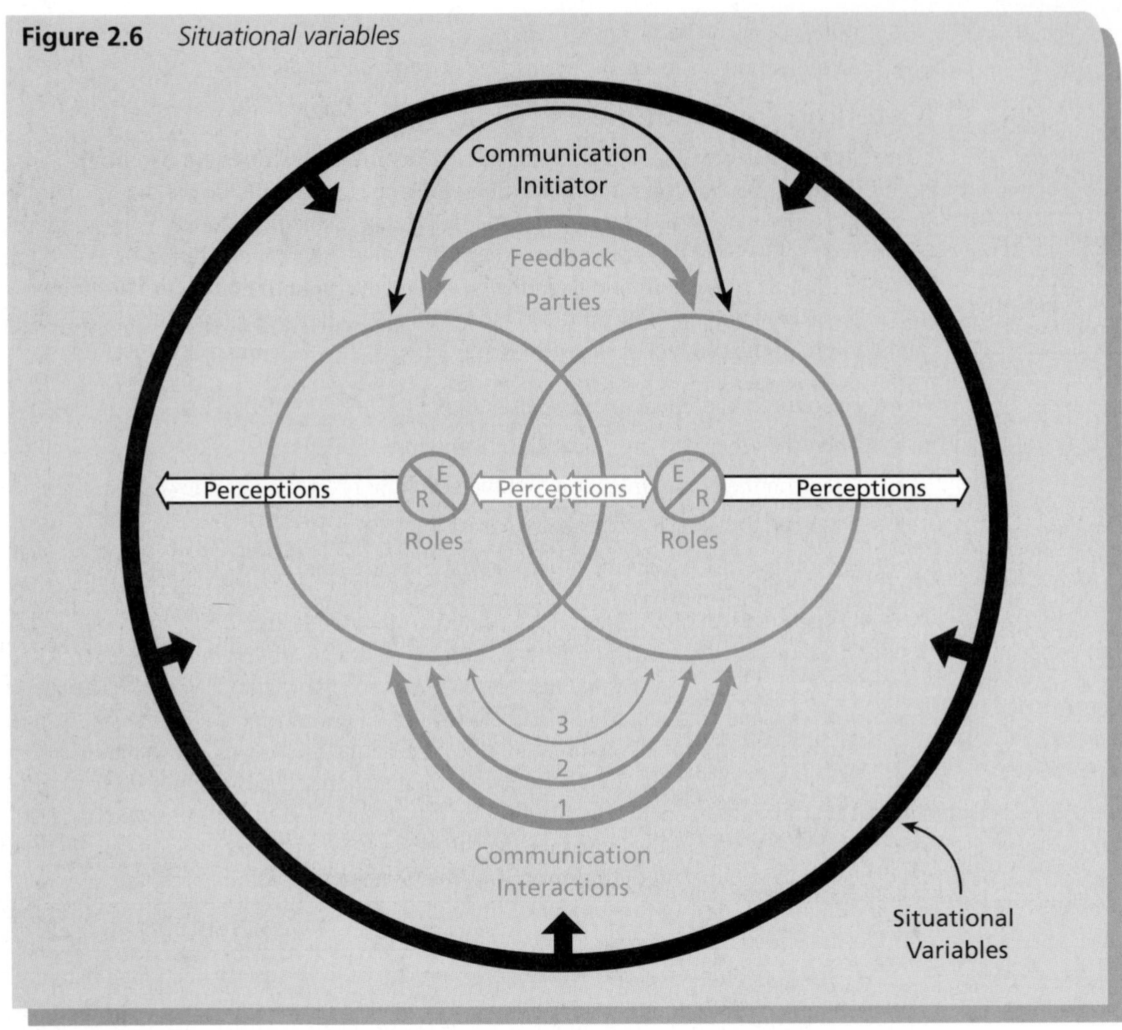

Initiating the Interview

Who initiates an interview and how may affect control, roles, and atmosphere.

Either party may initiate an interview, as shown by the arrows in Figure 2.6 that emerge from the top of the circle and touch each party. For example, you may walk into a professor's office to discuss an upcoming assignment, or a professor may call you in to discuss a research paper proposal. A technical support person may call you about updating the software on your computer, or you may call the support person about the need for updated software.

The situation often determines who initiates an interview and who must be interviewed. For instance, a recent fire in your apartment may require you to contact your insurance agent, and the insurance agent is likely to ask an insurance adjuster to interview you about the fire, its likely or determined causes, what you lost in the fire, and the fire department's efforts to extinguish it. Conversely, the person who initiates the interview affects the situation by determining how the contact is initiated.

You can affect the climate of the interview by initiating the interview directly rather than through a secretary, staff member, or friend. The climate will be more productive if you inform the other party about the nature, purpose, and use of the interview and initiate the interview in a positive and informative manner.

Perceptions

Each person comes to an interview with unique perceptions of the situation, including purpose, need, urgency, timing, place, and setting. Figure 2.6 symbolizes these perceptions by the arrows that run from each party to the situational circle. The interviewer may see the interview as a routine, everyday activity, nothing special or exciting, while the interviewee may see the interview as an extraordinary, once-in-a-lifetime event likely to affect career, advancement, marriage, financial plans, health, or social status. A recruiter, for example, may interview dozens of college seniors each day and perceive each interview as rather mechanical. A college senior, however, may perceive the interview as a long-anticipated opportunity. Medical examinations and television interviews are routine for physicians and journalists, but not for patients and respondents.

A party may see the interview as routine or an event.

Interview parties may see the setting quite differently. Supervisors may perceive their offices to be simple business locations, while their subordinates may see them as alien, off-limits environments, particularly if workers feel few of them ever come out as "happy campers." A professor may feel very relaxed sitting behind a desk, but a student may feel threatened when sitting in front of the desk.

Settings are seldom neutral.

Both parties have vested interests in the nature and outcome of interviews, but their goals may be quite different. A dentist may want to persuade you that an expensive crown is necessary for a fractured tooth, but you want to spend this money on a spring break trip. You may want to interview hurricane refugees still relocated in your city one year after the tragic event and see it as a good human interest story for the student newspaper. The refugees may not want to relive the tragedy or discuss it for the tenth time with a journalist.

Interview parties are most likely to communicate beyond Level 1 if they perceive the situation to be familiar rather than strange, informal rather than formal, warm rather than cold, private rather than open, and close rather than distant physically, socially, and psychologically. Organizations attempt to enhance concentration and motivation with well-lighted, pleasantly painted, moderate-sized rooms with comfortable furniture, temperature, and ventilation. Some attempt to create business and professional settings that resemble living rooms, dining rooms, family rooms, and studies to make interviewees feel more at home and thus more willing and able to communicate at Levels 2 and 3.

Perceptions are critical in moving beyond Level 1 interactions.

Time of Day, Week, and Year

Each of us has optimum times for interactions.

We tend to interact best at certain times of the day, week, and year. For instance, we might be morning, afternoon, or evening persons, meaning this is the optimum time for performance, production, communication, thinking, creativity, handling of conflicts, and dealing with important matters. It is unwise to address difficult issues or exchange important and extensive information just before lunch or late in the day or work shift when parties are mentally and physically tired. Moods tend to be dark and motivation low on Monday mornings and Friday afternoons. Holidays are good times for some interviews (sales, employment selection, journalistic) but bad for others (dismissals, reprimands, investigations, health care). Counselors note marked increases in crisis interviews with lonely people during family-oriented and happy seasons such as Thanksgiving, Christmas, and Passover. Police officers claim that full moons bring out strange behaviors in people.

Take into account events before and after interviews.

Be aware of events that precede or follow interviews. Wednesday morning may ordinarily be a good time for a supervisor or professor, but not *this* one because of a poor sales report or teaching evaluation. A student facing a major examination or a patient facing surgery may find it difficult to concentrate and answer questions. Threatened layoffs, personal problems, and organizational squabbles affect mood, expectations, concentration, and listening.

Place

We value and protect our turf.

Consider whose turf is best for the interview. For instance, you are likely to feel more comfortable and relaxed and less threatened in your home, room, office, or business. On the other hand, a neutral place might work best for a journalistic interview or in the prospective employer's office for an employment interview. We protect our turf. Think of your reactions when you walked into your room or office and found another person in your chair or at your desk or when you went to study in the library and another student chose a chair very close to yours. When one of the authors was head of a large academic department, he discovered that faculty often preferred to interact in their offices unless privacy was important or the issue was departmental rather than personal.

Don't underestimate the importance of place.

When possible, select the location most conducive to effective communication. The setting might be your place so you can feel more relaxed and "in charge," or because you have designed it with effective communication in mind, or you can exhibit a successful career or profession. The setting might be neutral such as a restaurant or conference room to avoid turf problems. Or it might be the other's residence because you want to talk about family concerns, the campus because you want a recruit to see its beauty and friendliness, or the other's place of business because you want to talk about business insurance or investment.

Surroundings

Surroundings help to create a productive climate.

Objects and decorations can create an appropriate atmosphere and interview climate. Trophies, awards, degrees, and licenses attractively displayed communicate achievements, professional credibility, and stature in a field. Pictures, statues, and busts of organizational leaders or famous persons communicate organizational and personal history, success, recognition, endorsement, and contacts. Models or samples may display and advertise state-of-the-art products and services. Colors of walls, types of carpeting, wall hangings, wallpaper, and curtains can provide a warm, attractive atmosphere conducive to effective communication.

Control noise to focus attention on the interaction.

Noise in an interview is anything that interferes with the communication process, including background noise, doors opening and closing, music, others talking, objects being dropped, and traffic. The interview may be interrupted by a ringing telephone, arrival of a faxed letter, or an e-mail message. People coming in and out of the room, walking by an open door, or asking for assistance are common distractions. The authors are surprised by the number of students who walk into their offices and interrupt conferences with students, almost as if their fellow students were invisible.

You generate a different kind of noise by coming to an interview fatigued, angry, overwhelmed with personal problems, or thinking about the next interview. You may be distracted by a headache, upset stomach, or cold. It is easy to look out a window at traffic, building construction, or scenery, or to concentrate on pictures, objects, furniture in the room, or the other party's mannerisms.

Come to each interview ready to communicate.

Eliminate negative influences of noise by selecting locations free of background noise or taking simple precautions: close a door, window, or curtain; take the phone off the hook; turn off a cell phone, television, or CD player. Inform others you do not wish to be disturbed. Limit self-generated noise by coming to each interview physically and psychologically ready to concentrate. Chapter 5 offers suggestions for note taking that avoids distractions and maintains the flow of communication.

Territoriality

We stake out physical and psychological space and resent those who invade it with their possessions, eyes, voices, or bodies. Think of how you have reacted to common invasions of territory:

Maintain an arm's length of distance between parties.

- Other students walking into a professor's office while you were interacting with the professor about a class problem.
- Diners at another table listening to your conversation with a prospective employer.
- Colleagues talking loudly at the next workstation when you were attempting to give information to a client.
- Persons who seated themselves at the same table while you were talking about a personal problem with a mentor.

Relationship affects territorial comfort zones.

Proximity of interview parties affects comfort level. We feel uncomfortable with persons who insist on talking nose-to-nose, and may react by backing up, placing furniture between us, or terminating the interview. Trenholm and Jensen write about "territorial markers" and use the term "personal space" to describe an "imaginary bubble" around us that we consider to be "almost as private as the body itself."[23] Others identify intimate distance (touching to 18 inches), personal distance ($1\frac{1}{2}$ to 4 feet), and social distance (4 to 12 feet).[24] Two to four feet—approximately an arm's length or on opposite sides of a table or desk—seems to be an optimum distance for most interviews. The next time you are in a library or airport, notice how people stake out their territory with coats, books, purses, and briefcases.

Relationship, particularly status, situation, and feelings of parties toward one another, influences the size of the bubble with which we are comfortable. High-status people stand or sit closer to low-status people, while low-status people prefer greater distances when dealing with superiors. We maintain a greater distance with a stranger than with close associates, peers, and friends. Some people want to "get in your face" when angry, while others widen the space because their anger is translated into distancing themselves from us physically and socially.

Age, sex, and culture influence territorial preferences.

The age, sex, and culture of the parties also determine space preferences. For instance, people of the same age stand or sit closer together than those of mixed ages,

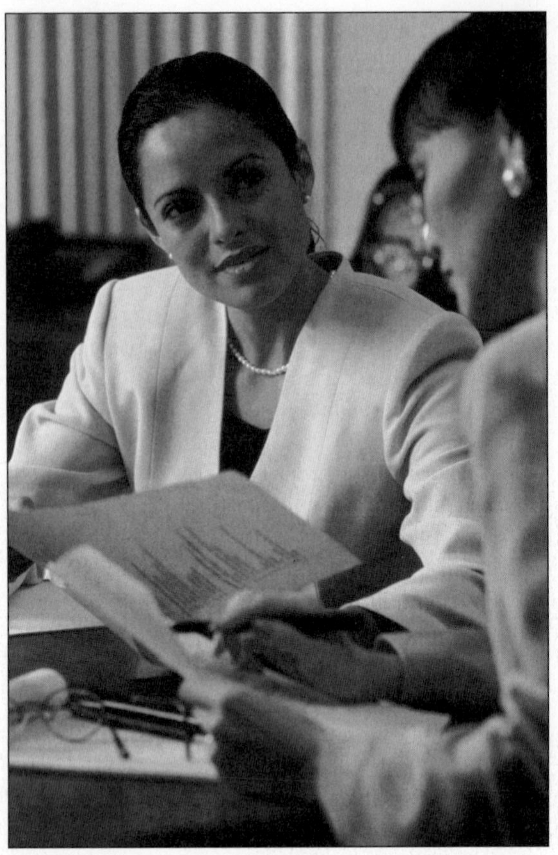
photo © Jose Luis Palaz, Inc./Corbis

A corner seating arrangement is preferred by many interviewers and interviewees.

particularly when the age difference is significant. All-male parties tend to arrange themselves farther apart than all-female or mixed-sex parties. North Americans prefer greater personal distances with other parties than do Middle Eastern and Latin American peoples. Many Arabs and Latin Americans see us as distant and cold, while we see them as intruding into our space. Northern Europeans tend to prefer greater personal distance than Southern Europeans.

Seating Arrangement

Where we sit and on what we sit is often determined by status, sex, furnishings, cultural norms, relationship between parties, and personal preferences. For example, a superior and a subordinate may sit across a desk from one another, arrangement A in Figure 2.7, with one sitting in a large leather swivel chair while the other sits on a simple wooden or clothcovered straight chair. This provides appropriate distance in a formal setting in which one party desires to maintain a superior position. Two chairs at right angles near the corner of a desk or table, arrangement B, creates a less formal atmosphere and a greater feeling of equality between parties. Students and staff have remarked to the authors that they prefer this arrangement with college professors and department heads or supervisors.

Seating may equalize control and enhance the interview climate.

You may remove physical obstacles and reduce the superior-subordinate atmosphere further by placing chairs at opposite sides of a small coffee table or by omitting the table altogether, arrangements C and D. A circular table, arrangement E, is growing in popularity, especially in counseling interviews or interviews involving more than two people, because it avoids a head-of-the-table position, allows participants to pass out materials, and provides a surface on which to write, review printed items, and place refreshments. The circular table or chairs around a small table works well for panel or group interviews. Arrangement F is most suitable when one or both parties consist of several persons.

Outside Forces

Although our primary concerns are the two parties in a specific situation, we must be aware of possible **outside forces** that may influence one or both parties before, during, and after the interview. Figure 2.8 indicates that common outside forces are family, associates, friends, employers, government agencies, and professional associations.

Figure 2.7 *Seating arrangements*

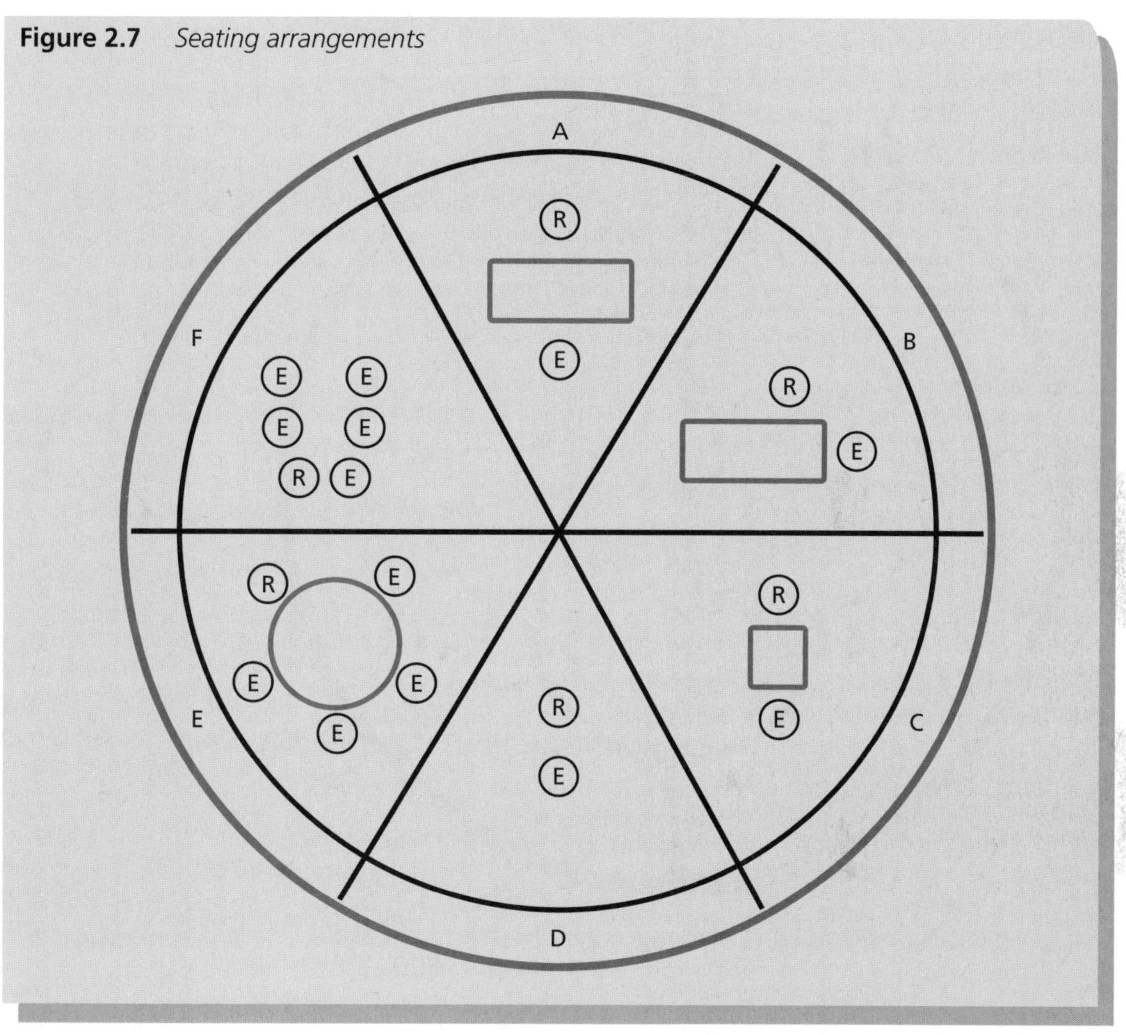

We are not really alone with the other party.

Many outside forces have input before the interview by providing guidelines for taking part in or conducting the interview. They may include topics to cover, structure to follow, questions to ask, answers to give, demands to make, or attitudes to assume. Some union contracts and corporate policies, for example, prescribe what questions can be asked and how they are to be phrased during employment interviews. No deviations or probing questions are permitted. In Chapters 7 and 8, we discuss how Equal Employment Opportunity (EEO) laws influence questions recruiters can ask and how applicants might respond in employment interviews.

Outside forces impact the interview when parties try to follow advice and guidelines from organizations, supervisors, and peers. For example, organizational policies may place restraints on the opening of the interview, the parties, perceptions, level of

Figure 2.8 *Outside forces*

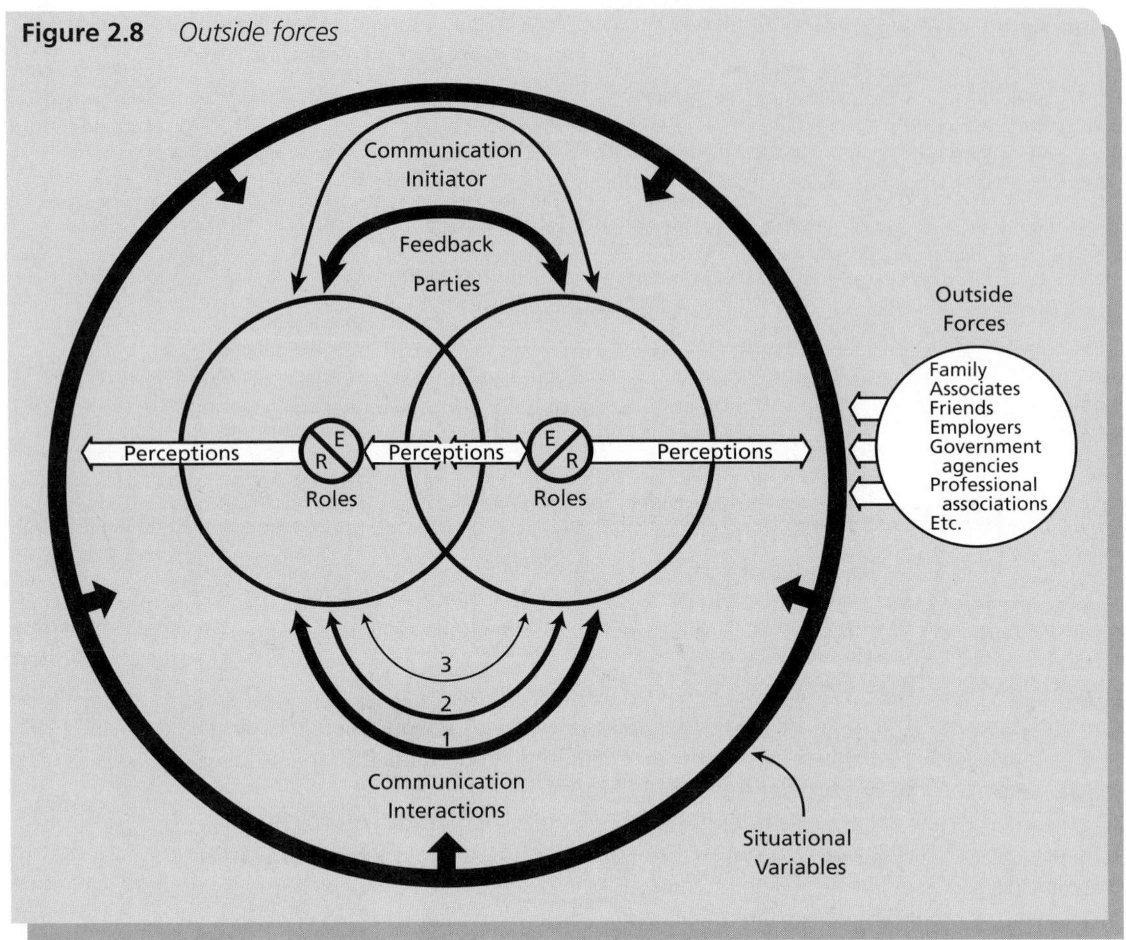

Outside forces determine roles in many interviews.

interactions, degree of self-disclosure, nature of messages, feedback, and interviewing approach. Policies often prescribe how we structure and conduct surveys, recruiting, performance review, counseling, and health care interviews.

Both parties may be concerned about post-interview reactions of outside forces. How will we report what took place, particularly answers, topics covered, demands, and agreements? For instance, interviewers may take hard lines in a negotiation or ask pressure questions during selection interviews because that is what their organizations demand. Interviewees may respond as outside forces have suggested or according to how they want the interview reported afterward. We may need to report that we "drove a hard bargain" when purchasing a new car, told a boss "where to get off," asked the questions we were told to ask, and demanded our money back. We may be cautious in interchanges because of possible lawsuits or grievances.

Be aware of how outside forces may affect your roles in a variety of interviews.

Know what advice you must take.

- What advice is wise to take?
- Which advice is appropriate for you, your position, and the situation?
- What advice must you take?
- How might your inclination to "satisfy the group" following an interview negatively affect the interview?

Be aware of outside forces impinging on the other party. This awareness will help to understand attitudes, responses, and behavior and avoid questions and topics that are off limits or demands that are impossible to grant. We often make demands and "let off steam" to organizational representatives on the telephone who have no authority to grant our wishes and who are not responsible for the problem. As bearers of bad news, they become the company's scapegoats and our targets.

Summary

In this chapter, we developed a summary model of the interpersonal communication process that contains the many interacting variables present in each interview: two parties, exchanging of roles, perceptions, levels of exchanges, verbal and nonverbal messages, feedback, listening, situation, and outside forces. Interviewing is a dynamic, complicated process between two complex parties operating with imperfect verbal and nonverbal symbols guided and controlled by perceptions and the situation. The ability to listen (for comprehension, empathy, evaluation, and resolution) and to employ silence strategically are often more important than what we have to say.

A thorough understanding of the process is a prerequisite for successful interviewing. Be aware that perceptions of self, the other party, how the other party sees us, and the situation are critical in determining how interviews progress and whether desired outcomes are achieved. Acknowledge and adapt to the influence of outside forces.

Interviewer and interviewee must be flexible and adaptable in choosing which approach to take (directive, nondirective, or a combination) not only because each party is unique and each situation is different, but because each party is molded and affected by demographics such as age, sex, race, and culture. In this chapter, we have tried to enhance your awareness of how demographics and culture affect self-esteem, disclosure, levels of communication, language, nonverbal communication, and territoriality. In the global village of the twenty-first century, we must be aware of how different people and different cultures communicate.

Key Terms and Concepts

The online learning center for this text features FLASHCARDS and CROSSWORD PUZZLES for studying based on these terms and concepts

Communication interactions
Complement
Control
Culture
Defensive climate
deceptively complex
Dialogic listening
Directive

- Feedback
- Initiating
- Interpersonal
- Levels of interactions
- Listening
- Noise
- Nondirective
- Nonverbal interactions
- Observing
- Outside forces
- Perceptions
- Personal space
- Politeness theory
- Process
- Proximity
- Reinforce
- Relational distance
- Relational history
- Self-concept
- Self-disclosure
- Self-esteem
- Self-identity
- Self-fulfilling prophecy
- Sex
- Silence
- Situation
- Substitute
- Supportive climate
- Territorial markers
- Territoriality
- Verbal interactions

An Interview for Review and Analysis

This interview is designed to incorporate all of the principles and theories presented in this chapter and to provide you with an opportunity to analyze them and determine how they affect the interview and the relationship between the two parties.[25] Begin by reading carefully the description of the two parties and the situation. Note the goal of this interview. Then, as you read carefully each interaction, think about the questions posed for review and analysis. Finally, what suggestions would you offer to the manager and Joe for handling such situations and for improving their interviewing skills?

Joe is a production supervisor with 20 years of experience and a good record. The plant manager is considering him for promotion and this interview is a first step in that process. It is exploratory rather than decision making. Company policy stipulates that employees are *not* to be informed when being actively considered for promotion, so Joe is unaware that a promotion may be in the offing. Company policy does allow mentioning overall considerations related to the current workforce situation and to established company criteria for promotions. Two hours prior to the interview, Joe received a call from the manager's secretary asking him to report to the manager. No reason is given. Joe enters the manager's office at 4:30 p.m. (his shift ends at 5:00 p.m.) and is seated across the desk from the manager.

What *perceptions* do Joe and the manager have of themselves, of one another, and of the situation? How would you assess the relationship between Joe and the manager? When, if ever, do the parties *exchange roles* of interviewer and interviewee? At which *communication levels* do most interactions occur? How do *words* influence the interview? How does *nonverbal behavior* affect the interview? Which *listening approaches* do Joe and the manager employ most often and with what effect? Which *interviewing approach* does the manager employ? How do *situational variables* influence this interview? What role, if any, do *outside forces* play in this interview?

1. **Manager:** Joe, come in. (smiling) Have a seat. It's been a while since we've had time for a chat.
2. **Joe:** (sitting facing the manager) Thank you, sir. (soft voice)
3. **Manager:** (serious facial expression and tone of voice) How are things moving along these days, Joe? *Everything* under control in your section?
4. **Joe:** Fine. No complaints. (fast speaking rate)

5. **Manager:** I'm *glad* to hear there are no *complaints*. (pause) You think you're doing okay?
6. **Joe:** As good as I know how, sir. (shifts weight in chair)
7. **Manager:** Good. (pause; looks Joe directly in the eyes) By the way, have you ever thought of uh, (pause) doing *something else?*
8. **Joe:** (pause; speaks slowly) Well (pause) uh, yes and no. I do like my job a lot. (rapidly)
9. **Manager:** Hmmm, I see. You don't want to change your job?
10. **Joe:** Uh (pause) no. (pause) I don't think so.
11. **Manager:** (looking closely at Joe; measuring his words) I see. Why do you want to stay on this job?
12. **Joe:** Well, I know the work real well. And everybody seems to like me.
13. **Manager:** Seems to like you? (looks Joe directly in the eyes)
14. **Joe:** Oh (pause) there may be one or two people who don't like me. But we manage to get along.
15. **Manager:** Some people don't like you, then? (sounds accusatory)
16. **Joe:** Well, I wouldn't exactly say *that*. Occasionally someone gets sore because I won't give him overtime.
17. **Manager:** That's the *only* reason?
18. **Joe:** Yes, sir! That's the only thing of importance I can think of. (firm voice, direct eye contact)
19. **Manager:** I see. (pause) Uh, Joe, did you ever think of (pause) *bettering* yourself?
20. **Joe:** Everyone wants to do better.
21. **Manager:** What do you mean by *that?*
22. **Joe:** Well, I mean, almost anyone can find ways to improve. (looks down)
23. **Manager:** You think, then, you could handle your job better?
24. **Joe:** Oh, there's always room for improvement. Do you have anything *specific* in mind, sir?
25. **Manager:** Joe, have you ever thought of bettering yourself on (pause) *another* job?
26. **Joe:** I like this job and company very much, sir! I know this job well, and you and the company have been very good to me.
27. **Manager:** I don't think you listened *carefully* to my question, Joe. Have you ever thought of *bettering* yourself on *another* job?
28. **Joe:** Well, everybody daydreams about how things might be at another company or even owning your own business. But I haven't given it much serious thought, really.
29. **Manager:** I take it, then, that you prefer definitely to stay on your *present job*.
30. **Joe:** Yes, sir. (pause) Do you have something in mind for another job *here,* sir? (rapid speaking voice)
31. **Manager:** Oh, don't worry about that, Joe. I'm glad we had time for this little chat. We'll have to get together again soon. Good luck. (shakes Joe's hand firmly without meeting his eyes)

Student Activities

1. Observe three face-to-face interactions (minimum length five minutes) between two men, between two women, and between a man and a woman. Look for similarities and differences in verbal and nonverbal communication. Which elements (sex, age, race, culture) do you believe influenced these interactions most?
2. Watch a televised news interview that lasts at least 10 minutes. Which communication level dominated the interview? How can you account for this? When was this level most dominant? What apparent effects did communication level have on the interview?
3. Visit three offices in which interviews routinely take place, such as a professor's office, a vice president's office, and an attorney's office. Which seem most comfortable and conducive to effective interviewing? What do the surroundings tell you about the people and the organization that created them? How would you recommend that they be changed for more effective interviewing?
4. Watch a C-SPAN or Sunday morning news show and study the language each party uses: ambiguities, jargon, slang, euphemisms, naming, and power words. How and why were these used? What communication problems did they create? How were theses problems resolved, if at all?

Notes

1. Robert S. Goyer, W. Charles Redding, and John T. Rickey, *Interviewing Principles and Techniques: A Project Text* (Dubuque, IA: Wm. C. Brown, 1968), p. 23.
2. John Stewart, ed., *Bridges Not Walls: A Book about Interpersonal Communication* (New York: McGraw-Hill, 2002), p. 22.
3. Stewart, p. 20.
4. Stewart, p. 33.
5. John Stewart and Carole Logan, *Together: Communicating Interpersonally* (New York: McGraw-Hill, 1998), p. 277.
6. Sarah Trenholm and Arthur Jensen, *Interpersonal Communication* (Belmont, CA: Wadsworth, 1996), p. 44.
7. Stewart and Logan, p. 257.
8. Diana K. Ivy and Phil Backlund, *Exploring Gender Speak: Personal Effectiveness in Gender Communication* (New York: McGraw-Hill, 1994), p. 219.
9. Stephen W. Littlejohn, *Theories of Human Communication* (Belmont, CA: Wadsworth, 1996), p. 262.
10. Laura K. Guerrero, Peter A. Andersen, and Walid A. Afifi, *Close Encounters in Relationships* (New York: McGraw-Hill, 2001), p. 46.
11. Michael Skube, "College Students Lack Familiarity with Language, Ideas," Lafayette, IN, *Journal & Courier,* August 30, 2006, p. A5.

12. Sik Hung Ng and James J. Bradac, *Power in Language: Verbal Communication and Social Influence* (Newbury Park, CA: Sage, 1993), pp. 45–51.

13. Guerrero, Andersen, and Afifi, pp. 297–98; Ivy and Backlund, pp. 163–165.

14. Julia T. Wood, "Gendered Interaction: Masculine and Feminine Styles of Verbal Communication," reprinted in Kathleen S. Verderber (ed.), *Voices: A Selection of Multicultural Readings* (Belmont, CA: Wadsworth, 1995), p. 24.

15. William B. Gudykunst, *Bridging Differences: Effective Intergroup Communication* (Newbury Park, CA: Sage, 1991), pp. 42–59.

16. Irving J. Lee, *How to Talk with People* (New York: Harper & Row, 1952), pp. 11–26.

17. Stewart, p. 129.

18. Stewart, p. 128.

19. Guerrero, Andersen, and Afifi, pp. 289–300.

20. Sarah Trenholm and Arthur Jensen, *Interpersonal Communication* (Belmont, CA: Wadsworth, 2000), pp. 61 and 366–368; Donald W. Klopf, *Intercultural Encounters* (Englewood, CO: Morton, 1998), pp. 232–233.

21. Stewart, p. 25.

22. Stewart, p. 220.

23. Sarah Trenholm and Arthur Jensen. *Interpersonal Communication,* 5th ed. (New York: Oxford, 2004), p. 57.

24. Stewart, pp. 84–85.

25. This interview is loosely based on pp. 24–25 in *The Executive Interview* by Benjamin Balinsky and Ruth Burger. Copyright 1959 by Benjamin Balinsky and Ruth Burger. It is reprinted by permission of HarperCollins.

Resources

Gudykunst, William B., and Young Yun Kim. *Communicating with Strangers: An Approach to Intercultural Communication*. New York: McGraw-Hill, 2003.

Lancaster, Lynne C., and David Stillman. *When Generations Collide*. New York: Harper Business, 2002.

Samovar, Larry A., and Richard E. Porter. *Communication between Cultures*. Belmont, CA: Wadsworth, 2001.

Stewart, John, ed. *Bridges Not Walls: A Book about Interpersonal Communication*. New York: McGraw-Hill, 2002.

Trenholm, Sarah, and Arthur Jensen. *Interpersonal Communication*. New York: Oxford, 2004.

Wood, Julia T. *But I Thought You Meant . . . Misunderstandings in Human Communication*. Mountain View, CA: Mayfield, 1998.

CHAPTER 3 Questions and Their Uses

Questions are tools for interviews.

As you read this chapter on questions and their uses, you may wonder why it's necessary to learn the names of so many different types of questions. After all, isn't a question merely a question? The answer is yes, but only in the same way that a golf club is a golf club, a screwdriver is a screwdriver, a knife is a knife, and a paint brush is a paint brush. There are many unique types of golf clubs, screwdrivers, knives, and paint brushes, and knowing which to choose for a particular task (driving, chipping, or putting for instance) enables you to perform a specific task *effectively* and *efficiently*. Knowing their names makes it easier to select the proper tool for the task you are confronting.

A question is any action that solicits an answer.

When you are involved in interviews, the tools of the trade are questions, a *question being any statement or nonverbal act that invites an answer or response.* Jamie McKenzie, editor of the educational technology journal *From Now On,* writes that "Questions may be the most powerful technology we have ever created." They "allow us to control our lives and allow us to make sense of a confusing world" because "they are tools that lead to insight and understanding."[1] Like all tools, questions have names, come in all shapes and sizes, have unique characteristics, perform specific functions, and enable you to perform interviewing tasks effectively and efficiently. This chapter focuses on types of questions, their uses, and common question pitfalls.

Questions have three essential characteristics.

Although the types and subtypes of questions may seem endless, each question has three essential characteristics.[2] The question is:

- Open or closed
- Primary or probing
- Neutral or leading

Open and Closed Questions

Open and closed questions differ in the amount of information they invite respondents to provide and the degree of interviewer control. The amount of information may range from one word to hundreds of words.

Open questions invite open answers.

Open Questions

Open questions are expansive, often specifying only a topic, and allow the respondent considerable freedom in determining the amount and kind of information to provide.

Highly Open Questions

Highly open questions have virtually no restrictions, such as:

Tell me about your experiences in Iraq.

What do you know about organic farming?

Tell me about your trip to Eastern Europe.

Moderately Open Questions

Moderately open questions have some restrictions but give respondents considerable latitude in their answers. The questions above might be narrowed, such as:

What was your housing like in Iraq?

What do you know about raising tomatoes organically?

Which sites did you visit in Poland?

Public opinion pollsters often hand a statement, picture, advertisement, or product offer to a person and then ask:

What comes to mind when you look at this accident picture?

How does this offer compare to the one for the product you usually purchase?

How would you react to this political ad that attacks an opponent?

Interviewees can volunteer and elaborate.

Open Questions Have Advantages

Open questions encourage respondents to talk and determine the nature and amount of information to give. Lengthy answers reveal what respondents think is important and motivate them to volunteer important information. Open questions communicate interest and trust in the respondent's judgment, are usually easier to answer, and pose less threat. Longer answers reveal a respondent's level of knowledge, uncertainty, intensity of feelings, perceptions, and prejudices.

photo © Michael Newman/Photo Edit

Open questions let the respondent do the talking and allow the interviewer to listen and observe.

Open Questions Have Disadvantages

A single answer may consume a significant portion of interview time because the respondent determines the length and nature of each answer. On the one hand, respondents may give unimportant or irrelevant information, and on

Interviewees can pick and choose, reveal and hide.

the other may withhold important information they feel is irrelevant or too obvious, sensitive, or dangerous. Keep respondents on track and maintain control by tactfully intervening to move on. Lengthy, rambling answers are difficult to record and process.

Restricted questions lead to restricted answers.

Closed Questions

Closed questions are narrow in focus and restrict the interviewee's freedom to determine the amount and kind of information to provide.

Moderately Closed Questions

Moderately closed questions ask for specific, limited pieces of information, such as:

What are your favorite television shows?

Which local restaurants do you go to most often?

What was your first reaction when you heard the news about 9/11?

Moderately closed questions often appear in recruiting interviews in which applicants are asked to identify specific skills or background information and in medical interviews in which patients are asked for critical information, such as:

In which computer software programs are you most proficient?

Which writing courses do you feel have prepared you best for a career in advertising and marketing?

Which prescriptions are you taking at present?

What did you have for dinner last evening?

Highly Closed Questions

Highly closed questions may ask interviewees to pick an answer.

Highly closed questions are very restrictive and may ask respondents to identify a single bit of information, such as:

When did you switch majors from technology to engineering?

How much are you asking for this used laptop?

How many hours did it take to fly to New Zealand?

Other highly closed questions ask respondents to select answers from a list, such as:

Which of these morning network news programs do you watch most often?

_____ *Good Morning America* on ABC
_____ *The Early Show* on CBS
_____ *Today Show* on NBC
_____ *American Morning* on CNN
_____ *Morning News* on Fox

Other highly closed questions may provide a list and a scale to choose from, such as:

> Your job has taken you to most of the major cities in Europe during the last five years. Listed on this card are major cities in Europe. Please rank them in order of preference with 1 being your most favorite, 2 being your next favorite, and so on:

London	1	2	3	4	5
Berlin	1	2	3	4	5
Madrid	1	2	3	4	5
Paris	1	2	3	4	5
Warsaw	1	2	3	4	5

Bipolar Questions

Bipolar questions offer polar opposites for answers.

Closed questions may be **bipolar** because they limit respondents to two polar choices. Some ask you to select an answer from polar opposites. For example:

Did you go to the morning or afternoon session?

Are you a Republican or a Democrat?

Are you a part-time or a full-time student?

Other bipolar questions ask for an evaluation or attitude. For example:

Do you like or dislike the proposed 9/11 memorial?

Do you agree or disagree with the president's position on Iraq?

Are you for or against the restaurant tax to fund the new stadium?

A yes or no question is likely to generate a yes or no answer.

The most common bipolar questions ask for yes or no responses. For example:

Are you going to vote tomorrow?

Do you live on campus?

Have you heard about the new health care proposal?

Closed Questions Have Advantages

Closed questions provide control and direction.

Closed questions permit interviewers to control the length of answers and guide respondents to specific information needed. Closed questions require little effort from either party and allow you to ask more questions, in more areas, in less time. And answers are easy to replicate, tabulate, and analyze from one interview to another. This is why surveys employ closed questions.

Closed Questions Have Disadvantages

Closed questions stifle volunteering.

Answers to closed questions often contain too little information, requiring you to ask several questions when one open question would do the job. And they do not reveal why a person has a particular attitude, the person's degree of feeling or commitment, or why this person typically makes choices. For instance, an interviewee may not know

Figure 3.1 *Question options*

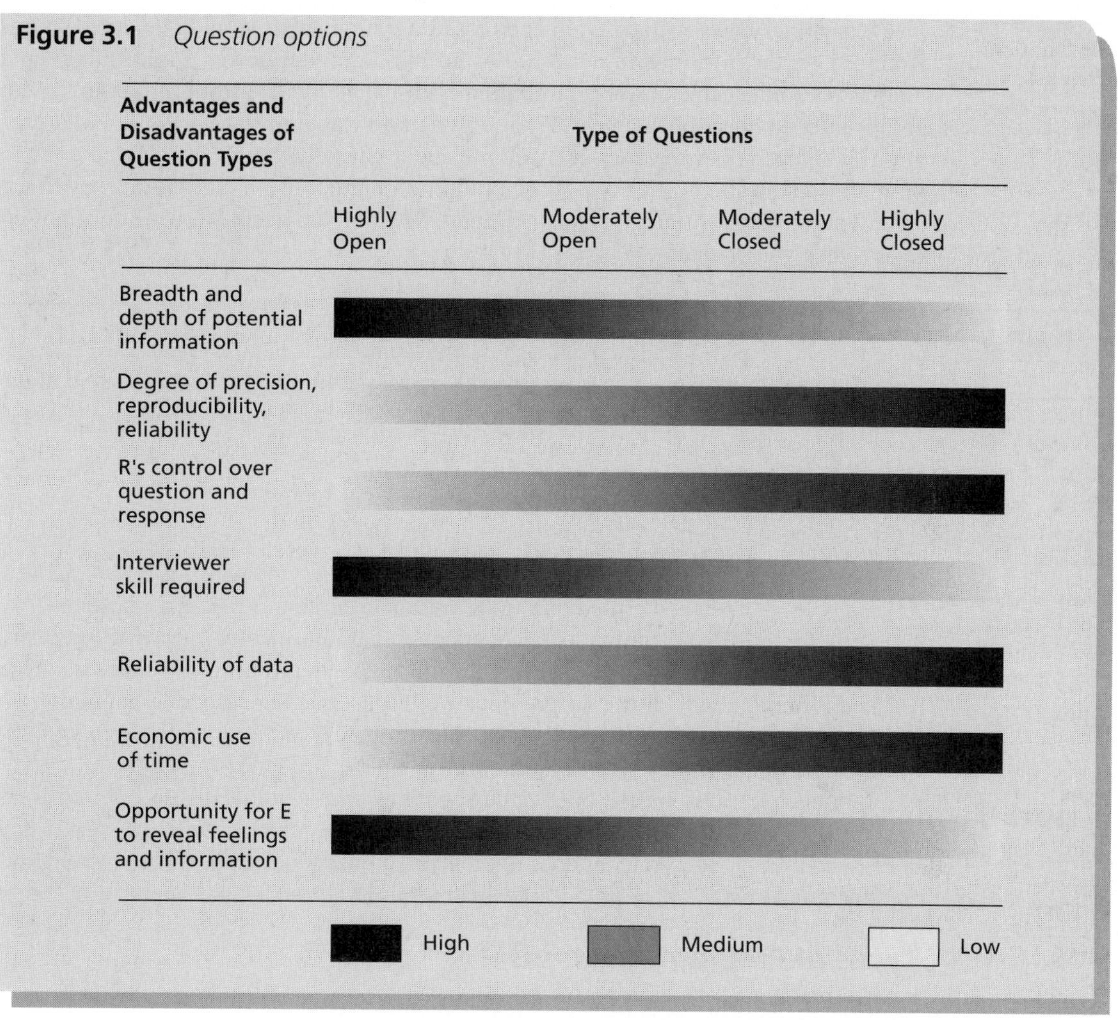

which products are American-made and which are foreign-made, or a person may purchase approximately the same amount of each. Interviewers talk more than interviewees when asking closed questions, so less information is exchanged. Interviewees have no opportunity to volunteer or explain information and can rate, rank, select an answer, or say yes or no without knowing anything about a topic.

Figure 3.1 illustrates the major advantages and disadvantages of open and closed questions. As you narrow a question, the amount of data decreases. As the amount of data decreases, your control increases, less time and skill are required, and the degree of precision, reliability, and reproducibility increases. On the other hand, as you open up a question, the amount of data increases and interviewees reveal knowledge level, understanding, reasons for feeling or acting, attitudes, and hidden motives.

Combinations often lead to the best results.

Many interviews include open and closed questions with varying degrees of constraint to get the information desired. For instance, an interviewer might follow up a bipolar question such as "Are you familiar with the new PowerPoint program?" with an open-ended question such as "What do you know about the new PowerPoint program?" An open question such as "Tell me about yourself," may be followed up with more closed questions such as, "When did you graduate from Nebraska?" "Tell me about your mission trip to Appalachia," and "Why did you decide to work for the Red Cross when you graduated?"

Primary and Probing Questions

Primary questions introduce topics or new areas within a topic and can stand alone even when taken out of context.

How did you become interested in owning a dude ranch?

Tell me about your internship with the CDC.

What training did you have before you purchased a motorcycle?

Primary questions make sense out of context.

All examples of open and closed questions presented earlier are primary questions.

Probing questions attempt to discover additional information following a primary question, so they are often called **probing** or follow-up, questions. They make no sense if asked without connection to a previous question. Imagine someone beginning an interview or topic by asking "What's your best estimate?" or "Tell me more about that" when you have not yet replied to a question.

Probing questions make sense only in context.

Probing questions may be open or closed. They enable you to dig deeper into areas and discover what an interview party may be implying or avoiding in answers. They are essential when a respondent does not reply to a question or appears to be giving incomplete, superficial, vague, suggestible, irrelevant, or inaccurate answers.

Types of Probing Questions

Silent Probes

Use a **silent probe** when an answer is incomplete or the respondent seems hesitant to continue. Remain silent for a few moments and use appropriate nonverbal signals such as eye contact, a head nod, sitting back in a chair, or a gesture to encourage the person to continue. Silence shows interest in what is being said and respect for the answer and the respondent. A person may become less defensive if you communicate disbelief, uncertainty, or confusion through a tactful, silent probe rather than words. An exchange might go like this:

Be patient and be quiet.

Interviewer: Why did you join the Air Force?

Interviewee: I like their uniforms best. (smiling)

Interviewer: (silence and smiling)

Interviewer: Actually, I have always been fascinated by airplanes and wanted to work with their armament.

Nudging Probes

A nudge replaces silence with a word or phrase.

Use a **nudging probe** if a silent probe fails or words seem necessary to get at what is needed. This question literally nudges the interviewee to reply or to continue with an answer. The nudging probe is usually simple and brief, such as the following:

I see.	And?
Go on.	So?
Yes?	Uh-huh?

A common mistake is the assumption that all questions must be multiple-word sentences. Instead of urging the respondent to continue through a simple verbal nudge, you may ask a lengthy probing question that stifles the interchange or a primary question that may open up a new area or topic, the opposite of what is needed. Valuable information may remain undetected.

Clearinghouse Probes

Ask rather than assume.

A **clearinghouse probe** is an essential tool for discovering whether a series of questions has uncovered everything of importance on a topic or issue. Clearinghouse questions encourage respondents to volunteer information you might not think to ask about and to fill in gaps your questions have missed. This probing tool literally clears out an area or topic, such as the following:

What else can you tell me about your interviewing experiences?

What have I not asked about graduate school that would be important for me to know?

Before moving on to the budget, is there anything else I need to know about staffing issues?

A good clearinghouse probe enables you to proceed to the next topic or series of questions, confident that you have gotten all important information. No one can anticipate or plan for all information a party might be willing to reveal. What is not asked may be more important than what is asked.

Informational Probes

Pry open vague, superficial, and suggestive answers.

Informational probing questions are important to get additional information or explanations. For example, if an answer appears to be superficial, begin a probing or follow-up question with phrases such as:

What are the implications you're referring to?

Tell me more about that incident.

What exactly did she say?

An answer may be vague or ambiguous, perhaps inviting a number of interpretations. Ask an informational probe such as:

When you say the crowd was "very large," what might that be in numbers?

What do you mean your report will be a "little late"?

How are you defining "marriage"?

An answer may suggest a feeling or attitude in addition to factual material, so ask an informational probe such as:

You appear to be angry about the changes I've made in your schedule.

Do I detect some fear about riding horses at the dude ranch?

How strongly do you feel about your reserve outfit being called up the third time for duty in the Middle East?

Restatement Probes

Restate or rephrase to get complete answers.

Respondents often do not answer the question that is asked or answer only a portion of the question. Rather than create a new probing question, restate all or part of the original question, perhaps using vocal emphasis to draw attention to the original concern. Rephrasing an original question is a tactful way to avoid embarrassing an interviewee. The following is a **restatement probe:**

Interviewer: How do you feel about the toll road being leased for a long time to an international investment group?

Interviewee: I'm more concerned about the new I-69 route.

Interviewer: That is another contentious issue, but how do you feel about the leasing of the toll road?

If a person seems hesitant to answer a question or answers only part of it, the question may be unclear or seem to demand what is not easy to provide. Restate the question in a clearer, easier to answer fashion. For example:

Interviewer: What is your philosophy of recruiting?

Interviewee: My *philosophy* of recruiting?

Interviewer: Yes, what do you believe are the fundamentals of recruiting?

If you ask a question with more than one part, a respondent may answer only one part. Restate the portion or portions left unanswered. For instance:

Interviewer: Tell me about your class reunion and your reactions?

Interviewee: I had more fun than I thought I would and reconnected with some old friends. We had a good time.

Interviewer: Tell me about the reunion.

Reflective Probes

Reflective questions verify and clarify.

A **reflective probe** reflects the answer just received to *verify* or to *clarify* it so you know you have interpreted it as the respondent intended. Make it obvious that the purpose is seeking verification and clarification, not attempting to lead or trap the interviewee into giving desired answers or to question her honesty or intelligence. Be tactful verbally and nonverbally. If an answer seems inaccurate (wrong date or figure, inaccurate quotation, mix-up in words), ask a reflective probing question such as the following:

The time was 12 *p.m.*?

That's the *area* code?

By late *last* century, you mean the *twentieth* century?

If unsure about what a respondent has said or implied, ask a reflective question to resolve uncertainty, such as the following:

Are you saying constitutional rights are expendable in the war on terrorism?

You're still thinking, then, about going to graduate school next fall?

Do I understand you to say you believe there are ghosts in O'Fallon Hall?

A reflective probe differs from a restatement probe in that the first seeks to clarify or verify an answer while the second seeks to obtain more information asked for in an initial question.

Mirror Probes

Mirror questions summarize to ensure accuracy.

The **mirror question** ensures that you have understood a series of answers or have retained information accurately. The mirror question is closely related to the reflective question, but the mirror question, rather than reflecting an answer just received, *summarizes* a series of answers or interchanges to ensure accurate understanding and retention. It may mirror or summarize a large portion or an entire interview. For example, a person may ask a mirror question to be certain of instructions, such as the following:

Let me check these directions to make sure I have them straight. We take I-95 out of Philadelphia to the Garden State Parkway in New Jersey. This will take us to I-87 in New York, and we take this north through Albany to New York 9N. We follow 9N through the village of Lake George and follow along the Lake George shoreline about 10 to 12 miles until we see the sign for the Northwoods Lodge. We turn right and the lodge is 300 yards down the lane.

An applicant might use a mirror question to be certain of the elements of an employment offer, such as:

This position, then, is a project engineer with your Dallas division. I would begin on June 1st and spend the first month in the division office getting acquainted with the area, the status of projects under construction, the project managers, and company policies and procedures. My starting salary would be $45,000 with an automatic 3 percent increase after the first year.

If asked properly, reflective and mirror questions can help you avoid errors caused by faulty assumptions, poor memory, or misinterpretations.

Skillful Interviewing with Probing Questions

The use of probing, questions separates skilled from unskilled interviewers and interviewees. The unskilled person sticks with a prepared list of questions, thinks ahead to

Skillful probing leads to insightful answers.

Be patient and be persistent.

the next question, anticipates questions prematurely, or is impatient. The skilled person listens carefully to each response to determine if the answer is satisfactory. If it is not, the questioner determines the probable cause within seconds and phrases an appropriate probing question. Skillful probing not only discovers more relevant, accurate, and complete information but may heighten the other party's motivation because the questioner is obviously interested and listening.

Probing questions may cause problems, however. Sometimes when a person does not respond immediately, we jump in with a probing question when none is needed. Phrase probing questions carefully and be aware of vocal emphasis. Stanley Payne illustrates how the meaning of a simple "Why" question can be altered by stressing different words.[3]

Why do you say that?

Why ***do*** you say that?

Why do ***you*** say that?

Why do you ***say*** that?

Why do you say ***that****?*

The "simple" why question may unintentionally communicate disapproval, disbelief, mistrust, or make the other party defensive and more reluctant to answer fully. A poorly phrased probing question may alter the meaning of the primary question or bias the reply. Be tactful and not demanding. When using reflective or mirror questions, try not to misquote or put words into the person's mouth.

Quiz #1—Supply the Probing Question

Supply an appropriate probing question for each of the following interactions. Be sure the question probes into the answer and is not a primary question introducing a new facet of the topic. Watch assumptions about answers, and phrase probing questions tactfully.

1. **Interviewer:** Define team work for me.

   Interviewee: (no response)

   Interviewer:

2. **Interviewer:** Are you going to get season basketball tickets this year?

   Interviewee: It depends.

   Interviewer:

3. **Interviewer:** What did you think of my sermon?

   Interviewee: It was good.

   Interviewer:

4. **Interviewer:** Tell me about your hometown.

   Interviewee: It was pretty small.

   Interviewer:

5. **Interviewer:** How do you feel about politicians?
   Interviewee: Don't ask.
   Interviewer:
6. **Interviewer:** In your opinion, who was the greatest NFL player of the past fifty years?
   Interviewee: Michael Jordan.
   Interviewer:
7. **Interviewer:** Are you thinking of going to Florida over spring break?
   Interviewee: I'm still paying off my car loan.
   Interviewer:
8. **Interviewer:** Are you planning to live off campus next year?
   Interviewee: I don't know.
   Interviewer:
9. **Interviewer:** How was your trip to Colorado?
   Interviewee: It was fabulous and then some.
   Interviewer:
10. **Interviewer:** Why did you decide to study civil engineering?
    Interviewee: I'd like to work outdoors.
    Interviewer:

Neutral and Leading Questions

Neutral questions encourage honest answers.

Neutral questions allow respondents to decide upon answers without overt direction or pressure from questioners. For example, in open, neutral questions, the interviewee determines the length, details, and nature of the answers. In closed, neutral questions such as bipolar questions, a person may choose between two equal choices: yes-no, approve-disapprove, agree-disagree. All questions discussed and illustrated so far have been neutral questions.

Leading questions direct interviewees to specific answers.

Leading questions suggest the answer expected or desired because the questioner leads the respondent toward a particular answer by making "it easier or more tempting for the respondent to give one answer than another."[4] A person merely agrees with the interviewer. This is called *interviewer bias*. Leading questions may be intentional or unintentional, implicit or explicit, verbal or nonverbal.

The varying degrees of leading and the distinction between neutral and leading questions are illustrated in the following questions.

Neutral Questions	Leading Questions
1. Do you like to ride roller coasters?	1. I assume you like to ride roller coasters.
2. Are you walking in the Hunger Hike?	2. You're walking in the Hunger Hike, aren't you?

3. How did this *Harry Potter* movie compare to the last one?	**3.** Didn't you like the last *Harry Potter* movie better than this one?
4. How do you feel about health food?	**4.** Do you dislike "health food" like most students?
5. What did you think of the diversity workshop?	**5.** What did you think of the ridiculous and insulting diversity workshop?
6. Have you ever tried drugs?	**6.** When was the last time you tried drugs?
7. Have you ever cheated on an exam?	**7.** Have you stopped cheating on exams?
8. Would you classify yourself as religious or secular?	**8.** Would you classify yourself as religious or an atheist?
9. How do you feel about the government listening to our telephone calls to stop terrorist plots?	**9.** Don't you think the government listening to our telephone calls allegedly to stop terrorist plots violates the Constitution?
10. Do you want a diet Coke?	**10.** I assume you want a diet Coke?

Interviewer bias leads to dictated responses.

Note that all 10 leading questions make it easier for a person to reply in a particular way. The potential for **interviewer bias** is obvious. The situation, tone of the interview, manner in which the question is asked, and relationship with the interviewer may influence the respondent's ability or willingness to ignore the direction provided. For instance, if you were in a nonthreatening, informal, pleasant situation with a friend or equal in an organizational or social situation, you might ignore or even object to a leading question. However, if you were in a threatening, formal situation with a superior, you might feel obligated to answer as the interviewer appears to dictate. At other times, you might go along with the direction because you want to be cooperative, avoid upsetting a person, or "not make a scene." If that's the answer a person wants, you give it, particularly when you do not care one way or the other.

An apparent bipolar question may in reality have only one pole.

The first four and the last leading questions are mild in direction. Each appears to be bipolar, to ask for a yes or no, agree or disagree response. However, the phrasing of each guides the respondent toward one pole; they are actually *unipolar* questions. You can avoid many leading questions by limiting the use of closed questions because open questions are less likely to be leading questions.

Respondents could ignore the direction of questions 1, 2, 3, and 10 if their relationship did not seem to depend on yes answers. Question 4 uses a bandwagon (follow-the-crowd) technique, and a respondent's answer might depend on past experiences with this interviewer and whether the respondent wants to go along with the majority. Question 10 suggests that the respondent will want a diet Coke. A person with ambivalent or apathetic feelings might just go along with the answer the interviewer seems to want.

Loaded questions dictate answers through language or entrapment.

Loaded Questions

Loaded questions are extreme leading questions. Questions 5 to 9 provide strong direction, virtual dictation of the correct answer; that's why they are called *loaded*

Figure 3.2 *Types of questions*

	Neutral		Leading	
	Open	**Closed**	**Open**	**Closed**
Primary	How do you feel about the new GPA requirement?	Do you approve or disapprove of the new GPA requirement?	Most good students favor the new GPA requirement; how do you feel about it?	Do you favor the new GPA requirement like most good students I've talked to?
Probing	Why do you feel that way?	Is your approval moderate or strong?	If you favor the new requirement, why did you vote against it?	I assume you favor the new requirement because you are graduating in two weeks?

questions. Questions 5 and 8 are loaded because of name-calling and emotionally charged words. In response to question 8, a person is likely to choose the least onerous of the choices provided, religious, because few Americans see themselves as atheists. Questions 6 and 7 entrap the respondent. Question 6 implies that the respondent has used drugs. Question 7 charges the person with cheating on exams. A yes or no may get the person in trouble. And question 9 places organizational or social pressure on the respondent to say yes.

Leading questions have legitimate functions.

Since leading questions, particularly loaded ones, have potential for severe interviewer bias, avoid them unless you know what you are doing! Introductory phrases such as "According to the law," "As we all know," "As witnesses have testified," and "As the Dean stated" may lead respondents to give acceptable responses rather than true feelings or beliefs. You can turn a neutral question into a leading question by the nonverbal manner in which you ask it. For example, you might appear to demand a certain answer by leaning toward the respondent, looking the person directly in the eyes, or raising an eyebrow. You might place vocal emphasis on a key word, such as:

Do you *like* that painting?

When did you *make an appearance* at the meeting?

You're going to select *her* for the opening?

Regardless of their potential for mischief, leading questions have important uses. Recruiters may want to see how interviewees respond under stress. Sales representatives use leading questions to close sales. Police officers ask loaded questions to provoke witnesses. Journalists ask leading questions to prod reluctant interviewees into responding. Counselors have discovered that a loaded question such as "When was the last time you got drunk?" shows that a range of answers is acceptable and that none will shock the interviewer.

Do not confuse neutral mirror and reflective probing questions with leading questions. Mirrors and reflectives may appear to direct respondents toward particular answers, but their purposes are clarification and verification, not leading or direction. If they lead by accident, they are failures.

Figure 3.2 compares types of questions available to interviewers and interviewees. Types include open and closed, primary and probing, and neutral and leading questions.

Quiz #2—Identification of Questions

Identify each of the following questions in four ways: (1) open or closed, (2) primary or probing, (3) neutral or leading, and (4) whether it is a special type of question tool: bipolar, loaded, nudging probe, clearinghouse probe, informational probe, restatement probe, reflective probe, or mirror probe.

1. On a scale of 1 to 5, with 5 being high, how would you rate the football coach?
2. You think, then, that you will consider graduate school when you graduate in May?
3. Tell me about your summer job at the dude ranch in Colorado.
4. That was really a stupid thing to do, wasn't it?
5. Uh huh?
6. When did you first join the Marines?
7. Did you take the GRE exam last week?
8. Tell me more about that.
9. Let's see if I understand your proposal correctly. I would pay the first month's rent on the condo and you would pay for moving in our furniture. We would split evenly the cost of a new hot tub and repainting the bedrooms. The current owner would replace the carpeting in the living room. Is that about it?
10. Don't you think you should start interviewing for positions *before* you graduate?
11. Do you take I-80 or I-70 when driving to Pennsylvania?
12. Which television reality shows do you like best?
13. What did you see when you came upon the accident?
14. Have you stopped padding your expense account?
15. **Interviewer:** How are your classes going?

    Interviewee: I've been having a great time playing intramural football, and the bar scene near campus is great. And I'm thinking about pledging a fraternity.

    Interviewer: And how are your classes going?

Common Question Pitfalls

Being aware of question tools and their uses is an important first step in learning to interview effectively and efficiently. The second critical step is knowing how to create and use questions to obtain free, accurate, honest, insightful, and thorough answers. A slight alteration in wording can change a question from open to closed, primary to probing, and neutral to leading.

Phrase questions carefully to avoid common pitfalls.

Because you often must create questions on the spot during the heat of an interview, particularly probing questions, it is easy to stumble into common **question pitfalls** without knowing it. These pitfalls include the bipolar trap, the open-to-closed switch, the double-barreled inquisition, the leading push, the guessing game, the yes (no) response, the curious probe, the quiz show, and the don't ask, don't tell question.

The Bipolar Trap

Avoid unintentional bipolar questions.

You fall into a **bipolar trap** whenever you ask a bipolar question designed to elicit a yes or no answer when you really want a detailed answer or specific information. This pitfall is obvious in questions such as "Do you know what happened at the meeting?" instead of "What happened at the meeting?" "Are you familiar with this incident?" instead of "What do you know about this incident?" Or "Do you approve or disapprove of heightened airport security?" If all you want is a yes or no, each is satisfactory, but none is likely to tell you much. Notice how little information is exchanged in this interaction:

Interviewer: Have you experienced any pains in your chest?

Interviewee: No.

Interviewer: Do you think your health is generally good?

Interviewee: Yes.

Interviewer: Any side effects from the cholesterol medicine?

Interviewee: No.

Bipolar questions assume there are only two possible answers and that the answers are poles apart: conservative–liberal, like–dislike, approve–disapprove, agree–disagree, high–low, yes–no. They do not allow for "undecided," "no opinion," or "don't know" answers or for degrees of awareness, liking, feeling, using, or knowing. The health care interviewer in the preceding example assumes that the patient knows what is meant by "chest pains," "generally good" health, and "side effects."

Eliminate bipolar traps by reserving bipolar questions for situations in which only a yes or no or a single word is desired. Begin questions with words and phrases such as *what, why, how, explain,* and *tell me about* that ask for detailed information, feelings, or attitudes. In general, avoid questions that begin with *do, can, have, would,* and *will.*

Think before asking and know when to stop asking.

The Open-to-Closed Switch

The **open-to-closed switch** question occurs when you ask an open question but, before the interviewee can respond, you rephrase it into a closed or bipolar question. This trap is readily apparent in interviews, such as:

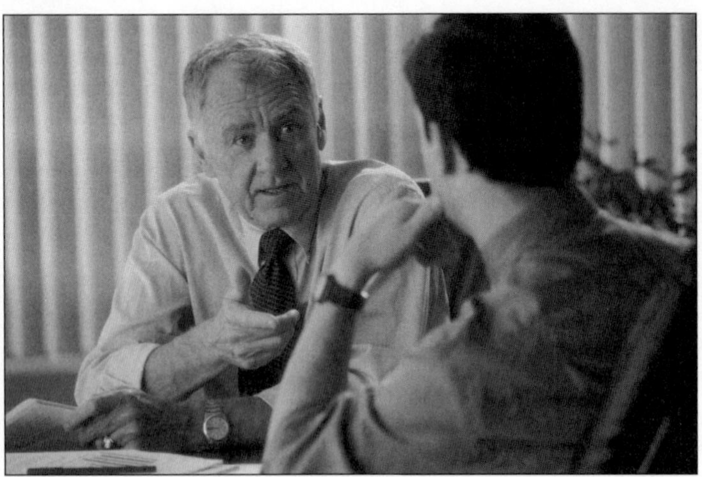
photo © Jose Luis Palaz, Inc./Corbis

How you ask a question may bias the answer you receive.

Tell me about your travel plans for the summer. Are you going to Europe again?

What did you do during homecoming last weekend? Did you go to the game?

Why did you choose a study abroad program in Poland? Was it because it was less expensive than France or Germany?

The open-to-closed switch occurs when you are still phrasing a question in your mind. This rummaging about for the right phrasing often changes a perfectly good open question into a narrow, closed question. The respondent is likely to address only the second question and often with a simple yes or no. Avoid the open-to-closed switch by preparing questions prior to the interview and thinking through questions before asking them.

The Double-Barreled Inquisition

Ask one question at a time.

The **double-barreled inquisition** question occurs when you ask two or more questions at the same time instead of a single, precise question. Double-barreled questions are common in interactions:

Did you like the Mediterranean cruise, and are you excited about taking another one?

Tell me about a typical day as a teaching assistant and why you decided to go to graduate school.

What types of fishing do you enjoy most and where do you go fishing most often?

Respondents are unlikely to remember or address all parts of double-barreled questions and will answer what they remember. Some will select the portion they want to answer and ignore the rest. Others will answer all parts but provide few details to avoid a long answer. Respondents may feel they are being subjected to a third-degree inquisition when asked a question such as, "Tell us what you owe in educational, car, mortgage, credit card, and personal loans." At the very least, the interviewer may find it necessary to repeat portions of the initial question to get all of the information wanted. At worst, the interviewer may be unaware of missing information and go to another primary question prematurely.

Avoid the double-barreled trap and its dangers by asking one question at a time. If you ask a double-barreled question, repeat the part the interviewee does not answer.

The Leading Push

Push only when there is a need to push.

The **leading push** occurs when you ask a question that suggests how a person ought to respond. The push may be intentional (you want to influence an answer) or unintentional (you are not aware of the push). It is easy to interject feelings or attitudes in questions through language and nonverbal signals, such as the following:

I really liked the show, didn't you?

You play the lottery *every day*?

Don't you think you should wear a helmet when riding your cycle?

You may not realize you have asked a leading push question and remain unaware that the interviewee may have given you a skewed answer to make you happy or to avoid a confrontation. Many people will go along with whatever answers you seem to want, particularly if you are in a superior role. Avoid the leading push trap and its dangers by phrasing questions neutrally and listening to each question you ask.

The Guessing Game

Don't guess; ask!

The **guessing game** pitfall occurs when you try to guess information instead of asking for it. Guessing is common in interviews, such as:

Did you purchase your interview outfit here in town?

Do you tend to order steak when eating at nice restaurants?

Is fire your greatest concern about living in an apartment complex?

Guessing is common in most interview settings: journalism, health care, recruiting, and investigations. Strings of closed, guessing questions fail to accomplish what a single open-ended question could do. Observe the failure of this guessing spree to gain simple information.

Interviewer: Is fishing your favorite pastime?

Interviewee: No.

Interviewer: How about hunting?

Interviewee: No, I don't like to hunt.

Interviewer: What about hiking?

Interviewee: Not really.

Interviewer: Well, what is your favorite pastime?

Interviewee: Sailing.

Guessing wastes time and energy when a single open question, such as the last one, will get the information needed quickly and efficiently. Avoid the guessing game pitfall by *asking* rather than *guessing* and relying on open-ended questions such as "Tell me about your favorite pastime."

The Yes (No) Response

The **yes (no) response** pitfall occurs when interview parties ask questions that have only one obvious answer, a yes or a no. Each of the following questions is likely to get a predictable response:

An obvious question will generate an obvious answer.

(asked of a student) Do you want to fail this course?

(asked of a sales person) Do you think this is a good digital camera?

(asked of an applicant) Do you think you can handle this job?

Avoid the yes (no) question pitfall by asking open-ended questions and by not asking the obvious.

The Curious Probe

Curiosity may be fatal to interviewers.

If every question you ask is relevant to your predetermined purpose, you will avoid **curious probes.** Do not ask for information you do not need and will not use. If an interviewee may perceive a question to be irrelevant, explain why it is important. The order of questions may result in perceived irrelevance. For example, ask for demographic data such as age, income, educational level, and marital status at the beginning if they are qualifying questions or at the end after you have established trust and have asked several relevant questions. Phrase questions carefully so the relevance of your question to this interview is clear to the interviewee.

As an interviewee, do not assume a question is irrelevant; the interviewer may have a legitimate and important reason for asking. Other cultures ask questions that might appear irrelevant to you but not to them. For instance, Japanese often ask personal questions early in interactions so they can learn important characteristics about the interviewee, including personality, knowledge, skills, and background. A Japanese party might ask where you were born, where you went to school, how you feel about Japanese food, what Japanese you speak, and what hobbies you have.

The Quiz Show

What does the interviewee know of relevance to this topic?

Interviews are not **quiz shows** with applicants, subjects, clients, employees, or patients serving as contestants. The parties you interview must have a store of knowledge that enables them to answer comfortably and intelligently. *Information level* is critical in interviews. Questions above a respondent's information level may cause embarrassment or resentment because no one wants to appear uninformed, ill-informed, uneducated, or unintelligent. On the other hand, questions beneath a respondent's level of information may insult his or her intelligence, wisdom, experiences, or status. Respondents may fake answers or give vague answers rather than admit ignorance.

Avoid the quiz show pitfall by asking for information in common categories or frames of reference such as pounds rather than ounces, cups rather than pots of coffee, or number of hours watching television per day rather than month or year. Determine if a respondent is a layperson, novice, or expert on the topic to avoid overly simple or overly complex words, explanations, requests. Do not assume respondents will have the information you want. Many of us are narrow specialists and know little about other areas of our fields, other fields, current events, or history.

Complexity vs. Simplicity

Questions should be simple, clear requests for reasonable amounts of information. Avoid overly complex questions that challenge respondents to figure out what you want. The following is a common type of survey question, often asked over the telephone:

> Now, I would like your opinion on some leading brands of coffee. I would like you to rate these brands by using the numbers from plus five to minus five. If you like the brand, give it a number from plus one to plus five. The more you like it, the bigger the plus number you should give it. If you dislike the brand, give it a number from minus one to minus five. The more you dislike it, the bigger the minus number you should give it. If you neither like nor dislike the brand, give it a zero.

If you must ask such a complicated question, use sample answers to explain the scale and give interviewees opportunities to try out the scale on noncoffee items to determine if they understand both the question and how to answer it correctly. If the interview is face-to-face, provide a small card containing the scale or answer options.

Phrase questions carefully and avoid a mixture of negatives, maybes, and positives in the same question. The following question illustrates this problem:

> Pick the most appropriate response. You feel that you understand each other, but you have never told them this.
>
> 1. You have never felt this way, or you have felt this way and never told them this.
> 2. You occasionally have felt this way, but you have never told them this.
> 3. You frequently have felt this way, but you have never told them this.

Imagine trying to answer this complex question in a typical interview or over the telephone.

Some questions seem simple enough, but they offer no obvious parameters or hints to guide the interviewee on what information is desired or how much information the interviewer desires. Common global questions such as "Tell me about yourself" or "Tell me about your country" pose difficult decisions to those who would reply. Where should they begin and end their answers? Is the interviewer interested in specific topics, happenings, or issues? Should they simply offer a few superficial facts or a brief summary, or should they give a lot of information on one or two areas? How lengthy and detailed should they make their answers? Should they ask if the interviewer has specific interests or an amount of information in mind? Obviously, the question itself need not be complex.

The Don't Ask, Don't Tell

Don't ask, don't tell questions delve into informational and emotional areas that many respondents may be incapable of addressing because of social, psychological, or situational constraints. We learn from an early age, for instance, that it is more socially acceptable to be humble than boastful. If an interviewer asks us to assess our beauty, intelligence, creativity, generosity, or bravery, we are likely to pose an "Aw shucks" attitude or say "Yes" with a flourish that treats our answer as a joke. We also learn that "there is a time and a place for everything," so we do not discuss certain topics in mixed groups, in public, or in political, religious, or social settings. Some areas are taboo in all but a few situations: sex, personal income, religious convictions, and certain illnesses.

Delve into inaccessible areas only when necessary.

As an interviewer, you should explain why such questions are essential to ask, and delay "touchy" or "taboo" questions until you have established a comfortable climate and positive relationship. Avoid the don't ask, don't tell pitfall by phrasing questions carefully to lessen social and psychological constraints and to avoid offending an interviewee.

Sex and cultural differences among respondents may affect social and psychological accessibility. Research indicates that women disclose more information about themselves, use more psychological or emotional verbs, discuss their personal lives more in business interactions, have less difficulty expressing intimate feelings, talk more about other people's accomplishments and minimize their own, and appear to be more comfortable when hearing accolades about themselves.[5] As discussed in Chapter 2, cultures also differ in readily accessible areas. It is always wise to learn as much as you can about an interviewee prior to an interview to determine what can and cannot be asked and how it should be asked.

Avoid common question pitfalls by planning most questions prior to the interview so you do not have to create them on the spot in the give-and-take of the interaction. When phrasing a question during an interview, think before uttering it, stop when you have asked a good open question instead of rephrasing it, use bipolar questions sparingly, ask only necessary questions, ask for information at the interviewee's level, avoid complex questions, and be aware of the accessibility factor in questions and answers. Above all, know the common question pitfalls well enough that you can catch yourself before tumbling into one.

Avoid pitfalls by preparing and thinking.

Quiz #3—What Are the Pitfalls in These Questions?

Each of the following questions illustrates one or more of the common question pitfalls: bipolar trap, open-to-closed switch, double-barreled inquisition, leading push, guessing game, yes (no) response, curious probe, complexity vs. simplicity, quiz show, and don't ask, don't tell. Identify the pitfall(s) of each question and rephrase it to make it a good question. Avoid a new pitfall in your revised question.

1. Tell me about the plane crash. Did you think you were going to die?
2. (asked of people on the street) What do you know about the EU's privacy directive?
3. Are you the most intelligent member of the team?
4. I understand you are from Wisconsin. Tell me about it.
5. You're following the new guidelines, aren't you?
6. Tell me about the hotel accommodations on Maui and what there was to do for children and adults.
7. (asked of a used car dealer) Are all of these cars carefully checked before you put them on the lot?
8. Do you approve or disapprove of the administration's immigration proposal?
9. Did you choose to study medicine because your mother and father are physicians?
10. (asked of an injured football player) Do you want to die?

ON THE WEB

Browse an Internet site to locate a variety of question-answer interactions that vary in intensity from happy to sad, cooperative to uncooperative, friendly to hostile, and understanding to patronizing. Identify the different types of primary and probing questions in these interactions. Which question pitfalls can you identify? Which of these pitfalls were accidental and which purposeful? Use search engines such as the Knight Ridder Newspapers (http://www.kri.com), CNBC (http://www.cnbc.com), and CNN (http://cnn.com).

Summary

Questions are the tools of the trade for both parties in interviews. If you know question types, unique uses, and advantages and disadvantages, you can develop considerable interviewing skill and enjoy the experiences.

You have a limitless variety of question tools to choose from, and each tool has unique characteristics, capabilities, and pitfalls. Knowing which question to select and how to use it is essential for interviewing effectively and efficiently. Each question has three characteristics: (1) open or closed, (2) primary or probing, and (3) neutral or leading. Open questions are designed to discover large amounts of information, while closed questions are designed to gain specific bits of information. Primary questions open up topics and subtopics, while probing questions probe into answers for more information, explanations, clarifications, and verifications. Neutral questions give respondents freedom to answer as they wish, while leading questions nudge or shove respondents toward answers interviewers want to hear.

Phrasing questions is essential to get the information needed. If you phrase questions carefully and think before asking, you can avoid common question pitfalls such as the bipolar trap, open-to-closed switch, double-barreled inquisition, leading push, guessing game, yes (no) response, curious probe, quiz show, complexity vs. simplicity, and don't ask, don't tell.

Key Terms and Concepts

The online learning center for this text features FLASHCARDS and CROSSWORD PUZZLES for studying based on these terms and concepts.

Bipolar question
Bipolar trap
Clearinghouse probe
Closed question
Complexity vs. simplicity
Curious probe
Don't ask, don't tell
Double-barreled inquisition
Guessing game
Informational probe
Interviewer bias
Leading push
Leading question
Loaded question
Mirror probe
Neutral question
Nudging probe
Open question
Open-to-closed switch
Primary question
Probing question
Question
Question pitfalls
Quiz show
Reflective probe
Restatement probe
Silent probe
Yes (no) response

An Interview for Review and Analysis

A student has decided to interview a friend of his parents for a field project assignment in an interviewing course. All he knows is that she was thought to be in the Air Force during World War II and had some interesting experiences. His goal is to get a woman's view of the war and military experience.

As you read through this interview, identify the questions as open or closed, primary or probing, and neutral or leading. Look for specific types of questions such as bipolar, loaded, silent probe, nudging probe, clearinghouse probe, informational probe, restatement probe, reflective probe, and mirror probe. Does the student stumble into common question pitfalls such as leading push, bipolar trap, yes or no response, open-to-closed switch, guessing game, double-barreled inquisition, curious probe, quiz show, complexity vs. simplicity, and don't ask, don't tell?

1. **Interviewer:** Mom has told me that you were in the Air Force during World War II. When did you enlist and what did you do?
2. **Interviewee:** Actually, I was a WAC.
3. **Interviewer:** A what?
4. **Interviewee:** A WAC. WAC stood for the Women's Auxiliary Corps. There was no Air Force until 1948.
5. **Interviewer:** Then, who flew the fighters and bombers?
6. **Interviewee:** They were the Army Air Corps, later to become the Air Force.
7. **Interviewer:** Oh, were the WACs the ones I've seen in pictures who gave food and coffee to troops on trains when they pulled into stations?
8. **Interviewee:** No. Those were volunteers from the Red Cross. I was a pilot.
9. **Interviewer:** What did you do as a WAC?
10. **Interviewee:** I was a pilot.
11. **Interviewer:** A pilot, wow. Did you shoot down any planes?
12. **Interviewee:** No.
13. **Interviewer:** Did you bomb cities in Germany? Or what?
14. **Interviewee:** No, I didn't bomb cities.
15. **Interviewer:** Did you fly air cover or maybe reconnaissance?
16. **Interviewee:** No. Women were not allowed to go into combat areas until just the past few years.
17. **Interviewer:** Then you delivered supplies?
18. **Interviewee:** No.
19. **Interviewer:** What did you do?
20. **Interviewee:** I spent most of the war ferrying bombers from plants and bases in the United States to bases in England.
21. **Interviewer:** What kinds of bombers?

22. **Interviewee:** Usually B17s and B24s.
23. **Interviewer:** Tell me about your experiences. Did you have any close calls?
24. **Interviewee:** Lots of them.
25. **Interviewer:** Were some pretty scary?
26. **Interviewee:** Yes.
27. **Interviewer:** Tell me about the scariest.
28. **Interviewee:** Well, we were in an unarmed B24 off the coast of Ireland and were attacked by some long-range German fighters. We lost two of our planes, and our Liberator was pretty shot up. British escort planes arrived just in time.
29. **Interviewer:** How many WACs were there and how many were killed and wounded during the war?
30. **Interviewee:** I don't recall.
31. **Interviewer:** What was the nightlife like in England? I've heard it was pretty wild.
32. **Interviewee:** I was engaged to a Marine fighting in the Pacific at the time.
33. **Interviewer:** Your nightlife was rather subdued, then?
34. **Interviewee:** Somewhat.
35. **Interviewer:** I'm sure patriotism was pretty strong among you pilots.
36. **Interviewee:** Not really.
37. **Interviewer:** It wasn't?
38. **Interviewee:** No. We had a job to do and we did it. There wasn't a lot of flag waving outside the states.
39. **Interviewer:** Is there anything else you would like to tell me about your experiences?
40. **Interviewee:** It was a different time from now. Nearly every family had someone in service, and most men and a great many women under 35 were in one service branch or another or working in the war plants. We placed life on hold and hoped for the best.
41. **Interviewer:** And you married your Marine after the war?
42. **Interviewee:** No.
43. **Interviewer:** Why not? Did you meet someone in the Army Air Corps?
44. **Interviewee:** Jim died in the invasion of Okinawa.
45. **Interviewer:** Oh. I'm, uh, sorry to hear that.
46. **Interviewee:** That's okay.
47. **Interviewer:** When and how did you meet Mr. Morosky?
48. **Interviewee:** In the early 1950s.
49. **Interviewer:** And when did you get married?
50. **Interviewee:** In 1956.
51. **Interviewer:** Well, that's all the questions I have. Thanks for your help with my project.

52. **Interviewee:** You're welcome. I haven't talked about the war for a long time.
53. **Interviewer:** Could you fill out this critique form and mail it to my professor?
54. **Interviewee:** Sure.

Student Activities

1. Watch an interview program on C-SPAN or an interview on sportingnews.com. Identify the types of questions asked. Which types of questions dominate? Which types of probing questions does the interviewer use? What question pitfalls can you detect?
2. Prepare two sets of 10 questions—one with all neutral questions and one with at least four leading questions. Interview four people, two with each list of questions. How did the answers vary to the neutral and leading questions? How did different people (age, gender, education, and occupation) react to leading and neutral questions?
3. Select a current local or national controversial issue and conduct two 8- to 10-minute interviews. Use only primary, open-ended questions in the first, and in the second, ask the same primary, open-ended questions plus probing questions. Compare and contrast the amount and nature of the information you attain in each interview.
4. Create a list of closed questions, including a number of bipolar questions, on a controversial issue. Interview three people, a friend or family member, an acquaintance, and a stranger. Which ones gave you closed, bipolar answers and which elaborated regardless of question types used? How can you explain the differences in the responses? What does this tell you about asking closed questions?
5. Tape-record a series of investigative interviews during a program such as *20/20*, *60 Minutes*, or *Dateline* and see if you can detect common question pitfalls. Which were intentional and which were unintentional? How did these affect the answers received? How did they appear to affect the climate of the interview?

Notes

1. Joyce Kasman Valenza, "For the best answers, ask tough questions," *The Philadelphia Inquirer,* April 20, 2000; http://www.joycevalenza.com/questions.html, accessed September 26, 2006.
2. See Stanley L. Payne, *The Art of Asking Questions* (Princeton, NJ: Princeton University Press, 1980), for an excellent discussion of types and uses of questions and difficulties in phrasing questions.
3. Payne (1980), p. 204.
4. Robert L. Kahn and Charles F. Cannell, *The Dynamics of Interviewing* (New York: John Wiley & Sons, 1964), p. 205.
5. Lillian Glass, *He Says, She Says: Closing the Communication Gap between the Sexes* (New York: Putnam, 1993), pp. 45–59.

Resources

A Questioning Toolkit, The Educational Technology Journal, 7, November–December, 1997; http://www.fno.org/nov97/toolkit.html, September 26, 2006.

Payne, Stanley L. *The Art of Asking Questions*. Princeton, NJ: Princeton University Press, 1980.

Types of Questions, http://www2.warwick.ac.uk/services/careers/undergrad/hunting/inttestass/interview/plan/, September 26, 2006.

What are the basic types of questions you can ask during an interview? http://scism.sbu.ac.uk/inmandw/tutorials/kaqa/qu7.htm, September 26, 2006.

Wood, Julia T. *But I Thought You Meant . . . Misunderstandings in Human Communication.* Mountain View, CA: Mayfield, 1998.

CHAPTER 4 Structuring the Interview

Since each interview has a predetermined and serious purpose, each has a degree of structure, the extent and nature of which are determined by purpose, length, and complexity. Different types of interviews (survey, recruiting, persuasion, counseling) may require a somewhat different structure, but fundamental principles and techniques apply to all. This chapter focuses on these principles and techniques and how they apply to the three major interview parts: opening, body, and closing.

Opening the Interview

It takes two parties to launch an interview successfully.

The few seconds or minutes of the opening are critical. What you do and say, or fail to do and say, influences how the other party perceives self, you, and the situation. The **opening** sets the tone for the interview and affects willingness and ability to go beyond Level 1 interactions. It may determine whether an interview continues or ends prematurely. The tone may be serious or lighthearted, optimistic or pessimistic, professional or nonprofessional, formal or informal, threatening or nonthreatening, relaxed or tense. A poor opening may lead to a **defensive climate** with superficial, vague, and inaccurate responses. If dissatisfied with the opening, a party may say no, walk away, close the door, or hang up the phone.

The primary function of the opening is to motivate both parties to participate willingly and to communicate freely and accurately. Motivation is a **mutual product** of interviewer and interviewee, so every opening must be a dialogue, not a monologue. It is *done with* the other party, not *to* the other party. Too often the interviewee is given little opportunity to say anything beyond single-word responses to opening questions such as "How are you this morning?" "Nice day, isn't it?" and "Got a minute?"

The Two-Step Process

The opening is a two-step process of establishing rapport and orienting the other party that encourages active participation and willingness to continue into the body of the interview. What is included and how content is shared depends upon interview type, the situation, relationship, and preference.

Establish Rapport

Rapport is a process of establishing and sustaining a relationship between interviewer and interviewee by creating feelings of goodwill and trust. You may begin with a self-introduction ("I'm Jessica McClone from technical assistance") or a simple greeting if the relationship is close ("Good morning, Jim") accompanied by appropriate nonverbal actions such as a firm handshake, eye contact, a smile, a nod, and a pleasant, friendly voice. The rapport step may proceed to personal inquiries ("How's your semester going?"). Small talk about the weather, mutual acquaintances, families, sports, or news events is common and often expected. Consider flavoring a personal inquiry and small talk with tasteful and appropriate humor.

Do not overdo small talk or compliments.

Customs of a geographical area, organizational traditions or policies, culture, status differences, relationship, formality of the occasion, interview type, and situation determine the appropriate verbal and nonverbal rapport-building techniques of each interview. Do not refer to strangers, superiors, or high-status persons by first names unless asked to do so. Limit humor or small talk when a party is busy or the situation is highly formal or serious. Overdoing sweet talk such as congratulations, praise, and expressions of admiration can turn off an interview party. Be sincere.

Orient the Other Party

Orientation is usually the second step in the opening. You may explain the purpose, length, nature of the interview, how the information will be used, and why and how you selected this party to interview. Study each situation carefully to determine the extent and nature of orientation that is essential.

Be careful of assuming too much or too little about the other party.

Do not assume that because you and the other party appear to be similar (sex, age, appearance, language, educational background, or culture) that you are similar in ways critical to the success of the interview. LaRay Barna warns that "The aura of similarity is a serious stumbling block to successful intercultural communication. A look-alike facade is deceiving when representatives from contrasting cultures meet, each wearing Western dress, speaking English, and using similar greeting rituals."[1] You may assume that you also share similar nonverbal codes, beliefs, attitudes, or values. "Unless there is overt reporting of assumptions made by each party, which seldom happens, there is no chance of comparing impressions and correcting misinterpretations." Be sure orientation is mutual so each knows the other and what to expect during the interview.

photo Digital Visions/Getty Images

What you do and say in the opening seconds sets the tone for the remainder of the interview.

Rapport and orientation are often intermixed and reduce **relational uncertainty.** By the end of the opening, both parties should be aware of important similarities, the desire of each to take part in the interview, degree of warmth or friendliness, how control will be shared, and levels of trust. An inadequate opening may mislead either party and create problems during an interview. Recall how angry you became when you discovered that an appeal for assistance from a stranger at your apartment door turned out to be a ruse to sell you magazine subscriptions.

The rapport and orientation steps are illustrated in the following opening.

1. **Interviewer:** Good morning, Josh. I see you're getting settled into your new office.
2. **Interviewee:** Hi Sarah. Yeah, I'm pretty well moved in, just a few boxes left.
3. **Interviewer:** How do the kids like their new schools?
4. **Interviewee:** Fine so far. Several of their classmates live in the neighborhood.
5. **Interviewer:** That's great. It's good to have you on the staff. I want to make arrangements for your new computer and software. We want to be sure you have everything you need as soon as possible, so I have some questions to ask before sending out orders.
6. **Interviewee:** Good. I'm anxious to get started, and I have a number of specific needs and concerns. Please have a seat.

Opening Techniques

Be creative when opening interviews, and always adapt to the interviewee and the situation rather than rely on a stock opening. The following **opening techniques** may build rapport, orient the other party, or serve as complete openings.

State the Purpose

This technique explains *why* you are conducting the interview.

Adapt the opening to each interviewee and situation.

Example: (a student to a professor) I've stopped by to talk to you about how I'm developing my outline for the midterm take-home paper. It's taking a long time to develop, and I'm still not sure I'm doing it the way you suggested in class.

There are occasions, however, when stating a detailed purpose would make its achievement difficult. This is the case in some research, survey, and sales interviews. You may need to withhold a specific purpose until later in the interview to get honest, unguarded answers, to motivate the interviewee to take part, or to avoid defensiveness.

Example: (an opinion poll for the Republican or Democratic Party three weeks prior to an election) I'm conducting a poll to determine how registered voters are leaning as the primary election approaches.

Summarize a Problem

Know when to end the opening and move on.

This technique is appropriate when an interviewee is unaware of a problem, vaguely aware of it, or unaware of details. Be sure the summary **informs** the interviewee but does not spill into the body of the interview.

Example: As you know, we began to outsource a lot of our photographic services about a year ago. At first this seemed to work quite well, but in recent months it has taken us longer and longer to get pictures, slides, and overheads prepared, cost has increased nearly 20 percent, and the quality has slipped. I'd like to talk to you about this situation.

Explain How a Problem Was Discovered

This technique explains *how* a problem was detected and perhaps *by whom*. Be honest and specific in revealing sources of information without placing the interviewee on the defensive.

> **Example:** Last night Gretchen came back to the building to pick up some materials for a presentation, and she discovered the front door propped open with a piece of wood, the printer room door open, and the graduate student computer lab unlocked. We obviously need to think about after-hours security.

Offer an Incentive or Reward

An incentive can be effective if it is appealing to the interviewee. It must be significant enough to make a difference and appropriate for the interview and situation. Because many sales pitches include a gift to motivate people to participate, it may become difficult to convince a respondent that you are conducting a research, journalistic, or survey interview if you offer an incentive.

> **Example:** I'm looking for students interested in taking part in a long-range study of college drinking habits, so I'm contacting first-year students such as you. My grant allows me to pay participants $5.00 for each weekly report they submit. Reports take about 15 minutes to complete.

Request for Advice or Assistance

Be sincere in offering incentives or requesting advice.

This is a common interview opening because help is often what an interviewer needs. Be sure the need is clear, precise, and one the interviewee can satisfy. Be sincere in asking for advice. Do not use this opening as a technique for another purpose such as networking, climbing the ladder, boosting one's ego, or "kissing up" to a superior.

> **Example:** Ralph, I'm lecturing tomorrow on the theory of cognitive dissonance in my persuasion course. Would you look over my outline and give me some pointers? I know you have done research on this theory.

Refer to the Known Position of the Interviewee

This technique identifies the interviewee's position on an issue or problem. Be cautious because a tactless or seemingly hostile reference to a known position may create a defensive attitude or antagonize the other party. A common problem is an inaccurate interpretation of the position.

> **Example:** Professor Knox, I know your position on extra credit work in your lecture course, but I would like to make a case for an exception.

Refer to the Person Who Sent You to the Interviewee

A referral is an excellent means of connecting positively with another party. Never use a person's name without permission to do so, and be sure the person you name did send you. Discover if the interviewee knows, respects, and likes the person you intend to name. It can be embarrassing or disastrous to discover after using a name that the interviewee does not recall or dislikes the reference.

> **Example:** I'm considering a career in labor–management relations, and my counselor, Jared Ortman, said you had spent nearly 20 years in such a career before coming to the College of Management.

Refer to Your Organization

Know what to do if references to an organization generate negative reactions.

Often you must refer to an organization you represent (company, hospital, government agency, church) to give you your identity. Your position with an organization may dictate whom you interview, when, where, and why. Realize that some interview parties will not be fans of your organization, particularly if you represent potential lawsuits, regulatory enforcement, or legal investigations.

> **Example:** (over the telephone) Good evening, is this Cynthia Dollar? . . . I'm Mike McMasters with the Mayor's commission on revitalizing old neighborhoods.

Request a Specific Amount of Time

Make an appointment for interviews of more than 5 or 10 minutes.

Ask for or state a realistic time, and by the end of this period, either complete the task or begin to close the interview. Give the interviewee an opportunity to continue the interview or to terminate it, perhaps arranging for another meeting. "Got a second?" is probably the most overused and misused interview opening.

> **Example:** Sean, do you have about 10 minutes to discuss the applicant who is joining us for lunch?

Ask a Question

Open-ended, easy to answer questions may enhance trust and begin to orient the interviewee. Common opening questions include:

> **Examples:** How did you hear about Whispering Pines Guest Ranch?
>
> What can I do to help with the Habitat for Humanity house our church is building?
>
> What are you looking for in study abroad programs?

Be careful of employing closed questions that can be answered with a quick no. Common closed, dead-end questions are:

> **Examples:** Can I help you?
>
> Do you need assistance?
>
> What are you looking for?

Many interviewees find questions with a single, obvious answer, yes-no questions, insulting.

Examples: Do you like my class?

Are we going to do anything important in class today?

Do you want a rewarding position?

These 10 opening techniques provide a variety of ways to open interviews effectively.

Use a Combination

Make the opening a dialogue between two parties.

Many openings include a strategic combination of techniques. Create an opening that is most appropriate for each interview and situation and avoid the temptation to use a standard or stock opening. We are all creatures of habit, and if a technique works well once, we may assume it is appropriate for a variety of situations. Above all, involve the interviewee in the opening. As an interviewee, insist on playing an active role from the beginning. Too many interviewers make the opening a monologue in which the interviewee is a mere bystander.

Nonverbal Communication in Openings

First impressions often determine the tone and flow of communication.

Verbal opening techniques must be accompanied by appropriate **nonverbal communication.** An effective opening depends upon *how* you look, act, and say *what* you say. Nonverbal communication is critical in creating a good first impression. It signals sincerity, trust and trustworthiness, warmth, interest, the seriousness of the interview, and the emotions being experienced.

Territoriality

Always knock before entering a room, even if the door is open, you are a superior, or you are in your own home, building, or organization. You are entering another's *space,* and any perceived violation of this territory is likely to begin an interview poorly. Wait until the other party signals to enter with a smile, head nod, wave, or pointing to a chair. Maintain good eye contact without staring because it shows trust and allows you to pick up nonverbal signals that say "come in," "be seated," "sit there," and "I'm interested/willing to talk to you."

Appearance and dress should send appropriate opening signals.

Appearance and Dress

Your appearance and dress contribute a great deal to first impressions. Both should communicate attractiveness, neatness, maturity, professionalism, and knowledge of what is appropriate dress for this interview and setting. Do not let physical appearance signal catastrophe when the interview will deal with routine matters, friendliness when you are about to discipline a person, warmth when you are angry, happiness when a major problem needs urgent attention, or closeness when you have never met.

Know when and with whom touch is appropriate.

Touch

If shaking hands is appropriate for the relationship and the situation, give a firm but not crushing handshake. Be careful of overdoing handshaking with acquaintances and colleagues or during informal interviews. Touching another on the hand, arm, or shoulder is generally appropriate only when both parties have an established and close relationship.

Reading Nonverbal Communication

Sex and culture regulate nonverbal communication in openings.

Do not underestimate the importance of verbal and nonverbal communication in openings, but do not read too much into simple words and nonverbal acts or try to read everyone the same. Even people of apparently similar backgrounds may differ significantly in communicative behavior.

Lillian Glass has catalogued 105 "talk differences" between American men and women in basic areas of communication: body language, facial language, speech and voice patterns, language content, and behavioral patterns. She has found that men touch others more often, tend to avoid eye contact and not look directly at the other person, sound more abrupt and less approachable, make direct accusations, and give fewer compliments.[2]

Americans share rules for greeting others, but these rules may not be shared with other cultures. Shaking hands, for instance, is a Western custom, particularly in the United States, so do not ascribe meaning to firmness or lack of firmness when interviewing persons from other cultures. They may see handshaking as merely a quaint Western custom of little importance. While Americans expect persons to look them in the eyes to exhibit trust, openness, and sincerity, other cultures consider such eye contact to be impolite and insulting. The United States is not a touching society, but do not be shocked if a party from Italy or Latin America touches you during an opening.

Quiz #1—Interview Openings

How satisfactory is each of the following openings? Consider the interviewing situation and type, the techniques used, and what is omitted. How might each be improved? Do not assume that each opening is unsatisfactory.

1. This interview is taking place at the front door of an apartment near a college campus. The parties have never met.

   Interviewer: Good afternoon, Ginny. (smiling, shakes hands vigorously) Got a couple of seconds?

   Interviewee: I'm studying for a final.

   Interviewer: Good. I'm conducting a survey about apartment conditions around the campus area and have a few questions. How long have you lived in this apartment?

2. This is a recruiting interview for a marketing position with a women's clothing chain.

   Interviewer: Hi. (shakes hands) I'm Janet Ho with Wilderness Casuals. Did you have a good drive down?

   Interviewee: Yes.

   Interviewer: Awesome. Well, let me begin by asking what you know about Wilderness Casuals.

3. This interview is taking place in a professor's office during her office hours. The student is one of nearly 300 in a large lecture course.

   Interviewer: Are we going to do anything important in class next Wednesday?

   Interviewee: Of course not!

   Interviewer: Oh, I didn't mean that we don't usually do important things in your class. I may be on a field trip with my botany class and didn't want to miss anything important.

4. This interview is taking place in the hallway near the U.S. Senate chamber between an ABC Capitol Hill correspondent and a senator. The senator is leaving the chamber to attend a subcommittee hearing on terrorism.

   Interviewer: Senator McCambridge! (waving and shouting) Would you comment on the chances of a terrorist attack during the fall election?

   Interviewee: We're going to be addressing that today.

   Interviewer: Are you concerned?

5. This interview is taking place between a manager and an assistant manager at a supermarket shortly before opening at 6:30 a.m.

   Interviewer: I saw Bill Dickens check in a few minutes ago. (serious tone of voice and frowning) Didn't you reassign him to the evening shift like I told you last week?

   Interviewee: Yes and no.

   Interviewer: Did you or didn't you?

   Interviewee: I'd like to talk to you about that.

The Body of the Interview

In a brief, informal interview, you may prepare little more than a few topic areas or questions and operate from memory or a piece of notepaper. For a longer, more formal interview, prepare a detailed outline of topics or carefully phrased questions. For formal interviews, such as surveys, prepare a schedule for the interview containing all questions and answer options.

Interview Guide

An interview guide contains topics, not questions.

An **interview guide** is a carefully structured outline of topics and subtopics to be covered during an interview. A guide helps you develop specific areas of inquiry, not a list of questions. This structure ensures coverage of all important topics and prevents forgetting important items during the heat of an interview. The guide may suggest follow-up questions and distinguish relevant from irrelevant information. It assists in **recording** answers and **recall** at a later date.

Outline Sequences

Since the interview guide is an outline, review the fundamentals of outlining learned over the years to impose a clear, systematic structure on each interview. **Outline sequences** are quite useful for interviews.

A **topical sequence** follows natural divisions of a topic or issue. For example, an interview during a search for a graduate school might include admissions criteria, areas of study, degree requirements, faculty, funding sources, and information on the school and university. The traditional **journalist's guide** consists of six key words: who, what, when, where, how, and why.

A **time sequence** treats topics or parts of topics in chronological order. For instance, an interviewer explaining a tour of Alaska might begin with air travel to Anchorage and then proceed with the bus trip to Denali National Park, train travel from Denali back to Anchorage, a bus trip to Seward where the party boards a cruise ship, and then the cruise south to Seattle with stops at Valdez, Skagway, Juneau, and Ketchikan.

Sequences help to organize topics and impose a degree of structure on interviews.

A **space sequence** arranges topics according to spatial divisions: left to right, top to bottom, north to south, or neighborhood to neighborhood. A student guide to a college campus might take you to a classroom building, the library, residence halls, athletic facilities, and recreational facilities.

A **cause-to-effect sequence** addresses causes and effects. For instance, what caused a serious decline in attendance at men's basketball games, an increase in alcohol abuse on campus, or the fact that fewer companies are taking part in job fairs on campus. An interviewer might begin with a cause or causes and then proceed to effect, or discuss an apparent effect and then move to possible causes.

A **problem-solution sequence** consists of a problem phase and a solution phase. You might discuss your grade with a professor first by identifying what you consider to be a serious problem and then by looking for solutions to improve quiz and exam scores. You might discuss a knee problem with a trainer and then ways to relieve the problem.

Developing an Interview Guide

Let's assume you are thinking about a safari to Kenya after graduating in May and before starting a position as a reporter with a Minneapolis television station. You have scheduled an interview with an experienced travel guide who is arranging his third safari to Kenya in May. First, decide on the major areas of information you want, such as the following topical sequence.

I. Cost
II. Kenya as a destination
III. Nature of the safari
IV. Requirements

Second, place possible subtopics under each major topic, such as the following:

A guide ensures the consideration of all important topics and subtopics.

I. Cost
  A. Transportation to and from the United States
  B. Housing
  C. Meals
  D. Souvenirs
  E. Tips

II. Kenya as a destination
   A. Safety
   B. Climate
   C. Topography
   D. Sites to see
   E. Animals

III. Nature of the safari
   A. Number of days
   B. Transportation in Kenya
   C. Housing in Nairobi and the bush
   D. People on the safari
   E. Meals
   F. Activities

IV. Requirements
   A. Language
   B. Immunizations
   C. Physical condition
   D. Clothing
   E. Equipment

Third, determine if there are subtopics of subtopics. For instance, you might want to know average temperature, typical breakfasts, safety from terrorists as well as animals, background of people on the safari, and specific types of clothing such as shoes, raingear, and hats. You may not know enough to develop subdivisions under some headings, or will discover subtopics as the interview progresses.

Interviews may include more than one sequence or none at all.

It is not unusual to employ more than one outline sequence in an interview. The sample outline is a topical sequence of major divisions, but a spatial sequence might be appropriate for subdivisions under housing.

Interview Schedules

A Nonscheduled Interview

After completing an interview guide, decide if additional structuring and preparation are needed. The guide may be sufficient, or you may transform all or part of it into questions. If you settle on a guide, you will conduct a **nonscheduled interview** with no questions prepared in advance. The nonscheduled interview is most appropriate when an interview will be brief, the information area is extremely broad, interviewees and information levels differ significantly, interviewees are reluctant to respond or have poor memories, or there is little preparation time.

A nonscheduled interview is merely an interview guide.

A nonscheduled interview gives you unlimited freedom to probe into answers and to adapt to different interviewees and situations because it is the most flexible of interview schedules. However, nonscheduled interviews require considerable interviewer skill and are difficult to replicate from one interview to another. You may have difficulty controlling for time limits. And interviewer bias may creep into unplanned questions. **Interviewer bias** occurs when interviewees respond in ways they think you want them to respond rather than reveal true feelings, attitudes, beliefs, or intentions.

A Moderately Scheduled Interview

A **moderately scheduled interview** contains all major questions with possible probing questions under each. The sentences and phrases in a guide become questions. The moderate schedule, like the nonscheduled interview, allows freedom to probe into answers and adapt to different interviewees, but it also imposes a greater degree of structure, aids in recording answers, and is easier to conduct and replicate. You need not create every question on the spot but have them thought out and carefully worded in advance. This lessens pressures during the interview. Since interview parties tend to wander during unstructured interviews, listing questions makes it easier to keep on track and return to a structure when desired. Journalists, medical personnel, recruiters, lawyers, police officers, and insurance investigators, to name a few, use moderately scheduled interviews. A moderately scheduled interview would look like this:

A moderately scheduled interview lessens the need for instant question creation.

I. Why did you choose to live in a residence hall?
   A. When did you decide to do this?
   B. Who influenced you most in your decision?
   C. What influenced you the most?
   D. How did you choose this residence hall?

II. What bothers you most about living in a residence hall?
   A. How about cost?
   B. How do you feel about having an assigned roommate?
   C. How do you feel about having a floor counselor checking on you?
   D. Is noise a problem?
   E. What do you think of the food selection in the dining court?

III. What are your future housing plans?
   A. Where do you think you will be living by your junior year?
   B. How might relationships affect your decision?
   C. You are close to the foreign language building; what if you changed majors or switched to another college on campus?
   D. How might increasing costs affect your decision?

A Highly Scheduled Interview

Highly scheduled interviews sacrifice flexibility and adaptability for control.

A **highly scheduled interview** includes all questions and the exact wording to be used with each interviewee. It permits no unplanned probing, word changes, or deviation from the schedule. Questions are usually closed in nature so respondents can give brief, specific answers. Highly scheduled interviews are easy to replicate and conduct, take less time than nonscheduled and moderately scheduled interviews, and prevent parties from wandering off to irrelevant areas or spending an inordinate amount of time on one or two topics. Flexibility and adaptation are not options, however. Probing questions, if any, must be planned. Researchers and survey takers use highly scheduled interviews such as the following:

I. Which problem pertaining to political campaigns concerns you the most?
   A. Why does this problem concern you the most?
   B. When did this problem begin to concern you?
   C. How do you think political parties and candidates should address this problem?
II. Do you believe this problem will be better or worse in this year's presidential campaign?
   A. (If the answer is better): Why do you feel it will be less of a problem this year?
   B. (If the answer is worse): Why do you feel it will be worse this year?
III. The majority of political candidates are using attack ads on television.
   A. Why do you think they are doing this?
   B. If you feel this trend will continue, why do you think so?
   C. How has your political consulting firm addressed this growing problem?

A Highly Scheduled Standardized Interview

Highly scheduled standardized interviews provide precision, replicability, and reliability.

The **highly scheduled standardized interview** is the most thoroughly planned and structured. All questions and answer options are stated in identical words to each interviewee who then picks answers from those provided. There is no straying from the schedule by either party. Highly scheduled standardized interviews are the easiest to conduct, record, tabulate, and replicate, so even novice interviewers can handle them. However, the breadth of information is restricted, and probing into answers, explaining questions, and adapting to different interviewees are not permitted. Respondents have no chance to explain, amplify, qualify, or question answer options. **Built-in interviewer bias** may be worse than **accidental bias** encountered in nonscheduled and moderately scheduled interviews.

Researchers and survey takers use highly scheduled standardized interviews because their procedures must produce the same results in repeated interviews by several interviewers. The following is a highly scheduled standardized interview:

I. Which of the following problems do you feel is the most important to you?
   A. More teaching assistants than faculty
   B. Classroom overcrowding
   C. Outdated labs and facilities
   D. Difficulty to get into required classes
   E. Tuition costs and fees
II. How likely is it that this problem will be resolved before you graduate?
   A. Highly likely
   B. Likely
   C. Unsure

D. Unlikely
E. Highly unlikely

III. Who do you think should determine the priority of problems?
A. Students
B. Professors
C. Provost
D. President
E. Alumni

IV. Rank order the solutions you would be willing to support to resolve this problem.
A. Tuition increase
B. A $1000 fee charged to all first-year students
C. Lab fees
D. Evening and/or Saturday classes
E. More large lecture courses

Each interviewing schedule has unique advantages and disadvantages. Your task is to choose the schedule best suited to needs, skills, type of information desired, and situation. Do not apply a favorite schedule to all interviews. A schedule designed for a survey would be a terrible schedule for an employment interview. Be aware of the options available and which one or ones seem most appropriate for each interview. Figure 4.1 summarizes the advantages and disadvantages of each schedule.

Combination of Schedules

Combined schedules enable interviewers to satisfy multiple needs.

Consider strategic combinations of schedules. For example, use a nonscheduled approach during the opening minutes, a moderately scheduled approach when it is necessary to probe and adapt to interviewees, and a highly scheduled standardized approach for easily quantifiable information such as demographic data on age, sex, religion, formal education, marital status, and organizational memberships. Although schedules are usually lists of questions, they may range from a topic outline to a manuscript. For instance, you might write major arguments for a persuasive interview, instructions for an information-giving interview, and the opening and closing for a survey interview.

Quiz #2—Interview Schedules

Which schedule would be most appropriate for each of the situations below: nonscheduled, moderately scheduled, highly scheduled, highly scheduled standardized? Explain why you would select this schedule.

1. You are a journalist interviewing a person who just escaped from a burning apartment complex.
2. As a member of the student government, you are conducting a survey of student attitudes toward the seating reserved for students behind the north goal in the basketball arena.
3. You are interviewing a professor to clarify the details of a field project assignment.

Figure 4.1 *Structural options*

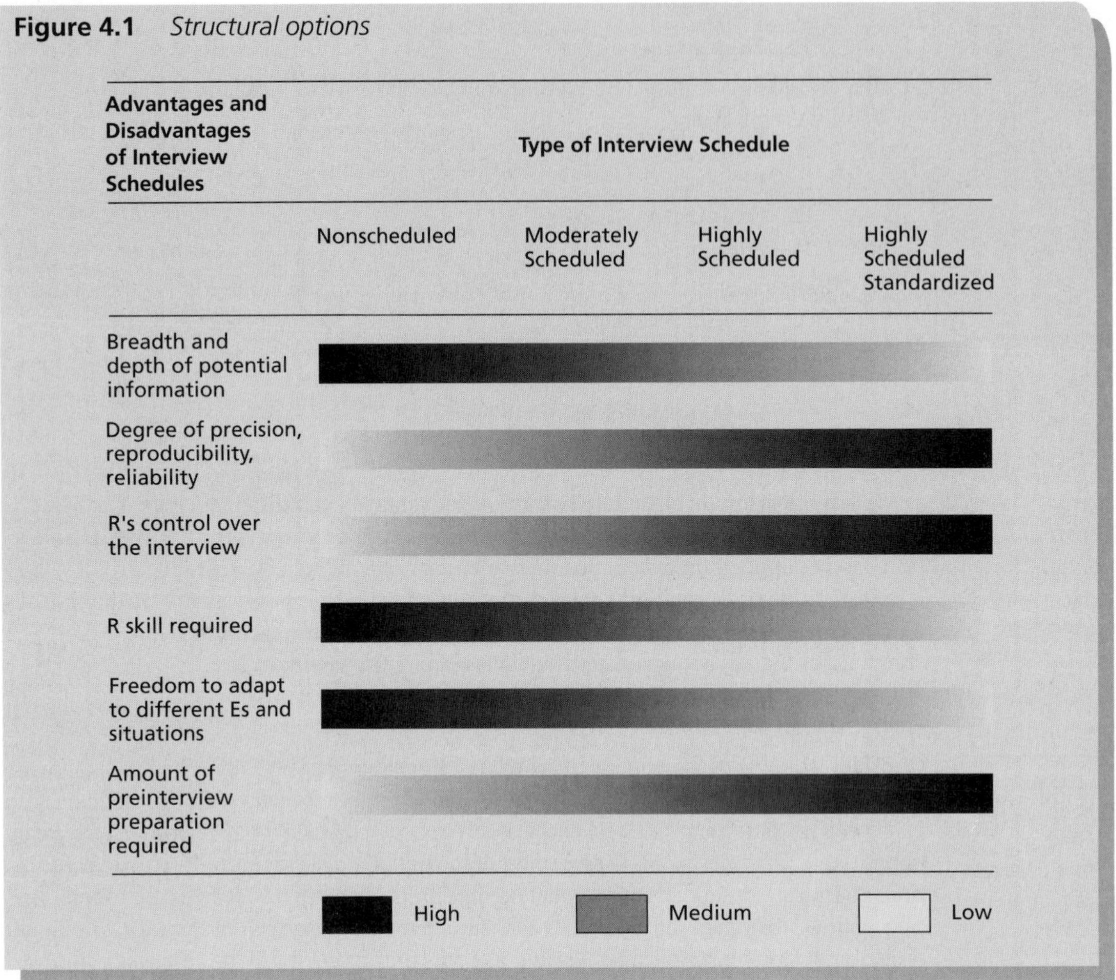

4. As a recent graduate of Mariana College, you have returned to campus to conduct recruiting interviews for your company.
5. You are conducting an interview with a grain farmer to persuade him to adopt no-till agriculture.

Question Sequences

In Chapter 3, we discussed a variety of question tools, and in this chapter we have introduced you to a variety of question schedules. It is now time to identify strategic use of question sequences. Common **question sequences** are tunnel, funnel, inverted funnel, hourglass, diamond, and quintamensional design.

Figure 4.2 *The tunnel sequence*

Open/closed questions Open/closed questions

Tunnel Sequence

A tunnel sequence works well with informal and simple interviews.

The **tunnel sequence,** sometimes called a *string of beads,* is a series of similar questions, either open or closed. Each question may cover a different topic, ask for a specific bit of information, or assess a different attitude or feeling. See Figure 4.2. This is a tunnel sequence.

I understand that you just got back from a vacation at a dude ranch.

1. Where was the ranch located?
2. What was the name of the ranch?
3. Who owns the ranch?
4. How long were you there?
5. What activities did you enjoy most?
6. Would you go back?

The tunnel sequence is common in polls, surveys, journalistic interviews, and medical interviews designed to elicit information, attitudes, reactions, and intentions. When the questions are closed in nature (perhaps a string of bipolar questions), information is easy to record and quantify.

Funnel Sequence

A funnel sequence works well with motivated interviewees.

A **funnel sequence** begins with broad, open-ended questions and proceeds with more restricted questions. See Figure 4.3. The following is a funnel sequence.

1. Tell me about your experiences in Afghanistan.
2. What were your most memorable experiences?
3. What areas did you operate in?
4. How long were you there?
5. Would you volunteer again if given the opportunity?

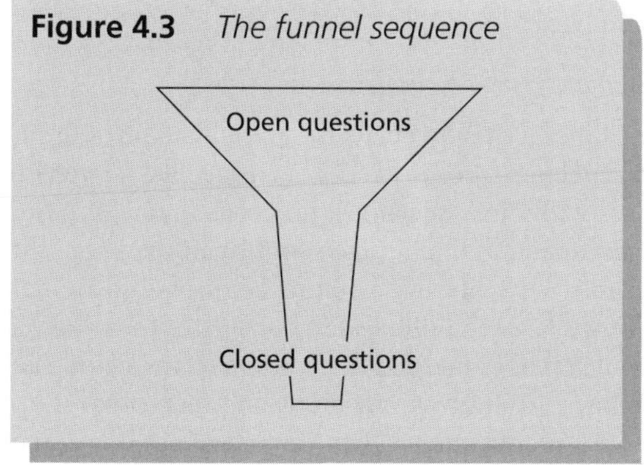

Figure 4.3 *The funnel sequence*

A funnel sequence that begins with an open-ended question is most appropriate when respondents are familiar with a topic, feel free to talk about it, want to express their feelings, and are motivated to reveal and explain attitudes. Open questions are easier to answer, pose less threat to respondents, and get people talking, so the funnel sequence is a good way to begin interviews.

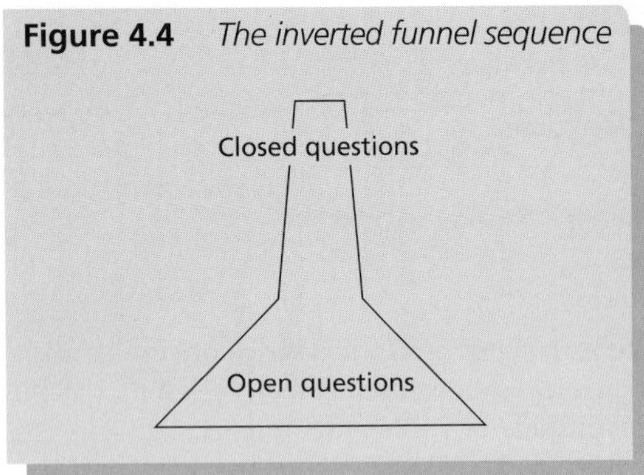

Figure 4.4 *The inverted funnel sequence*

The funnel sequence avoids possible conditioning or biasing of later responses. For example, if you begin an interview with a closed question such as "Do you think we should outlaw gay marriages?" you force a respondent to take a polar position that may affect the remainder of the interview and make the person defensive. An open question such as "How do you feel about gay marriages?" does not force respondents to take polarized positions and enables them to explain and qualify positions.

Inverted Funnel Sequence

The **inverted funnel sequence** begins with closed questions and proceeds toward open questions. It is most useful when you need to motivate an interviewee to respond or an interviewee is emotionally involved in an issue or situation. See Figure 4.4. The following is an inverted funnel sequence.

An inverted funnel sequence provides a warm-up time for those reluctant to talk.

1. **Interviewer:** You were the first to arrive on the scene?
2. **Interviewee:** Yes, I was.
3. **Interviewer:** That was about 2:35 p.m.?
4. **Interviewee:** Yes, about then.
5. **Interviewer:** And the car and semi were in the median?
6. **Interviewee:** Uh huh, they were on their sides facing in opposite directions.
7. **Interviewer:** Tell me what you saw.
8. **Interviewee:** Well, it was an awful, gruesome sight. The driver of the car was . . . (The interviewee goes into a lengthy, emotional account of the scene.)

The inverted funnel sequence is also useful when interviewees feel they do not know much about a topic or they do not want to talk. A respondent's memory or thought processes may need assistance, and closed questions can serve as warm-ups. Closed questions may work when open-ended ones might overwhelm a person. This sequence may end with a clearinghouse question such as "Is there anything else you would like to say?"

Figure 4.5 *The hourglass sequence*

Open questions

Closed questions

Open questions

Combination Sequences

Sometimes a situation calls for a combination of question sequences. For instance, the **hourglass sequence** begins with open questions, proceeds to one or more closed questions, and ends with open questions. It is employed when we wish to begin with a funnel sequence and then proceed in our line of questioning to an inverted funnel sequence. It is a combination that enables us to narrow our focus and then proceed to open it up once more when the interviewee or topic warrants it. See Figure 4.5.

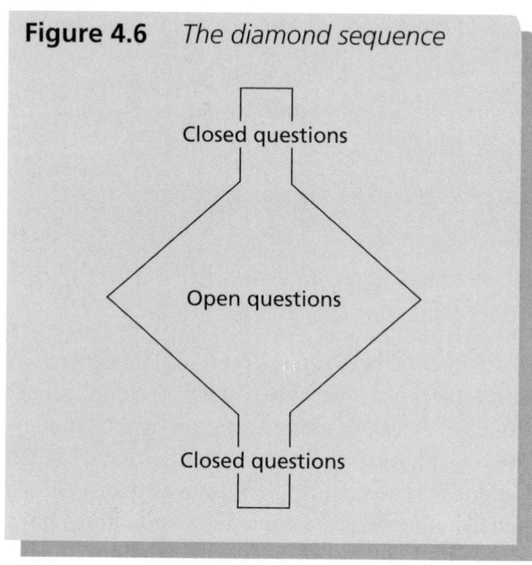

Figure 4.6 *The diamond sequence*

There is a second combination sequence that places funnel sequences top-to-top, what some writers call a **diamond sequence.**[3] This sequence enables interviewers to begin with closed questions, proceed to open questions, and end with closed questions. See Figure 4.6.

Each of these combination sequences offers different arrangements of open and closed questions that enable interviewers to approach specific interview situations and interviewees with greater flexibility and adaptability.

Quintamensional Design Sequence

George Gallup, the famous poll designer, developed the **quintamensional design sequence** to assess the intensity of opinions and attitudes.[4] This five-step approach proceeds from an interviewee's awareness of the issue to attitudes uninfluenced by the interviewer, specific attitudes, reasons for these attitudes, and intensity of attitude. For example:

The quintamensional design is effective at assessing attitudes and beliefs.

1. *Awareness:* What do you know about the proposed resumption of the military draft?
2. *Uninfluenced attitudes:* How might a military draft affect you?
3. *Specific attitude:* Do you approve or disapprove of resuming the military draft?
4. *Reason why:* Why do you feel this way?
5. *Intensity of attitude:* How strongly do you feel about this—strongly, very strongly, not something you will change your mind on?

You can use this sequence, or modify it by creating questions most suitable for specific interview situations.

Closing the Interview

The closing is an integral part of each interview, not something tacked on the end or an escape mechanism. Once you have asked or answered the last question, made your last point, or come to some sort of agreement with the other party, it is tempting to relax and feel the interview is complete. But an abrupt or tactless closing may undo the relationship established during the interview and agreements reached by making the other party feel like a discarded container—important only as long as needed.

Take your time and be tactful in what you say and do in the closing.

Functions and Guidelines for Closings

The **closing** has three primary functions.

First, the closing signals the termination of an interview but not a relationship. You may continue business, professional, social, and casual relationships with parties for years, and each interview creates or alters a relationship and sets positive or negative expectations about future interactions. Since many tasks require more than one

The closing often signals the continuation of a relationship.

interview to complete, a common element of closings is an agreement about when and where the next interview will take place:

> I see our time's up, and I have several more questions to ask; could we continue this interview when you get back from class?
>
> I'd like to keep track of your medical progress, so let's set another appointment early next week.
>
> The search committee has reviewed your application, and we would like you to come down for an interview. How about during your October break?

Simple phrases may communicate the likely interval between interviews. Phrases such as "See you" or "Until next time" signal short intervals. "Good-bye" and "So long" signal lengthy or forever intervals. "Let's stay in touch" and "Don't be a stranger" signal moderate intervals. "We'll be in touch" and "We'll call you" may signal the traditional "brush off" that means never. Be aware of cultural differences and expectations between parties that may lead to confusion about common closing phrases. People in other cultures have not understood that "We'll call you" is a brush off and have waited expectantly for calls.

Second, the closing may express supportiveness to enhance the relationship and bring the interview to a positive close. One or both parties may express appreciation, pleasure, or intention of future contacts. This is shown in the following interaction.

Interviewer: I really appreciate you taking the time to look over my outline for the midterm paper. It was taking a lot of time, and I wasn't sure I was doing it correctly.

Interviewee: I'm glad you stopped by because you were making the outline more difficult than it needed to be.

Interviewer: Thanks again for your help. I'll e-mail you if I have other questions.

A summary must reflect accurately the important elements of the interview.

Third, the closing may summarize the interview. Even when there is no systematic summary, either party may use the closing to bring the interview to an orderly ending and pull together issues, concerns, agreements, and information shared. Be sure the summary is accurate and addresses major areas of information, analysis, or agreement.

Rule number one for the closing, like the opening, is that it be a *dialogue,* not a monologue. Encourage the interviewee to take part through verbal and nonverbal signals. Be sincere and honest when closing an interview, and make no promises you cannot or will not keep. Don't rush the closing. The **law of recency** suggests that people recall the last thing said or done during an interview, so being rushed or dismissed with an ill-chosen phrase may jeopardize the interview's effects, your relationship, and future contacts with this party. The other party is likely to be observing and interpreting everything you say and do, and everything you *don't say* and *don't do,* until you are out of sight and sound. A slip of the lip or an inappropriate nonverbal act may negate all that you have accomplished prior to the closing. Leave the door open and set the groundwork for future contacts. If additional contact is planned, explain *what* will happen, *where* it will happen, *when* it will happen, and *why* it will happen. If appropriate, make an appointment before leaving. Don't introduce new topics or ideas when the interview has in fact or psychologically come to a close. Avoid **false closings** that occur when your verbal

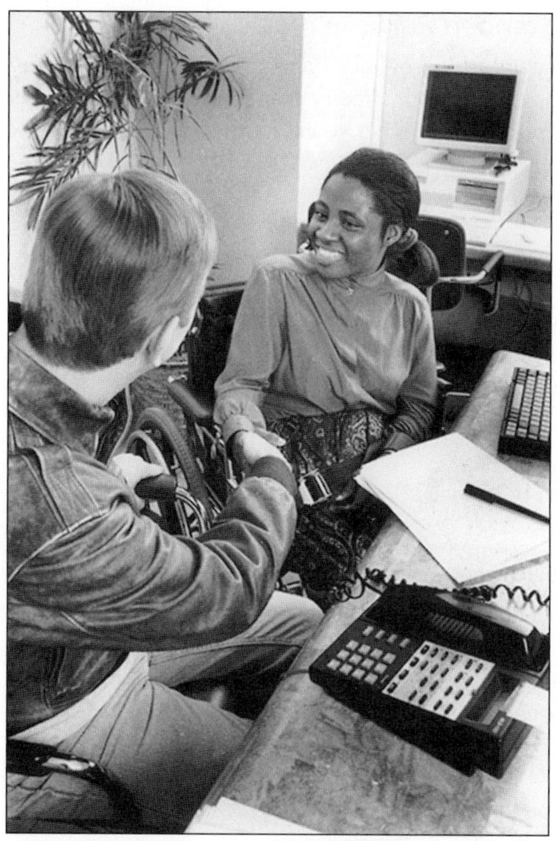
photo by Bob Daemmrich/Stock Boston

Remember that the interview is not completed until the interviewer and interviewee are out of sight and sound of one another.

and nonverbal messages signal the interview is coming to a close when it is not. Avoid what Irving Goffman has called **failed departures** that occur when you have brought an interview to a successful close and taken leave from the other party. Then a short time later you run into the party in the hall, parking lot, or restaurant.[5] The result is awkward because both of you have said your good-byes (after interviewing for a position, talking to a counselor, purchasing a product), and now you try to think of something appropriate to say when there is nothing to say. Practice situations to determine what you might say when this happens to avoid awkward and embarrassing moments.

Closing Techniques

Be creative and imaginative in closing interviews. Adapt each closing to the interviewee and the situation. The following techniques may serve as entire closings, begin the closing process, or complete the closing.

Offer to Answer Questions

Be sincere in your desire to answer questions and give the other party adequate time to ask them.

I'll be interested in hearing what you think about the new guidelines.

Do you have any questions about the implementation of Plan Q?

Do you have any questions before we end this videoconference?

Regardless of technique, involve the interviewee in the closing.

Do not give a brief answer to one question and then end the interview.

Use Clearinghouse Questions

A clearinghouse question allows you to determine if you have covered all topics, answered all questions, or resolved all concerns. Be sure the request is communicated as an honest and sincere effort to ferret out unaddressed questions, information, or areas of concern, not as a formality.

Questions, intentions, and inquiries allow you to close effectively.

Is there anything else you would like to add before we leave?

Are there questions I have not addressed?

Are there any problems we have not taken into consideration?

Declare Completion of the Intended Purpose

State that the task is completed. The word *well* probably signals more closings than any other word or phrase. When we hear it, we automatically assume that leave-taking is commencing and begin to wind things up. Is this what you want to happen?

That covers all of my questions.

Okay, that's a wrap.

That clarifies all of my concerns.

Make Personal Inquiries

Be genuinely interested in the other party.

Personal inquiries are pleasant ways to end interviews and to enhance relationships. They must be sincere and give the interviewee adequate time to address an inquiry or concern. Be sincerely interested.

When do you leave for your vacation in Venice?

How's your father doing?

Are you still planning to go to graduate school?

Make Professional Inquiries

Professional inquiries are more formal than personal ones, but they must be sincere and show genuine interest. We like persons who show interest in our careers.

How is your student teaching going at Westwood?

When does your term on the city council begin?

What are your plans for attending the Southwest Broadcasters convention?

Signal That Time Is Up

Do not rush the closing but end the interview when most appropriate.

This technique is most effective when a time limit was agreed to in advance or during the opening. Be tactful, and avoid the impression that you are running an interview assembly line.

I'm sorry, but I have a class in a few minutes.

Well, our time's up for today. How about meeting again this time next Wednesday?

You were kind enough to meet with me for a half-hour, and I've used up that time.

Explain the Reason for the Closing

Explain honestly why the interview must end. A phony-sounding reason can harm the interview and relationship.

I must close the interview because of a previous appointment.

I'm sorry, but I have another student waiting to see me at 10:45.

Our office closes in a few minutes.

Express Appreciation or Satisfaction

A statement of appreciation or satisfaction is a common closing because you have usually received something—information, assistance, evaluation, a story, a sale, a position, a recruit, time. Be sincere.

It has been great talking to you, and I really appreciate your help.

Thanks for your help.

I appreciate your willingness to listen to my problem.

Arrange for the Next Meeting

If a subsequent interview is necessary, arrange it now.

If appropriate, set up the next meeting or reveal what will happen next, including date, time, place, topic, content, or purpose.

I have some additional questions to ask; could we meet at the same time on Friday?

This has been a good start on this issue. How about getting together again on the 5th?

Could you come for a daylong interview at our regional office in Memphis on the 14th or 15th?

Summarize the Interview

A summary closing is common for informational, performance, counseling, and sales interviews. It may repeat important information, stages, and agreements or verify accuracy and agreement.

I'm glad we could get together before the board meeting on Wednesday. You will give the PowerPoint presentation on sales figures and marketing costs for the second quarter, and I will present our proposal for realigning the marketing districts. We will then discuss our concerns about trimming three staff positions at this time.

Nonverbal Closing Actions

In their classic study of leave-taking, Mark Knapp and his colleagues discovered that people employ a variety of **nonverbal closing actions.**[6]

- Straightening up in our seat.
- Leaning forward.
- Standing up or moving away from the other party.
- Uncrossing our legs.
- Placing our hands on our knees as if preparing to rise.
- Breaking eye contact.
- Offering to shake hands.
- Making hand movements.
- Smiling.
- Looking at a clock.

These nonverbal actions can signal when you want to close an interview or detect when another wants to close. Avoid sending unintentional closing signals. *Remember that any act may be interpreted in a meaningful way by the other party.* You may be unaware that you looked at a watch or leaned forward, or you may look at a clock to be sure you have adequate time remaining, but the other party may take these as leave-taking activities. As professors, we learned long ago not to look at our watches when talking with students in our offices. Students would immediately take this as a cue that we wanted them to leave. We have placed small clocks strategically on our desks so that students do not notice when we must check time for an upcoming class, meeting, or appointment.

Plan the closing as carefully as you do the opening and body of the interview.

Be aware of what words and actions are *saying* to the other party. Decide which closing techniques are most suitable. Your role in an interview and your relationship with the other party may require some techniques, rule out others, and determine who will initiate the closing and when. Often you will combine several verbal and nonverbal techniques into effective closings. For example:

> Well (closing a notebook), I think that answers all of my questions. (leaning forward and smiling) You've given me a lot of exciting information for my field project. (rising from the chair) I really appreciate your help. (shakes hands and looks the interviewee directly in the eyes)

Quiz #3—Interview Closings

How satisfactory is each of the following closings? Consider the interviewing situation and type, relationship, the techniques used, nonverbal communication, and what is omitted. How might each be improved? Do not assume each closing is unsatisfactory.

1. This is a recruiting interview taking place at KBRC-TV. The applicant is applying for a position as a meteorologist and recently graduated in agriculture from the state university. The applicant's experience is limited to the university's FM radio station.

   Recruiter: Okay, I think it's time for my next interview. (stands up) This has been informative.

   Applicant: I really enjoyed talking with you.

   Recruiter: Good. (shakes hands, does not look the applicant in the eyes) We'll be in touch. Good luck with your job search.

2. This is an academic counseling interview between a student and a counselor about academic progress.

   Counselor: Well (leaning forward), I'm glad to see that your grades are improving and you're moving through your required courses on schedule. I have another appointment in a few minutes.

   Counselee: Thanks. I've been working real hard.

   Counselor: (leaning back) What are your plans for specializing when you've completed the general requirements for the communication major?

ON THE WEB

This chapter has presented guidelines and techniques for developing effective openings and closings. Use the Internet to locate sample interviews on issues such as education, the economy, foreign affairs, and medicine. Critique the openings and closings used in these interviews. Two useful Internet resources for locating interviews are CNN (http://cnn.com) and C-SPAN (http://indycable.com/cabletv/comastindyupgrade/ch24.htm).

3. This is a journalistic interview between a television news reporter and a detective investigating a hit-and-run case near the airport.

Reporter: So you feel alcohol was probably involved in this case? And it's the third near the airport this year?

Detective: Yes we do.

Reporter: Back to you in the studio Liz.

4. This is a health care interview. Dave is having an eye examination following a severe infection the previous year.

Doctor: Your eye looks great, Dave. (looking at her watch) How's Dave Jr. doing in the Marines?

Patient: He's been in the Middle East in a pretty dangerous area for about five months.

Doctor: Uh huh. (opening the door) Be sure to see Tara at the front desk for your next appointment.

5. This is a sales interview at an electronics store. Melissa and Mark have been looking at 50″ plasma televisions.

Salesperson: We can make you a good deal on a 42″ Sony plasma TV.

Melissa: Well, we're sort of looking right now at 50″ sets.

Salesperson: Come back if I can be of help.

Mark: Thanks. See ya.

Summary

All three parts of each interview—opening, body, and closing—are vital to its success. Do not underestimate the importance of both words and nonverbal actions and reactions during all three stages. Be conscious of cultural differences that affect the meaning of actions such as handshaking, eye contact, voice, touch, and gestures.

The opening influences how both parties perceive themselves and one another. It sets the tone for the remainder of the interview, orients the interviewee, and influences the willingness of both parties to communicate beyond Level 1. The opening often determines whether the interview will continue or end prematurely. Select opening techniques most appropriate for each interview.

The body of the interview must be carefully structured with an appropriate sequence that guides the interviewer's questions, areas of information, or points systematically and allows the interviewee to understand where the interview is going and why. A nonscheduled interview is simply an interview guide with topics and subtopics an interviewer wants to cover. A moderately scheduled interview contains all major questions and possible probing questions under each. A highly scheduled interview includes all questions to be asked during an interview. A highly scheduled standardized interview contains all questions to be asked with prescribed answer options under each. Question sequences allow strategic structuring of questions within scheduled interviews.

The closing not only brings the interview to an end but may summarize information, verify agreements, arrange future contacts, and enhance relationships. A good closing should make both parties glad they took part and pleased with the results. Be sincere and honest. Do not rush the closing. Both sides should be actively involved in the closing.

Key Terms and Concepts

The online learning center for this text features FLASHCARDS and CROSSWORD PUZZLES for studying based on these terms and concepts.

Accidental bias
Built-in interviewer bias
Cause-to-effect sequence
Closing
Closing techniques
Combination schedule
Culture
Defensive climate
Diamond sequence
Failed departures
False closings
Funnel sequence
Highly scheduled interview
Highly scheduled standardized interview
Hourglass sequence
Interview guide
Interview schedules
Interviewer bias
Inverted funnel sequence
Journalist's guide
Law of recency
Moderately scheduled interview
Nonscheduled interview
Nonverbal communication
Noverbal closing actions
Opening
Opening techniques
Orientation
Outline sequences
Problem-solution sequence
Question sequences
Quintamensional design sequence
Rapport
Relational uncertainty
Space sequence
Territoriality
Time sequence
Topical sequence
Tunnel sequence

An Interview for Review and Analysis

This interview is taking place between a student and the director of security at Presbyterian Medical Center, a large, multiple-building complex near the center of a large city. The student is graduating next year in criminal justice and is considering law enforcement as a career. The director of security knows his mother, who is a registered nurse at Presbyterian Medical Center.

How satisfactory is the opening? Does the student employ one or more structural sequences? Which type of schedule does the student seem to employ? Does the student employ one or more question sequences? How satisfactory is the closing? How might nonverbal communication have influenced the opening, body, and closing?

1. **Student:** Good morning, Mr. Kim. Are you busy?
2. **Director:** No, I'm just sitting here. (laughs) What can I do for you?
3. **Student:** I called about my interest in a career in law enforcement. I think you know my mom.
4. **Director:** Maybe. (offers a seat) What's her name?
5. **Student:** Ashley Hardebeck. I'm Tim.
6. **Director:** Oh yes, I've known her for several years. How is she?
7. **Student:** She's doing fine. She's teaching some forensics science courses at Colby College.
8. **Director:** That sounds fascinating. Those CSI TV shows have really generated interest in forensic science. I'm willing to help you if I can.
9. **Student:** Thanks. (pause) As I mentioned on the phone, I'm a student in criminal justice and am considering a career in law enforcement.
10. **Director:** Uh huh. (laughs) And you want to know how I got here?
11. **Student:** Well, yeah, sort of. (appears nervous) How did you get started in law enforcement?
12. **Director:** My first job was as a night watchman at the courthouse. I was in criminal justice like you.
13. **Student:** Awesome! (sounds excited) How did you get this job?
14. **Director:** My grandfather was a county commissioner, and he set it up.
15. **Student:** Oh. And then what did you do after graduating?
16. **Director:** Well (pause), actually, I didn't graduate. I joined the Air Force after my sophomore year and chose air police.
17. **Student:** And then what happened?
18. **Director:** I served at bases in South Korea, Japan, and Alaska.
19. **Student:** What were your duties?
20. **Director:** Mainly security detail with some opportunities to do investigative work for a JAG unit.
21. **Student:** That sounds great. How long were you in the Air Force?
22. **Director:** Nearly eight years.
23. **Student:** And then what did you do?
24. **Director:** When I came home I became a deputy with the Sheriff's Department here in Lake County.
25. **Student:** And did you move up through the ranks?

26. **Director:** Yes, I became a sergeant within a few years.
27. **Student:** And when did you move into your current position?
28. **Director:** About three years ago. I retired after 20 years with the Sheriff's Department and wanted a less hectic career until retirement.
29. **Student:** I see. (looks at notes) Well, that's about all I need, I think.
30. **Director:** Good luck in your career decision. You can have a lot worse career than one in law enforcement.
31. **Student:** Why do you say that? (closes notebook and picks up a jacket)
32. **Director:** Well, it's an important role in society and can be very rewarding. Like all jobs, it can be boring at times, but there are some really exciting times as well.
33. **Student:** Tell me about some of these.
34. **Director:** The boring ones or the exciting ones?
35. **Student:** The exciting ones, of course.
36. **Director:** Several come to mind. There was the time in Korea when a North Korean agent breached our outer security fences. And I remember a time in Alaska when a moose showed up in the barracks area. And, of course, there were somewhat routine investigations of drug sales on base, drunken airmen coming from town, and—here at the hospital—a patient escaping from his room and running through the waiting room with his wide-open gown flapping around.
37. **Student:** Gee, you've had some interesting experiences. Thanks for your time. Could I come by again if I have some questions?
38. **Director:** Sure, but it would be best to set up an appointment.
39. **Student:** Okay.

Student Activities

1. Watch several television interviews, and observe how they are opened. Which techniques are most common? How are these techniques related to relationships, interview types, situations, and length of interviews? Which nonverbal actions did you observe, and how did these affect the openings? How effective were rapport-building and orientation?
2. Watch several television interviews, and observe how they are closed. Which techniques are most common? How are these techniques related to relationships, interview types, situations, and length of interviews? Which nonverbal actions did you observe, and how did these affect the closings? Were there any false closings and, if so, how did the parties handle them and bring interviews to a close?
3. Record a televised interview of at least 10 to 15 minutes in length. Construct an interview guide from it. Which structural sequences did the interviewer use? Which type of question schedule do you think the interviewer used? Which question sequences did the interviewer employ? How do you think interview type, situation, relationship between parties, and issue affected the interviewer's choices?

4. Conduct one interview over the Internet and one face-to-face in which you focus on interview structure. How did the Internet affect interactions, particularly during the opening and closing? What did you do differently when preparing for these two interviews? Which mode of interviewing did you find most appealing and most difficult?

Notes

1. LaRay M. Barna, "Stumbling Blocks in Intercultural Communication," in Larry A. Samovar and Richard E. Porter, eds., *Intercultural Communication: A Reader* (Belmont, CA: Wadsworth, 1988), pp. 323–324.
2. Lillian Glass, *He Says, She Says: Closing the Communication Gap between the Sexes* (New York: Putnam, 1993), pp. 45–59.
3. http://scit.wlv.ac.uk/university/scit/modules/cp4414/lectures/week3interview/sld021, accessed September 28, 2006.
4. George Gallup, "The Quintamensional Plan for Question Design," *Public Opinion Quarterly* 11 (1947), p. 385.
5. Erving Goffman, *Relations in Public* (New York: Basic Books, 1971), p. 88.
6. Mark L. Knapp, Roderick P. Hart, Gustav W. Friedrich, and Gary M. Shulman, "The Rhetoric of Goodbye: Verbal and Nonverbal Correlates of Human Leave-Taking," *Speech Monographs* 40 (1973), pp. 182–198.

Resources

Barone, Jeanne Tessier, and Jo Young Switzer. *Interviewing Art and Skill*. Boston: Allyn and Bacon, 1995.

Knapp, Mark L., Roderick P. Hart, Gustav W. Friedrich, and Gary M. Shulman. "The Rhetoric of Goodbye: Verbal and Nonverbal Correlates of Human Leave-Taking," *Speech Monographs* 40 (1973), pp. 182–198.

Krivonos, Paul D., and Mark L. Knapp. "Initiating Communication: What Do You Say When You Say Hello?" *Central States Speech Journal* 26 (1975), pp. 115–125.

Wilson, Gerald L., and H. Lloyd Goodall Jr. *Interviewing in Context*. New York: McGraw-Hill, 1991.

Zunin, Leonard, and Natalie Zunin. *Contact: The First Four Minutes*. London: Random House, 1986.

CHAPTER 5 The Probing Interview

The probing interview is the most common of interviews.

The **probing interview,** what we often think of as the **journalistic interview,** is the most common of all interviews because we experience them as interviewer or interviewee nearly every day. Journalists, as well as recruiters, police officers, counselors, supervisors, employees, consumers, professors, students, parents, and children, rely on probing interviews to obtain and impart all sorts of information, attitudes, opinions, and feelings. Probing interviews may be as brief and informal as a student inquiring about a grade after class or as lengthy and formal as a 30- to 40-minute interview between a journalist and CEO about a potential merger or a political consultant and a political candidate talking about the content of proposed campaign ads.

Regardless of length, formality, or setting, the **purpose** of the probing interview is to get relevant and timely information as accurately and completely as possible in the shortest amount of time. Gathering this information requires careful questioning, insightful listening and observing, and skillful probing into answers to dig beneath surface information for facts, examples, stories, explanations, attitudes, and reactions. Unfortunately, few of us are trained in interviewing. Chip Scanlan (author of *Reporting and Writing: Basics for the 21st Century*) writes that even "journalists get little or no training in this vital aspect of their job. Most learn by painful trial and error."[1]

Preparing the Interview

Successful probing interviews are thoroughly planned, sometimes rehearsed, and skillfully executed. There is no typical probing interview to serve as a model to follow because, as Eric Nalder the Pulitzer Prize winning chief investigative reporter for the *Seattle Times,* writes, they are as varied as the conversations we have and the people we talk to.[2] Preparation consists of determining a purpose, researching the topic, and structuring the interview. Scanlan describes interviewing as "a process, like writing, that involves a series of decisions and actions designed to get the best possible information."[3] The first step in this process is to determine your purpose.

Your purpose controls how you prepare and what you do in probing interviews.

Determining the Purpose

Begin by deciding exactly *why* you are going to conduct an interview. What is the end product? What kinds of information do you want: facts, opinions, feelings, expert testimony, eye witness accounts? A clear purpose is essential in determining the length and number of interviews, selecting interviewees, and deciding when and where to conduct interviews. Ken Metzler, a long-time professor of journalism at the University of Oregon, claims that when you know exactly what you want, "you're halfway there."[4]

The **situation** might constrict a purpose. For instance, if the setting is a news conference or briefing, the interviewee party may dictate the types and numbers of questions you can ask, information available, whether some topics will be off the record, quotations you can attribute to the interviewee, and when you may report certain facts and opinions. Situational factors such as seriousness of a problem, availability of sources, and recency of incidents may determine the urgency of interviews, how long you will have to conduct interviews, and what you can ask ethically and legally.

Researching the Topic

Be thoroughly briefed on the interview topic so you can determine what information and insights an interview can generate that are not readily available in other resources such as a course syllabus, books, journal articles, the Internet, library, annual reports, manuals and court documents. **Research** enables you to ask intelligent and insightful questions and avoid **false assumptions** about causes and effects, the willingness of a source to give important information, or the ability of a source to give information accurately. Some journalists recommend that research time should be 10 times the actual interview time.[5]

The Internet and databases are becoming essential resources for interviews.

Search through personal and organizational records, archives, and clipping files. Talk to colleagues and friends who have had occasion to study the topic or issue. Search through corporate, church, school, and courthouse records, publications, and documents. Visit the local or college library for reference works, atlases, almanacs, organizational and city directories, government documents, books, encyclopedias, professional journals, newspapers, periodicals, and biographical dictionaries. Browse the Internet. Some topics will take you to specialized libraries or computer databases devoted to law, medicine, former presidents, history, or technology.

Paying attention to omissions, dates, and interim events may help to focus your purpose.

While researching a topic or issue, pay attention to what is not included in available materials, such as explanations, interpretations of data, the many sides of an issue, attitudes, and feelings. How dated is available information? What has happened in the interim that might alter attitudes, preliminary data, or cherished dogma? What anecdotes and quotations might be important for a report or story?

Revealing that you have done your multifaceted homework is important. Eric Raymond and Rick Moen recommend that "when you ask your question, display the fact that you have done these things first; this will help establish that you're not being a lazy sponge and wasting people's time. Better yet, display what you have *learned* from doing these things. We like answering questions for people who have demonstrated they can learn from the answers."[6] On the other hand, ignorance or failure to do adequate homework may anger an interviewee, destroy your credibility, or embarrass you and your organization. There is no quicker way to lose the respect of an interviewee than an uninformed question or reaction. Don't try to impress a person with your knowledge of a topic but be prepared sufficiently to establish your credibility and show you understand the topic. Phrase initial questions to indicate your familiarity with an area such as science, medicine, technology, or history.

Show interest in me, and I'll show interest in you.

Evidence of research impresses interviewees, shows you cannot be easily fooled, and motivates people to respond more readily and in depth. We are flattered when

ON THE WEB

Use the Internet to research your college or one that you might select as a graduate or professional school. Focus first on the college or university, then on the school or college within this larger structure, and finally on the department. What kinds of information are readily available? How up-to-date is the information? What kinds of information are not included that you would have to discover through interviews with faculty or students?

others take the time to learn about us, our interests, fields, accomplishments, and opinions because we take pride in what we do and who we are. Know appropriate jargon and technical terms and use and pronounce them correctly. Know the respondent's name (and how it is pronounced), title, and organization. You should know if a person is a professor or an instructor, an editor or a reporter, a pilot or a navigator, and a doctor with a PhD, MD, DVM, DDS, DO, or EdD degree.

Structuring the Interview

Interview Guide

As you research a topic, jot down areas and subareas that might evolve into an **interview guide.** The guide may be an elaborate outline, major aspects of a topic, key words in a notebook, or the traditional journalistic interview guide.

- *Who* was involved?
- *What* happened?
- *When* did it happen?
- *Where* did it happen?
- *How* did it happen?
- *Why* did it happen?

Length, sophistication, and importance of the interview may dictate the nature of the guide.

Plan a structural sequence but remain flexible.

Refer to the structural sequences discussed in Chapter 4. Chronological sequences are particularly effective in moving through stories or happenings because they have occurred in time sequences. A logical sequence such as cause-to-effect or problem-to-solution is appropriate for dealing with issues and crises. A space sequence is helpful when an interview will deal with places. Remain flexible because few probing interviews go exactly as planned.

The Opening

Plan an **opening** that will establish an atmosphere of mutual trust and respect and create a positive relationship with the interviewee. Metzler recommends that we prepare "for 'small talk' or 'icebreaker' kinds of" questions and comments. Many of us are not good

A solid opening is essential in motivating an interviewee.

at such things without careful thought, or we might overprepare so they sound trite, mechanical, or staged. Do not be too familiar with the interviewee. Are you really on a first name or nickname basis? If you are a stranger, identify yourself, your position, and the organization you represent. Even if you are well known to another, explain *what* you wish to discuss and *why,* reveal how the information will be *employed,* and state *how long* the interview will take. Don't pull out a notebook or produce a tape recorder immediately because these can threaten the interviewee.

Consider an ice-breaker question about something you have noticed in the interviewee's office or about hobbies, interests, or a news item. Congratulate the person on a recent recognition or accomplishment. Insert something humorous that you discovered in your research or encountered in planning the interview. Refer tactfully to the interviewee's position on an issue. Ice-breaker questions and comments create interest in the interview and get people talking and ready to discuss substantive questions and issues. Don't begin with difficult or potentially embarrassing questions. Raymond and Moen warn, "Beware of asking the wrong question." Prepare the opening question carefully: "Think it through. Hasty sounding questions get hasty answers, or none at all. The more you do to demonstrate that having put thought and effort into solving your problem before seeking help, the more likely you are to actually get help."

Review the opening techniques discussed in Chapter 4 and select one or a combination best suited for this interview. Don't fall into the habit of using a stock opening for all occasions.

Design the opening to fit each occasion and interviewee.[7] A casual compliment, friendly remark about a topic or mutual friend, or a bit of small talk might create a friendly, relaxed atmosphere with one person and produce the opposite effect with a busy, hassled interviewee who neither likes nor has time for small talk. As we discussed in Chapter 1, establishing a positive relationship between interviewer and interviewee is critical to the success of every interview. Try to establish a "friendly conversational rapport, like old friends talking" without seeming to be too friendly or close. Enhance the relationship, but don't try to leap beyond it.[8] Avoid any semblance of artificiality in the opening.

Know what "off the record" means to both parties.

Be sure both parties have a mutual understanding of **ground rules** governing the interaction before proceeding past the opening. This is particularly important in investigative interviews conducted by police officers, journalists, and supervisors. If everything of importance is **off the record,** why conduct the interview? Make it clear there can be no retroactive off-the-record demands. Be sure both parties understand what "off the record" means. It may mean not naming the source or using information only as background. If a person does not want to be quoted, try to get agreement that quotations may be attributed to an unnamed source or worked into the text of a report without attribution.

A moderate schedule is a useful tool for long interviews.

Body

If the interview will be brief or you are highly skilled in conducting probing interviews and phrasing questions, you may prepare only a guide and conduct a nonscheduled interview. If not, develop a moderate schedule that turns topics and subtopics into primary questions and provides possible probing questions under each.

The moderate schedule eliminates the necessity of creating each question at the moment of utterance and allows you to phrase questions carefully and precisely. At the same time, the moderate schedule allows **flexibility** to delete questions or create new ones as the need or opportunity arises. For instance, you may accidentally discover an issue or topic not detected during research or planning that warrants a detour.

Interviewers often fear that if they digress from the planned schedule or guide, they will lose their train of thought and control of the interview. These risks are worth taking, and the moderate schedule minimizes them. You can return to your schedule and pick up where you left off. Thomas Berner recommends that if a good question comes up in answer to another question, jot it down in the margin of your schedule and return to it when most appropriate.[9] The freedom to adapt and improvise to each interviewee, situation, and response makes the moderate schedule ideal for probing interviews.

Closing

Abide by time limits.

End the interview when the information is attained or time runs out. If an interview is limited to 15 minutes, for instance, complete the interview in this time or prepare to close. Do not ignore the time limit or badger the person into continuing. The **interviewee** may grant additional time if you acknowledge that time is up and you need only a few more minutes. If not, close the interview positively and try to arrange for another one. Respect for the other party's time constraints will enhance the relationship.

Review the closing guidelines and techniques in Chapter 4, particularly clearinghouse probes. Be sure you understand the information you have received, can reproduce names, position titles, dates, quotations, and statistics accurately. Know how to reach the source if necessary. And make the closing a dialogue with the interviewee, not a monologue. **The interviewee should be an active party from opening through closing.** Always show appreciation for the interviewee's assistance. And remember that the interview is not over until both parties are out of sight and sound of one another. Look and listen for important information or insights during the closing moments when the interviewee's guard may be down. Journalist Pat Stith writes that "some of the best stuff you're going to get will come in the last few minutes, when you're wrapping up the interview, packing your stuff, getting ready to leave."[10]

Selecting Interviewees and Interviewers

Once you have determined a purpose, conducted the necessary research, and structured the interview, select interviewees and decide who should conduct the interviews.

Selecting Interviewees

Your purpose and situation may determine the party or parties you must interview: a wounded Marine, a witness to a tornado, the student government president, an eye surgeon who has developed a new laser procedure. At other times, you are free to select from among several students, politicians, witnesses, or members of the student government. Interviewees may need to be experts or merely lay persons with differing points of view. The interviewee may be the featured subject: an astronaut, survivor of an accident, member of congress, a religious figure from outside the United States. Use the following four criteria in selecting interviewees: level of information, availability, willingness, and ability.

Level of Information

Make sure your interviewee possesses the information you need.

The most important criterion is whether or not the person has the information needed. If so, what is the person's level of expertise through experiences, education, training, and positions? For instance, primary sources are those directly involved with the information you want, support sources are those with important connections to primary sources, and expert sources are those with superior knowledge or skills relating to the information you need.[11] Sometimes part of your purpose is to assess a person's level of expertise. As an oral historian, you may want to interview a person who was actively involved in developing the space shuttle, not merely an expert on the shuttle. As a journalist, you may need to interview a detective who was in charge of a murder investigation, not a bystander.

Raymond Gorden writes about **key informants** who can supply information on local situations, assist in selecting and contacting knowledgeable interviewees, and aid in securing their cooperation.[12] Discover who these people are and how they might assist in selecting respondents. A key informant might be a family member, friend, fellow member of a student organization, employer, or person being interviewed.

Availability

Do not assume a potential interviewee is unavailable; ask first.

A source might be too far away, available only for a few minutes when you need an in-depth interview, or unavailable until after a deadline. Consider the telephone, videoconference, or e-mail before giving up on a source. And never assume a person is unavailable. Stories abound among journalists and researchers about famous interviews that occurred merely because interviewers asked for interviews or were persistent in asking. You may talk yourself out of an interview by being certain the person will not talk—a self-fulfilling prophecy: "You don't have time to talk, do you?"

Consider a possible go-between, Gorden's key informant, such as a mutual friend or associate, an aide, or the public relations department. You might go to where a person works, lives, or plays rather than expect the person to come to you. Sometimes an interviewee will ask to see some or all of your questions in advance. Be careful of excessive demands about topics, questions, off-limit subjects, and off-the-record comments that may make the person no longer a viable party. Meeting such demands will destroy the spontaneity of the probing interview.

Willingness

Fear of what may be revealed in an interview might make participants reluctant.

Potential respondents may be unwilling to meet with you for a variety of reasons. They may mistrust you or your organization, profession, or position. They may fear that information they give will harm them, their organizations, or significant others, particularly because of inaccurate reporting, hidden agendas, or sensationalism prevalent in many news sources. They may feel the information you want is no one else's business or that it is unimportant and therefore a waste of time.[13] In short, a respondent may feel there is nothing in the interview that warrants the time and risks involved. Lawsuits materialize today over almost anything a person might say or not say, and organizations are particularly fearful of being sued for millions. They try to control the persons who can speak for them. Those who have dealt with the press and investigators relate times when they were misquoted, taken out of context, had information reported erroneously, or ended up being the focus of a report they thought was a study of many people.

You may have to convince interviewees that you can be trusted for confidentiality, accuracy, thoroughness, and fair reporting. People are likely to cooperate if they have an interest in you, the topic, or the outcome of the interview. Point out why their interests will be better served if information and attitudes are known. Sometimes you may have to employ a bit of arm-twisting such as "If you don't talk to us, we'll have to rely on other sources" or "The other parties involved have already told their sides of the incident. Are you certain you do not want us to hear yours?" Be careful of threats. They can ruin an interview, damage a relationship, and preclude future contacts. Few of us take threats lightly. Be wary of persons who are too eager to be interviewed. Consider their motivations and reputations.

Resort to arm-twisting as a last resort.

Ability

Is the potential interviewee able to transmit information freely and accurately? Several problems may make a person unacceptable: poor memory, failing health, state of shock, biases or prejudices, habitual lying, proneness to exaggeration or oversimplification, and repression of horrific memories. Elderly witnesses may remember events very differently than they really were. A father or mother grieving over the loss of a child (and confronted with tape recorders, interviewers, lights, and cameras) may be unable to focus on details. Interviewers often expect persons to relate minute details and exact timing of events that took place months or years before, when most of us have trouble recalling what we did yesterday.

Many potential interviewees are willing but unable.

If time permits, get to know interviewees ahead of time. Learn about their accomplishments, personalities, reputations, biases, interests, and interviewing traits. How skilled are they at responding to (and evading) questions? Many persons are interviewed daily, and a growing number have taken intensive courses in which they have learned how to confront interviewers of all types. Eugene Webb and Jerry Salancik write that the interviewer "in time, should know" a "source well enough to be able to know when a distortion is occurring, from a facial expression that doesn't correspond to a certain reply."[14]

Some interviewees study how to respond, evade, and confront.

Selecting Interviewers

Eric Nalder claims that the number one trait of an ideal journalist, or any probing interviewer, is curiosity about everyone and everything. Similarly, Ken Metzler claims "the best interviewers are those who enjoy people and are eager to learn more about the people they meet—and who are eternally curious about darned near everything." We would add that, along with curiosity, the interviewer should be friendly, courteous, organized, observant, patient, persistent, and skillful.

A situation may require an interviewer of a certain age, sex, race, ethnic group, religion, political party (or independent), or educational level. A 60-year-old interviewer might find it as difficult to relate to today's teenagers as a teenager would to the 60-year-old. A woman might confide more readily to a female interviewer than to a male interviewer. An interviewer of Arabic ancestry might be more effective with Iraqi immigrants because of common culture, traditions, and communication customs.

Status difference and similarity affect motivation, freedom to respond, control, and rapport.

Status difference or **similarity** between interviewer and interviewee may offer unique advantages for the interviewer. When an interviewer is *subordinate* to an interviewee (student to professor, hourly worker to manager, vice president to president):

- The interviewer does not have to be an expert.
- The interviewee will not feel threatened.
- The interviewee will feel freer to speak.
- The interviewee might want to help the interviewer.

Famous NBC news correspondent, anchor, and host David Brinkley remarked in a PBS interview that he welcomed the opportunity to meet with journalism students and young reporters in his office, to show them around the studio, and to discuss the academic background needed to be effective reporters.

When an interviewer is *superior* to the interviewee (captain to sergeant, CEO to division head, physician to nurse practitioner):

- The interviewer can control the interview.
- The interviewer can reward the interviewee.
- The interviewee may feel motivated to please the interviewer.
- The interviewee may feel honored to be a participant.

Some organizations give high-status-sounding titles to representatives to enhance their superior aura: chief correspondent rather than correspondent, vice president instead of sales director, editor rather than reporter, executive rather than supervisor.

Status is a critical criterion for some interviewees.

When the interviewer is *equal* to the interviewee (student to student, associate to associate, researcher to researcher):

- Rapport is easily established.
- There are fewer communication barriers.
- There are fewer pressures.
- A high degree of empathy is possible.

In many situations, we prefer to be interviewed by people similar to us in a variety of ways, including sex, age, education level, and professional field. Some interviewees will not grant interviews to organizations or people they perceive to be of lower status. If they are senior U.S. senators, for instance, they expect the newspaper or network to send its senior correspondent.

Be aware of the relational history of the parties.

Relationship of Interviewer and Interviewee

By the time you have researched and selected interviewees and interviewers, you should have an accurate picture of the **relationship** that will exist during the interview. Robert Ogles and other journalism professors note, for example, that journalistic interviews rely on "secondary relationships" that are nonintimate and limited to one or very few relational dimensions.[15] These dimensions tend to be more functional than emotional and rely on surface cues such as obvious similarities, appearance, and nonverbal behavior.

Many interviews, including some journalistic interviews, involve all of the relational dimensions discussed in Chapter 1. Be aware of perceived similarities and differences of both parties.

- To what extent does each want to be *included and involved* in this interview?
- How much do the parties *like and respect* one another?
- How much *control and dominance* is each party likely to exert or try to exert during the interview?
- What is the level of *trust between the parties?*

A positive relationship is critical to the success of even the simplest probing interviews because they tend to delve into beliefs, attitudes, values, feelings, and inner secrets.

Conducting the Interview

The purpose of a probing interview is to get in-depth and insightful information that only an interviewee can offer. It is essential, then, to get beyond superficial and safe Level 1 interactions to riskier and deeper Level 2 and Level 3 interactions. You must **motivate** an interviewee to disclose beliefs, attitudes, and feelings as well as unknown facts.

Motivating Interviewees

There are many reasons why a person might be reluctant to talk to you or to communicate beyond Level 1 if an interview takes place.[16] An interviewee may have been "burned" in previous interviews such as this one or by interviewers from your organization, by interviewers like you, or by you. Your negative or threatening reputation may precede you. An interviewee may see the interview as posing a risk to self-image, credibility with others, or to a career. Perhaps the interview is seen as an invasion of privacy or posing the danger of opening up areas the interviewee may prefer to remain forgotten or unknown. And the interviewee may simply not want to be interviewed on any subject. On the other hand, be careful of interviewees who appear to be too eager to take part and reveal secrets. They may be after publicity, exposure, an ego-trip, a chance to sell a product or idea, or to get even with someone or an organization.

Know what motivates each interviewee.

Interviewees are likely to communicate beyond Level 1 if you adhere to simple guidelines that follow the golden rule: *do unto others as you would have them do unto you.* This rule applies to the most difficult of interview situations. A report about interrogation interviews with insurgents in Iraq and Afghanistan noted that "the successful interrogators all had one thing in common in the way they approached their subjects. They were nice to them."[17] Parties are likely to communicate freely and accurately if they trust you to react with understanding and tact, maintain confidences, use the information fairly, and report what they say accurately and completely. Trust begins with the opening.[18] Ken Metzler recommends that we avoid the term *interview* and call it a

Trust is essential for probing interviews.

conversation, talk, discussion, or chat. He also advises us to "drop names" of people the interviewee respects that may serve as ice-breakers, credibility enhancers, and motivators. Come to the interview dressed appropriately for the situation and to show respect for the interviewee. Identify yourself, your organization, and the subject matter of the interview. Be honest in explaining your purpose, the nature of the interview, and how you will use the information you receive.

Don't have an *attitude.* From the opening until the interview ends, show sincere interest in and enthusiasm for the interviewee, the topic, and answers. Don't state or imply how you feel about answers and issues; be neutral. Control the interview without interrupting and look for natural pauses to probe or to ask primary questions rather than interrupt the interviewee. Ask questions rather than make statements. Be a good listener not only with your ears but your eyes, face, nods, and attentive posture. Metzler writes that, "It's not the questions you ask that make for a successful interview but the attention you pay to the answers you receive." Avoid tricks, gimmicks, and deceptions.

Asking Questions

Questions are not just the tools of the trade, but are critical in motivating interviewees to provide the information and insights needed. Unfortunately, interviewers tend to ask too many questions, and this limits their opportunities to listen, observe, and think. Too often interviewers are or appear to be arrogant or assume they "are *entitled* to an answer." Raymond and Moen declare that "You are not; you aren't, after all, paying for the service. You will earn an answer, if you earn it, by asking a substantial, interesting, and thought-provoking question—one that implicitly contributes to the experience of the community rather than merely passively demanding knowledge from others." Listen with empathy.

Ask Open-Ended Questions

Listening is as important as asking.

Open questions motivate and encourage interviewees to communicate, particularly in the opening minutes of probing interviews. Thorough answers to open-ended questions allow you to listen appropriately (for comprehension, empathy, evaluation, resolution) and observe the interviewee's mannerisms, appearance, and nonverbal communication. Listening and observing help determine the accuracy and relevance of answers and how the interviewee feels about the situation and the topic. A raised eyebrow or a slight hesitancy of a respondent from another culture, for instance, may signal that you used a slang phrase, colloquialism, or oxymoron with which this person is unfamiliar or that sounds strange.

Make the interviewee the star of the show.

Closed questions result in the interviewer talking more while listening and observing less. If you find yourself asking question after question and doing most of the work in an interview, you are asking too many closed questions and trying to guess information rather than ask for it. Be *patient* and *persistent.* Do not interrupt a respondent unless the person is obviously off target, evading a question, or promises to continue answering forever.

Ask Probing Questions

The flexible nature of the probing interview requires a full range of probing questions. Metzler writes that "probes—followup questions—are essential. Its seldom the first question that gets to the heart of the matter, it's the seventh, or maybe 16th-question you didn't know you were going to ask but have chosen to ask because of your careful, thoughtful listening." Use **silent** and **nudging probes** to encourage interviewees to continue. Many respondents state the first thing that comes to mind and stop. Silence or a simple nudge such as "Uh-huh" encourages them to continue. Use **informational probes** when you detect cues in answers or need additional information or explanation. They resolve superficial and suggestive answers. Use **restatement probes** when interviewees do not answer the question you asked. Use **reflective** and **mirror questions** to verify and clarify answers and to check for accuracy and understanding. Use **clearinghouse probes** before proceeding to new topics or closing the interview to be sure you have obtained everything of importance to your story or report. Metzler suggests asking **metaphorical questions,** such as "Governor, do you hope to hit a home run with this legislative proposal?" to motivate interviewees to expand answers in an interesting and understandable manner. You cannot plan for every piece of information or insight an interviewee might have. Some journalists advise that "even if you go into an interview armed with a list of questions, the most important probably will be ones you ask in response to an answer."[19]

Be an active listener, not a passive sponge.

When asking questions and probing into answers, be courteous, friendly, tactful, and nonargumentative. Do not debate a respondent. Be understanding when delving into sensitive or personal areas. Be prepared to back off if an interviewee becomes emotionally upset or angry. There are times when you need to pry into potentially embarrassing areas such as the nature of an illness, marital problems, organizational finances, or an arrest. Eric Nalder claims, "There are no embarrassing questions, only embarrassing answers."

Persistent probing is essential in probing interviews, but you must know when to stop. An interviewee may become agitated, confused, or silent if you probe too far. This exchange occurred between an attorney and a physician:[20]

Know when enough is enough.

Attorney: Doctor, before you performed the autopsy, did you check for a pulse?

Physician: No.

Attorney: Did you check for blood pressure?

Physician: No.

Attorney: Did you check for breathing?

Physician: No.

Attorney: So, then it is possible that the patient was alive when you began the autopsy?

Physician: No.

Attorney: How can you be so sure, Doctor?

Physician: Because his brain was sitting on my desk in a jar.

Attorney: But could the patient have still been alive nevertheless?

Physician: It is possible that he could be alive practicing law somewhere.

Be persistent and patient, but know when to stop. Listen, observe, and think.

Because probing interviews necessitate creating many questions on the spot, you may fall into the common question pitfalls discussed in Chapter 3. Review these carefully: the bipolar trap, the open-to-closed switch, the double-barreled inquisition, the leading push, the yes (no) response, the guessing game, the curious probe, the quiz show, the don't ask, don't tell, and complexity vs. simplicity. Remember the rules: think before asking, stop when you've asked a good question, and use bipolar or leading questions sparingly for specific purposes. Know the pitfalls well enough that you can catch yourself before stumbling into one. The following good and bad examples will sharpen question skills.

Even the most seasoned interviewer can stumble into a pitfall when unaware.

- The bipolar trap:

  Bad: Do you think gas prices will continue to increase through the summer?

  Good: What do you think will happen to gas prices through the summer?

- The open-to-closed switch:

  Bad: How do you think the economy will affect tuition? Will it cause it to increase substantially?

  Good: How do you think the economy will affect tuition?

- The double-barreled inquisition:

  Bad: What courses are you planning to take next fall and spring?

  Good: What courses are you planning to take next fall?

- The leading push:

  Bad: You're going to the job fair, aren't you?

  Good: What are your plans for the job fair?

- The guessing game:

  Bad: Did you change majors because of the math requirements?

  Good: Why did you change majors?

- The yes (no) response:

  Bad: Do you want to get fired?

  Good: How concerned are you about getting fired?

- The curious probe:

  Bad: (in a recruiting interview) What kind of music do you like?

  Good: What do you do to relax after a difficult day at work?

- The quiz show:

  Bad: (in an interview for an internship) Texas A&M is a land grant institution. Which president signed the land grant legislation into law?

  Good: What do you know about the history of Texas A&M?

- The don't ask, don't tell:

  Bad: Electronic cheating is becoming a serious problem on college campuses. Have you ever used electronic means to cheat on exams?

  Good: What experiences have you had with cheating in your classes?

- Complexity vs. simplicity:

  Bad: If you were the first to come upon the scene of an auto accident, would you continue on while using your cell phone to call 911, would you pull over with your flasher lights on while calling 911, would you stop in front of the accident and direct people away from the scene, or would you stop behind the accident and go immediately to the car to see if anyone needed help?

  Good: If you were the first to come upon the scene of an auto accident, what would you do first?

Make your questions brief, relevant, and clearly stated and then give the respondent your full attention. Journalist Melvin Mencher writes that "the point of the question is to induce the subject to talk. Complicated questions may overwhelm the source."[21] Avoid the *complexity vs. simplicity pitfall,* a problem that is exacerbated when a question is phrased poorly and with too much detail or too many options. We see this problem whenever we observe televised press conferences or congressional hearings. Cliff Stearns, U.S. Representative from Florida asked the following question during congressional hearings on the EU Data Protection Directive in 2001. The interviewee is Denis E. Henry, Vice President for Regulatory Law with Bell Canada.

> Mr. Henry, it seems like Canada has developed something with the participation of industry. So industry came in and participated in developing the code and practices, as I understand it, that is tailored to the different industry that applies. Did you find that industry's participation made it less burdensome? I mean, that relationship, did that make it palatable for them to take an all-encompassing law? I mean, you might give us just a little . . .

Henry cut in and answered the essence of the question before it became even more confusing.[22]

All rules are made to be broken, but you must know when and how.

Sometimes you need to break the rules to get information you want. It may be necessary to ask an obvious question even when you know the answer in advance, such as "I see you like to hike" when it is listed on an application form. Seemingly obvious questions can relax respondents by getting them to talk about things that are well known and easy to talk about and by showing interest in topics important to interviewees. A leading push such as "Come on, surely you don't believe that?" may provoke a respondent into an exciting and revealing interchange. Be very cautious when asking leading questions of children. Several studies have shown that children are susceptible to such questions because they "are very attuned to taking cues from adults and tailoring their answers based on the way questions are worded."[23] You might have to ask a double-barreled question at a press conference to get two or three answers because it may be the only question you are permitted to ask. You may ask a bipolar or a yes (no) response question because you need to have a yes or no for the record, a common need in medical interviews.

Know what you are doing and why.

Phrase questions carefully to avoid confusion. The following interaction between a patient and a physician illustrates the dangers of jargon and sound-alike words:

Physician: Have you ever had a history of cardiac arrest in your family?

Patient: We never had no trouble with the police.

Some interviewees will answer questions about which they have no knowledge, faking it rather than admitting ignorance. Others are experts on everything and nothing. Listen to call-in programs on radio to hear people make incredibly uninformed or misinformed claims, accusations, and observations. Sometimes interviewees will play funny games, such as this exchange that took place during an election campaign in New Hampshire:

Reporter: How are you going to vote on Tuesday?

Resident: How am I going to vote? Oh, the usual way. I'm going to take the form they hand me and put x's in the appropriate boxes (laughing).

Reporter: (pause) Who are you going to vote for on Tuesday?

Think before asking.

Think through questions carefully before uttering them to avoid embarrassments such as the following exchange between an attorney and a witness:

Attorney: Now, Mrs. Johnson, how was your first marriage terminated?

Witness: By death.

Attorney: And by whose death was it terminated?

Think before asking probing questions that you have not prepared or thought through in advance. For instance, Ken Metzler says we should avoid the "how do you feel about that" question because, "It's the most trite, overused question in American journalism and sources begin to hate it after time." He suggests a substitute such as, "What were you thinking when ____?" Not only is the "feel" question overused, but interviewees may respond with simple and meaningless answers such as, "Okay," "Sad," "Happy," "Not too bad," or "As might be expected." Other sources, however, refer to the *how do you feel* question as famous and infamous, noting that it remains a "standard tool" because it is useful and effective.[24] A rule of thumb is to use it for specific purposes in specific situations without relying too heavily on it as a staple.

Note Taking and Recording

Weigh carefully the pros and cons of note taking prior to the interview.

Some experts warn against taking too few or selective notes, while others say you should never take notes. Some recommend the tape recorder as the best way to record information, while others say recorders are intrusive and unreliable. The best advice is to select the means best suited to specific objectives, situation, interviewee, and question schedule. Use neither note taking nor recording equipment if either will inhibit the respondent from answering fully and truthfully. Extensive note taking or tape recording may be necessary during lengthy moderately scheduled interviews to help recall *exact* figures, names, and statements and *how* answers were given.

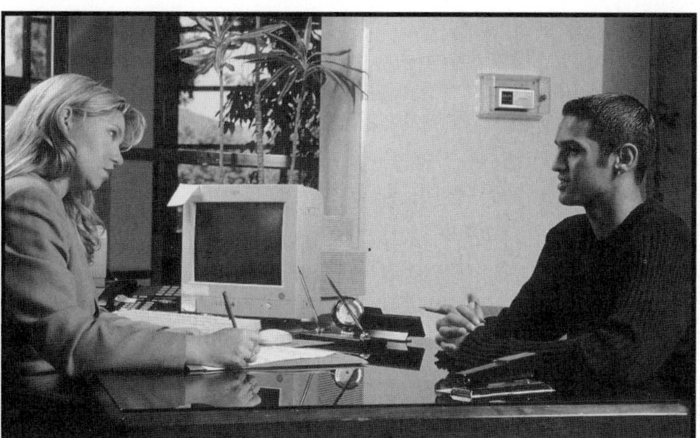

photo © Rachel Epstein/Photo Edit

Effective note taking entails maintaining eye contact as much as possible.

Note Taking

Note taking has three advantages. *First,* note taking increases your attention to what is being said and how. This enhanced attention shows respondents you are interested in what they are saying and are concerned about accuracy. William Zinsser writes that this direct involvement allows the interviewee to see you working and doing your job.[25] *Second,* when taking notes, you do not have to worry about a machine breaking down, running out of tape, or batteries going dead at a critical moment. *Third,* listening to entire recordings of interviews to pick out important bits of information is time-consuming, and transcriptions are costly in time and money. On the other hand, if you take notes according to the structure of the interview, you have your notes clearly organized when the interview ends.

Note taking should not threaten the interviewee.

Note taking also has disadvantages. You can rarely take notes fast enough to record exactly what was said, especially when a respondent speaks rapidly. It is difficult to concentrate on questions and answers and to maintain eye contact while writing notes, so you may fail to hear or probe into an answer because you are busy writing rather than listening. Note taking may hamper the flow of information because interviewees may become fearful or curious about what you are writing. Often people are reluctant to talk while you are writing or feel a break in communication while you are focusing on your pad instead of them.

In an in-depth interview with a newspaper publisher, one of our students discovered that whenever she began to write, the interviewee would stop answering until she stopped writing, apparently to let her catch up. Before long, he arranged his chair so he could see what she was writing. Follow these guidelines when taking notes during interviews.

- Preserve communication by taking notes as inconspicuously as possible and maintaining eye contact with the interviewee.
- Use abbreviations or a form of professional or personal shorthand so you do not have to write full words and sentences.
- Write down only important information, perhaps key words, to reduce the amount of note taking.
- Do not signal what you think is critically important or a "bombshell" quotation by taking notes frantically during a particular interaction. Wait until the interviewee is answering another question—perhaps a less important or "throwaway" question—before recording the answer or your reactions.

Maintain communication while taking notes.

- If the interviewee is speaking more rapidly than you can take accurate notes, ask the interviewee tactfully to slow down or repeat answers or use "stalling questions" such as "Tell me more about" that will provide time to get caught up.[26]
- Reduce interviewee curiosity or concern by asking permission to take notes, explaining why notes are necessary for both parties, and showing your notes occasionally to check accuracy. Eric Nalder says this tactic also allows interviewees to fill in blanks and volunteer information.
- Ensure accuracy of your notes by reviewing and typing them immediately after the interview to fill in the gaps, complete abbreviations, and translate your handwriting and shorthand.

Recording

Recording allows interviewers to listen and probe more effectively.

Recording also has advantages. *First,* a recorder enables you to relax and concentrate on what is being said and implied. You can then create effective probing questions. *Second,* you can hear or watch what was said and how it was said hours or days afterward instead of relying on memory. For example, the authors began to record student interviews in class because they discovered they had often missed important questions and answers while they were taking notes and filling out critique forms. *Third,* a recorder may pick up answers that were inaudible at the time. *Fourth,* a recorder gives you a completely accurate record of the content of the interview.

A recorder may add an intrusive element into the interview.

Recording has a number of disadvantages. *First,* recorders can malfunction or prove tricky to use. Batteries can go dead at the wrong time, and tapes can break or become entangled and disks can be defective. A number of our students have used tape recorders during lengthy interviews for class projects only to discover the tapes or disks were blank when they tried to review them later. *Second,* some people view recorders as intruders in intimate interviewing situations. *Third,* recordings provide permanent, undeniable records that threaten many people with unknown future consequences, so they fear or reject their use. Some interviewers such as police officers and insurance claims investigators are required to record interviews. *Fourth,* it takes a great deal of time to review a lengthy recording to locate facts, reactions, and ideal quotes while it may take only seconds to locate the same material in written notes.

Ask permission before using a recorder.

Follow these guidelines when recording interviews.

- Reduce interviewee fears and objections by asking permission, explaining why the recorder is advantageous to the interviewee, telling why you want or need to use a recorder and how the recording will be used, and offering to turn off the recorder when desired.
- Reduce mechanical difficulties by testing the recorder prior to the interview and taking extra batteries and cassettes.
- Be thoroughly familiar with the recorder and practice with it before the interview.
- Consider legal and communicative ramifications of using a hidden recorder or taping telephone interviews. The law generally allows one person to record another person without permission, but 11 states prohibit recording of conversations without consent of the interviewee: California, Florida, Georgia, Illinois, Maryland, Massachusetts, Montana, New Hampshire, Oregon, Pennsylvania, and Washington.[27]

Handling Difficult Situations

You will encounter many difficult and unexpected interviewing situations, but you can manage these situations if you plan in advance. Here are some suggestions for handling three situations.

A Sanitized versus a Real Setting

You may need to feel and experience before you can ask meaningful questions.

It is easier to interview persons in pleasant surroundings such as private offices, homes, parks, and restaurants than in real life settings where the action is. The field interview, however, is often essential to understanding an event, problem, or persons. Most memorable interviews take place at the scenes of hurricanes, terrorist bombings, fires, plant accidents, building sites, commencements, and labor strikes. Interviewers go into prisons, hospitals, nursing homes, factories, and neighborhoods or ride along with police officers, taxi drivers, EMTs, and salespersons to experience as well as interview. Eric Nalder claims that it is essential to interview people "at the place where they are doing the thing that you are writing about." It is important not only to *hear* answers but to *see* and get the *feel* of things. When Nalder was writing a book on oil tankers, for instance, a member of a crew told him he could not understand crews and oil tankers unless he was on board in the Gulf of Alaska during the violent seas of January "puking your guts out." He took this advice and got the most insightful interviews and feelings for his book because of his experiences and relationships with a crew.

Use good sense and good judgment in probing interviews.

In **unsanitized settings,** prepare for human suffering, destruction, filthy settings, and threats to health and safety. Be flexible in structure and questions. Be sensitive in questions and actions. Too often reporters, insurance investigators, and representatives of government agencies intrude into medical emergencies, catastrophes, and people's lives. Know where the interviewee's right to privacy and dignity begins.

The Press Conference or Group Interview

The interviewee usually controls the press conference.

The **press conference** or **group interview** severely limits interviewer control over the situation. The interviewee or a staff member may announce when and where the interview will take place and impose ground rules such as length and topics allowed. Protocol may enable the interviewee or a staff member to end the interview without warning, perhaps to avoid or escape a difficult exchange. You may or may not get to ask prepared questions or have an opportunity to probe into answers. Listen carefully to answers other interviewers receive because they might provide valuable information and suggest questions to ask.

Your relationship with the interviewee at a press conference is critical. If the interviewee likes, respects, and trusts you, you may be picked from among several interviewers to ask questions. If a relationship is hostile, an interviewee may refuse to recognize a person or give a vague, superficial, or hostile answer and turn quickly to another interviewer to evade follow-up questions. It may be necessary to ask a double-barreled question because it may be your only question opportunity.

The Broadcast Interview

The radio or television interview presents unique problems. Being on real or figurative stages may cause one or both parties to be extremely nervous or to engage in performing

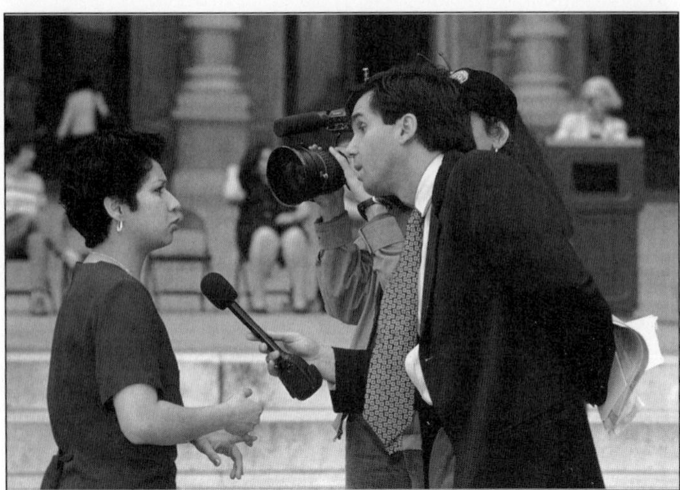
photo © Bob Daemmrich/The Image Works

The broadcast interview presents unique problems for both parties.

for audiences, cameras, and microphones. Become familiar with the physical setting, including possible seating for interviewer and the interviewee, audio and video equipment, technicians, and program format and purpose. Pay close attention to the briefing concerning time limits, beginning and closing signals, and microphone use, levels, and locations. Adequate preparation reduces nervousness and enhances efficiency and performance. In most broadcast interviews you need to obtain answers, statements, or pictures to replay over the air. By being on the air, or later in newspapers or on the Internet, there is an outside force, almost a third party, in broadcast interviews. This force or party is the viewer, listener, or reader, and some sources claim this makes the broadcast interview a "three-way interaction" because both interviewer and interviewee are aware of this party and may adapt questions and answers to it.[28]

Deadlines and extreme time limitations require questions that are direct, to the point, and moderately open. You may normally have several minutes, an hour, or more to discuss a problem with a source, customer, or employee, but a broadcast interaction may last no longer than seconds or a few minutes. Fred Fedler warns that "the live [broadcast] interview usually lasts just a few minutes and allows little chance to ask challenging questions."[29] Know questions well enough to ask them from memory or from a few small cards because forms or lists of questions may make noise or cast an awkward, amateurish, or unprepared appearance. If you want the interview to be spontaneous, do not provide questions prior to the broadcast.

Being familiar with the physical setting can avoid many surprises.

Some utterances and actions cannot be broadcast or may be embarrassing, such as profanities, obscene gestures, poor grammar, too many "uhs," "you knows," "know what I means," and excessive "blood and gore." Protestors have written profanities on their foreheads when they did not want to be on television. Some newspaper reporters, when being crowded out by cameras and microphones, shout obscenities to shut down their electronic counterparts and get closer to the action. A state legislator told one of the authors that he would purposely insert profanities into answers to prevent reporters from using them on the air.

Spontaneous questions generate spontaneous answers.

Those involved in broadcast interviews must also be aware of and skilled in "staging" interviews. For instance, framing shots is important, so the interviewer (or perhaps director) will decide whether the interviewer and interviewee will face the camera left or right, whether shots will be mid-shot or medium close-ups, and whether to select a sequence of shots. At the same time, the interview parties must make decisions about lighting, props, backgrounds, eyelines (interviewee's eyes level with the interviewer's), and studio setting. All of these decisions make the broadcast interview more complex than a simple face-to-face interview.[30]

The Videoconference Interview

As we mentioned in Chapter 1, the videoconference interview is becoming increasingly common as a means of communicating long distances quickly, efficiently, and inexpensively. Unfortunately, few interviewers or interviewees have training or experience in using or being subjected to video cameras. Videoconferences share similarities with face-to-face interviews, but there are differences we need to understand and practice. A Boston College Web site offers these suggestions for video interviewing.[31]

- **Hesitate slightly** before asking or answering questions because there is typically a slight delay in receiving the audio and video.
- **Look straight into the monitor** so you appear to be looking into the interviewer's or interviewee's eyes.
- **Focus on the interviewer or interviewee** so you can become comfortable with the video interview situation.
- **Avoid excessive motion or stiffness** so you appear relaxed and enjoying a pleasant conversation.
- **Speak naturally** without shouting because the microphone will pick up your voice, and you need not lean into the microphone to be heard.
- **Show energy and enthusiasm** through your voice and face (including smiling) because you will appear as a "talking head," no more than from the waist up.

Follow these simple rules, along with being thoroughly prepared, and the video conference interview will become a "normal" interview situation for both parties.

Handling Difficult Interviewees

Probing interviews delve into feelings, attitudes, and reasons for actions, so they may hit raw nerves and evoke reactions ranging from tears and hostility to an interviewee stopping the interview. The settings of disasters, crimes, election defeats, memorial ceremonies, deaths, and scandals are tense, emotional, and embarrassing. Be prepared to handle difficult interviewees in difficult situations. As journalist Bob Steele warns, "If we aren't proficient at asking the right questions at the right time, we'll miss on accuracy, fall short on context, and stumble on fairness."

Emotional Interviewees

Silence is often better than talk with emotional interviewees.

Respondents may burst into tears during interviews. The problem is not helped when friends, associates, or family exclaim, "Oh, God!" or "Now, stop that!" or when interviewers blurt out, "I know just how you feel." Reactions such as the following may help if they are tactful and sincere.

It's okay to cry.
Take your time.
Do you need a few minutes?

Remain silent until a person regains composure and is ready to continue. If you have a close relationship with an interviewee, you may hold the person's hand or place an arm across the shoulders as comforting gestures.

Treat others as you would like to be treated.

Be sensitive to people who have experienced tragedies and do not invade their privacy merely for pictures or tearful comments for news broadcast, data, or curiosity. How we broach a sensitive topic at a sensitive time is a serious ethical issue in journalistic and other probing interviews.[32] Reporters are infamous for asking a parent who has just lost a child in an accident, "How do you feel about your child's death?" or "Is the family devastated by this tragedy?" John and Denise Bittner suggest that you ask only direct and necessary questions at such times. "Remember, people in crisis situations are under a great deal of stress," they write. "A prolonged interview won't provide additional information; it will only upset people."[33] The dangers of insensitive interviewing were illustrated in late summer 2006 when a CNN interviewer grilled the mother of a missing boy on national television. She challenged her alibi, demanding to know where she was at the time, what she was doing, and why she wasn't providing specifics about stores she visited and items she purchased. Shortly after the interview, the mother committed suicide. Local media speculated that the CNN interviewer had "pushed her over the edge."[34]

Hostile Interviewees

If you detect hostility, try to determine if it is real or imagined. If it is real, discover why. A person may feel angry, depressed, helpless, or frightened because of circumstances beyond his or her control, and you become a convenient target for releasing feelings. Hostility may be toward you, your organization, your position or profession, or the way information may be used. Bad experiences with similar interviewers or ones from your organization may lead an interviewee to expect the worst from you. The person may simply be having a bad day because of small things—traffic, headache, a computer glitch, a late appointment.

A *nondirective interviewing approach* such as the following might reveal the source or cause of hostility and help to eliminate it:

You appear to be very angry this morning.
You seem very upset; would you like to talk about it?
Do I detect hostility toward this process?

Large male interviewers often appear threatening to interviewees.

Often you can avoid hostility by *not* making unwarranted demands, invading a person's territory or personal space, or allowing your physical presence and manner to appear threatening. You can reduce hostility or avoid creating it during interviews in several ways.

- Do not intentionally or unintentionally mislead the interviewee about who you are, what you want, why you want it, how you will use it, and whether the interviewee will be identified in your story or report.

- Substitute better sounding words for potentially antagonizing ones: aides for handlers, damage control for spin doctoring, negative campaigning for mudslinging.
- Use neutral, open-ended questions rather than leading and loaded ones.
- Remain silent to allow the interviewee to explain in depth and perhaps to blow off some steam.
- Proceed to a new topic.

Phillip Ault and Edwin Emery offer a simple rule: "Treat the average person with respect, and he [she] will do the same."[35]

Reticent Interviewees

Be prepared for the "silent types."

If a person seems unwilling or unable to talk, discover why. The person may be inhibited by you or your position, the situation, the topic, the surroundings, or other people nearby. Lack of privacy inhibits communication. Think of a time when you went to a professor or supervisor with a personal problem and the setting was a small cubicle or open area in which other persons could easily overhear. Many people are reticent around authority figures, supervisors, investigators, and journalists. Reticence may be a family or personal trait that has nothing to do with the interview and cannot be altered during the interview. Some people simply do not talk much.

Try these tactics when communicating with reticent persons. Use conversation starters by asking about pictures, awards, or arrangement of furnishings in the room, and begin with easy-to-answer questions about nonthreatening topics. Change your style from formal to informal or professional to close associate. If open questions are not generating in-depth answers, substitute closed questions (an inverted or hourglass question sequence) until the party is warmed up and more ready to talk. Use silence and nudging probes to keep the interviewee talking. No tactic can get some reticent people to talk openly and freely. They can outwait or outsilence the best of interviewers.

Talkative Interviewees

Controlling talkative persons may be more difficult than getting reticent ones to open up.

The *talkative interviewee* has the opposite tendencies of reticent ones. Some people love to talk to anyone at any time about anything. They give lengthy answers to closed questions. Responding makes them feel important, and they become too helpful. It may be difficult to turn them off or keep them on track.

Use highly targeted, closed questions that give talkative interviewees less verbal maneuverability and more direction. Look for natural openings or slight pauses to insert a question or redirect the interview such as:

Talking about George, did you . . .
I'm glad to learn that; now . . .
That's very interesting; now let's focus on . . .

Avoid obvious interruptions. A number of nonverbal actions may signal that you need to move on: looking at your notes, leaning forward, nodding your head as if to say

Be tactful and sensitive in using nonverbal signals.

"That's enough," stopping note taking, or glancing at your watch. Telephone and other electronic interviews pose unique problems because you have few nonverbal signals to halt answers, so interviewees tend to give long, rambling answers when responding over the telephone.

Evasive Interviewees

Discover why a person may be evasive.

Interviewees may try to evade questions that force them to reveal feelings or prejudices, make them take stands or give specific information, or may incriminate them in some way. Evasive strategies include humor, fake hostility, counter questions, ambiguous language, or rambling answers that never get to the point. Some interviewees will quibble over the wording of questions or the definitions of key words. A common tactic is to counter a question with a question, perhaps revolving the question onto the interviewer:

> Well, how would *you* answer that?
> What do *you* think we should do?
> Tell me about *your* private life.

Be patient and persistent.

Many interviewees will simply answer a question not asked but one they want to answer. You can deal with evasive interviewees by being prepared and persistent in questioning. For instance:

- Repeat or slightly rephrase a question.
- Laugh and continue with your questions.
- Go to other questions and come back to this one later.
- Resort to leading or loaded questions to evoke meaningful responses.

An evasive interviewee may be a dishonest one. Listen carefully to answers to determine if they square with the facts as you know them from your research and previous interviews. Observe nonverbal cues to detect dishonesty but be aware that clever respondents know how to *appear* honest, including excellent eye contact. Pat Stith writes that when an interviewee "says 'to be honest' or 'to be perfectly candid' the hair ought to stand up on the back of your neck. Almost always these phrases are followed by fibs."[36] Be trusting but be aware.

Confused Interviewees

Be understanding, helpful, and adaptive to confused interviewees.

Respondents may become confused by a topic, question, physical or mental state, or the situation. Be prepared to handle confused persons without embarrassing them or creating hostility. Restate a question tactfully or rephrase it. Return to the question later in the interview. Be conscious of jargon and similar sounding words. This exchange took place between an attorney and a witness.[37]

Attorney: Is your appearance here this morning pursuant to a deposition notice which I sent to your attorney?

Witness: No, this is how I dress when I go to work.

Be careful of nonverbal reactions. Broadcast journalists who get strange responses rarely exhibit a smile or shock when that happens. They go on to the next question or topic as if nothing embarrassing has happened.

Dissimilar Interviewees

Gender and cultural characteristics are generalities and may not apply to a particular interviewee.

Adapt carefully to interviewees who are dissimilar to you. Journalist Wendell Cochran asks us, "How do you deal fairly with someone whose views are anathema to you?"[38] One way to address this question is to observe interviews in the media (C-SPAN for instance) to see how interviewers deal with interviewees they clearly do not like such as those convicted of shooting children at a school, captured terrorists, CEO's who have deceived their workers and investors, or those with very different political, social, or religious beliefs. Previous chapters have identified important communicative characteristics unique to males and females and different cultures. Gender differences are important in probing interviews. For example, men tend to talk more, monopolize conversations, make more direct statements ("beat around the bush" less often), answer questions with declarations (while women tend to answer questions with questions), get to the point sooner in answers, and respond to questions with minimal responses (yeah, nope, fine, okay, sure). Many elderly respondents tend to be less trusting because of experiences and insecurity. However, they are often communication starved and may be *very* talkative in interviews.

Interviewers often stereotype ethnic groups such as Irish-Americans, Asian-Americans, African-Americans, Arab-Americans, and Hispanic-Americans and expect them to act in certain ways during interviews. They in turn may have developed solidarity through in-group codes, symbols, expectations, and enemies that outsiders neither share nor understand. Research indicates that African-Americans prefer indirect questions, consider extensive probing to be intrusive, and prefer more frequent and equal turn taking. Mexican-American respondents rely more on emotion, intuition, and feeling than midwestern European-Americans. Persons of rural backgrounds value personal know-how, skills, practicality, simplicity, and self-sufficiency more than those of urban backgrounds. Adapt questions and structure to different interviewees and be aware of gender and cultural differences to motivate interviewees and understand the answers received.

Preparing the Report or Story

The final stage in the probing interview is to prepare the necessary **report** or **story.** Review the information and observations obtained through one or more interviews to see if you have obtained the information necessary to satisfy your purpose. This means remembering interchanges, reading notes, and listening or viewing recordings. Sift through hundreds or thousands of words, statements, facts, opinions, and impressions to locate what is most important to include in a report or story. Check answers with other sources, especially if there is reason to suspect an interviewee gave inaccurate information.

Make it a habit to check all sources.

Once you know what you have obtained from the interview stage, editing begins. If the report is a verbatim interview for publication or dissemination, determine if grammatical errors, mispronounced words, expletives, slang, and vocalized pauses such as "uh," "and uh," and "you know" should remain. What about repetitious statements, long and rambling explanations, and simple, unintentional errors? Readers and listeners may enjoy the account with all of the warts showing, but both interview parties may be embarrassed and lose credibility. A relationship may be damaged beyond repair and place future interviews in jeopardy.

Be honest, accurate, and fair in reporting interview results.

Preface answers and questions so readers and listeners will have a clear understanding of each. Edit questions to make answers more pointed and meaningful. When quoting from notes or memory, strive for accuracy. Do not put words into an interviewee's mouth. Be sure proper qualifiers are included. Do not understate or overstate an interviewee's opinions, attitudes, intentions, or commitments. Be sure both questions and answers are reported in proper context.

The technical steps of report or story preparation are beyond the scope of this book (see the resources at the end of this chapter), but here are a few precautions.

- Remember the ground rules agreed to and what information is "off the record."
- Be careful of assumptions.
- Strive for accuracy and fairness in every fact and interpretation.
- Check carefully all sources and reports.
- Arrange information in order of importance.
- Use quotations to enliven and support the story or report.
- Include several points of view to achieve balance.

A few years ago Ted Mann, the former sports publicist for Duke University, picked up the morning paper and discovered to his surprise that he was dead. It had all started when a friend of a reporter who worked for a rescue squad told the reporter Mann had died. The reporter called the Mann home to verify the report, and the woman who answered the phone said, "Mr. Mann's not here. He's gone." The reporter assumed this phrase was a euphemism for dead and that the woman had verified Mann's death. He wrote an obituary on this false assumption.[39]

The Interviewee in the Probing Interview

Attention in interviewing books has historically focused on the interviewer because most readers and students are concerned with learning how to conduct interviews effectively. But all of us are interviewees at least as often as we are interviewers. Let's turn our attention, then, to becoming a more effective respondent in interviews.

Doing Homework

Get to know the interviewer as well as the interviewer knows you.

Before taking part in probing interviews, become thoroughly briefed on topics that might come up, including recent events, accidents, controversies, innovations, decisions, and laws. Have you played roles in any of these? Check organizations to be sure you understand organizational policies, positions, and involvements and what authority you have to speak for the organization or a subunit of that organization. Is there a more knowledgeable or authoritative person who should be the interviewee?

Learn everything available about the interviewer, including age, sex, ethnic group, education and training, special interests, and experiences. What are the interviewer's attitudes toward you, your organization, your profession, and the topic: friendly or hostile, trusting or suspicious, interested or disinterested. Do not assume the interviewer has little expertise in an area. Some reporters, for instance, have engineering, management, economics, or science degrees or have developed a high level of expertise on topics such as energy, stem cell research, or foreign policy. A mother of a hyperactive child may have become an expert on hyperactivity. A member of the clergy may have been an Air Force pilot before attending theology school. What is the interviewer's reputation for fairness and honesty? What questioning techniques does the interviewer usually employ?

Interviews often take place without warning. A person may call, stop by your office, appear at your front door, or approach you on the street. When this happens, be sure the opening reveals the identity of the interviewer, the interviewer's organization, length of the interview, information desired, and how the information will be used. A thorough opening, including small talk, orients you about the topic, purpose, and relationship and gives you time to think and prepare answers strategically.

Understanding the Relationship

Appreciate the impact of upward and downward communication in interviews.

The relationship between interviewer and interviewee is a major concern in probing interviews because one or the other is likely to be in a superior position: a young accountant interviewing the CFO or the president of the university interviewing a young assistant professor. This upward and downward communication may lead either party to be overawed by the other. Feelings of subordination, obligation, or flattery may lead you to answer any question asked, particularly in the presence of cameras, microphones, technicians, or audience. If there is a choice, determine whether to speak to a particular person at a particular time. Realize that refusals of interviews may lead interviewers to state ominously at a later date that "Margaret Adams was unavailable for comment" or "refused to talk to us." Such statements imply guilt, but may be preferable to foolish comments that become headlines.

Assess the relationship between parties prior to the interview for indicators of what might take place during the interview.

Understand the relationship prior to the interview.

- What is the relational history?
- How similar are the parties?
- How willing and eager are both parties to take part?
- How much control will you have?
- Do the parties perceive one another to be trustworthy, reliable, and safe?

Awareness of the Situation

Consider the situational variables that are likely to affect the interview. When will the interview take place? How might events prior to and afterwards affect the interview? Should you defer an interview until you are better informed and ready to manage difficult

Assess the many situational variables that will impact the interview.

questions? Where will the interview take place? What is the physical setting? Will an audience be present? If the interview will be broadcast, review the discussion presented earlier in this chapter. What outside influences must you take into account?

Consider establishing ground rules such as time, place, length, which topics are off-limits or off-the-record, and the identity of the interviewer. Be realistic in demands. If you demand that all important topics be off-limits, there is no interview. Occasionally you may require that questions be submitted in advance to prepare well-thought-out answers with accurate and substantial data. If Charles Gibson of ABC wants to interview you, you would be foolish to demand a different interviewer. How much control you have depends upon your importance as a source, your relationship with the interviewer, the situation, and how eager you are to serve as an interviewee.

Anticipating Questions

Be as prepared to answer as the interviewer is prepared to ask.

Anticipate questions and think through possible responses. For instance, what might be the most important information to divulge or conceal? How should you qualify answers? What evidence can you provide for assertions and claims? How might you reply to questions you cannot answer because of lack of information, need for secrecy, protection of sources, legal consequences, or organizational policies and constraints?

In this age of litigation and media involvement in every issue, increasing numbers of interviewees are undergoing training in how to handle questions. For instance, prosecutors, attorneys, and aides prepare witnesses and clients (including presidents of the United States and CEOs) to answer questions in court, congressional hearings, board meetings, and press conferences. Seek help if you are facing a difficult encounter with a trained and experienced interviewer.

Listening to Questions

While listening carefully to each question, follow several guidelines for responding effectively.

Listen and Think before Answering

Fully engage the brain before opening the mouth.

At scenes of accidents, crimes, or controversies, persons make statements they soon regret. African-Americans and Hispanic-Americans are often accused of crimes they did not commit because interviewees claimed to see a black or Hispanic man in the area where a crime took place. False statements and reports may lead to lawsuits, reprimands, or embarrassment. *Listen* carefully to what is being asked. Listen for words you do not know or may misinterpret. Listen for verbal and nonverbal cues that reveal feelings as well as facts.

Be Patient

Do not assume to know what a question is before it is completed. React only after fully hearing and understanding each question. Do not interrupt an interviewer because what the questioner is saying may help you understand the question and determine an answer.

Focus Attention on the Question of the Moment

Do not continue to replay a previous answer that is history or anticipate a future question because you will end up not hearing the current question.

Concentrate on Both the Interviewer and the Question

Watch for nonverbal signals that complement the verbal and reveal the interviewer's feelings, attitudes, and beliefs. Focus eyes and ears on the interviewer. This is particularly important in broadcast interviews that involve several persons, studios, cameras, monitors, and microphones and field interviews that involve spectators, noise, traffic, and distracting objects.

Do Not Dismiss a Question Too Quickly as Irrelevant or Stupid

The interviewer may have a very good reason for asking a question, and it may be one in a series leading up to a highly important question. An ice-breaker question, for instance, may not add much to the content of the interview but a great deal to the interaction between parties. An interviewer may be using an inverted funnel sequence, and you will get an opportunity to respond at length later.

Answering Strategically

Design answers carefully. A good answer is concise, precise, carefully organized, clearly worded, logical, well supported, and to the point. There are many strategies for responding to questions. Learn to use them as effectively as the question strategies we introduced in Chapters 3 and 4.

Becoming hostile reduces you to the level of the interviewer.

- Avoid defensiveness or hostility.
  —Give answers not sermons.
  —Give reasons and explanations rather than excuses.
  —Be polite and tactful in words and manner.
  —Use tasteful, appropriate humor.
  —Do not reply in kind to a hostile question or interruption.
- Share control of the interview.
  —Insist on adequate time to answer questions.
  —Do not allow the interviewer to "put words in your mouth."
  —Challenge the content of questions that contain unsupported assertions or inaccurate data or quotations.
  —If a question is multiple-choice, be sure the choices are fair and include all reasonable options.
  —Ask the interviewer to rephrase or repeat long, complicated, or unclear questions.
  —Answer a question with a question.
  —Search reflective and mirror questions for accuracy and completeness.
- Explain what you are doing and why.
  —Preface a lengthy answer by explaining why it must be so.
  —Preface an answer by explaining why a question is tough or tricky.
  —Provide a substantial explanation why you must refuse to answer a question or simply say "No comment."
  —Rephrase a question: "If what you're asking is . . ." or "You seem to be implying that . . ."

- Take advantage of question pitfalls,
  —Reply to the portion of a double-barreled question you remember and can answer most effectively.
  —Answer a bipolar question with a simple yes or no.
  —Reply to the open or closed portion of an open-to-closed switch question that is to your advantage.
- Avoid common question traps.
  —If a question is leading, such as "Don't you agree that . . . ," do not be led to the suggested answer.
  —If a question is loaded, such as "Are you still cheating on your taxes," be aware that either a yes or a no will make you guilty.
  —If an apparent bipolar question offers two disagreeable choices, such as "Did you go into medicine for the prestige or for the money," answer with a third option.
  —Watch for the yes-no pitfall, such as "Do you want to die," and answer or refuse to answer politely.
- Support your answers.
  —Use stories and examples to illustrate points.
  —Use analogies and metaphors to explain unknown or complicated things, procedures, and concepts.
  —Organize long answers like mini-speeches with an introduction, body, and conclusion.
- Open your questions positively rather than negatively. The authors of *Journalistic Interviews: Theories of the Interview* offer these examples of interviewee responses:[40]

Negative	**Positive**
You failed to notice	May I point out
You neglected to mention	We can also consider x, y, z
You overlooked the fact	One additional fact to consider
You missed the point	From another perspective

Summary

The probing or journalistic interview is the most common type of interview because it is used daily by persons ranging from journalists, police officers, and health care professionals to students, teachers, and parents. Length and formality vary, but the purpose and method are the same: to get needed information as accurately and completely as possible in the shortest amount of time. The means are careful questioning, listening, observing, and probing. Although preparation of an interview guide or schedule is important, the interviewer must remain flexible and adapt to each interviewee, situation, and response.

This chapter has presented guidelines for structured probing interviews that call for thorough preparation and flexibility.

Interviewees need not be passive participants in probing interviews. When given advance notice, interviewees should prepare thoroughly. They should share control with the interviewer and not submit meekly to whatever is asked or demanded. And they should know the principles and strategies of effective answers. Good listening is essential. The result will be a better interview for both parties.

This chapter has presented guidelines for preparing and participating in probing interviews. The nature of each stage will depend upon the situation and the relationship between the interviewer and interviewee.

Key Terms and Concepts

The online learning center for this text features FLASH CARDS and CROSSWORD PUZZLES for studying based on these terms and concepts.

Broadcast interview
Confused interviewees
Dissimilar interviewees
Emotional interviewees
Evasive interviewees
False assumptions
Hostile interviewees
Ice-breaker questions
Key informants
Metaphorical questions
Off the record
Press conference
Research
Reticent interviewees
Sources
Status difference
Strategic answers
Talkative interviewees
Unsanitized setting
Videoconference

A Probing Interview for Review and Analysis

The interviewer is part of a research team investigating how survivors of natural disasters cope during the first year following the event. She is interviewing a person who lost his home and adjacent small business when a massive tornado struck River Bend one year ago.

As you review this probing interview, ask such questions as, How satisfactory is the opening, including involvement of the interviewee? How well does the interviewer avoid common question pitfalls? How effectively does the interviewer listen and detect clues in answers? What areas of potentially valuable information does the interviewer discover and fail to discover? How satisfactory is the closing, including involvement of the interviewee? Which answer strategies does the *interviewee* employ and how effectively does the *interviewer* deal with them? How well does she manage to share control during the interview?

1. **Interviewer:** Good evening. I'm with the Kansas Storm Chasing Association that is studying how people cope with natural disasters, especially tornadoes. When I called Monday evening I said the interview would take about 15 to 20 minutes and that I would record it. Okay?
2. **Interviewee:** Okay.
3. **Interviewer:** First, tell me about that afternoon nearly a year ago. Were you aware a tornado was possible?

4. **Interviewee:** Yes.
5. **Interviewer:** Were you warned by siren or the broadcast media?
6. **Interviewee:** No.
7. **Interviewer:** How were you warned?
8. **Interviewee:** I was working in the shop. It was an unusually warm and muggy spring day with a cold front approaching from the north. Most of us in the Midwest know what that means, so we were keeping a wary eye on the sky.
9. **Interviewer:** Okay. When did you see the funnel cloud?
10. **Interviewee:** Around 4:30.
11. **Interviewer:** What did you see and hear?
12. **Interviewee:** Well, the first thing I noticed was how dark it got. It was like midnight, pitch-black. You couldn't see across the yard.
13. **Interviewer:** Uh huh.
14. **Interviewee:** I mean it was really dark, like being in a closet with the door closed. Almost like being in a cave.
15. **Interviewer:** I see. And what did you hear?
16. **Interviewee:** At first there was not a sound, not even a bird chirping. It was like death.
17. **Interviewer:** And then?
18. **Interviewee:** Then there was this terrible roar, sort of like—as I've heard others say—a hundred freight trains.
19. **Interviewer:** What was it like?
20. **Interviewee:** It was a massive, ugly boiling funnel coming right at us from across the river. I'll never forget that sight and sound. I thought we were all going to die. The newspaper pictures showed how terrible it was and many of us attending church the next day in the high school football stadium. Everything else was a mess. But we made it. As you can see, we've rebuilt the shop and the house is now about three-quarters done. We should be able to move back in about a month.
21. **Interviewer:** It's amazing that you survived and that you have been able to rebuild your lives so soon. What did you do when you saw the tornado coming across the river? Did you freeze for a moment?
22. **Interviewee:** If I had, I wouldn't be talking to you today!
23. **Interviewer:** What did you do?
24. **Interviewee:** I ran out of the shop and yelled for Megan; that's my wife. We grabbed the baby from its crib and headed to the basement of our home.
25. **Interviewer:** And then what did you do?
26. **Interviewee:** We got in the corner under a heavy workbench until this monster just tore everything up, even the floor.
27. **Interviewer:** Were you afraid?

28. **Interviewee:** Wouldn't you have been afraid at a time like that?
29. **Interviewer:** I'm sure I would. And the storm destroyed your house and your business?
30. **Interviewee:** Yes, everything was gone when we came out of the basement.
31. **Interviewer:** It's been nearly a year now. How have things worked out for you?
32. **Interviewee:** Okay, I guess.
33. **Interviewer:** Do you think about the tornado much?
34. **Interviewee:** Of course!
35. **Interviewer:** How so?
36. **Interviewee:** There are no trees.
37. **Interviewer:** I see. I'm sure you and your family tend to panic when the sky gets real dark in the spring.
38. **Interviewee:** Not panic, just cautious and prepared.
39. **Interviewer:** What about the new county warning system?
40. **Interviewee:** What about it?
41. **Interviewer:** Will it help the next time a tornado approaches?
42. **Interviewee:** I sure hope so!
43. **Interviewer:** Is there anything else you would like to tell me about the storm and its aftermath?
44. **Interviewee:** No. Well . . . no, I guess not. You have to experience it to understand.
45. **Interviewer:** Okay. I appreciate your willingness to talk to me about your experiences. Stay safe. Oh, where are you living now?
46. **Interviewee:** With friends in Hopewell about 10 miles from here.
47. **Interviewer:** Good. Thanks again.

Probing Role-Playing Cases

An Assault Case

You are a detective interviewing a female student who was attacked physically in a campus parking garage. She avoided serious injury when other students heard her yelling for help and chased off her attacker. This case seems similar to a number of attacks in parking garages throughout the area. You want to learn what the victim recalls about the attack and attacker, particularly things she may have recalled since her initial interview with police officers. The interview will take place in the interviewee's apartment.

A Veteran from the War in Iraq

You are a psychology student in a class focusing on the long-term effects of urban fighting on military personnel who have spent at least a year in such duty. You have been assigned to interview a local National Guard sergeant who spent fourteen months in Bagdad patrolling the streets and searching buildings for insurgents. He returned home a year ago to his wife and three children and, after a one-month leave and a brief stay at a VA hospital, resumed his position as an insurance sales representative. The interview will take place at a local Starbucks.

A Candidate for Congress

A recently retired Air Force colonel, who was a member of the famed Thunderbirds precision flying team, is openly considering a campaign for Congress. He has never been involved in politics or affiliated with a political party. Your editor has assigned you to interview the colonel as part of a special issue on the backgrounds of political candidates with no political experience. You will interview the colonel at the Experimental Aircraft Association Museum where he is signing autographs for his new book entitled *The Sky Is Not the Limit.* He has agreed to give you 15 minutes for the interview.

A Trip to Kenya

You have never traveled abroad, but you have always been fascinated with wild animal shows on television and thought it would be great to take a safari to Africa. A friend told you recently that she was taking a trip to Kenya at the end of the spring semester headed by a retired dean of the College of Liberal Arts. You have arranged an interview with this person for a Saturday morning at his home. You are excited and apprehensive about a safari in Kenya. You are concerned about possible terrorism or civil unrest in east Africa, the dangers of being so close to animals in the wild, cost, the long flight, and attitudes toward Americans.

Student Activities

1. Compare and contrast the sample attitude survey in Chapter 6 with the probing interview in this chapter. How are the openings similar and different? How are questions similar and different? What are the apparent question sequences? What schedules are used? How are the closings similar and different? What interviewing skills are required for the participants of each interview?
2. Interview a newspaper journalist and a broadcast journalist about their interviewing experiences and techniques. How does the nature of the medium affect interviewers and interviewees? How does the medium affect interview structure, questioning techniques, and note taking? What advice do they give about note taking and tape recording interviews? How do the end products differ? What constraints does each medium place on interviewers?
3. Attend a press conference in which one person is answering questions from several interviewers. How is this situation similar to and different from one-on-one interviews? What stated or implied rules governed this interview? What skills are required of interviewers and interviewee? How did the interviewee recognize interviewers? What answering strategies did the interviewee use? What questioning strategies did interviewers use?

4. A growing number of interviewers are turning to the Internet to conduct probing interviews. Develop a moderately scheduled 20-minute interview on a topic that will require fairly lengthy answers and then conduct one face-to-face interview and one over the Internet. Identify the advantages and disadvantages of each with respect to relationship building, communication interactions, depth of answers, self-disclosure, probing questions, spontaneity, and ability or inability to observe and hear the interviewee's answers.

Notes

1. Bob Steele, "Interviewing: The Ignored Skill," http://www.poynter.org/column.asp?id=36&aid=37661, accessed September 25, 2006.
2. Eric Nalder, *Newspaper Interviewing Techniques,* Regional Reporters Association meeting at the National Press Club, March 28, 1994, The C-SPAN Networks (West Lafayette, IN: Public Affairs Video Archives, 1994).
3. Steele.
4. Ken Metzler, Tips for Interviewing," http://darkwing.uoregon.edu/~sponder/cj641/interview.htm, accessed September 26, 2006.
5. Beverley J. Pitts, Tendayi S. Kumbula, Mark N. Popovich, and Debra L. Reed, *The Process of Media Writing* (Boston: Allyn and Bacon, 1997), p. 66.
6. Eric Steven Raymond and Rick Moen, "How to Ask Questions the Smart Way," http://www.catb.org/~esr/faqs/smart-questions.html, accessed September 26, 2006.
7. Henry Schulte and Michael P. Dufreshe, *Getting the Story* (New York: Macmillan, 1994), p. 24.
8. Metzler.
9. R. Thomas Berner, *The Process of Writing News* (Boston: Allyn and Bacon, 1992), p. 123.
10. Pat Stith, *Getting Good Stories: Interviewing with Finesse* (ProQuest Research Library, April 24, 2004), p. 2.
11. Pitts, Kumbula, Popovich, and Reed, p. 64.
12. Raymond L. Gorden, *Interviewing: Strategy, Techniques, and Tactics* (Homewood, IL: Dorsey Press, 1980), p. 235.
13. Fred Fedler, John R. Bender, Lucinda Davenport, and Paul E. Kostyu, *Reporting for the Media* (Fort Worth, TX: Harcourt Brace, 1997), p. 227.
14. Eugene C. Webb and Jerry R. Salancik, "The Interview or the Only Wheel in Town," *Journalism Monographs* 2 (1966), p. 18.
15. Robert Ogles is a professor of mass communication at Purdue University.
16. "Journalistic Interviews," http://www.uwgh.edu/clampitp/Interviewing/Interviewing%20lectures/Journalistic%20Interviews.ppt., accessed October 4, 2006.
17. Stephen Budiansky, "Truth Extraction," *The Atlantic Monthly,* June 2005, 32.

18. Carole Rich, *Writing and Reporting News: A Coaching Method* (Belmont, CA: Thomson/Wadsworth, 2005), p. 124; Berner, p. 127; The Missouri Group, *Telling the Story: Writing for Print Broadcast, and Online Media* (Boston: Bedford/St. Martin's, 2001), p. 51; Melvin Mencher, *Basic Media Writing* (Madison, WI: Brown & Benchmark, 1996), p. 231.
19. Missouri Group, p. 58.
20. Originally Cited in "The Point of View," a publication of the Alameda District Attorney's Office.
21. Mencher, p. 230.
22. "The EU Protection Directive: Implications for the U.S. Privacy Debate," Subcommittee on Commerce, Trade, and Consumer Protection, March 8, 2001, http://www.access.gpo.gov/congress/house.
23. "Leading Questions," http://www.mediacollege.com/journalism/interviews/leading-questions.html, accessed October 4, 2006.
24. "Open-Ended Questions," http://www.mediacollege.com/journalism/interviews/open-endedquestions.html, accessed October 4, 2006.
25. William Zinsser, *On Writing Well* (New York: Harper Perennial, 1994), p. 70.
26. Missouri Group, p. 58.
27. Carole Rich, *Writing and Reporting News: A Coaching Method* (Belmont, CA: Wadsworth, 1997), p. 110.
28. "Interview Structure," http://www.mediacollege.com/video/interviews/structure.html, accessed October 4, 2006.
29. Fedler, Bender, Davenport, and Kostyu, p. 224.
30. "Framing Interview Shots," http://www.mediacollege.com/video/interviews/framing.html, accessed October 4, 2006; "Composing Interview Shots," http://www.mediacollege.com/video/interviews/composition.html, accessed October 4, 2006; "Studio Interview Settings," http://www.mediacollege.com/video/interviews/studio.html, accessed October 4, 2006.
31. "Video Interviewing: Tips for Interviews Using Video Cameras," http://www.bc.edu/offices/careers/skills/intrerview/video/, accessed September 30, 2006.
32. Reporter and editor Wendell Cochran in Steele.
33. John R. Bittner and Denise A. Bittner, *Radio Journalism* (Englewood Cliffs, NJ: Prentice-Hall, 1977), p. 53.
34. Travis Reed, "Did TV Interview Lead Woman to Kill Herself?" http://www.suntimes.com/news/nation/52533,CST-NWS-grace14.article, September 14, 2006.
35. Phillip H. Alt and Edwin Emery, *Reporting the News* (New York: Dodd, Mead, & Co., 1959), p. 125.
36. Stith, p. 2.
37. William T. G. Litant, "And, Were You Present When Your Picture Was Taken?" *Lawyer's Journal* (Massachusetts Bar Association), May 1996.

38. Steele.

39. "Man Reads His Obituary in Paper," Lafayette, Indiana *Journal and Courier,* June 13, 1985, p. D4.

40. "EE's Perspective," http://www.uwgb.edu/clampitp/interviewing/interviewing%20Lectures/Journalistic%20Interviewsppt, accessed October 4, 2006.

Resources

Adams, Sally, and Wynford Hicks. *Interviewing for Journalists.* Florence, KY: Routledge, 2001.

Greaney, Thomas M. "Five Keys to a Successful Media Interview," *Communication World,* April–May, 1997, pp. 35–37.

Heritage, John. "Designing Questions and Setting Agendas in the News Interview," in *Studies in Language and Social Interaction,* Philip Glenn, Curtis LeBarob, and Jenny Mandelbaum, eds. Mahwah, NJ: Lawrence Erlbaum, 2002.

Metzler, Ken. *Creative Interviewing: The Writer's Guide to Gathering Information by Asking Questions.* Boston: Allyn and Bacon, 1996.

Metzler, Ken. "Tips for Interviewing," http://darkwing.uoregon.edu~sponder/j641/Interview.htm.

Rich, Carole. *Writing and Reporting News: A Coaching Method.* Belmont, CA: Thomson/Wadsworth, 2005.

Steele, Bob. "Interviewing: The Ignored Skill," http://www.poynter.org/column.asp?id=36&aid=37661.

CHAPTER 6 The Survey Interview

"Surveys reach out and touch everyone."

Thirty million survey interviews are conducted in the United States every year by some 2,000 research firms, federal and state governments, companies, universities, medical centers, political candidates, and others too numerous to mention. Most of us are involved in taking or conducting surveys on a regular basis.[1]

Manufacturers use surveys to gauge consumer desires and satisfaction. Advertisers use market research surveys to judge the effectiveness of campaigns. Politicians rely on polls to determine voter attitudes and personal popularity. Research organizations use surveys to measure public opinion and provide weekly reports on the ratings of presidents and Congress. Television networks conduct surveys to support news stories. Communication researchers employ surveys to determine the effectiveness of health care campaigns and teaching strategies. Students conduct surveys to determine which courses are most popular.

Survey interviews are neither flexible nor adaptable.

The survey is the most meticulously planned and executed of interviews because its purpose is to establish a solid base of fact from which to draw conclusions, make interpretations, and determine courses of action. When journalists conduct them, it's called **precision journalism.** While flexibility and adaptability describe the probing interview, **reliability** (assurance that the same information is collected each time in repeated interviews) and **replicability** (the ability to duplicate interviews regardless of interviewer, interviewees, and situation) describe the survey interview. Reliability and replicability are achieved through a systematic approach to preparing and conducting interviews and analyzing results.

Purpose and Research

Preparation for a survey begins by deciding what exactly is needed and why. The purpose is tied to research that will determine the topic areas, structure, questions, interviewees, and degree of precision.

Determining Purpose

Survey interviews have multiple purposes.

Earl Babbie writes that surveys have one or more of three purposes: to explore a topic or issue such as the war on terrorism, to describe a situation or event such as violence in sports, or to explain a phenomenon such as high gas prices.[2] Consider several factors when deciding whether a survey will have one, two, or three of these purposes.

- What types of information do you need: feelings, attitudes, facts, or statistics?
- How will you use the information you receive?

- How much time will you have for each interview?
- How soon must you complete the survey and present results?
- What are your research, financial, and personnel resources?
- What are your short- and long-range goals?

Longitudinal studies reveal trends and changes over time.

Many survey interviews are brief, four or five minutes, but research indicates that longer interviews cover more areas and are more reliable. A **cross-sectional survey** takes a slice of what is felt, thought, or known during a narrow time span and is used when you need to determine how interviewees are reacting at present to a scandal, accident, or proposed change. A **longitudinal survey** determines trends in feeling, thought, or knowledge over time such as throughout a medical advertising campaign, a military incursion, or students' tenure at a university.

Conducting Research

Don't assume adequate knowledge of a topic.

When you have a clearly defined purpose, investigate all aspects of the topic. Explore its past, present, and future as well as proposed and attempted solutions. Check resources such as organizational files and archives, correspondence and interviews with knowledgeable people, government documents, professional journals, books, previous surveys on this topic, the Internet, news magazines, and newspapers. Talk to people who have studied this topic or have been involved.

Don't waste time learning what you already know.

Research reveals information already available in other sources that need not be gathered in a survey. Become a mini-expert on the topic, particularly unique terminology and technical concepts. If you are going to deal with concepts such as stem cell research, third wave feminism, or the ethical and legal interrogation of prisoners of war, you must specify the meaning of these terms to the satisfaction of interviewees, readers, and users of the survey results. Research will reveal past attitudes and opinions and speculations about current attitudes and opinions. A thorough knowledge of the topic provides insights into the nature and size of the population you must sample, the complexities of the issue, and potential intentional and unintentional inaccuracies in answers during interviews.

ON THE WEB

Select a current international issue and do background research through the Internet. Use at least three different search engines, such as the United Nations (http://www.un.org), International Forum on Globalism (http://www.ifg.org/), global engineering (http://news.foodonline.com/pehanich/fpso11598.html). What types of information did you discover? What information is unavailable on the Internet? What does the search suggest for a survey on this issue: subtopics, areas of conflict, differing views of experts, public opinion, history of the issue, current developments?

Structuring the Interview

Once you have determined a precise purpose and conducted necessary research, develop a thoroughly structured interview.

Interview Guide and Schedule

A thorough interview guide is essential for survey interviews because the guide dictates the topics and subtopics to be covered and all primary and probing questions to be asked. Review carefully the suggestions for creating interview guides in Chapter 4.

A detailed guide is easily transformed into a scheduled format.

Begin an **interview guide** by listing major areas. For example, if you are planning to survey residents about the need for a new comprehensive hospital in the area, major topics might include experiences with and attitudes toward current hospitals, availability and nature of patient rooms, quality of physicians and nurses, medical specialties, cost of health care, trauma center, and location. If you are conducting a **qualitative survey,** in which you will present your "findings in textual form—usually words" you may develop a highly scheduled interview that includes open-ended questions, planned probes, and the possibility of unplanned probes that depend upon interviewee responses.[3] There is a degree of flexibility in questioning because you are more concerned about depth and revelation of information than with statistical compilation of data. The traditional interview guide (who, what, when, where, how, and why) may be adaptable to simple or qualitative surveys, but surveys often require a more detailed guide and schedule that ensures complete coverage of a topic or issue and means of organizing, reporting, and interpreting answers.

Standardization is essential for surveys.

The **quantitative survey,** in which you will present your "findings in numerical form—frequencies, averages, and so forth," is the most common because it enables many interviewers (1) to control hundreds or thousands of interviews with diverse interviewees in various settings and (2) to elicit answers that are easy to record, tabulate, and analyze.[4] The flexibility and adaptability of the qualitative survey may lead to difficulties in coding and tabulation of results, so interviewers often rely on a highly scheduled, standardized format that assures replicability of interviews and accurate compilation of findings.

The Opening

Although, as some would claim, "each interview is unique, like a small work of art . . . with its own ebb and flow . . . , a mini-drama that involves real lives in real time,"[5] each respondent must go through as identical an interview as possible. Write out the opening and recite it verbatim. The following opening includes a greeting, statement of purpose, a simple request, and qualifier questions. It may open a highly scheduled or highly scheduled standardized interview.

> Good evening, I'm ____________________, from Citizens for Better Schools, a grassroots group of residents like you who are working to improve our local public schools. The survey takes only about 10 minutes and will give you an opportunity to inform the school board and school administrators how parents of current and former students feel about our schools and the changes you would like to see take place to improve them. (GO TO FIRST QUESTION.)

1. Are you a resident of Mitchell? (IF YES, PLACE AN X BY THE ANSWER AND GO TO Q. 2. IF NO, TERMINATE THE INTERVIEW.)

   Yes ____1-1

   No ____1-2

2. Do you have children currently enrolled or who were enrolled in the past in the Mitchell public schools? (IF YES, PLACE AN X BY THE ANSWER AND GO TO Q. 3. IF NO, TERMINATE THE INTERVIEW.)

   Yes ____2-1

   No ____2-2

There are no ice-breaker questions or small talk in surveys.

This opening identifies the interviewer and organization and states a general purpose and length of the interview. Notice that the interviewee is not asked to respond. The interviewer moves smoothly and quickly from orientation to the first question without giving the respondent an opportunity to refuse to take part. The first two questions are employed to determine the interviewee's qualifications: a resident of Mitchell and parent of current or former students in the Mitchell public schools. Notice the survey provides instructions on the schedule for each interviewer to follow and has precoded each question for ease of tabulating results when the survey is completed.

In some surveys, the opening does not identify the group that is paying for the poll (the Democratic Party, Ford Motor Company, for instance) or the specific purpose (to determine which strategies to employ during a political or advertising campaign) because such information might influence how interviewees respond. When a newspaper such as the *New York Times* or the *Washington Post*, a cable or television network such as CBS or CNN, or a well-known polling group such as Harris or Gallup conducts a survey, the organization's name is used to enhance the prestige of the poll and the interviewer, to reduce suspicion that a candidate or corporation is behind the survey, and to motivate respondents to cooperate. In many surveys, interviewers must show identification badges or letters that introduce them or establish their legitimacy as survey takers.

Simple incentives reduce rejections.

If a survey deals with sensitive matters and information, provide effective assurances of confidentiality in the opening to improve the chances of accurate and complete responses. One study indicated that a simple prepaid, nonmonetary incentive (such as a ballpoint pen) made during the opening can increase response rates and result in greater completeness in answers during the early portion of survey interviews.[6]

The Closing

The closing is usually brief and expresses appreciation for the time and effort expended to aid the survey. For example:

> That's all of the questions I have. Thank you very much for your help.

If the survey organizer wants a respondent's telephone number to verify that a valid interview took place, the closing might be:

> That's all the questions I have. May I have your telephone number so my supervisor can check to see if this interview was conducted in the prescribed manner? (gets the number) Thank you very much for your help.

If you can provide respondents with results of a survey, common practice in medical research interviews, the closing might be:

> That's all the questions I have. Thank you for your help, and if you'll give me your address, I'll be sure that you receive a copy of the results of this study. (gets the address) Thanks again for your help.

Interviewees prefer anonymity.

Some interviewees will be reluctant to give their telephone numbers or addresses to strangers. Be prepared to back off from either request if the interviewee appears anxious, suspicious, or very reluctant. Do not sacrifice the rapport and goodwill you created during the interview. When one of the authors was conducting polls in his neighborhood for a political party, he discovered that many respondents were reluctant to give their telephone numbers for fear they would be targeted for calls from candidates during the campaign. With permission from the party, he stopped asking for telephone numbers, and closings went smoother.

Respondents may be curious about a survey or very interested in the topic and want to discuss it. This can be a good relationship builder and motivator for taking part in future surveys, but do so only if time permits, the interviewee will have no opportunity to talk to future interviewees, and the survey organization has no objections.

Survey Questions

Interviewers cannot make on-the-spot adjustments.

Create each question with great care because you cannot rephrase, explain, or expand on questions during interviews without risking the ability to replicate interviews, an essential element of surveys. In quantitative surveys, all question phrasing and strategic decisions are made in the planning stage; none on the spot. In qualitative surveys, all primary questions and the majority of probing questions are planned ahead of time. Any probing questions asked on the spot must be recorded exactly as asked so tabulation of results can be performed accurately. The goal is to perform the same interview over and over again.

Phrasing Questions

Every word in every question may influence results.

All interviewees must hear the same questions asked in the same manner; phrasing and nonverbal emphasis are critical. A slight change in wording or vocal emphasis on a word can generate different answers. For example, in a religious survey, interviewers asked one set of respondents, "Is it okay to smoke while praying?" Over 90 percent responded "No." When they asked another set of respondents, "Is it okay to pray while smoking?" over 90 percent replied "Yes." Although these questions appear to be the same, respondents interpreted them differently. The first sounded sacrilegious, lighting up while praying. The second sounded like a good idea, maybe even necessary. Recall the discussion of *why questions* in Chapter 3 that showed how emphasis could change the focus and meaning of simple questions. This is critical in surveys in which you are striving for replicability.

A single word might alter significantly how people respond to a question, thereby altering the results of a survey. Researchers asked the following question to one group of respondents:

> "Do you think the United States should allow public speeches against democracy?"

The results were "should allow" 21 percent and "should not allow" 62 percent. Then these researchers substituted a single word and asked respondents:

> "Do you think the United States should forbid public speeches against democracy?"

The results were "should not forbid" 39 percent and "should forbid" 46 percent.[7] Respondents obviously viewed the word "forbid" as a much stronger and more dangerous action than "not allow"—perhaps un-American—even though the effect of the governmental policy would be the same.

Adapt phrasing to all members of a target population.

Make each question clear, relevant, appropriate to the respondent's level of knowledge, neither too complex nor too simple, and socially and psychologically accessible. This is not a simple task when respondents may be of both sexes and differ widely in age, income level, education, intelligence, occupation, geographical area, and experiences. The increasing diversity of the American population may result in respondents being from several continents and cultures.

Be wary of negatively phrased questions.

Survey researchers warn against phrasing questions negatively because they can be misleading and confusing. For instance, Jack Edwards and Marie Thomas note that "a negative answer to a negatively worded statement may not be equivalent to the positive answer to a positively worded statement."[8] Even the explanation sounds confusing. They help by giving this example: "Disagreeing with the statement 'My work is not meaningful' does not necessarily mean that the same individual would have agreed with the statement 'My work is meaningful.' " They also note that forcing a respondent to disagree with a negative statement can be confusing. Think of the difficulties you've had with negatively phrased multiple-choice questions in examinations. Babbie warns that many respondents will fail to hear the word *not* in a question during an interview so those in favor of a statement such as "The U.S. should not build a missile defense system" and those who disagree may answer the same way.[9] "And," Edwards and Thomas warn, "you may never know which is which."

Sample Question Development

Many questions will evolve as you develop a schedule, particularly for a quantitative survey. Here is how what appears to be a simple question concerning air travel safety might evolve during preparation.

> How do you feel about the new government imposed restrictions on taking liquids aboard airplanes?

Keep recording of answers in mind when phrasing questions.

Take a closer look at this seemingly neutral question. "Government imposed" may bias the results because it may sound oppressive or tyrannical to some respondents. Government is once again imposing ridiculous restraints for no good reason. Many may not be aware of which liquids are banned or the amount allowed. The openness of the question may result in a wide range of answers, some positive ("It will make us safer," "I'm 100% for it," and "Anything to stop terrorism") and some negative ("What will they ban next, clothing," "Frustrated," "It's ridiculous"). Others may give lengthy answers for and against the new restriction that will create recording and coding nightmares.

Try a second version that closes up the question and eliminates *government imposed.*

Are you for, against, or have no feelings about the restrictions on taking liquids aboard airplanes?

For ________
Against ________
No feelings ________

This version eliminates the potential bias of the first (and resolves recording and coding problems), but it may be too closed for qualitative and quantitative purposes. Interviewees may not be simply for or against the restrictions or believe there should be exceptions or qualifications, perhaps allowing prescriptions or water. Intensity of feelings is not accounted for. The "No feelings" answer option may generate a great many undecided and don't know answers and either necessitate a lot of probing or reduce the impact of the question.

Develop a third version that allows for a degree of feelings and includes important notes on the extent of the restrictions.

Do you strongly agree, agree, disagree, or strongly disagree with the restriction on liquids that can be taken aboard airplanes to prescriptions and drinks purchased after going through security?

Strongly agree ________
Agree ________
Disagree ________
Strongly disagree ________
Undecided ________ (DO NOT PROVIDE UNLESS REQUESTED.)
Why? ________________________________
(ASK ONLY OF RESPONDENTS CHOOSING STRONGLY AGREE OR STRONGLY DISAGREE.)

This third option assesses intensity of feelings, is easy to record and code, leaves undecided as an unstated option, provides instructions for interviewers, and includes a built-in secondary "*Why*" question to discover reasons for strong approval or strong disapproval. The authors have discovered that those with moderate responses tend not to have ready explanations for agreeing or disagreeing, approving or disapproving, liking or disliking. They just have that general feeling.

Build in secondary questions for reasons, knowledge, level, and qualifiers.

Work with each question until it satisfies phrasing criteria and is designed to obtain the information needed. Careful phrasing avoids embarrassment, confusion, and inaccurate results. Later we will address the pretesting of surveys to detect potential problems with questions.

Question Strategies

Survey interviewers have developed question strategies to assess knowledge level, honesty, and consistency; reduce undecided answers; prevent order bias; and incorporate probing questions.

Filter Strategy

The **filter strategy** enables the interviewer to determine interviewee knowledge of a topic. For example:

Interviewer: Are you familiar with the modifications of the Homeland Security warning color code?

Interviewee: Yes, I am.

Interviewer: What are these modifications?

Don't take "yes" as the final answer.

If an interviewee says no, the interviewer will go to the next topic. If the interviewee says yes, the interviewer will ask the interviewee to reveal the extent and accuracy of knowledge. This follow-up question may discover that the respondent is confused or is misinformed. Many interviewees will say yes to bipolar questions, even when they have no idea what the interviewer is talking about, to avoid appearing ignorant or uninformed. The filter strategy ferrets out this tendency.

Repeat Strategy

The **repeat strategy** enables the interviewer to determine if an interviewee is consistent in responses on a topic, particularly a controversial one. You may ask the same question several minutes apart and later compare answers for consistency. A variation of this strategy is to disguise the question by rephrasing it.

5. Do you supervise your children's use of the Internet?
12. Do you give your children free access to the Internet?

Another example of a repeat strategy is to go from a moderately closed to a highly closed question, such as:

11. How often do you attend church?
18. I am going to read a list of frequencies of attending church during a year. Stop me when I read the frequency that describes how often you attend church:

Repeat questions must be essentially the same to determine consistency in answers.

Once a week ________
Twice a month ________
Once a month ________
Once every few months ________
A few times a year ________
Less than once a year ________

Do not make the repetition too obvious or near the initial question and be sure the rewording does not change the intent of the initial question.

Leaning Question Strategy

Many respondents are reluctant to take stands or make decisions, often because they do not want to reveal their feelings or intentions. Employ a *leaning* question, not to be confused with a *leading* question, to reduce the number of "undecided" and "don't know" answers. The following is a typical **leaning question strategy.**

7a. Which of the finalists for provost do you hope the Board of Trustees will select? (IF UNDECIDED, ASK Q. 7b.)

Sarak Kim ________
Joshua McDowell ________
Sam Weinberg ________
Shirley Berger ________
Undecided ________

7b. Well, which of the finalists do you lean toward at the moment?

Sarak Kim ________
Joshua McDowell ________
Sam Weinberg ________
Shirley Berger ________
Undecided ________

Leaning questions urge respondents to take a stand or make a decision.

The "undecided" option must remain in question 7b because an interviewee may be truly undecided at the moment. A variation of the leaning question is, "Well, if you had to choose today, how would you vote?" Clearly stated "undecided" and "don't know" options tend to invite large percentages of these answers, particularly when a question asks for criticism of people, organizations, or products. This is why many survey interviewers do not provide undecided or don't know options when asking an original question. Others recommend, however, that you always include "don't know" or "not applicable" answer options in all questions unless all interviewees will have a definite answer. They claim these options may reduce interviewee frustration and provide the most honest and accurate answers.[10]

Shuffle Strategy

The order of options in questions may affect interviewee selection. Research indicates that last choices in questions tend to get negative or superficial evaluations because interviewees get tired or bored and that interviewees also tend to select an option because it is the first mentioned or the last heard. The **shuffle strategy** varies the order of questions or answer options from one interview to the next to prevent **order bias.** The method of rotation is carefully explained when training interviewers to conduct a survey. Notice the built-in instructions to interviewers in the following example:

Now I'm going to read a list of vegetables, and I want you to tell me if you have a highly favorable, favorable, neutral, unfavorable, or highly unfavorable attitude toward each. (ROTATE ORDER OF THE VEGETABLES FROM INTERVIEW TO INTERVIEW. ENCIRCLE ANSWERS RECEIVED.)

Order bias is both fact and myth.

	Highly Favorable	**Favorable**	**Neutral**	**Unfavorable**	**Highly Unfavorable**
Carrots	5	4	3	2	1
Spinach	5	4	3	2	1
Corn	5	4	3	2	1

(*continued*)

	Highly Favorable	Favorable	Neutral	Unfavorable	Highly Unfavorable
Peas	5	4	3	2	1
Potatoes	5	4	3	2	1
Greenbeans	5	4	3	2	1
Asparagus	5	4	3	2	1

Potential order bias has resulted in strange events in politics, "persuasive" surveys, and advertising. A few years ago a political candidate in Indiana had his name changed legally so it would begin with A. This would place him at the top of the ballot on election day, the belief being that voters select the top names in lists of candidates. He lost, but his and similar actions have led states to shuffle names on ballots.

Chain or Contingency Strategy

Highly standardized and highly scheduled formats allow for preplanned probing questions that enable interviewers to probe into answers. This is called a **chain or contingency strategy** and is illustrated in the following series from a market survey. Notice the built-in instructions and precoding for ease of recording answers and tabulating data.

All probing questions in surveys are included in the schedule.

1a. During the past month, have you received any free samples of cereal? (PLACE AN X BY THE ANSWER RECEIVED.)

Yes ____ 1—ASK Q. 1b.
No ____ 2—ASK Q. 2a.

1b. Which cereal did you receive?

Quaker Oats ____ 1
Shredded Wheat ____ 2
Cheerios ____ 3
Puffed Wheat ____ 4
Frosted Flakes ____ 5
Raisin Bran ____ 6
Grape Nuts ____ 7
Other ____________ 8 (Please specify.)

1c. (ASK ONLY IF CHEERIOS IS NOT MENTIONED IN Q. 1b; OTHERWISE SKIP TO Q. 1d.)

Did you receive a free sample of Cheerios?

Yes ____ 1—ASK Q. 1d.
No ____ 2—SKIP to Q. 2a.

1d. Did you eat the free sample of Cheerios?

Yes ____ 1—SKIP to Q. 2a.
No ____ 2—ASK Q. 1e.

1e. Why didn't you eat the free sample of Cheerios?

____________ ____________ ____________

Replicability means to reproduce interviews.

The chain or contingency strategy allows interviewers to probe into answers while maintaining control of the process and ensuring that each interview is as identical as possible.

Question Scales

Survey interviewers have developed a variety of scale or multiple-choice questions that delve more deeply into topics and feelings than bipolar questions but still allow for ease of recording and tabulation of data.

Interval Scales

Likert scales provide a range of feelings, attitudes, or opinions.

Interval scales provide distances between measures. For example, **evaluative interval scales** (often called **Likert scales**) ask respondents to make judgments about persons, places, things, or ideas. The scale may range from five to nine answer options (five is most common) with opposite poles such as "strongly like . . . strongly dislike," "strongly agree . . . strongly disagree," or "very important . . . not important at all." Here is an example of an evaluative interval scale:

Do you strongly agree, agree, have no opinion, disagree, or strongly disagree with the NCAA's policy and actions toward college mascots that some groups have found to be offensive?

5 Strongly agree ________
4 Agree ________
3 Neutral ________
2 Disagree ________
1 Strongly disagree ________

Provide aids for interviewee recall of answer options.

Interviewers may provide respondents with cards (color-coded to tell them apart) for complex questions or ones with many choices or options. A card eliminates the faulty-recall problem that many respondents experience. They can study the answers or objects they are evaluating, rating, or ranking in some way without trying to remember all of the options given orally. Here is an example of card use:

Please use the phrases on this card to tell me how the recent television ads for the new Subaru Outback has affected your interest in visiting a Subaru dealer.

5 Increases my interest a lot ________
4 Increases my interest a little ________
3 Will not affect my interest ________
2 Decreases my interest a little ________
1 Decreases my interest a lot ________

Frequency scales deal with number of times.

Frequency interval scales ask respondents to select a number that most accurately reflects how often they do something or use something. For example:

How frequently do you eat at a restaurant?

More than once a week ________
Once each week ________

Every other week ________
Once or twice a month ________
Less than once a month ________
Never ________

Numerical scales deal with ranges.

Numerical interval scales ask respondents to select a range or level that accurately reflects their age, income, educational level, or rank in an organization. For example:

I am going to read several age groupings. Please stop me when I read the one that applies to you.

18–24 ________
25–34 ________
35–49 ________
50–64 ________
65 and over ________

Nominal Scales

Nominal scales deal with naming and selecting.

Nominal scales provide mutually exclusive variables and ask respondents to pick or name the most appropriate variable. These are self-reports and do *not* ask respondents to rate or rank choices or to pick a choice along an evaluative, numerical, or frequency continuum like interval scales do. Choices may be in any order. For example, you might ask:

Do you consider yourself to be a:

Democrat ________
Republican ________
Libertarian ________
Independent ________
Other ________

When you last watched a news program, was it on:

CBS ________
ABC ________
NBC ________
Fox ________
CNN ________
Other ____________________ (PLEASE WRITE NAME.)

In nominal questions, the options are mutually exclusive and include most likely options from which to choose. This is why "other" or "none of the above" is the final option in the examples. The respondent must be able to choose one of the named options or provide a name not listed.

Ordinal Scales

Ordinal scales ask for ratings or rankings.

All ordinal questions ask respondents to rate or rank the options in their implied or stated relationship to one another. They do not name the most applicable option as in interval and nominal scales.

A **rating ordinal scale** might look like the following:

During the past several years, you have flown abroad on several airlines. Please rate each as excellent, above average, average, below average, or poor.

SAS	Exc.	Abv. Av.	Av.	Bel. Av.	Poor
Quantas	Exc.	Abv. Av.	Av.	Bel. Av.	Poor
American	Exc.	Abv. Av.	Av.	Bel. Av.	Poor
Lufthansa	Exc.	Abv. Av.	Av.	Bel. Av.	Poor
Iberian	Exc.	Abv. Av.	Av.	Bel. Av.	Poor
British Air	Exc.	Abv Av.	Av.	Bel. Av.	Poor
Delta	Exc.	Abv. Av.	Av.	Bel. Av.	Poor

Notice that, unlike other scales that ask for a single response, this rating scale generates five answers, and respondents will consciously compare the seven airlines to one another in developing their answers. You might ask respondents to rank order options. A **ranking ordinal scale** might look like this:

On this card are the names of 10 corporations. Rank order them in terms of greatest contribution to the economy.

Corporation	Rank	Corporation	Rank
General Motors	____	Boeing	____
Pfizer	____	Ford	____
Wal-Mart	____	Sears	____
IBM	____	General Electric	____
US Steel	____	Proctor & Gamble	____

The following ordinal question asks respondents to select from among and rank order options.

On this card are several reasons cited frequently for granting school vouchers to poor grade school and high school students. Pick the three you think are most important and rank them in order of importance to you.

____ Fairness
____ Competition
____ Cost
____ Parental involvement
____ Reduction of union power
____ Higher quality education
____ Reduced government control

Bogardus scales measure effect of relational distances.

Bogardus Social Distance Scale

The **Bogardus Social Distance Scale** determines how people feel about social relationships and distances from them. The interviewer wants to know if a person's attitude or feeling changes as the issue comes closer to home. This scale usually moves progressively from remote to close relationships and distances to detect changes as proximity narrows. For example, you might use the following Bogardus Social Distance Scale to determine how interviewees feel about the increasing problem of disposing of solid waste materials.

1. Do you favor the development of new solid waste sites in the United States? ______ Yes ______ No
2. Do you favor the development of new solid waste sites in the southeast? ______ Yes ______ No
3. Do you favor the development of new solid waste sites in your state? ______ Yes ______ No
4. Do you favor the development of a new solid waste site in your county? ______ Yes ______ No
5. Do you favor the development of a solid waste site on the old Barkley farm a mile from here? ______ Yes ______ No

In many questions, respondents are safely removed from the attitude or feeling they are expressing about a product, issue, action, or person. The Bogardus Social Distance Scale brings an issue ever closer to home so it is no longer something impersonal or that affects others "over there."

Minimize guessing in surveys.

Question scales are designed to obtain a range of results and Level 2 and 3 disclosures, but many respondents try to "out psyche" survey takers. Students do this when taking standardized tests. For instance, respondents may try to pick "normal" answers in nominal and ordinal scales and safe, moderate, or middle options in interval scales. Rather than admit they do not know the correct answer, even when there is no correct answer, respondents may pick the option that stands out, such as the second in a list that includes 10 percent, 15 percent, 20 percent, 30 percent, and 40 percent. Respondents who first agree that a certain activity would make most people uneasy are less likely then to admit ever engaging in that activity and may attempt to change the subject.[11]

Anticipate confusion in scale questions.

Phrase scale questions carefully to avoid game playing, guessing, and confusion. Listen and observe reactions during pretesting interviews to detect patterns of responses, levels of interviewee comprehension, and hesitancy in responding. Long scales, complicated rating or ranking procedures, and lengthy explanations may confuse respondents, perhaps without either party realizing it at the time.

Question Sequences

Question sequences complement question strategies.

The question sequences discussed in Chapter 4 are suitable for survey interviews. The tunnel sequence is common in surveys when no strategic lineup of questions is needed. Gallup's quintamensional design sequence, or a variation of it, is appropriate when exploring intensity of attitudes and opinions. Funnel, inverted funnel, hourglass, and diamond sequences include open-ended questions, so answers may be difficult to record, code, and tabulate. This is taken into consideration for those doing qualitative surveys, because the wealth of information interviewers obtain from open questions is worth the problems involved. A study of the effects of question order suggests that general questions should come first followed by more specific questions. This is a funnel sequence.[12]

Selecting Interviewees

Select interviewees carefully because they are the sources of your data. The best schedule of questions will be of little help if you talk to the wrong people at the wrong time and in the wrong place.

Defining the Population

The first step in selecting interviewees is to define the **population** you wish to study. The population may be as small and similar as members of a youth soccer league or as large and diverse as those who attend religious services on a regular basis. You may be interested in a subset of a larger population such as all girls of a youth soccer league or all young adults from ages 21 to 25 who attend religious services on a regular basis. The identified population should include all persons who are able and qualified to respond to your questions and about whom you want to draw conclusions.

If a target population is small (members of a professional writing class or faculty of a college psychology department), you may interview all of them. Most surveys, however, deal with populations that far exceed time, financial, and personal limitations—the 35,000 undergraduate students at a university or all residents over the age of 18 in a city of 250,000. Dozens of interviewers could not reach, let alone interview, all of these people even if they had unlimited time and resources. Since you are often unable to interview all persons in a target population, interview a sample of them and extend findings to all of them.

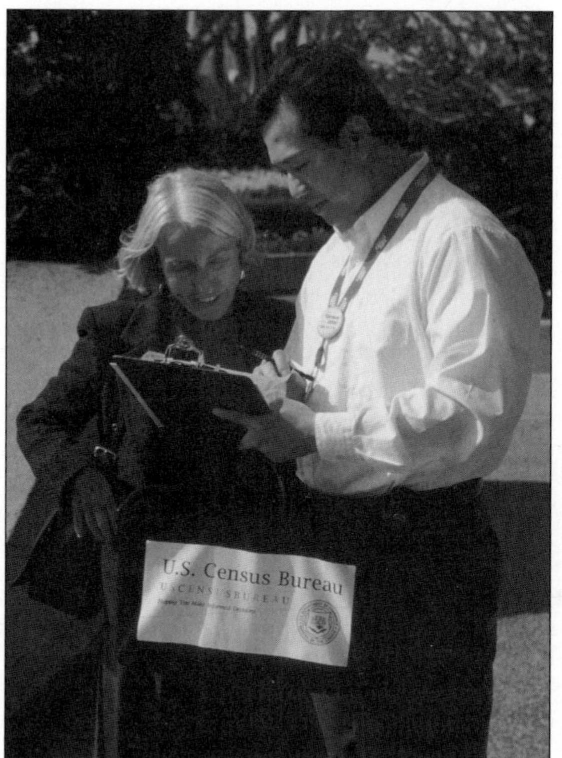

photo by Spencer Grant/Photo Edit

The first step in selecting interviewees is to define the population or target group you wish to study.

Sampling Principles

The fundamental principle is that a sample must accurately represent the population or target group under study. Old-time watermelon sellers practiced this principle when they carefully cut out a triangular plug from a watermelon. This plug was to show what the entire watermelon was like.

Each potential respondent from a defined population must have an equal opportunity of being selected. You must determine, then, the probability that each person might be selected to decide upon an acceptable **margin of error.** The precision of a survey is the "degree of similarity between sample results and the results from a 100 percent count obtained in an identical manner."[13] Most surveys attain a 95 percent **level of confidence,** the mathematical probability that 95 out of 100 interviewees would give results within 5 percentage points (margin of error) either way of the figures you would have obtained if you had interviewed the entire population. Survey results reported by NBC-Associated Press, CBS-*New York Times,* ABC-*Washington Post,* or Harris routinely state that a survey had a margin of error of 4 percent. This means that if 42 percent of respondents approve of the way the president is doing his job, the real figure might be as low as 38 percent or as high as 46 percent.

A sample is a miniature version of the whole.

A tolerable margin of error depends on the use of survey results. If you want to predict the outcome of an election or the effects of a new medical treatment, strive for a small margin of error, 3 percent or less. If you are conducting a survey to determine how employees feel about a new recreation facility, a higher margin of error is acceptable, 4 or 5 percent.

Margin of error determines the worth of a survey.

A sample is the actual number of persons interviewed.

Determine **sample size** by the size of the population and the acceptable margin of error. There is no magical formula for determining the number of interviewees. Some survey organizations produce accurate national surveys with a margin of error in the 3 percent range from a sample of 1,500. Standard formulas reveal that as a population increases in size, the percentage of the population necessary for a sample declines rapidly. In other words, you have to interview a larger percentage of 5,000 people than of 50,000 people to attain equally accurate results. Formulas also reveal that you must increase greatly the size of a sample to reduce the margin of error from 5 percent to 4 percent to 3 percent. The small reduction in the margin of error may not be worth the added cost of conducting significantly more interviews. Philip Meyer offers the following table that shows the sample sizes of various populations necessary for a 5 percent margin of error and a 95 percent level of confidence.[14]

Population Size	Sample Size
Infinity	384
500,000	384
100,000	383
50,000	381
10,000	370
5,000	357
3,000	341
2,000	322
1,000	278

Sampling Techniques

Size of sample is important, but how you take the sample is of utmost importance to the validity of a survey.

Random Sampling

Random sampling is like "drawing names from a hat."

Random sampling is the simplest method of selecting a representative sampling. For example, if you have a complete roster of all persons in a population, you place all names in a container, mix them thoroughly, and draw out one name at a time until you have a sample.

Table of Random Numbers

A more complicated random sampling method is to assign a number to each potential respondent and create or purchase a **table of random numbers.** With eyes closed,

In skip interval you select every *n*th name from a list.

place a finger on a number and read a combination up, down, across to left or right, or diagonally. Select this number as part of the sample or decide to read the last digit of the number touched (46) and the first digit of the numeral to the right (29) and thus contact respondent number 62. Repeat this process until you have the sample you need.

Skip Interval or Random Digit

In a **skip interval** or **random digit sampling,** you choose every 10th number in a telephone book, every fifth name in a roster of clients, or every other person who walks into a supermarket. The Random Digital Dialing system now in wide use for conducting surveys "randomly generates telephone numbers in target area-code and prefix areas," "gives every telephone number in the area an equal chance of being called," and ensures anonymity because no interviewee names are used.[15] This common sampling technique may have some built-in flaws. For instance, 15 percent or more of the population may have unlisted phone numbers, and an ever-growing number rely on cell phones. A voter, customer, or membership roster might be outdated. Time of day, day of the week, location of a strip mall, and stores in the mall may determine the types of persons available for interviews.

Stratified Random Sample

A stratified sample most closely represents the whole.

Random sampling procedures may not provide adequate representation of subgroups within a population. If a population has clearly definable groups (males and females; ages; education levels; income levels; and diverse cultural groups), employ a **stratified random sampling method.** This method allows you to include a minimum number of respondents from each group, typically the percentage of the group in the target population. For instance, if a targeted population consists of 52 percent women and 48 percent men, the survey sample would reflect these percentages.

Sample Point

A sample point is usually a geographical area.

A sample point represents a geographical area (a square block or mile, for instance) that contains specific types of persons (cattle farmers or retired persons, for instance). Instructions may tell interviewers to skip corner houses (corner houses are often more expensive) and then try every other house on the outside of the four-block area until they have obtained two interviews with males and two with females. This **sample point** or **block sample** gives the survey designer control over selection of interviewees without resorting to lists of names, random digits, or telephone numbers. The U.S. Department of Agriculture has used aerial photographs of farm areas and crops to determine which farmers to interview to determine the amounts of various crops planted and possible yields of these crops each year.

Self-Selection

Self-selection is the least representative of sampling methods.

The most inaccurate sampling method is **self-selection.** You see this method used nearly every day in radio and television talk shows and newscasts. Who is most likely to call C-SPAN, Rush Limbaugh, Larry King Live, or a television station? You guessed it—those who are very angry or most opposed to/most in favor of an action. Moderates rarely call or write. It is easy to predict how self-reporting surveys on gun control, abortion, and labor unions will turn out. Randomness and representation of diverse elements of a population disappear in self-selected samples.

Selecting and Training Interviewers

Creating a survey instrument and developing a careful sample of interviewees are critical, but so is selecting interviewers and training them to conduct the interviews properly.

Number Needed

You can rarely do it all by yourself.

If you plan to interview a small number of persons and the interviews will be brief, one interviewer may be sufficient. Most often you will need several interviewers, particularly when interviews will be lengthy, the sample is large, time allotted for completing the survey is short, and interviewees are scattered over a large geographical area. Large and difficult interviewing assignments result in serious interviewer fatigue and decline in motivation;[16] both will reduce the quality of interviews and the data received.

Qualifications

Interviewers must follow the rules.

A highly scheduled, standardized interview does not require the interviewer to be an expert on the topic or skilled in phrasing questions and probing into answers. It does require a person who can learn and follow guidelines, read the questions verbatim and effectively, and record answers quickly and accurately. If you are using a highly scheduled interview format that requires skillful, neutral probing into answers, interviewers must have the ability to think on their feet, adapt to different interviewees, handle unanticipated interviewee objections and concerns, and react effectively and calmly to strange answers. In this type of interview, professionally trained interviewers are more efficient and produce more accurate results.[17]

Personal Characteristics

Interviewer credibility is critical in surveys.

Interviewers who are older, have a nonthreatening demeanor, and have an optimistic outlook get better response rates and cooperation, regardless of their experiences. Age generates credibility and self-confidence, and optimism motivates interviewees to cooperate.[18] One study discovered that personality and attitude of the interviewer are the most important elements in shaping interviewee attitudes toward surveys.[19]

Interviewee Skepticism

Research studies report that nearly one-third of respondents believe that answering survey questions will neither benefit them nor influence decisions, that there are too many surveys, that surveys are too long, and that interviewers ask too many personal questions. Some 36 percent of respondents in one study said they had been asked to take part in "false surveys," sales or political campaign interviews disguised as informational surveys. Clearly, survey interviewers must be aware of relational dimensions such as warmth, involvement, dominance, and trust and make every effort to establish a positive relationship with each respondent by being friendly and relaxed and appearing to be honest and trustworthy.

Interviewees are increasingly wary of surveys.

Similarity of Interviewer and Interviewee

Similarity, but not a mirror image, may be important.

Similarity may be an important relational dimension in survey interviews. The interviewer should dress similar to interviewees because if interviewers *look like me,* I am more likely to cooperate and answer appropriately. An in-group relationship with the interviewee (black to black, senior citizen to senior citizen, Hispanic-American to Hispanic-American) may avoid cultural and communication barriers and enhance trust because the interviewer is perceived to be safe, capable of understanding, and sympathetic. It may be essential that interviewers are able to speak to interviewees in their own language, including dialects or regional differences.[20]

Training Interviewers

Provide training sessions and carefully written instructions for all interviewers, regardless of experience. Training results in greater use of appropriate probing questions, feedback, and giving instructions.[21]

Poor execution can undo thorough preparation.

During training sessions and developing written guidelines, discuss common interviewee criticisms of surveys and stress the importance of following the question schedule exactly as printed. Explain complex questions and recording methods. Be certain interviewers understand the sampling techniques employed. Emphasize the need to replicate interviews to enhance reliability and attain an acceptable margin of error and level of confidence. The following are typical instructions for interviewers.

Preparing for an Interview

Guard against interviewer bias.

Study the question schedule and answer options thoroughly so you can ask rather than read questions and record answers quickly and accurately. Dress appropriately, and be neat and well groomed. Do not wear buttons or insignia that will identify you with a particular group or position on the issue. This may bias responses. Choose an appropriate time of week and day.

Conducting the Interview

Be friendly, businesslike, and interested in the topic. Speak clearly, at a good pace, and loudly enough to be heard easily. Maintain eye contact and don't be afraid to smile. Ask all questions clearly, without hesitation, and neutrally.

Opening the Interview

You must motivate the interviewee from the moment the interview commences. State your name, identify your organization, and present your credentials if appropriate. Explain the purpose, length, nature, and importance of the study; then move to your first question without appearing to pressure the interviewee to take part.

Asking Questions

No question can be altered in any way.

Ask all questions, including answer options, exactly as worded. You may repeat a question but not rephrase it or define words. Do not change the order of questions or answer options unless instructed to do so. If you are doing a qualitative study, probe carefully into answers to obtain insightful and thorough answers free of ambiguities and vague references.

Maintain a pleasant "poker face" throughout.

Receiving Answers

Give respondents adequate time to reply, and then record answers as prescribed in your training and on the schedule. Write or print answers carefully. Remain neutral at all times.

Closing the Interview

When you have obtained the answer to the last question, thank the interviewee for cooperating and excuse yourself without being abrupt. Be polite and sensitive, making it clear that the interviewee has been most helpful. Do not discuss the survey with the interviewee.

Conducting Survey Interviews

With all preparation completed, it is essential to **pretest the interview** with a portion of the targeted sample to detect potential problems with questions and answer options.

Pretesting the Interview

Lack of pretesting invites disaster.

The best plans on paper may not work during real interviews. Conduct complete interviews, not merely specific questions. Try out the opening, questions, recording answers, and closing.

Leave nothing to chance. For instance, in a political poll conducted by one of our classes, students deleted the question "What do you like or dislike about your major?" because it took too much time, generated little useful data, and posed a coding nightmare because of diverse replies. When interviewees were handed a list of political candidates during another project and asked, "What do you like or dislike about . . . ?" many became embarrassed or gave vague answers because they did not know some of the candidates. This question was replaced with a Likert scale from "strongly like" to "strongly dislike," including a "don't know" option, and interviewers probed into reasons for liking or disliking only for candidates ranked in the extreme positions on the scale. Respondents tended to know something about candidates they strongly liked or strongly disliked. In a survey of mudslinging during political campaigns, one of the authors discovered that scale questions tended to confuse elderly respondents, so he added special explanations to complex questions.

Here are typical questions to ask when pretesting survey interviews:

Leave nothing unquestioned.

- Did interviewees seem to understand what was wanted and why?
- Did interviewees react hesitantly or negatively to any questions?
- Did questions elicit the kind of information desired?
- Were there problems recording answers?
- Can answers be tabulated easily and meaningfully?

Once you have studied the pretest results and made alterations in procedures, questions, and answer options, you are ready to conduct the full survey.

Interviewing Face-to-Face

Traditionally, the survey has been conducted face-to-face with an interviewee, what some call the "personal interview." This method obtains good response rates because of the personal touch. The interviewee can see, hear, and literally experience the interviewer. In some instances, they can feel, experience, or taste products in market surveys. It is easier for the interviewer to establish credibility through physical appearance, dress, voice, eye contact, and presentation of credentials. People tolerate longer interviews when face-to-face, and interviewers can focus on in-depth attitudes. Interviewers can also observe attitudes revealed through face, eye contact, and posture. And interviewers can target very specific audiences because it is easier to know who they are interviewing.

While the face-to-face interview has many advantages, it is very expensive and time-consuming. Face-to-face interviews require a considerable number of trained interviewers who may or may not obtain the representative sample the survey requires. And it's often difficult to do a survey that covers respondents in a wide geographical area.

Interviewing by Telephone

Telephone interviews may be inexpensive in money but costly in results.

A growing number of interviewers are turning to the telephone for easier, faster, and less expensive surveys.

Research on Using the Telephone

Some studies comparing telephone and face-to-face interviews suggest that the two methods produce similar results, with respondents giving fewer socially acceptable answers over the telephone and preferring the anonymity it provides (particularly in certain neighborhoods).[22] Other studies urge caution. One study discovered that many interviewers do not like telephone interviews, and this attitude may affect responses. Another found that fewer interviewees (particularly older ones) prefer the telephone. There is a lower degree of cooperation in telephone interviews.[23] People feel uneasy about discussing sensitive issues with strangers they cannot see, and it is difficult for interviewers to make convincing confidentiality guarantees when they are not face-to-face with respondents.[24] Add to these problems the growing number of persons with unlisted telephone numbers or relying on cell phones. Others are using answering machines, answering services, and call identifiers to filter out unwanted calls, including surveys. [25]

Advantages of the Telephone

Regardless of the potential problems, telephone surveys are becoming more frequent. A single face-to-face or "personal" interview may cost more than $100. Locating respondents at home is more difficult because fewer traditional homemakers exist and flexible working hours make it difficult to predict when a person will be home. Fewer than 50 percent of large city contacts consent to interview face-to-face. Many organizations want to interview persons over a wide geographical area, and the telephone allows them to interview people around the world without moving from an office or home.

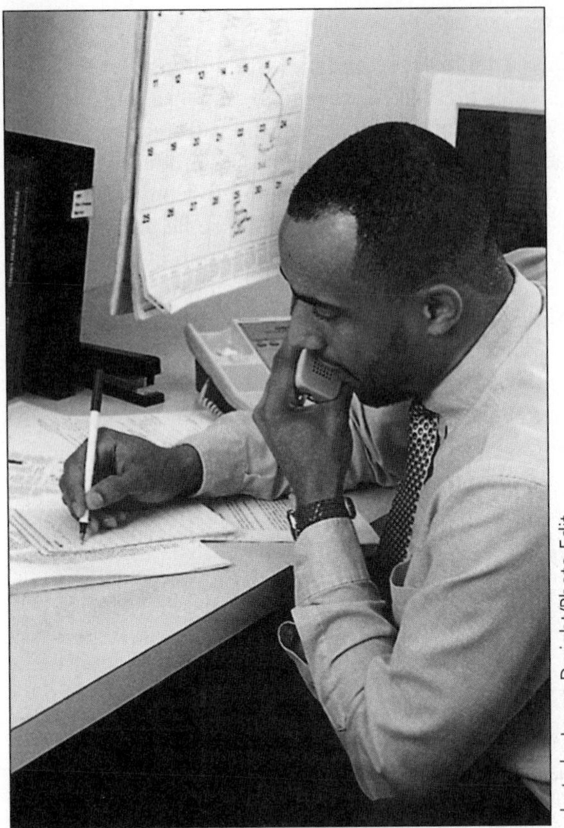

photo by Laura Dwight/Photo Edit

A growing number of interviewers are turning to the telephone for easier and less expensive means of conducting surveys and polls.

Opening the Telephone Interview

The majority of refusals in telephone survey interviews occur prior to the first substantive question: one-third in the opening seconds, one-third during the orientation, and one-third at the point of listing household members.

Speaking skills (pitch, vocal variety, loudness, rate, and distinct enunciation), particularly during the opening, seem to be more important than content. One study concluded, "Respondents react to cues communicated by the interviewer's voice and may grant or refuse an interview on that basis."[26] Telephone interviewers apparently must establish trust through vocal and verbal analogs to the personal appearance, credentials, and survey materials that enhance trust in face-to-face interviews.

How to Use the Telephone

The literature on survey interviewing contains important advice for would-be telephone interviewers. These guidelines are equally relevant to face-to-face interviews.

- *Do not give a person a reason or opportunity to hang up.* Develop an informal but professional style that is courteous (not demanding) and friendly (not defensive). Get the interviewee involved as quickly as possible in answering questions because active involvement motivates people to take part and cooperate.

Opening the telephone interview is critical.

Do nothing but ask and listen during telephone interviews.

- *Listen carefully and actively.* Give your undivided attention to what the interviewee is saying by not drinking, eating, sorting papers, or playing with objects on your desk. Don't communicate nonverbally with others in the room, and say nothing you do not want the interviewee to hear even if you believe you have the mouthpiece covered. Explain any pauses or long silences of more than a few seconds or signal you are listening with cues such as "Uh huh," "Yes," "Okay."
- *Use your voice effectively.* Talk directly into the mouthpiece. Speak loud enough, slowly, clearly, and distinctly because the interviewee must rely solely on your voice. State each answer option distinctly with vocal emphasis on important words and pause between each option to aid in comprehension and recall.
- *Use a computer-assisted telephone interview system* that enables you to dial random numbers quickly and to compile results within minutes of completing interviews.

Interviewing through the Internet

An increasing number of survey interviews are taking place through the Internet—e-mail, Web pages, and computer direct.[27] They are substantially less expensive and faster than either face-to-face or telephone surveys. Because they are highly flexible, Internet surveys can target specific populations over great distances. A major problem of survey interviews—interviewees attempting to give socially acceptable answers—is lessened because of the anonymity of the interview. Respondents may give more honest answers to sensitive topics. Unlike paper-and-pencil surveys, and even some face-to-face and telephone surveys, interviewees tend to provide more detail in answers to open-ended questions, perhaps because of the option to respond when it is most convenient to them.

On the other hand, the critical nonverbal communication that aids face-to-face and telephone interviews is lost when you use the Internet. Response rates may suffer because it is more difficult to establish the credibility of the survey and its source or to distinguish the survey interview from a slick telemarketer sales interview. While the Internet gives respondents time to think through answers, it also loses the spontaneity of interactions in face-to-face and telephone interviews, and it's nearly impossible to probe into answers or employ question strategies such as shuffle, leaning, and repeat. Since there is no way to tell who is replying to an Internet-based survey, the sample may be questionable. Evidence also indicates that completion rates are lower for lengthy surveys; respondents grow tired of the process and simply log off.

Coding, Tabulation, and Analysis

Once all interviews are completed, the final phase of the survey begins. This phase involves coding, tabulation, and analysis of the information received.

Coding and Tabulation

Begin the final phase of the survey by **coding** all answers that were not precoded, usually the open-ended questions. For instance, if question 20 is "You state that you drink at bars near campus every Thursday, Friday, and Saturday night. Why do you do this?" a variety of answers are possible. If 20 is coded #20, each answer might be coded 20 plus 1, 2, 3, etc.

20-1 All of my friends do it.
20-2 There's little else to do in this town.
20-3 It's fun.
20-4 You forget about the pressure of assignments and exams.
20-5 That's where you meet interesting men (women).
20-6 That's what college is all about.
20-7 I like beer.

Answers to open-ended questions may require analysis and structuring before developing a coding system. For example, in a study of voter perception of mudslinging in political campaigns, the interviewer asked, "What three or four words would you use

Record answers to open-ended questions with great care.

to describe a politician who uses mudslinging as a tactic?" Answers included more than 100 different words, but analysis revealed that most words tended to fit into five categories: untrustworthy, incompetent, unlikable, insecure, and immature.[28] A sixth category, "other" received words that did not fit into the five categories. All words were placed into one of these six categories and coded from one to six.

Analysis

Analysis is making sense of your data.

Once all answers are coded and the results tabulated, the **analysis** phase begins. This task can be overwhelming. One of the authors surveyed 354 clergy from 32 Protestant, Catholic, and Jewish groups to assess the interview training they had received during college and seminary and since entering the ministry.[29] The 48 questions in the survey times 354 respondents provided 16,992 bits of information. Attempts to compare respondents according to religious affiliation, years in the ministry, and demographic data such as age and geographical area produced hundreds of pages of computer printouts.

How can the survey interviewer handle massive amounts of information generated in most surveys? The late Charles Redding offered several helpful suggestions.[30]

- *Be selective.* Ask "What findings are likely to be most useful?" and "What will I do with this information once I get it?" If you have no idea, do not ask for it.
- *Capitalize on the potential of data.* Subject data to comparative breakdowns to discover differences between demographic subgroups.
- *Dig for the gold.* What is the really important stuff hidden within raw data and simple tabulations? For instance, in polls of registered voter attitudes, interviewers often discover that female respondents favor a candidate far less than male respondents and that Americans who have recently become citizens are likely to have very different views toward immigration than third or fourth generation Americans.
- *Look for what is missing.* What you do not find may be more important than what you do find. What information did you not obtain?

Know the limitations of your survey.

During analysis of data, ask a number of questions. What conclusions can you draw, and with what certainty? For what segment of a target population can you generalize? What are the constraints imposed by the sample, schedule of questions, the interviewing process, and the interviewers? Why did people respond in specific ways to specific questions? What unexpected events or changes have occurred since the completion of the survey that might make this survey dated or suspect? What should be done with the "undecided" and "don't know" answers or blanks on survey forms?

Be careful in using survey results.

Caution is essential for all survey takers. For example, journalists must be cautious when writing headlines and making predictions. Organizations must be cautious when basing policy decisions on survey results. Voters must be cautious when casting votes according to candidate-preference polls. You might subject data to a statistical analysis designed to test reliability and significance of data. Babbie and other research methodologists (see resources) provide detailed guidelines for conducting sophisticated statistical analyses.

When the analysis of data is complete, determine if the purpose and objectives of the survey are achieved. If so, what are the best means of reporting the results?

The Respondent in Survey Interviews

The proliferation of surveys ensures that interviewers will ask you to take part in them often. You may walk away from the market researcher at a mall, close your door to a political pollster, hang up the telephone on a person doing an attitude survey or refuse to reply to a Web survey. By doing so, however, you forfeit the opportunity to play an important role in improving products, selecting political candidates, influencing legislation, or bettering the community.

The Opening

Understand what a survey is all about before participating.

When asked to participate in a survey interview, take an *active* part in the opening. Discover by listening, observing and asking the identity of the interviewer, the organization the interviewer represents, why the survey is being conducted, how your answers will be used, how long the interview will take, and whether you will be identified in the results. Decide whether to take part after thorough orientation. If the interviewer does not provide important information, ask for it. For instance, when one of the authors was visiting his daughter and her family in Vancouver, Washington, more than 2,000 miles from home, he was approached in a shopping mall by a market researcher. The researcher explained who she was, what she was doing, and why she was doing it. She did not state he had to be a local resident. When asked if it made any difference that he was visiting from the Midwest, the interviewer said she wanted only those who regularly visited the mall. The interview was terminated.

The opening is also a critical time to determine if the interview is truly part of a survey or a slick sales effort under the guise of a survey. Is it a political preference survey or part of the persuasive campaign for a particular candidate or party? Be trusting but skeptical. When one of the authors recently answered the doorbell at his home, a person explained that he was conducting a religious survey, but a few targeted questions revealed the "survey" to be a clever "foot in the door" ruse to sell religious publications. The interview ended politely but abruptly.

The Question Phase

Listen perceptively.

Listen carefully to each question, particularly to answer options in interval, nominal, and ordinal questions. If a question or option is difficult to recall, ask the interviewer to repeat the question slowly. If a question is unclear, explain why and ask for clarification. Avoid replays of earlier answers, especially if you think you "goofed." Do not try to guess what a question is going to be from the interviewer's first words. You might guess wrong and become confused, give a stupid answer, or needlessly force the interviewer to restate a perfectly clear question.

Think before answering.

Think through each answer in order to respond clearly and precisely. Give the answer that best represents your beliefs, attitudes, or actions. Do not permit interviewer bias to lead toward the answer you think the interviewer wants to hear or how other respondents might answer.

You have rights as a respondent. For example, you can refuse to answer a poorly constructed or leading question or to give data that seems irrelevant or an invasion of privacy. Expect and demand tactful, sensitive, and polite treatment from interviewers.

Insist on adequate time to answer questions. If you have agreed to a 10-minute interview and the interview is still going strong at the 10-minute mark, remind the interviewer of the agreement and proceed to close the interview unless only a few more seconds are required. Remember, you can always walk away, close the door, or hang up the telephone. Survey interviews can be fun, interesting, and informative if both parties treat one another fairly.

Summary

The survey interview is the most meticulously planned and executed of interviews. Planning begins with determining a clearly defined purpose and conducting research. The purpose of all survey interviews is to establish a solid base of fact from which to draw conclusions, make interpretations, and determine future courses of action. Only then does the survey creator structure the interview and develop questions with appropriate strategies, scales, sequences, coding, and recording methods. Selecting interviewees not only involves delineating a target population to survey, but also involves choosing a sample of this population that represents the whole. The creator of the survey chooses sampling methods, determines the size of the sample, and plans for an acceptable margin of error. Each choice has advantages and disadvantages because there is no one correct way to handle all survey situations.

Survey respondents must determine the nature of the survey and its purposes before deciding whether to take part. If the decision is to participate, respondents have a responsibility to listen carefully to each question and answer it accurately. As a respondent, be sure you understand each question and its answer options. Demand enough time to think through answers. Feel free to refuse to answer obviously loaded or poorly phrased questions that require a biased answer or choosing among options that do not include how you feel, who you are, or what you do.

Key Terms and Concepts

The online learning center for this text features FLASHCARDS and CROSSWORD PUZZLES for studying based on these terms and concepts.

Bogardus Social Distance Scale
Chain or contingency strategy
Cross-sectional survey
Evaluative interval scale
Face-to-face interview
Filter strategy
Frequency interval scale
Internet interview
Interval scale
Leaning question strategy
Level of confidence
Likert scale
Longitudinal survey
Margin of error
Nominal scale
Numerical interval scale
Ordinal scale
Personal interview
Population
Qualitative survey
Quantitative survey
Precision journalism
Random digital dialing
Random sampling
Ranking ordinal scale
Rating ordinal scale
Reliability
Repeat strategy
Replicability
Sample point
Sampling principles
Self-selection
Shuffle strategy
Skip interval scale
Stratified random sample
Table of random numbers
Web survey

A Survey Interview for Review and Analysis

As you read through this survey schedule, notice the parts of the standard opening. See if you can identify question strategies (filter, repeat, leaning, shuffle, and chain), question scales (evaluative interval, frequency interval, numerical interval, nominal, ordinal, and Bogardus Social Distance), and question sequences (funnel, inverted funnel, tunnel, and quintamensional design). Notice the built-in probing questions, instructions for interviewers, precoding of answers, and inclusion of open questions. Note the simple, planned closing.

How might the opening be improved? How might the closing be improved? Are there problems with order and placement of questions, such as demographic data? How might questions be phrased more effectively? What problems might the open-ended questions pose for interviewers and interviewees? How could the interviewer make better use of question strategies and scales? Are the subtopics of the selected topic the most important? How adequate are recording techniques and instructions?

Issues Confronting the United States Today

(Speak to any person 18 years old or older who lives in the household.)

Hello, my name is ____________________ from Public Opinion Research, a nationwide survey research organization located in Philadelphia. The results of our study will be supplied to the public through the news media. We've been interviewing people in your neighborhood about current issues and would like to ask you a few questions.

1. I'm going to read you several age ranges. Stop me when I read the one that includes your age.

18–24	________	50–64	________
25–34	________	65 and over	________
35–49	________		

2. How often do you vote?

All elections ________
Most elections ________
Some elections ________
Occasional elections ________
Never ________

3a. Do you generally consider yourself a Democrat or a Republican? (*IF* INDEPENDENT, ASK Q. 3b.)

Democrat	________	Don't know	________
Republican	________	Refuse	________

3b. Well, do you generally vote for Democrat or Republican candidates for public office?

Independent/Democrat ________
Independent/Republican ________
Independent ________

4a. When you think of a serious problem facing the United States today, which problem comes to mind first?

____

4b. What do you think is the major cause of this problem?

____

4c. What are other possible causes of this problem?

____

____

5. Many people tell us that terrorism is the greatest problem facing the United States today. How would you rate the job the president is doing in addressing terrorism: excellent, good, average, not so good, poor? (CIRCLE ANSWERS IN THE SCALES PROVIDED AT THE END OF Q. 7.)

6. How would you rate the job Congress is doing in addressing terrorism: excellent, good, average, not so good, poor? (CIRCLE ANSWERS IN THE SCALES PROVIDED AT THE END OF Q. 7.)

7. How would you rate the job the Office of Homeland Security is doing in addressing terrorism: excellent, good, average, not so good, poor? (CIRCLE ANSWERS IN THE SCALES PROVIDED BELOW.)

	President	**Congress**	**Homeland Security**
Excellent	1	1	1
Good	2	2	2
Average	3	3	3
Not so good	4	4	4
Poor	5	5	5

8. Here is a card (HAND CARD TO INTERVIEWEE) that lists some of the problems people say the federal government must do something about. (ROTATE THE ORDER FROM ONE INTERVIEW TO THE NEXT.) Do you think the Republican or the Democratic Party is likely to address these problems most effectively?

	Rep.	**Dem.**	**Either**	**Neither**	**Don't know**
School funding	1	2	3	4	5
Drugs	1	2	3	4	5
Crime	1	2	3	4	5
Health care	1	2	3	4	5
Defense	1	2	3	4	5
Terrorism	1	2	3	4	5
Energy	1	2	3	4	5
Environment	1	2	3	4	5

9. Many people tell us they are concerned about the escalating price of gasoline. This card (HAND CARD TO INTERVIEWEE) lists several possible solutions to gasoline costs. Please tell me which one is closest to your feelings about a solution to this problem.

The federal requirements for miles per gallon per new vehicle must be increased substantially.	1
We need to build more refineries.	2
We need to drill for oil in the protected wilderness areas of Alaska and off the shore of Florida.	3
We should pressure our allies in the Middle East to increase the amount of oil they pump.	4
All gasoline should contain 10 percent ethanol to reduce dependence on foreign oil.	5

10. Many people we talk to feel that America is in a serious moral decline. This card (HAND CARD TO INTERVIEWEE) gives some causes people cite for America's morality problem. Which one of these reasons do you feel is the greatest cause of immorality? (RECORD ANSWER.) Which is the next most important cause? (RECORD ANSWER.) And which would be the next? (RECORD ANSWER.)

	First	**Second**	**Third**
Abortion	1	2	3
Same-sex marriage	1	2	3
Sexual promiscuity	1	2	3
Poverty	1	2	3
Immorality among leaders	1	2	3
Television	1	2	3
Outlawing prayer in schools	1	2	3
Failure of organized religion	1	2	3
Breakdown of the family	1	2	3
Drugs and alcohol	1	2	3

11. I'm going to read several proposed actions for strengthening the traditional family in America, and I would like you to tell me whether you strongly agree, agree, don't know, disagree, or strongly disagree with each. (RECORD ANSWERS ON THE SPACE BELOW AND ROTATE THE ORDER IN WHICH THE STATEMENTS ARE GIVEN FROM INTERVIEW TO INTERVIEW.)

a. We should outlaw abortion in this country.
b. We should make physical abuse the only grounds for divorce.
c. We should pass a constitutional amendment forbidding same-sex marriages.
d. Sex education should emphasize abstaining from sex until marriage.

e. Income tax laws should enable women to remain home with their children.
f. Adultery should be a felony in all 50 states.

	a	b	c	d	e	f
Strongly agree	1	1	1	1	1	1
Agree	2	2	2	2	2	2
Don't know	3	3	3	3	3	3
Disagree	4	4	4	4	4	4
Strongly disagree	5	5	5	5	5	5

12a. Are you familiar with the Patriot Act?

Yes ________ (IF YES, ASK Q. 12b.)
No ________

12b. What do you know about the Patriot Act?

____

____

13a. Scientists claim that stem cell research will lead to successful prevention or treatment of a wide variety of medical afflictions, such as Alzheimer's disease. Do you approve or disapprove of using stem cells that emanate from human embryos?

Approve ________ Disapprove ________

13b. Why do you feel this way?

____

____

13c. How strongly do you feel about this?

Strongly ________
Very strongly ________
Something about which you will never change your mind ________

14. With all of the focus on weapons of mass destruction in Iraq, there has been a renewed demand to dismantle our own, particularly highly dangerous nerve gas.

a. Would you be in favor of disposing of our nerve gas stockpiles?
Yes ________ No ________
b. Would you be in favor of disposing of these nerve gas stockpiles in your area of the country?
Yes ________ No ________
c. Would you be in favor of disposing of these nerve gas stockpiles in your state?
Yes ________ No ________

d. Would you be in favor of disposing of these nerve gas stockpiles in your county?
Yes _________ No _________

e. Would you be in favor of disposing of these nerve gas stockpiles near your city?
Yes _________ No _________

Now I would like to ask you some personal questions so we can see how people with different backgrounds feel about the issues facing the United States today.

15. Is your religious affiliation Protestant, Catholic, Jewish, Muslim, other, none?

Protestant _________
Catholic _________
Jewish _________
Muslim _________
Other _________________________ (WRITE NAME.)
None _________

16. What was the last grade level of your formal education?

0–8 years _________ 13–15 years _________
9 to 11 years _________ College graduate _________
12 years _________ Postgraduate _________

17. I'm going to read several income ranges. Stop me when I read the range that includes your current annual family income.

0 through $14,999 _________
$15,000 through $24,999 _________
$25,000 through $49,999 _________
$50,000 through $74,999 _________
$75,000 through $99,999 _________
Over $100,000 _________

That's all the questions I have. The survey results should be made public within five to six weeks.

Survey Role-Playing Cases

Grade Inflation

The interviewer is chairing a committee investigating the problem of grade inflation across disciplines on campus. Over the past 20 years, the average grade on campus has increased from a C or 2.25 on a 4.0 scale to slightly over a B or 3.05. There is growing concern that grades are not reflecting the quality of student work or distinguishing between levels of accomplishment in courses and majors. The committee's task is to interview a cross section of faculty and students to assess their opinions as to the causes of this rise in grades and its effects on faculty and students.

High Gas Prices

When the price of gasoline rose more than 45 percent over a three-month period, Stan Maguire, owner of Maguire Chevrolet, decided to aim all of his advertisements at this growing concern of car owners. Each ad has featured a different Chevrolet model and its city and highway gas mileage compared with comparable, competing models. He wants to know if the concern over mileage exceeds other major reasons for purchasing a new car such as style, power, seating, size, quality, and features. Stan has decided to hire your polling firm to contact people who purchase new cars every 3 to 5 years to assess their reasons for trading and buying particular brands and models and the possible effects of high gas prices.

A Social Service Survey

Your public relations class has taken as a client a recently created nonprofit service organization named Urban Community Care. The first task is to assess the service needs of the community, including homeless shelters, soup kitchens, child care facilities, substance abuse programs, a shelter for abused spouses, and a food pantry. This assessment will begin with a face-to-face survey of governmental, religious, educational, and social leaders to determine major needs and courses of action.

A Political Poll

You have volunteered to help the campaign of a former teacher who has decided to run for mayor of your city. This person was unopposed in the primary but faces stiff competition from an incumbent mayor running for a fourth four-year term. Your major goals early in the campaign are to determine degree of name recognition, problems of most concern to voters, degree of satisfaction with the incumbent, and potential role of political party affiliation. You will not conduct interviews but will create the schedule of questions and train a team of 10 interviewers.

Student Activities

1. Serve as a volunteer interviewer for a survey being conducted by a company, political party, government agency, or religious group. What instructions and training did you receive? How were interviewees determined? What problems did you encounter in locating suitable and cooperative interviewees? What problems did you have with the survey schedule? What is the most important thing you have learned from this experience? What advice would you give the organization you volunteered to serve?
2. Try a simple interviewer bias experiment. Conduct 10 short opinion interviews on a current issue, using an identical question schedule for all interviews. During five of them, wear a conspicuous T-shirt, button, or badge that identifies membership in or support of an organization that supports one side of the issue: a Republican elephant, a crucifix or a Star of David, an organization's logo, a product slogan. Compare results to see if your apparent identification with an organization on one side of the issue affected answers to identical questions.

3. Obtain a number of market survey and political poll schedules from your library, a professor, a survey organization, or political party. Compare and contrast these schedules. How are the openings similar and different? How are schedules and sequences similar and different? How are question strategies and question scales similar and different? How are closings similar and different? What surprises did you discover in your comparisons?
4. Conduct an interview with a person experienced in survey interviews. How does this person (or the person's organization) conduct background research? Create and pretest survey schedules? Determine the size of sample and sampling methods? Determine acceptable margins or error? Select and train interviewers? Use face-to-face, telephone, and Internet methods?

Notes

1. Paul Rosenfeld, Jack E. Edwards, and Marie D. Thomas, "Improving Organizational Surveys," *American Behavioral Scientist* 36 (1993), p. 414.
2. Earl Babbie, *The Practice of Social Research* (Belmont, CA: Wadsworth, 1995), pp. 84–86.
3. Leslie A. Baxter and Earl Babbie, *The Basics of Communication Research* (Belmont, CA: Wadsworth/Thomson, 2004), p. 22
4. Baxter and Babbie, p. 22.
5. http://www.socialresearchmethods.net/kb/interview.htm, accessed September 29, 2006.
6. Diane K. Willimack, Howard Schuman, Beth-Ellen Pennell, and James M. Lepkowski, "Effects of a Prepaid Nonmonetary Incentive on Response Rates and Response Quality in Face-to-Face Survey," *Public Opinion Quarterly* 59 (1995), pp. 78–92.
7. Stanley L. Payne, *The Art of Asking Questions* (Princeton, NJ: Princeton University Press, 1980), p. 57.
8. Jack E. Edwards and Marie D. Thomas, "The Organizational Survey Process," *American Behavioral Scientist* 36 (1993), pp. 425–426.
9. Babbie, p. 145.
10. Creative Research Systems, "The Survey System," file://C:DOCUME~1\stewart\LOCALS\Temp\G2BBVAF.htm, accessed September 29, 2006.
11. Norman M. Bradburn, Seymour Sudman, Ed Blair, and Carol Stocking, "Question Threat and Response Bias," *Public Opinion Quarterly* 42 (1978), pp. 221–234.
12. Sam G. McFarland, "Effects of Question Order on Survey Responses," *Public Opinion Quarterly* 45 (1981), pp. 208–215.
13. Morris James Slonim, *Sampling in a Nutshell* (New York: Simon and Schuster, 1960), p. 23.
14. Philip Meyer, *Precision Journalism* (Bloomington, IN: Indiana University Press, 1979), p. 123.

15. "Designing the Survey Instrument and Process," http://www.airhealthwatch.com/mdph_instrument.htm, accessed September 29, 2006.

16. Eleanor Singer, Martin R. Frankel, and Marc B. Glassman, "The Effect of Interviewer Characteristics and Expectations on Response," *Public Opinion Quarterly* 47 (1983), pp. 68–83.

17. Robin T. Peterson, "How Efficient Are Salespeople in Surveys of Buyer Intentions," *Journal of Business Forecasting* 7 (1988), pp. 11–12.

18. Singer, Frankel, and Glassman, pp. 68–83.

19. Stephan Schleifer, "Trends in Attitudes toward and Participation in Survey Research," *Public Opinion Quarterly* 50 (1986), pp. 17–26.

20. "Evaluation Tools for Racial Equity: Tip Sheets," http://www.Evaluationtoolsforracialequity.org/, accessed September 29, 2006.

21. Jacques Billiet and Geert Loosveldt, "Improvement of the Quality of Responses to Factual Survey Questions by Interviewer Training," *Public Opinion Quarterly* 52 (1988), pp. 190–211.

22. Theresa F. Rogers, "Interviews by Telephone and in Person: Quality of Responses and Field Performance," *Public Opinion Quarterly* 39 (1976), pp. 51–65; Stephen Kegeles, Clifton F. Frank, and John P. Kirscht, "Interviewing a National Sample by Long-Distance Telephone," *Public Opinion Quarterly* 33 (1969–1970), pp. 412–419.

23. Lawrence A. Jordan, Alfred C. Marcus, and Leo G. Reeder, "Response Style in Telephone and Household Interviewing," *Public Opinion Quarterly* 44 (1980), pp. 210–222; and Peter V. Miller and Charles F. Cannell, "A Study of Experimental Techniques in Telephoning Interviewing," *Public Opinion Quarterly* 46 (1982), pp. 250–269.

24. William S. Aquilino, "Interview Mode Effects in Surveys on Drug and Alcohol Use," *Public Opinion Quarterly* 58 (1994), pp. 210–240.

25. Michael W. Link and Robert W. Oldendick, "Call Screening: Is it Really a Problem for Survey Research," *Public Opinion Quarterly* 63 (Winter 1999), pp. 577–589.

26. Lois Okenberg, Lerita Coleman, and Charles F. Cannell, "Interviewers' Voices and Refusal Rates in Telephone Surveys," *Public Opinion Quarterly* 50 (1986), pp. 97–111.

27. Personal Surveys vs. Web Surveys: A Comparison," http://Knowledgee-base.supersurvey.com/in-person-vs-web-surveys.htm, accessed September 29, 2006; "The Survey System."

28. Charles J. Stewart, "Voter Perception of Mudslinging in Political Communication," *Central States Speech Journal* 26 (1975), pp. 279–286.

29. Charles J. Stewart, "The Interview and the Clergy: A Survey of Training, Experiences, and Needs," *Religious Communication Today* 3 (1980), pp. 19–22.

30. W. Charles Redding, *How to Conduct a Readership Survey* (Chicago: Lawrence Ragan Communications, 1982), pp. 119–123.

Resources

Baxter, Leslie A., and Earl Babbie. *The Basics of Communication Research.* Belmont, CA: Wadsworth/Thomson, 2004.

"Designing the Survey Instrument and Process," http://www.airhealthwatch.com/mdph_instrument.htm.

Fowler, Floyd J. *Survey Research Methods.* Thousand Oaks, CA: Sage, 2002.

Frey, James H. *How to Conduct Interviews by Telephone and In Person.* Thousand Oaks, CA: Sage, 1995.

Gubrium, Jaber F., and James A. Holstein, eds. *Handbook of Interview Research.* Newbury Park, CA: Sage, 2001.

Meyer, Philip. *Precision Journalism.* Lanham, MD: Roman & Littlefield, 2002.

Salant, Priscilla, and Don A. Dillman. *Conducting Surveys: A Step-by-Step Guide to Getting the Information You Need.* New York: Wiley, 1995.

CHAPTER 7 The Recruiting Interview

Recruiting new employees is a never-ending and critical task for every organization. Their futures depend upon it. But the task of attracting high quality employees is neither easy nor inexpensive. It is an elaborate courtship process fraught with all sorts of interpersonal problems and susceptible to bias and distortion. In spite of such problems, the interview remains a critical component of the selection process because we want to see and interact with future employees and colleagues.[1] You may not be heading toward a career in human resources but, regardless of your position, you will be involved in the hiring process for your organization, perhaps as early as the fall following your graduation. Many recent graduates are sent to their former schools and other campuses because they can identify readily with student recruits. This essential task has become even more difficult because of revolutionary changes in society, the work force, and the world of work.

Recruiting is expensive and complex.

The Changing World of Work

The world of work has changed dramatically in the past five years. Changes are not just in the global sense of work competition for manufacturing jobs but in the complexity of the work force. Competition in the workplace was at one time between Toledo and Pittsburgh, steel and automotive. Today the competition is between India and China, the European Union and Japan. This globalization is compounded by education, age, and ethnic considerations. As the work forces in many parts of the world have aged, there is a growing concern about how to involve the baby boomers and retirees so these forces can remain strong not only in numbers but in vibrancy. Society cannot afford to lose their experiential, intellectual, inventive, and critical contributions.[2]

Richard Fein writes, in his book entitled *The Baby Boomers Guide to the New Work Place,* that competition for skilled and nonskilled workers will be enormous in the not too distant future.[3] While there will always be competition for those with college degrees, competition will grow for nondegree positions. In his book entitled *America's Top 101 Jobs for People without a Four-Year Degree,* Michael Farr identifies 101 of the most popular nondegree jobs available today.[4] The competition for positions will result in increasing generational problems in the workplace. Lynne Lancaster and David Stillman explore the differing values, beliefs, and skills of workers in their 20s, 30s, 40s, and senior years in their book entitled *When Generations Collide.*[5] Issues such as loyalty, work ethic, people skills, and getting ahead cause conflicts between the generations and problems on the job.

Two additional problems for all potential employers are retirement and insurance. A few decades ago, people would join a company and receive a compensative insurance policy and the company's retirement plan. With the demise of the steel, heavy equipment, and automotive industries and the shrinking of manufacturing in general, workers today and in the future might have, at best, a 401K plan, be encouraged to have their own Roth IRA, or develop a personal retirement plan. Almost certainly they will need to furnish a portion of their health insurance. These changes have and will continue to affect the hiring process.

Knowledge, information, technology, medicine, and data are now where work and competition are anchored. This means that finding, recruiting, interviewing, evaluating, and retaining quality employees are an organization's biggest challenges.

Work, who does it, and how it is done have changed.

In his most recent and best book, *Re-Imagine,* Tom Peters warns that "if you don't like change, you'll like irrelevance even less."[6] He claims, "We are in a brawl with no rules." In his book, he explores the new global world, work and its context, and what *was* in the world of work and how it *is* now. Summary boxes in each chapter identify the characteristics of the past and present.

Peters believes that today "talent rules," so management must be obsessed with attracting talent.[7] The Boss 25 is a list of imperatives organizations must follow if they are going to compete in the twenty-first century. Others echo Peters' predictions. William Lewis writes that finding talent at a reasonable cost and developing that talent will be the ultimate difference between success and failure.[8] Doug Brown identifies six common traits to look for and argues that productivity, which encompasses technology and more people doing more things, along with outsourcing and elimination of unnecessary workers and supervisors, will lead to job recovery from the collapse of e-commerce and the global economic downturn.[9] Organizations will be seeking employees with specific skills and ones who can adapt to a broad range of duties.

Talent is the new gold standard.

Essential Applicant Skills

A search firm executive told the authors that "You can't know enough, learn enough, or experience enough" in a single interview. It is essential that recruiters become keenly aware of and probe into the skills, attitudes, and abilities that make an applicant an ideal fit for an organization and position. Organizations must provide candidates and recruiters with very specific skills, attitudes, and responsibilities. One senior manager said to your authors, "Anyone can buy technology, but the critical element in competing globally is the *people!*"

People hold the keys to success.

Employees in the future will need a number of basic skills and attitudes:[10]

- *Computer skills:* Every employee will deal with a wide range of computer technology, software, e-mail, Internet, and computer presentation skills. Boomers, seniors, and those with little training can attain computer skills from community colleges, senior clubs, and senior living centers.
- *Numbers skills:* Employees must be able to measure and compare products, services, costs, and profits. Many believe that if you cannot measure it (develop and apply a system of metrics), it's not getting done.

- *Problem solving attitudes and skills:* Many organizations operate with a very thin work force, so individuals must learn to resolve problems.
- *Strong interpersonal skills:* These skills are often referred to as "soft or weak skills," but nothing could be further from the truth. The abilities to deal with a wide range of individuals (of different age, education, and culture) are basic to success. Listening skills are essential.
- *Understanding culture and language:* In a global economy, the more you understand belief systems and language, the greater will be your ability to deal effectively with a wide range of people.

Flexibility and adaptability are essential.

- *Ability to deal with change and job ambiguity:* Changes in the nature of work, who does the work, and how an organization compensates for work will continue to evolve. Change in our lives will be constant.
- *Global and diverse perspective:* It used to be important to understand the differences between those from the South and the North, those from New England and the Atlantic states, and those from the West and Midwest. Today we must adapt to and understand those from Europe, the Far East, Near East, and Africa.
- *Customer and quality orientation:* Many people in the 1970s and 1980s laughed when someone said, "The Japanese make better cars." Toyota is rapidly becoming the world's largest automotive company, perhaps surpassing GM in less than 25 years. Quality and customer service are responsible.
- *Team player/group leader:* All of us will take on greater responsibility for the success of our position, group, unit, and product. Few of us will operate alone as in the past.

Where to Find Good Applicants

Merely publishing an opening is not sufficient.

Web sites have not replaced personal contacts.

The number and nature of sources available to locate good applicants is enormous. The Internet provides sources in virtually all fields from college graduates to senior citizens. Every university and college has its own Web site. Churches, senior citizen clubs, for-hire agencies, and placement services are readily available, most with Web sites.

Don't overlook traditional sources. Use your networks of colleagues, professional friends, ministers, and college professors. Keep a file of "potentials" you can refer to when necessary. College career centers and those of professional societies and ethnic organizations are excellent sources. Attend job fairs on campuses, at malls, and those coinciding with professional meetings and conferences.

A growing number of organizations, particularly in retail, are employing in-store terminals and kiosks to attract people who might not apply otherwise. This allows them to establish and update "a prospective database every minute the store is open" and to sort through applications to locate the most qualified applicants.[11]

There are literally hundreds of Internet and electronic sources available to locate quality applicants. Here are some key sources:

- Google/Expedia (http://www.google.com)
- Job Search (http://www.jobsearch.com)

- HeadHunter.net (http://www.headhunter.net)
- EONS, founded in 2006 by the creator of Monster.com (http://www.eons.com)
- MonsterTrak (http://www.monstertrak.com)
- Kennedy's Directory of Executive Recruiters (http://www.kennedyinfo.com/db/db_der_bas.html)
- Corporate Alumni Associations (http://www.corporatealumni.com)
- P.A.C.E., founded in 1992 to serve contract professionals, is good for older workers (http://www.pace.pros.com)
- Yahoo search engine (http://www.yahoo.com)
- Wall Street Journal search engine (http://wsj.com)
- My Career Builder (http://www.careerbuilder.com)
- Monster board career search (http://www.monster.com)
- Hot Jobs (http://www.hotjobs.com)

Most organizations are striving to diversify their workforces, particularly among ethnic groups, but few know how to locate or attract qualified minority applicants. Joyce Gioia offers these suggestions: advertise in ethnic media (such as alternate language newspapers, magazines, Web sites, radio, and television) and in movie theatres that attract a highly diverse clientele.[12] You need to think globally, Gioia writes, because recruiting employees from diverse ethnic groups "holds opportunities for companies beyond their wildest dreams."

Don't overlook your own Web site, because the vast majority of prospective applicants will check this site to determine if this is an organization they would find attractive. One study revealed that one in two potential applicants consider the employer's Web site to be "important" and that one in four would reject a potential employer on the basis of a poor Web site.[13] Your site should be easy to read, interesting, and sophisticated. A simple reality check is to log onto your site *as a potential employee* to see if it meets these criteria.

Preparing the Recruiting Effort

Since the recruiting interview will remain the central component of attracting and selecting employees, employers must approach the process systematically and learn how to prepare for, participate in, and evaluate it. Professionally conducted interviews not only select better employees but also present good impressions of organizations.[14] Begin your preparation with a thorough review of relevant **equal employment opportunity (EEO) laws.**

Reviewing EEO Laws

Since the 1964 Civil Rights Act and other appropriate laws were passed, a huge volume of case law has been developed around how and who you recruit and what being selected for employment means to the potential candidate and the organization. It is critical to review federal and state employment laws, and organizations should either hire or have available a specialist in employment law.

You do not want to be the cause of a lawsuit.

Although most relevant EEO laws have been on the books for decades, interviewers continue to violate them knowingly and unknowingly. A study reported in the *Wall Street Journal* found that 70 percent of 200 interviewers and recruiters for Fortune 500 companies, presumably among the best trained, thought at least five of 12 unlawful questions were "safe to ask."[15] And a survey of employers and applicants discovered that 12 percent thought it was acceptable to ask questions about political beliefs, 27 percent about family background, 30 percent about the candidate's spouse, and 45 percent about the candidate's personal life.[16] Ignorance or disregard of the law can lead to noncompliance and expensive, time-consuming, and embarrassing lawsuits against your organization. Cases may be tried by jury, and successful plaintiffs may receive back pay, benefits, compensation for lost future wages in lieu of reinstatement, and punitive damages.

EEO Laws to Know

Become acquainted with important EEO laws and executive orders that pertain to the employment selection interview. Federal EEO laws pertain to all organizations that deal with the federal government, have more than 15 employees, have more than $50,000 in government contracts, and engage in interstate commerce. Most organizations meet these criteria.

Know both state and federal EEO laws.

State laws may be more stringent than federal laws. The following are laws and executive orders you need to know.

- The Civil Rights Acts of 1866, 1870, and 1871 prohibit discrimination against minorities.
- The Equal Pay Act of 1963 requires equal pay for men and women performing work that involves similar skill, effort, responsibility, and working conditions.
- The Civil Rights Acts of 1964, particularly Title VII, prohibits the selection of employees based on race, color, sex, religion, or national origin, and requires employers to discover discriminatory practices and eliminate them. Congress created the Equal Employment Opportunity Commission to ensure compliance and is concerned with the results, not the intents, of hiring practices.
- Executive Order 11246, issued in 1965 and amended in 1967, prohibits discrimination and requires government contractors to take "affirmative action" to ensure that applicants are treated equally.
- The Age Discrimination in Employment Act of 1967 prohibits employers of 25 or more persons from discriminating against persons because of age.
- The Equal Employment Opportunity Act of 1972 extended the Civil Rights Act of 1964 to public and private educational institutions, labor organizations, and employment agencies.
- The Rehabilitation Act of 1973 orders federal contractors to hire disabled persons, and includes alcoholism, asthma, rheumatoid arthritis, and epilepsy.
- The Vietnam Era Veterans Readjustment Act of 1974 encourages employers to hire qualified Vietnam veterans, including those with disabilities.
- The Immigration Reform and Control Act of 1987 prohibits discrimination on the basis of citizenship.

Unintentional violations are still violations.

- The Americans with Disabilities Act of 1990 (effective July 25, 1992) prohibits discrimination against persons with physical or mental impairments that substantially limit or restrict the condition, manner, or duration under which they can perform one or more major life activities and requires reasonable accommodation by employers.
- The Civil Rights Act of 1991 (often referred to as the 1992 Civil Rights Act) caps compensation and punitive damages for employers, provides for jury trial, and created a commission to investigate the "glass ceiling" for minorities and women and rewards organizations that advance opportunities for minorities and women.
- The Family Medical Leave Act (effective in 1993) provides an extended time (12 weeks within any 12-month period or 1,250 work hours) for the birth of a child, care for an ill child, placement of a child for adoption or foster care, or care for a seriously ill spouse, child, or parent that prevents the employee from performing the functions of the job.
- The Uniformed Services Employment and Reemployment Act (USERRA) requires employers to reemploy, maintain salary levels, continue health benefits, accrue vacation and sick days, and maintain pension plans for those called into active military service. The Veterans Benefits Improvement Act of 2004 requires all employers to notify employees annually of their rights under USERRA.

Understanding and complying with these laws is good for business. For instance, studies indicate that aging baby boomers and senior citizens, rather than being a drag on organizations as previously thought, bring valuable experiences to positions; know what they can and cannot do; are willing to take the initiative; are loyal; exhibit a willingness to learn, adjust, and adapt as they have for many years; show patience and a willingness to "hang in there" when facing difficult situations and relationships; are good listeners; and have the ability to get the job done.[17] Firing these workers, or not hiring them in the first place, because of age is not only unlawful but will deprive your organization of valuable resources, particularly in a rapidly changing world of work.

Compliance with EEO Laws

BFOQs are the keys to non-discriminatory hiring.

Compliance with state and federal EEO laws and guidelines is relatively easy. Be sure that everything you do, say, or ask during the selection process pertains to **bona fide occupational qualifications (BFOQs),** requirements essential for performing a particular job. BFOQs usually *include* work experiences, training, education, skills, conviction records, physical attributes, and personality traits that have a direct bearing on one's ability to perform a job effectively. BFOQs usually *exclude* gender, age, race, religion, marital status, physical appearance, disabilities, citizenship, and ethnic group that have no bearing on one's ability to perform a job effectively.

Exceptions to laws and orders are made if an employer can demonstrate that one or more normally unlawful traits are essential for a position. For example, appearance may be a BFOQ for a modeling position, religion for a pastoral position, age for performing

EEO violations are easy to avoid.

certain tasks (serving alcohol, operating dangerous equipment), and physical abilities such as eyesight and manual dexterity for pilots.

A few simple guidelines will help you avoid most EEO violations and lawsuits.[18] First, meet the **test of job relatedness** by establishing legally defensible selection criteria. Second, be sure *all questions* are related to these selection criteria. Third, ask the *same questions* for all applicants for a specific position. If you ask certain questions only of female, disabled, older, or minority applicants, you are undoubtedly asking unlawful questions. Fourth, be cautious when probing into answers because a significant number of EEO violations occur in these created-on-the-spot questions. Fifth, be cautious of innocent chit-chat during the informal parts of interviews, usually the opening and closing or the minutes following the formal interview. This is when you are most likely to ask or comment about family, marital status, ethnic background, and nonprofessional memberships. Sixth, focus questions on what an applicant *can do* rather than on what an applicant *cannot do.* Seventh, if an applicant begins to volunteer unlawful information, tactfully steer the person back to job-related areas.

Focus on the positive, not the negative.

The Americans with Disabilities Act (ADA) of 1990 has created a whole new area of potential violations for the uninformed and unwary interviewer. Avoid violating this act, first, by not requiring a medical examination prior to a job offer and, second, by not asking about or commenting on:

- How the person became disabled.
- The nature of the disability.
- The severity of the disability.
- How the person can get to work.
- How the person will go to the bathroom.
- Conditions or diseases they have or have had.
- Past hospitalization.
- Past or current treatment for a mental condition.
- Past receipt of worker's compensation.

Treat applicants as you would want to be treated.

Some sources recommend shaking hands with a disabled applicant, not pushing a wheelchair unless asked, identifying yourself and others involved if the interviewee is blind, and using physical signals, gestures, facial expressions, and note passing if an applicant is deaf.[19] As a general rule, however, treat a disabled person the same as you treat everyone else.

Quiz #1—Testing Your Knowledge of EEO Laws

Test your knowledge of EEO laws and selection interviews by rating each question below as *lawful* (can be asked), *probably lawful* (may be asked under certain circumstances), or *unlawful* (cannot be asked).[20] Explain why it is lawful, probably lawful, or unlawful.

1. Can you speak Spanish?
2. Have you ever been arrested?

3. What does your wife do?
4. Did your hearing pose any problems for you today?
5. Tell me about your computer skills.
6. Are you a U.S. citizen?
7. Would you mind if I called you Peggy?
8. Tell me about a time when you handled an angry client.
9. Is there a significant other in the picture?
10. How long would you plan to work for us?
11. We've just promoted two people younger than you. How would this affect your interest in this position?
12. How did you lose your hand?
13. Any children in the offing?
14. Are you available to work on weekends?
15. What will you do if your husband gets transferred?

Keep Up to Date

Current information on EEO laws is essential.

Remain current on EEO laws, rules, and interpretations, and be aware of areas that can adversely affect the applicant and your recruiting efforts. Studies reveal that arrest records, age, disabilities, marital and family status, and religion are the unlawful areas probed into most often.[21] Keep these rules in mind when asking questions.

- Federal laws supersede state laws unless the state laws are more restrictive.
- The Equal Employment Opportunity Commission (EEOC) and the courts are not concerned with *intent* but with *effect.* Your organization may have to show that the "final decision maker deliberately disregarded any evaluations tainted" by stereotypical questions.[22]
- Advertise each position where all qualified applicants have a reasonable opportunity to learn about the opening: newspapers, placement centers, job fairs, organizational bulletin boards and publications, Internet, and professional journals.

Accepting or keeping unlawful information creates liability for the company even if the information was not requested.

- Your organization is liable if unlawful information is maintained or used even if you did not ask for it. Have a person not involved in the selection process review all applicant materials for potentially unlawful information such as personal data, pictures, and references.
- Do not write or take notes on the application form. In the past, some organizations used notes or codes to indicate race, ethnic group, age, and physical appearance of applicants.[23] Even doodling on an application form may appear to be a code.
- Pose highly similar or identical questions to all applicants.
- Three recent concerns have arisen in the law: domestic partners, same-sex marriage, and hearing as a disability. An appropriate response is, "We hire persons based on what they know and how well they can do the job, not on personal

preferences or disabilities." Organizations should be prepared to enhance volumes on phones and computers.

- The "at will doctrine"—the ability to hire and terminate at will—may be challenged in your state.[24] Evaluate new hires every three months to provide a record of performance should termination be necessary.

Developing an Applicant Profile

The profile must be a composite of BFOQs.

With EEO laws clearly in mind, conduct a thorough analysis to determine the knowledge, experiences, skills, and personal traits necessary to fill a position satisfactorily. You want to attract and hire "quality" employees, but the first step is to determine what you mean by quality.[25] From this analysis you should develop an **applicant profile** of the ideal employee for a position. All applicants are then measured against this profile.

- Observe employees in your organization who excel in their positions to identify key factors in their success.
- Develop a competency model of traits, skills, and motives from research on individuals who do the job well.
- Develop a profile by searching literature and interviewing incumbents, supervisors, and associates.
- Do a systematic study of outstanding people in the field.
- Analyze existing employee responses to performance questions to distinguish good from bad performance characteristics.

The profile is the ideal by which all applicants are measured.

A precise applicant profile will help you avoid EEO violations, enhance interviewing effectiveness, and improve hiring. Competency-based applicant profiles typically include specific skills, abilities, education, training, experiences, knowledge levels, personal characteristics, and interpersonal relationships. Each applicant is measured against this set of evaluative criteria in an effort to choose the person that comes closest to the ideal employee. The profile approach makes the selection process more objective, encourages all interviewers to cover the same topics and traits, and reduces the **birds of a feather syndrome** in which interviewers (often white, middle-class males) favor applicants who are most similar to themselves.

Some organizations, such as Bristol Myers, have begun to employ a **behavior-based selection** technique to ensure that each interviewer matches each applicant with the ideal employee profile.[26] Four principles underlie this technique:

Is past performance the best predictor of future performance?

1. Behavior that is observed can be read.
2. Behavior that is not seen must be probed for.
3. The best predictor of future behavior is past behavior.
4. Job-related behavior in the interview is a good indicator of future job performance.

The behavior-based selection technique begins with a needs and position analysis to determine which behaviors are essential for performing a particular job. The following behaviors might be important for a specific position:

achievement	dependability	oral communication
ambition	initiative	people-oriented
assertiveness	listening	responsibility
competitiveness	motivation	responsiveness

Can nondominant group applicants match your profile?

Regardless of the means you use, check each profile trait carefully. Is each trait essential for excellent job performance? For instance, is leadership necessary for an entry-level position? Can you measure the trait? Are you expecting recruiters to act as psychologists in assessing some traits? Will some traits adversely affect your organization's diversity efforts and discriminate unintentionally? For example, traits such as competitiveness, aggressiveness, direct eye contact, forcefulness, and oral communication skills may run counter to the upbringing and culture of many nondominant groups.[27] Remember, traits being sought must be position-related—BFOQs—and clearly defined so that all interviewers are looking for the same ones.

Once you have developed a careful applicant profile, you are ready to write a clear job description that "encapsulates requirements for a given position." Karen O'Keefe writes, "Ultimately, the job description is the inspiration for any subsequent interview so defining the position up front will make finding the right person for the job much easier."[28] Being underprepared may be the biggest mistake of interviewers.

Assessing What Applicants Want

Times and people are changing.

Once you complete an applicant profile, begin to plan interviews and select interviewers who are best able to determine if applicants meet the profile. Since recruiting interviews are as much about attracting as selecting outstanding employees, it is imperative that you understand the targets of your search.

What Do Applicants Desire in a Position and Career?

Young, college-educated applicants are very different from those of 10, 20, or 30 years ago. While they are very interested in career paths and steady employment, the thought of remaining with one organization until receiving the gold watch is not only unattractive but repulsive to some. They are also aware that it is unrealistic. Applicants are more interested in strong reputations than in brand name.

Salary and benefits are no longer the key factors in job attraction. Young applicants are more interested in stress training programs, mentoring, supervision, tuition assistance, and career development opportunities.[29] They want extensive information about positions and organizations prior to interviews.

Applicants are increasingly information-driven.

The new workforce fully understands that diversity is reality. They expect and welcome working with a range of educations, ages, races, and ethnic groups. Political and geographical boundaries pose few obstacles since many have traveled, studied, or worked abroad. The infamous glass ceiling for females and minorities is cracked or nonexistent in many fields and organizations.

What Do Applicants Desire in an Interviewer?

Today's applicants have very clear preferences in interviewers. Applicant decisions are significantly affected by their satisfaction with the communication that takes place, and their attraction to the interviewer is the strongest predictor of their attraction to an organization.[30] They view the recruiter's behavior as a model of what to expect from the employer, so a negative experience may eliminate an organization from further consideration.

The recruiter is the organization in the applicant's eyes.

Applicants expect interviewers to be friendly, attentive, sensitive, warm, honest, enthusiastic, straightforward, personable, and genuinely interested in them. They do not want to be pressured or interrupted. They prefer interviewers to act and talk naturally without reading questions, being stuck to a schedule, or giving canned presentations.

Select recruiters with applicant traits in mind.

Applicants want interviewers to be professionals who know what they are talking about. In one survey, 93 percent reported they like to meet with and learn the experiences of relatively new employees rather than veteran representatives determined to sell their organizations.[31] Nondominant group applicants (women, minorities, lower class) report they are more comfortable and communicate more openly with and feel better understood and evaluated by interviewers more like them. Unfortunately, this openness and relief may turn to confusion, anger, and guarded interactions if they feel scrutinized by "one of their own."[32]

During interviews, today's applicants want interviewers to ask them relevant, open questions and give them opportunities for self-expression. They like interviewers to offer limited self-disclosures, not to the point of shifting the focus away from the applicant.[33] And applicants want detailed information that is relevant to the position and organization.

Obtaining and Reviewing Information on Applicants

With planning completed and the recruitment effort under way, you need to develop a "sense of the professional and personal qualities of each job applicant."[34] This entails gathering as much information as possible through application forms, resumes, letters of recommendation, and objective tests.

Application Forms

Modify application forms to fit the applicant profile.

Design the **application form** with the applicant profile in mind. Avoid traditional categories that violate EEO guidelines such as sex, age, race, ethnicity, marital status, physical characteristics, arrest records, type of military discharge, and request for a picture. Include a few open-ended questions similar to ones you will ask during the interview. Be sure to provide adequate space for applicants to answer all questions thoroughly. Look for what is and is not reported on the form, how applicants respond to open-ended questions, and gaps in dates of employment and education

Resumes

Review each resume carefully in advance. Patricia Buhler writes that "reading the resume for the first time in front of the applicant sends a clear message about a lack of preparedness and a lack of importance."[35] Delete any unlawful information from the resume (picture, age, marital status, religious organizations, and so on) before any person involved in the recruitment effort can see it. If you keep this information (even though you did not request it), you can be held liable for possible discrimination based upon it.

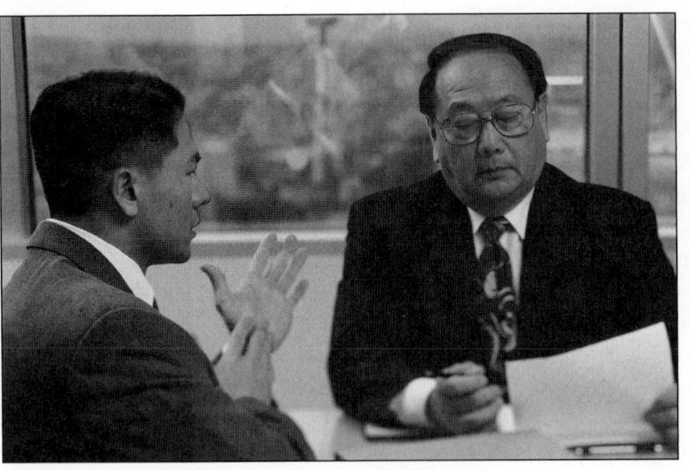
photo by © Keith Brofsky/Photodisc Guen/Getty Images

Review the applicant's credentials prior to the interview so you can devote full attention to the applicant during the interview.

Begin your analysis by, first, noting how well the applicant's career objective meets the applicant profile. If it does so, then assess how well the applicant's education, training, and experiences complement the stated career objective and the applicant profile. Look for what *is* and what *is not* included on the resume, a grade point average for instance.

Be aware that many applicants exaggerate their qualifications and experiences on resumes. In a survey on Careershop.com, 73 percent of applicants admitted that they lied on their resumes. Common deceits were inflating job titles, years of work, experiences, education, and current salary. The most common, however, was leaving out items that might appear unfavorable to a recruiter.[36] You are in an age of gamesmanship, so you must know how the game is being played by a significant percentage of applicants to hire the best qualified applicants.[37]

Some applicants do not match their resumes.

Some companies use electronic systems to screen resumes. Resume scanning systems sort out applicants based on key words or skills listed in the system by a hiring manager or human resources department. Two popular systems are Restrac and Resumix. You can purchase inexpensive scanning software packages over the Internet, but their flexibility and accuracy are questionable.

Consider a scanner if you attract hundreds of applicants.

If your organization receives large volumes of resumes for positions or is hiring a large number of workers, scanning systems are worth the cost. They are also of value if your organization has a central human resources structure that selects candidates for regional or multiple divisions at international locations. A scanning system can save time, sort through and store a large volume of resumes, and enable you to scan the pool again if the need arises.

Scanners may encourage gamesmanship by applicants.

There are disadvantages to using scanning systems. For example, if an excellent candidate uses "personnel" instead of "human resources" or "purchasing" instead of "procurement/materials management," the candidate may be eliminated from the system and sent a rejection letter. The result is the same if an applicant's degree abbreviations do not match those in the system. Your system may identify candidates who know the system or operable key terms or jargon rather than the best qualified. Include key scannable terms in your advertisements and recruiting literature so all candidates are playing on the same field.

The cover letter is often your first opportunity to "see" an applicant.

Cover Letters

Review each **cover letter** carefully. What does it reveal about career goals and qualifications? How well is it adapted to your position and organization, or is it a "To Whom It May

Concern" all-purpose letter? Does it reveal interest in the position and your organization? Is it written professionally? Is it free of spelling, grammatical, and punctuation errors?

Letters of Recommendation and References

Review **letters of recommendation** with skepticism because nearly all are written by friends or admirers. They rarely contain negative information. Letters do reveal people an applicant knows who will write letters and add bits of information about how well the applicant fits the profile.

References are usually persons applicants choose carefully to guarantee a favorable recommendation. Calls to references, however, allow you to ask open-ended questions and probe into answers to get beyond the superficial or guarded words and phrases of the letter. Unfortunately, fears of lawsuits have led many organizations to formulate policies that allow them to give you nothing more than the dates on which the applicant attended school or was employed. Many organizations require interviewers to get permission from applicants before contacting letter writers or references. Be aware of all organizational policies pertaining to recruiting. Bob Ayrer recommends calling references once a short list is determined and picking out those with a medium range relationship to the applicant—"not close enough to lie for them, but close enough to have an opinion" of the applicant's worth.[38] He claims neighbors and coworkers are usually truthful.

Fears of lawsuits are hampering reference checks.

Tests

A growing number of organizations are using testing as a supplement in the recruiting process. Some sources claim that the behavioral interview can be very effective, but it is even more effective "when combined with employment tests, many of which are now administered online."[39] Adam Agard writes: "The best way to increase the chances of finding the ideal employee is to test the applicant for the required skills before conducting the interview. And the best way to do this is with software specifically designed for skills testing."[40] Be sure any test you employ is job-related, has been validated on a cross-section of the population, and is nondiscriminatory. If a test screens out one group more than another (more women than men, more black Americans than white Americans, more Hispanic than European-Americans, more older applicants than younger applicants), do not use it.[41] Tests fall into three categories.

All tests must be carefully pretested.

Basic Skills Tests

Basic skills tests measure mathematics, measurement, and reading or spelling skills. The use of calculators and computers has created problems with simple math. Poor reading and spelling skills are posing major problems when individuals or teams are asked to write up problems on their machines or with their groups. Some tests describe a basic problem and then ask the applicant to write five to seven sentences describing the problem. Examiners or test monitors look for spelling, sentence structure, verb tense, and readability using a common formula.

Basic skills appear to be declining when they are more important than ever.

Personality Tests

Personality tests attempt to assess the people skills of applicants. An insurance institute claims its personality test is very successful in assessing the personality traits of applicants and predicting sales success. Organizations use the Myers-Briggs and the Wilson Analogy tests to identify personality type and the thinking skills of applicants.[42]

Honesty Tests

Honesty tests may appear intrusive, but they are here to stay.

Honesty tests designed to assess ethics, honesty, and integrity entered the scene in the 1990s. There is a growing concern in the United States over the apparent lack of ethics and honesty among all types of people, including highly respected professionals. The recruiting process is no exception. The rapid growth in technology has made available a wide range of information that can be duplicated, stolen, sold to the competition, or destroyed. Product liability, risks, and lawsuits for negligent hiring make it important to hire honest employees.

Concerns about Honesty Tests

A task force of the American Psychological Association reviewed over 200 studies and concluded that honesty tests identify individuals who have a high propensity for stealing in the workplace.[43] But critics wonder about applicants who fall into the moderate to low ranges. Robert Fitzpatrick, a Washington attorney who specializes in employment law, warns, "While they [honesty tests] might screen out some undesirable job candidates, they also screen out [like the old polygraph tests] a tremendous percentage of perfectly honest, upstanding citizens."[44] And Wayne J. Camara warns that "an honest applicant may not be the best qualified. Poor performance may mean greater losses than theft."[45]

The Use of Interviews

Probing deeply into answers is essential in assessing honesty.

Because the federal government has greatly limited the use of the polygraph in recruiting and many states have prohibited written honesty tests, organizations have turned to so-called **integrity interviews** to assess the honesty or integrity of prospective employees.[46] One study recommends that truth can best be determined through an analysis and comparison of factual information about the applicant, an honesty test, and a thorough probing interview.[47] This study concludes that an accurate reading of the applicant's verbal and nonverbal reactions to questions can help separate truth from deception. Truthful applicants tend to acknowledge the probability of employee theft, reply without hesitation, reject the idea of leniency for dishonesty, and expect favorable test results. Interviewers have reported a strange phenomenon called *outguessing* in which applicants cheerfully admit to unethical activities because they believe they are normal and "everyone does it."[48]

Two formats are used most frequently. The first consists of highly structured interviews that focus on ethics and integrity by delving into previous work experience directly related to the position available. Work-related questions result in applicants having positive feelings toward the integrity interview and the organization.

Focus on real or hypothetical work situations.

Second, if previous work experience is unavailable, the interviewer poses situational questions using specific dimensions of ethical and honest behavior. Donna Pawlowski and John Hollwitz have developed a structured situational interview "based on the assumption that intentions predict behaviors."[49] Interviewers ask interviewees to respond

ON THE WEB

Integrity interviews are becoming more common during the selection process as employers attempt to assess the integrity of potential employees in an age when honesty often seems the exception rather than the norm. Many employers and researchers are raising serious questions about the accuracy and value of honesty tests in the employment selection setting. Search the Internet for discussions of the uses and concerns raised by written and oral honesty tests. These sources should get you started on your search: Infoseek (http://www.infoseek.com), PsycInfo (http://www.psycinfo.com), The Monster Board (http://www.monster.com/), CareerBuilder (http://www.careerbuilder.com/), and PsychLit (http://www. psychlit.com/).

to hypothetical scenarios and employ a 5-point scale with an agreed upon definition of the dimension. Other dimensions are relationship manipulation, interpersonal deception (lying), security violation (giving out trade secrets), and sexual harassment (telling dirty jokes or displaying nude pictures).

Benefits of Previewing Applicants

Doing your homework leads to more effective interviews.

Previewing information on the applicant should give you a fairly clear notion of your relationship with the applicant by revealing how much each of you wants to take part in the interview, the degree of interest, and how control is likely to be shared. It is your first opportunity to determine how well the applicant matches your organization's unique culture.[50] The preview also reveals areas to probe during the interview, perhaps comparing oral and written answers to similar questions. Fredric Jablin and Vernon Miller discovered that employers who review applicant credentials thoroughly tended to ask more questions, a wider variety of questions, and to probe more into answers.[51] The result is a better determination of how well each applicant fits the position you are trying to fill.

Structuring the Interview

Once you have obtained extensive information on applicants, you can focus attention on structuring the interview.

The Opening

Involve the applicant in the opening.

As we have stated often in this book, the opening is a critical part of each interview. It sets the tone for the interview and creates the all-important first impression of you and your organization.

Establishing Rapport

Begin the recruiting interview by greeting the applicant by name in a warm, friendly voice and with a firm but not crushing handshake to create **rapport.** Introduce yourself and your position with the organization. Do not ask the applicant to call you by first name if this is a first interview because few applicants will feel comfortable doing so.

Rapport building is particularly important in cross-cultural interviews. Establish a relationship "that is based on trust, understanding, and acceptance" from the first moments of the interview, and bear in mind "that speaking the same language does mean sharing the same culture."[52]

Do not delay the inevitable.

If appropriate, engage in a bit of small talk about a noncontroversial issue, but do not prolong casual conversation or fall into overworn questions such as "What do you think of this weather?" and "How was your trip?" They elicit few meaningful responses and add nothing to your rapport with the applicant. Prolonged idle chatting may heighten tension rather than reduce it by creating anxiety and suspense.

Orientation

Proceed to the orientation phase of the opening in which you tell the applicant how the interview will proceed. Traditionally this has meant:

- Questions from the recruiter.
- Information about the position and the organization.
- Questions from the applicant.

Be systematic and creative.

Some interviewers, however, begin with applicant questions and then proceed to their questions. Others give information first, but this delays active involvement of the applicant in the interview and may communicate that the recruiter intends to dominate the interview. You might tell the applicant how long the interview will take and approximately how long you will devote to each part. If the interview is taking place during an on-site or plant trip, provide the applicant with an agenda for the visit and the names and positions of people who will be involved in the selection process.

Share control with the applicant.

While the traditional approach has been interviewer-controlled, some recruiters are recommending an interviewee-controlled approach. For instance, Bob Ayrer, who specializes in hiring salespersons, recommends an extensive orientation period. "At this point SHUT UP!" he writes. "Allow the prospective salesperson to take control (that is what you are hiring them to do in the field, isn't it?)"[53]

The Opening Question

The transition from the opening to the body of the interview is usually the **opening question.** This open-ended, easy-to-answer first question gets the applicant talking about a familiar subject (education, experiences, background, recent internship, and so on). It sets the proper tone for the interview—the applicant talking and the recruiter listening and observing.

Begin with an open question, but not too open.

Plan the opening question carefully, and do not fall into the rut of always starting with the same question. Adapt it to what you have learned in previewing information on each applicant. The most common opening question, "Tell me about yourself," is so open that applicants often do not know where to begin or how much information to give. Do they start with birth, grade school, high school, college, or current/recent positions? Do they talk about family, hobbies, education, work experiences, major events? Such highly open, generic questions neither relax applicants nor get applicants talking

Do not set up the applicant for an early failure.

about meaningful subjects. A better opening question is "Give me some idea of your recent duties (or responsibilities) in your current position."

Do not put the applicant on the spot too early because interviewers tend to put more weight on negative information, and the earlier it comes in the interview, the more devastating it may be. Pose an easy-to-answer, reasonably open question to get the applicant ready and able to answer more difficult questions. A common question is "What is the favorite part of your current position?"

The Body of the Interview

Unstructured interviews do not recruit top-quality applicants.

Authorities differ on how structured the body of the recruiting interview ought to be, but research indicates that the validity of recruiting highly qualified applicants is most successful when organizations utilize highly structured formats.[54] All agree that the old "seat of the pants," "off the top of the head," and "my gut tells me" interviews lead to numerous hazards. Some authorities state bluntly that "a typical interview—unstructured, rambling, unfocused—tells the interviewer almost nothing about job candidates."[55] For instance, interviewers talk more than applicants in unstructured interviews rather than the 80 percent for applicants (some prescribe 95 percent) to 20 percent for recruiters rule of thumb. Interviewers tend to make their decisions within the first four minutes, long before answers to critical and thought-provoking questions. They cover factual and biographical information that is readily available on application forms and resumes. And interviewers are more susceptible to stereotyping and biases and more likely to ask questions that violate EEO laws.

Highly Structured Interviews

Highly structured interviews are more reliable but less flexible and adaptable.

A growing number of sources are advocating highly scheduled interviews in which all questions are prepared and tested ahead of time and posed to each applicant without variation. Highly structured interviews are more reliable because all applicants are asked the same or very similar questions and employers must pay close attention throughout the interview instead of the first few minutes. Organizations may employ a highly structured interview centered on specific traits in the applicant profile (interpersonal skills, computer expertise, team experience) or an interview guide (can the person do the job, will the person do the job, will the person fit into the organization).

Fit or match with the position and organization is a growing emphasis because organizations are discovering that well-qualified applicants who do not match the organization's culture result in poor performance and high turnover rate. Some cover specific topics such as company environment, management influence, and coworkers.

Behavior-based methods focus on job-related skills.

Behavior-based selection techniques are becoming very common. An organization develops a highly structured interview that provides for skillful patterning and selecting of questions, recording of responses, and rating of applicants on behaviorally defined dimensions. In the following example, the interviewer would employ a five-point scale to rate each answer according to the degree to which it exhibits or gives information about one or more behaviors: 5 = strongly present and 1 = minimally present.

Rating	Behavior	Question
_______	Initiative	Give me an example of when you have resolved conflicts between employees.
_______	Energy	How many times have you done this?
_______	General intelligence	What was the outcome?
_______	Decisiveness	How did you feel about the results you got?
_______	Adaptability	When faced with intransigence, what did you do?

Build in insightful secondary questions.

While listening to the answer to the first question, for example, you would be looking for the kinds of conflicts the applicant has addressed and their complexity. Preplanned probing questions probe deeper into the experience, including methods used, and success the applicant had in resolving them. The answer may reveal a number of other characteristics such as communication ability, sensitivity, fairness, and ability to follow prescribed procedures.

Moderately Structured Interviews

Highly scheduled interviews have significant limitations.

The majority of recruiters, including the authors, recommend a moderately scheduled interview. While the highly scheduled interview may lessen the influence of stereotypes, recruiter-applicant dissimilarity, and the possibility of lawsuits for EEO violations, it has several shortcomings:[56] It enhances recruiter control and may be detrimental to underrepresented group members. The applicant has little opportunity to introduce job-related information. Recruiters have little or no opportunity to adapt to specific applicants, to probe into answers, or to share information when thought necessary. The organization dominates what should be a mutual activity between recruiter and candidate.

Place the applicant in realistic work settings.

William Kirkwood and Steven Ralston argue that the highly structured interview bears little resemblance to situations applicants will face on the job. Thus, the interviewee is unable to demonstrate and the recruiter is unable to observe the applicant's skills in realistic settings.[57] Any process that stifles the recruiter's ability to probe into answers is likely to result in fewer insights into the applicant as a person and potential employee. The moderately scheduled interview allows both parties the flexibility necessary for meaningful interactions and a maximum of self-disclosure.

Question Sequences

Select one or more **question sequences** appropriate for the interview and the applicant; normally this means funnel or tunnel sequences. Interviewers tend to use the inverted funnel sequence by asking closed primary questions during the early minutes of the interview and open-ended probing questions in the later minutes.[58] The inverted sequence enables recruiters to test applicants and then switch to a funnel sequence with applicants they perceive to be most qualified.

Get the applicant talking as quickly as possible.

Since applicants tend to give short answers to closed questions while they feel out the interviewer and longer answers and more information to open questions, interviewers may make snap judgments within the first few minutes of interviews based on very little information. Also, the best way to relax an applicant is to get the person talking. Begin with a funnel or tunnel sequence to get the interviewee talking, relaxed, and giving maximum information.

Closing the Interview

The closing must sustain the positive tone of the interview.

If you have the authority to hire on the spot (rare in most interviews), either offer the position or terminate further consideration. If you do not have hiring authority or do not want to make an immediate decision, explain specifically what the applicant can expect after the completion of the interview. For example:

> Allison, it's been a pleasure talking with you this morning. (pause to let the applicant talk) As you know, we are interviewing students on several campuses for this position in finance at ZYC Industries. We plan to invite three or four candidates to our office in St. Cloud for additional interviews. We will notify you within the next 10 days to let you know whether we will ask you to come to St. Cloud. If you need to contact me, here is my card with office telephone number and e-mail address. Do you have any final questions or concerns?

Do not encourage or discourage applicants needlessly.

Be straightforward with applicants. If you have many excellent applicants for a position, do not give each the impression that he or she is at the top of the list. If you know an applicant will not be considered further, do not "string the person along" with false hope. Let the individual down gently.

And watch what you do, say, and ask following the formal closing as you walk with the person to the door or to the parking lot, or escort the person to meet another member of your organization. These informal times can lead to EEO violations. Do not do or say anything that adversely affects the relationship you have developed carefully during the interview.

Make decisions and notify all applicants as soon as possible.

Follow up on all prospects. If possible, have all letters signed by you or your representative. A personal touch, even when rejecting an applicant, can maintain a feeling of goodwill toward you and your organization.

Conducting the Interview

Take care to establish an environment that is conducive to sharing information and disclosure of feelings and attitudes. It should be a comfortable, quiet, and private location. Prevent interruptions. Turn off telephones, cell phones, computers, and beepers. Close office doors. Provide seating that maximizes interpersonal communication. Approach each interview in a positive manner, realizing that it is likely to be a major event in the applicant's life (even if routine for you), a public relations opportunity for your organization, and a critical part of attracting and selecting productive employees for your organization. Patricia Buhler writes: "The interview is a two-way street. While the interviewer is screening applicants for fit with the organization and the position, the applicant is 'interviewing' the company for fit as well. The interview, then, should also be viewed as a public relations tool." She warns that "Bad publicity travels quickly."[59] Give the impression that this interview is your day's top priority.

You are your organization.

Applicants make no distinction between you and your organization. They are more likely to accept offers if you are perceived to be a good representative of your organization. Remember that you are recruiting as well as appraising applicants. Be open and honest with each interviewee. Give a realistic picture of the position and organization. Some sources advocate a **conscious transparency** in which organizations share information with applicants, explain the purpose of questions, provide a less defensive climate, and promote unrestricted dialogue between interview parties.[60]

Nontraditional Interviewing Approaches

Applicants and recruiters prefer the traditional one-on-one interview.

Organizations are experimenting with nontraditional approaches. For instance, a **team, panel,** or **board** of two to five persons may interview an applicant at the same time. In some situations, panel members divide up the applicant's resume and application form with one member asking about previous work experiences, a second asking about education and training, a third asking about technical knowledge, and a fourth asking about specific job-related skills. Although some research indicates that the panel is more effective in predicting job performance than the traditional one-on-one interview and preemployment tests, applicants and interviewers tend to prefer the traditional approach.[61] A panel or team would be advisable when conducting cross-cultural interviews to enhance communication and understanding and to eliminate possible bias.

Some organizations use a **chain format** in which a human resources person may take 20 minutes getting a general impression of the applicant's skills and then pass the applicant on to another person who probes into technical knowledge. This person may then pass the applicant to a third person who probes into specific job skills. After one to three interviews, the human resources person may pick up the applicant along with written evaluations and either terminate consideration of the applicant or close the interviewing process in an upbeat manner to keep the applicant interested in the position.

Stifle any signs of competition in seminar interviews.

Other organizations are using a **seminar format** in which one or more recruiters interview several applicants at the same time. This approach is subject to the pitfalls of individual interviews (if only one interviewer is present), but it takes less time, allows the organization to see several applicants at the same time, and may provide valuable insights into how applicants work with one another in a team effort. If conducted with skill, applicants will not see the interview as a competition but as an opportunity to build upon others' comments and reveal their experiences and qualifications.

Asking Questions

The opening question gets the body of the interview and questioning under way. Questions are your primary tools for obtaining information, assessing how well the applicant matches the applicant profile and fits with your organization, and discovering what the applicant knows about the position and organization.

Keep your questions open-ended.

Questions should be open-ended, neutral, insightful, and job-specific. Open-ended questions encourage applicants to talk while you listen, observe, and formulate effective probing questions. Applicants give longer answers to open-ended questions and feel greater interview satisfaction with interviews that are dominated by open-ended primary and probing questions.[62]

Common Question Pitfalls

Recruiters often create or rephrase questions to detect relevant behaviors and probe for details, clarity, and implied meanings. This spontaneity makes the interview a lively conversation but makes them susceptible to a number of common question pitfalls identified in Chapters 3 and 5.

Be on guard for pitfalls in primary and secondary questions.

- Bipolar trap

  Have you worked in teams before?

- Open-to-closed switch

  Tell me about your study abroad semester at St. Andrews in Scotland. Did you study the economic effects of the European Union on Scotland?

- Double-barreled inquisition

  Tell me about the co-op program in engineering and the company you worked for.

- Leading push

  You have experience with basic spreadsheets, don't you?

- Guessing game

  Did you change majors from management to psychology because of the math requirements?

- Yes (no) response

  Do you feel you are ready for this position?

- Curious probe

  How did your parents feel about your attending college 2,000 miles from home?

- Quiz show

  You're in agricultural economics. Do you know what the South's main cash crop was before the Civil War?

- Don't ask, don't tell

  Do you see yourself as the best student coming out this year from the Academy?

Evaluative responses will lead to safe, superficial answers.

There are three question pitfalls that are particularly relevant to the recruiting interview. Recognize and avoid them.

1. *The evaluative response:* The interviewer expresses judgmental feelings about an answer that may bias or skew the next response.

   That wasn't very wise was it?

2. *The EEO violation:* The interviewer asks an unlawful question.

   Do you consider yourself a religious person?

Do not ask for information you already have.

3. *The resume or application form question:* The interviewer asks a question that is already answered on the resume or application form.

   What professional organizations do you belong to?

Quiz #2—What Are the Pitfalls in These Questions?

Each of the following questions contains one or more common employer question pitfalls: bipolar trap, open-to-closed switch, double-barreled inquisition, leading push, guessing game, curious probe, quiz show, don't ask, don't tell, evaluative response, EEO violation, yes (no) response, and resume-application question. Identify the pitfall in each and rewrite it to make it a good question without stumbling into another pitfall.

1. Do you feel you can handle this job?
2. Where did you get your civil engineering degree?
3. Do you have problems getting around in that wheelchair?
4. Tell me about your position at McWilliams. Were you in charge of marketing to high school students?
5. Did you take the pass/fail option in your electives because they were difficult courses?
6. You're willing to work on the midnight to eight shift, aren't you?
7. Leaving your last position without another offer wasn't a good idea, was it?
8. What would you guess is the average salary of CEOs in this field?
9. Have you worked in teams?
10. Tell me about your internship at Dow and your research appointment in biochemistry.

Traditional Questions

The following are **traditional recruiter questions** that avoid pitfalls and gather important job-related information.

- Interest in the organization

  Why would you like to work for us?
  What materials have you read about our organization?
  What do you know about our products and services?

- Work-related (general)

  Tell me about the position that has given you the most satisfaction.
  How have your previous work experiences prepared you for this position?
  What did you do that was innovative in your last position?

- Work-related (specific)

  Describe a typical strategy you would use to motivate people.
  What criteria do you use when assigning work to others?
  How do you follow up on work assigned to subordinates?

- Teams and team work

  How do you feel when your compensation is based in part on team results?
  What does the word *teamwork* mean to you?
  How would you feel about working on cross-functional teams?

- Education and training

  What computer programs do you know?
  What in your education has prepared you for this position?
  If you had your education to do over, what would you do differently?

- Career paths and goals

  If you join us, what would you like to be doing five years from now?
  How do you feel about the way your career has gone so far?
  What are you doing to prepare yourself for advancement?

- Performance

  What do you believe are the most important performance criteria for a project engineer?
  All of us have pluses and minuses in our performance. What are some of your pluses (minuses)?
  How do you make difficult decisions?

- Salary and benefits

  What are your salary expectations?
  Which fringe benefits are most important to you?
  How does our salary range compare to your last position?

- Career field

  What do you think is the greatest challenge facing your field?
  What do you think will be the next major breakthrough in your field?
  How do you feel about environmental regulations in your field?

The major problem with traditional or standard questions is that applicants are familiar with them and have prepared answers in advance. Do not avoid such questions, but be ready to probe into answers to get beneath the prepared surface answers to Level 2 and 3 answers.

Nontraditional Questions

The trend is toward on-the-job questions.

The most important trend in questioning is the introduction of behavior-based interviews predicated on the principle that the best predictor of future behavior is past behavior. A variety of question strategies attempt to determine how an applicant has handled or will handle work-related situations. These questions also enable interviewers to counter impression management tactics used by nearly all applicants such as self-promotion (designed "to evoke attributions of competence") and ingratiation (designed "to evoke interpersonal liking and attraction"). Both of these tactics have proven to be "positively related to interviewer evaluations."[63]

Past Experiences

Traditionally, interviewers conducting behavioral-based interviews have asked questions about past experiences in which applicants have handled situations that are related to the position. For instance, recruiters may ask:[64]

Tell me about an idea of yours that was implemented primarily through your efforts.

How did you handle a past situation when the rules were changed at the last minute?

Tell me about your most difficult relationship with a team member and how you handled it.

Describe a time when you experienced a setback in a class, in a sport, or on the job and how you handled it.

Tell me about a situation when you had to handle an irate customer or client.

Give me an example of an unpopular idea you had to sell to fellow workers.

Be prepared for coached applicants.

Unfortunately, applicants have gotten wise to past experience questions and are often coached on how to respond. Even worse, some applicants are making up impressive stories to satisfy recruiters. For instance, when MBAs were asked to tell about a time when they faced a challenge, six gave identical answers about serving on a fund-raising committee. Later investigation revealed that none of the six had even been on such a committee.[65]

Behavioral-based questions have other problems.[66] Experienced applicants have a wealth of examples from which to draw, while soon-to-be college graduates and those with little experience have few. Behavioral questions favor those who can tell good stories in a positive and likeable manner. They may measure social skills and storytelling rather than intelligence and ability to perform well on the job.

"Drill down for details," not to see if an applicant is lying necessarily but to get important details and insights into the applicant's experiences. Also, be prepared to react if you get information you do not want or need and may violate EEO laws. Rochelle Kaplan relates an incident in which an applicant replied to a question about the greatest challenge in undergraduate studies by stating: "Coming out as a gay male to my friends and family."[67] Other applicants have delved into religion and politics.

Critical Incidents

Critical incident questions assess how applicants would handle real work situations.

In **critical incident questions,** recruiters select actual critical incidents that are occurring or have occurred on the job within their organizations and ask applicants how they would handle or would have handled such incidents. For instance:

We are experiencing a growing problem of waste in our milling operation. How would you handle this if we hired you?

Last year we encountered a lot of strife among our sales staff. If you had been with us, what would you have done?

Like many firms, we are experiencing a decline in sales of our personal computers. What would you suggest we do about it?

Hypothetical Situations

Hypothetical questions are often criticized because of their misuse in the past when recruiters asked seemingly silly questions such as: "If you were a vegetable, which vegetable would you be?" "If you could become a famous American from the past, who would you be?" "How would you go about counting all of the golf balls in the United States?"[68] Hypothetical questions, like critical incident questions and case questions, can be valuable tools in the recruiting interview. Justin Menkes writes that questions such as these are useful because they "raise questions and situations that the candidate has never confronted" and for which the candidate cannot be prepared in advance.[69]

In hypothetical questions, a recruiter creates highly realistic but hypothetical situations and asks applicants how they would handle each.

Suppose you are suspicious that some workers are doctoring their time cards. What would you do?

If your company suddenly announced the closing of your facility by January 1, what would you do?

If a female employee came to you claiming sexual harassment, how would you handle it?

A Case Approach

A case approach is the most realistic on-the-job question format.

In a case approach, an applicant is placed into a carefully crafted situation that may take hours to study and resolve. It could be a personnel, management, design, or production problem. Some are elaborate simulations that require role playing and may involve several people, including other applicants.

All on-the-job questions (past experiences, critical incidents, hypothetical situations, case studies) are based on the belief that the best way to assess ability to perform a job is to observe the applicant doing the job. Many applicants can tell you about the theories and principles they would use, but they are unable to put these theories and principles into practice. It is one thing to say how you might confront a hostile employee but quite another to do it.

Do not settle for Level 1 interactions.

Regardless of the questioning methods you use, design the questioning phase of the interview to explore how well the applicant meets the ideal employee profile and fits into your organization. Probe for specifics; explore suggestions or implications in responses; clarify meanings with reflective probes; and force the applicant to get beyond safe, superficial Level 1 responses to reveal feelings, preferences, knowledge, and expertise.

Use all available tools to get the information necessary to select the best applicants. **Remember there are always two applicants in each interview, the real and the make-believe.** Your task is to determine how much of what you see and hear is a facade and how much is genuine. Get beneath the surface of rehearsed and planned answers to find the real person.

Be responsive without talking.

Listen carefully to all that *is* said and *is not* said. Silent and nudging probes are effective because applicants feel less threatened and more respected when interviewers respond with simple verbal and nonverbal signals and do not interrupt them. Avoid becoming a cheerleader by saying "Good!" or "Awesome!" after every answer. Applicants will come to expect the praise and become concerned if it stops.

Giving Information

Giving information is an essential ingredient in successful interviews. Information before and during the interview is a major determinant of applicant satisfaction, along with the process and attitude toward the organization.

Information is the primary interest of applicants.

Before you begin to give information, however, ask applicants two important transition questions: *"What do you know about this position? What do you know about our organization?"*

Answers to these questions show, first, how much homework the applicant has done, thus revealing the applicant's level of interest and work ethic. And, second, they tell you what the applicant already knows about the position and organization so you can begin where the person's knowledge leaves off. This prevents you from wasting valuable interview time giving information the applicant already has or is readily available on your Web site.

Give adequate information to facilitate the **matching process** between the organization and the applicant. Information about your organization's reputation, organizational environment, the position, and advancement opportunities tend to be the most important factors in acceptance of job offers. Tell applicants what a typical workday would be like. Compare your organization to your competitors', but do not be negative.

Minimize "you" in the interview.

Sell the advantages of your position and organization. Do not exaggerate, intentionally hide negative aspects of the position or organization, or inflate applicant expectations. These practices result in high rates of employee dissatisfaction and turnover. Avoid gossip. Do not talk too much about yourself, a common problem in selection interviews.

While you want to inform applicants thoroughly, do not allow your information giving to dominate an interview. Some studies have found that applicants speak for only 10 minutes in a typical 30-minute screening interview.[70] Reverse this figure, because you will learn more about the applicant by listening than by talking. Review the guidelines for information giving in Chapter 13 and follow these suggestions for information giving.

Rule #1: Keep your ears open and your mouth shut.

- Practice good communication skills because applicants may judge the "authenticity" of information by how it is communicated verbally and nonverbally.
- Encourage applicants to ask questions about information you are giving so you know it is being communicated accurately and effectively.
- Do not overload applicants with information.
- Organize your information systematically and logically.

Evaluating the Interview

Record your impressions and reactions immediately.

The growing recommendation that recruiters take notes during interviews was enhanced by a recent study that discovered traditional note taking increased recall and judgment accuracy.[71] If you have taken notes, review them carefully, and then record your reactions to each applicant as soon as possible after each interview. Build in time between interviews for this purpose. Many organizations provide recruiters with standardized evaluation forms to match applicants with the applicant profile for each position. If the

Figure 7.1 *Interview evaluation report*

Interview Evaluation Report

Applicant ______________________ Position ______________________

Interviewer ______________________ Date__________ Location __________

	Excellent	Very Good	Good	Unsatisfactory
Interest in this position	___	___	___	___
Interest in the company	___	___	___	___
Fit with this position	___	___	___	___
Education and training	___	___	___	___
Experiences	___	___	___	___
Adaptability	___	___	___	___
Analytical ability	___	___	___	___
Self-confidence	___	___	___	___
Enthusiasm	___	___	___	___
Communication skills	___	___	___	___
Professional appearance	___	___	___	___

General comments and reactions: ______________________________________

____

Do you favor an offer? ____ Yes ____ No ____ Undecided

Overall rating: Unfavorable 1 2 3 4 5 6 7 8 9 10 Favorable

interview is a screening interview, decide whether to invite the applicant for a second round of interviews. If the interview is a determinate interview, decide whether to make an offer or send a rejection letter (the infamous "ding letter").

The **interview evaluation** often consists of two parts: a set of standardized questions and a set of open questions. See the sample interview evaluation form in Figure 7.1. The standardized part should consist of bona fide occupational qualifications for each position and be extensive enough to allow you to determine how well the applicant matches these qualifications. Do not allow gender, age, ethnic, or racial biases or preferences to enter into your evaluation. Focus on the applicant's qualifications, not irrelevant factors. A study at the University of North Texas revealed that recruiters often chose applicants on the basis of voices and regional accents. Those identified with specific regions by accent were less likely to be chosen for "high profile jobs" and more likely to be assigned, if hired, to lower-skilled and lower-contact positions.[72]

The following are typical open-ended questions in postinterview evaluations:

- What are the applicant's strengths for this position?
- What are the applicant's weaknesses for this position?
- How does this applicant compare to other applicants for this position?
- What makes this applicant a good or poor fit with our organization?

Use the evaluation stage to assess your interviewing skills and performance. The following are typical self-evaluation questions:

Assess the performance of both interview parties.

- How successfully did I create an informal, relaxed atmosphere?
- How effectively did I encourage the applicant to speak openly and freely?
- How thoroughly did I explore the applicant's qualifications for this position?
- How effectively did I listen?
- How adequate was the information I provided on the position and organization?
- Did the applicant have adequate time to ask questions?
- How well did I respond to the applicant's questions?
- How effectively did I close the interview?

Summary

The recruiting interview can be an effective means of selecting employees, but it takes preparation that includes becoming familiar with state and federal EEO laws, developing an applicant profile, obtaining and reviewing information on applicants, and developing a carefully structured interview. Preparation must be followed by a thoroughly professional interview that includes an effective opening, skillful questioning, probing into answers, thorough information giving, honest and detailed answers to questions, and an effective closing. You must practice effective communication skills that include language selection, nonverbal communication (silence, voice, eye contact, facial expressions, posture, and gestures), listening, and empathy.

When the interview is concluded, conduct evaluations of the applicant and yourself. The first focuses on the applicant's suitability and fit and the second on your effectiveness as recruiter and evaluator.

Key Terms and Concepts

The online learning center for this text features FLASH CARDS and CROSSWORD PUZZLES for studying based on these terms and concepts.

Applicant profile
Basic skills tests
Behavior-based selection
Birds of a feather syndrome
Board interview
Bona fide occupational qualification (BFOQ)
Conscious transparency
Cover letters
Critical incident questions
EEO laws
Honesty tests
Integrity interviews
Interview evaluation
Job fairs
Matching process

A Recruiting Interview for Review and Analysis

In this interview, Victor Ransom is applying for an entry-level position in public relations with Dodge, Smiley, and Shine, an agency that divides its clients equally among health care facilities and political candidates. Teresa Valdez is one of the agency's college recruiters. The interview is taking place at the campus career center.

How satisfactory are the rapport and orientation stages of the opening? How well do the employer's questions meet EEO guidelines and avoid common question pitfalls? How effectively does the employer *probe into* and *react* to answers? What evidence is there that the employer has an ideal applicant profile in mind? How adequate is the employer's information giving? Does the employer control the interview too much, too little, or about right? How satisfactory is the closing?

1. **Recruiter:** Good morning. I'm Teresa Valdez.
2. **Applicant:** Hi.
3. **Recruiter:** Please call me Terri.
4. **Applicant:** Okay. I'm Vick.
5. **Recruiter:** Your semester going okay?
6. **Applicant:** Yes. It's been one of my easier semesters.
7. **Recruiter:** Well, let's get started. I'm going to ask you some questions about you and your interests; then I will tell you a bit about Dodge, Smiley, and Shine; and finally, I will answer any questions you have for me. Okay?
8. **Applicant:** Sure. I've been looking forward to this interview for some time.
9. **Recruiter:** Good. First of all, why did you switch majors from management to public relations and political science?
10. **Applicant:** Well . . . when I came to school, I started in management because my dad said that would be the best major to get a job in business. I soon learned that management was too theory- and mathematics-oriented for me, and some of my friends in public relations said it was interesting and business-oriented. So that's why I switched.
11. **Recruiter:** Very good. How people-oriented are you?
12. **Applicant:** Well, it seems like my whole life has been centered around people. Through my school activities and the things I have done, I see that I am a very people-oriented person. I can't explain why; I just enjoy working with people.
13. **Recruiter:** Excellent. Tell me what enables you to work well with people?
14. **Applicant:** Well, I come from a large Catholic family; I have three brothers and four sisters. It seems like the Ransoms and the Kowalskis, my mother's side of the family, were always getting together for reunions and the like. And my neighborhood in Chicago had all kinds of people from all over the world, not to mention some very interesting characters. I learned to understand different people and to speak a little of several languages.
15. **Recruiter:** Awesome. How about internships?

16. **Applicant:** Yes. As I mention in my resume, I had an internship during the school year with our intercollegiate athletics department, and this past summer I had an internship in London.
17. **Recruiter:** Tell me about the most difficult people situation you had to deal with during one of your internships.
18. **Applicant:** Okay. That was when I was assigned as a team leader to design new brochures for the football program. The other team members were students like myself but were more interested in being around the players and coaches than in getting public relations experience. We quickly fell behind schedule.
19. **Recruiter:** What did you do?
20. **Applicant:** Well, I called an emergency meeting, explained our responsibilities, and set tight deadlines for each aspect of the project. I warned that we would meet in the evenings and on weekends if necessary. We got the job done on time.
21. **Recruiter:** Excellent! How do you feel your personal qualities and characteristics, as well as experiences, will help you in a public relations agency?
22. **Applicant:** I feel these equip me to work in many areas of public relations. Specifically relating to Dodge, Smiley, and Shine, I feel they are going to help me in working with small businesses.
23. **Recruiter:** What are some of your personal qualities and characteristics we would find helpful?
24. **Applicant:** Well . . . I'm outgoing . . . and . . . I like people . . . and I find it easy to communicate with people in many settings.
25. **Recruiter:** Very good. And what about your experiences?
26. **Applicant:** As I've mentioned, my internships gave me some great experiences, and I had a problems class in PR in which we worked with a nonprofit client. Of course, my classes gave me some great experiences.
27. **Recruiter:** I see. Victor, why are you interested in a position with us?
28. **Applicant:** My majors in public relations and political science have prepared me well for a position in a public relations agency like yours. It is a growing agency in a very competitive field that is changing rapidly from individual PR consultants and public relations only to large agencies that deal with both public relations and advertising. I think this will be exciting because I also have some background and interest in advertising.
29. **Recruiter:** I noticed that in your letter and resume. So why should we choose you over other applicants?
30. **Applicant:** That's a tough question. I feel that my internship experiences and ability to work with all kinds of people should place me at the top of most applicant lists.
31. **Recruiter:** Let me tell you a little bit about Dodge, Smiley, and Shine. We were founded in 1990 when three nationally known PR consultants, Sam Dodge, Rebecca Smiley, and Nate Shine, decided to combine their efforts into a single agency. We currently have health care and political clients throughout the Southeast. Our income places us among the top three agencies in this area, and we are clearly the fastest growing. Do you have any questions for me?

32. **Applicant:** Yes. The stock market has fluctuated tremendously during the last several months. How is this going to affect your health care and business accounts?
33. **Recruiter:** We have not been affected like many agencies because we are well diversified. Health care will continue growing as our population increases and ages, and there are political candidates who face elections nearly every year.
34. **Applicant:** I know Dodge, Smiley, and Shine is expanding throughout the Southeast. What about other areas of the country?
35. **Recruiter:** We are recruiting heavily right now because we are moving people around the agency and planning to open a major office in Washington, D.C., by early next year.
36. **Applicant:** That sounds great. I would like to know more about your training program.
37. **Recruiter:** Well, it's basically an orientation program. We assume people we hire are ready to go from day one. You'd be meeting people, getting familiar with our policies, procedures, and client base.
38. **Applicant:** That's all the questions I have. I would like to say Ms. Valdez that I'm very interested in Dodge, Smiley, and Shine.
39. **Recruiter:** Very good. I should be getting in touch with you by e-mail no later than the 15th of this month. I notice that you will be available after June 1 and have no specific location preference on your application.
40. **Applicant:** That's correct, but the new Washington office sounds awesome.
41. **Recruiter:** You should hear from me within two weeks. If not, give me a call or e-mail me at either of these numbers on my business card.
42. **Applicant:** Okay.
43. **Recruiter:** We'll be in touch. Have a good day.
44. **Applicant:** Thanks.

Recruiting Role-Playing Cases

A Public Relations Position

Your public relations firm has created a new area that specializes in repairing the image of individual and corporate clients who have been accused of unlawful, unsocial, injurious, or unethical acts. An increasing number of these clients—companies, politicians, entertainers, sports figures, and charitable organizations—are turning to you to help them defend themselves effectively and thus to repair or maintain their images and credibility. The person you wish to hire must be a college graduate who has taken courses in public relations, persuasion, and image repair strategies and has experiences working with clients with image problems. The applicant has impressive academic credentials, including an M.A. in public relations, but little experience except a one-semester internship.

A Management Position

You have an opening for a manager at one of the five Charlie and Bill Brewpubs you own near college campuses in the Southwest. The position requires a degree in management or organizational supervision, knowledge of the restaurant industry, and the ability to talk easily and persuasively with employees, suppliers, and customers. Charlie and Bill Brewpubs offer bonuses based on profits and opportunities for upper management. The applicant has a degree in restaurant and hotel management and has worked at an Applebee's near campus for the past three years. During a brief telephone conversation, the applicant seemed interested, pleasant, easy to talk to, and familiar with restaurants located near campuses. However, it is unclear if the applicant will be available by June 1 when you hope to have the new manager in place.

A Meteorologist

You are the new owner-manager of radio station WIPZ in a city of 90,000. This station has changed owners a number of times and, with each new owner, there has been a new format: classic rock, pop, jazz, country and western, a mixture of everything, and talk. The weather department has been the one consistently bright spot in WIPZ because it has retained two veteran meteorologists and the community has been very supportive. Retirements are now threatening the quality of the weather department. You want to hire a first-rate meteorologist who can develop good relationships with the local officials, police agencies, civil defense, and schools and do occasional in-depth reports. The applicant's background and sample tape are impressive, but the applicant is a recent college graduate whose experience has been at the college radio station. You are not sure the applicant is ready to jump into a commercial station and meet your high expectations.

Student Activities

1. A few years ago Home Depot advertised for 7,000 senior citizens to work in its retail stores. This appears to be a trend across the country. Contact six local businesses and ask what their policy is toward hiring senior citizens and how many they employ. Most important, discover why they have hired seniors when only a few years ago seniors were virtually unemployable.
2. Many managers believe that attitude is everything. Contact your campus career center and ask for permission to pose two questions to a dozen recruiters: What two positive attitudes would you like to see each candidate display in interviews? What one attitude is a real turnoff?
3. Contact a number of recruiters from different companies or organizations and ask them to discuss the pluses and minuses of "senior citizen" employees. Probe for specifics, including examples without names. What changes have they seen in such employees during the past 10 years.
4. Contact a number of recruiters from different companies and organizations and ask them to discuss the relationship pluses and minuses between baby boomers and younger workers. How tolerant are they of one another? What can each teach and learn from the other?

Notes

1. Patricia M. Buhler, "Interviewing Basics: A Critical Competency for All Managers," *Supervision* 66 (March 2005), pp. 20–22; Adam Agard, "Pre-employment Skills Testing: An Important Step in the Hiring Process," *Supervision* 64 (June 2003), pp. 7–8.
2. Jeffrey E. Garten, "Keep Boomers on the Job," *BusinessWeek Online,* November 14, 2005, http://www.businessweek.com, accessed September 11, 2006; "Retiring Baby Boomers: The Work Force of Tomorrow," *BusinessWeek Online*, October 17, 2000, http://www.businessweek.com, accessed September 11, 2006.
3. Richard Fein, *Baby Boomers Guide to the New Work Place* (New York: Taylor Trade Publishing, 2006).
4. Michael Farr, *America's Top 101 Jobs for People without a Four-Year Degree* (Indianapolis, IN: JIST Works, 2005).
5. Lynne C. Lancaster and David Stillman, *When Generations Collide* (New York: HarperBusiness, 2002).
6. Tom Peters, *Re-Imagine: Business Excellence in a Disruptive Age* (London: Dorling Kindersley, 2003), pp. 18 and 81.
7. Peters, p. 241.
8. Edward L. Gubman, *The Talent Solution: Aligning Strategy and People to Achieve Extraordinary Results* (New York: McGraw-Hill, 1998); Meglian Stromberg, "Winning the Talent War: How to Hire," *Professional Builder,* June 2003, p. 54; William W. Lewis, *The Power of Productivity: Wealth, Poverty, and the Threat to Global Stability* (Chicago: The University of Chicago/McKinsey and Company, 2004).
9. Doug Brown, "Six Common Traits Employers Look For in an Interview," *Fort Worth Business Press,* June 13, 2004, p. 7.
10. Rick Archer, "Hiring Is More Than Just Interviewing Candidates," *Fairfield County Business Journal,* April 5, 2004; Alison Aprhys, "Seven Deadly Interview Sins," *Australian CPA* 72, August 2002, pp. 48–49; Anthony O'Donnell, "'Suitable' Job Candidates," *Insurance and Technology,* September 2002.
11. Roger Herman and Joyce Gioia, "You've Heard of E-Business . . . How About E-Recruiting?" The Workforce Stability Institute, http://www.employee.org/article_you_heard_of_e-business.html, accessed September 14, 2006.
12. Joyce Gioia, "Special Report: Changing the Face(s) in Your Recruiting Efforts," Workforce Stability Institute, http://www.employee.org/article_changing_the_face.html, accessed September 14, 2006.
13. Joyce Gioia, "Are Prospective Applicants Saying 'No'—Based on Your Website?" Workforce Stability Institute, http://www.employee.org/article_prospective_saying_no.html, accessed September 14, 2006.
14. Michael A. McDaniel, Deborah H. Whetzel, Frank L. Schmidt, and Steven D. Mauer, "The Validity of Employment Interviews: A Comprehensive Review and Meta-Analysis," *Journal of Applied Psychology* 79 (1994), pp. 599–616.

15. Junda Woo, "Job Interviews Pose Risk to Employers," *The Wall Street Journal,* March 11, 1992, pp. B1 and B5.

16. Clive Fletcher, "Ethics and the Job Interview," *Personnel Management,* March 1992, pp. 36–39.

17. Roger Herman, "Older Workers—A Hidden Treasure," Workforce Stability Institute, http://www.employee.org/article_older_workers_hidden_treasure.html, accessed September 14, 2006; "Old, Smart, Productive," *BusinessWeek Online,* June 27, 2005, http://www.businessweek.com, accessed September 11, 2006.

18. Phillip M. Perry, "Your Most Dangerous Legal Traps When Interviewing Job Applicants," *Law Practice Management,* March 1994, pp. 50–56; Stephen Sonnenberg, "Can HR Legally Ask the Questions That Applicants with Disabilities Want to Be Asked?" *Workforce,* August 2002, pp. 42–44; Susanne M. Bruyere, William A. Erickson, and Sara VanLooy, "Comparative Study of Workplace Policy and Practices Contributing to Disability Nondiscrimination," *Rehabilitation Psychology* 49 (2004), 28–38.

19. "Etiquette for Interviewing Candidates with Disabilities," *Personnel Journal* supplement, September 1992, p. 6.

20. According to Rochelle Kaplan, legal counsel for the College Placement Council, no question is technically unlawful. The use of a question may be unlawful because courts assume that if you ask such a question, you will use it for unlawful purposes.

21. Perry (1994), pp. 50–56; Phillip M. Perry, "Foolproofing the Job Interview," *Folio,* January 1, 1993, pp. 83–84.

22. Heather K. Gerken, "Understanding Mixed Motives Claims under the Civil Rights Act of 1991: An Analysis of Intentional Discrimination Claims Based on Sex-Stereotyped Interview Questions," *Michigan Law Review* 91 (1993), pp. 1824–1853.

23. Buhler.

24. Meredith P. Cook, "High Court Ruling Shifts 'at Will' Employment Rules," *New Hampshire Business Review,* May 3, 2004, p. 29A.

25. Kevin Wheeler, "Interviewing Doesn't Work Very Well," *Electronic Recruiting Exchange,* http://www.ere.net, accessed September 14, 2006.

26. George F. Dreher, Ronald A. Ash, and Priscilla Hancock, "The Role of the Traditional Research Design in Underestimating the Validity of the Employment Interview," *Personnel Psychology* 41 (1988), pp. 315–327.

27. Patrice M. Buzzanell, "Employment Interviewing Research: Ways We Can Study Underrepresented Group Members' Experiences as Applicants," *Journal of Business Communication* 39 (2002), pp. 257–275.

28. Karen O'Keefe, "Five Secrets to Successful Interviewing and Hiring," http://www.writingassist.com, accessed September 14, 2006.

29. Troy Behrens, "How Employers Can Ace Their Campus and Site Interviews," *Journal of Career Planning & Employment,* Winter 2001, pp. 30–32.

30. Steven M. Ralston and Robert Brady, "The Relative Influence of Interview Communication Satisfaction on Applicants' Recruitment Decisions," *Journal of Business*

Communication 31 (1994), pp. 61–77; Camille S. DeBell, Marilyn J. Montgomery, Patricia R. McCarthy, and Richard P. Lanthier, "The Critical Contact: A Study of Recruiter Verbal Behavior during Campus Interviews," *The Journal of Business Communication* 35 (1998), pp. 202–224.

31. Behrens, pp. 30–32.

32. Patrice M. Buzzanell, "Tensions and Burdens in Employment Interviewing Processes: Perspectives of Nondominant Group Applicants," *Journal of Business Communication* 36 (1999), pp. 134–162.

33. DeBell, Montgomery, McCarthy, and Lanthier, pp. 204–224.

34. "Hiring: An Expert Explains How to Choose the Best Applicant," *Effective Manager* 6 (1982), pp. 4–5.

35. Buhler.

36. Wayne Tomkins, "Lying on Resumes Is Common; Catching It Can Be Challenging," Lafayette, Indiana *Journal and Courier,* September 1, 2000, p. C7.

37. Landy Chase, "Buyer Beware: How to Spot a Deceptive Sales Resume," *New Orleans City Business,* November 4, 2002, p. 22.

38. Bob Ayrer, "Hiring Salespeople—Getting behind the Mask," *American Salesman,* December 1997, pp. 18–21.

39. Stephanie Clifford, Brian Scudamore, Andy Blumberg, and Jess Levine, "The New Science of Hiring," *Inc* 28 (August 2006), pp. 90–98, http://www.wf2la7.webfeat.org, accessed September 13, 2006.

40. Agard.

41. Rochelle Kaplan, "Do Assessment Tests Predict Behavior or Screen Out a Diverse Work Force?" *Journal of Career Planning & Employment,* Spring 1999, pp. 9–12.

42. Patrick H. Raymark, Mark J. Schmit, and Robert M. Guion, "Identifying Potentially Useful Personality Constructs for Employee Selection," *Personnel Psychology* 50 (1997), pp. 723–736.

43. Wayne J. Camara, "Employee Honesty Testing: Traps and Opportunities," *Boardroom Reports,* December 15, 1991.

44. Carol Kleiman, "From Genetics to Honesty, Firms Expand Employee Tests, Screening," *Chicago Tribune,* February 9, 1992, p. 8-1.

45. Camara.

46. Donna R. Pawlowski and John Hollwitz, "Work Values, Cognitive Strategies, and Applicant Reactions in a Structured Pre-Employment Interview for Ethical Integrity," *The Journal of Business Communication* 37 (2000), pp. 58–75.

47. Anita Gates, "The Secrets of Making a Good Hire," *Working Woman* 17 (1992), pp. 70–72.

48. Pawlowski and Hollwitz, pp. 58–75.

49. Pawlowski and Hollwitz, p. 61.

50. Louis Rovner, "Job Interview or Horror Movie?" *Occupational Health & Safety,* February 2001, p. 22.

51. Fredric M. Jablin and Vernon D. Miller, "Interviewer and Applicant Questioning Behavior in Employment Interviews," *Management Communication Quarterly* 4 (1990), pp. 51–86.

52. Choon-Hwa Lim, Richard Winter, and Christopher C.A. Chan, "Cross-Cultural Interviewing in the Hiring Process: Challenges and Strategies," *The Career Development Quarterly* 54 (March 2006), p. 267.

53. Ayrer, pp. 18–21.

54. Arthur H. Bell, "Gut Feelings Be Damned," *Across the Board,* September 1999, pp. 57–62; Allen I. Huffcutt and Winfred Arthus, "Hunter and Hunter (1984) Revisited: Interview Validity for Entry-Level Jobs," *Journal of Applied Psychology* 79 (1994), pp. 184–190; Karen I. van der Zee, Arnold Bakker, and Paulien Bakker, "Why Are Structured Interviews So Rarely Used in Personnel Selection?" *Journal of Applied Psychology* 87 (2002), pp. 176–184.

55. Clifford, Scudamore, Blumberg, Levine.

56. Buzzanell, pp. 134–162.

57. William G. Kirkwood and Steven M. Ralston, "Inviting Meaningful Applicant Performances in Employment Interviews," *The Journal of Business Communication* 36 (1999), p. 66.

58. Craig D. Tengler and Fredric M. Jablin, "Effects of Question Type, Orientation, and Sequencing in the Employment Screening Interview," *Communication Monographs* 50 (1983), pp. 245–263.

59. Buhler.

60. Kirkwood and Ralston, pp. 69–71.

61. Marlene Dixon, Sheng Wang, Jennifer Calvin, Brian Dineen, and Edward Tomlinson, "The Panel Interview: A Review of Empirical Research and Guidelines for Practice," *Public Personnel Management* 31 (2002), pp. 397–428.

62. Jablin and Miller, pp. 51–86; Gerald Vinton, "Open versus Closed Questions—an Open Issue?" *Management Decision* 33 (1995), pp. 27–32.

63. Aleksander P. J. Ellis, Bradley J. West, Ann Marie Ryan, and Richard P. DeShon, "The Use of Impression Management Tactics in Structured Interviews: A Function of Question Type," *Journal of Applied Psychology* 87 (2002), pp. 1200–1208.

64. Randy Myers, Interviewing Techniques from the Pros," *Journal of Accounting* 202 (August 2006), pp. 53–55; "Using Behavioral Interviewing to Help You Hire the Best of the Best," *HR Focus* 81 (August 2006), p. 56; "Interview Tips and Best Practice," *Healthcare Registration,* October 2006, pp. 7–9.

65. Jim Kennedy, "What to Do When Job Applicants Tell . . . Tales of Invented Lives," *Training,* October 1999, pp. 110–114.

66. Justin Menkes, "Hiring for Smarts," *Harvard Business Review* 83, November 2005, pp. 100–109.

67. Kaplan, pp. 9–12.

68. Myers.

69. Menkes.

70. Thomas Gergmann and M. Susan Taylor, "College Recruitment: What Attracts Students to Organizations?" *Personnel* 61 (1984), pp. 34–36; Fredric M. Jablin, "Organizational Entry, Assimilation, and Exit," *Handbook of Organizational Communication* (Beverly Hills, CA: Sage, 1987).

71. Catherine Houdek Middendorf and Therese Hoff Macan, "Note-Taking in the Employment Interview: Effects on Recall and Judgments," *Journal of Applied Psychology* 87 (2002), pp. 293–303.

72. "If They Say Tomato, and You Say To-Mah-To, What Then?" Workforce Stability Institute, http://www.employee.org/article_tomato.html, accessed September 14, 2006.

Resources

Farr, Michael. *America's Top 101 Jobs for People without a Four-Year Degree.* Indianapolis: JIST Works, 2005.

Fein, Richard. *Baby Boomers Guide to the New Work Place.* New York: Taylor Trade Publishing, 2006.

Fields, Martha R. A. *Indispensable Employees: How to Hire Them/How to Keep Them.* Franklin Lake, NJ: Career Press, 2001.

Lancaster, Lynn C., and David Stillman. *When Generations Collide: Who They Are, Why They Clash, and How to Solve the Generational Puzzle.* New York: HarperBusiness, 2002.

Miller, Michael. Expedia: *The Ultimate Google Resource.* Indianapolis IN: Que, 2007.

CHAPTER 8 The Employment Interview

The world of work has changed dramatically.

Welcome change and diversity.

Times and attitudes change.

Through much of the twentieth century, people looked for *jobs*, often with the organization that had employed their fathers, uncles, and grandfathers. It was to be a lifetime commitment on the parts of employee and employer, and both were most likely males. Those who thought of *careers* rather than *jobs* were typically interested in law, medicine, education, and engineering. They advanced through experience and further education, licenses, and certificates. Learning was a lifetime expectation and commitment. Women were limited to nursing and teaching careers and to retail and secretarial jobs. Racial and ethnic minorities had to choose among low-level jobs.

Today the world of work is a very different place. The knowledge generation is here, and there are fewer and fewer jobs available for high school graduates and dropouts beyond the minimum wage service sector. The key word is *career,* and a lifetime of education and training is the norm. The workforce looks very different. Your coworkers and supervisors may be female (now half or more of all workers), over 65 (there will be 70 million workers over that age by 2010–2012), Hispanic-American (15 percent of the population and growing), African-American (12 percent of the population), or Asian-American (10 percent of the population).

Diversity and economic productivity have created a clash of belief systems. Lancaster and Stillman describe four basic belief systems that are alive and thriving in the workplace.[1]

- *Traditionalists:* employees with their "heads down" and an onward and upward attitude live out a work ethic shaped during the Great Depression.
- *Baby boomers:* 80 million vacillate between their overwhelming need to succeed and their growing desire to slow down and enjoy life.
- *Generation Xers:* try to prove themselves constantly yet dislike the image of being overly ambitious, disrespectful, and irreverent.
- *Millennials:* new to the workforce, mix savvy with social conscience, and promise to change the business landscape.

Choosing a Career Path

Choosing a career is a daunting task in an age when new career paths are being created and old ones are disappearing at an increasing rate. Some segments of the market have moved ahead of others because of changes in our nation's demographics, technology, and the global economy. Here are some market trends:

- *Health care in every form:* therapy, nursing, home health care, senior complexes, long-term care facilities.
- *Hospitality management:* cruising, travel, resorts, lodging, restaurants.
- *Technology:* computers, cell phones, automotive, technical and science writing.
- *Education:* every level of teaching from pre-school to graduate school, online and distance learning, service learning, training.
- *Engineering:* mechanical, electrical, chemical, robotics.

Select the best path for you.

The sooner you determine your interests, the greater are the opportunities to develop appropriate courses of study and attain necessary experiences in the form of internships, full- and part-time positions, and observations. As Peter Drucker would say, "If you don't know where you're going, any path will get you there."

So how do you locate these paths? Every Barnes and Noble and Borders bookstore has numerous books and resources on careers. So do college and professional career centers. The Myers-Briggs Personality Indicator will enable you to identify your interests and talents. Alan B. Bernstein has authored a system that identifies some 40 career profiles that provide educational needs, training, career statistics, and a color-coded organization that will enable you to identify needs, desires, and aspirations. Edgar Schein, a well-known management consultant, has a more simplified approach called "Career Ameliors." You can take this individually or in groups. Most college career centers have computer programs that will enable you to match yourself with a wide variety of careers, many you've never heard of.

Analyzing Yourself

You cannot sell you if you don't know you.

Once you have identified one or more careers that interest you, the next step in locating and obtaining the position you want is a thorough and insightful **self-analysis.** First, you must *know yourself* so you can determine which positions and which organizations are ideal for you. And second, nearly all interview questions will be aimed at discovering who *you* are, what *you* can do, and how well *you* fit a specific position within an organization. You cannot answer questions insightfully and persuasively if you don't know who you are.

Questions to Guide Your Self-Analysis

Self-analysis may be painful because few of us want to probe deeply and honestly into our strengths and weaknesses, successes and failures. No one needs to see your self-analysis but you, so be painfully honest with yourself. The following questions can serve as guides.[2]

- What are your *personality* strengths and weaknesses?

Reliability	Values
Motivation	Maturity
Open-mindedness	Flexibility
Adaptability to change	Ability to accept criticism
Integrity	Moral standards

Assertiveness	Ambition
Self-control	Work under pressure

- What are your *intellectual* strengths and weaknesses?

Intelligence	Ease of learning
Organizing	Analyzing
Creating	Evaluating
Planning	Reasoning

- What are your *communicative* strengths and weaknesses?

Oral communication skills	Written communication skills
Listening skills	Interpersonal skills
With superiors	With subordinates
With coworkers	With persons of different sex, age, race, ethnic group, nationality

- What have been your *accomplishments* and *failures*?

Academic	Extracurricular activities and hobbies
Work	Professional
Goals set and met	

Focus on strengths and weaknesses.

- What are your *professional strengths* and *weaknesses*?

Education	Training
Experiences	Specific skills
Talents	

- What do you want in a *position* and *organization*?

Responsibility	Contact with people
Independence	Authority
Type of work	Security
Prestige of organization	Variety
Decision making	Benefits
Coworkers	Income

- What are your *most valued needs*?

Family	Home
Possessions	Free time
Relationships	Recreation opportunities
Geographical location	Prestige
Recognition	Success

- What are your *professional interests*?

  Short-range goals Long-range goals
  Advancement Recognition
  Growth

Why and how have you made past decisions?

- Why did you attend ______________ college/university and how happy are you with this decision?
- Why did you major in ______________ and how happy are you with this decision?
- Why did you accept positions at (1) ______________, (2) ______________, (3) ______________?
- Why did you leave (1) ______________, (2) ______________, (3) ______________?
- What is your tolerance of risk? For instance, over the past several years, organizations have attracted bright, young employees with low take-home pay but large stock options. Many have found themselves with stock worth only pennies. Analyze your ability to deal with risk. Stock options and stock purchase plans are common forms of compensation, but consider the take-home pay and benefits (health insurance, profit-sharing, retirement, 401(k) in addition to stock plans.

By the time you answer these questions thoroughly and honestly, you should know who you are, what you are qualified to do, what you would like to do, and what you want in life. Above all, you will "have identified what sets you apart from other candidates" so you can present your uniqueness through your resume and cover letter and during interviews.[3]

Doing Your Homework

Once you know yourself thoroughly, start your homework. **Research** your field or fields, the organizations to which you will apply, the positions for which you will apply, current events, and the interviewing process.

Research Your Field

Knowing your field is essential for selecting organizations and scheduling interviews.

Discover your field's history, developments, trends, areas of specialization, challenges, current and future problems, and employment opportunities. What education, training, and experiences are essential for entering this field? Develop a mature, realistic perception of what your field is like and what people do during typical workdays.

There are published and Internet resources on nearly every major career field from acting and advertising to visual arts and writing that will aid your research. Some sources are:

Career Opportunities Directory Volume II: Business Administration

Marketing and Sales Career Directory

National Directory of Corporate Training Programs

Peterson's Job Opportunities for Business and Liberal Arts Graduates

Monster Careers: How to Land the Best Job of Your Life

Web sites by Career Field (http://www.denison.edu/**career/career**_resources/**careerfield**.html)

Career Center (http://www.career.berkeley.edu)

SearchingCareers.org.

Natural Resources Stewardship Career Field (http://www.nps.gov/training/nrs/nrshome.htm)

Advertising, Marketing, Promotions, Public Relations, and Sales Managers (http://www.bls.gov)

Wetfeet.com

Online.onecenter.org

Employers expect you to be acquainted with organizational life and have positive attitudes toward a career in business, management, teaching, health care, law, engineering, journalism, or whatever career you choose. They expect you to know why you want to enter a field. Interview friends and professionals about their fields. Internships, cooperative arrangements, part-time positions, observational visits, and volunteer activities are excellent ways to discover what a field is all about.

Research Organizations

Learn everything you can about each organization to which you apply. Your investigation should focus on its leaders and staff, products and services (old and new), geographical locations, expansion or downsizing plans, potential mergers, competitors, and financial status. Discover the organization's reputation in the field, particularly with its own employees, customers, clients, patients, or students.

Research enables you to answer and ask questions insightfully.

Only through careful research can you answer a critical interview question, *Why do you want to work for us?* And only through research can you determine if your personality and interests are a good fit with the organization's culture.

You can discover information about organizations by writing to the organization or by talking to current and former employees and clients, professors, and friends. An organization's publications, Web site, recruiting literature, and annual reports are valuable sources of information. See if there is a mission statement or strategic plan available. Current employees can identify the kinds of persons and the specific skill sets their employers are looking for. Check the library for sources such as the following:

The Career Guide: Dun's Employment Opportunities Directory

Job Choices

Information is available if you know where to look.

Dictionary of Professional Trade Organizations

Encyclopedia of Business Information Sources

Encyclopedia of Careers and Vocational Guidance

Occupational Outlook Handbook

Open the Book: How to Research a Corporation

Standard and Poor's Corporation Records
Thomas Register of American Manufacturers
Ward's Directory of Public and Private Corporations

Do not overlook the growing number of databases, many on CD-ROM. Resources include American Business Disc, Company ProFile, Disclosure Database, Dun's Electronic Business Directory, Dun's Million Dollar CD-ROM Collection, and ABI/Inform Ondisc.[4] The article "50 Places to Launch a Career" by Lindsey Gerdes identifies the best places for new college graduates.[5]

Research the Recruiter

It may be difficult to research the person or persons who will conduct your interview because you may not know the identity of the interviewer or interviewers until an interview begins. If you do know the identity of the person ahead of time, talk to friends, associates, professors, career center personnel, and members of the interviewer's organization to discover the interviewer's position, professional background, organizations to which the interviewer belongs, personality, and interviewing characteristics. An interviewer may have a dry sense of humor, come from a different culture, or be "all business." It helps to know such characteristics ahead of time.

When possible, get to know the interviewer ahead of time.

Research the Position

Learn everything you can about the position for which you are applying. Your research should include responsibilities, duties, necessary skills, required education, training, experiences, type of supervision, advancement potential, amount of travel involved, locations, organizational culture and climate, job security, fringe benefits, training programs, salary and commissions, relocation possibilities and policies, rate of turnover, co-workers, and starting date.

How closely do you and the position fit?

A thorough knowledge of the position for which you are applying prepares you to answer questions effectively, ask meaningful questions, and determine if you, the position, and the organization are a good *fit.* A number of authorities recommend that, besides the usual research sources, the applicant should arrive for the interview a few minutes early to determine "how well a potential employer fits an individual's work style and career goals."[6] Observe the dress of employees, office interiors (including whether employees are allowed to decorate their offices), whether there is a break room and how it is outfitted, how employees interact with one another and supervisors, the makeup of the workforce, level of technology, and if senior managers are located near their staff.

The position search model in Figure 8.1 will help you analyze each position and determine if it suits your needs and desires.

Research Current Events

Keep abreast of what is happening in the world and in your field.

Keep up to date with what is going on in the world. *Newsweek, Time, BusinessWeek, Fortune, The Wall Street Journal,* and online news sources and versions of newspapers are excellent sources of current world developments. Employers expect mature applicants to be aware of what is going on around them and in the world—local, state, national, international. They expect you to have formed intelligent, rational positions on important issues.

Figure 8.1 *The cash position search model*

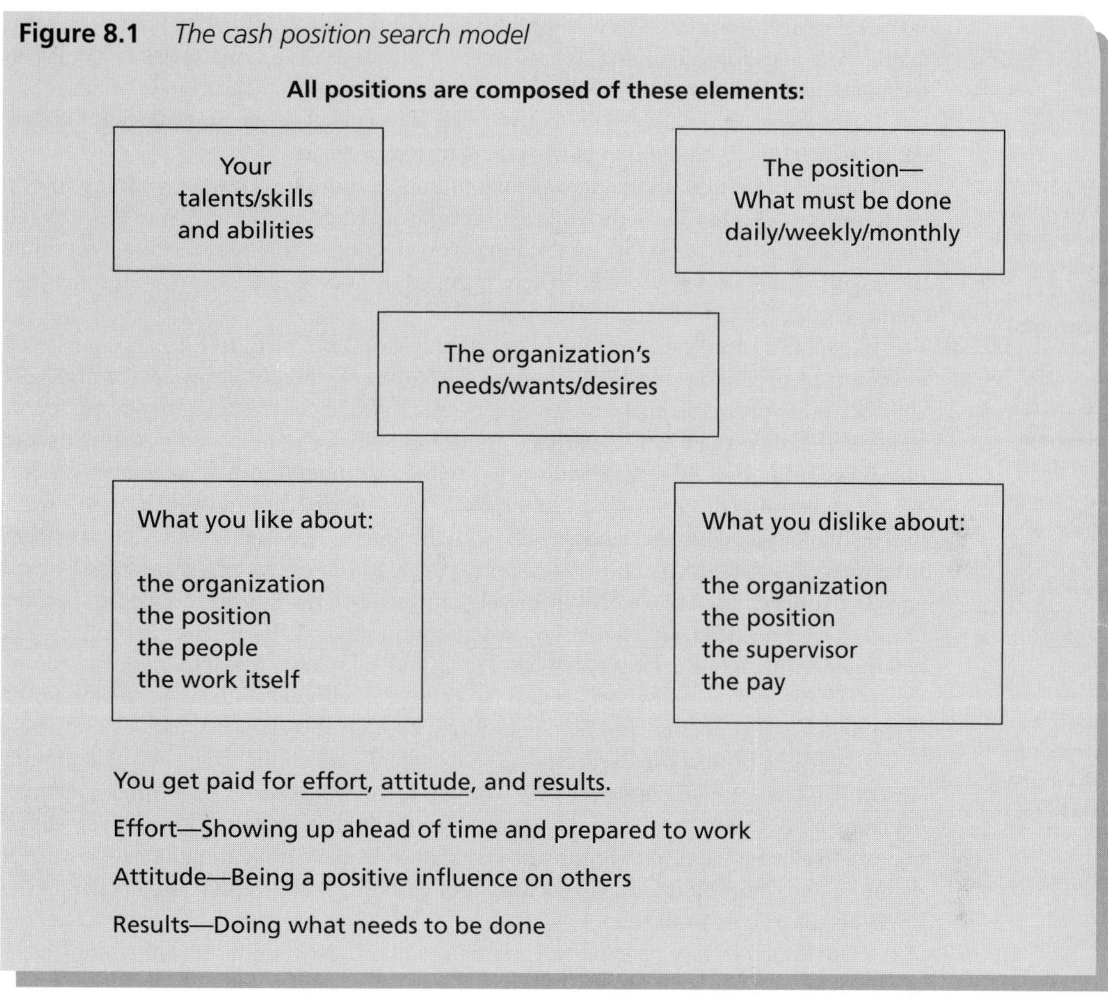

All positions are composed of these elements:
Your talents/skills and abilities
The position— What must be done daily/weekly/monthly
The organization's needs/wants/desires
What you like about:
the organization
the position
the people
the work itself
What you dislike about:
the organization
the position
the supervisor
the pay
You get paid for effort, attitude, and results.
Effort—Showing up ahead of time and prepared to work
Attitude—Being a positive influence on others
Results—Doing what needs to be done

Be well informed on all current events that may affect your field or profession. What are the trends, changes, and mergers that may influence your employment decision? For instance, if you are going into the pharmaceutical field, be aware of any controversies concerning new drugs and costs. If you are interested in working for an organization with facilities in India, be aware of American and organizational relations with India and how Indian culture differs from American culture.

Research the Interview Process

Learn everything you can about what happens during interviews. Read Chapter 7 on the recruiting interview that will give you insights into what to expect in interviews. Talk to friends and acquaintances who have recently been through the interviewing process, professors who are involved in interviewing and keep track of what is taking place in their fields, and recruiters. There are a growing number of Web sites that can be helpful, including www.references-etc.com, www.interviewcoach.com, and www.asktheinterviewcoach.com.[7] Ask questions such as: "What kinds of questions do recruiters ask?" "What do recruiters look for in answers?" "What turns recruiters off?" "What kinds of questions should you ask?" "How likely is it that you will face a panel or seminar situation?" "How are subsequent interviews different from the screening interview?"

Rely on no single source about employment interviews.

There is no single or standard means of conducting interviews, so talking to one person, even a highly skilled corporate recruiter, will give you only one view of the process. That is why many of us teaching interviewing skills do not bring a recruiter to class to "show how it is done." There is no single source that can speak for the hundreds of variations in selection interviews.

Telephone interviews are a common means of screening applicants.

Expense, a more rapid response to openings, and the need to fill many positions have forced organizations to implement a number of screening processes and new approaches. Some companies employ video- or telephone conferencing so several representatives of the organization, perhaps at different sites, can talk with you at the same time.[8] Recordings allow representatives to review your interview at their convenience.

Because of cost and a shortage of applicants in critical fields such as information technology and engineering, you may go through only two interviews, a **screening interview** with reference checks, transcripts, drug test, and a Myers-Briggs assessment and then a **determinate** (decision-making) **interview.** Do not be shocked if you are asked to take a drug test. This is becoming commonplace. IQ tests or predictors can be a plus for persons seeking entry-level positions who have few experiences and on-the-job skills because these tests reveal "executive intelligence" that can substitute for experiences and skills that will come quickly with most positions.

Expect a variety of tests in many fields.

Integrity or **honesty tests,** discussed in Chapter 7, are common in areas that require security and safety. An employer may ask you to answer a series of written questions (as many as 40 to 80) or go through a preemployment interview dealing with degrees of honesty. Be honest and forthcoming because all of us have done things that, by a strict definition, are morally or ethically wrong. For example, have you taken pencils, paper, or printer cartridges from school or office?

Expect the unexpected.

Your research may produce surprising results. For example, recent studies have revealed the following: 50 percent of "speech acts" in a sample of interviews were declarative statements rather than questions and answers. Most interviewers have no training in interviewing. In a study of 49 interviews, 10 interviewers did not give applicants opportunities to ask questions. Interviewers are increasingly viewing the interview as a *work sample* and look for relevant job behaviors from applicants. They usually have three questions in mind: can you do the job, will you do the job, and how well will you *fit* into the organization? Employers also want to see **evidence** that you have researched their organizations and positions prior to interviews—that you have done your homework.

Integrity is essential for all positions.

When supervisors at Hughes Aircraft were asked to list behaviors and information they looked for when interviewing applicants, they produced a pyramid (see Figure 8.2) with the most important behaviors and information at the bottom, as foundations, and the least important at the top.[9] Many observers were shocked by the apparent unimportance placed on specific abilities related directly to education and training. The supervisors explained that **integrity** was most important because a highly trained and skilled employee without honesty, morals, and sincerity will quickly become a detriment to organizations,

Figure 8.2 *Criteria for evaluating applicants*

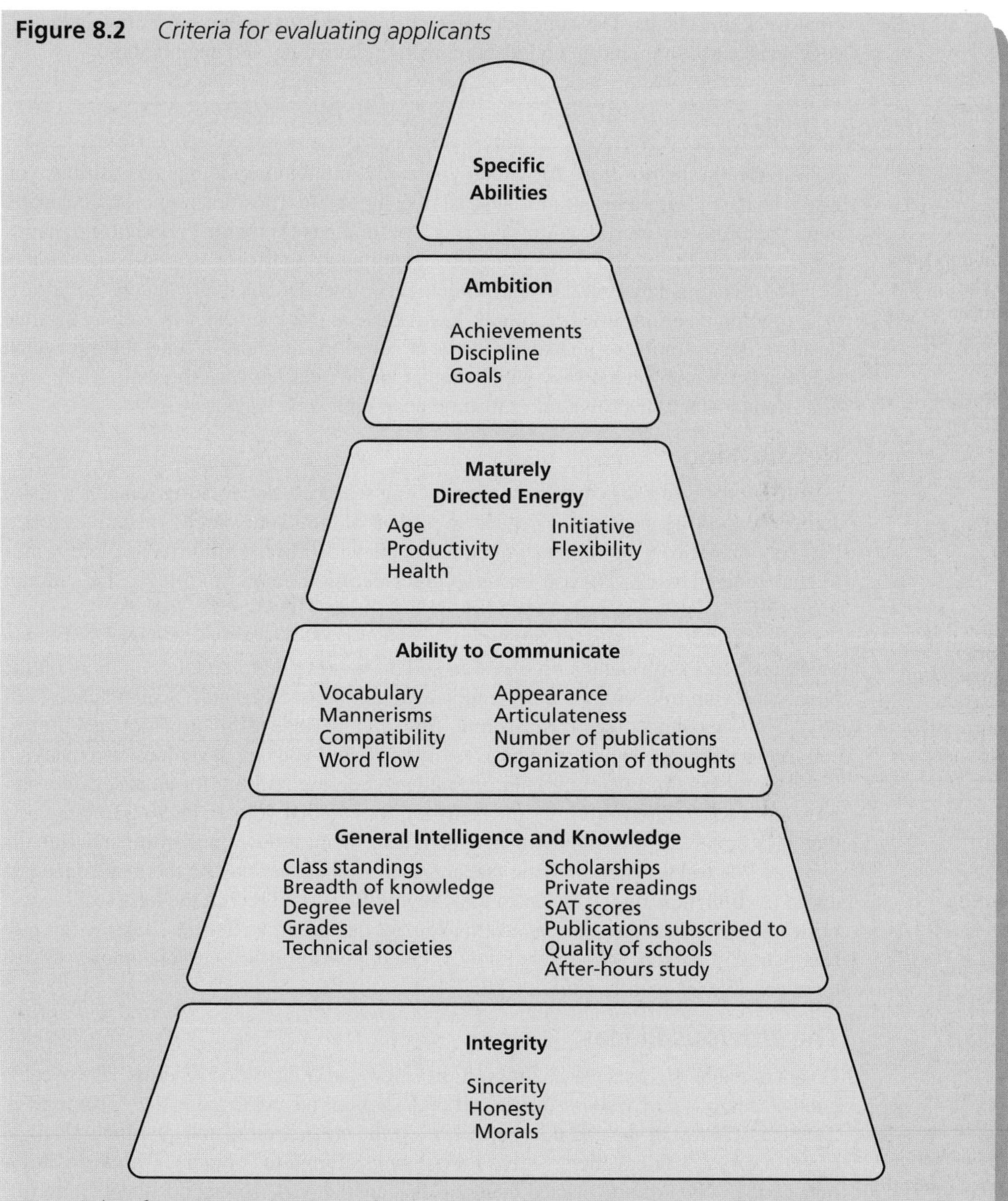

Note: Taken from "Toward More Productive Interviewing," by Robert A. Martin. Copyright May 1971. Reprinted with the permission of *Personnel Journal,* Costa Mesa, CA.

employees, and clients. The same holds true, they argued, for employees narrow in knowledge, unable to communicate orally and in writing, immature, and unambitious.

Conducting the Search

Be selective in the positions for which you apply, but choose a range of positions you would be happy with. For instance, instead of being set on a position as a cost accountant, public relations director, or editorial writer, try for a position with a good firm or newspaper, with the hope of moving into cost accounting or a director's or op-ed position.

You may have to start at the bottom to get to the top.

The changing labor market is leading to recommendations that you consider a part-time or temp position in which to gain experience and work your way into a full-time position. For example, some teachers serve as substitute teachers or time-share in which they teach a class for a half-day while another teacher teaches the other half. They hope this arrangement will evolve into full-time positions.

Networking

Despite all the electronic sources for conducting searches, **networking** remains a major source for locating positions. Fifty-seven percent of human resources executives report they rely on networking to locate qualified applicants.[10] Many students use internships to start their networks. If you make a career decision early in college, the summer internship may serve as entry into a full-time position.

Leave no potential source off your network tree.

Here are suggestions for beginning a network. Take a sheet of paper and begin a **network tree** with names on one side and addresses and telephone numbers on the other. Start your tree with the most readily available sources: friends, acquaintances, relatives, family connections, former employers, alumni, internship directors, and professors. Your primary contacts may be as many as 50, but you can never have too many.

Call the person in slot number one and say you are looking for a *career opportunity,* never a *job*. The word *job* signals the impression that you are looking for anything that pays money. If this contact gives you a lead, write it down under this individual's name so you can recall who made the suggestion. The *who* may be the major factor in a lead's willingness and enthusiasm to help you. Be sure to record the lead's full name, position, and telephone number. If this contact has no opportunities, ask for three or four names of persons who might know of career possibilities. Everyone knows at least three possible leads if they think a bit.

The Obvious Places

Do not overlook obvious places for positions. Newspaper classified sections have become good places to locate positions because if organizations advertise there, their opening will meet the EEO test of making it known to those who are interested and qualified. *The Wall Street Journal* is an excellent source for openings around the country. Check organizational bulletin boards and printed materials that announce personnel openings. Subscribe to professional publications such as *The Chronicle of Higher Education* that include ads for a variety of positions.

The personnel office is not the starting point for salaried and professional positions.

Approach organizations directly to see if they have current or future openings. Contact human resources departments primarily for hourly and temporary positions.

Specific departments of organizations usually conduct the searches for salaried and professional positions. Try to locate persons in charge of searches.

The Placement Agency or Service

Your campus career center does more than schedule interviews.

The **placement agency** or service is still an important source. A perusal of Google will enable you to select from a wide variety of agencies, services, and centers. Almost every college and university has a free agency for students and alumni. These agencies not only provide contacts for on-campus interviews but offer counseling services that will help you analyze yourself (including the careers you seem most interested in and qualified for), discover career fields, obtain information on organizations and positions, develop resumes, and write cover letters.

Other placement services are associated with professional organizations or specific career areas. For instance, check into specialized resources for health care professionals, teachers, management majors, communication majors, civil engineering majors, and so on. The cost is minimal.

Percentage agencies will help to place you for a fee, often a percentage of your first year's salary, payable upon assuming a position they helped you obtain. Most of these agencies have **fee-paid positions,** which means that an organization has retained them on a fee basis to locate quality applicants. You pay nothing. If you use a percentage agency, be aware that they may charge a registration fee to process your credentials.

If it sounds too good to be true, it probably is.

Most agencies are ethical and want to find excellent positions for their clients, but use reasoned skepticism. If they want a great deal of money in advance just to process your resume or make claims of placing nearly all of their applicants in very high-paying positions, go elsewhere. Be careful of agencies that want to produce videotapes and other expensive credentials for you. Check an agency thoroughly before making any monetary commitment or signing any contract.

Publications

Publications are still valuable in the computer age.

There are publications in your college career center or library that will guide you to career opportunities and services. *BusinessWeek* has identified 50 organizations (including Disney, Goldman Sachs, and Lockheed Martin) where you can develop a career.[11] *Jobs,* published annually and written by Kathryn and Ross Petras, contains some 600 pages of addresses, toll-free numbers, and industry groupings. At the beginning of each industry grouping is a brief employment history, the best bets for growth

ON THE WEB

Select a position you will be interested in when you complete your education or training. Search at least three Internet resources to discover the availability of such positions, geographical areas in which they are located, organizations that are seeking to fill them, and the nature of the positions being offered. Check resources such as Job Hunt (http://www.job-hunt.org), CareerBuilder Center (http://www.careerbuilder.com), MonsterTrak (http://www.monstertrak.com). After collecting this information, develop a list of interview questions to which you would need answers before making a decision to accept one of these positions.

and job opportunities, and names of associations, directories, and professional journals for that grouping. This source is ideal for entry-level positions.

The Kennedy Publications are helpful for those with 10 or more years of experience, particularly their *Executive Directory of Search Firms* and *Directory of Executive Recruiters* (published annually). Other Kennedy publications include *Consultants News, Executive Recruiter News, Directory of Management Consultants,* and *Directory of Outplacement Firms*.

Career Communication Incorporated publishes sources such as the *Job Market Directory National Edition.* This large format paperback provides general career information helpful to those getting their first positions and those recently terminated. This directory includes job market data; federal, state, and city job centers; nontraditional training; and employment programs serving women. A spin-off publication entitled *Job Hotlines USA* lists 1,000 organizations that post openings by telephone, including banks, hospitals, insurance companies, school districts, and colleges. Their most helpful publication is the *Job Hunters Yellow Pages* that includes more than 15,000 employment agencies and services.

Search printed materials for career opportunities and resources.

The Internet

The Internet is growing rapidly into a major source for positions and tips on how to obtain them. Colleges and other organizations are using Web pages to advertise positions and seek high quality applicants. You should check an up-to-date copy of *The Guide to Internet Job Searching,* compiled by Margaret Riley Dikel, Frances Rodney, and Steve Oserman, and published by VGM Career Horizons. Here are leading Web sites and addresses.[12]

Learn to use the Internet efficiently and effectively.

- Newbie-U (New User University) http://www.newbie-u.com
- *America's One Stop Career Center System* http://www.ttrc.doleta.gov/onestop
- Monster.com is one of the largest sites on the Internet and provides excellent resume formats, job sources, and advice. http://www.monster.com
- My Search Associations lists more than 2,000 associations. http://www.myjobsearch.com/network/associations
- The Riley Guide (http://www.rileyguide.com) and the Minorities Job Bank (http://www.minorities-jb.com) are excellent sources for women, minorities, and the disabled.
- Govbot provides easy access to most searchable databases for government Web sites. http://ciir2c.s.umass.edu/govbot
- Hot Jobs http://www.hotjobs.com
- American Job Bank http://www.amj.dm.us
- Job Bank USA http://www.jobbankusa.com
- My Job Search http://www.myjobsearch.com

Know how to make the most of job fairs.

Career Fairs

Career fairs held on your campus or around the country are excellent for networking and making contacts with organizations for internships and postgraduate employment. Many are limited to specific majors or areas such as liberal arts, engineering, or agriculture,

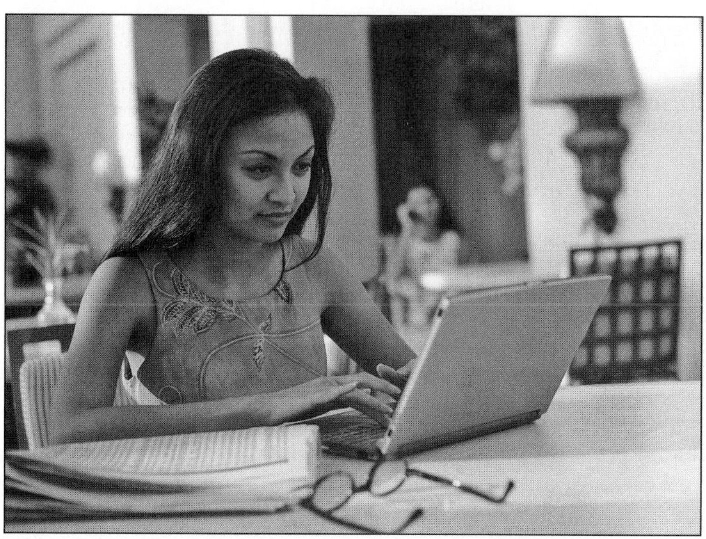
photo by © Royalty-dee/Corbis

Use the Internet to search for positions and conduct research on organizations.

while others are open to all fields of interest. Some large companies conduct their own career fairs. Listed below are contacts for information on fairs:

Career Fairs International
311 S. Wacker Drive, Suite 4550
Chicago, IL 60606
Phone (312) 697-4717
Fax (312) 697-4769

American Job Fairs
Phone (516) 681-9200

Job fairs (http://www.TargetedJob**Fairs**.com)

Job fairs by year (http://www.careerbuilder.com)

Few recruiters at job fairs are interested in conducting formal interviews, but they do have clear expectations of applicants who stand out in the crowd. A recent survey revealed that the majority of recruiters want students to have hard copies of their resumes, expect students to have a clear career focus or objective, and expect some type of follow-up from students. The worst mistake a student can make is to walk up to a recruiter at a job fair and ask,[13] "What are you hiring for?"

Preparing Credentials

Once you have analyzed yourself thoroughly, completed your homework, and searched for positions, it is time to prepare your credentials. These consist of resumes, portfolios, and cover letters.

Resumes

No single resume is suitable for all positions.

Prepare different resumes for each type of position for which you apply. The **resume** is your *silent sales representative,* and it is most persuasive when it is tailored to the skills and expectations of positions and appears to be highly professional.

Your resume is the first opportunity for a recruiter to *see* you. Since most recruiters will spend only two to four minutes scanning each resume, yours must gain and maintain **positive attention** if you hope to get beyond the application stage in the selection process. James Campion recommends that you "think like the boss" if you want the job.[14] Would *you* hire *you*?

Make it easy for interviewers to locate you.

Content of Resumes

Place your *full name* at the top center of the page in bold print. Use no nicknames.

Provide one or two *complete addresses* (with zip codes), telephone numbers (with area codes), an e-mail address, and fax number so the employer can reach you easily and quickly. If you list a campus telephone, provide a date when it will no longer be operable.

Phrase career objectives with great care.

Your **career objective** usually comes next. This is critical if the employer does not have a cover letter from you or chooses to review resumes alone. The majority of employers will read no further if your career objective does not fit the opening or is unimpressive. Impressive career objectives are:

- Career rather than job oriented.
- Brief and precise.
- Targeted to a specific type of position.
- Not self-centered.

Your educational record is most important for your first position.

If you are just completing your education or training and your work experiences are minimal or unrelated to the position, your educational record usually comes next. In a survey of 188 college recruiters conducted by John Cunningham, 57 percent preferred education to be listed first, even when the college applicant had significant work experiences.[15] List your degrees or training in reverse chronological order so the employer can detect quickly what you are *doing now* or what you recently completed. List degree, diploma, or certificate, date of graduation or completion, school, location of the school if name is insufficient for accurate identification (many universities have multiple campuses and there are several universities called Loyola), and majors and minors. You might provide a selective list of courses relevant to the opening, particularly if you are short on experience. However, courses often take up too much space and reveal the obvious. List your grade point average (GPA) if it is a B or better, and be sure you indicate the numerical system used at your college, for example: 3.35 (4.0 scale) or 3.35/4.0. Do not use abbreviations for courses, majors, or degrees. An interviewer may not know if Eng. refers to English or engineering. And be sure to list relevant certificates or licenses.

Relevant experiences can set you apart from the crowd.

After education and training, if you have selected this order, present your relevant experiences for the specific position for which you are applying. If you entitle this section "experiences," you can include more than work or salary earning situations, an advantage if you are young and just completing your education or training. Volunteer activities may be relevant and impressive. A recent study revealed that recruiters rate the following as *very important* or *above average* in importance in selecting employees:[16]

Job-related work experiences	88%
Leadership roles in student organizations	86%
Paid, job-related experiences	79%
Member of preprofessional organizations	73%
Experience in volunteer community service	58%

Types of Resumes

If you are developing a **chronological format,** the most common form of resume, list your experiences (including internships, co-op arrangements, assistantships, unpaid positions, organizational activities) in *reverse* chronological order so the employer can see quickly what you have been up to most recently. See Figure 8.3 for a sample chronological format resume.[17] List organization, title of your position or positions, dates, and above all, what you did in each position. Emphasize the skills and experiences most relevant for the opening. Studies indicate that the primary concern of interviewers is applicant achievement and accomplishment. Use action verbs, such as the following, to show you are a *doer:*

Be honest when constructing your resume.

Action verbs can show you are a doer.

Administered
Advised
Arbitrated
Arranged
Built
Budgeted
Coached
Consulted
Counseled
Created
Designed
Directed
Edited
Eliminated
Evaluated
Facilitated
Fashioned
Formulated
Founded
Generated
Improved
Increased
Instructed
Led
Maintained
Managed
Modified
Negotiated
Operated
Organized
Oversaw
Performed
Persuaded
Planned
Recommended
Reconfigured
Researched
Sold
Solved
Supervised
Tested
Trained
Updated
Wrote

If you are developing a **functional format,** most appropriate for creative positions and those in which writing is important, place your experiences under headings that highlight your qualifications for the position (see Figure 8.4). Typical major headings are management, sales, advertising, training, counseling, team building, organizational development, recruiting, finance, teaching, administration, supervision, project manager, and marketing. You can include a variety of experiences from different positions, internships, and organizations under each heading, a major advantage when you have had few paying positions or positions directly related to the opening. Be sure to use action verbs when identifying your experiences, such as "Wrote press releases for . . ." and "Developed training modules for . . ." Do not include too many headings and subheadings.

If you are using a chronological format, the next section may list relevant organizational memberships and activities, including college, professional, and community. Be selective. High school activities are excluded for college graduates, and college activities will be excluded after a few years in your career. It is a continual updating process. A long list of organizations without leadership roles is likely to give a negative impression. Show you are a doer. Include honorary organizations such as Phi Beta Kappa and Golden Key, and provide a brief description of organizations with which the interviewer might be unfamiliar.

Leadership, not membership, impresses interviewers.

Figure 8.3 *Chronological resume*

Joshua H. Mullins

Campus Address	Permanent Address
2712 Dodge Street	706 Hard Rock Creek
West Lafayette, IN 47906	Chatham, IL 62629
(765) 743-1213	(217) 973-2044
Email: jhmul@dodge.com	
Fax: (765) 743-1112	

Objective: A management position requiring strong interpersonal and communication skills.

Education: **Purdue University**

Bachelor of Science Degree, May 2008
Major: Management
Minor: Organizational Communication
GPA: 3.25/4.0 (Overall) 3.45/4.0 (Major)

Experience: **Guest Relations Intern**—Summer 2007

Six Flags Great America, Gurnee, IL

- Evaluated and replied to guest concerns
- Provided assistance to guests

Public Relations Assistant—Summer 2006

Illinois Department of Tourism, Springfield, IL

- Created and implemented PageMaker charts
- Edited brochures of fall festivals
- Updated records on attendance at festivals
- Composed letters for Director of Public Relations

Computer Skills: WordPerfect 6.0, Windows 2005, PageMaker, Lotus 1-2-3, World Wide Web, Home Page, PowerPoint

Activities: **President**—Travel Club, 2006–2007

- Conducted monthly meetings
- Chaired Travel Planning Committee
- Developed Web page for the Travel Club

Activities Director—Management Student Council, 2005–2006

- Planned monthly meetings
- Arranged for guest speakers
- Organized field trips

Figure 8.4 *Functional resume*

Judy Rutledge
7125 W. Lamar Parkway
Philadelphia, PA 19122
(215) 678-2456
Email: jrut@temple.com
Fax: (215) 678-2225

Objective: Assistant director

Education: **Temple University**
Bachelor of Arts, June 2008
Major: Radio, Television, Film
Minor: Theatre
GPA: 3.1/4.0 (Overall) 3.75/4.0 (Major)

Experience:

Management

- Developed operating budgets for student productions.
- Supervised the staff of a student production.
- Provided liaison between students and faculty.

Production

- Scheduled television programming for a BS station.
- Directed radio and television commercials.
- Produced and directed basketball half-time television shows.

Writing

- Developed equipment manuals for the television studios.
- Assisted professor in writing a textbook for the production sequence.
- Wrote advertising copy for student productions.
- Wrote press releases and brochures for productions.

Work Experience:

Merchandising Associate October 2007–June 2008
Home Depot, Philadelphia, PA

Showroom Sales Associate May 2006–August 2007
Macy's, Pittsburgh, PA

Honors:

- Outstanding Television Documentary
- Superior Achievement Award for Public Relations Announcement
- Dean's List, Temple University
- Who's Who Among American College Students

If you are using a functional format, you may list organizations or include them within various major headings under experience. A functional format may include this section or blend it within your skills and experiences. Realize that your outside activities can indicate motivation, communication skills, ability to work with people, work ethic, and ability to lead. Employers are concerned about narrow specialists.

Select the resume format best suited to you.

A chronological format, such as the one in Figure 8.3, has a number of advantages. It is easy to write and organize, emphasizes experiences, is most common, and is easy for an employer to scan for relevant experiences.

A functional format, such as the one in Figure 8.4, also has a number of advantages. It focuses attention on relevant skills to match the ideal applicant profile, dates are less important, and seemingly unrelated positions and education are not highlighted. A functional resume does not repeat the same skills and experiences under different positions, so it can be tighter and shorter. Most resumes today are blends of the two formats, as is apparent in Figures 8.3 and 8.4.

Exclude items that might lead to EEO violations.

Do not include the following in your resume: references; political, religious, or ethnic memberships or activities; a picture; or personal data such as age, marital status, parental status, height, and weight. You do not break any laws if you include these items, but you are providing information apart from bona fide occupational qualifications and assuming that an employer may hire you from unlawful criteria. Realize that you may *not* get a position because of this information.

Regardless of the type of resume format you select, follow these rules when selecting content:

Pay attention to content and appearance.

- Be accurate and honest.
- Do not repeat the same information.
- Be precise and persuasive.

Lying on Resumes

It is estimated that one in six college students lie on resumes and application forms, most often claiming experiences they have not had, courses they have not taken, and graduation indexes they have not achieved. Students are far from being the only ones who lie on resumes. So-called "edu-fibs" appear on resumes from CFOs, CEOs, poet laureates, and big-time college football coaches. Michael Josephson, president of the Josephson Institute of Ethics, warns that "Lies are like potato chips. You can't tell just one."[18] Some estimate that 35 percent of job seekers lie on their resumes, including falsified job titles, previous salaries, graduate degrees, responsibilities, accomplishments, and employment dates.[19] For instance, executive assistants often claim to be human resource directors.

Some applicants have something to hide, but most believe that a little "puffery," a euphemism for lying, will help them get a position and advancement. Employers and ethicists agree that this is a **bad idea** with potentially **bad results.** One source warns that "When fitted onto resumes, falsehoods can sit undetected indefinitely. Or, they can detonate at any moment, proving fatal to careers and credibility."[20] Scott Reeves writes bluntly: "A solid resume will get you in the door. A lie on the resume will get you kicked down the stairs."[21] Remember the Hughes Aircraft pyramid that contains *integrity* as the foundation stone for top applicants and employees.

It is not difficult to unmask lies on resumes. Your resume and application form may not match. Your references may reveal the truth about your education, experiences, and positions. Jim Barnhill, a specialist in human resources recruitment, claims that "If you don't have the experience, you can't speak intelligently about the topic."[22] Behavioral based questions are designed to get beneath surface answers and claims on resumes. If these don't do it, an honesty test is likely to reveal your "edu-fib" for what it is—dishonesty that may affect not only you but the organization you work for in the future. As Reeves advises, "Here's today's lightning bolt insight: Don't lie on your resume."

Mechanics of Resumes

Make your resume easy to review.

Proofread your resume with great care.

Do not overlook the effects of appearance and layout. Have your resumes professionally printed on white, off-white, light gray, or light beige bond paper. Pay attention to how the resume is blocked so it looks neat, attractive, organized, carefully planned, and uncrowded. Employers like *white space* on resumes, so indent sections carefully, double space parts, and leave at least one inch margins all around. Center your name at the top in bold letters so it stands out. Use different printer fonts so headings guide the reader through important information about you. Employers prefer resumes with bullets that separate and call attention to important information because this helps them scan the resume more efficiently. If you provide two addresses, place one on each side under your name. If you provide one address, place it in the center or on the right side away from staples and paper clips. Be sure to use perfect grammar, select wording carefully, check spellings and grammar, and proof for errors.

Most employers prefer a single page resume. A two-page resume may be acceptable, however, if it is less crowded and provides valuable information about experiences, skills, awards, and organizational activity and leadership that will not fit on a single page. If you develop a two-page resume, consider having it printed front to back on one sheet of paper because a second page may get misplaced or ripped off when your resume is taken from a file or briefcase. Be sure you signal with a page number or notation that there is more on the back. If you prepare two pages, be sure your name is repeated at the top on the left and a page number is on the top right.

The Electronically Scanned Resume

Some organizations use electronic systems to scan resumes. Those who do so tend to have large numbers of openings that attract large numbers of applicants. The scanner saves time and money.

If one of your resumes is likely to be electronically scanned, follow some basic rules. Figure 8.5 is a scannable resume. Use white paper. Employ only one or two print fonts. Do not use underlining. Be sure your resume contains up-to-date terms, labels, and names the scanner is programmed to detect. Some employers scan career objectives to sort resumes into files for different positions, so be sure to have a clearly identifiable career objective.

The following are examples of correct and incorrect terms for scannable resumes:

Yes	No
human resources	personnel
administrative assistant	secretary

Figure 8.5 *Scannable resume*

Nathan Mason
1408 E. Main Street
Norwalk, Ohio 23320
Home Phone (614) 796-4420
Email: masonn@aol.com
Fax: (614) 796-4400

Objective: To obtain a position in retail store management and merchandising

Experience:

2006–2008 Regional Store Manager and Buyer

- Manager of 5 regional stores in Northwestern Ohio
- Buyer of all retail shoes sold in the store
- Design specific store displays in line with corporate guidelines and plans
- Directly supervise 9 employees—5 full-time, 4 part-time
- Indirectly supervise 4 managers, 4 assistant managers, and 37 part-time employees
- Responsible for all financial and sales reporting and verifications

2005–2006 Assistant Manager, Payless Shoe Source
349 Erie Street
Sandusky, Ohio

- Promoted from Associate to Assistant Manager, Spring 2005

2004–2005 Sales Associate

- Worked full-time from 2004 to promotion in 2005
- Responsible for weekly inventory for 3 departments (men's, children's, and athletic)

2001–2004 Part-Time Sales Associate

- Hired full-time in fall of 2001

2000–2001 Pizza Hut Host and Server

- Part-time during the year and 2 summers full-time

Education: B.S. in Marketing and Merchandising, Ohio University, 2001

- Member, American Marketing Association
- Vice President, Retail Management Club

Terms and labels are critical in scannable resumes.

sales associate	sales clerk
information systems	data processing
environmental services	housekeeping
accountant	bookkeeper
facilities engineering	maintenance
inside sales	customer relations

Most organizations reject candidates that have less than 50 percent of the required skills. Avoid frustration by not applying for positions unless your qualifications and the position are an obvious match.

Many organizations are now accepting or asking for resumes to be sent electronically to save time and to create electronic files of applicants. Be sure your software system will send your resume in an attractive format. Instructors and students at some universities have reported that organizations have requested all applicant files be sent on CD-ROMs. Paper files are unacceptable. On the other hand, many organizations are being inundated with hundreds of e-resumes from unqualified applicants and those failing to state the specific position for which they are applying. They find such resumes to be sloppy, impersonal, and mass-mailed rather than customized for a particular position with a particular organization. Often they include attachments that are difficult to open or read. Unless told to do otherwise, include a cover letter that clearly identifies the position you are applying for and stresses how you are a good fit. Always bring copies of your cover letters and resumes to the interview so they are available if requested.

Online Resumes

As the Internet became more and more a part of our everyday lives, it was inevitable that organizations and entrepreneurs would create online sites for posting resumes and seeking positions. The advantages are that it is easy and you have the potential of reaching a wide variety of potential employers in many career fields worldwide. Here are a few of the common online resume posting services:

Monster Jobs—Get Work (http://www.monster.com)

Resumes Online: Posting Your Resume (http://www.jobsearchtech.about.com)

Post Resume Online (http://www.languagejobs.org)

Resume Posting Services (http://www.jobsearchabout.com)

The Job Bank (http://www.jobbank.com)

Use online services with caution.

Unfortunately, the ease of posting resumes online has made applicants easy prey for unscrupulous Web searchers who act as fake employers to take your money and your identity. Heather Galler of Carnegie Mellon University has developed a computer program called "Identity Angel" that searches online job boards for what she calls the "holy trinity" of information thieves love to attain: name, address, and Social Security number. If it locates such information, it sends a warning to the potential target of online thieves and frauds.

Galler offers these suggestions:[23] First, read the privacy policy carefully to determine how long your resume will be active and how you can delete it. "If there's no privacy policy, forget it." Second, be aware of fake recruiters, particularly if they ask for a drivers license or other personal information under the pretense of needing this for background checks. Ask the "recruiter" for references and check to see if they are members of local or national recruiter's associations. Third, set up an alternative e-mail address, use a cell phone, and provide a P.O. box as your address for job hunting. Fourth, if you want to see if your personal information is online, type in your name and the last four digits of your Social Security number. By providing more information, you may outsmart yourself because thieves can use spyware to get more of your personal information.

The Portfolio

Your portfolio shows you in action.

Portfolios are essential if you are in fields such as photography, advertising, public relations, art and design, journalism, architecture, teaching, and professional writing. Your **portfolio** should be a small yet varied collection of your best work. Organize your portfolio thematically. Make it visually attractive. Have excellent copies of your work—not faded, soiled, marked-up, or wrinkled samples. Employers want to see how well you write, design, photograph, edit, and create, and the well-designed and presented portfolio is the best means of doing this.

If you are going into broadcasting, your portfolio is likely to be an audio or videotape of selections that illustrate your best oral and video work. Quality, not quantity, is what sells. The portfolio is an ideal way to exhibit your skills and experiences.

Some colleges and universities are encouraging or requiring students to create electronic portfolios that can include a wide variety of materials in an attractive, compact, and highly usable package. In addition to revealing what a candidate has done and can do, the e-portfolio demonstrates knowledge of and ability to apply new technologies.

The Cover Letter

The all-purpose form letter is rarely taken seriously.

Your **cover letter** may open the employment door by showing *interest* in the position, the organization, and its products or services. Make the recruiter want to read your resume by making a pleasant and professional impression.

Send an *original* cover letter along with each resume to any lead that might prove fruitful. Form cover letters or ones aimed at a number of positions impress no one. You must tailor letters to each position and organization.

Whenever possible, address your letter to a *specific person* who will be actively involved in the selection process. "To whom it may concern" letters rarely get responses. Sending a letter to a person uninvolved in recruiting will, at best, delay reaching the correct person. Be sure your letter has the correct and complete address.

Design and target letters to specific positions and organizations.

The letter should be brief, usually three or four paragraphs, and never more than one page. Figures 8.6 and 8.7 illustrate typical cover letters. As with the resume, the cover letter must be neat, be printed on bond paper, have at least one-inch margins, be phrased in the employer's language, and look professional with no typos, misspellings, grammatical errors, or punctuation errors.

Specify the position in which you are interested and why. Reveal how you discovered the opening and what you know about the organization. Explain how your

Figure 8.6 *Sample cover letter*

3379 North Cumberland Avenue
Athens, GA 30601
January 14, 2008

Ms. Elizabeth George
The Westin Peachtree Plaza
Atlanta, Georgia 30343

Dear Ms. George,

Professor John Williams at the University of Georgia has informed me that the Westin Peachtree Plaza will soon be hiring managers for its expanded convention and resort programs. I have attended several conferences held at the Peachtree and have always been impressed with its facilities, services, and staff. Since my career goal is to manage convention and resort facilities at a major hotel, I am very interested in the possibility of interviewing for a position with you.

My academic program in Hotel, Institutional Management at the University of Georgia has given me a firm foundation in labor-management relations, marketing, property management, computer systems, and communication. This background will enable me to work effectively with employees, guests, the public, and organizations interested in holding conventions at the Westin Peachtree Plaza. In addition, my summer internship at the Hyatt-Regency in Louisville and the Opryland Hotel in Nashville have provided me with experiences in managing conventions, customer relations, and the operations of large hotels.

I would thoroughly enjoy an opportunity to talk with you about how my training and experiences have prepared me for a position with the Westin Peachtree Plaza. Since Athens is only a short drive from Atlanta, I could come for an interview at your convenience.

I look forward to hearing from you.

Sincerely,

Diana Johnson

Enclosure: resume

Figure 8.7 *Sample cover letter*

321 Ferguson Road
Santa Clara, CA 95052
September 21, 2008

Mr. Lou Gaffney
Motorola Energy Products Division
4412 Industrial Avenue
Mundelein, IL 60019

Dear Mr. Gaffney:

I am writing in response to your advertisement in *The Wall Street Journal* for an industrial engineer with 3–5 years of experience and a background in sonic welding.

It is my understanding that the Energy Division is a spin-off division of the Cellular Phone Division and supplies batteries for that division.

My B.S. degree is in industrial engineering from the University of California at Los Angeles (UCLA). I have spent the last three years working at Mattel Toys providing engineering support for their mini-toy division (matchbox cars), which uses Unitek Sonic Welders.

I look forward to discussing the opportunity that this position affords someone with my qualifications and experiences. Please feel free to contact me at my home telephone number because my answering machine is on 24 hours a day.

Sincerely,

Robert J. Jeffries

Enclosure: resume

education and training, experiences, organizational memberships, and activities make you an ideal fit with the applicant profile. You can refer to your resume, but do not merely repeat it. The goal is to persuade the recruiter that you are well suited for *this position* with *this organization* at *this time*.

Show interest and enthusiasm or do not apply.

Emphasize your *interest* in and *enthusiasm* for this position with this organization. Show that you have researched both thoroughly. If you reveal that you know little about the position or organization or communicate lack of interest, your application is dead upon arrival.

Close the cover letter by restating your interest in the position and organization. Ask for an interview and state when you might be available for an interview. If, for instance, you will be in the Salt Lake City area where the organization is located during the third week of April, state your willingness to meet with them at that time.

If a position is listed on a Web site or in a newspaper or journal, use the ad's language. Do not merely repeat the words but show you fit the requirements. Use the cover letter to sell the skills, abilities, and experiences you possess that make you a good match for the position. Be positive and to the point.

Personal Web Sites, Pages, and Blogs

Many applicants, like potential employers, create Web sites for personal use and as a supplement to the standard resume and portfolio. These can be effective means of selling you and your potential if they are done carefully and you follow the guidelines offered in this chapter and elsewhere for creating your credentials. Most of you will prepare these with care to present a professional and mature image and to show your creative, technical, and writing abilities.

Your private notes and thoughts are public.

The most potentially dangerous sites to you as an applicant are the highly popular social networking sites such as Facebook, MySpace, TagWorld, Bebo, Blogger, Flickr, Friendster, Orkut, Linkedin, Ryze, and Monster. A great many college students and others, often with humorous and personal intent (a diary to share with family or friends), include pictures of themselves drinking excessively or in sexually explicit poses, profanity, stories of sexual escapades and drunken parties, and threats that may impress someone of their age but not potential employers. Many blog users may feel that these "social" sites are safe, private, easy to delete, irrelevant to their professional lives, and unknown to potential employers. The sites are part of their own world.[24] **Wrong!**

Virtually anyone can access your blog site with a little effort and discover your personal life and, once discovered, it becomes public knowledge and impressions. Students have been suspended, expelled, refused admission to graduate school, and dropped as hot job prospects because of what they included in their sites and blogs. Interested parties can access your site even after you have attempted to delete it. One source warns that, "The Web may seem ephemeral, but what you casually post one night might just last a digital eternity."[25] Employers are concerned about how applicants will fit into their culture, perform maturely on the job, and present a positive image in the organization, community, and field. Materials on your blog may present a highly negative image to them and make you appear to be a questionable hire.

Recruiters are aware of and do check your sites.

Not long ago many recruiters and employers were unaware of blog sites. This is no longer the case. A study by Kimberly Shea and Jill Wesley of Purdue University's Center for Career Opportunities discovered that over a third of recruiters routinely run applicant names through search engines to discover what is "out there." Nearly half use some sort of technology to screen applicants. Some 75 percent of recruiters indicated that what they found did influence their decisions, 50 percent negatively.[26] In spite of these figures, over 50 percent of students believe recruiters do not check such sites as Facebook. A growing number of recruiters are employing college students and interns to search sites their peers use routinely. Shea and Wesley remind students that "You are responsible for your personal marketing campaign." They ask, "Would you be willing to share your Web site/blog/Facebook profile with your grandparents?"

Creating a Favorable First Impression

As you approach the interview, realize that your **attitudes** are a critical ingredient in your success or failure.[27] Be thoroughly prepared. Anxiety is heightened when you feel you do not know enough about the position or the organization, are unready to answer tough questions, and do not know what questions to ask. If you feel you are not going to do well in an interview, you won't.

Avoid self-fulfilling prophecies.

Approach the employment interview for what it is, a sales process, and you are the product. Know yourself thoroughly.[28] If you cannot sell you to you, how can you sell you to the recruiter? Be *positive* about yourself, current and past employers, associates, professors, and clients. Be professional and ethical throughout the interview. Never bad-mouth others or reveal confidences. One study revealed that good **first impressions** lead interviewers to show positive regard toward applicants, give important job information, sell the organization to them, and spend less time gathering information.[29]

If the interview will be over the telephone, avoid common "interruptions" such as flushing toilets, cleaning dishes, barking dogs, and answering e-mail messages.[30] Find a quiet place and give your full attention to the interview interaction. Avoid the cell phone if possible because the signal may fade and it's often difficult to hear clearly on cell phones.

Relationship of the Interview Parties

Know how and when to share control of the interview.

Assess the *relationship* that is likely to exist between you and the interviewer. How will control be shared? Degree of control is often determined by the job market and the organization's need to fill the position. *Successful applicants* dominate interviews but also know when to let the interviewer control the conversation. *Unsuccessful applicants* are submissive or try to dominate when the employer clearly wants to do so.

Do you want to take part in this interview? You may find it difficult to "get fired up" for an interview if you have been turned down a number of times during previous months or you are not really interested in this position or organization. For instance, you may be interviewing for a sales position only because you cannot get into management.

Understand and adapt to the relationship with the recruiter.

What degree of liking (mutual trust, respect, friendship) is there between you and the interviewer as revealed in previous encounters, telephone contacts, and letters? How similar are you to the interviewer in age, sex, race, ethnic group, background, education, and profession, and how might these similarities affect the interview positively and negatively? Research reveals that the same-race effect remains in selection interviews. Candidates racially similar to interviewers (black and white) receive higher interviewer ratings.[31]

Dress and Appearance

Dress for a formal business occasion.

Dress and *appearance* are critical elements in a favorable first impression. In a survey of college recruiters, 95 percent cited professional image as *important* and 61 percent as *very important*.[32] They see clothes and accessories as "making a strong visual statement" that suggests confidence and "gives the interviewee a competitive edge." While many companies are now promoting business casual at the workplace, 81 percent of respondents in this survey prefer formal business attire for formal interviews "to see how applicants would present themselves in a business meeting or presentation." Mary Dawne Arden, an executive coach and president of Arden Associates in New York, states that "No one can fault you for being too formal in an interview. But being sloppy, or even too casual, will kill your prospects."[33]

The following are five common mistakes men and women make.[34]

Men

1. Dirty and wrinkled clothes that do not fit properly.
2. Shirts that are too tight at the collar or around the waist.
3. Dirty hands, nails, or hair.
4. Shoes wrong color for clothes or dirty and scuffed.
5. Wrong style for body shape.

Women

1. Too much or inappropriate jewelry.
2. Too much or too little makeup, particularly overpowering perfume.
3. Scuffed or inappropriate shoes.
4. Clothing inappropriate for the workplace.
5. Ill-fitting clothing.

Neatness costs nothing and pays dividends.

Your budget may limit the clothing you have to wear, but there is no excuse for dirty hands, nails, and hair or rumpled, dirty, and inappropriate attire. Be sure you hair is neatly combed or brushed and trimmed. Beards and mustaches are generally acceptable but should be neat and trimmed. There are many printed sources and Web sites that offer tips on dressing for success, including www.menswearhouse.com, www.quintcareers.com/dress_for_success.html, and www.collegegrad.com/book/15-5.shtml.[35]

Advice for Men

Be on the conservative side in dress and appearance.

Standard interviewing apparel for men is a dark suit (blue, gray, black, charcoal) with a white or pastel solid shirt and a contrasting but not "wild" tie. The rule of thumb is to wear conservative, professional, and formal apparel to the interview, even if the interviewer (who has a job by the way) may be dressed informally.

Try the sit-down test to check for fit. Almost anyone can wear clothes that are a bit too tight when standing, but sitting down quickly reveals if the jacket, waistband, seat, or collar is too tight or the shirt gaps at the waist. Insert one finger into the collar of your shirt. If the collar is too tight, you need a larger shirt; if it is too loose, you need a smaller shirt to avoid the sloppy look of a drooping collar.

Coordinate colors carefully.

Be sure shoes are clean and polished. Wear dark socks that complement your suit and cover at least half a leg so when you sit down and cross your legs, no skin is visible. Tie size and age depend upon what is in style, but it is always safe to wear a wide stripe, polka dot, or conservative pattern tie that is blue, red, gray, or burgundy.

When in doubt, ask for help.

Men also need to choose clothing that is appropriate for their body shapes: regular, thin or slender, heavy or muscular, and tall or short. For example, a heavy, muscular male should not wear large plaids, thick stripes, or bright colors. Better choices are dark shades with pinstripes. For less formal settings, such as dinner during the interviewing process, you might wear a blue blazer with light gray or tan slacks. A thin or slender male may wear a greater variety of clothing, and some plaids might add size and depth to the physical appearance.

Jewelry for men should be minimal and professional. A gold or silver watch, rather than a plastic one, and a gold or silver ballpoint or fountain pen, rather than plastic, are more impressive. One or more earrings may negatively affect some interviewers but, if earrings are important to you, you may want to take the risk.

Advice for Women

Appearance should not call attention to itself.

Makeup, hairstyle, and clothing are personal decisions that reveal a great deal about your personality—who you are, your self-concept, and what you think of others. Take them seriously. No makeup is probably too little, but if makeup calls attention to itself, it is too much. Recruiters suggest small (not dangling) earrings with one per ear, one ring per hand, and no bracelets. Coloring is essential, and a cosmetic counselor can help determine what is professionally appropriate for you.

Select a business suit or jacket with a skirt rather than slacks. Pantsuits are generally acceptable, but it would be wise to ask the prospective employer if a pantsuit is appropriate before wearing one to a formal interview. A conservative jacket that is not too informal and an appropriate length skirt give a professional rather than a casual appearance. Wear a conservative blouse that matches the suit. Low, comfortable pumps are more appropriate than high heels or flats.

Provocative clothing can end your candidacy.

Try the sit-down and one-finger-in-the-collar tests recommended for men. Avoid "see through" blouses or ones with plunging necklines. Avoid short skirts and ones with long slits. If you must tug at your skirt when you sit down, it is too short. Wear clear or plain color stockings appropriate for your outfit. In all matters of clothing, be neat, clean, comfortable, and professional.

Nonverbal Communication

Nonverbal communication, such as voice, eye contact, gestures, and posture, are important ingredients throughout selection interviews.[36] Scott Reeves reports a typical example in which an applicant looked very strong on paper but "offered a dead-fish handshake, slouched and fidgeted in his chair, failed to make eye contact with the interviewer and mumbled responses to basic questions." He was not hired.[37] Arden cites a study that found "a first impression is based on 7% spoken words, 38% tone of voice and 55% body language."[38] Interviewers react more favorably toward applicants and rate them higher if they smile, have expressive facial expressions, maintain eye contact, and have clear, forceful voices. Although technology plays important roles in the employment process, recruiters continue to interview applicants because they prefer "high touch" to "high tech" when selecting people who will join and influence the futures of their organizations. They want to see, hear, and observe them in action.

Be alive and dynamic.

Dynamism and energy level are communicated through the way you shake hands, sit, walk, stand, gesture, and move your body. Use a firm but not crushing handshake. Try to appear (and be) calm and relaxed, but sharp and in control. Avoid nervous gestures, fidgets, movements, and playing with pens or objects on the interviewer's desk. Respond crisply and confidently but with no sign of arrogance. When replying to questions, maintain eye contact with the recruiter. If there are two or more recruiters in the room, glance at the others when answering a question but focus primarily on the questioner, particularly as you complete your answer.

Good communication skills are important in all positions.

Speak in a normal conversational tone with vocal variety that exhibits confidence and interpersonal skills. Interviewers prefer standard or prestigious accents. If English is your second language or you have an accent developed since birth, work on your accent and pronunciation so interviewers can understand you clearly and effectively. Realize that the interviewer may be wondering how the organization's staff, clients, customers, or others will be able to understand you if hired.

Do not hesitate to pause before answering difficult critical incident and hypothetical questions, but be aware that frequent pauses may make you appear hesitant, unprepared, or "slow." Interviewers interpret pauses of one second or less as signs of ambition, self-confidence, organization, and intelligence.

Arrival and Opening

Arrive for the interview a few minutes ahead of time. If you cannot be on time for the interview, will you be on time for work? Is this a sign of the importance you place on this interview? Do not arrive too early. The employer may have other tasks to perform or interviews to conduct and does not want to assign staff to entertain you until the scheduled interview time. Be courteous to everyone you meet.

Be on time and ready to interact.

Greet the employer pleasantly and dynamically. Do not use the interviewer's first name unless invited to do so. Sit when asked to do so and never sit down before the interviewer does. Be an active participant during the opening, avoiding a string of yes and no answers. You will become more relaxed once you get into the flow of the interview, so respond to opening, ice-breaker questions as you would in any normal conversation. How you handle yourself during the first few minutes with a stranger tells the interviewer a great deal about your interpersonal communication and people skills.

Answering Questions

Decisions are made on the total interview.

Although dress, appearance, and nonverbal communication are important ingredients in the selection process, do not overestimate their importance. A number of studies suggest that the final decision is most often based on a combination of verbal and nonverbal impressions, with a combination of interviewing skills, background, and experiences accounting for most successful searches.[39]

Preparing to Respond

Be ready and eager to answer questions effectively. Nervousness is natural and will disappear if you concentrate on answering questions confidently and thoroughly. All successful applicants are prepared to handle frequently asked questions such as:[40]

Be ready to handle traditional questions.

- Tell me about yourself.
- Why do you want to work for us?
- What are your greatest strengths? Weaknesses?
- What are your short-range career goals? Long-range goals?
- Why did you leave your position with __________?
- What did you like best in your position at __________? Like least?

- Why should we select you over the other applicants for this position?
- What do you know about our organization?
- Tell me about your experiences in working on teams.
- What do you do when you're not studying?

These traditional questions continue to play major roles in selection interviews, particularly during the opening minutes. Interviewers use them to get applicants talking and to learn about them as human beings and budding professionals.

As we discussed in Chapter 7, however, the nature of questioning in employment interviews has changed. Interviewers are asking more challenging questions about your experiences in specific situations (behavior-based questions) and placing applicants in **joblike situations** to see how they might fit in and function as employees. The philosophy is simple: employers can determine best how applicants might operate in specific positions by placing them in these positions during the interview process. Task-oriented questions assess thinking and communication abilities and reveal how well you can operate in stressful or surprise situations. Here are common on-the-job question strategies:

Welcome on-the-job questions to show what you can do.

- *Behavior-based questions:*

  Tell me about a situation in which you had to deal with an angry client.

- *Current critical incident questions:*

  "We are facing a situation in which we . . . If you were on our team, what would you recommend we do to resolve this situation?"

- *Historical critical incident questions:*

  "Two years ago we had a conflict between . . . If you had been the supervisor in this situation, what would you have done?"

- *Hypothetical questions:*

  "Suppose you had a customer who claimed his computer hardware was damaged in shipment. How would you handle this?"

  "If we hired you and you saw one of our employees, perhaps a supervisor, doing something you considered unethical, what would you do?"

- *Task-oriented questions:*

  "Here's a sheet of paper. Write a policy statement for the assignment of overtime." Interviewers have been known to take out a ballpoint pen and say to an applicant not interviewing for a sales position, "Sell this to me."

- *Past experience questions:*

  "Tell me about a time when you have operated as part of a team to solve a vexing technical problem."

"Tell me about the most difficult decision you have ever had to make and how you went about making the decision."

Many employers are requiring would-be teachers to teach, salespersons to sell, engineers to engineer, managers to manage, and designers to design. Job simulations, role-playing, presentations, and day-long case studies challenge applicants to demonstrate their knowledge, skills, experiences, maturity, and integrity.

Responding: Successful Applicants

Listen, think, and then answer.

Successful applicants *listen* carefully to the *whole question* without interrupting or trying to second-guess the interviewer. They *think* before replying, and then give answers that are succinct, specific, and to the point of the question. Many applicants miss the mark of questions, such as in the following example:

1. **Recruiter:** Why would you like to work for Preston & Associates?
2. **Applicant:** I've been interested in advertising since a summer job I had with P.J. Cline after my freshman year. It's an exciting and ever-changing field.

This applicant emphasizes interest in the field of advertising, but does not address the question "Why Preston & Associates?"

Effective answers are long on substance and short on puffery.

Present carefully organized responses with clear arguments, relevant content, good grammar, and action verbs that show you are a doer. Be aware of common words and how to use them correctly. Michael Skube, who teaches journalism, discovered that these simple and common words stumped many college students: impetus, ramshackle, lucid, advocate, derelict, satire, brevity, novel, and afflicted vs. afflict.[41] He calls them "potholes in exchanges," and recruiters are turned off by them. Use professional jargon when appropriate. If you are short of actual work experiences, provide relevant illustrations from other experiences. If you are asked a question about working in teams, realize that the recruiter is likely to be listening to the pronouns you use. If you work well in teams, you will speak of *us* and *we;* if you work better alone, you will speak of I and me.[42]

Be honest. Any hint of dishonesty, insincerity, unethical behavior, or evasion is fatal. Do not reply with canned answers, prepared and rehearsed in advance to sound good. A skilled recruiter will see through your answer or destroy it with a single, well-placed probing question, such as:

1. **Recruiter:** Why are you interested in construction management?
2. **Applicant:** I believe it would be an exciting, stimulating, and rewarding career.
3. **Recruiter:** How would it be stimulating?
4. **Applicant:** Well, uh, it would be challenging with each project being different.
5. **Recruiter:** Tell me about these challenges.

Do not play act; act yourself.

Remember, there is *no correct answer* for each question. Five different recruiters asking the same question may be looking for somewhat different answers.

Be enthusiastic and dynamic. Be interested in the position and organization and show it. Speak positively about your experiences. Successful applicants demonstrate the characteristics of the interviewer's ideal applicant profile through communication skills, answers, and actions.

Accept responsibilities for past actions. Give *reasons,* not *excuses.* Blame yourself for mistakes, not others. Show in everything you do and say that you are a mature man or woman, not an immature boy or girl.

Good recruiters detect phoniness.

Answer questions thoroughly, but know when to stop talking. Knowing when enough is enough is particularly difficult during conference calls because you do not have the usual interviewer nonverbal cues (leaning forward, looking at notes, facial expressions, gestures) present in face-to-face interviews to tell you when to stop.

Successful applicants know when to follow up questions with questions. If you are asked a vague question or one you do not understand, paraphrase it in your own words or ask tactfully for clarification. Recruiters assume applicants understand questions unless they state otherwise.

Be informed before replying.

If you are asked a difficult critical incidents, hypothetical, task, or problem-solving question, think your answer through carefully and consider the ramifications of your response for you and the organization. For example, you might ask about organizational policies or legal constraints that have a bearing on the problem. Ask for additional details you need to know before framing a response. Ask what authority you would have in this situation. Asking for such information will impress the interviewer with your professionalism and understanding of organizational situations and caution about acting with haste. Ralston, Kirkwood, and Burant write that these behavioral questions require applicants to tell stories, and these stories are critical to successful interviews. They list a number of criteria for good stories.[43] Is the story internally consistent? Is the story consistent with the facts the recruiter holds to be true? Is the story relevant to the question asked and the applicant's claim? Does the story provide details that support the claim? How does the story and how it is told reflect the applicant's beliefs and values?

Responding: Unsuccessful Applicants

Unsuccessful applicants play passive, limited roles in openings and closings. They seem unable to identify with the needs and interests of the employer, partly because they know little about the position or organization. They appear uncertain about the kinds of positions they want and where they hope to be in 5 or 10 years. As a result they fail to show interest in and qualifications for the position and organization. In the end, they do not ask for the position.

Unsuccessful applicants seem evasive in answers and use less active, concrete, and positive language and technical jargon that would exhibit experiences and knowledge of the field and position. They give brief answers that indicate they are nonassertive. Their answers contain:

Poor applicants are passive and cautious.

- *Qualifiers* such as "perhaps" and "maybe."
- *Meaningless slang* such as "you know" and "know what I'm sayin."
- *Nonfluencies* such as "ummm" or "uhh."
- *Vagueness* such as "and stuff like that" or "and that sort of thing."

Too often unsuccessful applicants answer before thinking about what they are saying. For instance, when asked "Why should I hire you?" one applicant answered that he could be a great asset to the company softball team while another replied that he was bored watching TV.[44] Some applicants seem to volunteer interview ending comments. For example:[45]

- "Sorry for yawning, I usually sleep until my soap operas are on."
- "I am quitting my job because I hate to work hard."
- "My resume might make it look like I am a job hopper. But I want you to know that I never left any of those jobs voluntarily."

Think before making comments or answering questions, and then *word* each very carefully.

Avoid doing weird or impolite things during interviews. Here are a few examples that have happened during interviews and were immediate turnoffs.

- An applicant put his feet on the recruiter's desk.
- An applicant stretched out on the floor to fill out the application form.
- An applicant wore a Walkman and said she could multitask during the interview.
- An applicant said she had not had lunch and proceeded to eat a hamburger and fries during the interview.
- When a recruiter asked an applicant to tell him about his hobbies, the applicant stood up and danced around the office.
- An alarm clock went off in an applicant's briefcase. After he shut it off, he asked the recruiter to hurry with his questions because he had to leave for another interview.

You may not be guilty of such interview improprieties, but you may commit common ones. In a survey of 188 college recruiters, John Cunningham discovered a number of ways applicants can "slip up" during interviews.[46] Notice how they summarize (in a negative way) the suggestions presented in this chapter.

Know what not to do during interviews, and then do not do it.

1. Lacking in awareness about the company and position.
2. Showing no interest or enthusiasm.
3. Lying or telling the recruiter what you think he or she wants to hear.
4. Exhibiting poor communication skills.
5. Being too money oriented.
6. Having unclear or unrealistic goals.
7. Not having relevant experience.
8. Having no campus involvement.
9. Presenting a poor appearance.
10. Not having any questions to ask.

11. Exhibiting a bad attitude.
12. Being inflexible.
13. Arriving late for the interview.
14. Having poor listening skills.
15. Being arrogant or cocky.

Unlawful Questions

Do not be surprised by unlawful questions.

Many applicants, particularly women, are still asked unlawful questions even though federal and state laws have existed for decades and most organizations train employees to follow EEO guidelines when interviewing applicants. Violations range from mild infractions such as "What does your husband do?" to sexual harassment. Some are accidental during informal chatting with applicants and some are due to curiosity, tradition, lack of training, and ignorance of the laws.

Regardless of why recruiters may violate EEO laws and guidelines, unlawful (or as some prefer "inappropriate") questions pose serious dilemmas for applicants. If you answer an unlawful question honestly and directly, you may lose the position for an unlawful reason. If you refuse to answer an unlawful question (almost impossible to do graciously), you may lose a position because you appear to be uncooperative, evasive, or "one of those."

Review EEO laws and your rights.

Be prepared to answer unlawful questions *tactfully* and *effectively*. First, review the EEO laws and quiz in Chapter 7 so you can determine when a question is and is not unlawful.

Quiz #1—Which Questions Are Unlawful and Why?

For instance, if you were a female college student interviewing for a manager position with a restaurant-bar such as T.G.I. Friday's, Applebee's, or Texas Road House, which of these questions would be unlawful? Why would they be unlawful?

1. Would you be able to work on weekends?
2. How long would you expect to work for us?
3. When do you hope to graduate from Tech?
4. Tell me about your experiences at McDonald's.
5. Do you smoke?
6. Do you have a significant other?
7. Which religious holidays do you observe?
8. Have you ever committed a felony?
9. How would you handle a customer who insisted on smoking in a non-smoking area?
10. Do you have any medical conditions that might affect your work here?

Second, be aware of tricks recruiters use to get unlawful information without appearing to ask for it.[47] For example, a low-level clerk may ask you which health

Beware of recruiter tricks to get unlawful information.

insurance plan you would choose if hired, and your answer may reveal that you are married and have children, that you are a single parent, or that you have a serious medical problem. During lunch or dinner or a tour of the organization's facilities when you are least expecting and prepared for serious questions, an employer may address an unlawful area indirectly. For instance, an employer, perhaps a female, may probe into child care under the guise of talking about their own problems: "What a day! My daughter Emily woke up this morning with a fever, my husband is out of town, and I had an eight o'clock conference downtown. Do you ever have days like this?" You may begin to tell problems you have had with your children or family members and, in the process, reveal a great deal of irrelevant, unlawful, and perhaps damaging information without knowing it. Employers have learned how to get unlawful information through lawful questions. Instead of asking, "Do you have children?" an employer asks, "Is there any limit on your ability to work overtime (evenings, weekends, holidays)?" Others use coded questions and comments.

- "Our employees put a lot into their work" means "Older workers like you don't have much energy."
- "We have a very young staff" means "You won't fit in."
- "I'm sure your former company had its own corporate culture, just as we do here" means "Hispanics need not apply."
- "We are a very traditional company" means "We don't hire women beyond clerical staff."

Consider your needs and desires before responding.

Third, determine how important the position is for you. How much do you want and need it? Your primary goal is to get a good position, and if you are hired, you may be able to change organizational attitudes and recruiters' practices. You cannot do anything from the outside. If one or more questions are gross violations, consider not only refusing to answer the question but reporting the recruiter to his or her superior or to career center or employment agency authorities. If this person is typical of the organization or a person you would report to directly if hired, you might be wise to look elsewhere. If not, you may discount the problem or report your experience with a human resources manager once hired.[48]

Fourth, practice using a variety of answer tactics. For example, try a tactful *refusal* that is more than a simple "I will not answer that question because it is unlawful."

Be tactful!

1. **Interviewer:** How old are you?

   Interviewee: I don't think age is important if you are well qualified for a position.

2. **Interviewer:** Do you plan to have children?

   Interviewee: My plans to have a family will not interfere with my ability to perform the requirements of this position.

3. **Interviewer:** What do you do on Sunday mornings?

   Interviewee: If working on Sundays or weekends is a requirement of this position, I would prefer to discuss that after we determine whether or not I am the person you want for this position.

Use a *direct, brief* answer, hoping the interviewer will move on to relevant, lawful questions.

1. **Interviewer:** What does your wife do?

   Interviewee: She's a pharmacist.
2. **Interviewer:** Do you attend church regularly?

   Interviewee: Yes, I do.

Pose a *tactful inquiry* such as the following that skirts the question and attempts to guide the recruiter away from the unlawful inquiry with a job-related question.

1. **Interviewer:** What does your husband do?

   Interviewee: He's in construction. Why do you ask?
2. **Interviewer:** You seem confined to a wheelchair; how might this affect your work performance?

   Interviewee: I am quite mobile in my chair. How is my disability relevant for a position as a computer software designer?
3. **Interviewer:** How do you normally vote in presidential elections?

   Interviewee: I always vote for the candidate that seems to be best qualified. How do you encourage your staff to get involved in community activities?

Try to *neutralize* the recruiter's obvious concern.

1. **Interviewer:** Do you plan on having a family?

   Interviewee: Yes, I do. I'm looking forward to the challenges of both family and career. I've observed many of my women professors and fellow workers handling both quite satisfactorily.
2. **Interviewer:** Who will take care of your children while you are at work?

   Interviewee: Our children will attend good day care centers and preschools until they are in the primary grades.
3. **Interviewer:** What happens if your husband gets transferred or needs to relocate?

   Interviewee: The same that would happen if I would get transferred or asked to relocate. We would discuss location moves that either of us might have to consider and make the best decision.

Make unlawful questions work for you.

Try to *take advantage* of the question to support your candidacy.

1. **Interviewer:** Where were you born?

   Interviewee: I am quite proud that my background is ___________ because it has helped me work effectively with people of diverse backgrounds.
2. **Interviewer:** How would you feel about working for a person younger than you?

   Interviewee: I have worked for and with people younger and older than I am. This has never posed a problem for me because I admire competence regardless of age.
3. **Interviewer:** Are you married?

Interviewee: Yes, I am, and I believe that is a plus. As you know, studies show that married employees are more stable and dependable than unmarried employees.

You might try what Bernice Sandler, an authority on discrimination in hiring, calls a **tongue-in-cheek test response** that sends an unmistakable signal to the recruiter that he or she has asked an unlawful question. This tactic must be accompanied by appropriate nonverbal signals to avoid offending the interviewer.

Be careful when being clever.

1. **Interviewer:** Who will take care of your children?

   Interviewee: (smiling, pleasant tone of voice) Is this a test to see if I can recognize an unlawful question in the selection process?

2. **Interviewer:** How long do you expect to work for us?

   Interviewee: (smiling, pleasant tone of voice) Is this a test to see how I might reply to an unlawful question?

Asking Questions

While applicants check lists of employer questions and mull over appropriate and effective answers, too few spend more than a few minutes planning questions *they* will ask. Most recruiters will give you an opportunity to ask questions and some may begin selection interviews with applicant questions.

Guidelines for Asking Questions

Asking good questions results in more than information.

Your questioning portion of the interview is a critical time not only to get information to help you make an important life decision but to reveal preparation, maturity, professionalism, interests, motivation, and values. You control this part of the interview, so make the most of it.

Ask insightful and mature questions.

A major and common mistake is not having any or having too few questions to ask. Your questions can help persuade the interviewer that you are an ideal person for this position and organization or destroy the favorable impression you made during the opening and while answering questions.

If you had a number of questions prepared when you arrived but the interviewer has answered all of them during the information-giving portion of the interview, resist the urge to ask a question just to ask a question. There is a good likelihood it will be a poor question.

Successful applicants ask probing questions.

Successful applicants tend to ask more questions than unsuccessful applicants. And the questions of successful applicants are open-ended and probe into the position, the organization, and the recruiter's opinions to get complete and insightful answers. Unsuccessful applicants ask closed questions and miscellaneous information questions, much of which is available in organizational literature or on the Web.

Review the guidelines presented in Chapter 3 for effective questions. There are some specific guidelines for employment questions.

- Avoid the "me . . . me . . . me . . ." syndrome in which all of your questions inquire as to what you will get, how much you will get, and when you will get it.

Ask your most important question first.

- Avoid questions about salary, promotion, vacation, and retirement during screening interviews and never pose them as your first questions.
- Do not waste time asking for information that is readily available in the organization's publications, on the Internet, or in the library.

Question Pitfalls

When asking questions, you are acting as a probing interviewer, and you may be prone to tumble into the common question pitfalls discussed in previous chapters: double-barreled, curious probe, leading, yes/no response, bipolar, guessing game, and open-to-closed switch.

Quiz #2—Applicant Questions and Common Question Pitfalls

Identify the pitfall(s) in each question below and rephrase it to make it a good question. Avoid a new pitfall in your revised question.

1. Do you encourage employees to find new ways to perform assigned tasks?
2. Tell me about your orientation and training programs.
3. Did you close your plant in Frankfort because of its age?
4. You reward innovative ideas, don't you?
5. Are you a progressive company?
6. Tell me about the new operation in Phoenix. Is it similar to the one in Portland?
7. When did you start with the company?
8. Do you pay on commission?
9. What are your future expansion and consolidation plans?
10. I assume you reward staff according to their performance.

In addition to common question pitfalls, applicants have some pitfalls of their own. These tend to be centered on common wording that can produce a negative impression at a critical time late in the employment interview.

Quiz #3—Applicant Pitfalls

Prepare a schedule to avoid question pitfalls.

Rephrase each bad question below to make it a good question.

1. *The have to question* may sound like you will be an unhappy and uncooperative employee.

   Bad: Would I have to travel much?
   Good:

2. *The typology question* focuses on type rather than explanation that is desired.

   Bad: What type of training program do you have?
   Good:

3. *The pleading question* (often a series of them) seems to beg for answers.

   Bad: Could you please tell me about your plans for the Des Moines facility?
   Good:

4. *The little bitty question* may indicate lack of interest in detailed information, perhaps asking a question merely to ask a question.

   Bad: Tell me a little bit about your operation in Cleveland.
   Good:

5. *The uninformed question* may exhibit lack of maturity or background study prior to the interview.

   Bad: Tell me about benefits and stuff like that.
   Good:

How you ask may be more important than what you ask.

Take the time to prepare a moderate schedule of questions in advance so you have questions phrased effectively and ordered according to importance. Do not place a critical question fifth or sixth on your list because you may not get the opportunity to ask five or six questions in a 20- to 25-minute interview, particularly if your questions are open-ended and you probe into answers.

Sample Applicant Questions

The following sample applicant questions show interest in the position and the organization, are not overly self-centered, and meet question guidelines:

Adapt your questions to each position and organization.

- Describe your ideal employee for me.
- Tell me about the culture of your organization.
- How does your organization encourage employees to come up with new ideas?
- How much choice would I have in selecting geographical location?
- What is a typical workday for this position?
- What is the possibility of flexible working hours?
- How does your organization evaluate employees?
- What characteristics are you looking for in applicants for this position?
- How might your organization support me if I wanted to pursue an MBA?
- How often would I be working as part of a team?
- What, in your estimation, is the most unique characteristic of your organization?
- How might an advanced degree affect my position in your organization?
- Tell me about where other persons who have held this position have advanced within the organization.
- What do you like most about working for this organization?
- Tell me about the merger with TelEx.
- I noticed in *The Wall Street Journal* last week that your stock has risen almost 4 percent during this economic downturn. What explains this increase?

- Tell me about the people I would be working with.
- Tell me about your training program.
- What major departmental changes do you anticipate during the next five years?
- What is the most important criterion for selecting a person for this position?

The following questions may help with a variety of positions in new and startup organizations:

- Which of your products are most in demand?
- Who are your major competitors?
- How much collective experience do your top officers have in the field?
- What are your plans for going public?
- Who are the major regulators of your business?

The Closing

Be aware of everything you say and do.

The closing stage of the employment interview is usually brief, rarely more than a few minutes. Do not say or do something that will detract from an impressive performance. Take an active part in the closing. Express your interest in the position and organization. And discover what will happen next and when and whom you should contact and how if you need to get in touch about the position.

There is a major rule for all interview closings, "It's not over 'til it's over." If any member of the organization walks you to the outer office, the elevator, or the parking lot, the interview is not over. If a person takes you on a tour of the organization or the area, it is not over. If a person takes you to lunch or dinner, it is not over. The employer is likely to note everything you do and say. Positions are lost because of the way applicants react during a tour, converse informally, meet other people, eat dinner, or handle alcoholic beverages.

Evaluation and Follow-Up

Assume that a second interview, plant trip, or offer might come in the near future. Write down notes about the information the recruiter provided and the answers to your questions. What do you know and what don't you know that would be important in making a decision? Make a list of the pros and cons of the position and the organization.[49] Talk about the situation with people who know you, the organization, and/or the career field. Do not make a hasty decision one way or the other.

Remember: the interview is more art than science.

Following each interview, do a thorough review with the goals of repeating strengths and eliminating weaknesses in future interviews.[50] Be careful not to overreact to your impressions and the interviewer's feedback. Your perceptions of what happened during an interview, how the interviewer reacted, or what nonverbal actions meant may be greatly exaggerated. Do not believe you can assign specific meanings to each verbal and nonverbal signal.

Ask questions such as the following during your post-interview evaluation:

Be thorough in your debriefing.

- How adequate was my preparation: background study, resume, cover letter?
- How effective was I during the opening?
- How appropriate were my dress and appearance?
- What opportunities to sell myself did I miss?
- How thorough and to the point were my answers?
- How well did I adapt my questions to this organization and position?
- How effectively did I show interest in this organization and position?
- Did I obtain enough information on this position and organization to make a good career decision?

Quality applicants write thank-you notes.

Be sure to follow up the interview with a brief, professional letter thanking the interviewer for the time given you. Some applicants believe erroneously that promptness is more important than content and fire off letters with little thought. For instance, Lisa Ryan, managing director for recruiting at Heyman Associates of New York, tells the story of walking a person to the elevator and finding an e-mail thank-you note waiting for her when she returned to her office moments later. The candidate had e-mailed her from the elevator. She recommends that "you want to put some substance into your thank-you note."[51] Emphasize your interest in this position and organization. The thank-you letter provides an excuse to contact the interviewer, keeps your name alive, and includes additional information that might help the organization decide in your favor. And, after all, it is the polite thing to do. Like your cover letter, be sure your word choice, grammar, spelling, and punctuation are excellent.

Handling Rejection

Every applicant will face rejection letters, even after they have felt an interview went well. Potential employers reject applicants for a variety of reasons, often because of fit or because another applicant has a valued experience or skill. They may interview dozens of people for a single position and must make difficult choices. Sometimes you will never hear from a company again and are left to wonder what happened and why.

Learn from rejections.

How you handle rejections may influence your attitudes, and these attitudes may lead to further rejections. One writer warns: "**Don't be a victim.** The worst thing tired and frustrated job seekers can do is to conclude that employer reps and hiring managers are out to get them, that the job search process is out of their control, and that they're the victims of some evil, monolithic power."[52] Avoid the attitude that you are perfect, so anyone who rejects you is stupid or evil.

Use each interview as part of the learning process. Ask what you might do differently in the next interview. How did you handle behavioral-based questions and critical incident questions? What was the nature of the questions you asked? How might you have prepared more thoroughly? What did you do that might have turned the recruiter off? Was this a position for which you were highly qualified, or was it a stretch?

Summary

Technology has allowed us to communicate instantly and to send and check information immediately. The scanning of resumes and the use of the Internet as sources for positions and resume storage are changing the face of searching for positions. Personality, integrity, and drug tests are adding a new dimension to the process.

We have become a part of the global economy and are undergoing a second industrial revolution moving from a manufacturing to a service- and information-oriented society. The best positions in the future will go to those who understand and are prepared for the selection process. You must know yourself, the position, and the organization in order to persuade an employer to select you from hundreds of other applicants. The job search must be extensive and rely more on networking and hard work than merely appearing at your college career center for an interview. Your resumes and cover letters must be thorough, professional, attractive, adapted to specific positions with specific organizations, and persuasive.

Interviewing skills are increasingly important because employers are looking for employees with communication, interpersonal, and people skills. You can exhibit these best during the interview. Take an active part in the opening, answer questions thoroughly and to the point, and ask carefully phrased questions about the position and the organization. Take an active part in the closing, and be sure the interviewer knows you want this position. Close on a high note.

Follow up the interview with a carefully crafted thank-you letter that expresses again your interest in this position and organization. And do an insightful post-interview evaluation that addresses strengths and weaknesses with future interviews in mind.

Key Terms and Concepts

The online learning center for this text features FLASHCARDS and CROSSWORD PUZZLES for studying based on these terms and concepts.

Appearance
Arrival
Attitudes
Career fairs
Career objective
Chronological format resume
Cover letter
Determinate interview
Electronically scanned
Fee-paid positions
First impression
Follow-up
Functional format resume
Honesty tests
Joblike situations
Networking
Network tree
Nonverbal communication
Percentage agencies
Placement agency
Portfolio
Relationship
Research
Resume
Screening interview
Self-analysis
Successful applicants
Universal attitudes
Universal skills
Unsuccessful applicants

An Employment Interview for Review and Analysis

This interview is between a senior in computer technology and a college recruiter for Software Specialties, Inc., a firm that creates computer software for the aircraft industry. SS has been growing rapidly as more sophisticated aircraft have come on line and security against terrorism has become a critical concern since 9/11.

How active and effective is the applicant during the opening? What image does the applicant present during the interview? How appropriate, thorough, to the point, and persuasive are the applicant's answers? Has the applicant done adequate homework? How persuasively does the applicant demonstrate an interest in and fit for the position as a production supervisor for SS? How well do the applicant's questions meet the criteria presented in this chapter? How active and effective is the applicant during the closing?

1. **Recruiter:** Good afternoon, Carolyn. (shaking hands) Please be seated.
2. **Applicant:** Thanks.
3. **Recruiter:** I hope you have had a chance to meet some of our people here at the computer science job fair.
4. **Applicant:** Yes, I have.
5. **Recruiter:** Good. And you've had an opportunity to look through some of our materials?
6. **Applicant:** Yes.
7. **Recruiter:** Good. I want to talk to you for about 20 to 25 minutes. Let me begin by asking why you chose computer science at Texas Tech.
8. **Applicant:** I've always been a Tech fan, and I wanted to go to a large university close to home.
9. **Recruiter:** And why computer technology?
10. **Applicant:** Well, during my freshman year, I realized that I was both hands-on and theory-oriented. The computer technology program is very hands-on. After taking some CS classes and talking to students and faculty, I decided to switch majors.
11. **Recruiter:** Describe what you would consider to be an ideal position for you.
12. **Applicant:** I guess it would be like my internship with Microsoft. It would give me an opportunity to work on interesting projects, do some troubleshooting, and stuff like that.
13. **Recruiter:** Tell me about the most difficult situation you have ever faced.
14. **Applicant:** It was when my father had a heart attack during my sophomore year.
15. **Recruiter:** How did you handle it?
16. **Applicant:** I leaned sort of on my mom and my older sisters.
17. **Recruiter:** And?
18. **Applicant:** Dad got better and we have been closer than ever.
19. **Recruiter:** How about geographical location?
20. **Applicant:** I like to travel and find people very friendly everywhere. Know what I mean?
21. **Recruiter:** What experience have you had working with teams?
22. **Applicant:** Quite a bit actually.
23. **Recruiter:** Tell me about some of these experiences.
24. **Applicant:** I was involved in teams and group work in most of my CT classes. And I worked with teams quite often during my internship.

25. **Recruiter:** Tell me about a difficult team project.

26. **Applicant:** Well, that was in a design class, and the group was not getting the job done. I had to step in and take charge by calling meetings, assigning specific tasks, and things like that.

27. **Recruiter:** And then?

28. **Applicant:** I managed to meet the deadline and get an A– on the project.

29. **Recruiter:** Why would you like to work for SS?

30. **Applicant:** Well, everything I have read indicates that you are one of the fastest growing computer software companies, and I'm really interested in developing software for aircraft and national security.

31. **Recruiter:** Anything else?

32. **Applicant:** Yes. You're located in the Northwest near some great ski resorts.

33. **Recruiter:** That's true. Why should we hire you for this position?

34. **Applicant:** Well, I have received an excellent education at Tech, and I think my experiences have prepared me for this job.

35. **Recruiter:** What do you know about SS?

36. **Applicant:** Not a great deal. You were originally started by Robert Cabrini. You went public in the early 90s and formed Software Specialties, Inc. You now have facilities in Oregon, Washington, and Nevada.

37. **Recruiter:** We have nearly 1,500 employees. We have facilities in the states you named and have plans for a facility near Boston. What questions do you have?

38. **Applicant:** What is the salary range for this position?

39. **Recruiter:** It would depend upon the location, but we are very competitive with the industry.

40. **Applicant:** Tell me a little bit about the stock-sharing plan mentioned in one of your brochures.

41. **Recruiter:** After you've been with us for six months, you are eligible to purchase stock in the company. We believe this is a good way for all of us to have a stake in what we do.

42. **Applicant:** Would I have to relocate very often?

43. **Recruiter:** Not really.

44. **Applicant:** Tell me about the culture of SS. Do you have a diverse research staff?

45. **Recruiter:** Yes we do. In fact, our research staff includes people from 12 different countries. Any other questions?

46. **Applicant:** None right now.

47. **Recruiter:** Good. We hope to make a decision in about two or three weeks. It's been good talking with you and getting acquainted.

48. **Applicant:** Thanks for the interview.

49. **Recruiter:** You're welcome. I'll be in touch.

Employment Role-Playing Cases

A Career in Computer Games Technology

You are a recent graduate with a degree in computer science and media technology and design. Although you are confined to a wheelchair because of a swimming accident while in high school, you have managed to get around a large university campus for four years and played in a wheelchair basketball league. Your interest is in computer games design and technology, and you are applying for a position that would require you to travel to a variety of locations in the United States and Japan to confer with other designers and check out technological developments.

Managing a Corporate Farm

You grew up on a 700-acre grain farm in eastern Kansas and will graduate this spring in the animal science department at Kansas State University. Since there is no opportunity to manage the family farm and your interests are in livestock rather than grain, you are interviewing recruiters for corporate farms. You have an appointment with a recruiter for Prairie Farms, a corporation that owns both grain and livestock farms through the Midwest and Southwest. The opening is for a manager of Bar Y farms in South Dakota that includes herds of beef cattle and bison. It is a major supplier for specialty steak restaurants in the Midwest, particularly Omaha, Kansas City, Minneapolis, and Chicago.

A New-Car Salesperson

You are in your late 20s and have worked for six years as a salesperson of women's clothing in a major department store. You have a very good record, and many of your customers seek you out for help with purchases. After becoming dissatisfied with your salary and no opportunity for advancement, you have decided to interview for a position as a new-car salesperson. You have an interview with the owner of a large dealership that includes Pontiac and BMW brands.

A Public Relations Position

You recently graduated from college with a major in general communication rather than a specialty because you weren't sure what you wanted to do. The position you are applying for is with a public relations and advertising agency. Its advertisement specified a degree and experience in public relations. While you only took one introduction to public relations course in college, you have worked with local politicians on their campaigns and with the intercollegiate communications office. You helped write press releases and organize events.

Student Activities

1. Contact 7 to 10 organizations and ask for their policies on hiring Baby Boomers and seniors over 60. Follow these up with brief interviews about their experiences with older workers, including advantages and disadvantages.

2. Visit your college career center to discover the services and materials they offer. How do they counsel students who are trying to determine careers they might be interested in and qualified for? How can they help you arrange and prepare for interviews?
3. Take the Myers-Briggs Personality Indicator. How do the results compare to your self-perceptions. How might these results help determine career paths and positions?
4. Experience not only is a good teacher but is critical in attracting top organizations in your field. Select five organizations and check their Web sites for internship possibilities. If they address internship possibilities, what information do they provide? How qualified are you for them?

Notes

1. Lancaster and Stillman, "Where Jobs Are," *BusinessWeek*, March 22, 2004, pp. 36–37.
2. Lois Einhorn, *Interviewing . . . A Job in Itself* (Bloomington, IN: The Career Center, 1977), pp. 3–5; Charles J. Stewart, *Interviewing Principles and Practices: Applications and Exercises* (Dubuque, IA: Kendall/Hunt, 2003), pp. 105–108.
3. J. Craig Honaman, "Differentiating Yourself in the Job Market," *Healthcare Executive,* July–August 2003, p. 66.
4. Reid Goldsborough, "Job Hunting on the Internet," *Link-Up,* November–December 2000, p. 23.
5. Lindsey Gerdes, "50 Places to Launch a Career," *BusinessWeek,* September 18, 2006, p. 64.
6. Chuck Paustian, "What's Not Said Makes a Difference," *Marketing News,* April 2001, p. 13.
7. "The Interview Expert's Web," *Canadian HR Reporter,* October 6, 2003, p. 20.
8. Rene Jackson, "Nailing the Interview," *Nursing Management,* October 2003, pp. 6–8.
9. Robert A. Martin, "Toward More Productive Interviewing," *Personnel Journal* 50 (1971), pp. 359–362.
10. Catherine Smith MacDermott, "Networking and Interviewing: An Art in Effective Communication," *Business Communication Quarterly,* December 1995, pp. 58–59.
11. Gerdes, p. 64.
12. For listings of Internet resources, see John R. Cunningham, *The Inside Scoop: Recruiters Tell College Students Their Secrets in the Job Search* (New York: McGraw-Hill, 1998), pp. 45–58; Michael Gowan, "Find the Right Job Online," *PC World,* February 2001, pp. 135–144; and Goldsborough.
13. Amber Palomares, "Employer Expectations of Students Attending Job Fairs," *Journal of Career Planning & Employment,* Winter 2000, pp. 20–23.
14. "Extra Touches Help Resume Dazzle," Lafayette, Indiana, *Journal and Courier,* May 21, 1995, p. C3.

15. Cunningham, p. 68. See also Kevin Hutchinson and Diane S. Brefka, "Personnel Administrators' Preferences for Resume Content: Ten Years After," *Business Communication Quarterly,* June 1997, pp. 67–75.

16. Robert Reardon, Janet Lenz, and Byron Folsom, "Employer Ratings of Student Participation in Non-Classroom-Based Activities: Findings from a Campus Survey," *Journal of Career Planning and Employment,* Summer 1998, pp. 37–39.

17. We wish to thank Rebecca Parker, Department of Communication, Western Illinois University, for assisting us with the sample chronological and functional resumes included in Figures 8.3 and 8.4.

18. Kris Frieswick, "Liar, Liar—Grapevine—Lying on Resumes," *CFO: Magazine for Senior Financial Executives,* http://www.findarticles.com, accessed October 2, 2006.

19. Scott Reeves, "The Truth About Lies," http://www.forbes.com, accessed October 2, 2006.

20. "Lying on Resumes: Why Some Can't Resist," *Dallas Morning News,* The Integrity Center, http://www.integctr.com, accessed October 2, 2006.

21. Reeves, "The Truth About Lies."

22. Reeves, "The Truth About Lies."

23. Annette Bruzzeze, "Online Resumes Can Trigger Identity Theft," *Journal & Courier* (Lafayette, Indiana), August 30, 2006, p. D3.

24. Justin Pope, "Colleges Add Net Behavior to Orientation," *Journal & Courier* (Lafayette, Indiana), August 3, 2006, p. A4.

25. Brad Stone, "Web of Risks," *Newsweek,* August 28, 2006, p. 77.

26. Kimberly Shea and Jill Wesley, "FaceBook, and Friendster, and Blogging—Oh My! Helping Students to Develop a Positive Internet Presence," Center for Career Opportunities, Purdue University, unpublished manuscript, 2006.

27. Benjamin Ellis, "The Four A's of the Successful Job Search," *Black Collegian,* October 2000, p. 50.

28. Shannon L. Hatfield, "Interviewing as a Sales Process," *Afp Exchange,* January–February 2002, pp. 66–67.

29. Thomas W. Dougherty, Daniel B. Turban, and John C. Callender, "Confirming First Impressions in the Employment Interview: A Field Study of Interviewer Behavior," *Journal of Applied Psychology* 79 (1994), pp. 659–665.

30. Sarah E. Needleman, "Four Tips for Acing Interviews by Phone," *The Wall Street Journal,* http://www.career;journal.com, accessed September 11, 2006.

31. Amelia J. Prewett-Livingston, Hubert S. Field, John G. Veres III, and Philip M. Lewis," Effects of Race on Interview Ratings in a Situational Panel Interview," *Journal of Applied Psychology* 81 (1996), pp. 178–186.

32. Karol A. D. Johansen and Markell Steele, "Keeping Up Appearances," *Journal of Career Planning & Employment,* Summer 1999, pp. 45–50.

33. Scott Reeves, "Is Your Body Betraying You in Job Interviews?" http://www.forbes.com, accessed October 20, 2006.

34. Richard J. Ilkka, "Applicant Appearance and Selection Decision Making: Revitalizing Employment Interview Education," *Business Communication Quarterly,* September 1995, pp. 11–18.

35. Thomas Pack, "How to Dress for Success," *Information Today,* December 2003, pp. 37–38; Alicia Griswold, "How to Dress the Part," *Adweek,* May 19, 2003, p. 37; Bill Leonard, "Casual Dress Policies Can Trip Up Applicants," *HR Magazine,* June 2001, pp. 33–35; "Dressing for the Job Interview," January 28, 2004, www.careerbuilder.com.

36. Ronald E. Riggio and Barbara Throckmorton, "The Relative Effects of Verbal and Nonverbal Behavior, Appearance, and Social Skills on Evaluations Made in Hiring Interviews," *Journal of Applied Psychology* 18 (1988), pp. 331–348; Lisa Frederiksen Bohannon, "Is Your Body Language on Your Side?" *Career World,* November–December 2000, pp. 21–23.

37. Reeves, "Is Your Body Betraying You in Job Interviews?"

38. Reeves, "Is Your Body Betraying You in Job Interviews?"

39. Ann Perry and Caren Goldberg, "Who Gets Hired: Interviewing Skills Are a Prehire Variable," *Journal of Career Planning & Employment,* Winter 1998, pp. 48–52.

40. Olivia Crosby, "Employment Interviewing: Seizing the Opportunity and the Job," *Occupational Outlook Quarterly,* Summer 2000, pp. 14–21.

41. Michael Skube, "College Students Lack Familiarity with Language, Ideas," *Journal & Courier* (Lafayette, Indiana), August 30, 2006, p. A5.

42. Julia King, "Looking for a New Job? Watch Your Behavior." *Computerworld,* May 12,1997, pp. 67–68.

43. Steven M. Ralston, William G. Kirkwood, and Patricia A. Burant, "Helping Interviewees Tell Their Stories," *Business Communication Quarterly,* September 2003, pp. 8–22.

44. "Why Should I Hire You?" *Afp Exchange,* November–December 2003, p. 8.

45. "Run That One by Me Again: You Did What at Your Last Job?" *Barron's,* January 13, 2003, p. 12.

46. Cunningham, p. 184.

47. William Poundstone, "Why Are Manhole Covers Round (and How to Deal with Other Trick Interview Questions)," *Business,* July 2003, p. 14.

48. Kris Maher, "The Jungle: Focus on Recruitment, Pay and Getting Ahead," *The Wall Street Journal,* January 26, 2003, p. B6.

49. Rebecca Ann Beach, "Interviewing 101," *Family Practice Management,* January 2001, pp. 38–41.

50. Mary Frances Lyons, "Post Interview Debriefing: What Hiring Organizations Say about You," *Physician Executive,* January–February 2001, pp. 69–72.

51. Kris Maher, "The Jungle: Focus on Recruitment, Pay and Getting Ahead," *The Wall Street Journal,* January 14, 2003, p. B10.

52. "Job Seekers, Take Heart—and Control," *BusinessWeek Online,* http://www .businessweek.com, accessed September 11, 2006.

Resources

Enelow, Wendy S., and Shelly Goldman. *Insider's Guide to Finding a Job*. Indianapolis, IN: JIST Works, 2005.

Kay, Andrea. *Life's a Bitch and Then You Change Jobs,* New York: Stewart, Tabori, and Charing, 2005.

Martin, Carole. *Perfect Phrases for the Perfect Interview*. New York: McGraw-Hill, 2005.

Wall, Janet E. *Jobseekers Online Goldmine*. Indianapolis, IN: JIST Works, 2006.

Yate, Martin. *Knock'Em Dead: The Ultimate Job Seekers Guide*. Adam, MA: Adam Media Corp., 2006.

CHAPTER 9 The Performance Interview

Assumptions about workers and work have changed.

The world of work has changed immensely since the mid-twentieth century when manufacturing dominated and brawn rather than brains prevailed. Pay and benefits were simple and straightforward, much like the work millions of employees performed in the office and on the plant floor. Performance expectations and measures were equally simple, often with union contracts stipulating each. Today the world of work is much different, and so is the performance review interview.

New Visions for New Organizations

Employee leadership and initiative are essential in the new world of work.

Peter Senge took Peter Drucker's **knowledge workers** and placed them within the **learning organization.** Employee leadership is necessary not only because of the elimination of layers of management but because of teams (many of them self-directed) and explosive technology needs, demands, and leaders.[1] Stephen Covey, Terrence Deal, John Kolter, and Jon Katzenbach have identified the qualities, skills, and abilities necessary to lead teams to peak performance.[2] Phrases such as "creating the high performance organization" and "high performance teams" have populated management literature for more than 20 years and summarize the performance expectations most organizations have for employees today.

Compensation has become more than salary and fringe benefits.

E-commerce has taken some old and previously reserved compensation methods and made them available to all employees, including stock options, bonuses, and profit sharing. For example, to reduce *cash-burn,* a new term for spending more and going into debt beyond generated income, employees in many dot-com companies are paid partly in stock. Compensation, measurement, and performance are tied to coaching and improved performance.[3] Each group, level, department team, and individual has metrics (measures) by which performance is gauged. Achievement of the organization's strategic goals and objectives is often the basis for compensation. It is a balanced scorecard approach.[4]

The **balanced scorecard approach** is best illustrated in Robert Kaplan and David Norton's book entitled *The Strategy-Focused Organization.* The basic framework from which the scorecard flows is seen in the Kaplan-Norton model in Figure 9.1.[5]

The goal is to achieve a balance among all facets of the organization.

With fewer management levels, increased competition, and rapid technological development that make changes in products and services nearly overwhelming, the use of separate programming structures in organizations no longer makes sense. The idea that a balance must be struck between an organization's performance, products, processes, customers, and finances at every level within the organization means that performance and its measurement are keys at every level and involve every process in the organization.

Figure 9.1 *The balanced scorecard as a strategic framework for action*

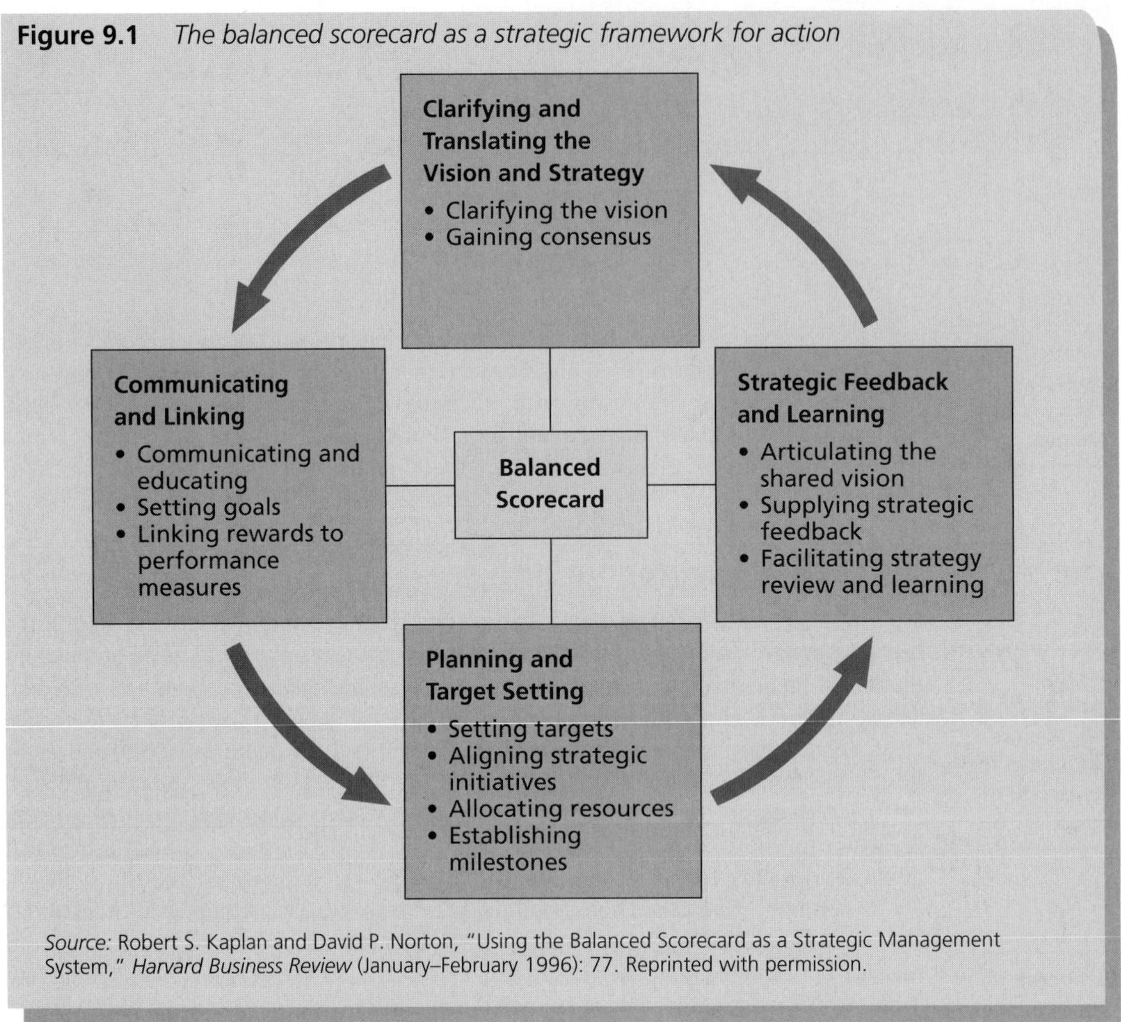

Source: Robert S. Kaplan and David P. Norton, "Using the Balanced Scorecard as a Strategic Management System," *Harvard Business Review* (January–February 1996): 77. Reprinted with permission.

An organization may take a number of paths to maintain this critical balance. Figure 9.2 portrays five paths to this balance presented in Katzenbach's book *Peak Performance*.[6] The Katzenbach model encompasses every kind of organization in today's world of work.

Performance is the key to new thinking.

The new philosophies do not signal that working 24/7 with your beeper and cell phone and laptop ready to receive e-mail has made work less demanding than under the managers of old. One realization has reverberated throughout organizations in both economic upturns and downturns: people's performance makes the difference. A senior executive from a major high-tech organization recently told one of the authors on the way to a speech before a large group of graduate students: "Today everyone has the same computers, technology, and buildings, so the major difference is people and their creative contribution. My job is to attract, develop, empower, and retain the best minds and creative spirits that I can find."

Figure 9.2 *Characteristics of the five balanced paths*

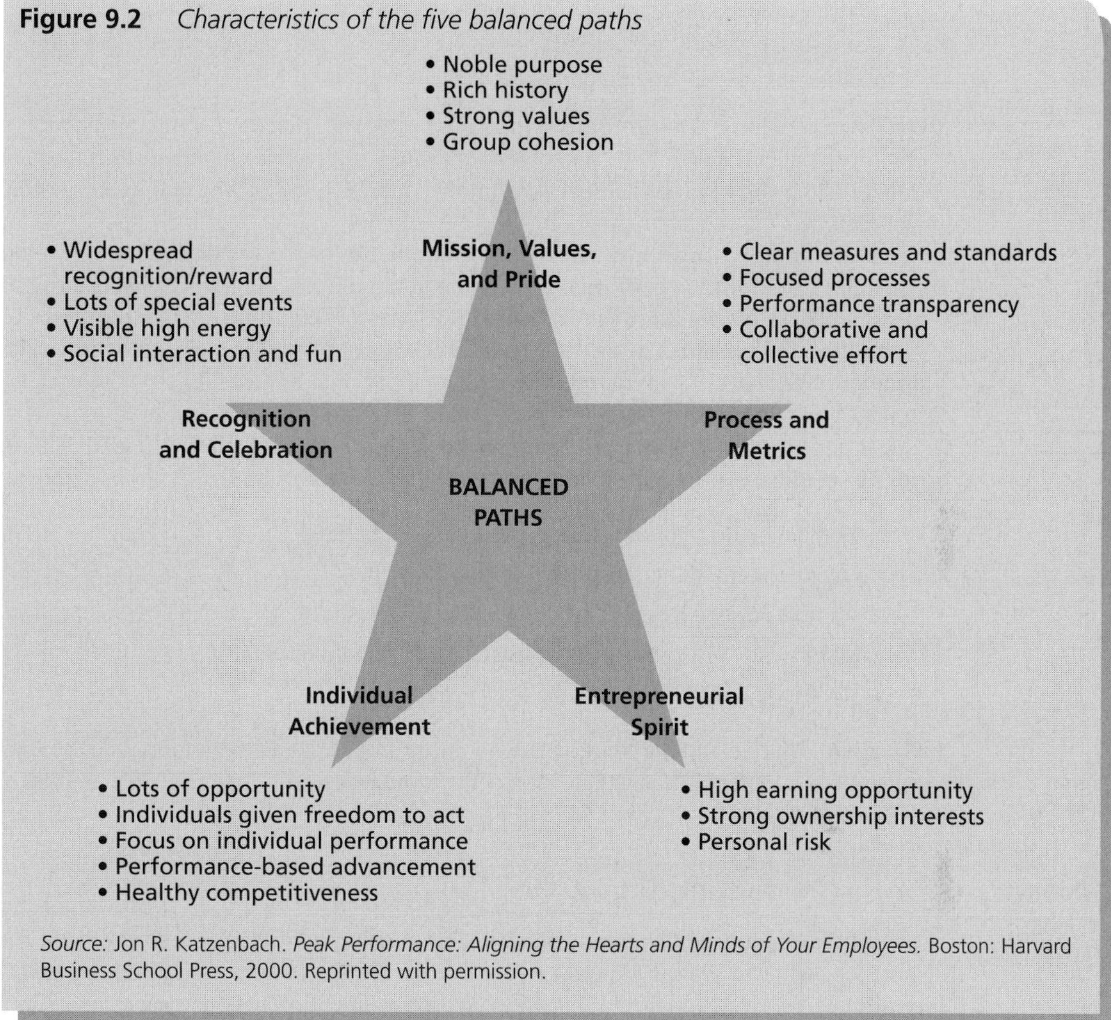

Source: Jon R. Katzenbach. *Peak Performance: Aligning the Hearts and Minds of Your Employees.* Boston: Harvard Business School Press, 2000. Reprinted with permission.

But how do you develop, empower, and retain these minds and creative spirits? A major focus is on the traditional performance review interview, what until a few years ago was called the "appraisal interview." It was highly *judgmental,* focused on the *past* rather than the future, was *tied directly* to salary, and was *boss controlled.*[7] It was a hated annual or semi-annual "tooth-pulling" that was dreaded by both parties.

Development rather than judgment is key to the performance review.

Along with a new vision for organizations and emphasis on development has come a new vision for the performance interview, what management consultant Garold L. Markle calls "catalytic coaching." He defines catalytic coaching as:

> A comprehensive, integrated performance management system built on a paradigm of development. Its purpose is to enable individuals to improve their production capabilities and rise to their potential, ultimately causing organizations to generate

> better business results. It features clearly defined infrastructure, methodology and skill sets. It assigns responsibility for career development to employees and establishes the boss as developmental coach.[8]

Catalytic coaching is future rather than past centered, places responsibility on the employee rather than the boss, and deals with salary indirectly. The manager is a coach rather than evaluator. Markle declares that this approach spells "the end of the performance review" as we have known it.

Later in this chapter, we will review a number of processes designed to develop employees and enhance performance, and the notion of coaching will be a centerpiece of each. These processes range from the old 1-page checklist with 5-point scales to group coaching sessions after each team process or event. The amount of time, the number of individuals involved, and the depth of data and feedback vary widely. Regardless, the employee review-development processes are aimed at improving individual performance. Former pro-football coach Don Shula and player Ken Blanchard offer a set of basic principles that appropriately spell out coach.[9]

- Conviction driven—Never compromise your beliefs.
- Overlearning—Practice until it's perfect.
- Audible ready—Respond predictably to performance.
- Consistency of leadership—Consistency in performance.
- Honesty based—Walk the talk.

What both Markle and the Shula-Blanchard duo emphasize is the importance of commitment to excellence, honesty, responsibility, and teamwork that result in a high level of performance.

Preparing for the Performance Interview

Use of teams, restructuring, and intense competition have heightened the need for more frequent and improved performance interviews, discussions, and coaching/development. A recent study found that frequent communication between supervisors and employees results in more favorable job-related performance ratings.[10]

Create a supportive climate that involves the interviewee.

Organizations are increasingly conducting various forms of performance interviews on a more frequent basis and are connecting them closely to developmental and coaching plans. Regardless of frequency or connections, however, employees prefer a **supportive climate** that includes mutual trust, well-defined job descriptions, subordinate input, and a planning and review process. They want to be treated sensitively by a supportive, nonjudgmental interviewer. Employees want to contribute to each aspect of the review, get credit for their ideas, know what to expect during the interview, have the ability to do what is expected, receive regular feedback, and be rewarded for a job well done.

Attack the problem, not the person.

As an interviewer, you can create a relaxed, positive, and supportive climate by continually monitoring the employee's progress, offering psychological support in the forms of praise and encouragement, helping to correct mistakes, and offering substantial feedback.[11] Base your review on performance, not on the individual. Provide performance-related information and measure performance against specific standards agreed upon during the previous review. Studies reveal that subordinates see supervisors as helpful, constructive, and willing to help them solve performance-related problems when these supervisors encourage them to express their ideas and feelings and to participate equally in performance review interviews.[12]

"Too seldom" is a common complaint.

Providing feedback on a regular basis, literally as a day-to-day responsibility, can avoid formal, once-a-year "tooth-pulling" reviews dreaded by both parties. Evaluate poor performance immediately before damage to the organization and the employee is irreparable. Avoid surprises during the interview caused by withholding criticisms until the formal review session. And be sure to conduct as many sessions as necessary to do the job right.

Training and effectiveness are inseparable.

Training interviewers is essential for successful reviews. Interviewers must know how to create a genuine dialogue with interviewees. Strive to be a good listener by not talking when the other wants to talk and by encouraging the employee to speak freely and openly.[13] Be an active listener who asks appropriate and tactful questions, not a passive listener who just lets the other party talk with little guidance or support. Playing the role of evaluator will reduce the two-way communication process and negatively affect a relationship that is critical to the review process. Subordinates perceive interviewers who have learned how to handle performance-related information, assign goals, and give feedback to be equitable, accurate, and clear during performance interviews.

Be careful of judging what you cannot measure.

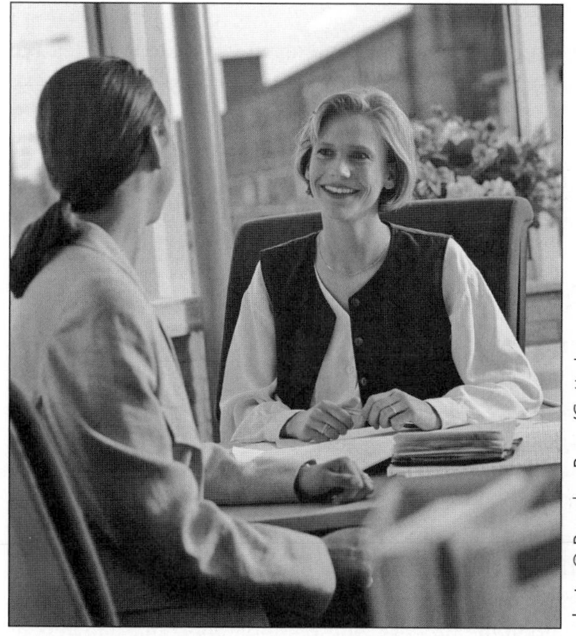

photo © Benelux Press/Getty Images

Supervisors at all levels have found it useful to talk periodically with each subordinate about personal and work-related issues.

Reviewing Rules, Laws, and Regulations

Each interview must be thoroughly researched and prepared. Begin by reading your organization's regulations and policies for reviewing employees performance. Then turn to laws, specifically Title VII of the 1964 Civil Rights Act as amended, and Equal Employment Opportunity Commission (EEOC) guidelines and interpretations. Be careful of assessing traits such as honesty, integrity, appearance, initiative, leadership, attitude, and loyalty that are difficult to judge objectively and fairly.

All aspects of the employment process, including hiring, promoting, transferring, training, and discharging, are covered by civil rights legislation and EEO guidelines. Laws do not require performance reviews, but ones conducted must be standardized in form and administration, measure work performance, and be applied equally to all employees. Compensation based on gender, race, age, or ethnic group is unlawful.

Changing demographics have led to changes in methods and assumptions.

The rapidly changing demographics of the workforce require a keen familiarity with EEO laws, the nature of the review interaction, and questionable assumptions that have governed organizational interactions for too long. Increasing numbers of the disabled, females, and minorities are entering the workforce. Review carefully the EEO laws outlined in Chapter 7.

Age will play an ever-greater role as baby boomers turn 50 and 60 in ever-greater numbers.

Goodall, Wilson, and Waagen warn that communication between "superiors" and "inferiors" in the review process leads to ritual forms of address "that are guided by commonly understood cultural and social stereotypes, traditional etiquette, and gender-specific rules."[14] If this is so, do not be surprised if performance interviewers violate EEO laws and guidelines. The American workforce is increasingly older, and some authorities predict that age discrimination will be the most prominent area of litigation in the twenty-first century. Contrary to popular assumptions, older workers perform better than younger workers.[15]

Selecting an Appropriate Review Model

To meet EEO guidelines and conduct fair and objective performance-centered interviews, theorists and organizations have developed a number of models during the past 20 years. All competency-based models establish competencies, set goals and expectations, monitor performance, and provide feedback.[16]

Person-Product-Service Model

The P-P-S model focuses on competencies.

According to the **person-product-service model,** managerial competencies lead to effective behaviors which then lead to effective performance. A competency may be a motive, trait, skill, aspect of self-image, social role, or body of knowledge that leads to effective performance. Supporters of this model argue that reviews of persons in terms of competencies have two major advantages: a single competency is manifest in several different actions and a manager's particular behavior is affected by several competencies.

Behaviorally Anchored Rating Scales (BARS) Model

The BARS model focuses on skills.

In the **behaviorally anchored rating scales** (BARS) model, skills essential to a specific job are identified through a job analysis, and standards are set, often with the aid of industrial engineers. Typical jobs for which behaviors have been identified and standards set include telephone survey takers (at so many telephone calls per hour), meter readers for utility companies (at so many meters per hour), and data entry staff or programmers (at so many lines of entry per hour). Job analysts identify specific skills and weigh their relative worth and usage. Each job has specific measurable skills that eliminate game-playing or subjective interpretation by interviewers.

Employees whose interviewers use BARS report high levels of review satisfaction, feel they have greater impact upon the process, and perceive their interviewers as supportive.[17] They know what skills they are expected to have, their relative worth to the organization, and how their performance will be measured. However, not every job has measurable or easily identifiable skills, and arguments often arise over when, how, and by whom specific standards are set. One study suggests that using the behaviorally anchored rating scale model results in more accurate performance ratings than does using a mixed standard scale model.[18]

Management by Objectives (MBO) Model

The **management by objectives** (MBO) model involves a manager and a subordinate in a mutual (50-50) setting of results-oriented goals rather than activities to be performed. Advocates of the MBO model contend that behaviorally based measures can:

The MBO model focuses on goals.

- Account for more job complexity.
- Be rated more directly to what the employee actually does.
- Minimize irrelevant factors not under the employee's control.
- Encompass cost-related measures.
- Be less ambiguous and subjective than person-based measures.
- Reduce employee role ambiguity by making clear what behaviors are required in a given job.
- Facilitate explicit performance feedback and goal setting by encouraging meaningful employer-employee discussions regarding the employee's strengths and weaknesses.

The MBO model applies four criteria to each position: quality, quantity, time, and cost.

The MBO model classifies all work in terms of four major elements: inputs, activities, outputs, and feedback.[19] Inputs include equipment, tools, materials, money, and staff needed to do the work. Activities refer to the actual work performed. Outputs are results, end products, dollars, reports prepared, or services rendered. Feedback refers to subsequent supervisor reaction (or lack of it) to the output. Figure 9.3 shows how the four major work elements interact. If you serve as a performance review interviewer using an MBO model, keep several principles in mind.

1. Always consider quality, quantity, time, and cost. Almost any job can be measured by these four criteria. The more of these criteria you use, the greater the chances that the measurement will be accurate. If you want to measure the effectiveness of a recruiter, for instance, you might count the number of interviews conducted by that recruiter per hire. By comparing the number of interviews per hire, you obtain the quality and quantity measure needed. You can calculate the cost in terms of time taken to fill a position, and measure quantity and quality by noting the number of people hired who received outstanding performance ratings.
2. State results in terms of ranges rather than absolutes. Whether you use minimum, maximum, or achievable, or five- or seven-point scales, allow for freedom of movement and adjustment. Do not try to fine-tune the performance measure at the start, but begin with a broad range you can adjust as the performance period continues.

Do not consider too many objectives.

3. Keep the number of objectives few and set a mutual environment. If you are measuring a year's performance with quarterly or semiannual reviews, measure no more than six to eight major or critical aspects of performance. Positions such as research or development may have only one objective. The agreed-upon objectives should cover about 70 percent of the work. Keep 30 percent in reserve to measure performance of assignments that come up unexpectedly.

Figure 9.3 *MBO performance appraisal model*

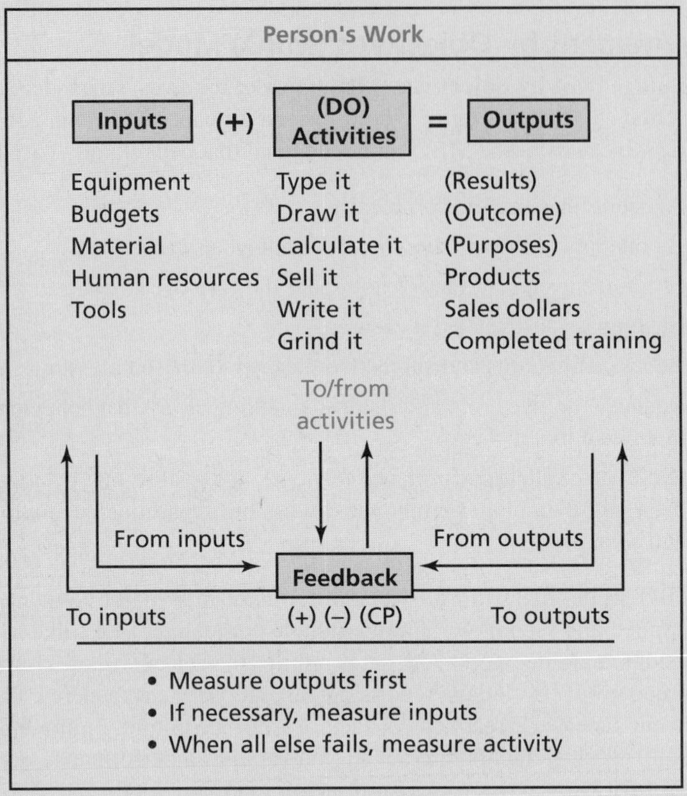

Beware of setting complex objectives.

4. Try for trade-offs between mutually exclusive aims and measures. An objective that is too complex may be self-defeating. For example, if you attempt to reduce labor and decrease cost at the same time, you may create more problems than you solve. Job performance is somewhat like performance in sports—when you concentrate on one aspect of the game, other parts may deteriorate.
5. When the value of the performance is abstract, initiate practices that make it measurable. Measuring may be difficult. In a legal department, you might measure performance in terms of the number of cases won or lost or in terms of dollars lost to the organization.

Anyone or anything that works can be measured.

6. If you cannot predict conditions on which performance success depends, use a floating or gliding goal. As one part of the target grows or moves, the other part does the same. This comparative measure works, for example, with production changes when people say, "You can't measure us because the production schedules change so often." Measure the amount produced versus the amount scheduled.

Universal Performance Interviewing Model

William Cash has developed and tested a **universal performance interviewing model** in more than 40 organizations. This model begins with four basic questions that are followed by six important words.

1. What is not being done that should be?
2. What expectations are not being met at what standard?
3. Could the person do it if he or she really wanted to?
4. Does the individual have the skills to perform as needed?

The UPI model focuses on performance and work requirements.

Too often personality clashes, prejudices, or politics result in unfair interviews that lead to termination. If an interviewer says "I do not like how she is doing . . ." or "I cannot put my finger on it, but he is just not doing . . . ," the four questions set up in columns on a blank piece of paper can serve as guidelines for fairness and comparisons of one employee to another. The interviewer must be able to specify what is missing or not being done well, such as "She does not fill out the customer complaint form when she is on the telephone and often leaves off the customer's number." This is feedback that can lead to change.

Understand why performance is lagging.

Narrow each problem to a coachable answer. Maybe no one has emphasized that getting 100 percent of customers' numbers at the beginning of calls is critical because the customer number drives the system and makes it easier to access billing or other pieces of information under that number. Perhaps the employee cannot type fast enough to enter the number. Maybe the employee knows the customer's number by heart and intends to place it in the correct position on the screen after the customer hangs up. The observation judgment dilemma has always been a problem for performance reviewers. A problem like the above may only require a quick reminder and not a lengthy discussion.

The four questions in conjunction with six key words shown in Figure 9.4 allow interviewers to make a number of observations about performance. This model can be employed with others (such as the popular 360-degree review process) or with separate observations by supervisors, peers, and customers (internal and external) that can be compared to one another for consistency, trends, and rater reliability.

Use UPI in conjunction with other models.

An 11-by-14 sheet of paper with the four questions in columns can provide the bases for quarterly or annual reviews or brief coaching sessions. Many organizations are eliminating the annual performance review and replacing it with a coaching process that takes place weekly for production workers and monthly for professionals. A summary session may be done quarterly with an annual review to set goals for the coming year, review progress, and look at developmental needs.[20]

Reviews must recognize excellence as well as problems.

Once you have answered the four basic questions, start on the model with *keep.* When an employee is doing something well, make sure the person knows you appreciate a job well done. Start with keep and then go to *stop,* followed by *start, less, more,* and finishing with a time frame for improving performance. The word *now* emphasizes the importance of making appropriate changes immediately. Performance problems do not resolve themselves. Define *now* in terms of weeks or perhaps months. Be specific.

Figure 9.4 *Six key words in the universal performance interviewing model*

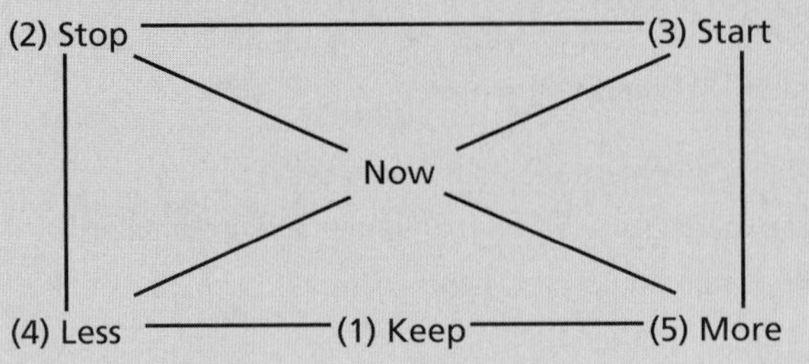

Play the role of coach rather than evaluator or disciplinarian.

The universal performance interviewing model enables you as coach to start with positive behavior you wish the employee to maintain, followed immediately by behaviors you wish corrected now. This begins the interview on a positive note. Your *stop* list should be the shortest and reserved for behaviors that are qualitatively and procedurally incorrect, place an employee at risk, or are destructive to others in the workplace.

The interviewer can present each of the four questions and the six words at different verbal and nonverbal levels, including hints, suggestions, and corrections. For example, the interviewer might say:

I want you to stop doing . . .	You must do more of . . .
You must stop doing . . .	You must do less of . . .
I want you to start doing . . .	You must do . . . now.

Many highly sophisticated systems spend too much time on the analytical end and little time on specific behavior to be altered and how. If you cannot provide a specific alternative behavior, there is no need for a performance review.

Don't turn a mole hill problem into a mountain.

Let's use the customer service representative mentioned earlier as an example. Assume that the representative knows many customer numbers because of the frequency of calls from them and has the numbers memorized. She thinks it is unnecessary to log each number into the system until she has finished discussing specific problems with customers. After all, she often has several lines ringing and wants to get to other customers as quickly as possible because of the four-ring objective—every incoming call must be answered within four rings. She is above average (4 on a 5-point scale). Use one of the following styles to present the problem without making it a bigger problem.

Hint and suggest before correcting.

- *Hint:* (smiling pleasantly) I noticed you were busy this morning when I stopped by to observe you. I just thought it might be easier for you to record each customer's number while the person is at the beginning of your conversation.
- *Suggestion:* (neutral facial expression and matter-of-fact vocal inflections) Just one little idea came to mind from my observation this morning. I'd like to see you try to record each customer's number early so it doesn't get lost in the shuffle of answers to other callers, and you won't forget to record it.

- *Correction:* (stern voice and face) Based on my observation this morning, you must be sure to record each customer's number before you do anything else on the system for that number. This number drives our entire system, and problems result when a number is not recorded immediately.

The purpose of every performance interview is to provide accurate feedback to the employee about what must be altered, changed, or eliminated and when. Most employees want to do a good job, and the performance mentor or coach must provide direction. Imagine if the following comments were made to our customer representative:

Think before commenting.

- **Interviewer:** (matter-of-fact face and voice) You need to get better on that system.
- **Interviewer:** (uncaring) I would like to see some improvement before I observe you again.
- **Interviewer:** (uncaring and angry) After my observation this morning, what do you think I found wrong with your performance?

What is the improvement hinted at or demanded? Such "feedback" neither identifies the problem nor provides suggestions for resolving the problem. The interviewee is likely to be confused and angry.

Vague comments and suggestions may harm relationships and fail to improve performance.

This brings us to another part of the model that is crucial in performance interviews. The two Ss are *specific* and *several* and are important in every review session. Performance interviews must not be guessing games. The two Ss enable interviewers to provide specific examples to show the problem is not a one-time incident but a trend.

Our three examples above violate both Ss because they are neither specific nor several. Example one does not reveal what or how much. This is why measurement—an established yardstick—of clearly established objectives is so important. Example two is similar to example one. And example three does nothing to improve performance and may retard an ongoing relationship. The two Ss are important because they indicate the severity and frequency of an error or behavior and whether a lengthy exploration or brief on-the-job adjustment is most appropriate.

Figure 9.5 includes all parts of the universal performance interviewing model. This model allows you to measure or observe on-the-job behavior and either compare it to goals or quickly correct the smallest error.

The 360-Degree Approach

The 360-degree approach involves multiple observers.

Richard Lipsinger and Anntoinette Lucia provide the most complete book on the **360-degree approach** to performance review.[21] The basic differences between the old check sheet followed by the annual review and the 360 degree are the number of people involved, the collection of data, and the use of data during the interview for improvement in performance.

Each firm employs a somewhat unique 360-degree process, questionnaires, and interview schedules, but we can describe the general tests used. The employee in question works with his or her supervisor to select a number of evaluators, such as a direct supervisor, staff at the same level as the employee, colleagues, and individuals from departments the employee interacts with on a regular basis. The performance review,

Figure 9.5 *The universal performance interviewing model*

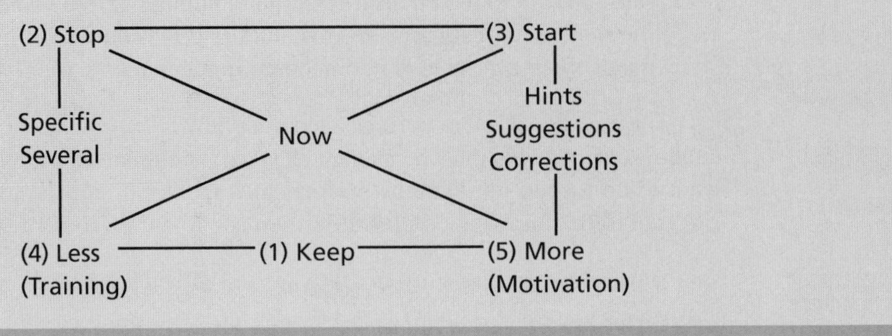

The interviewee plays a role in selecting evaluators.

The 360 approach uses a group feedback interview.

like employee selection, is becoming a group process that requires team and interpersonal skills. Questionnaires covering skills, knowledge, and style are sent to each of the evaluators. The completed questionnaires are summarized and, in some cases, scores are displayed on a spreadsheet. The manager selects individuals from the original group to serve as a panel to conduct a feedback interview. The interviewer/facilitator may take the raw data from the questionnaires and interview the evaluators. The employee receives the data in advance of the meeting. Each participant is asked to come with coaching or behavior change input. The purpose of the session is not to attack, blame, or hurt the employee but to provide objective, behavior-based feedback with suggestions where necessary for improvement. The employee may not need much improvement, so compliments are acceptable.

The interviewer/facilitator may ask the employee to start the meeting with reactions to the data. The interviewer/facilitator's role is to ask open questions with neutral probes. For example:

Employ open questions and probe into answers.

- Tell me about your responsibilities in SAP training.

  Tell me more.

  Explain it to me.

  Describe your frustrations with the consultants' training manual.
- If you were going to take on a similar project, what would you do more or less of?
- When you identified those people in __________________ department as "rockheads," what did you mean?

  How did they behave?

  What did they say?

  What did they do?

A plan for improvement is essential.

Once the feedback session is completed, the interviewer/facilitator and employee formulate a plan for improvement. This would probably be a person's direct supervisor. If not, the team would develop improvement goals and objectives.

The use of **multisource feedback** for employee development works best in organizations that use a goal-setting process from the top down.[22] Goal-setting, positive feedback from several perspectives, and a plan to improve make multisourcing a productive experience.[23] This approach has advantages and disadvantages, however.

Advantages

Be aware of pluses and minuses of each review model.

- The single process is useful for both improvement and development.
- Questionnaires and interviews provide objective data and the feedback needed for employee development.
- Raises and bonuses are not based on a single performance, so a poor supervisor will not prevent employee development.
- The employee has control over who gives feedback.
- The employee reads, hears, and discusses the data, so data are more than numbers on a form.
- The process provides documentation for dealing with performance problems.

Disadvantages

- It takes a great deal of time and training.
- It is costly.
- It may give more feedback than some people can handle.
- It may be seen as the employee's turn in the middle to be shot down.
- Follow-up coaching is necessary to assure that necessary change occurs.

Garold Markle writes that the 360-degree approach is highly inefficient because it is enormously time consuming on the part of both interviewer and interviewee and takes weeks or months in turnaround time. This delay may result in both parties forgetting what they had to say during the process. In spite of these problems, he recommends that it remain a part of the organization's review kit.[24]

Force Choice Distribution

The **force choice distribution method** is sometimes referred to as the *ABC method* or *GE approach.*[25] Large organizations have used it most often.

Force choice ranks employees into group by grades.

In its simplest form, employees are ranked into three or four groups according to the sales dollar, return of budget, or another clearly measurable goal. The top 5 to 20 percent receive an A that entitles them to a raise, bonus, or prize such as a car or trip. The next 20 to 30 percent receive a B that denies them a bonus but grants a raise that might equal the cost of living. The next 20 percent receive a C that places them on an improvement program. The bottom 5 to 15 percent are terminated. If a person receives two grades of C within a two-year period, the person is terminated.

Companies such as Ford, General Electric, Intel, Hewlett-Packard, and others listed among *Fortune*'s most admired companies have used variations of this performance review approach. For example, one year, Ford gave 20 percent As, 80 percent Bs, and

ON THE WEB

As you begin to think seriously about specific careers and organizations, investigate how organizations assess the performance of employees. Use the Internet to discover the types of performance review models used by employers in which you have a career interest. Access two types of resources. First, research employers through general resources such as Career Builder (http://www.careerbuilder.com), Monster-Trak (http://www.monstertrak.com/), and Monster (http://www.monster.com/). Second, check the Web sites of specific organizations such as Price Water-house (http://www.pw.com/mcs), Ford (http:// www.ford.com/), and Electronic Data Systems (http://www.eds.com).

Organizations use a variety of percentage systems.

10 percent Cs. The next year they gave only 5 percent Cs. GE employs 20 percent, 80 percent, and 10 percent categories. Hewlett-Packard and Microsoft use a 1–5 scale with 5 being the highest level. According to Jack Walsh, "Not removing the bottom 10% . . . is not only a management failure but false kindness as well."[26]

The movement toward clear measurements at all levels and in all job markets makes a force choice distribution method more acceptable.

Those arguing for this approach note that numbers don't lie; an employee can either do the job or not. They claim poor performers pull everyone down and are in either the wrong position or the wrong organization. If the competition maintains only the best, we must follow suit.

Weigh the advantages and disadvantages of the force choice model.

Those arguing against force choice approach claim it discriminates against older workers and blames workers for the failure of management. Numbers, they argue, do not measure attitudes, helpfulness to customers and colleagues, and effectiveness in teams. Many factors beyond the control of the employees may determine numbers, such as changes and assignment of territories, projects, budgets, and economic times. This system fosters an unhealthy climate of competition among employees.

Select the method best suited to your situation.

The authors do not recommend a particular performance review approach. You need to be aware of the nature and advantages of a variety of methods. Then you should select a method best suited to the goals of your organization, the type, or types, of work that is done, and the skills and competencies needed to achieve organizational goals.

Conducting the Performance Interview

Do your homework.

Regardless of the review model you select, you must do thorough homework. Study the employee's past record and most recent performance evaluation. Review the employee's self-evaluation. Understand the nature of the employee's position and work. Pay particular attention to the fit between the employee, the position, and the organization. Identify in advance the primary purpose of the interview, especially if it is one of several with an employee. Prepare possible questions and forms you will use pertaining to measurable goals.

Select and understand the perspective of the interview.

Know yourself and the employee as persons. For example, will you approach the interview from an appraisal or a developmental perspective? From an **appraisal perspective,** you see the interview as required and scheduled by the organization, superior-conducted and directed, top-down controlled, results-based, past-oriented, concerned with *what* rather than *how,* adversarial, and organizationally satisfying. By contrast, from a **developmental perspective,** the interview is initiated by individuals whenever needed, subordinate-conducted and directed, bottom-up controlled, skill-based, now- and future-oriented, concerned with *how,* cooperative, and self-satisfying.[27] We strongly urge you to select a developmental approach, Markle's "catalytic coaching," rather than an appraisal approach.

Relationship influences both parties and the nature of the interview.

Understand the relationship that is likely to exist between you and the employee. What is your relational history? Are you the best person for the interviewer role, or would the interviewee prefer someone else? How motivated is each party to take part in the process? How will control be shared? Research reveals that two or more employers often evaluate the same employee differently because their relationships differ.

Schedule the interview several days in advance so that both parties can prepare and the employee realizes it is not a spur-of-the-moment crisis or problem interview. Prepare a possible action plan to be implemented following the interview.

Opening the Interview

Climate and atmosphere are critical.

Put the interviewee at ease with a pleasant, friendly greeting. Get the person seated in an arrangement that is nonthreatening and not superior-subordinate. Fear of what performance interviews might yield "interferes with communication between interviewer and interviewee and keeps the review process from achieving its full potential."[28]

Be prepared but flexible in opening the interview.

Establish rapport by supporting the employee and engaging in a few minutes of small talk. Do not prolong this stage. Orient the employee by giving a brief outline of how you want to conduct the interview. If there is something the employee would rather talk about first, do so. An alteration of your interview plan is worth the improved communication climate. Encourage the employee not to wait for a turn or the correct moment to ask a question or bring up a topic but to participate actively throughout the interview.

Discussing Performance

Communication skills are critical to successful performance interviews. Be aware of your own nonverbal cues and observe those emanating from the interviewee. As noted in Chapter 2, it is often not so much *what* is said but *how* it is said. Listen carefully to the interviewee and adapt your listening approach to the changing needs of the interview, listening for comprehension when you need to understand, for evaluation when you must appraise, with empathy when you must show sensitivity and understanding, and for resolution when developing courses of action to enhance performance.

Use all of your listening skills.

"Be an active listener" is good advice and common sense, but Goodall, Wilson, and Waagen warn that interviewers must know *why* they are listening actively: "Motives may include a desire to exhibit efficient appraisal behavior, to show a concern for the interviewee's well-being, or to collect evidence of talk that may be used for or against the subordinate at a later date."[29] The first two are positive, but the third may be detrimental both to the interview and future interactions with the interviewee.

Feedback is central in performance interviews.

Maintain an atmosphere that ensures two-way communication beyond Level 1 by being sensitive, providing feedback and positive reinforcement, reflecting feelings, and exchanging information. Feedback may be your most important skill. Use a team of interviewers rather than a single interviewer. Research indicates that the panel approach produces higher judgment validation, better developmental action planning, greater compliance with EEO laws, more realistic promotion expectations, and reduced perception of favoritism.

Develop a true dialogue with the interviewee.

Make discussing performance an opportunity for full and open discussion between both parties aimed at improving individual and organizational performance. Keys to the success of the appraisal interview are your abilities to communicate information effectively and encourage open dialogue. Strive to be a counselor, coach, or partner in career management and development.

Discuss the interviewee's total performance, not just one event or a specific portion of the review period. Begin with areas of excellence so you can focus on the person's strengths. Strive for an objective, positive integration of work and results. Cover standards that are met and encourage the interviewee to identify strengths. Communicate factual, performance-related information and give specific examples.

Excessive and prolonged praise may create anxiety and distrust because employees not only expect but desire to discuss their performance weaknesses. An employee who receives no negative feedback or suggestions of ways to improve will not know which behavior to change. Discuss needed improvements in terms of specific expected behaviors in a constructive, nondirective, problem-solving manner. Employees are likely to know what they are not doing satisfactorily, but unlikely to know what they should do differently. Let the employee provide much of the input. Probe tactfully and sensitively for causes of problems.

Strive for a balance between praise and criticism.

Do not heap criticism upon the employee. The more you point out shortcomings, the more threatened, anxious, and defensive the employee will become. As the perceived threat grows, so will the person's negative attitude toward you and the review process. Where comments, suggestions, and criticisms are concerned, it is often not what is intended that counts but what the other party believes is intended. If a fault cannot be corrected by positive suggestions, do not mention it during the interview.

Know how to conduct performance interviews.

Terry Lowe identifies seven ways to ruin a performance review.[30] For instance, the **halo effect** comes about when an interviewer gives favorable ratings to all job duties when the interviewee excels in only one. The **pitchfork effect** leads to negative ratings for all facets of performance because of a particular trait the interviewer dislikes in others. The **central tendency** causes interviewers to refrain from assigning extreme ratings to facets of performance. The **recency error** occurs when an interviewer relies too heavily on the most recent events or performance levels. The length of service of an interviewee may lead the interviewer to assume that present performance is high because performance was high in the past. The **loose rater** is reluctant to point out weak areas and dwells on the average or better areas of performance. The **tight rater** believes that no one can perform at the necessary standards. And the **competitive rater** believes than no one can perform higher than his or her levels of performance.

Use question tools to gain and verify information.

Summarize the performance discussion and make sure that the employee has had ample opportunity to ask questions and make comments before establishing goals. Use reflective probes and mirror questions to verify information received and feedback given. Use clearinghouse questions to be sure the employee has no further concerns or comments.

Setting New Goals and a Plan of Action

Focus on the future and not the past.

Goal-setting is the key to successful performance reviews and should constitute 75 percent of the interview. Focus on future performance and career development rather than dwelling on the past. Be an advisor, supporter, and facilitator—a coach—rather than a judge. Hill writes that "Although it is important to evaluate on the basis of past performance, it is just as important to anticipate future growth, set goals, and establish career paths."[31]

Follow these guidelines when discussing and setting goals in performance review interviews.

The interviewee must be an active participant.

- Review the last period's goals before going on to new ones.
- Never intentionally or unintentionally impose goals.
- Avoid either/or statements, demands, and ultimatums.
- Make goals few in number, specific, well-defined, practical, and measurable.
- Feedback combined with clear goal-setting produces the highest employee satisfaction.
- Avoid ambiguous language in goals such as teamwork, cooperation, unity, and group effectiveness.
- Do not make the goals too easy or too difficult.
- Encourage the employee to suggest and agree on programs for improvement.
- Do not directly relate improved performance to salary increases.
- Decide upon follow-up procedures and how they will be implemented.
- Both employer and employee must be able to determine when goals have been accomplished and why.

Close with the perception that the interview has been valuable for both parties.

Closing the Interview

Do not rush the closing. Be sure the interviewee understands all that has transpired. Conclude on a note of trust and open communication. End with the feeling that this has been an important session for interviewee, interviewer, and the organization. If you have filled out a form such as the one in Figure 9.6, sign off the agreements. If organizational policy allows, permit interviewees to put notes by items they feel strongly about. Provide a copy of the signed form as a record of the plan for the coming performance period.

The Employee in the Performance Review

Do a self-evaluation before the interview.

As an employee, prepare by reviewing the objectives you were to reach during the period and the standards by which your performance will be measured. Make a list of your accomplishments and problem areas. Analyze the causes of your strengths and weaknesses and be prepared to respond to possible corrective actions with ideas to improve on your own. Self-criticism often softens criticism from others.

Figure 9.6 *Performance appraisal review form*

Name: ____________	**Date of Appraisal:** ____________
Performance Expectations	Performance Accomplishments
Employee Signature ____________	Employee Signature ____________
Supervisor Signature ____________	Supervisor Signature ____________
Manager Review ____________	Manager Review ____________

Understand your relationship with the interviewer and his or her performance review style. Check into the interviewer's mood prior to the interview. Be aware that sexual harassment occurs in organizations and that employees who have submitted to it tend to be judged more harshly than those who have resisted when such cases come to trial.

Approach the interview with a positive attitude.

At least half of the responsibility for making the interview a success rests with you. Approach the performance interview as a valuable source of information on prospects for advancement, a chance to get meaningful feedback about how the organization views your performance and future, and an opportunity to display your strengths and accomplishments. Be prepared to give concrete examples of how you have met or exceeded expectations. Prepare intelligent, well-thought-out questions. Be ready to discuss career goals.

Avoid unnecessary defensiveness.

When taking part in the interview, maintain a productive, positive relationship with the interviewer. Do not defend yourself unless there is something to be defensive about. If you are put on the defensive, maintain direct eye contact and clarify the facts before answering charges. You might ask, "How did this information come to your attention?" or "What are the exact production figures for the third quarter?" This gives you time to formulate thorough and reasonable responses based on complete understanding of the situation. Answer all questions thoroughly. Ask for clarification of questions you do not understand. Offer explanations, not excuses. Assess your performance and abilities reasonably, and be honest with yourself and your supervisor. Realize that what you are, what you think you are, what others think you are, and what you would like to be may describe different people.

A good offense is better than a good defense.

The performance review interview is not a time to be shy or self-effacing. Mention achievements such as special or extra projects, help you have given other employees, and community involvement on behalf of the organization. Be honest about challenges or problems you expect to encounter in the future. Correct any of the interviewer's false impressions or mistaken assumptions. Do not be afraid to ask for help.

If you are confronted with a serious problem, discover how much time is available to solve it. Suggest or request ways to solve your differences as soon as possible. The interviewer is not out to humiliate you, but to help you grow for your own sake and that of the organization. Keep your temper cool. Telling your supervisor off may give you a brief sense of satisfaction, but after the blast, the person will still be your supervisor and the problem will be worse. Do not try to improve everything at once. Set priorities with both short- and long-range goals.

Leave your temper at the door.

As the closing approaches, do not be in a hurry. Summarize or restate problems, solutions, and new goals in your own words. Be sure you understand all that has taken place and the agreements for the next review period. Be certain that the rewards fit your performance.[32] Close on a positive note with a determination to meet the new goals.

The Performance Problem Interview

When an employer has problems with an employee, the situation today is handled as a performance problem that requires coaching. The negative connotation and implication of discipline implies guilt, and organizations are reluctant to imply guilt.

The need for discipline has become a performance problem.

Determining Just Cause

Whether a contract is implied or in writing, an employer must show just cause to terminate an employee who is not in a probationary period or designated as a temporary or contract worker. Just cause means fair and equitable treatment of each employee in a job class. Many organizations are using behavioral selection interview processes and behavioral performance reviews to provide documentation in case a performance problem arises. This typically involves a team. A number of interviewers or reviewers provide more and better insights, spread the blame among several members of the organization, and should termination occur, make it difficult for the dismissed employee to counter four, five, or six points of view.

The following tests of just cause are tests that come from union contracts and attorneys involved in termination cases.

Know what constitutes a just cause.

- *Did the employee violate reasonable rules or orders?*

  For instance, if an employee has been working on a specific machine, his or her supervisor may request the employee to move to a similar piece of equipment until the current one undergoes needed repairs. If the employee refuses this request, you have grounds for discharge.

- *Was the employee given clear and unambiguous notice?*

  If an employee has been with your organization for six months to a year, follow an oral warning with a written warning within a short time.

Treat all employees fairly and equally.

- *Was the investigation timely?*

  In most union contracts and employee appeals policies, a specific length of time and procedures are outlined for investigating performance problems. *Timely* usually means within one to three days. If there is a refusal to work or a confrontation, the supervisor or manager may want to have a witness present and obtain a written statement from this witness.

- *Was the investigation conducted fairly?*

  Did the supervisor interview all parties involved? Did the supervisor obtain all necessary documentation? If there is a union contract, was a union representative included in all interviews or discussions?

- *Were all employees given equal treatment?*

  "Equal treatment under the law" means that each organizational investigation of performance problems is conducted in exactly the same manner.

- *Is there proof and documentation that a performance problem has occurred?*

  Most failures are due to a supervisor's unwillingness to take the time to write down the problem and obtain necessary records before disciplinary action or termination occurs. You need three things for termination: documentation, documentation, documentation.

The punishment must fit the infraction.

- *Is the penalty fair?*

  The longer an employee is with an organization, the longer the termination process. Union contracts and organizational policies usually have designated steps before an employee can be disciplined or terminated. If an offense is minor, a day off without pay or a written warning may be appropriate. A number of infractions within a short time may end in termination. Punishment should be progressive rather than regressive.

Preparing for the Interview

Practice before conducting the real thing.

Prepare for performance problem interviews by taking part in realistic role-playing cases. These rehearsals can lessen anxiety and help you anticipate employee reactions, questions, and rebuttals. The variety of situations and interviewees encountered can help you refine your case-making, questioning, and responding while sticking to the facts and documenting all claims with solid evidence.

Role-playing cases, literature reviews on performance problem situations, and discussions with experienced interviewers will help you learn what to expect. For example, Monroe, Borzi, and DiSalvo discovered four common responses from subjects occurred in 93 percent of incidents.[33]

Be prepared for common reactions and responses.

1. *Apparent compliance:* overpoliteness and deference, apologies, promises, or statements of good intentions followed by the same old problem behaviors.
2. *Relational leverage:* statements that they have been with the organization longer than the interviewer and therefore know best, that they are the best and you can't fire or discipline them, reference to friends or relatives within the organization, or reference to your close relationship to them.
3. *Alibis:* claims of tiredness, sickness, being overworked, budget cuts, family problems, it's someone else's fault, or poor instructions or information.
4. *Avoidance:* disappearing on sick leave or vacation, failure to respond to memos or phone calls, or failure to make an appointment.

What evidence do you have of the infraction?

Review *how* you know the employee has committed an infraction that warrants an interview. Did you see the infraction directly, as in the case of absenteeism, theft, poor workmanship, intoxication, fighting, harassing another employee, or insubordination? Did you find out indirectly through a third party or by observing the results (such as lateness of a report, poor quality products, or goals unmet)? Were you anticipating an infraction because of a previous incident, behavior, or stereotype? For example, African-Americans and other minorities are often watched more closely than others because supervisors believe they are more likely to violate rules. On the other hand, supervisors tend to be lenient with persons they perceive as likable, similar to themselves, or possessing high status or exceptional talent. Supervisors may avoid confronting persons they know will "explode" if confronted. Not confronting is the easy way out.

Distinguish between the severity of infractions.

Next, decide whether the perceived problem warrants a confrontation or punitive action. Absenteeism and low performance are generally considered more serious than tardiness and horseplay. Try to determine the cause of the infraction because this will affect how you conduct the interview and what action to take. For example, interviewers are more likely to fire, suspend, or demote employees when they believe poor work is due to lack of motivation or drive rather than lack of ability or technical competence.

Learn why an infraction has occurred.

Review the employee's past performance and history. The two basic reasons for action are poor performance or a troubled employee. When a person's performance gradually or suddenly declines, the cause may be motivational, personal, work-related, or supervisory. Drops in performance may be indicated by swings in the employee's behavior. For example, a friendly employee may suddenly become nasty, aggressive, or uncooperative. Keep an eye on performance indicators such as attendance, quality or quantity of work, willingness to take instructions, and cooperation with others.

A troubled employee may have an alcohol or drug dependency, a marital disturbance, problem with a child, or an emotional problem such as depression. An employee may be stealing from your organization to support a gambling habit, drug or alcohol addiction, or a boyfriend or girlfriend. These employees need counseling, not discipline.

For principles applicable to the performance problem interview, review the performance portion of this chapter and Chapter 12 on the counseling interview. Consider the relational dimensions discussed in Chapter 1 on interviews. Often neither

Relational dimensions are critical in performance problem interviews.

party wants to take part, and as supervisor, you may have delayed the interview until there is no other recourse and multiple problems have piled up. As a specific problem comes to a head, you and the employee may come to dislike and mistrust one another, even to the point of verbal and nonverbal abuse. Both may see one another as very dissimilar. Your options are generally the most potent, unless the employee is very valuable to your organization at this time. Trust, cooperation, and disclosure are difficult to attain in a threatening environment.

Keeping Self and the Situation under Control

Uncontrolled anger can destroy an interaction.

You are the supervisor, and while you want to head off a problem before it becomes critical, you must not lose your temper or let the situation get out of hand. Never conduct a performance problem interview when you are angry. You will be unable to control the interview if you have difficulty controlling yourself.

When one or both parties may have difficulty containing their anger and perhaps animosity, follow these suggestions.

- *Hold the interview in a private location.* Performance problem interviews are often ego shattering, so do not worsen the situation by reprimanding the employee in the presence of peers. Meet in a place where you and the employee can discuss the problem freely and openly.
- *When severe problems arise, consider delaying a confrontation and obtaining assistance.* For example, if two employees are caught fighting on a dock, have them report to your office or send them home and talk with each the next day. Let all tempers cool down. Depending on the situation, you may want to consult a counselor or call security before acting.

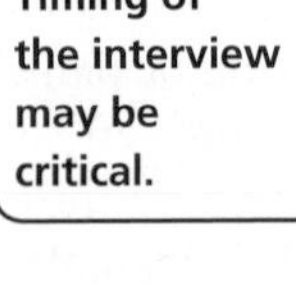

Timing of the interview may be critical.

- *Include a witness or union representative.* The witness should be another supervisor because using one employee as a witness who might testify against another employee is dangerous for all parties involved. If the union contract or organizational policies spell out the employee's right to representation, be sure to follow this procedure to the letter.

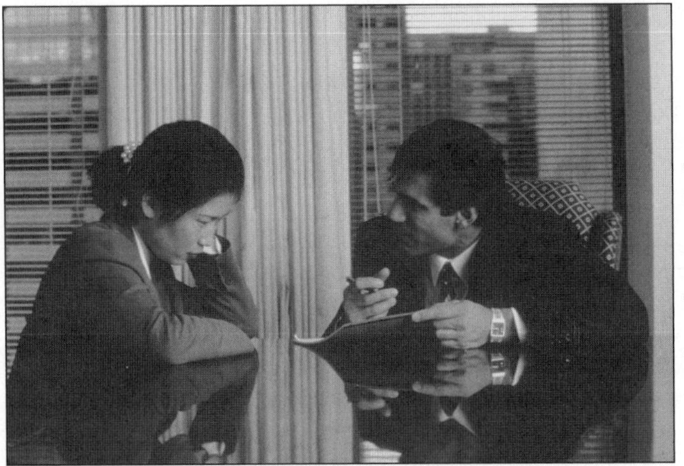

photo by Bill Lai/The Image Works

Never conduct a performance review interview when you are angry, and conduct the interview in a private location.

Focusing on the Problem

Deal in specific *facts,* such as absences, witnesses to the event, departmental records, and previous disciplinary actions. Do not allow the situation to become a trading contest: "Well, look at all the times I have been on time" or "How come others get away with it?" Talk about this situation and this employee.

Deal with facts rather than impressions and opinions.

- *Record all available facts.* Unions, EEOC, and attorneys often require complete and accurate records. Take detailed notes, record the time and date on all material that might be used later, and obtain the interviewee's signature or initials for legal protection. A **paper trail** may be critical for future interactions.
- *Try not to be accusatory.* Avoid words and statements such as troublemaker, drunk, thief, and liar. As a supervisor, you cannot make medical diagnoses of alcoholism or drug addiction, so do not use these terms.

Avoid unsupported accusations.

- *Preface remarks carefully.* For example, you may begin comments with phrases such as "According to your attendance report . . . ," "As I understand it . . . ," and "I have observed . . ." These phrases force you to be factual and keep you from accusing an employee of being guilty until proven innocent.

Ask questions that draw out the interviewee.

- *Ask questions that allow the person to express feelings and explain behavior.* Begin questions with "Tell me what happened . . . ," "When he said that, what did you . . . ," "Why do you feel that . . . ?" Open-ended questions allow you to get facts as well as feelings and explanations from the employee. Strive to establish the facts of the case and reach a common agreement with the employee regarding the alleged problem.

Avoiding Conclusions during the Interview

Do not verbalize conclusions during the interview. A hastily drawn conclusion may create more problems than it solves. Some organizations train supervisors to use standard statements under particular circumstances. If you are sending an employee off the job, you may say:

Be slow to draw conclusions.

"I do not believe you are in a condition to work, so I am sending you home. Report to me tomorrow at . . ."

"I want you to go to medical services and have a test made; bring me a slip from the physician when you return to my office."

"I'm sending you off the job. Call me tomorrow morning at nine, and I will tell you what action I will take."

The last statement gives you time to talk to others about possible actions and provides a cooling-off period for all concerned.

Closing the Interview

Conclude the interview in neutral. If discipline or termination is appropriate, do it. Realize, however, that delaying action may enable you to think more clearly about the incident. Be consistent with organizational policies, the union contract, this employee, and all other employees. Refer to your organization's prescribed disciplinary actions for specific offenses. Theft, except under unusual circumstances, is usually grounds for dismissal, while employees with alcohol and drug problems may be counseled the first time and fired the second time. Apply all rules and actions equally to all employees.

Summary

Review an employee's performance on the basis of standards mutually agreed upon ahead of time. Apply the same objectives equally to all employees performing a specific job. Research and good sense dictate that performance, promotion, and problem issues are discussed in separate interview sessions. Performance review interviews should occur at least semiannually, while promotion, salary, and performance problem interviews usually take place when needed. Deal with performance problems before they disrupt the employee's work or association with your organization. Select a performance review model most appropriate for your organization, employees, and positions.

For both employer and employee, flexibility and open-mindedness are important keys in successful performance review interviews. Flexibility should be tempered with understanding and tolerance of individual differences. The performance process must be ongoing, with no particular beginning or end. Supervisors and subordinates are constantly judged by the people around them. By gaining insights into their own behavior and how it affects others, both parties can become better persons and organization members.

Key Terms and Concepts

The online learning center for this text features FLASHCARDS and CROSSWORD PUZZLES for studying based on these terms and concepts.

360-degree approach
Balanced scorecard approach
Behavior based feedback
Behaviorally anchored rating scales
Catalytic coaching
Central tendency
Competitive rater
Force choice distribution
Halo effect
Just cause
Loose rater
Management by objectives
Multisource feedback
Person-product-service
Pitchfork effect
Recency error
Supportive climate
Tight rater
Universal performance interviewing model

A Performance Interview for Review and Analysis

Med-Tech manufactures a variety of electronic monitors and diagnostic tools used in hospitals and clinics throughout the United States. It has grown in 10 years from a staff of 10 to more than 150, many of whom are engaged in assembling the complicated monitors and tools that rely heavily on microchips and tiny circuits. Peter McBride is the manager of production, and Cindy Tiller is a production supervisor who has worked at Med-Tech for three years.

How effective is the opening in rapport building and orientation and involving the production supervisor? Is the climate supportive or defensive? How effectively do manager and production supervisor deal with positive aspects of performance before getting to negative aspects? Does either party dominate a specific phase of the interview? How effectively do the parties set goals for the next review period? How effectively is the interview closed? How skilled is the manager, as a coach?

1. **Interviewer:** Hi Cindy; have a seat.
2. **Interviewee:** Thanks. It's good to get off my feet for a bit.
3. **Interviewer:** I'm sure it is. We've really been busy the past six months. How's the family?
4. **Interviewee:** They're fine thanks. Mindy enters kindergarten this fall and Sarah is totally involved in gymnastics.
5. **Interviewer:** That's great. Anything special you would like to mention before we get started?
6. **Interviewee:** No . . . not really. Things are going pretty well.
7. **Interviewer:** Great. Let's think back to three months ago when we last talked and set some objectives for this quarter. Our major goals were quality improvement, meeting production quotas, and being on time with orders.
8. **Interviewee:** Yeah. That's what I recall as our major goals, but we were also concerned about turnover of associates.
9. **Interviewer:** That's right, and as I look over the figures, we have lost only one associate when we had been averaging five or more. Good job. That's amazing with the competition for skilled production people.
10. **Interviewee:** Thanks. I'm pleased with the quality and commitment of our associates.
11. **Interviewer:** Production looks good overall, pretty much on target.
12. **Interviewee:** I think a lot of that is due to the stability of our staff. I've had to do a lot less training and correcting this quarter. As you can see also, quality has improved so we do not have to return monitors and the new diagnostic tools to the line for corrections. That speeds things up.
13. **Interviewer:** Very good. I'm quite pleased.
14. **Interviewee:** I thought you would be. It's certainly made my life easier.
15. **Interviewer:** did notice one problem however. Line three seems to be slower than the other five lines.
16. **Interviewee:** That's true, but we've made our deadlines in spite of this minor problem.
17. **Interviewer:** Yes, you've met deadlines, but your overtime budget is up 12 percent from the previous quarter.
18. **Interviewee:** I've had to keep some associates past their eight hours from time to time.
19. **Interviewer:** Why is that?
20. **Interviewee:** Well . . . some associates are faster than others in assembling the new micro circuits and chips.
21. **Interviewer:** Uh huh? Is this a problem with a number of associates?
22. **Interviewee:** Oh no. Not many.
23. **Interviewer:** How many are slow enough to create an overtime problem?
24. **Interviewee:** Only one.
25. **Interviewer:** And this one is . . . ?

26. **Interviewee:** April Proctor.
27. **Interviewer:** What is April's problem? Have you worked with her to increase her speed and efficiency?
28. **Interviewee:** Yes, but that's not the problem.
29. **Interviewer:** And the problem is . . . ?
30. **Interviewee:** She's getting rather severe arthritis in her hands and fingers and is having difficulty maneuvering elements, particularly in the new monitors. Sometimes she can't come to work at all.
31. **Interviewer:** Have you reported this to the HR department? It seems to me that either she can do the job assigned or not.
32. **Interviewee:** I understand that, but she's been a loyal employee since Med-Tech was founded and her husband has been laid off for nearly a year.
33. **Interviewer:** Well, I certainly don't want to appear hard-hearted, but we're not a charity. How about the three of us meeting on Wednesday morning at around 9:00 to evaluate her situation. Perhaps we could transfer her to another position that would pay about the same.
34. **Interviewee:** That sounds good. I'll talk to her this afternoon.
35. **Interviewer:** I appreciate your wanting to protect a loyal employee, but these situations cannot continue when there's no way to improve them. Since everything else seems to be in order, let's continue with the same goals for the next quarter. Keep up the good work.
36. **Interviewee:** Thanks. I'll see you on Wednesday.

Performance and Problem Role-Playing Cases

A Sales Representative

The interviewer is sales manager for KXWP-TV located in a suburb of Las Vegas. She is conducting a semiannual performance review with a sales associate who joined the station's sales staff two years ago. At first the associate was consistently near or at the top of all sales associates, and sometimes setting new records for sales at KXWP. Within the last few months, however, his sales have slipped considerably. There are rumors that he has a gambling problem and has been seen at casinos when he was supposed to be meeting with advertising clients. The sales manager's task is to discover reasons for declines in sales and to get the associate back on track without confronting him with unproven rumors. She has been reluctant to play detective.

A Soccer Coach

The interviewer is the athletic director at Central High School and reviews the performance of each head coach prior to and after each season. The interviewee is the varsity soccer coach who has been head coach for three years after serving two years as an assistant. The team had a typical season record of eight wins and seven losses, but expectations were high this year because nearly all starters were seasoned seniors. Some parents have complained to the athletic director that the coach often benched the best players for "minor infractions" that would be ignored anywhere else. The coach has exhibited little patience for "whining" players and parents.

A Troubleshooter

The interviewer is the vice president of a large paper products manufacturer that has plants throughout the United States and in several other countries. He oversees plant managers and engineering troubleshooters who travel weekly to different plants to resolve production problems, set up and troubleshoot new computer systems, and train personnel in operating new production equipment. The interviewee, a former plant manager, is an excellent troubleshooter, but he is becoming unhappy with the constant travel and being away from his family. This performance interview is aimed at keeping the interviewee happy and on the job as well as reviewing performance.

A Borderline Performer

The interviewer is the manager of a clothing department in a major department store. The interviewee is a young married employee with two small children. When she is at work, she does an average job. She anticipates problems, thinks of various solutions, and is professional in dress and manner. However, about every three or four weeks, she has what is laughably called in the department a "mommy problem." Reasons or excuses abound: one of her children is sick, the babysitter is late, her husband is out of town, and so on. She is late so often by several hours that five months into the year she has used up all of her sick days and two vacation days. She obviously needs coaching. The interviewer must determine what questions to ask during the performance review and which key points he could make to let her know without question that her tardiness is unacceptable.

Student Activities

1. Arrange an interview with the human resources director of a medium to large company. Ask questions such as: "Which performance review system or systems do you use, and how did you select them?" "How do you train performance interviewers to be coaches rather than judges?" "How do you deal with compensation during performance reviews?" "How do you coach employees about retirement plans and options?"
2. Compare and contrast Garold Markle's "catalytic coaching" approach to performance review with the traditional balanced scorecard approach, the behaviorally anchored rating scales model, the management by objectives model, and the universal performance interviewing model. How might the catalytic coaching approach alter each and improve each?
3. Radio Shack recently laid off several hundred workers by e-mail. How might this impersonal method of informing employees affect future performance review interviews? Consider organizational environment, relationship building, choice of performance review models, and matters of loyalty.

4. Contact 3 to 5 organizations (for-profit and not-for-profit) and ask them for their philosophy of performance review and the resulting methods of compensation. Do they use individuals, groups, or both as a means of rewarding and paying for performance? Do they use profit sharing, stock options, direct cash payments, or other forms of compensations?

Notes

1. Peter Senge, *The Fifth Discipline: The Art & Science of the Learning Organization* (New York: Doubleday, 1990); Jon R. Katzenbach and Douglas K. Smith, *The Wisdom of Teams* (New York: HarperCollins, 1993); Jon R. Katzenbach and Douglas K. Smith, *The Discipline of Teams* (New York: John Wiley & Sons, 2001); Peter Drucker, *The Post-Capitalist Society* (New York: Harper-Business, 1993); and Jeffrey Pfeffer and Robert I. Sutton, *The Knowing-Doing Gap: How Smart Companies Turn Knowledge into Action* (Boston: Harvard Business School Press, 2000).
2. Stephen Covey, *The Seven Habits of Highly Effective People* (New York: Simon Schuster, 1989); Terrence E. Deal and Allan Kennedy, *The New Corporate Cultures: Revitalizing the Workplace after Downsizing and Mergers and Re-engineering* (New York: Persius Books, 1999); Jon R. Katzenbach, *Peak Performance: Aligning the Hearts and Minds of Your Employees* (Boston: Harvard Business School Press, 2000).
3. Edward E. Lawler III, "Reward Practices and Performance Management System Effectiveness," *Organizational Dynamics* 32 (2003), pp. 396–404.
4. Abdrea Gumbus, Dorothy E. Bellhouse, and Bridget Lyons, "A Three Year Journey to Organizational and Financial Health Using the Balanced Scorecard: A Case Study at a Yale New Haven Health System Hospital," *Journal of Business & Economic Studies* 9 (2003), pp. 54–64.
5. Reprinted with permission from Robert S. Kaplan and David P. Norton, "Using the Balanced Scorecard as a Strategic Management System," *Harvard Business Review,* January–February 1996, p. 77.
6. Reprinted by permission from Jon R. Katzenbach, *Peak Performance: Aligning the Hearts and Minds of Your Employees* (Boston: Harvard Business School Press, 2000).
7. Garold L. Markle, *Catalytic Coaching: The End of the Performance Review* (Westport, CT: Quorum Books, 2000), p. 5.
8. Markle, p. 4.
9. Taken from *Everyone's a Coach* by Don Shula and Ken Blanchard. Copyright 1995 by Shula Enterprises and Blanchard Family Partnership. Used by permission of Zondervan Publishing House (http://www.zondervan.com).
10. K. Michele Kacmar, L. A. Witt, Suzanne Zivnuska, and Stanley M. Gully, "The Interactive Effect of Leader-Member Exchange and Communication Frequency on Performance Ratings," *Journal of Applied Psychology* 88 (2003), pp. 764–772.
11. O. L. Hill, "Time to Evaluate Evaluations," *Supervisory Management,* March 1992, p. 7.
12. Ronald J. Burke, William F. Weitzell, and Tamara Weir, "Characteristics of Effective Employee Performance Review and Development Interviews: One More Time,"

Psychological Reports 47 (1980), pp. 683–695; H. Kent Baker and Philip I. Morgan, "Two Goals in Every Performance Appraisal," *Personnel Journal* 63 (1984), pp. 74–78.

13. "Guidelines for Conducting the Performance Interview," http://www.lcms.org, accessed December 19, 2006.

14. H. Lloyd Goodall, Jr., Gerald L. Wilson, and Christopher F. Waagen, "The Performance Appraisal Interview: An Interpretive Reassessment," *Quarterly Journal of Speech* 72 (1986), pp. 74–75.

15. Gerald R. Ferris and Thomas R. King, "The Politics of Age Discrimination in Organizations," *Journal of Business Ethics* 11 (1992), pp. 342–350.

16. David Martone, "A Guide to Developing a Competency-Based Performance-Management System," *Employment Relations Today* 30 (2003), pp. 23–32.

17. Stanley Silverman and Kenneth N. Wexley, "Reaction of Employees to Performance Appraisal Interviews as a Function of Their Participation in Rating Scale Development," *Personnel Psychology* 37 (1984), pp. 703–710.

18. Phillip G. Benson, M. Ronald Buckley, and Sid Hall, "The Impact of Rating Scale Format on Rater Accuracy: An Evaluation of the Mixed Standard Scale," *Journal of Management* 14 (1988), pp. 415–423.

19. This model and explanation come from a booklet prepared by Baxter/Travenol Laboratories entitled *Performance Measurement Guide*. The model and system were developed by William B. Cash, Jr., Chris Janiak, and Sandy Mauch. The model is reprinted with permission of Baxter/Travenol, Deerfield, Illinois.

20. Jack Zigon, "Making Performance Appraisals Work for Teams," *Training,* June 1994, pp. 58–63.

21. Richard Lipsinger and Anntoinette D. Lucia, *The Art and Science of 360 Feedback* (San Francisco: Jossey-Bass, 1998).

22. Anthony T. Dalession, "Multi-Source Feedback for Employee Development and Personnel Decisions," in *Performance Appraisal: State of the Art in Practice,* James W. Smitter, ed. (San Francisco: Jossey-Bass, 1998).

23. Nathalie Towner, "Turning Appraisals 360 Degrees," *Personnel Today,* February 17, 2004, p. 18.

24. Markle, pp. 76, 78.

25. Matthew Boyle, "Performance Reviews: Perilous Curves Ahead," *Fortune,* May 28, 2001, pp. 187–188.

26. Boyle, pp. 187–188.

27. From a speech to a client briefing on September 30, 1983, in San Francisco by Buck Blessing of Blessing and White, Inc., a leading international career development company.

28. Goodall, Wilson, and Waagen, pp. 74–87; Arthur Pell, "Benefiting from the Performance Appraisal," *Bottomline* 3 (1996), pp. 51–52.

29. Goodall, Wilson, and Waagen, p. 76.

30. Terry R. Lowe, "Eight Ways to Ruin a Performance Review," *Personnel Journal* 65 (1986), pp. 60–62.

31. Hill, p. 7.

32. Tanya N. Ballard, "Performance Pay Pitfalls," *Government Executive,* December 2003, p. 16.

33. Craig Monroe, Mark G. Borzi, and Vincent DiSalvo, "Conflict Behaviors of Difficult Subordinates," *Southern Communication Journal* 54 (1989), pp. 311–329.

Resources

Markle, Garold L. *Catalytic Coaching: The End of the Performance Review.* Westport, CT: Quorum Books, 2000.

Miller, John G. *The Question Behind the Question: Practicing Personal Accountability in Life.* Denver: Denver Press, 2001.

Osteen, Joel. *Your Best Life Now: 90 Devotionals for Living Your Free Potential.* New York: Warner Faith, 2005.

Philly, Robin L., and Gregory Northercraft. *Get Paid What You're Worth.* New York: St. Martin's Griffin, 2000.

Shepard, Glenn. *How to Be the Employee Your Company Can't Live Without.* New York: John Wiley, 2006.

Thaler, Linda Kaplan, and Robin Koval. *The Power of Nice.* New York: Currency Doubleday, 2006.

CHAPTER 10 The Persuasive Interview: The Persuader

Persuaders exchange information to influence, not to inform.

In early chapters on probing and survey interviews, we emphasized the need to be neutral and to avoid interviewer bias. The goal was to avoid influencing how an interviewee might answer a question. In the last three chapters, we covered interviews that contained *elements of persuasion*—to convince recruits to join our organization, to convince recruiters to employ us, to convince employees that they are valuable assets to our organizations who can achieve even more with us, and to convince employers that we are making important contributions to their organizations. In future chapters on counseling and health care, we will again address persuasive elements. In each situation, however, the critical task is to gather and give information; persuasion is secondary.

We cannot avoid persuasion in our society.

Unlike these chapters, this chapter and the next one focus on interviews in which the essential goal or purpose is not merely to share information accurately but to *persuade*—to influence—how an interviewee *thinks, feels, and/or acts*. Too often when we think of a *persuasive interview,* we think first of a *sales* interview in which one party is trying to sell a car, insurance policy, computer, sweat suit, football tickets, or HDTV to another party. Selling something is a common persuasive purpose, but there are many others, including recruiting students to a sorority or fraternity, raising funds, campaigning for votes, collecting for charities, obtaining permission to use a university vehicle, presenting a proposal to a supervisor, converting a person to our religious faith, or trying to persuade a professor to raise a grade. It's a rare day in which we do not take part in a variety of interviews, perhaps none of them dealing with sales. The pervasiveness of persuasion in our lives has led Roderick Hart, a professor of communication at the University of Texas, to claim that "one must only breathe to need to know something about persuasion."[1]

The Ethics of Persuasion

Whenever we attempt to change or reinforce another's way of thinking, feeling, or acting, we take on a serious ethical responsibility. As Isocrates in ancient Greece wrote more than two thousand years ago, it is not enough to learn the mere techniques of persuasion; we must also learn and practice basic ethical standards, including honesty, fairness, and sincerity.[2]

Unfortunately, today as in ancient Greece, the practice of ethics leaves a great deal to be desired.[3] It is estimated that one in six college students lie on their resumes or application forms when seeking employment. In a recent survey of cheating among

Ethics is a growing concern in society.

college students, 78 percent reported that they had cheated on some form of assignment.[4] But students are far from alone in violating ethical standards. Virtually every profession has published codes of ethics, but they are violated so often that most of us are skeptical when dealing with them. A survey of attitudes toward American professions indicated that fewer than 20 percent of us perceive car sales representatives, advertising practitioners, insurance sales persons, lawyers, union leaders, and real estate agents to be ethical and honest. Only health care professionals score consistently above 50 percent.[5] Survey results are comparable in other countries. For instance, Australians rate the honesty of car sales representatives at 3 percent, real estate agents at 10 percent, business executives at 15 percent, and advertising people at 10 percent.[6] If we are going to be successful persuaders, particularly in the one-to-one situation of the interview, interviewees must see us and our persuasive efforts as meeting high ethical standards. Let's begin by determining what is meant by ethical and then we can move to a code of ethics that should guide our efforts.

What Is Ethical?

Richard Johannesen, a recognized authority in the ethics of persuasion, writes that "**Ethical issues** focus on value judgments concerning degrees of right and wrong, goodness and badness, in human conduct."[7] Notice the word *degrees.* There appear to be few absolutely and universally unethical behaviors. Situations in our complex world often appear to be so unique that ethical principles are inappropriate or useless.

When do we cross ethical boundaries?

Some theorists and practitioners argue that persuaders ought to determine the ethics of their efforts according to the *end* being sought, while others claim we must judge the *means* used to reach the end. Some argue that ethics are determined by prevailing conduct in a society or personal conscience, and others argue that ethics are clearly stated in legal statutes and religious documents such as the Bible, Torah, and Koran. Some argue that life is gamelike, with a buyer-beware attitude, while others argue that anything that dehumanizes or cheapens persons is unethical.

Is the effort to influence the lives of others inherently unethical?

A confounding problem is who will make the judgments concerning degrees of right and wrong, goodness and badness, means and ends? Every rule seems to have justified exceptions and to pose more questions than answers. For example, withholding evidence may be bad if a person is selecting an organization to join or an investment to buy but good if health or security is at stake. We may resent a persuader trying to scare us into a decision through fear appeals and then use the same appeals when persuading a child not to get in a car with a stranger. Virtually every strategy and tactic discussed in this chapter, even careful analysis and adaptation to the interviewee, may be identified as *manipulative* and, therefore, unethical.

Fundamental Ethical Guidelines

Although there may be no single code of ethics applicable to all persuasive interviews and acceptable to all interview parties, fundamental guidelines for both parties exist. Gary Woodward and Robert Denton identify these when they write that "ethical communication should be fair, honest, and designed not to hurt other people."[8]

When you are planning to take part in persuasive interviews as an interviewer, ask yourself these fundamental questions:

- Who are you, including social status, position held, and level of expertise?
- Who is your interviewee, particularly the person's degree of vulnerability and the potential seriousness of results?
- How adequate is the content you are preparing, including fair selection of language and tactics, accurate and adequate evidence, and honest claims?
- How open will you be with this person, including revelation of your motives, balance of original ideas with adaptation to this person and situation, and belief in what you advocate?
- Are you innocent of violating fundamental ethical standards, including intent to deceive, adherence to agreed upon standards, and willingness to fulfill commitments and promises?

Ethics is the foundation of persuasion.

Kenneth Andersen writes that "although we do not wish to force a given system of values or ethical code upon the reader, we do argue that he [she] has a responsibility to form one. We believe that it is desirable both for the immediate practical reasons of self-interest and for more altruistic reasons that a person accept responsibility for what he [she] does in persuasion both as receiver and as source."[9] The age-old "golden rule" is an excellent guideline for ethical conduct: "Do unto others as you would have them do unto you." For instance, would you want an interviewer to lie to you, use fictitious evidence, hide ulterior motives, employ racist or sexist language, pretend dangerous consequences are minimal or nonexistent, or play tricks with language?

What are the implications of the golden rule?

If each of us were to treat others as we wish to be treated, few unethical practices would occur in persuasive interviews.

Preparing for the Interview

Although success is never ensured in a persuasive interview, the possibility of success is enhanced considerably if your persuasive effort meets five interrelated conditions.

1. *Your proposal must create or address an urgent need or one or more desires or motives.* If the interviewee sees no need or has no desire, persuasion will not occur.
2. *Your proposal and you as an interviewer (including your profession and organization) must be consistent with the interviewee's values, beliefs, and attitudes.* Lack of compatibility, trust, or respect will result in lack of persuasion.
3. *Your proposal must be feasible, practical, workable, or affordable.* Possibility is a critical factor in persuasion.
4. *Your proposal's advantages must outweigh its disadvantages. Every proposal generates objections, sometimes stated and sometimes not.* You must recognize and neutralize them.
5. *No better course of action is available.* You must show your proposal is the best among possible choices.

Mutual trust is essential.

You can meet these five conditions only if you spend time and energy preparing for each persuasive interview.

Sources

As you strive to learn everything you can about the other party, do not overlook any potentially valuable source of information. What do you know from previous contacts with members of this party? What information is included in your personal or organizational files? What can other people tell you about this party? What information is included in church, school, professional, and community directories? Check personal and organizational Web sites. How, when, where, and under what circumstances has the interview party expressed interest in this issue, problem, or proposal? When insufficient information is available or you have no opportunity to study the other party ahead of time, use the first few minutes of the interview to discover important information by *observing* the interviewee's physical makeup, dress, manner, and attitudes; by carefully *asking questions* into background, interests, attitudes, and purposes of this meeting; and by *listening* insightfully to what the party says and does not say. If the party consists of more than one person, try to determine who is the leader, who will make important decisions, and who is in need.

Do your homework.

Analyzing the Other Party

The other party in a persuasive interview typically consists of only one, two, or three people. While this is a great disadvantage in numbers when compared to persuasion through public addresses or the mass media, you have the distinct advantage of being able to *tailor* your persuasive effort to specific human beings. Speeches and the mass media require a generic approach to persuasion that is "sort of adapted" to a diverse audience, most of whom have little or no interest in your proposal. Begin your tailoring by seeking answers to four questions.

Tailoring requires knowing.

1. What is the makeup of the other party?
2. What does the other party know?
3. What does the other party believe?
4. How does the other party feel?

Physical and Mental Characteristics

Consider potentially relevant physical characteristics such as age, gender, race, culture, size, health, disabilities, and physical appearance. Although any one of these characteristics may be central in a persuasive effort (choice of college, medical insurance, retirement plan, clothing, religious affiliation), it is foolhardy and insulting to assume, for instance, that all elderly persons are gullible, all Hispanic-Americans are recent illegal immigrants, or all blonds are dumb.

Avoid stereotyping other human beings.

Level of intelligence may make interviewees more or less receptive to your message. Research indicates, for instance, that highly intelligent interviewees are more influenced by evidence and logical arguments but tend to be highly critical and therefore more difficult to persuade.[10]

Socioeconomic Background

Review important socioeconomic data including the interviewee's memberships because attitudes are strongly influenced by the groups people belong to or aspire to.

Memberships may be powerful outside forces.

The more attached people are to groups, the less they are persuaded by efforts that conflict with group norms. Investigate the interviewee's occupation, income, avocations and hobbies, superior/subordinate relationships, marital status, dependents, work experiences, and geographical background because these affect frames of reference—ways of viewing people, places, things, events, and issues.

Culture

You will need to understand cultural differences that may affect persuasive efforts. For instance, some cultures consider bribery a normal part of business. Others feel it is necessary to give gifts as part of the process. Bargaining is an essential part of persuasion in many cultures, often preceded by a relationship-building period over dinner or tea. In the United States, as the saying goes, time is money, so Americans expect people to be on time or within a very few minutes of the time set. In Great Britain, however, it is considered "correct" to be 5 to 15 minutes late, and in Italy a person may arrive two hours late and not understand why you are upset.[11]

Values/Beliefs/Attitudes

Each culture has a set of generally accepted **values**—fundamental beliefs about ideal states of existence and modes of behavior that motivate us to think, feel, or act in particular ways.[12] Values are the foundations for our specific beliefs and attitudes. The following scheme of values includes those central to the American value system.

Values are the "hot buttons" we push in persuasive interviews.

Survival Values

Peace and tranquility	Preservation of health
Personal attractiveness	Safety and security

Social Values

Affection and popularity	Generosity
Cleanliness	Patriotism and loyalty
Conformity and imitation	Sociality and belonging

Success Values

Accumulation	Material comfort
Ambition	Pride, prestige, and social recognition
Competition	Sense of accomplishment
Happiness	

Independence Values

Equity and value of the individual	Freedom from restraint
Freedom from authority	Power and authority

(continued)

Progress Values

Change and advancement	Quantification
Education and knowledge	Science and secular rationality
Efficiency and practicality	

As you read through this list of American values, recall recent experiences urging you to contribute to the state police program for summer camps, help the children in Haiti, or replace cable with satellite TV. Appeals of these persuaders may have centered on values such as prestige, generosity, considerateness, security, belonging, peace, and salvation. Determine which values are most relevant to this party in this situation, with this issue.

Political, economic, social, historical, and religious **beliefs** emanate from values. You need to determine which of these beliefs relate to a topic and proposal. If equity and value of the individual are important values, a party is likely to support equal rights and opportunities for women, African-Americans, and Hispanics. If education and knowledge are important values, a party is likely to support increased funding for schools, give to college fund-raising campaigns, and be interested in books and computer databases.

Values are the foundations of our belief systems.

Attitudes are relatively enduring combinations of beliefs that predispose you to respond in particular ways to persons, organizations, places, ideas, and issues. If you are a conservative, you are likely to react predictably to things you consider to be liberal. The reverse is true if you are a liberal. Attitudes come from beliefs that come from cherished values. Determine the interviewee's probable attitude toward the need or desire you will develop and the proposal you will make.

Attitudes tend to predict actions.

Persuasion theorists from Aristotle in ancient Greece to present day have claimed that the interviewee's attitude toward the interviewer (ethos, credibility, image) is the most important determinant of success.[13] It's critical, then, that you assess the other party's attitudes toward you, your profession, and the organization you represent. Researchers have identified a number of dimensions that determine your credibility with an interviewee. These include *trustworthy/safe* (honest, sincere, reliable, fair), *competent/expert* (intelligent, knowledgeable, good judgment, experienced), *goodwill* (caring, other-centered, sensitive, understanding), *composure* (poised, relaxed, calm, composed), and *dynamic/energetic* (decisive, strong, industrious, active).[14] Think of your previous experiences with this party. Recall the discussion of attitudes a few pages ago that identified low-credible and high-credible professions. If a party dislikes you, distrusts your organization, or sees your profession as dishonest or untrustworthy, you will not succeed without altering these attitudes during the interview. To create and maintain high credibility with another interview party, your appearance, manner, reputation, attainments, personality, and character must communicate trustworthiness, competence, caring, composure, and dynamism. We tend to react more favorably to highly credible interviewers who are similar to us in important ways and appear to share our values, beliefs, and attitudes. While we want interviewers to be similar to us, we also expect them to be wiser, braver, more knowledgeable, more experienced, and more insightful.[15] Consider all of these factors prior to the interview.

Low credibility may undermine the best effort.

Perceived similarities may enhance receptivity.

Figure 10.1 *The relationship of values, beliefs, and attitudes*

Values } Beliefs } Attitudes } Judgment/Action } Persons / Places / Things / Ideas / Acts

What, then, is the significance of the relationship of values, beliefs, and attitudes in persuasive interviews? As indicated in Figure 10.1, the process begins with values (our fundamental beliefs about existence and behavior), that lead to *specific beliefs* (judgments about what is probably true or believable), that form *attitudes* (organizations of relevant beliefs that predispose us to respond in particular ways), that result in *judgment or actions* toward persons, places, things, ideas, proposals, and acts.

As you prepare for a persuasive interview, consider the other party's probable attitudes along an imaginary scale from 1 to 9 with 1, 2, and 3 indicating strongly positive; 4, 5, and 6 indicating neutrality or ambivalence; and 7, 8, and 9 indicating strongly negative.

Strongly for			Undecided/neutral			Strongly against		
1	2	3	4	5	6	7	8	9

Know what is possible, likely, and impossible.

From what you have learned about the interviewee, where along this scale is this person's attitude likely to rest? If on positions 1 or 2, little persuasive effort may be required. If on positions 8 or 9, persuasion may be impossible beyond a small shift in feeling or thinking. If the attitude is on positions 4, 5, or 6, theoretically you should be able to alter ways of thinking, feeling, or acting with a good persuasive effort. This may not be the case, however, if an interviewee is strongly committed to remaining neutral, undecided, or noncommital.

Emotions

How we feel may determine what we do.

Emotions, sometimes called feelings or passions, significantly influence how interview parties think, feel, and act. Those involved in sales, recruiting, fund-raising, and campaigning often refer to emotions, along with values, as the "hot buttons" you need to discover and push if you hope to be persuasive. Some emotions are necessary for *survival*. Try to determine if the other party is fearful or secure, angry or calm, hateful or loving. Other emotions are necessary for *social involvement*. Does the other party feel ashamed or proud, guilty or innocent, sad or happy, vindictive or forgiving, indifferent or sympathetic? In short, you must be aware of the other party's mood, why the party feels that way, and how it is likely to affect the interview.

Analyzing the Situation

The interview situation is a context of persons, relationships, motives, events, time, place, and objects.

The "why" of the interview may vary significantly between parties.

Atmosphere

Study carefully the atmosphere in which the interview will take place. Know why the interview is occurring at this time: a regularly scheduled event, an emergency, a moment of opportunity, a major event, or merely routine? Will it be hostile, friendly, ambivalent, or apathetic?

Timing

Timing may be everything.

Timing is often critical. When would be an ideal time to conduct the interview? How close to this ideal is the time you have chosen? For instance, a few semesters ago one of our students came in during the last week of the semester and stated in his opening, "You told us to come see you if we got into grade trouble before it was too late." For this student, it was very late. On the other hand, a college student may wait until after a parent's annual bonus before discussing law school. What events have preceded this interview such as visits from your competitors? Few of us would want to be the fourth employee of the day to ask for a raise from an employer who has just discovered a serious financial problem. What events will take place following the interview, such as a competing fund-raiser, an annual sale, a budget meeting, visit by a competitor? Certain times of the year (vacation time, tax time, Christmas season) are great for some interviewers and terrible for others.

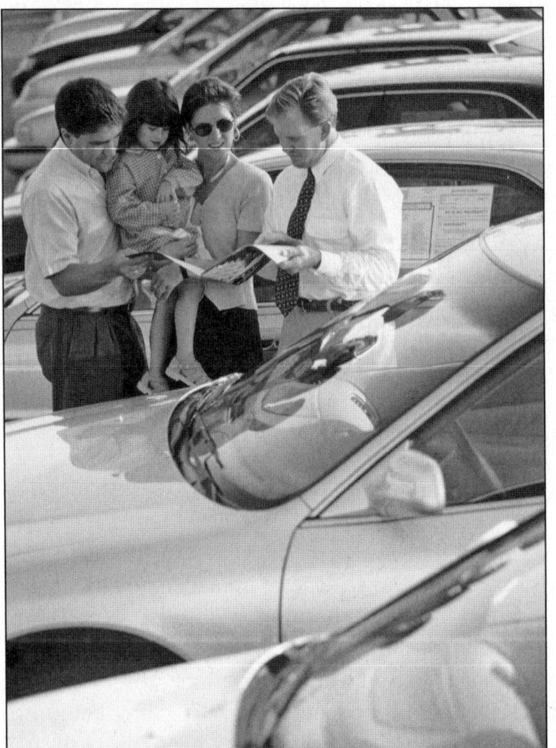

photo Arthur Tilley/Getty Images

The persuasive situation is a total context of persons, relationships, events, time, place, and objects.

Physical Setting

Consider carefully the physical setting of the interview. Try to provide for privacy and to control interruptions, especially telephone calls. Make an appointment if possible because it is often difficult to guess how much time an interview will take.

Will you be the host (the interview is in your office or residence); a guest (the interview is in the interviewee's place of business or residence); or on neutral ground (a conference room, restaurant, hotel, club)? If you are trying to recruit a student for your university, you might prefer to get the interviewee on campus during a beautiful day when everything is green

On whose turf will the interview take place?

and in bloom, perhaps following a sports victory. If you are selling a life insurance policy, you might want the interview to take place in the interviewee's home surrounded by family members, furnishings, and valued possessions the family would want protected in case of a medical emergency or death.

Outside Forces

Consider the influence of **outside forces.** For instance, organizational or professional policies may prescribe what you can and cannot do in sales interviews. You may be trying to convince a friend to attend your college while another college is actively recruiting this person with scholarship money. Mom and dad may want the interviewee to attend their alma mater. A significant other may want the interviewee to attend a local community college. Awareness of outside influences may determine how you open an interview, select appeals and evidence, develop proposals, and address counter-persuasion.

Researching the Issue

Outside influences may wage counter-persuasive efforts.

Be the best informed, most authoritative person in each interview. Investigate all aspects of the topic, including events that may have contributed to the problem, reasons for and against change, evidence on all sides of an issue, and possible solutions. Search for solid, up-to-date information that will help persuade the interviewee that your proposal is the best for a need or desire. You are taking part in a persuasive interview, not giving a speech to an audience of one, so the interviewee can demand support, challenge assumptions, generalizations, and claims, and ask for documentation of a source at any moment during an interview. Parties are impressed with persuaders who reply to inquiries with facts and documentation rather than generalities and evasions. Try to determine what the other party knows about the issue and what the party's attitudes are toward the issue and its possible solutions.

You must have the facts and know how to use them.

Sources

Do not overlook any potentially valuable source of information and evidence: the Internet, e-mail, interviews, letters, pamphlets, questionnaires, surveys, unpublished studies, reports, newspapers, periodicals, professional journals, and government documents. Do not forget your own experiences and study. Check carefully all sources available to the interviewee.

An overlooked source may be the most important.

Types of Evidence

Search for a variety of evidence to support the need and proposal. Collect *examples,* both factual and hypothetical, that may illustrate points you will make. People like good *stories* that make problems seem real. Gather *statistics* on relevant areas such as inflation, growth rates, expenses, benefits, insurance coverages, profits and losses, causes and effects. Collect *statements* from acknowledged *authorities* on the topics as well as *testimonials* from those who have joined, attended, purchased, signed, or believed. Look for *comparisons and contrasts* between situations, events, proposals, products, and services. Locate clear and supportable *definitions* for key terms and concepts.

Gather and use a variety of evidence.

The effect of a well-supported interview lasts longer than a poorly supported one.

Here are suggestions for seeking and employing information you discover. Distinguish *opinion* (something that is assumed, usually cannot be observed, can be made at any time, and either is or should be believed tentatively) from *fact* (something that can be or has been observed, is verifiable, and is thought of as securely established). Present your evidence effectively, including thorough documentation of your sources: identifications and backgrounds of authorities or witnesses, when research occurred, and where the evidence was reported. Solid evidence, the substance of your persuasive interview, enhances the long-term effect of your interview that is particularly important if a decision will not be made for weeks or months.

Planning the Interview

Only after analyzing the interviewee, studying the situation, and researching the issue are you ready to plan the interview. Begin by determining your purpose.

Determining Your Purpose

Be realistic but not defeatist.

Be realistic. If you know the interviewee will be a hard sell because of a value, belief, and attitude system, then your purpose may be only to influence thinking or feeling in minor ways. Just to get the interviewee to think about an issue or to admit there might be a problem may be a major success for a first interview. Later interviews might move the interviewee toward a more significant change or action. On the other hand, if an interviewee contacts you and tells you he or she wants to change cell phone companies or is interested in an investment, you can move quickly through need and desire to solutions with a good chance of success.

Be realistic in the goals you set for each interview. Be aware that major changes often come in increments and a series of interviews. Do not give up too quickly or assume after one interview that an interviewee is not interested or will not change. Some authorities on sales interviews claim that it typically takes five contacts before a sale is made. Be prepared to be patient.

Selecting and Developing Main Points

Do not make the need too complicated.

Select points or reasons to establish a need or desire. Do not rely on a *single* reason or point. The interviewee may see little urgency in a problem that seems so simple or unidimensional or find it relatively easy to attack or reject *only* one point. Research indicates that more points also enhance the effectiveness of persuasion over time.[16] On the other hand, six or eight points are likely to make an interview too long or very superficial as you try to rush through so many points. An interviewee may become overloaded with information and complex arguments and end up confused or bored.

Know the strength of each point and introduce It strategically.

As you select and develop your points or reasons for a change, ideally three or four, determine the strength of each for this interviewee in this situation. This will help you to decide the order in which you present points. Let's assume that you know a top recruit to your college would most likely rank reasons in this order: available majors, academic reputation, and financial aid. Research indicates that introducing your strongest point first or last (available majors) is about equal in effect. It might get lost in the middle of the interview. If there's any possibility of the interviewee terminating the interview before you can present all of your points, start with your strongest point.

Developing Main Points

It is not enough to know which points or how many to develop in an interview or in which order to present them. You must develop each point into what the other party will see as valid and acceptable patterns. The most effective interview is a carefully crafted blend of the logical and the psychological. There are choices to make.

Arguing from accepted belief, assumption, or proposition involves three explicitly stated or implied assertions (statements you believe and clearly want others to believe). For instance, a health care interviewer might argue this way:

Your assertions must lead to your conclusion.

Assertion #1: Persons with high cholesterol levels have a significantly greater chance of having strokes or heart attacks.

Assertion #2: Your cholesterol level is very high, in the 260 range.

Conclusion: You are in serious danger of a stroke or heart attack.

The interviewer need not state all three parts of this pattern if the other party is likely to provide the missing assertion or conclusion. Your argument rests on the first assertion that is the critical belief, assumption, or proposition.

Arguing from condition is based on the assertion that if something does or does not happen, something else will or will not happen. You might reason this way with a roommate:

Assertion #1: If we don't cut down on electricity and gas, we are not going to be able to pay the rent.

Assertion #2: I don't see us doing anything to conserve.

Conclusion: I don't think we're going to have enough money to pay the rent on the 15th.

Weigh conditions carefully and be able to support them effectively.

Arguing from two choices is based on the assertion that there are only two possible proposals or courses of action. You delete one by establishing that it will not work or resolve a problem, and conclude the obvious. For example:

Assertion #1: I think you have two choices for graduate school in environmental communication, the University of Utah or Texas A & M University.

Assertion #2: The person you want to study with recently moved to A & M.

Conclusion: I think you should select A & M.

This argument rests, first, on being able to limit the choices and, second, convincing the interviewee that one is unacceptable so yours is the only one remaining.

Your evidence must warrant your conclusion.

Arguing from example leads to a generalization about a whole class of people, places, things, or ideas from a sample of this class. For instance, an interviewer attempting to "sell" a person on trucks that use alternative fuels might argue like this:

Sample: In a recent EPA study of 1,000 pickup trucks that used propane, ethanol, and biodiesel rather than gasoline, researchers discovered that the trucks had more horsepower, fewer engine problems, and 29 percent lower fuel cost.

Conclusion: You ought to purchase a pickup that uses alternative fuels because they are the best buy.

The sample, as in the survey interview that relies on sampling, is critical in argument from example.

Arguing from cause-effect is related to example because interviewers often use a sample as proof of a causal relationship. Unlike the argument from example that leads to a generalization, this argument attempts to establish what caused a specific effect. For instance:

Beware of false causes.

Evidence: A study of 50 accidents on or near campus that involved student drivers revealed that more than half had been drinking prior to the accidents.

Conclusion: Alcohol clearly is the cause of most student accidents.

You must convince the other party that the evidence leads to the major or single cause of a recognized effect.

Arguing from facts is the attempt to reach a conclusion that explains best a body of facts. This is how real detectives and those in who-done-it books and television shows argue when attempting to prove who committed a crime. For instance:

Facts: He was seen in the area on September 21 prior to the break-in at the computer lab in Yung Hall and has no alibi for the evening. On the 25th he attempted to sell two laptops on his Web site. When we searched his apartment, we found three laptops and other hardware that were stolen from Yung Hall on the 21st.

Conclusion: He took the computers from Yung Hall.

Unlike argument from example, the interviewer in this case is arguing from a variety of facts, not a sample of one class of things.

Arguing from analogy occurs when you point out that two things (people, places, objects, proposals, ideas) have important characteristics in common and draw a conclusion based on these similarities. For example, a coach might argue like this:

How similar are the similarities?

Points of comparison: This team reminds me of the one that went undefeated in 1987 and won the Orange Bowl. Like this team, the quarterback was a real leader and true Heisman candidate. His offensive line protected him extremely well, and the defense made sure the offense was on the field longer than anyone else. Above all, they operated as a team and not individuals. And they were coachable.

Conclusion: I think this team will go undefeated and compete successfully in a BCS bowl.

The number and significant similarities are critical in developing and selling this argument.

Selecting Strategies

When you think theories, think strategies.

Once you have determined a purpose and goals, chosen main points, and developed these points into persuasive argument patterns, select psychological strategies that will make them persuasive. Theorists have developed a number of theories both to explain how persuasion comes about and to prescribe how persuaders might bring about changes in thinking, feeling, and acting. Theories are efforts to explain complex human activities such as persuasion through careful observation of what happens in the real world.

Identification Theory

Kenneth Burke, arguably the leading rhetorical theorist of the past century, claims that we persuade by identifying with the other party. We must strive to establish **consubstantiality** (a substantial similarity) with the interviewee. The overlapping circles representing the interview parties in the model developed in Chapter 2 are based on Burke's notion that to communicate or persuade, you must talk the other party's language "with speech, gesture, tonality, order, image, attitude, *identifying*" your ways with theirs.[17]

There are several ways you can identify with a persuadee.[18] You may establish common ground by *associating* yourself with groups to which you both belong, common cultural heritage, programs you support, or regional identification. You may reverse this tactic by *disassociating* yourself from groups, cultures, programs, and regions the interviewee opposes or is separated from. You may identify through *appearance* and *visual symbols* such as dress, hairstyle, makeup, jewelry, political buttons, and religious symbols such as a cross, Star of David, or crescent. You may identify through *shared language* such as professional jargon, slang, colloquialisms, and in-group words and phrases. You may identify by selecting *content* and appealing to *values* that are important to the interviewee. It's important that you strive for real identification, not a fabrication to initiate the change you desire.

Appearances are important in perceiving common ground.

Balance or Consistency Theory

Balance and consistency theories are based on the belief that human beings strive for a harmonious existence with self (values, beliefs, and attitudes) and experience psychological discomfort (dissonance) when aspects of existence seem inconsistent or unbalanced.[19] You may experience source-proposition conflict when you like persons but detest their positions on issues or dislike persons but favor their products or services. You may experience attitude-attitude conflict when you oppose government involvement in your life but want the government to outlaw hate speech and require prayer in the public schools. You may experience perception-perception conflict when you see New York as a great place for vacation but dangerous for tourists. And you may experience a behavior-attitude conflict when you believe strongly in law and order but break the speed limits and use a fake ID to get into a bar.

Not all interviewees are happy with harmony.

As a persuader, you may create psychological discomfort (dissonance) by attacking a source or pointing out attitude, perception, and behavioral conflicts. Then you show how the interviewee can bring these inconsistencies into balance by providing changes in sources, attitudes, perceptions, and behaviors. If you detect that an interviewee is experiencing psychological discomfort, you may bring about balance or consistency by helping the interviewee to see no inconsistency, perceive the inconsistency to be insignificant, or to tolerate inconsistency.

An interviewer may create or resolve dissonance.

Inoculation Theory

Inoculation theory is based on the belief that it may be more effective to prevent undesired persuasive effects from occurring than trying damage control afterward.[20] For example, a few years ago one of the authors received a telephone call from the

An inoculation strategy immunizes an interviewee from future persuasion.

state police. The caller warned him of solicitors who were claiming to be representatives of a state police sponsored charity for children and related what they were telling potential contributors. The caller for the state police hoped the preemptive call would prevent the author from being victimized and maintain the credibility of legitimate state police charities.

This strategy forewarns interviewees. Sometimes the interviewer will expose the interviewee to small doses of a potential persuader's language, arguments, and evidence so the interviewee can resist the effort. Or the interviewer might provide arguments and evidence the interviewee may use to mount an effective countereffort if confronted by an interviewer against whom he or she is being immunized.

Induced Compliance Theory

There are many ways to trigger self-persuasion.

According to **induced compliance theory,** you can change an interviewee's thinking, feeling, or acting by inducing them to engage in activities counter to their values, beliefs, and attitudes.[21] Participation in counteractivities may bring about self-persuasion. It is important to apply enough pressure so interviewees will comply with your request without feeling they have no choice. If they feel coerced, they are unlikely to change thinking, feeling, or acting.

There are a variety of ways to induce compliance. You might induce an interviewee to *espouse* a belief or attitude counter to what they hold to understand, even appreciate the other side of an issue, such as a liberal position on sex education or a conservative position on health care reform. You might induce an interviewee to *take part* in an activity to which they are unaccustomed or unattracted, such as going to a religious service or helping at a homeless shelter. You might induce an interviewee to *play an opposite role,* such as a superior instead of a subordinate or teacher instead of a student. You might induce a party to act to *receive a reward* or *avoid a punishment,* such as tickets to a concert or a speeding ticket.

Psychological Reactance Theory

Restricting behavior may lead to persuasion or resentment.

According to **psychological reactance theory,** people react negatively when someone threatens to restrict or does restrict a behavior they want to engage in.[22] They may come to value the restricted behavior, such as renting R-rated videos, more and want to engage in it more than they normally do. People may devalue alternatives because they feel they are stuck with these alternatives instead of preferring them. Such people may resent the restricting agent.

Many organizations produce limited editions of books, stamps, coins, and cars to enhance demand for them. Tickets to the NCAA basketball Final Four become of great value because they are scarce. Interviewees may be in favor of giving to the college development fund or joining their athletic booster clubs until they feel they are being forced to do so.

Whenever possible avoid real or perceived pressure on the other party to think, feel, or act differently. Make your proposal attractive, make scarcity or a deadline known without appearing to threaten, develop a serious need without excessive appeals to fear, and try to offer choices.

Conducting the Interview

With thorough analysis of the interviewee and situation, research of the issue, and careful planning completed, you are now ready to conduct the interview. As you approach the interview, remember to be flexible, adaptable, and cautious about assumptions. You are conducting an interview, an interaction between two parties, not writing an essay or giving a speech to one. Plan how you will involve the interviewee from the first seconds of the interview.

Opening the Interview

Do not use routine openings even for routine interviews.

Design your opening to gain attention and interest, establish rapport, and motivate the interviewee to take part. The major advantage of the interview over public or mass persuasion is the opportunity to tailor your message to a single person or party. It is important to adapt the opening to each interviewee and setting. Resist the temptation to rely on a standard or traditional formula that may be inappropriate for a particular interviewee.

If the opening fails, there may be no body or closing.

Some writers estimate that "roughly 75 percent" of all sales representatives "fail in the attention step."[23] Think of the openings in the numerous sales calls made to your home and how you reacted. Persuaders trying to convince you to give to a charity are often trained to recite a prescribed opening regardless of your age, sex, income, background, or level of interest. You may dislike this charity; it makes no difference to the persuader. Little wonder that only about one in a hundred of these cold calls to homes is successful.

Review the opening techniques and principles discussed in Chapter 4. Select one or more techniques most suitable for this party and situation. Begin with a warm greeting and use the interviewee's name. If the person is a stranger, do not make your greeting sound like a question: "Good evening, Mrs. Walsh?" This suggests that you are unsure of the person's name or identity, unsure of yourself, and not well prepared.

If you know the interviewee well enough and both the situation and your relationship warrant it, use the person's first name. As a general rule, do not greet a stranger, superior, or person in a formal setting by first name or nickname unless you are asked to do so. On the other hand, being both somewhat formal and somewhat informal at the same time has its hazards. If, for example, callers greet the authors of this text as "Charles" or "William," they know neither of us well enough to use our first names.

Neither rush nor prolong the opening.

It may be necessary to introduce yourself (name, position, title, background), your organization (name, location, nature, history, products, services), and the purpose of the interview. Orientation is essential when there is no relational history between parties and no appointment or arrangements are made ahead of time.

You may begin with sincere personal inquiries about family or mutual friends or small talk about the weather, sports, highway construction, or campus facilities. Do not prolong this rapport stage. Be conscious of the interviewee's situation and preferences. If a person replies immediately after the greeting, "What can I do for you?" this signals that the person wants to get down to business.

Cultures differ in amount of acceptable small talk and socializing. Most Americans want to "get to the point" and "get the job done." Japanese and other cultures desire

Reduce reticence by involving the interviewee immediately and often.

to get acquainted, to follow "interaction rituals," and to go slower in making commitments and decisions.[24] Do not prolong the rapport stage, but be sure it is appropriate.

Involve all members of the other party from the start so each person will play an active role throughout the interaction. Persuasion is not something you do *to* a person but *with* a person. Be cognizant of cultural differences. American persuaders and persuadees, particularly males, tend to take turns unevenly during interactions and to speak at length during each turn. Japanese and others take turns evenly and make shorter statements.

The opening should be a good fit with the whole interview.

The opening should create mutual interest in the interview and establish trust and degree of affection or liking between the parties. Each party should understand the purpose of the interview and how they will share control.

Creating a Need or Desire

You will create a need or desire by developing in detail the three or four points you selected in the preparation stage. Introduce them in the order you have determined will be most effective, strongest point first or last with weaker points in the middle.

Develop One Point at a Time

Explain a point thoroughly. Provide sufficient evidence that is factually based, authoritative, recent, and well documented. Use a variety of evidence (examples, stories, authority, statistics, comparisons, definitions) so the interviewee is neither buried under an avalanche of figures nor bored with one story after another. Incorporate the values, beliefs, and attitudes most important to this interviewee.

Encourage Interaction and Interviewee Involvement

Don't lecture; interact.

This is an interview, not a speech. You are more likely to persuade if the interviewee is actively involved in the interaction. Stress how each point affects this interviewee's needs and desires.

Do not go to your next point until there has been some sort of agreement. With one point developed and agreed upon, move to point two, then three, and so on. Do not rush through a point or jump to the next one if the interviewee raises objections or poses questions. Move on when the interviewee seems ready to do so. Be patient and persistent.

Use Questions Strategically

Questions play unique roles in persuasive interviews.

Although you will rarely come to a persuasive interview with a schedule of questions, questions serve a variety of functions in persuasive interviews. Some sales professionals believe you should never *tell* when you can *ask* because this involves the interviewee as an active participant rather than a passive recipient. But you cannot rely solely on questions, particularly when a party sees no need and has no idea of options available once a need or desire is established.

Use questions to analyze the interviewee.

Information-Gathering Questions

If you have had little opportunity or success in analyzing an interviewee ahead of time, employ questions to ascertain an interviewee's background, needs, desires, values, beliefs, and attitudes. Ask questions to determine knowledge level and to draw out unstated concerns and objections. Listen carefully to responses and probe for accuracy and details. For example:

- How often do you replace your laptop?
- What do you know about Timeline Investments?
- What experiences have you had with international carriers?

Verification Questions

Questions can clarify and verify interactions.

Use reflective, mirror, and clearinghouse probing questions to check the accuracy of your assumptions, impressions, and information obtained before and during an interview. For instance, you may assume you have answered an objection satisfactorily or gotten an agreement when you have not. Be certain an interviewee understands what you are saying and grasps the significance of your evidence or points. Silence on the interviewee's part can indicate confusion or disagreement as well as understanding and agreement. For example:

- We are in agreement, then, with the long-term care benefits of this plan?
- My impression is that you are most concerned about security on our downtown campus.
- Does that answer your concern about travel reimbursement?

Encouraging Interaction Questions

Questions can stimulate interactions.

Use questions early in interviews to serve as a warm-up and tone-setting phase so that questioning, talking, and answering become natural for the interviewee. This climate encourages the interviewee to play an active role in the interview. Interviewees will feel freer to ask questions and provide meaningful feedback once they are an active part of the process and understand that you want them to. Employ questions to discover how a quiet or noncommittal interviewee is reacting. For example:

- How was the tour of our facilities?
- What were your reactions to the new look of the alumni magazine?
- What are your thoughts about leasing rather than buying an RV?

Attention and Interest Questions

Questions can sustain attention and interest.

Attention and interest questions keep the interviewee tuned in and alert to what you are saying. Many interviewees are busy or preoccupied with other concerns and their minds may wander. Use interesting, challenging, and thought-provoking questions to maintain interest and attention. For example:

- Remember when you had that accident in the Nevada desert?
- What would you do if someone stole your credit cards?
- How would you react if the school board decided on a redistricting plan that would send your children to the new elementary school five miles from here instead of Homestead just three blocks from here?

Agreement Questions

Questions can attain agreements and commitments.

Employ questions to obtain small agreements that will lead to bigger agreements. For instance, getting agreement after each point leads to agreement at the end of your need so you can move effectively to establishing criteria for solutions. Do not ask for agreement or commitment before you have developed or supported a point thoroughly. Too many persuaders think a barrage of generalizations and claims proves a point or need. It does not. Use a yes-response question (often in the form of a statement) to control the interview and lead to agreement if asked at the right time—after thorough development of one or more points and small agreements. For example:

- This seems to be an ideal time to act, doesn't it?
- I know you realize that cutting staff is the only way to balance the budget.
- Do you want to lose this account?

Objection Questions

Do not try to substitute questions for substance.

Use objection questions to respond tactfully to objections and to draw out unstated questions and objections. The goal is to get them on the table at the proper time. These questions can also discover what an interviewee knows about an issue and reveal the importance or reasons behind objections. For example:

- I know that "timing is everything" in campaigns, but can we just ignore the attacks on your agenda until after the state convention in August?
- I understand you have lots of questions when making a decision like this, but what concerns you most?
- You say that cost is a major concern, but what have you paid in repairs alone during the past year?

Questions can be valuable tools in persuasive interviews if asked tactfully and strategically. Don't ask questions prematurely that call for agreements when you have established nothing upon which to agree. Use leading and loaded questions sparingly because interviewees are turned off by high-pressure tactics. A series of questions is not enough to persuade. You must present good reasons supported by information and evidence.

Adapting to the Other Party

Tailor each part of the persuasive interview to the values, beliefs, and attitudes of the interviewee. Determine the probable disposition of the interviewee, and then select appropriate tactics and strategies.

The interviewee may see no personal need or relevance.

Indecisive, Uninterested Interviewees

If an interviewee is likely to be indecisive, uninterested, or uncertain, you may need to educate the person to see the reality and urgency of the problem, issue, or need. Use opening techniques that get the interviewee's attention and generate interest in the seriousness of the situation. Then lead off with your strongest point and provide a variety of evidence that informs as well as persuades and shows why the issue is of critical importance to this interviewee. Use questions to draw out feelings and perceptions, and involve the interviewee in the interaction.

Avoid real or perceived pressure, but reveal the urgency of the problem and the necessity of acting *now*. You may use moderate fear appeals to awaken the interviewee to dangers to self, family, or friends. Include appeals to values such as preservation of health, safety and security, freedom from restraint, ownership, and value of the individual. And show *how* this person can make a difference in solving or reducing the problem or danger.

Hostile Interviewees

Do not assume there will be hostility.

If an interviewee will be or appears to be hostile, be sure your anticipation or impression is accurate. Do not mistake legitimate concerns or objections or a gruff demeanor for hostility. If a person is truly hostile, determine why; then consider a common ground approach.

- A **yes-but approach** begins with areas of agreement and similarity and gradually leads into points of disagreement. The strategy is to lessen hostility and disagreement later by establishing common ground early on.
- A **yes-yes approach** hopes to get a party in the habit of agreeing so the party will keep on agreeing when you reach apparent disagreements.
- An **implicative approach** withholds an explicit statement of purpose or intent to avoid a knee-jerk negative reaction from the interviewee. You hope interviewees will see the implications of what you are saying and proving, perhaps feeling they came up with the concerns and solutions.

You must get to the point in a reasonable amount of time.

Regardless of the common ground approach, listen, be polite, and avoid defensiveness or anger when working with hostile interviewees. Hostility often results from lack of information, misinformation, or rumors. Respond with facts, expert testimony, examples, stories, and comparisons that clarify, prove, and resolve issues between parties. Be willing to accept minor points of disagreement and to admit your proposal is not perfect; no proposal is. Employ **shock-absorber** phrases that reduce the sting of critical questions: "Many residents I talk to feel that way, however . . ." "That's an excellent question, but when you consider . . ." "I'm glad you thought of that because . . . ."

Closed-Minded and Authoritarian Interviewees

Select evidence most appropriate for each party.

A **closed-minded or authoritarian interviewee** relies on trusted authorities and is more concerned about who supports a proposal than the proposal itself. Facts alone, particularly statistics, will not do the job. You must show that the interviewee's accepted authorities support your persuasive efforts. The closed-minded and authoritarian person has strong, unchangeable central values and beliefs, and you must be able to identify yourself and your proposal with these values and beliefs.

Do not bypass hierarchical channels or alter prescribed methods. Authoritarians react negatively to interviewers who don't belong or appear to be out of line, and may demand censure or punishment for appearing to violate accepted and valued norms.[25] Be sure you know the party you are dealing with and adapt accordingly.

Skeptical Interviewees

The interviewee may be skeptical because of a low opinion of you, your profession, or your organization. Begin the interview by expressing some views the interviewee holds—a yes-but or yes-yes approach. Maintain positive nonverbal cues such as a firm handshake, good eye contact, a warm and friendly voice, and appropriate appearance and dress. If the interviewee feels you are young and inexperienced, allude tactfully to your qualifications, experiences, and training and provide substantial and authoritative evidence. Be well prepared and experienced without bragging and avoid undue informality and a cocky, egotistical attitude. If the interviewee sees you as argumentative, avoid confrontations, attacks on the person's position, and demands. If the interviewee thinks you are a know-it-all, be careful when referring to your qualifications, experiences, and achievements. If the interviewee has concerns about your organization, you might withhold its name until you have created personal credibility with the interviewee. If the name must come out early in the interview, try to improve its image by countering common misperceptions, relating how it has changed, or identifying its strengths. On occasion, you may have to distance yourself from some elements or practices of the organization.

Image or credibility may be the major cause of failure.

Shopping-Around Interviewees

Many interviewees shop around before making a major purchase or decision. This means they will face **counterpersuasion** from other interviewers. When meeting with a shopper or an undecided interviewee, forewarn and prepare the interviewee. Provide the interviewee with supportive arguments, evidence, and responses to questions or points likely to be raised in encounters with others. Give small doses of the opposition's case (inoculation theory of persuasion) to show the strengths and weaknesses of both sides.

Be prepared for interviewees facing counter-persuasion.

Develop a positive, factual, nonemotional, approach that addresses the competition when necessary but dwells primarily on the strengths of *your* position and proposal.

Intelligent, Educated Interviewees

The highly **intelligent or educated interviewee** tends to be less persuasible because of knowledge level, critical ability, and faculty for seeing the implications behind arguments and proposals. Research indicates that such interviewees "are more likely to attend to and comprehend the message position but are less likely to yield to it."[26] For example, they are likely to see through the good guy–bad guy approach used in many sales situations, such as when the sales representative must get approval from the owner or manager for the deal he or she is trying to get for you.

A two-sided approach addresses but does not advocate each side.

When working with highly intelligent and educated interviewees, support all of your ideas thoroughly, develop arguments logically, and present a two-sided approach that weighs both sides of issues. Minimize emotional appeals, particularly if the interviewee is neutral or initially disagrees with your position and proposal. Encourage the interviewee to ask questions, raise objections, and be an active participant.

If an interviewee is of low intelligence or education, develop a simple, one-sided approach to minimize confusion and maximize comprehension. A complex, two-sided approach and intricate arguments supported by a variety of evidence may confuse the interviewee. Use examples, stories, and comparisons rather than expert testimony and statistics. Appeal to basic emotions: anger, fear, pity, and pride.

Presenting the Solution

When you have developed the need, summarized your main points, and gotten important agreements, both parties are ready to consider possible solutions.

Establishing Criteria

Establishing criteria is natural but often unconscious.

Begin the solution phase of your interview by establishing criteria (requirements, standards, rules, norms, principles) that any solution should meet. If the interviewee is obviously ready to move into this phase of the interview before you have presented all of your points, move on. Students who come to the authors to persuade them to extend the deadline for an assignment, make up a quiz, or write a letter of recommendation often continue to persuade after the authors have agreed to the request. They are determined to complete their case.

Establish a set of criteria *with the interviewee* for evaluating all possible solutions to the need that you have established. This process comes natural to us, but we often do not write down a list of specific criteria. For example, when selecting a college major, you may have considered courses, core requirements, specialties, careers, faculty, availability of internships, and marketability when you graduate. Even in simple decisions such as selecting a place to eat, you have criteria in mind, such as type of food and beverage, cost, distance, location, atmosphere of the restaurant, music, availability of large screen television for watching a football game, and preferences of other interview parties. Use this natural process in persuasive interviews.

All criteria are not created equally.

As you think of criteria prior to the interview and develop them with the interviewee during the interview, realize that not all criteria are of equal importance to the interviewee. For example, admissions directors at state universities have found that quality of school is the most important criterion for out-of-state applicants while cost is number 1 and quality is number 2 for in-state students. The situation can influence criteria. For instance, cost may override all other criteria during economic recessions.

Criteria are designed to evaluate and to persuade.

Establishing a set of criteria with the interviewee involves the interviewee in the process and shows that you are attempting to tailor your proposal to his or her needs, desires, and capabilities. The criteria phase provides a smooth transition from the need to the solution and reduces the impression that you are overly anxious to sell your point. Agreed-upon criteria enable you to build on a foundation of agreements, provide an effective means of comparing and assessing solutions, and deal with objections.

Considering the Solution

Seeing is believing.

With a need established and criteria agreed upon, present your solution in detail. Do not assume the other party will understand the details and nature of the solution you have in mind unless this has become clear during your pre-interview research or earlier in the interview. It's best to err on the side of too much information rather than not enough.

If you will consider more than one solution, deal with one at a time. Explain your solution in detail and use whatever visual aids might be available and appropriate: booklets and brochures, drawings and diagrams, graphs, letters, pictures, slides, computer printouts, sketch pads, swatches of materials, objects, and models. Some sources claim that interviewees remember only about 10 percent of *what they hear* but 50 percent of *what they do* and 90 percent of *what they both see and do.*[27]

Approach the solution in a positive, constructive, and enthusiastic manner. Believe in what you are presenting and show it. Emphasize the strengths and benefits of your proposal rather than the weaknesses of the competition. Avoid **negative selling** unless the competition forces you to do so as a matter of self-defense. I am likely to be more interested in the advantages of your proposal than the disadvantages of another.

Help interviewees make decisions that are best for them at this time. Encourage the interviewee to ask questions and be actively involved. Use repetition, what one writer calls the "heart of selling," to enhance understanding, aid memory, gain and maintain attention, and make the interviewee aware of what is most important.[28] Educate interviewees by informing them about options, requirements, time constraints, and new features.

Handling Objections

You cannot address an objection you do not hear.

Nothing is more threatening to an interviewer than the thought of the interviewee raising unexpected or difficult objections. But you should encourage the interviewee to do so because objections voice the need for more information or clarification and reveal the interviewee's concerns, fears, misunderstandings, and misinformation.

Do not assume agreement because an interviewee does not raise questions or objections. Watch for nonverbal clues such as restlessness, fidgeting, poor eye contact, raised eyebrows, confused expressions, signs of boredom, or silences. Find out what is taking place within.

Possible objections are numerous and often issue, goal, situation, and party specific. Five are most common and generic to persuasive interviews.

Anticipate common objections.

- *Procrastination: Never do today what you can put off until tomorrow.*
  Let me think about it.
  I've still got three weeks before that paper is due.
  My old truck is doing fine, so I'll wait awhile.
- *Money: That's a lot of money.*
  That copier model is too expensive for us.
  I didn't expect remodeling to cost that much.
  That's pretty expensive for a week on the beach.
- *Tradition: We've always done it this way.*
  That's just the way we've always done business.
  We've always attended the First Baptist Church.
  My grandfather chose that line of clothing when he opened the business in 1924.

- *Uncertain future: Who knows what tomorrow will bring.*
  My job is rather iffy right now.
  The economy is struggling, so I'm reluctant to hire new staff.
  At my age, I don't buy green bananas.
- *Need: What's the problem?*
  We've got good investments, so we don't need life insurance.
  I think the current mayor is doing a good job.
  We haven't had much crime around here, so I don't think we need a home security system.

How to Approach Objections

As you anticipate objections to eliminate surprises, think about handling each objection as a series of steps.

Meeting objections requires thought, understanding, tact, and substance.

Plan how to respond to reduce the danger of being put on the spot.

Listen carefully, completely, and objectively, never assuming you understand the other person's point or concern until you have heard it.

Clarify the objection, making sure you understand exactly what it is and its importance before you respond.

Respond appropriately, diplomatically, tactfully, and professionally. Never treat an objection as if it is frivolous. *If it is serious to the interviewee, it is serious.*

There are four common strategies for handling objections.

Minimize the Objection

Reduce the importance of the objection.

Minimize an objection by restating it to make it seem less important or by comparing it to other weightier matters. Providing evidence may reduce the importance of the objection, as in the following example:

1. **Interviewee:** We've always thought it would be great to live in the downtown of a large city in a loft like this, but we're afraid of the crime rate in downtown areas.
2. **Interviewer:** That was true a few years ago, but crime is declining in the centers of cities and spreading to outlying areas where there are fewer police officers. For example, in this area during the past three years, robberies and theft have declined by 23 percent, assaults by 43 percent, and shootings have all but disappeared. At the same time, in the outlying areas of this city, robberies and theft have increased by 27 percent, assaults by 12 percent, and shootings by 15 percent.

Capitalize on the Objection

Take advantage of the objection.

Capitalize on an objection by using it to *clarify* your own points, *review* the proposal's advantages, *offer* more evidence, or *isolate* the motive behind the objection. Convert a perceived disadvantage into an advantage. For example:

1. **Interviewee:** We'd like to purchase a house instead of continuing to pay rent on an apartment, but with the economy and layoffs we're afraid to take the risk.

2. **Interviewer:** Actually, this is an ideal time to buy a home because the interest rates are the lowest they've been for over 30 years and sales are great. You would have little problem selling your home with a margin of profit if that were to become necessary. You're losing a lot of money in rent payments.

Deny an Objection

Deny an objection *directly* or *indirectly* by offering new or more accurate information, by introducing new features of your proposal, or by showing how circumstances have changed. You cannot deny an objection by merely denying it, however. If you say it isn't so, *prove it.* Here is an example of denying an objection.

If you deny it, you must prove it isn't so.

1. **Interviewee:** I've heard the Citizen's Action Coalition is tied in with anti-gun groups and plans to raise property taxes.
2. **Interviewer:** We're not involved in the gun or property tax issues. In fact, many of our members are hunters and gun collectors. Three are actively involved in competitive skeet and trap shooting. You may have seen Karen McBride's name in the sports pages last fall as state champion in skeet shooting. Our concerns are with clean air and water and less dependence on fossil fuels. We want citizens like you to place pressure on Congress to toughen and enforce laws that will enable us to breathe easier and live longer. Property taxes are not the way to further these causes.

Confirm an Objection

Confirm an objection by agreeing with the interviewee. It is better to be honest and admit problems than to offer weak defenses. Here is a confirmation tactic:

Do not try to deny the undeniable.

1. **Interviewee:** Why should I pay $2,300 for a laptop when I can buy a desktop for less than $1,000?
2. **Interviewer:** Yes, laptops are a lot more expensive than desktops, but a laptop provides unique advantages. You can take the laptop anywhere with you: your apartment, the library, classroom, home during weekends, even coffee shops.

Closing the Interview

Approach the closing positively and confidently. Do not pressure the interviewee or appear too anxious for a final agreement. Interviewers often hesitate to close, fearing they may fail to persuade, while interviewees fear they will make a wrong decision. Sales professionals, for instance, cite hesitation to ask for a sale as the major cause of failure to sell.[29]

Both parties may fear the closing.

The closing of the persuasive interview usually consists of three stages: (1) trial closing, (2) filling out the contract or agreement, and (3) leave-taking.

Trial Closing

Begin the closing as soon as possible. Do not continue talking if the interviewee is sold on your proposal. You may talk yourself out of an agreement by giving the interviewee more opportunities to generate reasons not to be persuaded.

As you approach the end of the solution phase of the interview, watch and listen for verbal and nonverbal cues that the interviewee is moving toward a decision. Verbal cues include questions and statements such as "How soon will the new software be available?" "The idea appears sound." "This looks like a great tour of Ireland." Nonverbal cues include enthusiastic vocal expressions, head nods, and smiles. Two interviewees may exchange glances at one another as if to verify interest or agreement or begin handling brochures, pictures, or written reports.

Know when to stop talking.

Ask yes-response and leading questions to verify that the interviewee is ready to close: "I'm sure you can see this is the best way to go." "You want the safest SUV for your family, don't you?" "Do you want to face a negligence lawsuit?" After you ask a trial closing question, *be quiet!* Give the interviewee time to think and self-persuade. Silence communicates confidence in the interviewee and gives the party an opportunity to ask questions or raise objections not yet brought out or answered fully. Often interviewees just want final verification that they are doing the right thing.

Probe insightfully and cautiously into negative responses.

If you get a no to your trial closing question, discover why. Perhaps you need to review the criteria, compare advantages and disadvantages of acting now, or provide more information. Often an interviewee is simply not ready to act. Perhaps fear of possible consequences and how others will react (outside forces) overcomes the need or desire.

If you get a yes to your trial closing question, make a statement that will lead into the contract or agreement stage: "We can sign off on this today." "We can have this equipment installed within two weeks." "It would be a relief to have this lawsuit settled."

Contract or Agreement

Once you have completed a successful trial closing, move to the contract or agreement stage. This is a critical time in the interview because the other party knows the closing and a commitment are coming and may be frightened or anxious. Be natural and pleasant. Maintain good communication. Review the closing techniques and principles discussed in Chapter 4. There are a variety of closing techniques appropriate for the contract or agreement stage.

- An *assumptive close* addresses part of the agreement with a phrase, such as "I assume from our previous contacts that you prefer . . ."
- A *summary close* summarizes agreements made as a basis for decisions.
- An *elimination of a single objection close* responds to the single objection that stands in the way of an agreement, such as "Well, I can understand your reluctance to leave a position you're comfortable with, but think of the new challenges and rewards at the Omaha office.
- An *either-or close* limits the interviewee's choices, then shows that the solution you advocate has the most advantages and the fewest disadvantages.

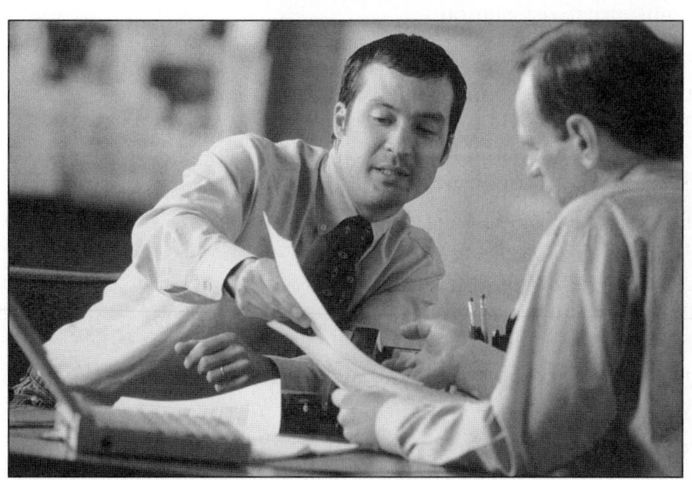
photo by Bruce Ayres/Getty Images

The contract or agreement stage is critical because the interviewee knows a commitment is imminent.

Select closing techniques most appropriate for this interview and interviewee.

- An *I'll think it over close* acknowledges the interviewee's desire to think about a decision, but tries to discover the level of interest and why the interviewee is hesitating. For example, "Just to clarify things, which part of this proposal do you want to think over?"
- A *sense of urgency close* stresses why an interviewee should act now. For example, "You must agree to this buy-out plan by the first of the month."
- A *price close* emphasizes the savings possible or the bottom line of the offer. For example, "This is the lowest price we have ever had on a 42″ plasma HDTV-capable widescreen monitor."

Leave-Taking

Leave-taking should reinforce all you have accomplished.

When the contract or agreement is completed, no agreement or contract can be reached, or another interview is necessary, conclude pleasantly and positively. Do not make the **leave-taking** phase **abrupt** or **curt.** You may undo the rapport and trust you worked so hard to establish by communicating to interviewees they were of value only as long as they were potential clients.

The verbal and nonverbal leave-taking techniques discussed in Chapter 4 may be adapted or combined to suit each interview. Above all, be sincere and honest in this final closing phase. And make no promises you cannot or will not keep because of personal or authority limitations, organizational policies, laws, or time constraints.

Summary Outline

The following outline summarizes the elements in the developmental structure of a persuasive interview that covers both need/desire and solution.

I. Opening the interview
  A. Select the most appropriate techniques from Chapter 4.
  B. Establish rapport according to relationship and situation.
  C. Provide appropriate orientation.

II. Creating a need or desire
  A. Provide an appropriate statement of purpose.
  B. Develop a need point-by-point with maximum involvement of and careful adaptation to the other party.
    1. Use appropriate argument patterns
    2. Provide a variety of evidence.
    3. Employ effective strategies.
    4. Appeal to important values and emotions.
    5. Obtain overt agreements as you proceed, being sure to point out how the interviewee party is involved or must be concerned.
  C. Summarize the need or problem and attain overt agreements from the interviewee.

III. Establishing criteria
  A. Present the criteria you have in mind, explaining briefly the rationale and importance of each criterion.

B. Encourage the interviewee to add criteria.
C. Involve the interviewee in the discussion of criteria.
D. Summarize and get agreement on all criteria.

IV. Presenting the solution
A. Present one solution at a time.
1. Explain the solution in detail using visual aids when possible.
2. Evaluate the solution using agreed-upon criteria.
B. Respond to anticipated and vocalized objections.
C. Get agreement on the appropriateness, quality, and feasibility of the preferred solution.

V. Closing the interview
A. Begin a trial closing as soon as it seems appropriate to do so.
B. When the trial closing is successful, move to a contract or agreement with the interviewee.
C. Use appropriate leave-taking techniques discussed in this chapter and Chapter 4.

You need not develop all parts of this outline in every interview. For instance, if an interviewee agrees with the need or problem prior to the interview, merely summarize the need in the opening and move directly to criteria. An interviewee, for instance, may see the need but not agree with your proposed solution. Or an interviewee may feel any move now is impossible because of financial or other constraints. Feasibility would be the central concern of this interview, not need or a specific proposal.

There is no set pattern for all persuasive interviews.

In other persuasive situations, the interviewee may like your proposal but see no need to take action at this time: the computer is still working, business is still good, no serious health problem has occurred, or retirement is still decades away. You would devote nearly all of your interviews with such persons to establishing urgent needs or desires.

ON THE WEB

Assume you are going to purchase a new car upon graduation. You want to be thoroughly informed and prepared when you contact sales representatives so you can make an intelligent decision and get a good deal. Use the World Wide Web to access information on brands, models, features, comparative prices, and assessments by automotive experts. Sample manufacturer sites are Toyota (http://www.toyota.com), Acura (http://www.acura.com), Mazda (http://mazdausa.com), Buick (http://www.parkavenue.com), and Chrysler (http://www.chryslercars.com). What information is readily available on the Internet, and why is this so? What information is not included on the Internet, and why is this so? What are common persuasive tactics used on the Internet? What questions does your research suggest you pursue during interviews?

Summary

Good persuasive interviews are ones in which both parties are actively involved, not speeches given to an audience of one but interpersonal interactions in which both parties must speak and listen effectively. The guiding principle is that persuasion is *done with* not *done to* another party.

Good persuasive interviews are honest endeavors conducted according to fundamental ethical guidelines. They are not games in which the end justifies the means or *buyer beware* is a guiding principle. The appeal should be to both the head and the heart rather than relying on emotional hot buttons that will override critical thought and decision making.

Good persuasive interviews are carefully researched, planned, and structured, yet they remain flexible enough to meet unforeseen reactions, objections, and arguments. The goal is to adapt the persuasive effort to *this persuadee* rather than create a generic interview minimally adapted to a broader audience or clientele. The persuader develops, supports, and documents important reasons for a change in thinking, feeling, or acting and presents a detailed solution that meets criteria agreed upon by both parties. Except in simple efforts, persuasion is seldom a "one-shot" effort but entails several contacts in which the persuader and persuadee reach incremental agreements.

Key Terms and Concepts

The online learning center for this text features FLASHCARDS and CROSSWORD PUZZLES for studying based on these terms and concepts.

Agreement questions
Analyzing the interviewee
Arguing from accepted belief
Arguing from analogy
Arguing from cause-effect
Arguing from condition
Arguing from example
Arguing from facts
Arguing from two choices
Atmosphere
Attention and interest questions
Attitudes
Attitude-attitude conflict
Balance or consistency theory
Behavior-attitude conflict
Beliefs
Closed-minded or authoritarian interviewee
Closing
Consubstantiality
Contract or agreement closing
Criteria
Culture
Dissonance
Encouraging interaction questions
Ethics
Evidence
Hostile interviewee
Identification theory
Implicative approach
Indecisive interviewee
Induced compliance theory
Information-gathering questions
Intelligent interviewee
Interrelated conditions
Leave-taking
Motives
Objection questions
Objections
One-sided approach
Opening
Outside forces
Psychological discomfort
Psychological reactance theory
Physical and mental characteristics
Physical setting
Shock-absorber phrases
Shopping-around interviewee
Situation
Skeptical interviewee
Socioeconomic background
Solution
Source-perception conflict
Structure
Timing
Trial closing
Two-sided approach
Values
Verification questions
Yes-but approach
Yes-yes approach

A Persuasive Interview for Review and Analysis

This interview is between Josh Molinsky, a member of the County Council, and Susan Dawson, president of the Chamber of Commerce, in which Josh will attempt to convince Susan of the need to implement a highly controversial Local Option Highway User Tax, better known as a wheel tax. Susan has expressed concerns about the need for such a tax and the potential negative impact of this tax on businesses located or doing business in the county, particularly if surrounding counties do not adopt a wheel tax. Josh feels that Susan's support is critical in selling the idea of a user tax to other segments of the community and hopes this interview will be a first step in changing her mind. No action is desired.

How thoroughly has the interviewer done his homework, including analyzing the persuadee? How does the relationship of the parties affect the interview? How satisfactory are the opening, need, and closing? How satisfactory is the evidence in support of reasons for a change? How effectively does the persuader respond to objections and questions?

1. **Interviewer:** Good morning, Susan. (cheerful and smiling) How are the kids?
2. **Interviewee:** Hi Josh. They're fine, thanks. (shakes his hand) Jamie will graduate from high school in a few weeks.
3. **Interviewer:** That's great. I can remember when she was a preschooler. How was the state Chamber of Commerce convention last week in Columbus?
4. **Interviewee:** It was a wonderful opportunity to share ideas and talk about the business climate in our communities and some of the problems communities across the state are having.
5. **Interviewer:** I always find the sharing of ideas and concerns at conventions to be helpful. Just to discover you're all in the same boat helps at times.
6. **Interviewee:** That's true. (looks at her watch) What can I do for you?
7. **Interviewer:** Did the Local Option Highway User Tax come up during your meetings?
8. **Interviewee:** Yes, it did. (frowning) It's not very popular among Chamber members or in their communities. Is that what you want to talk to me about? I know the County Council is considering it soon.
9. **Interviewer:** Yes, that's why I'm here this morning. I'm well aware of the unpopularity of the so-called wheel tax. Letters to the *Constitution* and call-ins on local radio shows are running 3 to 1 opposed to the idea. As you know, several of us on the County Council feel it's the lesser of two evils.
10. **Interviewee:** Uh huh. And what does that have to do with me or the Chamber of Commerce?
11. **Interviewer:** Well . . . frankly . . . we feel it is essential to have you aboard on this issue if we're going to sell it to business leaders and employers.
12. **Interviewee:** That's not going to happen until our members change their minds, which is unlikely. You see . . .
13. **Interviewer:** (cuts in) I'd like to explain why we've changed our minds during the past year and maybe why you might change yours.

14. **Interviewee:** Okay. I'm willing to listen, but that's it.
15. **Interviewer:** Good. As you know, we hoped the state legislature this year would provide supplemental appropriations and perhaps a small increase in the gas tax to provide needed highway funding. Because of opposition to raising taxes of any kind and then the catastrophic increase in gas prices this past summer, the legislature did neither. We're now in a bind with new projects and necessary repairs far exceeding the funds available.
16. **Interviewee:** I think, in times like this, that all agencies will have to live within their means. Even if that seems painful to some.
17. **Interviewer:** I guess it depends upon who's feeling the pain, or "whose ox is being gored" so to speak.
18. **Interviewee:** I don't follow that metaphor at all. All of us were gored at the pump and all of us felt the pain of fill-ups.
19. **Interviewer:** Well, the Chamber has been pushing the county to make Karber Road four lanes instead of two because of the rapidly growing development on the south side. The cost of this improvement, with necessary curbs, sidewalks, and storm sewers, will be more than $1 million per lane per mile. This limits us to a quarter-mile of a four-lane Karber Road per year. That's a long time to complete this much-needed five-mile stretch of road.
20. **Interviewee:** I think it's time to prioritize projects. Those of us in *business* (vocal emphasis) have to do that all the time.
21. **Interviewer:** And so do those of us in government positions. The problem is that many projects seem to be at the top of the priority list. For instance, the Karber Road project is highly important, but so are the replacement costs of 15 bridges in the area that the state is demanding we repair or replace. The cost is more than a million a bridge just for repair work.
22. **Interviewee:** Well, those could be at the top of the county's list.
23. **Interviewer:** (sounds exasperated) Yes, we could, but the average life for a paved road is about 15 years, and a great many new roads built in the county in the booming 1990s are reaching that age. Do you know what it costs just to repave a road?
24. **Interviewee:** No (laughing), but I'll bet you're going to tell me.
25. **Interviewer:** That's right. (not smiling) Last year it cost $25,000 to resurface a mile of road that required no other repairs. Since we rely primarily on asphalt that is oil based, the cost this year with the 44 percent rise in oil prices is likely to exceed $30,000 a mile, not including the gas increases for running our equipment.
26. **Interviewee:** I can appreciate this fact, but you'll just have to delay some resurfacing until the economy improves.
27. **Interviewer:** That *sounds* (vocal emphasis) like a good idea until you figure in the added cost of a deteriorated road that requires more than resurfacing. The cost could jump to $50,000 a mile. We have over $650 million invested in county roads.
28. **Interviewee:** Josh, it's priority again. Prioritize the important projects and reduce or eliminate other costs.

29. **Interviewer:** Okay, that sounds like *good business* (vocal emphasis). We can do this by eliminating culvert repairs, guardrail improvements, signage, snow plowing, salting of icy roads, mowing during the summer, picking up dead animals, and patching of potholes. Would you and county residents be in favor of this after the first snowfall or severe damage to tires and suspensions because of potholes and ruts?
30. **Interviewee:** I'm not proposing the elimination of these *essentials* (vocal emphasis).
31. **Interviewer:** I see. Then these are top priority items, too?
32. **Interviewee:** Okay, Josh, I see some of what you're saying. There seem to be a lot of high priority items. But a wheel tax would burden our county residents but not those driving in from surrounding counties.
33. **Interviewer:** (sounding incredulous) You're president of the Chamber of Commerce, and you're concerned about those who bring their business and their money into this county?
34. **Interviewee:** Of course not (sounds a bit testy). We have many programs designed to encourage working and shopping here. I'm just concerned about fairness.
35. **Interviewer:** Me too, but short of tollbooths on every road, there is no way to charge a road tax on those coming in, and we both agree we want them to continue coming in.
36. **Interviewee:** That's not what I had in mind. It's ridiculous.
37. **Interviewer:** Real or imagined tollbooths won't be necessary because I suspect that surrounding counties will soon have a Local Option Highway User Tax of their own. In fact, Jefferson and Henry counties to our west will institute such a tax this fall. Like us, they see no other choice.
38. **Interviewee:** Well, you've made some good points. I'm not sure I'm sold on the idea of a new tax yet, but I'd like to think about it and then talk to you about the nature of the tax plan you would initiate, such as a sunset provision that would end it after a few years.
39. **Interviewer:** That's all I wanted to do this morning, to encourage you to consider the idea and the problems we face. How about meeting on Thursday morning around 9:00?
40. **Interviewee:** That time is open on my calendar, but I'd like to see a breakdown of the highway budget for this year before then to see where our road money is going.
41. **Interviewer:** The County Council committee on option taxes is meeting Wednesday night, and I might have some ideas to share the next morning. I'll get you a copy of the budget.
42. **Interviewee:** Okay. See you then.

Persuasion Role-Playing Cases

Acquiring a Commuter Airline Service

The interviewer is the manager of a university-operated airport that has provided commercial passenger service to the area since the 1950s. Unfortunately, the convenience and limo service every two hours to an international airport just 65 miles away and the cost of commuter airline tickets have resulted in several airlines coming and going over the years because of lack of passengers. Nighthawk Air is the only airline continuing to serve the airport with two morning and two afternoon flights to Lambert Field in St. Louis. It has announced that it will discontinue service on December 1. The interviewer is scheduling interviews with several commuter airlines in an effort to persuade them to replace Nighthawk Air in December.

The interviewee is Chief of Operations for Eastern-Southern, a four-year-old commuter airline serving Delaware, Maryland, Virginia, and North Carolina. Their long-range plans are to extend service to Pennsylvania and Ohio. Competition from large airlines and a steep rise in fuel bills have made these plans tenuous at best. She is willing to listen to the interviewer from a service area that might be in their future, but she is well aware of the number of airlines that have come and gone from his airport. There would have to be guarantees of reasonable passenger numbers and some financial incentives. The interviewer has a good background in the aviation industry but little management experience or success in selling commuter service to his campus and community.

Development of Three Resort Complexes

The interviewer is one of several people who have formed Resorts Unlimited to develop resorts in the Upper Peninsula (UP) of Michigan, which has suffered severe economic problems and unemployment since the copper and iron ore mines closed during the 1970s and 1980s. Resorts Unlimited wants to create several resorts in the hills and along the lakes of the UP that have remained undeveloped and populated by people who prefer the solitude of the area and the pristine condition of the lakes. Fishing and hunting are excellent because few tourists have invaded the area. The interviewer is trying to convince three families—the Lindbergs, Petersens, and Johnsons—to join the consortium or to sell their land to the consortium so it can build three resorts that will attract year-round tourists who enjoy hunting, fishing, and winter sports.

The interviewees (one each from the Lindberg, Petersen, and Johnson families) want the area to stay as it has in the five generations they have lived on their property or in the area. They are aware of the economic problems of the area but feel efforts should be directed toward restarting the mines or attracting companies willing to build on the old mine sites. They fear that resorts will permanently destroy the area as they have known it for generations. They think the interviewer is more interested in the profit from hoards of tourists at resorts than in resolving the area's economic plight. Most of the new jobs created would be low-paying service positions. Above all, the interviewer is from the Lower Peninsula, an outsider who does not appreciate the unique history and characteristics of the UP.

Adoption of the New Line of Clothing

The interviewer is 24 years old and is the assistant manager of Abbey's, a women's clothing store in a shopping mall close to a college campus. The three lines of clothing and the selection of jewelry clearly appeal to "mature" women in their late 30s and older, not the college customer but her mother. The interviewer wants to persuade the owner–manager to eliminate at least one line of clothing and replace it with one or ones that will attract the teenage and young adult clientele. The selection of jewelry would be mixed in appeal. The interview is taking place in the interviewee's office at 8:00 before the shop opens at 9:30.

The interviewee has owned Abbey's for nearly six years and has been pleased with sales and the number of repeat customers she attracts. Ego involvement is high because the interviewee personally selected the shop's brands and jewelry and travels to Chicago, San Francisco, and New York to make stock selections. The interviewer is seen as a very hard worker with excellent communication skills but highly interested in her own tastes in clothing and jewelry. She is part of her generation, but this does not prevent her from interacting with and selling to women several years older. The interviewee sees her shop as one of the few in the mall that appeals to women her age rather than "teenyboppers."

A Vacation Home in the Poconos

The interviewer is a real estate sales representative for Mountain View Realty in the Pocono Mountains a few hours north of Philadelphia. During the past several months, he has been working with the Kabara family, who are looking for a vacation home in the area, preferably on or near a large lake. The Kabaras have four children, ages six to twelve, and are anxious to purchase a home so all of their children will have years to enjoy it. Unfortunately, they have been unable to locate a suitable home. Mountain View Realty has recently purchased several two-acre lots in a heavily wooded area with access to a nearby lake. He wants to persuade the Kabara family to build a log home on one of these lots.

The interviewees have not given much thought to building a home, particularly since they still have less than fond memories of building their current home eight years ago. The wife manages a restaurant, and the husband is a chemical engineer for a pharmaceutical company. Their combined income should make the investment of nearly $400,000 feasible if they encounter no financial difficulties. Two of their children have been diagnosed with learning disabilities and recently enrolled in expensive private schools in Philadelphia. They would like to find a house they can move into without the building headaches. They like the realtor but see him as too eager at times to make a sale.

Student Activities

1. Locate a professional (sales representative, recruiter, fund-raiser) who conducts persuasive interviews on a regular basis and spend a day on the job with this person. Observe how this person prepares for each interview, selects strategies, opens interviews, develops needs and solutions, closes interviews, and adapts to interviewees.
2. Visit two different establishments (such as a department store, car dealer, travel agent, or real estate representative) with persons who wish to make persuasive transactions. Observe a persuasive interview in each establishment. How much information about the person did the interviewer get before making a presentation or suggestion? How did the person's personal characteristics such as age, sex, race, culture, dress, physical appearance, and apparent degree of wealth seem to affect these interactions? Which values did the interviewers appeal to?
3. Interview a college coach who actively recruits high school students for his or her program. Probe specifically into how the coach adapts to each recruit's needs and desires. What kinds of information does the coach provide? What "hot buttons" does the coach try to push, and how does the coach determine these are the ones to

push? How does the coach handle objections? When and how does the coach try to close persuasive efforts?

4. Select a person you either admire or dislike—a casual acquaintance, fellow student or worker, relative, national figure. Make a list of descriptive adjectives (such as honest/dishonest, competent/incompetent, trustworthy/untrustworthy) that you think describe this person. Which of these traits are important facets of credibility? How was this image formed in your mind? What could this person do to alter this image in your mind?

Notes

1. Roderick P. Hart, "Teaching Persuasion," *Teaching Communication: Theory, Research, and Methods,* John A. Daly, Gustav W. Friedrich, and Anita L. Vangelisti, eds. (Hillsdale, NJ: Lawrence Erlbaum, 1999), p. 133.
2. Isocrates, "Against the Sophists," in *The Rhetorical Tradition: Readings from Classical Times to the Present,* Patricia Bizzell and Bruce Herzberg, eds. (New York: Bedford/ St. Martins, 2001), pp. 72–75.
3. "Ethics Endorsed as Skill for 21st Century," Lafayette, Indiana, *Journal and Courier,* January 31, 1996, p. A5.
4. Melanie Butler, Tiffani Ridley, and Mary Allen, "The Demographics of Cheating in College Students," http://www.psich.org/pubs/articles/article_324.asp, accessed October 21, 2006.
5. "Public Ranks Professions by Their Ethics and Honesty," http://globalethics.org/ newsline/members/issue.tmpl, accessed October 21, 2006.
6. Morgan Poll, http://roymorgan.com/news/polls/2005/3938, accessed October 21, 2006.
7. Richard L. Johannesen, "Perspectives on Ethics in Persuasion," in Charles U. Larson, *Persuasion: Reception and Responsibility* (Belmont, CA: Thomson/Wadsworth, 2004), p. 27.
8. Gary C. Woodward and Robert E. Denton, Jr., *Persuasion and Influence in American Life* (Long Grove, IL: Waveland Press, 2004), p. 339.
9. Kenneth E. Andersen, *Persuasion: Theory and Practice* (Boston: Allyn and Bacon, 1971), p. 327.
10. Deirdre Johnston, *The Art and Science of Persuasion* (Madison, WI: Brown & Benchmark, 1994), p. 185; Sharon Shavitt and Timothy Brock, *Persuasion: Psychological Insights and Perspectives* (Boston: Allyn & Bacon, 1994), pp. 152–153.
11. Michael Argyle, "Intercultural Communication," in Larry A. Samovar and Richard E. Porter, *Intercultural Communication: A Reader* (Belmont, CA: Wadsworth, 1988), pp. 35–36.
12. Milton Rokeach, *Beliefs, Attitudes, and Values* (San Francisco: Jossey-Bass, 1968), p. 124.
13. Aristotle, *Rhetoric,* W. Rhys Roberts, trans. (New York: The Modern Library, 1954), Bk. I, Chap. 2, p. 25.

14. Robert H. Glass and John S. Seiter, *Persuasion, Social Influence, and Compliance Gaining* (Boston: Pearson, 2007), p. 77; Charles U. Larson, *Persuasion: Reception and Responsibility* (Belmont, CA: Thomson/Wadsworth, 2007), pp. 276–277.

15. Woodward and Denton, pp. 110–118; Omar Swartz, *Persuasion as a Critical Activity* (Dubuque, IA: Kendall/Hunt, 2001), pp. 75–76.

16. O'Keefe, p. 186.

17. Kenneth Burke, *A Rhetoric of Motives* (Berkeley, CA: University of California Press, 1969), p. 55.

18. Burke, pp. 21–45; Charles J. Stewart, Craig Allen Smith, and Robert E. Denton, Jr., *Persuasion and Social Movements* (Prospect Heights, IL: Waveland Press, 2001), pp. 152–160.

19. Woodward and Denton, pp. 147–151; Larson, pp. 90–93.

20. Kathleen Kelley Reardon, *Persuasion in Practice* (Newbury Park, CA: Sage, 1991), pp. 54–55; Daniel J. O'Keefe, *Persuasion: Theory and Practice* (Newbury Park, CA: Sage, 1990), pp. 179–181; Erin Alison Szabo and Michael Pfau, "Nuances of Inoculation: Theory and Applications," in *The Persuasion Handbook: Development in Theory and Practice,* James Price Dillard and Michael Pfau, eds. (Thousand Oaks, CA: Sage, 2002), pp. 233–258.

21. O'Keefe, pp. 71–77.

22. Michael Burgoon, Eusebio Alvaro, Joseph Grandpre, and Michael Voulodekis, "Revisiting the Theory of Psychological Reactance," in *The Persuasion Handbook: Development in Theory and Practice,* James Price Dillard and Michael Pfau, eds. (Thousand Oaks, CA: Sage, 2002), pp. 213–232.

23. James F. Roberson, H. Lee Mathews, and Carl G. Stevens, *Selling* (Homewood, IL: Richard D. Irwin, 1978), p. 109.

24. William B. Gudykunst and Tsukasa Nishida, *Bridging Japanese/North American Differences* (Thousand Oaks, CA: Sage, 1994), pp. 68–73.

25. Stewart, Smith, and Denton, pp. 83–87; Robert N. Bostrom, *Persuasion* (Englewood Cliffs, NJ: Prentice-Hall, 1983), pp. 181–182.

26. Shavitt and Brock, pp. 152–153.

27. Larson, p. 295; Woodward and Denton, pp. 386–389.

28. Tom Hopkins, *How to Master the Art of Selling* (Scottsdale, AZ: Champion Press, 1982).

29. Lee Iacocca, *Iacocca: An Autobiography* (New York: Bantam Books, 1984), p. 34.

Resources

Brennan, Charles D. *Sales Questions That Close the Sale: How to Uncover Your Customer's Real Needs*. New York: AMACOM, 1994.

Dillard, James Price, and Michael Pfau, eds. *The Persuasion Handbook: Developments in Theory and Practice*. Thousand Oaks, CA: Sage 2002.

Glass, Robert H., and John S. Seiter. *Persuasion, Social Influence, and Compliance Gaining*. Boston: Pearson, 2007.

Larson, Charles U. *Persuasion: Reception and Responsibility*. Belmont, CA: Thomson/Wadsworth, 2007.

Woodward, Gary C., and Robert E. Denton. *Persuasion and Influence in American Life*. Long Grove, IL: Waveland Press, 2004.

CHAPTER 11 The Persuasive Interview: The Persuadee

In Chapter 10, we emphasized that persuasion is *done with* not *to* another party. It is a mutual activity in which both parties must play active and critical roles. It literally takes two to tangle.

Be an active participant.

Since we often find ourselves in the persuadee role as customer, client, student, contributor, voter, or recruited, we must understand the process that is taking place and be responsible, informed, active, and critical participants. We cannot afford to be passive and ignorant of the process because the results are likely to be important to us, our family, our associates, and our organization. A good offense is often the best defense, but this defense must be tempered first with ethical responsibilities.

Be a Responsible Participant

Both parties share ethical responsibilities.

Since the persuasive interview is a mutual activity, both parties share ethical responsibilities. Richard Johannesen writes, for instance, that "As receivers and senders of persuasion, we have the responsibility to uphold appropriate ethical standards for persuasion."[1] Herbert Simons suggests, "In your role as communicator and recipient of persuasive messages, ask yourself: What ethical standards should guide my conduct in this particular case? What should I expect of others?"[2] As noted in Chapter 10, there appear to be few universally accepted ethical standards applicable to all complex persuasive interviews that inevitably deal with degrees of right and wrong, good and bad. There are, however, fundamental ethical standards that can serve as guidelines when you are a persuadee.

Be Honest

We know when we are being honest.

Most of us assume that we are basically honest in our dealings with others but admit that we do tell "little, white lies" from time to time, particularly when we don't initiate the persuasion process. We tell a telemarketer that a significant other is not home when the person is sitting right next to us, tell a sales associate that we are "just browsing" when we are active shoppers, and tell a caller from a charity that "we gave at the office." Is it really dishonest to pretend to be a customer or client to get information for a class project, a free ride in a luxury sports car, or a free sample? These may not do much harm, and indeed may be expected by some persuaders, but persuasive interviews can be productive only if you are willing to exchange accurate information, answer questions truthfully, and admit motives, weaknesses, lack of information, and lack of training. Simons suggests two questions to assess your honesty: "How will

I feel about myself after this communicative act? Could I justify my act publicly if called on to do so?"[3]

Be Fair

Relationships can grow or wither during interviews.

If you follow the golden rule, "Do unto others as you would have them do unto you," fairness will not pose a problem. For instance, ask real and fair questions. Avoid stockpiling grievances and objections until late in an interview and then dumping them on the persuader. Don't drag in irrelevant, trivial, or far-fetched ideas or arguments that detract from the quality of the interview and disadvantage the other party.[4] Disagreements, even very strong and emotional ones, are common in persuasive interviews, but avoid name-calling and other tactics that may have a negative impact on not only this interaction but your long-term relationship with this party.

Be Skeptical

Be skeptical but open to change and actions.

You are responsible for a reasoned skepticism about assertions, claims, and promises. Too often we are more interested in quick fixes, good deals, good news, and something-for-nothing than in thoroughly analyzing needs and weighing competing solutions. Don't be gullible. As the saying goes, "If it sounds too good to be true, it probably is." Con artists would become extinct if we all became critical consumers. Scams work because we are willing accomplices, often because of simple greed. We think we are getting a deal-of-a-lifetime on a like-new BMW with only 12,000 miles on the odometer, a new roof from materials left over from another job, a great job in a foreign country, or an investment in a start-up electronics firm. Remember the "buyer beware" notion of ethics because you're the buyer.

Listen, question, and analyze.

Be Thoughtful and Deliberate in Judgment

Listen, question, analyze, synthesize, and then decide whether to accept or reject a person, idea, or proposal.[5] Raise critical objections and demand responses backed by solid evidence. Research indicates that interviewees are frequently more interested in appearances than substance. For instance, if we like the interviewer (often because of appearance and dress), we assume the proposal is logical and acceptable.[6] If a claim appears to agree with our values, beliefs, and attitudes, we may accept it regardless of how it was reached. Unfortunately, the appearance of logic or reasoning may be more important than the substance of it. And we often see no difference between biased and unbiased sources or between sources such as supermarket tabloids and *The Wall Street Journal* or *The New York*

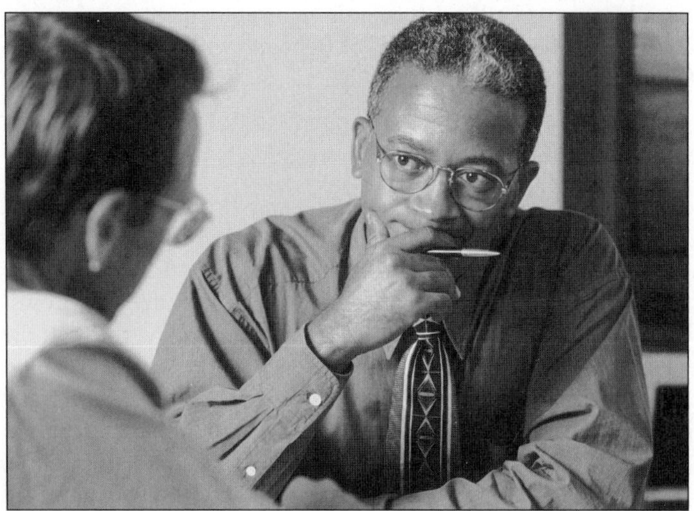

photo by Paul Barton/Corbis

Listen, question, analyze, and synthesize before acting.

Times. Johannesen claims that "an essential element of responsible communication, for both sender and receiver, is the exercise of thoughtful and deliberate judgment."[7]

Be Open-Minded

Open-mindedness is not gullibility.

Being open-minded does not mean that you have no strong beliefs or commitments to positions and organizations. It means that you should not automatically assume certain persuaders (because of profession, religion, race, age, sex, or culture) are untrustworthy or incompetent, that you do not automatically reject proposals from groups you oppose, or that you do not automatically reject proposals that challenge your own. "Be open to dissent and opinions of others" and strive to limit defensiveness and ego involvement.[8]

Be Responsive

Feedback is essential to the process.

Provide thorough verbal and nonverbal feedback to persuaders so they understand your needs, limitations, and perceptions of what is taking place and being agreed to. Let them know what you are thinking and how you are reacting. There is no substitute for being actively involved in the interview from opening through closing. Johannesen writes that "persuasion can be seen as a transaction in which both persuaders and persuadees bear mutual responsibility to participate actively in the process."[9]

Be an Informed Participant

Many persuaders are thoroughly versed in the art and science of persuasion and understand how attitude and behavioral changes are likely to come about. Few share this knowledge because we have only recently begun to prepare people to be intelligent consumers of persuasion. It is important for you to know the "tricks of the trade" to *inoculate* yourself from unwanted persuasive effects.

Psychological Strategies

We may act automatically during persuasive interviews.

Many persuaders rely upon strategies that are designed to create psychological discomfort—dissonance—that leads persuadees to alter ways of thinking, feeling, and/or acting.[10] For instance, they know that **standard/learned principles** automatically guide many of our actions and decisions. Most of us believe, for example, that:

You get what you pay for.

If it's expensive, it's good quality.

Sales offer bargains and save us money.

If an expert says so, it must be true.

If it's in print, it's true.

If it meets industry standards, it's safe.

Upscale retailers depend on these standard/learned principles to move expensive, high-quality items ranging from jewelry to automobiles. One of the authors remembers working at a supermarket while in college. The manager wanted to move bunches of radishes late one Saturday, so he raised the price from 2 for 19 cents to 10 cents a bunch with a sale sign. They sold out in a matter of minutes.

Look for real differences

In the **contrast principle,** persuaders know that if a second item is fairly different from the first in attractiveness, cost, or size, it seems *more different* than it actually is. If I want to rent you an apartment, I may show you a real dump first and then a somewhat better apartment next. You are likely to jump at the chance to rent the second. The same strategy works with persons: introduce an ugly or obnoxious person first and a somewhat homely person next. If I can sell you an expensive suit first, then expensive ties, shirts, and belts seem inexpensive in comparison. The same principle applies to automobiles and expensive accessories. If you pay $30,000 for an SUV, a $350.00 towing package doesn't sound too bad.

We feel obligated to return favors.

The **rule of reciprocation** instills in us as persuadees a sense of obligation to repay in kind what another provides. For instance, studies show that if a person gives you a free soft drink and then asks you to buy a raffle ticket, you feel obligated to buy the ticket even though it may cost more than the soft drink. This process is at work every time you open your mail and discover yet another packet of personalized address labels. You are likely to send in a donation or not use the labels even though you did not request them. If you use the labels and do not send in a donation or accept the coke and then decline the request to purchase a raffle ticket, you may experience psychological discomfort and fear shame or disapproval if someone discovers your action.

One concession deserves another, or not.

In a **reciprocal concessions** strategy, we feel a sense of obligation to make a concession when another has made one to us. Parties employ this psychological strategy in labor–management negotiations when one party, for example, concedes on health care and the other then feels obligated to concede on overtime or retirement benefits. It is common in legal interviews, sales transactions, and recruiting. You encounter this strategy in everyday interactions such as when a roommate agrees not to come in late on weekdays and you then offer to limit the amount of time a friend spends in the room. A time-honored concession takes place on high school and college campuses when one party offers to provide the car and the other feels obligated to pay for the gas.

Persuaders may ask for a lot and settle for less.

Persuaders employ a **rejection then retreat** strategy when a first proposal is exaggerated just enough to make a second more acceptable. The idea is that after you reject the first you will feel both obligated and somewhat relieved to agree to the second. One study, for example, discovered that if Boy Scouts asked persons to purchase $5.00 circus tickets and were turned down, the same persons were likely to say yes to a second proposal of a $1.00 chocolate bar. The Boy Scouts gained either way, and the persuadees felt good about helping out for a lesser amount. One of the authors experienced this strategy recently when he received a call from his alma mater. The student caller asked, "Can we put you down for a $500.00 donation this year?" When the answer was a stunned "No," the student then asked, "Can we put you down for the $100.00 you gave last year?" The answer was a relieved "Yes," and the caller got a donation. Sales persons often start with the top of the line and then retreat *if* necessary.

A relatively new strategy is called **undercover** or **stealth marketing.** A persuader party, often of two or more persons, pretends to be a friendly, disinterested party and anything but a sales representative. For example, two people appearing to be tourists or visitors ask a person passing by if she will take their picture. The cooperative passerby agrees and just happens to notice that the couple has a very interesting and attractive digital camera. She asks about it and the party, who just happen to be undercover sales reps for this camera company gladly comply. The persuadee has no idea that a sales interview is taking place.

Be a Critical Participant

As we have emphasized throughout this chapter, you must be a critical participant in the persuasive interview, not a passive bystander listening to a persuasive speech to an audience of one. Silence alone is not enough. Be ethical, knowledgeable, and critical. Challenge psychological and language strategies and the substance of interviews, including the logical strategies and evidence interviewers employ to alter or strengthen the way you think, feel, and act. Let's turn first to language strategies.

Language Strategies

Seek the meanings of symbols.

Woodward and Denton write that language "is far more than a collection of words and rules for proper usage. Language is the instrument and vehicle of human action and expression."[11] Skilled persuaders are keenly aware of the power and manipulation of verbal symbols for both good and ill, but too many of us see these symbols as merely words and rules. Larson warns that "as receivers, we need to get to the bottom of persuasive meanings; carefully analyzing the symbols used or misused by persuaders can help us get there."[12] An important first step in this analysis is to identify common language strategies.[13]

Framing and Reframing

Jargon is not harmless.

Persuaders use language to frame or construct the way we see people, places, things, and objects. For instance, **jargon** (sometimes called bureaucratese because bureaucrats use it so frequently) substitutes peculiar words for common words. While some jargon seems harmless enough (schedule irregularity for airline flight delay), others can hide the truth (culturally deprived environment for slum or terminological inexactitude for lie), make something sound more technical than it is (wood interdental stimulator for toothpick or emergency exit light for a flashlight), more valuable than it is (garment management system for one hook and two hangers), or less severe (collateral damage for the killing of civilians during military actions). Woodward and Denton warn that jargon may "require special interpretations and make us dependent on attorneys [physicians, engineers, professors, consultants] for help, advice, and action."[14]

Ambiguities say little but sound like a lot.

Persuaders employ **strategic ambiguities,** words with multiple or vague meanings, when they want to avoid specific definitions or explanations. They hope different persuadees will interpret the words according to their specific needs or perceptions without asking embarrassing, negative, or insightful questions. If a politician claims to be a conservative or moderate, what exactly is this person? What is a lifetime guarantee or a limited warranty? What is an affordable apartment or a top salary? What is free-range poultry or poultry raised the old-fashioned way? What is a natural food bar or low carb ice cream? Studies show that we will pay a premium price for lite, diet, natural, and low carb products without knowing exactly how these differ from ones that are not and what positive and negative effects they may produce.

photo by IT International, Ltd. Stock Photo

Look beyond words and pictures in weighing alternatives.

Persuaders employ **imagery**—essentially word pictures—that contains multisensory words to color what we have experienced, will experience, may experience, or experience indirectly. A representative of a travel agency, with the aid of leaflets, posters, and Web sites, will help us visualize skiing in the mountains of Switzerland, visiting the Aztec ruins in Mexico, surfing on the beaches of Hawaii, seeing the wildlife of Kenya, or enjoying the theatre in New York. There will not be a discouraging word or warning about the dangers or downsides of these destinations. On the other hand, a persuader might employ the same tactics to paint a negative picture complete with apocalyptic images and dire predictions if we vote for a political opponent, purchase a competing product, join a different religious group, accept a football scholarship with another school, or travel to Egypt instead of Greece. There will not be an encouraging word or compliment about the advantages or upside of these actions.

Imagery substitutes for experiences.

Euphemisms, as we mentioned in Chapter 2, are efforts to substitute *better sounding* words for common words. Cadillac was the first to substitute pre-owned for used cars. You might find an inexpensive interview suit but not a cheap one and purchase it from a sales associate rather than a clerk. A lifelike Christmas tree sounds better than a fake or artificial one. Women's sizes is a common substitution for large women sizes, and you will not find petite sizes in a men's department. You might order a lite beer at your favorite campus hangout, but would you order a diet beer? Persuaders know that we are attracted by pleasant sounding words, names, and labels. Powder room *sounds better* than toilet or john.

Euphemisms replace substance with sound.

Differentiation is not merely an attempt to find a better sounding word but to alter how we see *reality*. For example, when an animal rights advocate wants us to become animal guardians instead of animal owners, this person wants to alter how we see our relationship with our pets. Calling female members of an organization women is not merely "political correctness"—a euphemism—but an effort to change perceptions of the abilities, capabilities, and maturity of women compared to girls. When President George W. Bush insisted on calling suicide bombers in the Middle East homicide bombers, White House spokesman Ari Fleischer explained to reporters that "these are not suicide bombings. These are not people who just kill themselves. . . . These are people who deliberately go to murder others, with no regard to the values of their own life. These are murderers."[15] The purposes of euphemisms and differentiation are very different because the first merely wants something to *sound better* while the second wants to change our *visions of reality*.

Words may alter reality.

Appealing to the People

For many of us, the majority rules.

Persuaders use the historic faith of Americans in the rule and wisdom of the majority, following Abraham Lincoln's adage that you can fool all of the people some of the time and some of the people all of the time, but you can't fool all of the people all of the time. The ***ad populum*** tactic appeals to or on behalf of "the people" or the majority. We frequently hear persons claim that because the majority of Americans favor amending the Constitution to allow prayer in the public schools, to protect the flag, or to outlaw same-sex marriages, Congress should pass these amendments immediately. On campuses we hear pleas on behalf of the students, faculty, administration, staff, and athletic teams, the claim always being that the majority of each desires or needs assistance, recognition, or new policies. Rarely are more than a few of each quoted or the opposition given much attention.

Have an inquiring mind.

Persuaders employ the **bandwagon tactic** when they urge persuadees to follow the crowd, to do what everyone else is doing. They appeal to our desire to belong and to conform. Often there is a note of urgency: "Students are really signing up for this spring break trip, so you'd better get your money in." Listen for important qualifiers such as nearly, probably, almost, and majority. Ask for numbers or names of those who have signed a petition, agreed to a change, or joined an organization. Be cautious of phrases such as experienced investors, people in the know, and those who are on the move that are designed to pressure and flatter.

Simplifying the Complex

Fear of chain reactions may stifle any action.

Many persuasive interviews involve complex organizational, social, religious, legal, economic, and environmental issues, so persuaders may employ tactics to reduce problems, issues, controversies, and situations to their simplest elements. One such tactic is the **thin entering wedge,** also known as the **domino effect** or the **slippery slope.** The persuader claims that one decision, action, or law after another is leading toward some sort of disastrous consequences. Talk to a person who is against censorship, gun control, or same-sex marriages, and you are likely to hear how censorship of books in public schools is one more step toward censoring all reading materials, how the registration of handguns is yet another step toward outlawing and confiscating all guns, and how same-sex marriage is a slippery slope toward the destruction of the home and the family. Look for evidence of a related, intentional string of actions that are tipping dominos, producing wedges, or sliding down a dangerous slope.

Slogans are clever phrases and more.

Slogans or **tabloid thinking** is common in all forms of persuasion, including interviews. They are clever phrases that encapsulate positions, stands, or goals, and nearly every organization uses them to alter our ways of thinking, feeling, or acting. One of the most famous was General Electric's "Progress is our most important product." Current ones include Armstrong's "Your ideas become realities"; Toyota's "Get the feeling"; Microsoft's "Your potential. Our passion"; and Lowe's "Improving home improvement." Organizations change slogans to communicate different notions of themselves. For example, when Purdue University replaced "Discover Purdue" with "Purdue: It's Happening Here," President Martin Jischke explained that "there is a tremendous amount of excitement around campus. . . . I think this theme is just trying to capture that sense of energy, momentum and pride that we have at Purdue."[16] Discover what these slogans mean and if they truly represent an organization or campaign.

Polarizing limits our choices and our thinking.

Persuaders simplify by **polarizing** (sometimes called **bifurcation**) organizations, people, positions, and situations by claiming there are only two. Common claims include, you're either a conservative or a liberal, you're either with us or against us, you're either for abortion or for life, and Ziebart's original slogan "It's us or rust." A few years ago, Marine Corps recruiters on campus divided all students into two types: dreamers who think of nothing else but getting their degrees and realists who think of taking exciting college credits that will enable them to achieve a good job and good life. Do all college students fit into these neat categories? Are we really either conservative or liberal rather than some of each, or do we fall somewhere in the middle?

Dodging the Issue

Attacking a source does not address the issue.

Persuaders may employ a variety of tactics to dodge critical issues, questions, or objections. ***Ad hominem*** (sometimes called getting personal) enables a persuader to dodge undesired challenges by discrediting a source because of age, culture, sex, race, affiliation, or past positions, statements, or claims. A parent may have told you as a child to "just consider the source" when someone called you a name or questioned a belief. A source, even one with a spotty record for accuracy or authoritativeness, may be on target this time. Insist that the persuader address the issue, point, or substance, not the source alone.

Sharing guilt does not remove guilt.

All of us have used the ***tu quoque*** tactic since childhood. It attempts to dodge an issue or objection by revolving it upon the challenger or questioner. Remember when you exclaimed "You're one too," "It takes one to know one," or "So do you" in response to another's charge or challenge? These are classic *tu quoque* responses. If you question a political candidate about taking money from special interests, the person may likely reply, "All politicians take money from special interests" or "Your candidate has accepted money from labor unions and trial lawyers."

Blaming others is an attempt to dodge responsibility.

Persuaders try to dodge issues by **transferring guilt** to others by making the accuser, victim, or questioner the guilty party. Cheating on an exam is the professor's fault; failing to report all income on a tax report is the IRS's fault; parking illegally is the college's fault for not providing enough parking places. Defense attorneys turn victims of crimes into the guilty parties, particularly in rape or abuse cases. Do not allow the persuader to attribute all guilt to others without addressing your questions, concerns, and objections.

Logical Strategies

The logical and psychological are inseparable.

As we pointed out in Chapter 10, persuaders understand that it is not enough to know which reasons to develop and in what order to introduce them. They need to develop them into what you will see as valid and acceptable patterns. The most effective interview is a carefully crafted blend of the psychological and the logical. It is not enough to introduce you to psychological strategies and tactics; it is equally important that you be able to recognize and challenge common logical patterns, the ways persuaders attempt to *reason* with us.[17]

Recall that **reasoning from example or generalization** is a statement about the distribution of some characteristic among the members of a whole class of people, places, or things. It's often based on a sample of this class, so recall the principles and

Always check the sample from which generalizations come.

methods of sampling discussed in Chapter 6 on survey interviewing. For instance, a college basketball recruiter might tell a high school student and his parents that a recent survey of intercollegiate athletes at his institution found that 84 percent completed their degrees within five years, so this is the place to play sports and succeed academically. This 85 percent figure consists of a recent sample of individual athletes from different sports, and the coach generalizes to all basketball players. If you recognize this pattern, inquire about the amount and nature of the sample. Are these typical or unusual classes? How, when, and where was the sample selected? What exactly is the persuader asserting about this sample?

Beware of a *hasty generalization* in which the persuader generalizes to a whole group of people, places, or things from one or a few examples. For instance, you've heard people claim that your campus had major alcohol problems because of the students they observed after a football game or that you had great school spirit because of students they saw wearing school colors during homecoming. People have warned you about dining at a particular restaurant because they had a bad meal there once or praised Chrysler products because they owned one or two in the past.

Be careful of coincidences seen as causes.

Reasoning from cause-to-effect is a statement indicating what caused an observed effect. It may appear similar to reasoning from example because interviewers often use a sample as proof of a *causal* relationship, but it does not *generalize*. For instance, a persuader might argue that a study of 300 students who had left campus during their first semester found the majority had lived alone in a residence hall or apartment. Therefore, living alone is a major cause of college dropouts. Ask a number of questions when persuaders employ causal reasoning. Was this cause able to generate this effect? Was this cause the only or the major cause? Think of the many alleged causes you have heard for the failure of marriages, high gas prices, juvenile crime, and diseases such as cancer and Alzheimer's. What evidence does the persuader offer to establish this causal link?

Just because B followed A, it does not mean that A caused B.

Beware of the ***post hoc* fallacy** or **scrambling cause-effect** that argues simply because B followed A, A must have caused B. For instance, I got the flu the day after I got that flu shot, so the shot gave me the flu. You mistake coincidences for causes, such as when you wash your car and it rains 15 minutes later or you get a good golf score whenever you wear a lucky shirt or blouse.

Be a super-sleuth when encountering hypotheses.

Reasoning from fact or hypothesis is a statement that explains best the available evidence. It is the best accounting or explanation for a body of facts and is the type of reasoning sleuths use in murder mysteries—the "whodunits" of television and book fame. For instance, a construction manager might reason that the new intersection will be completed before classes begin in August because the lanes have been poured, the curbs are in, sidewalks are well under way, landscaping is progressing because of the good weather, and signage will be delivered within a week. Ask these questions when listening to an argument from facts. How frequently is this hypothesis accurate with this evidence? Is this body of facts sufficient to warrant this claim? What evidence would make this hypothesis more or less convincing—the famous "smoking gun"? How simple is the hypothesis because the more complex it becomes, the greater the risk of it being inaccurate?

Reasoning from sign is a statement that two or more variables are related in such a way that the presence or absence of one may be taken as an indication of the presence

A sign may have many meanings or no meanings.

or absence of the other. For example, you may note that the flag on the post office is at half-mast and reason that someone of importance must have died. You may observe the absence of a ring around the moon and reason that tomorrow will be without rain. Be careful of concluding too much from signs. For instance, a few years ago one of the authors noted a large number of people standing outside of the arena during a basketball game and thought there must be a bomb scare. The answer was simpler. The university had recently instituted a no-smoking policy for the arena and many people were smoking outside the arena during halftime. Ask these questions when hearing an argument from sign. What is the relationship between the variables? Is the presence or absence verifiable? What is the believability or reliability of the sign?

Look for important differences as well as important similarities.

Reasoning from analogy or comparison is a statement that two people, places, or things share a number of characteristics and then makes a claim about one of them. It is based on the assumption that if the two have many similarities, they will share others. For instance, a salesperson might argue that since a moderately priced SUV has many of the same features as a luxury SUV (V8 engine, room for six adults, equal cargo space, video system for rear seat occupants, leather seating, and four-wheel drive), you should lease the less expensive SUV because it is of the same quality. Ask these questions when a persuader makes comparisons. How similar are the similarities? Are enough points of comparison provided? Are critical points of similarity given?

Beware of a *false analogy*. A persuader may compare two unlike people, places, or things to make an illogical claim. For instance, you hear sports analogies applied to everything from clergy and politics to sales campaigns and equal rights. Persuaders compare education of students to selling products to consumers or making widgets. A political candidate recently remarked to one of the authors that competition between public and private schools through a voucher system would enhance the education of students because that is how we improved the making of automobiles.

Identify the major assertion upon which the argument rests.

Reasoning from accepted belief, assumption, or proposition involves three stated or implied assertions. For instance, a physician might argue that persons who smoke have a significantly greater chance of having heart attacks and strokes. Since you smoke, you are likely to have a heart attack or stroke. The recommendation may be a newly developed medicine. The strength of this reasoning rests on the strength or acceptance of the assertions, some of which may remain unstated. For instance, your physician may let you provide the part about how likely you are to suffer a heart attack or stroke or that people who smoke are prone to these. Ask these questions. Do you accept the assertions as stated or implied? Does the conclusion necessarily follow from the assertions?

"If" arguments may ignore obvious or unpredictable conditions.

Beware of arguments based on **self-evident truths** that claim questions or issues are not arguable because they are settled by rule or fact. Political and religious liberals and conservatives, for example, have many beliefs and attitudes they feel cannot be questioned or disputed. They are fact because the Bible, the Constitution, the courts, or trusted authorities say so.

Reasoning from condition is based on the assertion that if something does or does not happen, something else will or will not happen. For instance, a supporter of a wheel tax might argue that if we don't pass a wheel tax the roads in the county will deteriorate and result in accidents, damaged vehicles, and reduced economic development.

Since the county commissioners will vote for the tax, the roads will be first-rate and the county and its residents will be safer and gain economically. The central focus is the word *if*. Ask these questions of conditional arguments. Do you accept the condition? Is this the only condition? Is this the major condition?

Two-choice arguments work only when we accept these two choices.

Reasoning from two choices is based on the assertion that there are only two possibilities in a situation. The persuader removes one possibility, and it stands to reason that there is only one acceptable or likely possibility—the remaining one. For instance, a college recruiter might argue that you have only two choices to study engineering in the state, the state university or the institute of technology. Since tuition at the institute is more than $25,000 a year, the logical choice is the state university. When presented with two choices, ask these questions. Are these the only two choices? Are these the major choices among several choices? Do you agree with the elimination of choice A or B?

Beware of the *false dichotomy* that reduces a complex issue or process into two sides or alternatives. This is essentially the polarizing or bifurcation tactic discussed earlier. Most complex issues are multiple-sided, not two-sided.

Evidence

Look very closely at the evidence persuaders offer (or do not offer) to gain attention and interest, establish credibility and legitimacy, support arguments, develop a need, and present a solution.[18] They may give examples, tell stories, cite authorities or witnesses, make comparisons and contrasts, present statistics, and define key terms. Use these questions to assess the acceptability of the persuader's evidence.

Assess the reliability and expertise of sources.

- *Is the evidence trustworthy?* Are the persuader and the persons and organizations being cited unbiased and reliable? Are the sources of the evidence (newspapers, reports, Internet, publications) unbiased and reliable?
- *Is the evidence authoritative?* What are the training, experience, and reputation of the authorities or witnesses being cited? Were they in positions to have observed the facts, events, or data?
- *Is the evidence recent?* Is it the most recent available? Are newer statistics or findings available? Have authorities changed their minds?
- *Is the evidence documented sufficiently?* Do you know where and how the statistics or results were determined? Who determined them? Where and when were they reported?
- *Is the evidence communicated accurately?* Can you detect alterations or deletions in quotations, statistics, or documentation? Is the evidence cited in context?

Insist on both quantity and quality of evidence.

- *Is the evidence sufficient in quantity?* Are enough authorities cited? Enough examples given? Enough points of comparison made? Adequate facts revealed?
- *Is the evidence sufficient in quality?* Are opinions stated as facts? How satisfactory is the sample used for generalizations and causal arguments? Does proof evidence (factual illustrations, statistics, authority, detailed comparisons) outweigh clarifying evidence (hypothetical illustrations, paid testimonials, figurative analogies, and metaphors)?

Be an Active Participant

Be an active and critical player in the interview.

Play an active role in every persuasive interview in which you take part. Each interview has the potential of altering or reinforcing the way you think, feel, or act, including the money you spend, the votes you cast, the relationships you establish or maintain, the possessions you protect, the work you do, and the life you lead.

Use a variety of questions during each of the interview stages. Informational questions enable you to obtain information and explanations, probe into vague and ambiguous words and comments, and reveal feelings and attitudes that may lie hidden or merely suggested. Reflective, mirror, and restatement questions enable you to be certain about what the other party is saying, what you and the other party are agreeing to, and what commitments each party is making. Remember, there are no foolish questions, only questions you foolishly fail to ask.

The Opening

Play an active role in the opening because it initiates the persuasive process.

Be alert and active from the first moments of each interview. If the interview is a "cold call" on the telephone or in person in which you have no time to prepare, use carefully phrased questions to discover the identity, position, and qualifications of the persuader. Discover the real purpose and intent of the interview; it's often not what the persuader wants you to think. As the sports metaphor goes, use the opening to "level the playing field" so you can play an active, critical, and informed role in the interview. It all starts with the opening.

Too many persuadees play passive roles during openings. Here is a typical example from a recent interview in one of our classes. The persuadee is head of surgery at this hospital, believes in following strict hierarchies with surgeons at the top, and is all business.

Persuader: Dr. Smalley, I'm Lilly McDowell, one of the surgical supervisors.

Persuadee: Hi Lilly, have a seat.

Persuader: I'd like to talk to you about the problems we are having with surgical patients after they leave the hospital and a solution to this problem.

Persuadee: Okay.

Persuader: Well, we have discovered that . . .

The persuadee does not exhibit his personality or attitudes and learns little about the persuader, the purpose of this interview, how long it will take, or the nature of the problem. He allows the persuadee to launch into the need without question.

Creating a Need or Desire

Ask questions, challenge arguments, and demand solid evidence.

A persuader may attempt to conduct an unstructured interview without a clear purpose and in which the need is a collection of generalizations and ambiguous claims with no clear points that establish a need or desire. When this happens, insist on a point-by-point development with each point crafted carefully and logically, supported with adequate evidence, and adapted to *your* values, beliefs, and attitudes. Beware of common argument fallacies and tactics that dodge careful reasoning and your questions and objections. Persuaders may attempt to introduce another point rather than address your concerns about this point. Insist on answers to your questions and objections and get agreements before delving into another point.

Weigh evidence carefully and be on guard against psychological strategies designed to manipulate your reactions and make you feel obligated to reply in kind. Do not tolerate smears, innuendos, or half-truths aimed at the competition, what is often called negative selling in sales interviews and mudslinging in political interviews. Insist on getting agreements on the need before going into criteria or a solution.

Establishing Criteria

Criteria enable you to weigh solutions.

As we discussed in Chapter 10, establishing criteria with the interviewee that any solution should meet is a critical part of the persuasion process. Insist that the persuader develop criteria with you. Persuaders often come to interviews with a list of criteria they feel are important. This is ideal, but be sure these are presented clearly and that they include all criteria you feel are important. Do not hesitate to rephrase criteria, add criteria, or insist on a rationale for each.

Presenting the Solution

Be sure the solution meets the need and is the best available.

A persuader may assume or pretend that there is only *one* solution to the need or desire you have agreed upon. There is rarely only one solution, merely the one the persuader prefers or is trying to sell to you. Insist upon a detailed presentation of each possible solution. Ask questions and raise objections. Be sure the criteria are applied equally to each solution to determine which is best for you in this situation. Ask for clarifications of terminology, particularly if the persuader is using jargon with which you are unfamiliar. If possible, insist on seeing, feeling, hearing, and experiencing the product or proposal. There are no good substitutes for driving a car, trying on a suit, playing a musical instrument, touring an apartment, attending a church service, or visiting a college campus.

When you have agreed upon a solution or course of action, beware of "add-ons" such as guarantees, rebates, accessories, processing fees, and commitments. These may be costly when added up or time-consuming when looked into. The persuader may hope that since you have made the *big* decision, you will readily agree to *small* decisions—the contrast principle discussed earlier. What are you getting that's "free?" A common periodical sales technique is to offer you five magazines for free; all you have to do is pay for handling and mailing fees that incidentally may add up to hundreds of dollars a year.

The Closing

Take your time when making a final decision.

Do not be rushed into making a decision or commitment. You have little to gain and much to lose through haste. A common tactic is to create a psychological reaction by claiming the possibility of censorship or the scarcity of a product. An organization may produce a limited number of books, coins, cars, or positions to make them more in demand. You must act quickly before it is too late or an agency steps in to prevent you from acting.

Do not hesitate to take time to think about a decision, literally to sleep on it. Be sure all of your questions and objections have been answered satisfactorily. Be fully aware of the possible ramifications of your decision. Consider getting a second or third opinion. Talk to persons who have relevant expertise or experiences. Check out competing products, candidates, offers, and programs. Shopping around is wise before committing yourself. For instance, when coming to a new community, many people will check out several neighborhoods before buying a home or renting an apartment. Similarly, visit several college campuses before deciding where to pursue a degree; attend a number of church services before deciding which church to join; try out several laptops before deciding which to purchase.

Summary

Good persuasive interviews involve the interviewee as a responsible, informed, critical, and active participant who plays a central role, not a passive recipient of a persuasive message. It is a mutual activity in which both parties play active and critical roles. Interviews are interactions in which interviewees act ethically, listen critically, ask insightful questions, raise important objections, challenge evidence and arguments, recognize common tactics for what they are, and weigh proposals according to agreed upon criteria.

Key Terms and Concepts

The online learning center for this text features FLASHCARDS and CROSSWORD PUZZLES for studying based on these terms and concepts.

Ad hominem
Ad populum
Attitudes
Bandwagon tactic
Beliefs
Bifurcation
Bureaucratese
Buyer beware
Contrast principle
Differentiation
Dissonance
Domino effect
Ethics
Euphemisms
Evidence
Fairness
False dichotomy
Framing and reframing
Hasty generalization
Honesty
Imagery
Jargon
Language strategies
Logical strategies
Name-calling
Open-minded
Polarization
Post hoc fallacy
Psychological discomfort
Psychological strategies
Reasoning from accepted belief, assumption, or proposition
Reasoning from analogy or comparison
Reasoning from cause-to-effect
Reasoning from condition
Reasoning from example or generalization
Reasoning from fact or hypothesis
Reasoning from sign
Reasoning from two choices
Reciprocal concessions
Rejection then retreat
Rule of reciprocation
Scrambling cause-effect
Self-evident truths
Slippery slope
Slogans
Standard/learned principles
Stealth marketing
Strategic ambiguities
Symbols
Tabloid thinking
Thin entering edge
Transferring guilt
Tu quoque
Undercover marketing
Values

A Persuasive Interview for Review and Analysis

This interview is between Shawn Chan, a sales representative of a fire equipment manufacturer and the Director of Public Safety, Donica Timberhoff, in Brooktown, a city of 30,000 in an area prone to grass fires on its perimeter and fires in older homes in its center. The interviewer has been in Brooktown on several occasions in the past, visited several fire stations, and talked to a number of firefighters. Two months ago he talked to Donica at the Southwest Firefighters Convention in Portland, Oregon, about a number of recently developed pieces of equipment. This interview is a first step in a process that not only includes the Director of Public Safety but also the Public Safety Board, Fire Chief, and city council. The interview is taking place in the Director's office.

What role does the interviewee play in the opening, including the summary of the problem discussed during an earlier interaction between the parties? How does the relationship between the parties affect the opening and summary? Since persuasion is done with and not to an interviewee, how mutual is this interview? How active and critical is the interviewee in developing a set of criteria for evaluating solutions, analyzing evidence, weighing the proposed solution, and applying the agreed-upon criteria? How effective is the interviewee's use of questions concerning language and logical strategies?

1. **Interviewer:** Good afternoon, Donica. I'm Shawn. We met at the Southwest Firefighters Convention a couple of months ago.
2. **Interviewee:** Shawn?
3. **Interviewer:** Oh, Shawn Chan of ACE Fire Equipment in Vancouver, Washington.
4. **Interviewee:** Oh yes, I remember our conversation now about replacing some of our older equipment. Please have a seat.
5. **Interviewer:** That's correct. You invited me to come talk to your Fire Chief and some of his men and to look over your equipment. Well, I've done that and thought we might talk a bit about your needs and possible actions.
6. **Interviewee:** I'm always glad to talk to equipment representatives because we are constantly reviewing our needs and looking to the future. You understand, of course, that I am only part of the chain of command in making major purchases such as a new truck?
7. **Interviewer:** Of course. Your equipment is well maintained and, for the most part, is in good condition. I'm impressed with your fire department staff and leadership.
8. **Interviewee:** I'm glad to hear that and that we do not have serious needs.
9. **Interviewer:** Well, there is a problem with your pumper equipment, particularly the 1961 LaFrance. It's simply not adequate for fighting the grass and brush fires you have nearly every year in late summer and early fall. I believe you ought to replace it sooner than later.
10. **Interviewee:** What does that mean? Chief Yosef has not mentioned any problem this serious.
11. **Interviewer:** I discovered several potential problems. For example, the water pump needs a complete overhaul because records show that it's pumping well-below the level required for fighting serious grass fires.

12. **Interviewee:** Our mechanical shop is very good and should be able to refurbish the water pump. What do you mean by "potential" problem and "well-below"?
13. **Interviewer:** It's pumping at 550 gpm and should be in the 900 to 1,100 range. I doubt that you can repair this pump.
14. **Interviewee:** What is "gpm," and why is that?
15. **Interviewer:** Oh, gallons per minute. LaFrance stopped making parts for the pump in 1991.
16. **Interviewee:** Well, we'll see what we can do about used parts. In the meantime, we can use it at the Central Station to fight small house fires that do not require so much water. Is that the only problem?
17. **Interviewer:** No; reliability is another concern. Some of the firefighters mentioned that the LaFrance averages only a couple of trips before it needs some mechanical attention. This downtime could be critical during the grass fire period.
18. **Interviewee:** Sometimes our crews exaggerate a bit when they would like to have a shiny new truck from which to operate. I would like to get along for another three to five years before we have to purchase a new pumper. As I said, we could move it to Central.
19. **Interviewer:** I can understand your feeling, but I think you're living dangerously with such an unreliable truck as a key piece of equipment. And there's another problem.
20. **Interviewee:** Another one?
21. **Interviewer:** Yes, the Chief tells me that the city has been thinking about replacing the small emergency truck purchased from the Air Force 10 years ago.
22. **Interviewee:** That's correct. It's not large enough to carry all of the emergency equipment we have and the need for ever-increasing PI calls.
23. **Interviewer:** I noticed that in your records, along with the fact that a pumper is often called to the scene of PI emergencies. That means you have two units and crews tied up at many accidents, doubling the cost and lessening your ability to fight two emergencies at once.
24. **Interviewee:** We can't do too much about that because gasoline spills are common in PIs.
25. **Interviewer:** Well, we have started building a single unit suitable for rescue and pumper duties.
26. **Interviewee:** I didn't know there was such a unit.
27. **Interviewer:** I think it's just the solution for you. Here, let me show you the specifications for the ACE 2000 combo unit.
28. **Interviewee:** I'm not sure we have a problem that warrants a new truck at this time. Certainly we're not going to be in a position to make a purchase for at least several months.
29. **Interviewer:** I understand. Let me show you some of the specs on the ACE 2000.
30. **Interviewee:** I'm sure they're impressive, but we need to consider our specific needs before looking at any solution, particularly one that seems best for grass fires and PI cases. We do have a major need to fight fires in older homes in the city center.

31. **Interviewer:** Okay, let's list some of these requirements. I think it should be easy to maintain, capable of fighting brush fires, and large enough to carry both fire and emergency equipment. Now, the ACE 2000 . . .

32. **Interviewee:** (cutting in) Any unit must meet *all* of our specifications and needs, some of which may be unique to a small town fire department.

33. **Interviewer:** What do you have in mind?

34. **Interviewee:** Well, it must be compatible with our current equipment. Maintenance must be simple and cost-effective. The unit must be financially feasible for our tax base. And a unit must be available for our inspection and testing.

35. **Interviewer:** The ACE 2000 is very easy to maintain and is compatible with most older units made by other manufacturers. And the cost is well within reason.

36. **Interviewee:** That's reassuring but not convincing. What are the data?

37. **Interviewer:** We put the ACE 2000 through tests that meet or exceed industry standards and did not put it on the market until we were certain that it would meet or exceed purchaser expectation. Believe me, this is an excellent truck in quality and cost. It is now Board Certified by Firefighters International.

38. **Interviewee:** We will need some hard facts to support your claims. What about compatibility?

39. **Interviewer:** We would match this truck to your existing equipment. Just call Chief Bodie in Warren County. He was one of the first to try out, and purchase, the ACE 2000. It is a superb unit for fighting grass and brush fires.

40. **Interviewee:** You seem to ignore our need to fight house fires in the city center.

41. **Interviewer:** I'm sorry. I assumed that if it was excellent at one, it would be excellent for another. Would you like for us to prepare a contract that would include all of the specifications and detailed item-by-item costs?

42. **Interviewee:** We're no where near the contract stage. Out of curiosity, what does the ACE 2000 run for?

43. **Interviewer:** Just under $380,000.

44. **Interviewee:** Wow! That's way out of our league.

45. **Interviewer:** But that unit would come fully equipped—jaws of life, radio system, automatic transmission, foam guns, a Cummins diesel engine, dual pumping systems, the works. It will do what two of your trucks do now.

46. **Interviewee:** We'd have to have a lot of two-truck and emergency runs to make up that cost. We're not ready to move on a purchase, but I will ask the Chief to draw up a list of specifications. I'll talk to the Public Safety Board and the City Council to see what they think; then I'll send our specifications to you to consider.

47. **Interviewer:** That's great. I'm confident we can get together on this before you face a major equipment crisis.

48. **Interviewee:** Thanks for coming in. I'll get in touch when we have something to talk about.

Persuasion Role-Playing Cases

A New Computer Security Program

After selling and servicing computer software and hardware for a number of companies for the past 20 years, the interviewer has designed a security software package on her own time that she is convinced is far superior to any on the market. She believes the Department of Homeland Security will become a major client. Unfortunately, she is generally unknown in the industry and does not have the personal funds to develop, test, and market the package. She has decided the solution is to persuade a major software firm to purchase her security program and provide her with 15 percent royalties from sales of the program.

The interviewee is the Vice President for Development at Maxware, a computer program developer. He and his researchers have been working on a software security package but have had continuing problems. They contracted with several hackers to test their XF-34 system, and the hackers managed to break into systems protected by the XF-34 within a matter of days. He's skeptical that a private person with a sales and service background could do what he and his researchers have been unable to do, but he's willing to listen.

A New Type of Seed Corn

The interviewer is a sales representative for Harvest Gold Hybrids that has a new type of seed corn on the market that has proved in tests to be quite effective in fighting wireworms. The intent of this new hybrid seed is to prevent wireworms from getting into seed in the field before it has a chance to sprout. He first met the interviewee, a farmer-owner of a 2000-acre grain farm in western Ohio, when he was a college intern with Harvest Gold Hybrids. He's now in his second year as a sales representative for Harvest Gold and knows wireworms are a problem in this area.

The interviewee used Harvest Gold Hybrids in the past but switched to Premium Hybrids three years ago to fight wireworms more effectively. His success has been better but not where he would like it to be. He vaguely remembers the interviewer and is aware that he is quite young and new to the seed market and sales. Although he is willing to talk about the new hybrid, he generally prefers to see what his neighbors experience with new products before he buys in. Why change before you are certain what you are changing to?

Preserve a Historical Theatre

The Grand Theatre was built in downtown Wattsbury in 1930 in the then popular art deco style and was a popular destination for moviegoers until it closed in 1990. Since then it has deteriorated nearly to the point of no return with a leaky roof, damaged marquee, and crumbling facade. The interviewer purchased the building for $70,000 but needs at least $1 million to restore it to its glory days and turn it into a dinner theatre with both film and live entertainment. She is contacting the director of the State Department of Historic Preservation to obtain a grant to initiate restoration work.

The director of the State Department of Historic Preservation has read the persuader's prospectus for a dinner theatre in the old Grand Theatre building and is sympathetic. However, the director is swamped with proposals to preserve old theatres and hotels in the state and has limited funds that enable him to support only a few projects each year. A major concern will be the persuader's plans to raise funds in addition to a possible SDHP grant to complete the project.

Need for Additional Staff

The interviewer is director of human resources for Olympic Sports, Inc., a small chain of comprehensive sporting good stores in the Southeast. Until recently Olympic Sports faced no significant competition from other large sports stores and had reduced staff at all stores to the bare minimum to remain profitable during a severe three-year economic downturn. Its staff had traditionally trained and served in a single area such as fishing, guns, hunting, trapping, golf, tennis, and clothing. They were known for their expertise. Now staff alternate from one area to another, sometimes during the same day, and find it difficult to know the merchandise or specific sports. The director has made an appointment with the CEO to propose hiring additional staff to return the chain to its previous level of staff expertise. A major motivation is the arrival of several Bill's Sporting Goods mega-stores in the area. Their advertisements emphasize service and experts in every area of every store.

The CEO is aware of the arrival of the new competition but feels now is not the time to take on expensive staff and to increase the budget, which would inevitably affect prices. The best way to fight this competition is to remain lean and sustain its longtime slogan: "Nobody beats our prices, nobody." The CEO respects the director of human resources, who is a great people person but not a numbers person.

Student Activities

1. Go with a person who is in the process of making a major purchase: auto, home, boat, piano, jewelry. See if you can detect the use of psychological strategies by the persuader: standard/learned principles, the contrast principle, the rule of reciprocation, reciprocal concessions, and rejection then retreat.
2. Virtually every family has one or more members who are famous for driving hard bargains and getting better deals than anyone else. Identify such a person in your family and go with this person to a persuasive interview; it need not be a sales situation. Observe the roles the person plays in the opening, how the person handles the need or desire the persuader is trying to create, the information the person obtains and the objections and questions raised about the solution, and how the person negotiates a final decision. If the person uses threats such as leaving, going to competitors, or not making any decision, how do they affect the interview and how does the persuader react to them?
3. Go to the Internet and observe the use of language strategies designed to entice you to purchase products and services. How do they communicate urgency and scarcity? What functions do jargon, euphemisms, and strategic ambiguities play? How do they make complex problems, issues, and decisions appear simple? Which logical strategies are most common, and how can you explain this?

4. Review this chapter and other sources on ethics and develop a code of ethics for persuadees. What difficulties did you encounter? How is your code similar and different from one you might create for persuaders? How appropriate is it for varying interview situations?

Notes

1. Richard L. Johannesen, "Perspectives on Ethics in Persuasion," in *Persuasion: Reception and Responsibility* by Charles U. Larson (Belmont, CA: Thomson/Wadsworth, 2004), p. 27.
2. Herbert W. Simons, *Persuasion in Society* (Thousand Oaks, CA: Sage, 2001), p. 374.
3. Simons, p. 374.
4. Johannesen, p. 32.
5. Gary C. Woodward and Robert E. Denton, Jr., *Persuasion and Influence in American Life* (Long Grove, IL: Waveland Press, 2004), p. 348.
6. James Price Dillard and Michael Pfau, eds., *The Persuasion Handbook: Developments in Theory and Practice* (Thousand Oaks, CA: Sage, 2002), pp. 4–14.
7. Johannesen, p. 28.
8. Woodward and Denton, p. 348.
9. Johannesen, p. 31.
10. Kelton V. Rhoads and Robert B. Cialdini, "The Business of Influence: Principles That Lead to Success in Commercial Settings," in *The Persuasion Handbook: Developments in Theory and Practice,* James Price Dillard and Michael Pfau, eds. (Thousand Oaks, CA: Sage, 2002), pp. 514–517; Robert B. Cialdini, *Influence: Science and Practice* (New York: HarperCollins, 1993), pp. 19–44.
11. Woodward and Denton, p. 53.
12. Larson, pp. 103–104.
13. See Woodward and Denton, pp. 52–81; Larson, pp. 118–146.
14. Woodward and Denton, p. 73.
15. *Journal and Courier*, (Lafayette, Indiana) April 13, 2002, p. A4.
16. *The Exponent*, (West Lafayette, Indiana) August 22, 2003, p. B1.
17. See Woodward and Denton, pp. 85–106; Larson, pp. 184–215.
18. See Simons, pp. 167–171.

Resources

Cialdini, Robert B. *Influence: Science and Practice*. Boston: Allyn and Bacon, 2000.

Dillard, James Price, and Michael Pfau, eds. *The Persuasion Handbook: Developments in Theory and Practice*. Thousand Oaks, CA: Sage, 2002.

Larson, Charles U. *Persuasion: Reception and Responsibility.* Belmont, CA: Thomson/Wadsworth, 2007.

Seiter, John S., and Robert H. Gass, eds. *Perspectives on Persuasion, Social Influence, and Compliance Gaining.* Boston: Pearson Education, 2007.

Woodward, Gary C., and Robert E. Denton, Jr. *Persuasion and Influence in American Life.* Long Grove, IL: Waveland Press, 2004.

CHAPTER 12

The Counseling Interview

When a co-worker, friend, family member, student, supervisor, club member, neighbor, or client approaches you in person or on the telephone and states, "I've got a problem," "I need some advice," "I need some help," or simply "Got a few minutes," you are likely to find yourself in the role of counselor in a counseling interview. It is an everyday activity in which nearly all of us take part in one role or the other. Unfortunately, few of us are trained counselors and, in many fields where counseling is frequent—ministry, medicine, teaching, law, management, and funeral service—training is minimal at best. Fortunately, the *lay counselor* has proved to be remarkably successful, as is seen in countless campus and urban crisis centers. People seeking help trust persons like themselves who are open, nonthreatening, and willing to listen.[1] Because of this tendency, you need to understand how to approach and conduct counseling interviews.

Be a helper, not a problem solver.

This chapter introduces you to the counseling interview, perhaps the most sensitive of interviews because it occurs when persons feel incapable or unsure of themselves and how to address a *personal* problem—work performance, grades, finances, relationship, health. Merely asking for assistance may be a blow to a person's ego and pride because we are taught to be independent, to "stand on our own two feet," to be a man or woman, and to solve our own problems. The goal of the counseling interview is to *assist* another person in gaining insight into and coping with a problem; it is not to *resolve* the problem for this person.

Trust may overcome lack of expertise.

This chapter serves as an introduction to the principles of counseling interviewing so you can work more effectively with those who come to you for assistance with day-to-day problems in their personal and work lives. **It is not to train you to be a psychotherapist or to handle critical problems such as drug or alcohol abuse, severe psychological problems, or legal issues.** Approach each counseling interview systematically with considerable attention to preparation and planning.

Preparing for the Counseling Interview

Begin preparation with a detailed and insightful analysis of the interview parties, focusing as much on yourself as the other party. You will have difficulty understanding and helping others if you do not know yourself and the party coming to you for help.

Do not stray beyond your level of expertise.

Analyzing Self

Have a realistic understanding of your counseling skills. Do not try to handle situations for which you have neither the experience nor the training. Know when to refer the interviewee to a person with greater skills and expertise. Keep up to date in your field, including research, trends, and changes. Know how other people (particularly the interviewee) view you and your position, organization, and profession.

Assess how your personality characteristics match those of effective counselors. Research indicates that qualities intrinsic to the personalities, attitudes, and nonverbal behavior of counselors—rather than sex or ethnic group membership, largely account for counseling effectiveness.[2] However, a recent study of white racial identity in counseling interviews recommended that counselors "who are racially unaware must obtain sufficient training to aid them in becoming multiculturally competent." This training should "emphasize racial and cultural self-awareness, knowledge about other racial and cultural groups in the context of interpersonal interactions (e.g., counseling relationships), and skill development in terms of intervening with clients in a culturally appropriate manner."[3]

Know yourself before trying to help others know themselves.

Be open-minded, optimistic, serious, self-assured, relaxed, and patient. Do not be argumentative or defensive. Counselors have higher credibility with clients if they share beliefs in the causes of the person's problem.[4]

Be people-centered to be sensitive to the interviewee's needs. Communicate understanding, comfort, reassurance, and warmth. Above all, show you understand the interviewee's situation and feelings. Feel comfortable with disclosing your motives, feelings, values, beliefs, and attitudes. An interviewer's self-disclosure of personal experiences and background helps the interviewee gain insights and new perspectives for making changes because of an equalized relationship and reassurance.[5]

Good problem solvers may be poor counselors.

Do not dominate interpersonal interactions, but have a sincere desire to help others. Be people-oriented rather than problem-oriented. Unfortunately, most education and professional training are geared toward solving problems with the emphasis on taking charge and doing it yourself. In most counseling interviews, however, problems are attached to people who need assistance, not prescriptions, in solving the problems themselves. Counselors tend to be less open and to provide less feedback in these situations.[6]

Assess your intellectual, communicative, and emotional strengths. Are you imaginative and analytical? Are you a good listener and skilled in verbal and nonverbal communication? How comfortable are you when people reveal personal and embarrassing problems and incidents or express intense emotions such as sorrow, fear, and anger?

Analyzing the Interviewee

Review everything you know about the interviewee preferably before the interview: age, ethnicity, education, work history, academic record, family background, group memberships, medical and psychological histories, test results, previous counseling sessions, and information about past problems and solutions. Talk to people (instructors, supervisors, family members, friends, acquaintances, counselors, and fellow workers) who may have insights into the person and why the person needs assistance.

Be informed but keep an open mind.

Be careful of information from other sources. Think of times when you formed a negative, defensive, or wary attitude toward a supervisor, roommate, or professor because of what other people told you. You may have found the person to be just the opposite: helpful, friendly, and understanding.

Be aware of past, present, and future events.

Consider how past events or current happenings might affect the interviewee: death in the family, recent divorce of parents, failing grade, potential job change or loss. An interviewee might be concerned about the future: pending graduation, marriage, surgery, job search, or retirement. We are often held hostage by the past and future to the point where we cannot thrive in the present.

What is your relationship with the interviewee? Consider the critical dimensions of relationships discussed in Chapter 1: similarity, inclusion/involvement, affection/liking, control/dominance, and trust. What social or professional relations do you have in common? What values, beliefs, and attitudes do you share? Under what circumstances and how effectively have you counseled this person before? How much do you trust one another? How will control be shared? One study found that those not yet contemplating change (compared to those who were contemplating change, already engaged in change, or maintaining previous changes) have significantly lower expectations of help and the interviewer's acceptance, genuineness, and trustworthiness.[7] Other studies have shown that when there is a match of worldviews between interviewer and interviewee, particularly agreement on the causes of problems, good working relationships are established and interviewees feel more understood. On the other hand, a mismatch may hinder the relationship, particularly when counseling Asian-Americans.[8]

If you know an interviewee thoroughly prior to the interview, you may anticipate and respond effectively to common questions and comments. The following are ones we have all heard (and used) at one time or another:

Be prepared for rejections of offers to counsel.

If I need help, I'll let you know.

I can take care of myself.

I need to get back to work.

Why should I discuss my personal problems with you?

You wouldn't understand.

Don't tell Mom and Dad.

Just tell me what I should do.

No one knows how I feel.

You don't know what it's like being a student (parent, patient, teenager).

Get off my back.

I can't afford to take time off.

The more thoroughly you have analyzed the interviewee, the more likely you will know *why* a person is reacting in a particular way and how you might reply effectively.

Listen rather than talk.

An interviewee may ask for help without notice or explanation. When there is no warning and you have no relational history with this party, rely on your training and experiences to discover what is bothering the person and how you might help. Do not assume you know why a person is calling, showing up at your door, or bringing up a topic. Listening, particularly during the opening minutes, is critical in the counseling interview.

Selecting an Interviewing Approach

After carefully analyzing yourself and the interviewee, determine an appropriate interviewing approach. Chapter 2 introduced you to two fundamental approaches, *directive* and *nondirective* and their advantages and disadvantages. The sensitive and potentially explosive nature of the counseling interview necessitates a careful selection of interview approach.

Directive Approach

When using a **directive approach,** you control the structure of the interview, subject matter attended to and avoided, pace of interactions, and length of the interview. You collect and share information, define and analyze problems, suggest and evaluate solutions, and provide guidelines for actions. In brief, the directive interviewer serves as an expert or consultant who analyzes problems and provides guidelines for actions.

Know when to maintain control and when to let go.

The interviewee is more of a reactor and recipient than an equal or major player in the interaction. The directive approach is based on the assumption that the interviewer knows more about the problem than the interviewee and is better suited to analyze it and recommend solutions. The accuracy of this assumption, of course, depends upon the interviewer, the interviewee, and the situation.

Nondirective Approach

Is the interviewee capable of or willing to take control?

In the **nondirective approach,** the interviewee controls the structure of the interview, determines the topics, decides when and how they will be discussed, and sets the pace and length of the interview. The interviewer assists the interviewee in obtaining information, gaining insights, defining and analyzing problems, and discovering and evaluating solutions. The interviewer listens, observes, and encourages but does not impose ideas.

The nondirective approach is based on the assumption that the interviewee is more capable than the interviewer of analyzing problems, assessing solutions, and making correct decisions. After all, the interviewee must implement recommendations and solutions.

The accuracy of this assumption, like the directive assumption, depends on the interviewer, interviewee, and situation. The interviewee may know nothing about the problem or potential solutions, or worse, may be misinformed about both.

Do not assume the problem is lack of information.

The interviewee's problem may not be lack of information or misinformation. The person or party may not be capable of visualizing a current or future problem or making sound decisions. Or the person may be hopelessly confused about what to do or how to do it. The interviewer must serve as an objective, neutral referee, presenting pros and cons of specific courses of action. Distinguish between when you are serving as expert advisor and when, perhaps subtly and unintentionally, you are imposing personal preferences.

On the other hand, the interviewee may prefer a directive (highly structured) approach. A study of Asian-American students discovered that when career counselors used a directive approach, students saw them as more empathetic, culturally competent, and providing concrete guidance that produced immediate benefits.[9]

Combination of Approaches

Be flexible in choosing and changing approaches.

Many counseling interviewers employ a combination of directive and nondirective approaches. You may, for instance, begin with a nondirective approach to encourage the interviewee to talk and reveal the problem and its causes. Then you may switch to a more directive approach when discussing possible solutions or courses of action. A directive approach is best for obtaining facts, giving information, and making diagnoses, while a nondirective approach tends to open up large areas and bring out a great deal of spontaneous information.

Selecting the Setting

Do not underestimate the importance of location and seating.

Consider carefully the climate and tone of the interview. Both will affect the levels of communication that will take place and the willingness of both parties to disclose feelings and attitudes.

Provide a climate conducive to good counseling—a quiet, comfortable, private location, free of interruptions. You cannot expect an interviewee to be open and honest and communicate at Levels 2 and 3 if other employees, students, workers, or clients can overhear the conversation. Select a neutral location such as a restaurant, lounge, park, or organization's cafeteria where the interviewee might feel less threatened and more relaxed. Some interviewees feel comfortable or safe only on their own turf, so consider meeting in the person's room, home, office, or place of business.

A round table is a traditional arrangement for problem solving.

When possible, arrange the seating so that both interviewer and interviewee are able to communicate freely. Studies suggest that the **situation** is the most important variable in determining level of self-disclosure and that an optimal interpersonal distance is 3.5 feet. Review the discussion of seating arrangements in Chapter 2. Many students and others comment that an interviewer behind a desk makes them ill at ease, as though the "mighty one" is sitting in judgment. They prefer to sit in a chair at the end of the desk—at a right angle to the interviewer—or in chairs facing one another with no desk in between.

Arrangements of furniture can contribute to or detract from the informal, conversational atmosphere so important in counseling sessions. Many counseling interviewers are discovering that a round table, similar to a dining room or kitchen table, is preferred by interviewees because it includes no power or leader position. Interviewees seem to like this arrangement because they have often handled family matters around the dining or kitchen table.

Photo by Robin Nelson Photo/Edit

Provide a climate conducive to effective counseling, which is a quiet, comfortable, private location, free of interruptions.

Structuring the Interview

As you begin to plan the interview and determine how you will structure it, keep some important principles in mind. Realize that you are "investing in people" and that people can change, grow, and improve. You must be able to accept the person as the person is, so don't approach the interview as an opportunity to remodel an individual to your liking. The counseling interview may include confrontations over perceptions, points of view, and courses of action. It is a learning process for both parties and is unlikely to be a one-shot effort.[10]

The Opening

Want to help and show it.

The first minutes of a counseling session set the verbal and psychological tone for the remainder. Design the opening with care. Greet the interviewee by name in a warm, friendly manner, being natural and sincere. Show you want to be involved and to help. Do not be condescending or patronizing. You might want to say, "It's about time you showed up!" or "What have you done this time?" Stifle your frustration or irritation. Accept the interviewee as he or she is.

Initial Comments and Reactions

Do not try to second-guess the interviewee's reason for making an appointment or dropping by. It is natural and tempting to make such statements as:

I can't talk to you about your personal problems.

Are you still fighting with your roommate?

I assume you want to be excused from class again.

I suppose this is about money.

I know why you're here.

A person may not have initiated this interview for any of these reasons but may feel threatened or angry by your comment and attitude. At the least, your interruption and comment may ruin an opening the interviewee has prepared that would have revealed the primary purpose.

Be tactful and neutral but not indifferent.

Avoid tactless and leading reactions all too common in interactions with family members, friends, and associates. All of us have been on the receiving end of such statements as:

Why did you pierce your tongue?

You look awful.

You've been turning work in on time, haven't you?

Looks like you've put on a few pounds.

When did you get red hair?

Such comments and questions can destroy the climate and tone necessary for a successful counseling interview.

Rapport and Orientation

Accept seemingly irrelevant opening comments.

The counseling interview often consumes considerable time getting acquainted and establishing a working relationship. This time may be necessary even when your relationship with the interviewee has a long history. Your relationship history may be a positive or a negative for an interview because both parties monitor previous interactions and enter a new exchange with high or low expectations. This history may be a critical factor in extent of self-disclosure. The counseling interview is often more threatening than other interactions. An interviewee may begin by talking about the building, your office, books on the shelves, pictures on the walls, the view out the window, the weather, a recent event, or sports unrelated to the interview topic and purpose. Be patient. The interviewee is sizing up you, the situation, and the setting and is, perhaps, building up the nerve to introduce the issue of concern.

The **rapport** stage, in which you establish a feeling of goodwill with the interviewee, is your chance to show attention, interest, fairness, willingness to listen, and ability to maintain confidences. You can discover the interviewee's expectations and apprehensions about the interview and attitudes toward you, your position, your organization, and counseling sessions in general.

Encouraging Self-Disclosure

Disclosure of information, beliefs, attitudes, concerns, and feelings usually determines the success of the counseling interview. In fact, self-disclosure is a major factor in the interviewee's decision to seek or not seek help.[11] Studies have shown that "self-disclosing is a very complex process that involves intricate decision making."[12] The climate conducive for this disclosure begins during the opening minutes of the interaction. If the climate is positive and aids in creating a trusting relationship, the disclosure process that may initially generate shame and anxiety because the person is seeking help will ultimately engender "feelings of safety, pride, and authenticity and the perception that keeping secrets inhibits" the helping process "whereas disclosing produces a sense of relief from physical as well as emotional tension."[13]

Self-disclosure varies from person to person.

Some factors may be beyond your control. Females tend to disclose significantly more about themselves and their problems than do males, especially on intimate topics such as sex, and a person's self-disclosure history often affects disclosure in other interviews.[14] Males often have psychological defenses to protect themselves from feelings of weakness and to restrict emotional reactions.[15]

Culture may also play a role in determining level of self-disclosure. For instance, a study of African-Americans engaging in counseling at a community health agency discovered that African-Americans in this setting "engaged in an ongoing assessing process. Initially, they assessed client-therapist match [white or black], which was influenced by three factors: salience of Black identity, court involvement, and ideology similarity between client and therapist. These clients then assessed their safety in therapy and their counselor's effectiveness simultaneously." They used this information to "monitor and manage their degree of self-disclosing along a continuum."[16] Another study supported the importance of counselor self-disclosure in cross-cultural counseling—particularly their reactions to and experiences of racism or oppression. Such counselor self-disclosure typically improved the counseling relationship and made clients feel more understood.[17]

Encourage interviewee disclosure, for example, by disclosing your own feelings and attitudes, ensuring confidentiality, and using appropriate humor.[18] Although full self-disclosure is usually a desirable goal, an interviewee might be less tense and more willing to talk to you by hiding some undesirable facets of themselves.[19]

When you initiate a counseling session, state clearly, precisely, and honestly what you want to talk about. If there is a specific amount of time allotted for the interview, make this known so you can work within it. The interviewee will be more at ease knowing how much time is available. Quality is more important than the length of time spent with an interviewee.[20] Attire and role behavior significantly affect the interviewee's perceptions of attractiveness and level of expertise and determine how closely the person will be drawn to you and the level of self-disclosure.

Work within a known time frame.

The Body of the Interview

Although there is no standard structural format for counseling interviews, Echterling, Hartsough, and Zarle's **sequential phase model** is applicable to most counseling situations.[21] They originally developed it for handling calls to campus and community crisis centers. Figure 12.1 illustrates the sequential phase model.

Figure 12.1 *Phases of counseling interviews*

Affective	Cognitive
1. Establishment of a helpful climate *a.* Making contact *b.* Defining roles *c.* Developing a relationship	2. Assessment of crisis *a.* Accepting information *b.* Encouraging information *c.* Restating information *d.* Questioning for information
3. Affect integration *a.* Accepting feelings *b.* Encouraging feelings *c.* Reflecting feelings *d.* Questioning for feelings *e.* Relating feelings to consequences or precedents	4. Problem solving *a.* Offering information or explanations *b.* Generating alternatives *c.* Decision making *d.* Mobilizing resources

The affective or emotional phases, boxes 1 and 3, involve the interviewee's feelings of trust in the counselor, feelings about self, and feelings about the problem. A nondirective approach is usually best for the affective phases of the interview.

Feelings play central roles in counseling interviews.

The cognitive or thinking phases, boxes 2 and 4, involve thinking about the problem and taking action. A directive or combination approach is usually best for **cognitive phases.**

The typical interview begins with establishing rapport and a feeling of trust (phase 1), proceeds to discovering the nature of the interviewee's problem (phase 2), probes more deeply into the interviewee's feelings (phase 3), and comes to a decision about a course of action (phase 4). Except in emergencies, do not move from phase 1 to phase 4, or omit phase 3, without careful thought. If you do not discover the depth of the interviewee's feelings, you may not understand the problem or possible solutions.

Do not expect to move through all four phases in every counseling interview or to proceed uninterrupted in numerical order. You may go back and forth between phases 2 and 3, or between 3 and 4, as different aspects of the problem are revealed or disclosed, feelings increase or decrease in intensity, and a variety of solutions are introduced and weighed. Unless the interviewee wants specific information (where to get medical assistance, how to drop a course and add another, how to get an emergency monetary loan), you may not get to phase 4 until a second, third, or fourth interview. Be patient!

Enable the interviewee to relate the problem.

When rapport is established and orientation completed, let the interviewee begin with the topic that seems of most interest, particularly if the interviewee initiated the contact. This is the first step (as seen in the sequential phase model) toward discovering the precise nature of the problem and why a person has been unable to face or resolve it. Do not rush the interviewee. People will usually tell you what they want you to know when they are ready to do so.

If it becomes obvious early on during the interview that this problem is beyond your level of expertise in counseling or beyond your knowledge level, refer the interviewee to a more appropriate person for counseling. This is not a sign of weakness but of counseling maturity on your part. Keep an important rule in mind—strive to do no harm.

Do not charge in with solutions as soon as you think you have discovered the problem. Observe the interviewee's nonverbal cues carefully because apparently insignificant cues may reveal inner feelings and their intensity. If you initiated the contact or the interviewee seems incapable of getting to the point, you may cautiously guide the interviewee toward discovering the nature of the problem.

Closing the Interview

Closing the counseling interview is vital. If interviewees feel they have imposed on you or been pushed out the door as though on an assembly line, progress made during the interview may be erased, including the relationship fostered so carefully throughout.

Involve the interviewee as an active participant in the closing.

The verbal and nonverbal leave-taking actions discussed in Chapter 4 explain how interviews are closed both consciously and unconsciously. Decide which means or combination of means best suits you and the other party.

The interviewee should be able to tell when the closing is commencing. Don't begin new topics or raise new questions. Don't expect to meet all expectations or finish with a neat solution, but be content that you have stirred thought and enabled the interviewee to discuss problems and express feelings. Leave the door open for further interactions.

The Telephone Interview

A great many counseling interviews take place over the telephone, often over a cell phone while one or both parties are walking to class, driving to work, having dinner, working in an office, or relaxing after class or during a vacation. Crisis centers have used telephones effectively for many years.

Telephone interviews are common because they are inexpensive, convenient, allow for anonymity (may be "safer" than a face-to-face interaction), can give one a sense of control (you can hang up at any time), and can take place over long distances and at any time of the day or night. Unfortunately, telephone interviews may come at very inconvenient times when a counselor is too busy to talk, is in a different time zone, or is counseling another person. This often happens during our office hours. The telephone also invites "multitasking" because a party can do other things while "listening" to you.

A recent study of telephone counseling revealed that respondents found "telephone counseling was helpful for both global and specific improvement and that they were satisfied with the counseling they received. Respondents also rated the counseling relationship and level of interpersonal influence similar to face-to-face counseling studies measuring the same attributes."[22] The authors of this study noted the absence of visual contact between interview parties and recommended training for counselors to use their voices as substitutes for place, clothes, nonverbal cues such as eye contact and gestures, and physical appearance.

Evaluating the Interview

Review all you did and did not do and accomplish.

Think carefully and critically about the counseling interviews you take part in. Only through perceptive analysis will you begin to improve your helping interactions with others. Be realistic. They are interactions between complex human beings, at least one of whom has a serious problem and may not know or admit it.

Remember that your perceptions of how the interview went and how the interviewee reacted may be exaggerated or incorrect. You will be greatly surprised by your successes and your failures in attempting to help others. Some of each are short-lived.

The following questions may serve as guides for your post-interview evaluations.

Preinterview Preparation

How prepared were you for this interaction?

How thoroughly did I review available materials concerning the interviewee before the interview?

How effectively did I assess how I communicate and come across with others, particularly this party?

How thoroughly did I review questions I might ask to get necessary information and make informed decisions?

How thoroughly did I review questions the interviewee might ask, and how I might respond?

How successfully did I prepare a climate and setting in which openness and disclosure would be fostered?

Structuring the Interview

How effective was the opening?

How effectively did I blend directive and nondirective approaches?

How effectively and completely did I explain all options?

How effective was the closing?

Interviewing Skills

How skillful were my question techniques?

How appropriate were my responses and reactions?

Which skills need more work?

How was the pace of the interview—too fast or too slow?

How effectively did I motivate the interviewee to communicate at Levels 2 and 3?

How effectively did I listen for comprehension, empathy, evaluation, and resolution?

Counseling Skills

How well did I adapt to this party and situation?

How effectively did I help the interviewee gain insights and make decisions?

How effectively did I discover the real problem?

Did I make promises I will not be able to keep?

Did I agree with the interviewee when I should have disagreed?

How did my responses, feedback, and presentation of recommendations enhance the likelihood of interviewee compliance?

Conducting the Interview

Although you will play many roles in each counseling interview, five dominate: listening, observing, questioning, responding, and informing.

Listening

Focus on the interviewee and the interviewee's problem.

Listening (for comprehension, empathy, evaluation, and resolution) is the most important skill to master. To get to the heart of a problem, you must give undivided attention to the interviewee's words and their implications and to what is intentionally or unintentionally left unmentioned. Be genuinely interested in what the person is saying.

Do not interrupt or take over the conversation. Beware of interjecting personal opinions, experiences, or problems. Too often, for example, a person may want to talk about a serious illness of a father or mother, but the counselor takes over with a story about his or her own family illness.

If the interviewee pauses or stops talking for a few moments, do not chatter to fill in the silence. Use silence to encourage the interviewee to continue talking. Review Chapter 2 for uses of silence and listening principles. Rebecca Leonard suggests several nonverbal behaviors that communicate a willingness to listen: lean toward and face the other person squarely, maintain good eye contact, and reflect attention through facial expressions.[23] Interviewees tend to interpret smiles, attentive body postures, and gestures as evidence of warmth and enthusiasm.

Observing

Look for nonverbal signals but interpret them cautiously.

Observe how the interviewee sits, gestures, fidgets, and maintains eye contact. Pay attention to the voice for loudness, timidity, evidence of tenseness, and changes. These observations provide clues about the seriousness of the problem and the interviewee's state of mind. Deceptive answers may be lengthier, more hesitant, and characterized by longer pauses. Research indicates that people maintain eye contact longer when they lie.

If you are going to take notes or record the interview, explain why, and stop if you detect that either activity is affecting the interview adversely. Many people are hesitant to leave a taped record that others might hear. They are willing to confide in you, not others.

Questioning

Do not ask too many questions.

Although questions play important roles in counseling interviews, asking too many questions is a common mistake. Questions may interrupt the interviewee, change topics prematurely, and break the flow of self-disclosure. Numerous questions reduce the interviewee to a mere respondent and may stifle the interviewee's own questions.

Keep your questions open-ended.

Open-ended questions encourage interviewees to talk and express emotions. Both are very important for phases 2 and 3. Ask one question at a time because double-barreled questions result in ambiguous answers with neither portion answered clearly and thoroughly. Use encouragement probes such as:

And?	I see.
Uh-huh?	Go on.
Then what happened?	And then?

Use *informational probes* for clarification, explanation, and more in-depth information. For example:

Tell me why you think that happened.

How exactly did she react to your comments?

What do you mean he "overreacted" during this incident?

Tell me more about your confrontation with Professor Barger.

The *clearinghouse probe* can assure that you have obtained all necessary information about an incident or problem. For instance:

What if anything happened after that?

Have you given me all of the important details?

Is there anything else you would like to talk about?

Have I answered all of your questions about a communication major?

Phrase all questions with care.

Avoid **curious probes** into feelings and embarrassing incidents, especially if the interviewee seems hesitant to elaborate. Beware of questions that communicate disapproval, displeasure, or mistrust and make the interviewee less open and trusting. Avoid leading questions except under unusual circumstances. Be careful of *why* questions that appear to demand explanations and justifications and put the interviewee on the defensive. Imagine how an interviewee might react to questions such as, *Why* weren't you on time? *Why* did you do that? *Why* confront Doug? *Why* do you think that? Review the question tools discussed in Chapter 3 and the probing skills discussed in Chapter 5 for questioning guidelines useful in counseling interviews.

Responding and Informing

Selecting appropriate responses to questions and information requests may be difficult. A client-centered approach will help.

A client-centered approach focuses the interview on the interviewee.

A Client-Centered Approach

Turner and Lombard summarize a **client-centered approach** in Figure 12.2 that shows the information potentially available to the interviewer and the ways the interviewer might respond.[24] These types of information and responses may occur in any of Echterling, Hartsough, and Zarle's four interaction phases. Turner and Lombard say the interviewee is likely to talk about (1) objects, events, ideas, concepts, and so on, (2) other people,

Figure 12.2 *Information and responses in counseling interviews*

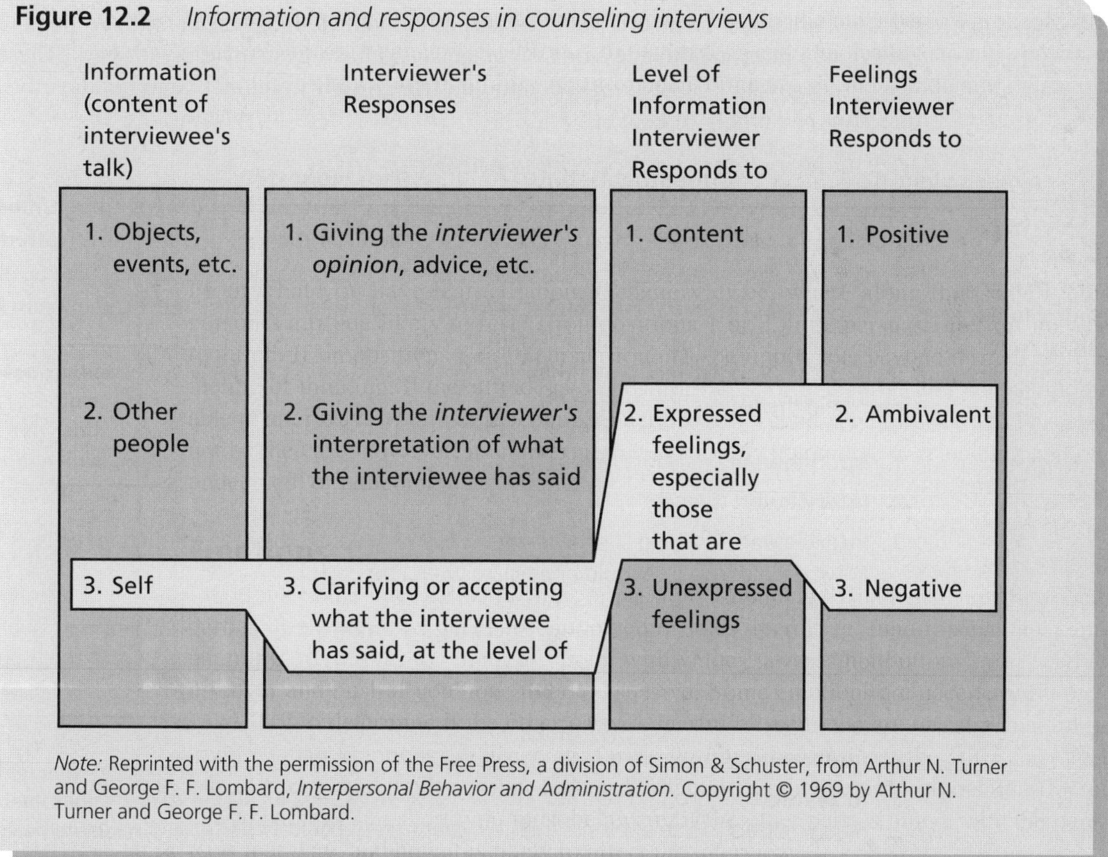

Information (content of interviewee's talk)
Interviewer's Responses
Level of Information Interviewer Responds to
Feelings Interviewer Responds to
1. Objects, events, etc.
1. Giving the *interviewer's opinion*, advice, etc.
1. Content
1. Positive
2. Other people
2. Giving the *interviewer's* interpretation of what the interviewee has said
2. Expressed feelings, especially those that are
2. Ambivalent
3. Self
3. Clarifying or accepting what the interviewee has said, at the level of
3. Unexpressed feelings
3. Negative

Note: Reprinted with the permission of the Free Press, a division of Simon & Schuster, from Arthur N. Turner and George F. F. Lombard, *Interpersonal Behavior and Administration.* Copyright © 1969 by Arthur N. Turner and George F. F. Lombard.

Center the interview on this interviewee, no one else.

or (3) self. Respond to what the interviewee is saying about **self** because self is the primary focus of counseling interviews.

You may respond to information on self by (1) giving opinions, advice, or suggestions, (2) interpreting what the interviewee is saying, or (3) accepting or clarifying "what the client has been saying from the client's own frame of reference." With these choices, **accept or clarify** what the interviewee has been saying about self, maintaining focus on the interviewee.

You may respond to the interviewee's talk about self at the level of (1) content, (2) expressed feelings, or (3) unexpressed feelings. Respond to **expressed feelings** the interviewee is willing and able to reveal and apparently believes are important.

Expressed feelings provide a fourth decision. Should you respond to feelings that are (1) positive, (2) ambivalent, or (3) negative? Turner and Lombard recommend that you respond to **ambivalent and negative feelings** rather than to positive ones to gain insights into the interviewee's problem.

Turner and Lombard provide guidelines but not a formula.

Turner and Lombard's suggestions are not fixed rules. The interviewee, the situation, and the phase of the interview will determine what kinds of information become available and which ones have priority. Phase 4 in Echterling, Hartsough, and Zarle's sequence may require advice rather than clarification of what the interviewee has said, but use Turner and Lombard's suggestions as guidelines. Interviewers may respond to interviewee information, questions, comments, and feelings in a variety of ways. These responses may be placed along a continuum from highly nondirective to nondirective, directive, and highly directive.

Highly Nondirective Reactions and Responses

Highly nondirective reactions give total control to the interviewee.

Highly nondirective reactions and responses encourage interviewees to continue commenting, analyze ideas and solutions, and be self-reliant. The interviewer offers no information, assistance, or evaluation of the interviewee, the interviewee's ideas, or possible courses of action. Highly nondirective reactions and responses are used in phases 1, 2, and 3 of the interaction phase model.

Remain silent to encourage interviewees to continue or to answer their own questions, as in the following example:

1. **Interviewee:** I may just resign.
2. **Interviewer:** (silence)
3. **Interviewee:** Well, I'd like some encouragement sometime instead of complaints. Maybe someone else would appreciate what I do.

Encourage interviewees to continue speaking by employing semi-verbal phrases, such as the following:

1. **Interviewee:** Nothing seems to work out the way I want it to.
2. **Interviewer:** Um-hmm.
3. **Interviewee:** I thought the new hours would work best for the family, but that has made matters worse at work. Then I thought that I could work three days a week at home, but the kids are constantly interrupting me. So I decided to . . .

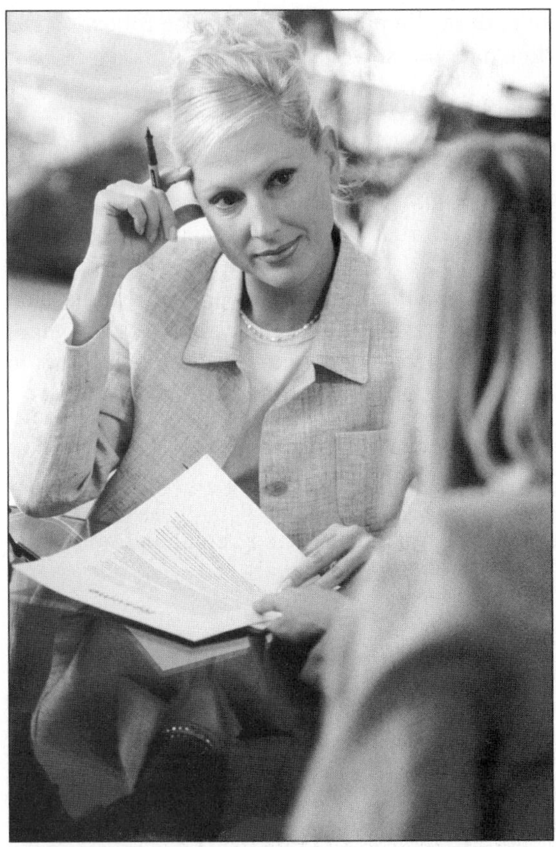

Review the interviewee's file prior to the interview so you can devote full attention during the interview.

When reacting and responding in a highly nondirective manner, be aware of your *nonverbal behaviors*. Face, tone of voice, speaking rate, and gestures must express sincere interest and reveal a high level of empathy. Show you are listening. Interviewees look for subtle as well as overt signs of approval or disapproval, interest or disinterest. For instance, Ruth Purtilo discusses five kinds of smiles: I know something you don't know; poor, poor you; don't tell me; I'm smarter than you; and I don't like you either.[25]

Holding one's hand or a simple touch may reassure a person and show you care and understand.

Simple nonverbal reactions such as rolling your eyes, raising an eyebrow, crossing your arms, and sitting forward on your chair may adversely affect an interview. Do not prolong silence because it will become awkward for both parties. If an interview party seems unable to continue or to go it alone, switch to more appropriate responses.

A variety of question techniques may serve as highly nondirective responses. Silent, nudging, and clearinghouse probes are quite useful. You may restate or repeat an interviewee's question or statement instead of providing answers or volunteering information, ideas, evaluations, or solutions. The goal is to urge the person to elaborate or come up with ideas alone.

Silence has its limits.

1. **Interviewee:** I'm stumped.
2. **Interviewer:** What have you tried?

You may *return* a question rather than answer it. The purpose is to encourage the interviewee to analyze problems and select from among possible solutions. A return question looks like this:

Use questions that force the interviewee to formulate answers and solutions.

1. **Interviewee:** Should I ask for my old job back?
2. **Interviewer:** How do *you* feel about doing that?

Do not continue to push a decision back if you detect that the individual has insufficient information or is confused, misinformed, genuinely undecided, or unable to make a choice.

You might *invite* the interviewee to discuss a problem or idea. The following is a typical invitation question in counseling interviews.

1. **Interviewee:** I'm beginning to doubt that I can handle this.
2. **Interviewer:** Want to talk about it?

The invitation question asks if the person is *willing* or *interested* in discussing, explaining, or revealing. The interviewer does not intrude with more demanding questions such as, "Tell me about it" or "Such as?"

Reflective and mirror questions are valuable techniques to make sure that you understand what the interviewee has just said or agreed to. As discussed in Chapter 3, reflective questions are designed to *clarify* and *verify* questions and statements, not to lead a person toward your preferred point of view. Here is a reflective response.

Use questions to determine what a person is and is not saying.

1. **Interviewee:** I first noticed a change in our relationship in January?
2. **Interviewer:** That was right after the all-night, New Years eve party?

Reflective questions require careful listening and a concerted verbal and nonverbal effort not to lead the interviewee.

Nondirective Reactions and Responses

Be an informer rather than a persuader.

Nondirective reactions and responses inform and encourage. No imposition of either information or encouragement is intended. These reactions occur primarily in phase 4 but may appear in phase 2. The following is an example of information giving.

1. **Interviewee:** What are my options?
2. **Interviewer:** You could take the course pass/fail so you would only need a C grade, or you could still drop the course with a passing grade.

Be specific in answers whenever possible. If you do not have the information, say so and promise to get it or refer the interviewee to a better-qualified source. Encourage and reassure the interviewee by noting that certain feelings, reactions, or symptoms are normal and to be expected, such as the following:

1. **Interviewee:** I seem to lose my temper over things that never used to bother me.
2. **Interviewer:** I believe that is all part of the pressure you are under for taking on too many projects at the same time.

A thoughtless comment or two can damage a relationship.

There are quick ways to lose the trust and respect of an interviewee facing a difficult situation. You may give unrealistic assurances such as, "There's nothing to worry about," "I'm sure everything will be just fine," or "Everything works for the best." You may preach to the person with "in the old days" comments such as, "You think you have it tough? When I was your age, I had to . . ." or "When we were first married, we faced . . ." Avoid clichés "like the plague."

Every cloud has a silver lining.

We all have to go sometime.

It's always darkest before the dawn.

It could have been worse.

No pain, no gain.

You're lucky; why, I know a person who . . .

Be careful of falling into the *we* trap. Think of when you experienced these all too common *we'isms* from counselors, teachers, health care providers, and parents:

How are *we* doing this afternoon?

We can handle it?

Let's take it one day at a time.

Are *we* ready for the exam?

You may have felt like shouting, "What do you mean *we*? I'm the one taking the test (getting the shot, undergoing therapy, overcoming grief)!"

Directive Reactions and Responses

Directive responses advise and evaluate but do not dictate.

Directive reactions and responses go beyond encouragement and information to mild advice and evaluations or judgments. Directive reactions are employed primarily in phases 2 and 4. In the following interchange, the interviewer supports the interviewee's ideas and urges action:

1. **Interviewee:** I don't think I can ride a horse at my age.
2. **Interviewer:** Why not give it a try?

A second type of directive response mildly questions the interviewee's comments or ideas. Be tactful and cautious.

1. **Interviewee:** I can't tell mom and dad I'm dropping out of college and joining the Army.
2. **Interviewer:** You haven't discussed this with them?

In a third type of directive response, the interviewer provides information and personal preference when asked, such as:

1. **Interviewee:** Would you go through the ROTC while in college if you were planning to join the Air Force when you graduated?
2. **Interviewer:** Yes, I would. You would be commissioned a second lieutenant the day you graduated and could go right on active duty as an officer.

Directive reactions and responses may challenge an interviewee's actions, ideas, or judgments, or urge the person to pursue a specific course or to accept information or ideas. Both are mild, however. Employ directive responses only if nondirective responses do not appear to be working.

Highly Directive Reactions and Responses

Reserve **highly directive reactions and responses** for special circumstances. Suggestions and mild advice are replaced with ultimatums and strong advice that should be reserved for phase 4. The following are examples of highly directive responses and reactions:

1. **Interviewee:** I can pass this lecture class without attending lectures because the professor doesn't take attendance.

   Interviewer: Then how can you explain a failing grade at midterm?

2. **Interviewee:** I don't know how to develop a Web page.

   Interviewer: Then it's time you learned. We are offering a short course starting next Thursday. Sign up for it today.

Exhaust all less directive means first.

Highly directive responses are most appropriate for simple behavioral problems and least appropriate for complex ones that are based on long-time habits or firmly held beliefs and attitudes. Try to be a helper, not a dictator, because the change or solution must come from the interviewee. You can rarely force people to comply with instructions and regimens, even when you have the authority or power to punish or fire them.

Interviewer reactions and responses may enhance self-disclosure during interviews, so it is important that you select appropriate directive and nondirective responses.

- Use highly directive responses only after you have established a close relationship with the interviewee.
- Do not be shocked by what you hear, or do not show it.
- Prepare carefully to reduce surprises and make extreme or unusual reactions or comments less likely to shock you.
- Do not try to dodge unpleasant facts.
- Be honest and tactful.
- Let your voice, facial expressions, eye contact, and gestures communicate a relaxed, unhurried, confident, warm, and caring image.
- Create a good working relationship with the interviewee.
- Release tensions with tasteful and tactful humorous interventions and responses.
- Talk as little as possible, and do not interrupt the interviewee.
- Listen empathically.

Know when to become more or less directive.

Research reveals interviewees who receive positive feedback comply more with the interviewer's requests and recommendations, return more often for counseling, and arrive earlier. These findings led the researcher to conclude that, "How interviewers respond seems to make a crucial difference."[26] Another study discovered that interviewees are more likely to implement interviewer recommendations when there is a good match between the recommendation and the problem, the recommendation is not too difficult to implement, and the recommendation is built on the interviewee's strengths.[27]

ON THE WEB

Selecting counseling approaches and responses most appropriate for a particular interviewee and problem may be critical to the outcome of the interview. Philosophies and practices differ among counselors and counseling agencies. Use the Internet to explore the interviewing approaches currently advocated and illustrated by researchers, practitioners, and agencies when dealing with a variety of clients and problems. Useful sources are the Pamphlet Page (http://uhs.uchicago.edu/scrs/vpc/virtulets.html), the Counseling Center Village (http://ub-counseling.buffalo.edu/ccv.html), and Counseling and Psychological Services at Purdue University (http://www.purdue.edu/caps).

Summary

You take part in a counseling interview whenever you try to help a person gain insights into a physical, career, emotional, or social problem and discover ways to cope. The counseling interview may be the most sensitive of interview settings because it usually does not occur until a person feels incapable of handling a problem or a counselor decides that a helping session is needed.

Preparation helps to determine how to listen, question, inform, explain, respond, and relate to each interviewee. No two interviews are identical because no two interviewees and situations are identical. Thus, many suggestions but few rules are available for selecting interview approaches, types of responses, questions, and structures.

Key Terms and Concepts

The online learning center for this text features FLASHCARDS and CROSSWORD PUZZLES for studying based on these terms and concepts.

Client-centered approach
Cognitive phase
Compliance
Curious probes
Directive approach
Directive reactions
Expressed feelings
Highly directive reactions and responses

A Counseling Interview for Review and Analysis

This counseling interview is between Zach Mendoza, a machinist at Attica Automotive that makes parts for several automobile manufacturers, and Shirley McNulty, a consultant for start-up businesses and adjunct professor in the School of Management at Wesleyan University. Attica Automotive has been restructuring and downsizing because many of its auto customers are doing the same, and Zach sees the end coming since the company has been making "retirement" and "buy-out" packages available to long-time employees like him. He wants to talk to Shirley about starting his own small business—a life-long dream—with one of these packages. He met Shirley a few years ago when she taught an employment interviewing and career workshop at the local Carnegie Library. The interview is taking place at the O'Malley Irish Pub recently started by a former Attica production supervisor.

How effectively does the instructor handle the opening? Which approach or approaches (directive, nondirective, or a combination) does she use? How appropriate is this choice? How effectively does the instructor meet the four phases of counseling interviews? How appropriate are the instructor's reactions, responses, and questions? At which levels of disclosure (1, 2, or 3) are the student's revelations? How effective is the instructor as a listener? How adequate is the closing?

1. **Interviewee:** Hi Professor McNulty, I really appreciate your willingness to talk to me about my start-up business idea.
2. **Interviewer:** Hi, Zach, and please call me Shirley. I remember you from my workshop at the library.
3. **Interviewee:** I'm glad you remembered me—Shirley. That was a great workshop, and it got me started thinking seriously about a new career, a change in my life.
4. **Interviewer:** Uh-huh?
5. **Interviewee:** I'm sure you've seen the news reports about the very real possibility that Attica Automotive will be closing or at least greatly reducing its workforce. The "handwriting's on the wall," so to speak.
6. **Interviewer:** Yes, I've been following the news accounts and have been talking to Attica about doing some interview training for its personnel. Like you, I think Attica is going to move to Mexico or combine with a firm in Michigan.
7. **Interviewee:** I'm glad you see it as I do. Well . . . I've been thinking about taking one of the "buy-out" offers that will amount to about $75,000. This would give me a chunk of money to invest or start my own business. What do you think?
8. **Interviewer:** About these two choices?
9. **Interviewee:** Yes, but mainly about starting my own business.
10. **Interviewer:** That can be expensive and risky. What did you have in mind?
11. **Interviewee:** Well . . . (very excited) I've always wanted to open a fly fishing shop that also provided guide services.
12. **Interviewer:** I see.
13. **Interviewee:** I've fished since I was a kid and really know the lakes and streams around here. Fly fishing is a hobby that I would like to make into a career. I am good at it and know how to make really effective flies. I could fish every day of the week and never get tired of it.
14. **Interviewer:** That sounds like a great hobby, but running a business can't be a hobby. It takes long hours, often seven days a week, requires business training and experience, and demands a lot of money up front.
15. **Interviewee:** That's why I haven't made the leap before now—the money problem. But now I will have $75,000 from Attica and I have about $25,000 in savings. One hundred thousand dollars will buy a lot of flies, rods, reels, equipment, and clothing. Outfits such as vests, waders, hats, rain gear, and all that should be big sellers.
16. **Interviewer:** Um-hmm. And where will you locate your new enterprise?

17. **Interviewee:** Well, at first I thought I would operate out of the house, but then my wife and the zoning people nixed this. So I've been looking at one of those storefronts downtown. They would give Stony Creek Outfitters a nice, old fashioned flavor. And the one I've looked at has a loft that would be great for displays.
18. **Interviewer:** That sounds very exciting, and I see you've already picked out a name.
19. **Interviewee:** Yes, what do you think? Stony Creek just east of town is great for fly fishing in the spring and summer with some great small mouth bass fishing.
20. **Interviewer:** What would the rent be on the downtown site?
21. **Interviewee:** Only about $1,800 a month for the first two years? I could swing that and draw on the $75,000 buy-out in the early stages.
22. **Interviewer:** And how much would it cost to remodel the space and loft to make it attractive and ready for business?
23. **Interviewee:** Maybe $10,000 to $12,000 for materials. My brother-in-law Hector is a great carpenter.
24. **Interviewer:** And what about furniture, display cases, clothes racks, and those sorts of things?
25. **Interviewee:** Hey, I've given this careful thought. We could get lots of those things at flea markets and estate sales.
26. **Interviewer:** So, what is a good estimate of the total start-up costs, including rent on the space until you can get it up and running?
27. **Interviewee:** Well . . . I haven't come up with a final figure yet but, hey, I will have $100,000 in the bank.
28. **Interviewer:** Do you recall what I said in the workshop about small business failures?
29. **Interviewee:** It was fairly high.
30. **Interviewer:** Yes it is. Some 95 percent of new small businesses fail during the first year.
31. **Interviewee:** Well, I'm not going to be one of them. I have a great plan.
32. **Interviewer:** I see. Do you intend to be in the store eight hours a day, seven days a week?
33. **Interviewee:** Oh no. I'm not going to get in that rut. I will need to try out a lot of streams around the state and up into Michigan and down into Kentucky and Tennessee. And then, of course, I will be providing expert guide service.
34. **Interviewer:** Who will run the store when you're not there?
35. **Interviewee:** I know some fly fishers in the area and a lot of young people from my stints as a baseball and football coach. They would find this fun to do.
36. **Interviewer:** Work and Fun often don't match. And how much would you pay for your helpers?
37. **Interviewee:** Oh, some might volunteer a bit of time, and the youngsters would work for about seven or eight dollars an hour.
38. **Interviewer:** Uh-huh.

39. **Interviewee:** I know what you're thinking, that there's more to it than I think. I know I can do this.
40. **Interviewer:** What about taxes, insurance, benefits, competition . . .?
41. **Interviewee:** I can take care of these things. I'm a fast learner.
42. **Interviewer:** Zach, would you do me a favor? A couple of years ago I went trout fishing in the north Georgia mountains with my two sons. We used Unicoi Outfitters in Helen, Georgia. They have a beautiful shop and retail store right on the Chattahoochee River. Drive down there some weekend and talk to them about your plans. See what they have to say. You'll enjoy the beautiful drive and talking to the owners and their guides. Hey, you might even get to do some great trout fishing. I caught a $7\frac{1}{2}$ pound rainbow.
43. **Interviewee:** That does sound like a good idea. We don't have too many outfitters around here, especially specializing in fly fishing. Most people do spin casting.
44. **Interviewer:** Good. I can get you their address and phone number. Promise me you'll do that before getting too far into your plans and bank account.
45. **Interviewee:** Okay, sure. But I'm going to do this. It's the right time. I can feel it.
46. **Interviewer:** Feelings are good; facts are excellent. It's been good talking to you Zach. I wish you the best.
47. **Interviewee:** Thanks for meeting with me Shirley. Maybe you'll be my first customer.
48. **Interviewer:** Maybe. Fly fishing is fun. Think about how you're going to convert all of those spin casters into fly fishing enthusiasts.
49. **Interviewee:** Yeah, I'll think about that. Maybe I can covert a bunch of them.

Counseling Role-Playing Cases

A Paper from the Internet

The interviewer has the reputation of being a good teacher and counselor. As he was grading term papers in his Civil War history course, he became suspicious of a paper that seemed beyond the level of undergraduate work. He browsed the Internet and came up with a paper that is remarkably similar to the one handed in to him. He has decided to call the student in to talk about the paper and its similarity to one on the Internet. The interviewer knows the interviewee very well and has had him as a student in two previous history courses. He finds it hard to believe that the student handed in someone else's work, but the facts seem to speak for themselves.

The interviewee is a last-semester junior in college and has never been accused of cheating before. He is minoring in history and considers his relationship with the interviewer to be excellent. He realizes that the interviewer thinks he cheated on the paper, but he does not think he has done anything wrong. He is proud of his paper.

Dating and Religion

The interviewee is 22 years old and a student at the University of South Dakota. She has been dating a classmate for several months, and both are beginning to get serious about a future together. She is Catholic and he is Jewish, and their religious faiths are very important to them. While neither sees religion as a major problem, neither of them is willing to change faiths or to commit themselves to raising future children in the other's religious tradition.

The interviewee has decided to meet with a neighbor back home, Sheri Prohofsky, during Thanksgiving break to get some suggestions. Sheri is married with three children, and her husband is Jewish. She and her husband have seemed to work out their religious differences quite well with each remaining active in their church and temple. They have allowed their children to decide which faith tradition they will follow.

A Graduate School Decision

The interviewee is a second semester junior in college and has been planning to enter the job market in human resources. Because he has a 3.85/4.0 grade point average and has worked on research projects with two faculty members, friends and family members are urging him to consider going to graduate school after he graduates. Some are pushing an MBA while others are suggesting an MS as preparation for work toward the PhD and perhaps a college teaching career. He doesn't know what to do and wonders whether he should work for a few years before considering a graduate program.

The interviewer is a professor of management and has taught the interviewee in two human resources courses. She has both an MBA and PhD and worked in industry before and after the master's degree. The last time she talked to the interviewee he was excited about job fairs to be held on campus early in the fall.

Too Much Debt

The interviewee is 25 years old and graduated from college two years ago in social work. While in college, she relied heavily on credit cards and loans to cover tuition, fees, books, and living expenses. She believed that once she graduated, she would be able to pay off the loans and reduce the credit card debt. Her starting salary was not what she expected, and the cost of living in the Santa Barbara area has resulted in more loans and credit cards that are almost maxed out. Some medical problems have resulted in missed work and significant out-of-pocket costs. She is desperate. She has decided to seek out a friend who is a financial aid counselor at her alma mater.

The interviewer is 35 years old and sees young and old people who have gotten themselves caught in the easy credit trap. She worked with the interviewee when she was a student and knew that she might be facing future problems because she had to finance nearly all of her college.

Student Activities

1. Visit a crisis center in your community or on your campus. Observe how volunteer counselors handle telephone counseling. Talk with counselors about their training techniques and self-evaluations. How does telephone counseling differ from face-to-face counseling?
2. Interview three different types of counselors, such as a marriage counselor, a student counselor, a financial counselor, or a legal counselor. How are their approaches and

techniques similar and different? What kinds of training have they had? How much training do they consider essential? In their estimation, what makes a "successful" counselor?

3. Pick one of the counseling role-playing cases and develop a complete approach to the case, beginning with setting and furniture arrangement. How would you begin the interview? What questions would you ask? How much would you disclose about yourself—training, background, experiences, and so on? What kinds of reactions and responses would you use? What solution would you suggest? What would you do and not do to aid interviewee compliance? How would you close the interview?
4. Interview an athletic, academic, or student services staff member who counsels students every day. Talk to this person about how different cultures (African-American, Asian-American, Hispanic-American, Arab-American), nationalities (United States or international students), ages, and genders necessitate differences in counseling approaches. How has the counselor's culture, nationality, age, or gender affected counseling interviews in the past? What suggestions does this person have for you as a lay counselor?

Notes

1. Donald R. Atkinson, Francisco Q. Ponce, and Francine M. Martinez, "Effects of Ethnic, Sex, and Attitude Similarity on Counselor Credibility," *Journal of Counseling Psychology* 31 (1984), pp. 589–591.
2. Barbara Goldberg and Romeria Tidwell, "Ethnicity and Gender Similarity: The Effectiveness of Counseling for Adolescents," *Journal of Youth and Adolescents* 19 (1990), pp. 589–603.
3. Madonna G. Constantine, Anika K. Warren, and Marie L. Miville, "White Racial Identity Dyadic Interactions in Supervision: Implications for Supervisees' Multicultural Counseling Competence," *Journal of Counseling Psychology* 52 (2005), p. 495.
4. Roger L. Worthington and Donald R. Atkinson, "Effects of Perceived Etiology Attribution Similarity on Client Ratings of Counselor Credibility," *Journal of Counseling Psychology* 43 (1996), pp. 423–429.
5. Sarah Knox, Shirley A. Hess, David A. Petersen, and Clara E. Hill, "A Qualitative Analysis of Client Perceptions of the Effects of Helpful Therapist Self-Disclosure in Long-Term Therapy," *Journal of Counseling Psychology* 44 (1997), pp. 274–283.
6. Mary Ann Hoffman, Clara E. Hill, Stacey E. Holmes, and Gary F. Freitas, "Supervisor Perspective on the Process and Outcome of Giving Easy, Difficult, or No Feedback to Supervisees," *Journal of Counseling Psychology* 52 (2005), pp. 3–13.
7. William A. Satterfield, Sidne A. Buelow, William J. Lyddon, and J. T. Johnson, "Client Stages of Change and Expectations about Counseling," *Journal of Counseling Psychology* 42 (1995), pp. 476–478.
8. Bryan S. K. Kim, Gladys F. Ng, and Annie J. Ahn, "Effects of Client Expectation for Counseling Success, Client-Counselor Worldview Match, and Client Adherence to

Asian and European American Cultural Values on Counseling Process with Asian Americans," *Journal of Counseling Psychology* 52 (2005), pp. 67–76.

9. Lisa C. Li and Bryan S. K. Kim, "Effects of Counseling Style and Client Adherence to Asian Cultural Values on Counseling Process with Asian American College Students," *Journal of Counseling Psychology* 51 (2004), pp. 158–167.

10. "Effective Counseling," http://www2.ku.edu/~coms/virtual_assistant/via/counsel.html, accessed October 12, 2006; "Counseling Interviews," http://www.uwgb.edu/clampit/interviewing/interviewing%20lectures/counseling%Interviews%.html, accessed October 12, 2006.

11. David L. Vogel and Stephen R. Wester, "To Seek Help or Not to Seek Help: The Risks of Self-Disclosure," *Journal of Counseling Psychology* 50 (2003), pp. 351–361.

12. Earlise C. Ward, "Keeping It Real: A Grounded Theory Study of African American Clients Engaging in Counseling at a Community Mental Health Agency," *Journal of Counseling Psychology* 52 (2005), p. 479.

13. Barry A. Farber, Kathryn C. Berano, and Joseph A. Capobianco, "Client's Perceptions of the Process and Consequences of Self-Disclosure in Psychotherapy," *Journal of Counseling Psychology* 51 (2004), pp. 340–346.

14. Timothy P. Johnson, James G. Hougland, and Robert W. Moore, "Sex Differences in Reporting Sensitive Behavior: A Comparison of Interview Methods," *Sex Roles* 24 (1991), pp. 669–680; Judy Cornelia Pearson, Richard L. West, and Lynn H. Turner, *Gender and Communication* (Madison, WI: Brown & Benchmark, 1995), pp. 149–152.

15. James R. Mahalik, Robert J. Cournoyer, William DeFranc, Marcus Cherry, and Jeffrey M. Napolitano, "Men's Gender Role Conflict and Use of Psychological Defenses," *Journal of Counseling Psychology* 45 (1998), pp. 247–255.

16. Ward, p. 471.

17. Alan W. Burkard, Sarah Knox, Michael Groen, Maria Perez, and Shirley A. Hess, "European American Therapist Self-Disclosure in Cross-Cultural Counseling," *Journal of Counseling Psychology* 53 (2006), p. 15.

18. Bryan S. K. Kim, Clara E. Hill, Charles J. Gelso, Melissa K. Goates, Penelope A. Asay, and James M. Harbin, "Counselor Self-Disclosure, East Asian American Client Adherence to Asian Cultural Values, and Counseling Process," *Journal of Counseling Psychology* 50 (2003), pp. 324–332.

19. Anita E. Kelly, "Clients' Secret Keeping in Outpatient Therapy," *Journal of Counseling Psychology* 45 (1998), pp. 50–57.

20. Paul R. Turner, Mary Valtierra, Tammy R. Talken, Vivian I. Miller, and Jose R. DeAnda, "Effect of Session Length on Treatment Outcome for College Students in Brief Therapy," *Journal of Counseling Psychology* 43 (1996), pp. 228–232.

21. Lennis G. Echterling, Don M. Hartsough, and H. Zarle, "Testing a Model for the Process of Telephone Crisis Intervention," *American Journal of Community Psychiatrists 8* (1980), pp. 715–725. see also Meredith Glick Brinegar, Lisa A. Salvi, William B. Stiles, and Leslie S. Greenberg, "Building a Meaningful Bridge: Therapeutic

Progress from Problem Formulation to Understanding," *Journal of Counseling Psychology* 53 (2006), pp. 165–180.

22. Robert J. Reese, Collie W. Conoley, and Daniel F. Brossart, "Effectiveness of Telephone Counseling: A Field-Based Investigation," *Journal of Counseling Psychology* 49 (2002), pp. 233–242.

23. Rebecca Leonard, "Attending: Letting the Patient Know You Are Listening," *Journal of Practical Nursing* 33 (1983), pp. 28–29; Ginger Schafer Wlody, "Effective Communication Techniques," *Nursing Management,* October 1981, pp. 19–23.

24. Reprinted with permission of the Free Press, a Division of Simon & Schuster from *Interpersonal Behavior and Administration* by Arthur N. Turner and George F. F. Lombard. Copyright 1969 by Arthur N. Turner and George F. F. Lombard.

25. Ruth Purtilo, *The Allied Health Professional and the Patient: Techniques of Effective Interaction* (Philadelphia: Saunders, 1973), pp. 96–97.

26. Peter Chang, "Effects of Interviewer Questions and Response Type on Compliance: An Analogue Study," *Journal of Counseling Psychology* 41 (1994), pp. 74–82.

27. Collie W. Conoley, Marjorie A. Padula, Darryl S. Payton, and Jeffrey A. Daniels, "Predictors of Client Implementation of Counselor Recommendations: Match with Problem, Difficulty Level, and Building on Client Strengths," *Journal of Counseling Psychology* 41 (1994), pp. 3–7.

Resources

Cormier, L. Sherilyn. *Counseling: Strategies and Interventions.* Boston: Pearson Allyn and Bacon, 2005.

Hill, Clara E. *Helping Skills: Facilitating Exploration, Insight, and Action.* Washington, DC: American Psychological Association, 2004.

Nelson-Jones, Richard. *Basic Counseling Skills: A Helper's Manual.* Thousand Oaks, CA: Sage, 2003.

Okun, Barbara F. *Effective Helping: Interviewing and Counseling Techniques.* Pacific Grove, CA: Brooks/Cole, 1997.

Sugarman, Leonie. *Counseling and the Life Course.* Thousand Oaks, CA: Sage, 2004.

CHAPTER 13 The Health Care Interview

While *some of you* may be planning careers as health care providers, *all of you* will take part in health care interviews on a regular basis because of common illnesses and increasing emphasis on preventive medicine and the early detection of potentially life-threatening medical problems. These interviews vary from routine physical checkups and stitches following an accident to major surgery and treatments for heart disease and AIDS. You may arrange an interview days, weeks, or months in advance or without warning because of an accident or virus. These interactions are often tense and emotional involving the embarrassment of a gynecological or testicular examination or fear of the unknown. They may be single, brief consultations or one of dozens over many years. Regardless of the reason or timing, interpersonal communication is at the heart of every health care interview.

Health care interviews deal with the ordinary and the extra-ordinary.

This chapter deals initially with how both parties have traditionally viewed the health care interview, the changing role of communication in health care, and how provider and patient can contribute to a productive relationship that promotes a collaborative effort to diagnose and treat medical problems to the satisfaction of both parties. Then it addresses the major parts of health care interviews: the opening, getting information, giving information, counseling, persuading, and the closing.

Changing Views on the Health Care Interview

During the nineteenth century when health care providers could do little scientifically to combat germs and bring people back to health, they established relationships by being available and through caring and listening skills. The physician in a one-horse buggy making house calls and sitting by a person's bed throughout the night remains in our collective memory, magnified and glorified by motion pictures and television.

The Provider's View

During the twentieth century as science and technology enabled physicians to attack germs that cause diseases, caring and listening seemed less important and, for a time, scientific language, manner, and procedures brought new respect to medical professionals. Unfortunately, this biomedical model also brought a power imbalance between patient and provider.[1]

Views of health care continue to evolve.

Providers viewed most medical visits as routine and, as most of us do in routine situations, assumed their behavior was appropriate and their interpretations were accurate. They were scientists who diagnosed and resolved medical problems and effective communication, if it was given any thought, was taken for granted. Nurses, for instance, reported that they communicated effectively verbally and nonverbally even when they were observed not to do so.[2] Providers assumed that they would acquire necessary "interpersonal skills through role-modeling or by trial and error without exposure to a formal teaching program."[3] When training did take place, "too much emphasis" was "given to the content of the interview and not enough to the process of the interview."[4]

Task orientation fosters relational distance.

Health care providers learned from training, role models, peer pressure, and the actions and comments of superiors that they were to be in control at all times. Many were understandably reluctant to share this control with patients and their families or with other professionals, particularly nurses, emergency medical technicians, or staff members who were lower in the medical hierarchy. To maintain control, often under difficult and emotional circumstances, providers adopted a professional distance or impersonal attitude toward patients and associates. In a recent article on medical errors, Charles Lauer related an instance when a surgeon operated on a woman's foot instead of doing the scheduled tonsillectomy. Seven members of the surgical team wondered why the surgeon was operating on the foot but were afraid to speak their minds and run the risk of angering the person in a power position.[5] Providers tend to be busy, task-oriented individuals who are reluctant to waste time on seemingly inconsequential chats with patients. Time was critical. The desire was to diagnose and treat the disease quickly and efficiently and to move to the next patient.

The Patient's View

Patients feel vulnerable.

Patients viewed medical visits "with apprehension and uncertainty, especially if they normally" experienced good health.[6] Facing the unknown or an uncertain future frightened patients and affected their perspectives. As Dean Barnlund writes, "To be uninformed is to be communicatively impotent, and this dependent state is not one mature people tolerate gracefully."[7] They were openly admitting that their health problems were beyond their control and they had to turn to others for help. Life itself often appeared out of control, and patients felt exceedingly vulnerable because they were without the security of homes, jobs, routines, and normal relationships. They found themselves in threatening environments, deprived of their dignity, autonomy, authority, and freedom. It seemed dangerous to displease medical authorities in any way.

The setting is threatening and demeaning.

When placed in seemingly helpless positions, patients were disappointed with themselves and felt guilty, weak, and inadequate. A common response was change in personality, self-image, and identity. They reacted to altered and threatening circumstances in a variety of ways. Many became self-centered and developed unrealistic expectations of health care providers from receptionists to physicians. Some became overly conservative, rigid, and suspicious. They saw small incidents they would have ignored when well as affronts or signs of rejection. Others reacted angrily and lashed out at providers. Still others withdrew into themselves or became overly dependent. Some wanted to remain ill to get attention, escape the world, or achieve personal ends.

Unlike the provider who focused on diagnoses, technology, and treatment, the patient focused on being ill and the care received. Good care was equated with personal treatment, interpersonal communication, and relationship building. Consumers became increasingly dissatisfied with medical care and the communication that accompanied it.

In one study, 39 percent expressed dissatisfaction with nurses, 36 percent with physicians, and 44 percent with receptionists and nontechnical personnel.[8] Experts claimed most malpractice cases were due to poor communication. As early as 1979, the American Board of Internal Medicine identified poor interviewing skills as critical in health care delivery and patient satisfaction.[9]

The Emerging View

Perceptions of health care are undergoing rapid change in the twenty-first century. Health care educators and providers are beginning to see and espouse the importance of a collaborative partnership, a mutual participation in health care. The emphasis is on patients and providers as "coagents in a problem-solving context."[10] Advocates of co-agency contend that when patients are more actively involved as partners, rather than passive bystanders, they are more satisfied with their care, receive more patient-centered care such as information and support, are more committed to treatment regimens, have a stronger sense of control over their health, and experience better health.[11]

Collaboration is critical in health care.

The goal of the health care interaction is to "develop a reciprocal relationship, where the exchange of information, identification of problems, and development of solutions is an interactive process," a reciprocal rather than an authoritative relationship.[12] Researchers claim that "the physician–patient relationship is the most critical component of the health care delivery process."[13] For instance, Gary Kreps concludes that relationship "facilitates exchange of relevant health information, coordination of efforts, and provision of emotional support between interdependent health care consumers and providers."[14]

Creating a Collaborative Relationship

If a collaborative relationship is the key to health care interviews, how can this relationship be established and maintained, particularly since it is constantly being redefined and adjusted through interactions? Although it takes two parties to form a productive relationship, providers and patients continue to believe the provider has the burden to make the relationship work.[15]

photo by Michael Newman/PhotoEdit

The development of positive relationships between health care providers and receivers is essential for effective communication and health care.

Sharing Control

A sharing of control is the difficult first step in forming a collaborative relationship. Traditionally, power and authority have been seriously lopsided in the health care interview. The provider is highly trained, sees the situation as routine, speaks in scientific terms and acronyms few patients understand, appears to be in control of self and the situation, is emotionally uninvolved, and is fully clothed in a suit or uniform. Control gravitates to the provider because this party chooses and controls the setting, timing, and structure of the interview. Closed questions, limited reactions, changing of topics, and interruptions signal who is in charge. When patients challenge this situation, providers may quickly reassert their "authorial presence" or ignore the challenge.[16]

Both parties must share control.

On the other hand, the patient (literally one who bears or endures pain or suffering with composure and without complaint) is typically uninformed, sees the situation as a crisis, is emotionally involved, has little medical knowledge, has little control over what happens in an unfamiliar and threatening environment, and may be partially nude, highly medicated, or in severe pain. Patients are partly to blame for the parent–child relationship that may exist in the interview by dutifully taking on a subordinate role in the relationship and remaining compliant.[17] They often fail to ask questions at critical times during interviews. Although the patient usually is or appears to be compliant, many have subtle control strategies. They may change topics, ask numerous questions, give short, unrevealing answers to open questions, withhold vital information, or talk incessantly. Others demonstrate relational power through silence rather than conversational dominance. Patients may agree with providers during interviews and then ignore prescriptions, regimens, and advice afterward.

Patients must be active and responsive.

While there appears to be considerable agreement on what constitutes competent physician communication, there has been little evidence of what constitutes competent patient communication. A recent study revealed that "From the physician's perspective, the communicatively competent patient is well prepared," "gives prior thought to medical concerns," educates him/herself about the illness, comes to the interview with an agenda, and remains focused on it, provides "detailed information about his or her medical history, symptoms, and other relevant matters," and seeks information by asking questions about the diagnosis and treatment.[18] The patients' perspective in this study mirrored the physicians'. While these results are very encouraging, this study also discovered that there was not "a significant correlation between perceptions of competence and patients' actual discourse, that "perceptions of communication in a medical interview do not necessarily match what is actually said." What physicians and patients think they see and hear often does not match reality.

Both parties in the health care interview must negotiate and share control "as partners striving for a common goal."[19] As a provider, develop positive relational climates by showing interest in the patient's lifestyle, nonmedical concerns, and overall wellbeing. Supportive talk that includes statements of reassurance, support, and empathy demonstrates interpersonal sensitivity and sincere interest in the patient as a person.

Empathy is "an essential element of the physician-patient relationship," and a showing of empathy increases patient satisfaction and reduces time and expense. Carma Bylund and Gregory Makoul write that "Empathy is not just something that is 'given' from physician to patient. Instead, a transactional communication perspective informs us that the physician and patient mutually influence each other during the interaction."[20] They discovered that while some patients provided repeated opportunities for empathic responses, others provided little or none. When patients did so, physicians in their study "had a clear tendency for acknowledging, pursuing, and confirming patients' empathic opportunities." This is a positive trend in physician-patient interactions.

It takes two to form an effective relationship.

Encourage the patient to express ideas, expectations, fears, and feelings about the medical problem and value the patient's expertise. The goal is to treat one another as equals. As a patient, come to the interview well informed about the health problem and ready to provide detailed information as honestly and accurately as possible, express concerns, respond effectively to the provider's questions, and state your opinions, suggestions, and preferences. Don't be overawed by the surroundings, technology, or status of the provider. Accept reality as it is, not as you would like it to be, listen openly and perceptively, be careful of assumptions, and speak up when you have questions about words, diagnoses, or recommendations.

Reducing Relational Distance

Dwell on similarities, not differences.

Patient-centered care (PCC), in which patient "needs, preferences, and beliefs are respected at all times," is a growing movement in the United States[21] that can advance if both parties share control and actively seek to reduce relational distance. While both parties are unique in some ways, they share many perceptions, needs, values, beliefs, attitudes, and experiences. Both are real persons, not medical magicians or miracle workers and not disease carriers or chronic whiners. Both strive to maintain dignity, privacy, self-respect, and comfort. Provider and patient can build relationships by working to understand and identify with one another.

While medical personnel can reduce relational distance by not hiding behind uniforms, expertise, and policies, patients can do the same by not hiding behind hospital gowns, ignorance, and their medical conditions. Neither party should push the relationship too quickly, but each can reduce emotional distance by encouraging two-way dialogues about feelings rather than one-way monologues about technical matters. They must make efforts to know and understand one another.

Enhance relationships through understanding.

Medical education programs are encouraging students to spend a day lying in a hospital bed or using a wheelchair or crutches to experience the feelings of helplessness and dependency patients experience. Some medical schools are replacing vinyl models with mock patients, sometimes medical students, to assess competence and compassion. Few patients understand the working lives of health care professionals, but it would be immensely productive if they strived to do so, perhaps merely by observing carefully the routines and actions of personnel in the facilities visited or by talking to providers about what they do on a daily basis. Mutual understanding reduces relational distance. Zakus and others suggest five ways providers and patients can enhance relationships: try to be relaxed, confident, and comfortable; show interest in the patient or provider as an individual; maintain objectivity; be sincere and honest; and maintain appropriate control during the interaction.[22]

Appreciating Diversity

While the goal is to reduce relational distance, diversity among patients and providers is a reality both parties must recognize and address. We understand intuitively that patients, particularly those from other cultures, experience and react differently to health care interviews, but few of us are aware that providers also experience stress and anxiety when dealing with different types of patients and those from other cultures.[23]

Sex

Age and sex influence communication and treatment.

Sex may make a difference in the health care interview. Women tend to be more concerned about health than men and are more verbal during interactions. This may be a learned difference because more health care information in the media is aimed at women than men. Women spend more communication time with providers and are more active communicators during these visits, but their providers take their concerns less seriously. On the other hand, male patients tend to be more domineering than females regardless of the sex of the provider.[24] A by-product of more females entering the fields of obstetrics and gynecology is the significant percentage of women patients choosing female physicians. This has led male physicians to work on improving their interpersonal communication skills.[25]

Age

Age is becoming a growing factor as life expectancy increases and the baby boomer generation reaches retirement age. Older patients are more reluctant to "challenge the physician's authority" than younger patients, often with good reason. Providers who are mostly under 55 are "significantly less egalitarian, less patient, and less respectful with older patients," perhaps reflecting society's changing attitudes toward "aging" and the wisdom of our elders. Providers are "less likely to raise psychological issues with" older patients.[26] Younger patients are more comfortable with "bothering" health care providers and less awed by authority and credentials. If a patient is incapacitated, often because of age, it may be wise to involve a surrogate (spouse or child) or a health care proxy who may have important information to share with the physician and be able to collaborate about the patient's care.[27]

Culture

There are approximately 47 million people in the United States who speak a language other than English at home, and this does not include the millions of international travelers who come to the United States each year.[28]

Health communication differs in the global village.

Globalization and its accompanying cultural differences affect interpersonal communication in many ways. African-American and Puerto Rican patients have indicated that their race, ethnicity, and lower economic status impacted negatively on their information seeking (particularly HIV-related information) and health care.[29] Patients of a lower social class may be openly reluctant to challenge physicians so they attempt to control the relationship.[30] Arab cultures practice close proximity and kissing among men; both actions may be seen as offensive in American or European health care interactions. Native American and Asian cultures prize nonverbal communication, while American and German cultures prize verbal communication. Many societies, particularly Asian, are less assertive.

Kreps and Thornton have identified the differences in medical philosophies in different countries and suggest the difficulties these might pose for nonnative health care providers and patients:[31]

- French physicians tend to discount statistics and emphasize logic.
- German physicians tend to be authoritarian romantics.
- English physicians tend to be paternalistic.
- American physicians tend to be aggressive and want to "do something."

All of these differences affect communicative roles and control sharing in medical interviews. Providers must be culturally sensitive to differences in reporting pain, understanding informed consent, using appropriate language, and disclosing information that may rely on cultural knowledge, modesty, and comfort. Alice Chen, in an article entitled "Doctoring Across the Language Divide," relates an instance when she was treating a Muslim woman and ordered an X ray to assess for arthritis. A male X-ray technician wanted to lift up the horrified woman's hijab so he could position the equipment properly. Chen referred her to a different facility with a notation that the patient needed a female technician.[32] For example, while only 59 percent of emergency room patients understand what they are told, the figure is significantly lower for Spanish-speaking patients.[33]

Stereotypes

"Good" patients get better health care.

Stereotypes affect the way providers see and treat patients. Many are labeled as emotionally disturbed, having personality disorders, being childlike, and lacking in knowledge, understanding, and intelligence because of the way they look or respond to unclear language and frightening situations. Provider perception of the patient as a childlike dependent is often revealed in condescending attitudes and baby talk with adults. One study indicated that 20 percent of staff interactions in nursing homes qualifies as *baby talk,* a speech style common when speaking to infants that has a "slower rate, exaggerated intonation, elevated pitch and volume, greater repetition, and simpler vocabulary and grammar.[34] Other health care providers use *elderspeak* when addressing older adults. Examples include "Hi *sweetie*. It's time for *our* exercise," "Good girl. You ate all of your dinner," and "Good morning *big guy.* Are *we* ready for *our* bath?" The results of such "inappropriately intimate and childish" baby talk and elderspeak may be "decreased self-esteem, depression, withdrawal, and the assumption of dependent behaviors congruent with stereotypes of frail elders." Although the physician or nurse may call the patient by first name or nickname, the patient nearly always refers to the provider as "the EMT," "the nurse," doctor, or Miss.

Providers have traditionally had positive attitudes toward middle-aged patients and negative attitudes toward others such as adolescents. The stereotypical *good patient* is cooperative, quiet, obedient, grateful, unaggressive, considerate, and dispassionate. *Good patients* tend to get better treatment than *bad patients.* Patients seen as lower class tend to get more pessimistic diagnoses and prognoses. Overweight patients are deemed *less* likable, seductive, well educated, in need of help, or likely to benefit from help and *more* emotional, defensive, warm, and likely to have continuing problems. One writer concludes that "it is not so much the patient's needs but the doctor's individuality that determines the form of the doctor–patient relationship."[35]

Creating and Maintaining Trust

Trust is a critical factor in health care interactions because they deal with intimate and sensitive personal information and must maximize self-disclosure. Level 1 exchanges elicit little information or insight from either party. Trust comes about when both parties "see one another as legitimate agents of knowledge and perception."[36] Breaches of confidentiality, a fundamental right of patients, may lead to discrimination, economic devastation, or social stigma. Trust is destroyed and with it any hope of building or maintaining a productive relationship the parties may have nurtured for months or years. Breaches of confidentiality may be intentional or unintentional and occur in many places: elevators, hallways, cafeterias, providers' offices, hospital rooms, cocktail parties, or over the telephone, particularly the ubiquitous cell phone. Confidentiality is often breached because providers talk or ask questions so loudly that roommates, visitors, others waiting to be treated, and those in hallways can overhear interactions. Maria Brann and Marifran Mattson relate an instance in which a patient tried to keep the reason for her appointment confidential by handing the provider a written note; the provider insisted that the patient read the note aloud. In another situation, a patient tried to answer confidential questions quietly; the provider proceeded to ask questions about her situation in a loud voice.[37] Solutions to breaches in confidentiality are rather simple: talk and answer questions in soft tones, exchange information only with providers who have a need to know, and conduct interactions (particularly over the telephone) in private, audibly secure locations.

Confidentiality and trust go hand in hand.

Trust is established in the early minutes of interviews when each party is feeling out the other to determine if this is a person they can trust. It is further negotiated as both parties "enact behaviors" that construct "shared expectations of a trusting relationship."[38] Humor, for instance, can "facilitate positive patient–provider interactions" and "create a patient-centered environment" that affects "patients' positive attitude and happiness."[39] The results are positive perceptions of caregivers that enhance trustworthiness and lead to better health outcomes, increased compliance with providers' advice, and fewer malpractice suits.[40] Spontaneous humor is most effective. Health care providers can also enhance trust through supportive talk that increases patient participation in interviews and by eliciting full disclosure of information, clarifying information, and assessing social and psychological factors involved in illness.

Providers and patients co-create trust.

Opening the Interview

The opening of the health care interview, when and where it takes place, and who initiated it have significant impact on the remainder of the interview. Neither party should see it or dismiss it as routine.

The opening sets the tone for the entire interview.

Enhancing the Climate

The provider should create an atmosphere in which the patient feels free to express opinions, feelings, and attitudes—even ones with which the provider might disagree. Though both parties rely heavily on interviews to get and give information and provide counsel, the process is often taken for granted and they fail to realize that cooperation is essential for sharing information and attitudes toward courses of action. True collaboration leads to information exchange, greater patient satisfaction, and compliance with instructions.

Location and setting promote collaborative interactions.

When possible, select a comfortable, attractive, quiet, nonthreatening, and private location free of interruptions in which interactions will remain confidential. Simply close the door so no one else can overhear the conversation that takes place. Check out a typical pediatrics area and one for adults of all ages and conditions. The first is designed thoughtfully in every detail (pictures, aquarium, toys, plants, books) for the young patient and parents to minimize fear and anxiety and maximize cooperation and communication. The second is likely to be a stark treatment room that contains a variety of medical gadgets and a small stack of ancient magazines of little interest to anyone. The dentist treatment room may be the worst. This is not a relaxing setting but one that it likely to increase anxiety and tension.

Being Sensitive and Personal

Employ individualized rather than routine opening approaches. Adapt to each patient. In a study of provider-patient satisfaction, Mohan Dutta-Bergman discovered that "open physician-patient communicative style is not the universal solution to patient needs. Instead, the fundamental message that emerges from this research is the need for tailoring the health care providers' communicative styles depending on the needs of the patient."[41] Be aware of communication apprehension common in medical interviews, particularly ones dealing with sensitive and embarrassing topics. You can reduce apprehension by carefully explaining procedures, being attentive and relaxed, treating patients as equals, and talking to them in their street clothes rather than backless hospital gowns or seminudity.

Use the opening to reduce apprehension.

As the provider, open the interview with a pleasant greeting and by introducing yourself and position if you are unacquainted with the patient or family. Realize that if you address the patient by first name (Hi Sally) while you address yourself by title (I'm Dr. Percifield), you are creating a superior-to-subordinate relationship from the start. If you are acquainted with the other party, open with a personal greeting that acknowledges this relationship. As a patient, return the greeting and take an active part in the opening.

Establishing rapport through a bit of small talk can enrich the relationship and help both parties relax. Rapport building and the ensuing orientation phase are strengthened if the provider reviews the patient's file before entering the examination room so the interview can begin on a personal and knowledgeable level. We are impressed and feel we are not merely a number when a provider remembers our school, academic major, occupation, hobbies, recent travel experiences, and family situation. Neither rush nor prolong rapport building unless trust is low because both parties are looking for sincere interest and prefer to get to the point after a brief, pleasant orientation.

Neither rush nor drag out the opening.

If a patient has been waiting for some time because you are behind schedule or you are late for an appointment with a provider, apologize for the inconvenience and explain the reason for it. Simple politeness—treating people the way you want to be treated—can defuse an angry or impatient interviewee or interviewer and show you value their time and are sensitive to the person's perceptions and needs. Judith Spiers has shown the relevance of *politeness theory* and how it can improve communication in the health care interaction. She writes that:

Politeness breeds politeness.

> Politeness is used primarily to ease social interaction by providing a ritualistic form of verbal interaction that cushions the stark nature of many interactions such as requests, commands, or questioning. Politeness provides a means for covering embarrassment, anger, or fear in situations in which it would not be to one's advantage to show these emotions either as a reflection of one's self or because of the reaction of the other.[42]

Spiers offers excellent advice on how to help health care receivers "save face" in a threatening situation over which they have little control.

Adapting the Opening

The content of the opening after greeting and a brief pleasantry depends on who initiated the interview. The initiation process affects orientation, the nature of questions, and who initially controls the interview content.

When a patient initiates an interview without explanation, the provider's opening question is most likely to be a "general-inquiry" question such as, "What brings you in this morning?" "What seems to be the problem?" or "What can I do for you today?" If a patient has mentioned a reason when making an appointment or told the physician's assistant or nurse about a problem, the provider's opening question is likely to be a "confirmatory" question such as, "I understand you're having some sinus problems today?" "What kind of difficulties are you having with your knee?" or "Tell me about the stress you are experiencing." A second type of confirmatory question focuses on specific symptoms, such as, "Is the pain mainly on the left side of your head? or "Does the dizziness occur most often when you focus rapidly on near and far objects and then near objects again?" John Heritage and Jeffrey Robinson discovered that general-inquiry questions elicit longer problem presentations, including more current symptoms. On the other hand, the more restrictive (closed), second form of confirmatory question constitutes "a method for initiating problem presentation and distinctively communicates physicians' readiness to initiate, and enforce the initiation, of the next phase of the visit: information gathering."[43] The physician takes control and dictates where the interview is heading.

The opening must fit the situation.

Be careful of open-to-closed switch questions that focus on a narrow issue: "What problems are you having with your back? Are you experiencing pain in the lower back?" or "Tell me about the stress you're facing. Does it have to do with your mother's failing health?" The patient orients the provider by providing a self-diagnosis ("I've got the flu"), a list of symptoms ("I've got a terrible headache and am having trouble breathing"), or a contextualization ("It started last night after I ate dinner at O'Shayes and attended the West Side football game").[44] The provider should employ a multiple-turn interaction that encourages the patient to provide a full narrative of relevant events, type and duration of symptoms, attempts at self-medication, and previous related problems or occurrences. A premature diagnosis or formulation of a treatment

Get the whole story.

plan will lead to patient dissatisfaction and a breakdown in meaningful interaction. One study revealed that 77 percent of providers do not fully elicit the patient's reason for the visit.[45]

If the provider initiated the interview, the opening question may be broad such as "How has your health been during the past year?" or specific such as "Have you experienced any side effects from the medication for your cholesterol?" What takes place after the opening question depends upon the reason for the visit. If it is an annual routine checkup, the provider is likely to orient the patient as to what will take place and then launch into the body of the interview with questions and examinations. If it is a follow-up session, the provider is likely to move to the body of the interview with a series of questions directed toward a specific problem or results of a previous treatment such as surgery. The opening is likely to be brief.

Orient the patient.

Getting Information

Health care providers and patients devote significant portions of interviews seeking vital information about problems, causes, treatments, and necessary changes in lifestyle. In fact, information exchange is a major component of competence in provider–patient interactions. This is not an easy task, so we will begin first by identifying barriers to sharing information and second by offering suggestions for getting information effectively and efficiently.

Barriers to Getting Information

Do not assume patients will provide accurate information.

Physical and emotional factors may make it difficult for patients to recall or articulate information accurately and completely. Their main concern is discovering why they are ill rather than what they can do about it. Frightened and anxious patients leave out significant parts of their medical histories or intentionally minimize symptoms to get a good diagnosis. On the other hand, some overestimate the risk of a problem. For instance, research indicates that "many women overestimate their percentage risk of breast cancer, even after they have received careful estimates from health care professionals." They resist the information received.[46] One way to reduce this problem appears to be a "social comparison strategy" in which subjects were asked to compare their risk to others. However, even after counseling using this strategy, women continued to see their risk as "50 percent when the actual risk was closer to 14 percent."[47] Mothers recall only about half of their children's major illnesses. When patients feel ashamed or embarrassed, they may camouflage the real problem and make allegorical statements such as, "You know how teenagers are."

Depth of self-disclosure, often with Level 1 interactions dominating the interview, will remain shallow if the patient does not trust the provider or strict confidentiality is impossible because of the setting. A patient may give short answers in hopes of ending an uncomfortable interview. And some will give answers they think providers want to hear to please them or avoid bad news.

Ask obviously relevant questions as soon as possible.

The traditional history-taking portion of interviews is often longer than discussions of diagnostic and prognostic issues and creates many problems. The manner tends to be impersonal, and the numerous questions may have little or nothing to do with the patient's current problem or concern. As a patient remarked after such an experience, "He spent so long on things not wrong with me—two pages of lists—that it made me feel the interview had nothing to do with my illness at all."[48] Patients in great pain or psychological discomfort may become angry or numbed by endless, closed questions, what one researcher calls "negative weakening." One of the authors witnessed this wearing down process while visiting a family member in a nursing home in Florida. An elderly, ill, confused, and angry patient had just been admitted to the same room as the author's mother-in-law. Two medical personnel entered soon thereafter and began to ask a lengthy list of questions. Many would have taxed a medically fit person, and it did not take long before the patient was exhausted and obviously confused. The interview droned on, even though one of the questioners remarked to the other, "I don't know why we don't do this over two or three days. It's not like she's going anywhere." The interview continued with diminishing returns.

Weigh the ability of patients to respond.

A series of rapid-fire closed questions (sometimes referred to as the Spanish inquisition approach) clearly sets the tone for the relationship: the provider is in charge, wants short answers, is in a hurry, and is not interested in explanations. One study revealed that 87 percent of questions were closed or moderately closed and that 80 percent of answers provided only solicited information with no volunteering.[49] Providers control interactions through closed questions, content selection, and changing of topics.

Provider dominance deadens interactions.

Many health care providers assume familiarity with medical *jargon* and *acronyms* that are useful only for interactions with other medical professionals. The following exchanges illustrate patient misunderstanding of jargon and the dangers of bipolar questions.[50]

- **Provider:** Have you ever had a history of cardiac arrest in your family?
- **Patient:** We never had no trouble with the police.
- **Provider:** Multiple births?
- **Patient:** (after a long pause) I had a retarded child once. (perhaps thinking multiple meant Siamese twins)
- **Provider:** Do you have dentures?
- **Patient:** No. I have schizophrenia.

What if each patient had answered yes or no? The providers would not have detected any problems. One study discovered that 20 percent or more of respondents did not know the meaning of such common terms as abscess, sutures, tumor, and cervix, and the percentages escalated with more uncommon words such as edema and triglyceride. Persons over 65 are less knowledgeable than ones between 45 and 64, and more educated respondents are most familiar with medical terms.[51]

Explain medical terms and procedures.

Ambiguous questions pose equally serious problems. During most interviews, providers routinely ask questions such as: Do you have regular bowel movements? Do you feel tired? Are you ever short of breath? Any chest pains? What does *regular* mean? Who doesn't feel *tired*? Who hasn't been *short of breath* from time to time or experienced an occasional *chest pain*? Patients seldom ask for clarification or repetition of questions or terminology. They feel it is the provider's responsibility as the expert and one in charge.[52]

Ask focused, explicit questions.

Ways to Improve Information Getting

There are many ways to improve information getting in the health care interview. The key is to find ways to foster exchanges between the two parties that create a collaborative effort. Providers should promote turn-taking so patients will feel free to ask questions, provide more details, and react to what they are saying. Simple techniques can do this: pauses, eye contact, nodding the head, and using verbal signals to invite interactions instead of monologues. Be careful of verbal routines that give patients false cues for turn-taking. These include "Okay?" "Right?" and "Uh-huh" that only appear to invite reactions. Patients see them as false cues that invite agreement, not questions or competing notions.

Encourage turn-taking.

Asking and Answering Questions

Providers may use a funnel sequence that begins with open-ended questions and gradually narrows to specific symptoms, diagnoses, and treatments. Open questions communicate interest in what the patient has to say, encourages lengthy, revealing responses, and shows trust in the patient as a collaborator to provide important information, including information for which the provider might not think to ask. Such questions are free of interviewer bias and invite rather than demand answers, thus giving patients a greater feeling of control.

The funnel sequence gives a sense of sharing control.

Use an inverted funnel sequence with caution because closed questions asked early in an interview may set a superior-to-subordinate tone and communicate the desire of the provider to seek brief answers and maintain control. Patients are likely to give short answers that reveal little information and easily hide fears, feelings, and symptoms they are reluctant to share. By the time the provider reaches the open questions in the sequence, patients may be unable or unwilling to adjust to the new expectations and continue with brief answers.

As providers and patients ask and answer questions, they should listen carefully and actively for hidden as well as obvious requests and responses. Listen for evidence of confusion, hesitation, apprehension, or uncertainty. Patients should write lists of questions prior to interviews when they can think through concerns without the pressure of interactions with providers. Don't hesitate to ask for a repeat or rephrasing of an unclear question. You cannot reply sufficiently if you do not understand what is being asked.

Vary listening approaches.

Telling Stories

What patients want most is an opportunity to tell their stories, and these narratives are "essential to the diagnostic process" and the most efficient approach to eliciting necessary information.[53] Gary Kreps and Barbara Thornton, for example, write that:

> Stories are used by consumers of health care to explain to their doctors or nurses what their ailments are and how they feel about these health problems. . . . By listening to the stories a person tells about his or her health condition, the provider can learn a great deal about the person's cultural orientation, health belief system, and psychological orientation toward the condition.[54]

Other researchers emphasize the collaborative nature of effective storytelling and reception. Susan Eggly writes that both parties must cocreate the illness narrative so they can influence one another and shape the narrative as it is told.[55] She identifies three types of stories: "narratives that emerge through the co-constructed chronology of key events, the co-constructed repetition and elaboration of key events, and the co-constructed interpretation of the meaning of key events." An important reason for collaboration in storytelling is that patients routinely omit valuable information from narratives because they do not know what is important, do not feel safe in revealing some details, or assume the provider would not be interested.[56]

Encourage storytelling and listen.

Health care providers should avoid unnecessary interruptions during narratives and answers, especially when patients become overwhelmed with emotion. The success of the interview may be due to the number of words the provider does *not say* or the numbers of questions *not asked*. Some researchers use the phrase "empathic opportunity terminator" to identify interactions that redirect interviews and cut off further revelations of patients' emotional concerns.[57] For example, in the first interaction below, the physician changes the subject.

The less you talk, the more you may say.

Patient: I'm in the process of retiring . . .

Physician: You are?

Patient: Yeah. I'll be 66 in February.

Physician: Do you have Medicare?

In this next interaction, the physician retreats to an earlier, less emotional concern.

Patient: And right now I'm real nauseous and sick. I lost 10 pounds in six days.

Physician: Okay. And you lost 10 pounds.

Patient: And I'm getting, and I'm getting worse. I'm not getting any better.

Physician: Okay . . . and right now you are not able to eat anything, you said?

Older patients tend to give significantly longer presentations and narratives than younger patients, but they did not reveal more current symptoms. They do offer more information about a symptom, "engage in more painful self-disclosure," and disclose more about seemingly irrelevant matters such as family finances.[58] Providers need to be patient and to probe for relevant specifics and explanations. Caplan, Haslett, and Burleson write that "It is particularly critical to understand how communication processes change and how older adults communicate their concerns and feelings."[59] They discovered that when older patients discussed a loss in later life, they "shifted from a primarily factual mode (what the loss was, how the loss occurred, etc.) to more of a focus on the impact of this loss on their lives (e.g., handling new tasks and expressions of emotions)." They cite research that "physicians are often unmotivated to talk about patients' worries or emotional concerns" and recommend that caregivers "consider encouraging elderly patients to reminisce and help focus their attention on coping and adaptation. Messages could also be targeted for elderly adults, depending on an individual's current location in the coping process."

Listening, Observing, and Talking

As a provider, be patient and use nudging probes to encourage interviewees to continue with a narrative or answer. Avoid irritating interjections such as *right, fine, okay,*

Be patient and persistent.

and *good.* Avoid guessing games. Ask, "When does your back hurt?" not "Does it hurt when you first get up? When you stand a lot? When you sit for a while?" Avoid double-barreled questions such as "And in your family, has there been high blood pressure or strokes? Diabetes or cancer?" What would a yes or no answer mean? Is the patient saying yes or no to each of the health problems or to the last choice? Employ reflective and mirror questions to check for accuracy and understanding. Listen for important cues in answers, what patients are suggesting or implying verbally and nonverbally. As a provider or patient, you may have to make it clear to parents, spouses, relatives, or friends present that the patient must answer questions if physically and mentally able to do so.

Both parties must learn to *listen* and *observe* as well as *talk.* Active interviewees volunteer more information and opinions and understand more clearly what is taking place, experience a better medical outcome, and are more satisfied with health care. Leading questions such as "You're staying on your diet, aren't you?" signal that you want agreement, a yes answer, and that is likely what you will get even if it's false. They foster passive, agreeable patients. At times, however, you may need to use leading questions to persuade patients to follow regimens and take medicines properly and faithfully. Annette Harres discusses the importance of "tag questions" to elicit information, summarize and confirm information, express empathy, and provide positive feedback.[60] Examples are "You can bend your knee, can't you?" "You've been here before, haven't you?" "I'm sure it's been a very difficult adjustment since your husband Paul died."

Use leading questions with caution.

Addressing the Language Barrier

Health care professionals have long recognized that "**communication** breakdowns are the most common root cause of **health errors** that harm patients," and this problem is exacerbated by an estimated "95 million people" who "do not have the fundamental literacy skills in English to understand even the most basic" health information such as how and when to take medication.[61] Nearly half of this number have little or no command of the English language. The misinterpretation of a single word, such as "irritate," may lead to delayed care, medical errors, and malpractice lawsuits. Declining quality of health care, patient satisfaction, efficient use of resources, and cost will grow as the language barrier among the elderly, immigrants, and international visitors increases in the coming years.[62]

Health care providers have tried a variety of solutions, some successful and some not. For example, family and friends may speak the patient's native language or be more fluent in English, but they may not repeat all of a provider's questions or explanations or be able to translate or explain medical terms accurately into the patient's native language or at the patient's level of understanding.[63] Children as interpreters pose problems because their command of the parents' native language may be minimal, "their understanding of medical concepts tends to be simplistic at best," and "parents can be embarrassed or reluctant to disclose important symptoms and details to their child."[64] Volunteers may be readily available in many communities but lack training as interpreters and in health care terms, practices, and procedures.

Successful programs have included comprehensive interpreter services in a language such as Spanish, creation of a course to teach Spanish to health care professionals, and use of specific phrases in Spanish to assess acute pain.[65] Such programs are limited, of course, to a single language, common though it may be. Some large medical facilities include a number of interpreters who are fluent in languages they encounter most often. Telephone interpreter services such as the AT&T Language Line provide interpreters in many languages but are costly "and frustratingly inadequate when difficult cultural or interpersonal issues arise."[66] A variation of this model would be a national system of interpreters fluent in many languages and trained in health care, similar to the one operated by the Australian government on a 24/7 basis.

Giving Information

Nearly every health care interview involves giving information that is essential for the provider and patient to understand, remember, and act upon. As noted earlier, patients provide information when they answer questions and tell stories that explain their medical conditions. Providers explain the nature and causes of medical problems, prescribe medications, and detail regimens that must be followed carefully to resolve problems without causing others.

Patients remember little and follow less.

Giving information is a deceptively difficult process, however. One study revealed that within 10 to 80 minutes, less than 25 percent of patients remembered everything they were told, and patients who remembered most had received only two items of information. Another discovered that within a short time, 10 patients showed significant distortions of information received and 4 showed minimum distortions.[67] Although patients forget and distort information, they cite insufficient information more than any other aspect of medical care.

Causes for Loss and Distortion of Information

There are three root causes for failure to give and to recall information accurately in the health care setting: attitudes of medical providers, problems of patients, and ineffective transmission methods. Information giving must be a collaborative effort.

Attitudes of Providers

Both parties contribute to loss and distortion.

Health care providers tend to place greater emphasis on getting information than giving it even though the strongest predictor of patient satisfaction is how much information is given on a condition and treatment. In a typical 20-minute interview, less than 2 minutes is devoted to information giving. Providers may be reluctant to provide information because they do not want to get involved, fear patients' reactions, feel they (particularly nonphysicians) are not allowed to give information, or fear giving incorrect information. Nurses, for instance, often have insufficient data about a patient's condition or are uncertain about what a physician wants the patient to know or has told the patient.

Beware of faulty assumptions.

Providers underestimate the patient's need or desire for information and overestimate the amount of information they give. A study of cancer patients revealed that barely over 50 percent of those who wanted a *quantitative* prognosis got one and over 60 percent of those who did not want a *qualitative* prognosis got one.[68] Many providers assume patients understand what they tell them, including information laced with medical jargon and acronyms, and take few steps to verify these assumptions. Metaphors such as "We're turning a corner," "There's light at the end of the tunnel," and "The Central Hospital family is here to help" require patients to complete the implied comparison, and the result may be confusion and anxiety rather than comfort and reassurance. Providers tend to give more information to specific types of patients, regardless of the illness or its severity. For instance, they provide more information and elaborate explanations to educated, older, and female patients.

According to conventional wisdom, people with health-related decisions actively seek information on the Internet, in the press, on television, and through interpersonal contacts and weigh their options carefully. They trust a variety of sources. This is true for so-called "seeker patients" with higher educations and incomes, who are younger, and who are actively involved in interpersonal networks. They are "health conscious" and like the active "involvement in the processing of information."[69] It is not true for so-called "nonseeker patients" who are older, have less education, and come from low-income groups. They "intentionally avoid information that may cause them anxiety or stress."[70] Nonseekers place most trust in their physicians as sources of information but may be reached through passive media outlets such as radio and television.

Problems with Patients

Patients may hear what they want to hear.

Patients' illnesses, fears, anxieties, and suspicions affect their ability to hear, listen, comprehend, and remember. They may protect themselves from unpleasant experiences by refusing to listen, or they may interpret information and instructions according to their personalities. For instance, if a provider says, "You have six months to a year to live," a pessimist may tell friends, "I have less than six months to live," while an optimist may relate cheerfully, "The doctor says I might live for years." Patients may desire information and want the provider to make decisions so they have someone to blame if something goes wrong.

Use acronyms cautiously.

Patients often do not understand or comprehend information because they are untrained or inexperienced in medical situations. Older patients have less knowledge and understanding of medical situations and greater difficulties in giving information.[71] Few interview settings are as replete with communication-stifling gadgets, smells, noises, and goings-on. Patients are bombarded with unfamiliar acronyms (IV, EKG, D & C, pre-op, chemo) and jargon (adhesions, contusions, nodules, cysts, benign tumors, diuretic, and metastases). The names of pharmaceuticals are nearly impossible to pronounce and remember, let alone understand. A recent study by Hagihara, Tarumi, and Nobutomo investigated the all too common phenomenon in which physicians' and patients' understanding and evaluation of medical test results and diagnoses differ markedly. They recommend that "To avoid either a failure on the part of the patient to understand the explanation, or a patient misunderstanding the physician's explanation, physicians should pay more attention both to the topic under discussion and to their patients' questions and attitudes."[72]

Authority and setting may stifle collaboration.

The aura of authority may inhibit patients from asking for clarification and explanation. For example, a woman who did not understand what *nodule* meant did not ask questions "because they all seem so busy, I really did not want to be a nuisance . . . and anyway she [nurse] behaved as though she expected me to know and I did not want to upset her."[73] The strange setting combined with hope for a favorable prognosis leads patients to oversimplify complex situations or interpret information as not really aimed at them. Others are afraid they will appear stupid if they ask questions that reveal they do not understand words, explanations, problems, or procedures. For a variety of reasons, "patients routinely pass up, or actively 'withhold,' an opportunity to" ask about "the nature of the illness, its relative seriousness or the course it is likely to follow."[74]

A little knowledge can be dangerous.

Many of us rely on **lay theories** that influence how we communicate and interpret health problems. Common "theories" include: All *natural* products are healthful. If I no longer feel bad, I do not need to take my medicine. If a little of this medicine helps, a lot will do more good. If this medication helped me, it will help you. And radiation and chemicals are bad for you. Katherine Rowan and Michele Hoover write that "scientific notions that contradict these and other powerful lay theories are often difficult for patients to understand because patients' own lay alternatives seem irrefutably commonsensical."[75]

Ineffective Methods

Employ more than one medium.

Information is lost or distorted because of ineffective transmission methods. For instance, providers often rely on a single medium. They use oral information giving, but research reveals that about one-third of patients remember oral diagnoses while 70 percent recall written diagnoses.[76] Oral exchanges are often so brief and ambiguous that they are confusing or meaningless. A provider made this comment: "Now, Mr. Brown, you will find that for some weeks you will tire easily, but you must get plenty of exercise."[77] How long is "some weeks"; what does "tire easily" mean; and how much is "plenty of exercise"? Michael Cohen and Neil Davis relate numerous problems with information exchanges.[78] For example, a nurse coming on duty on a ward asked a patient if he was Mr. Thomas, and the patient replied "Wright." Mr. Wright received Mr. Thomas's medication. Incomplete and carelessly written messages produce similar mistakes. A physician treating a patient for a painful right ear wrote a prescription with "R" and "ear," leaving out the period. The person administering the medication read the directions as "rear" and the patient received the medication in his rectum.

Avoid information overload.

Health care providers routinely *overload* patients with data, details, and explanations far beyond their abilities to comprehend and recall. Ley discovered that within a few hours 82 percent of patients could recall two items of information, but the percentage dropped to 36 percent for three or four items, 12 percent for five or six items, and 3 percent for seven or more items.[79] Ley also noted that providers tend to give diagnostic information before instructions. Not surprisingly, patients remember diagnostic information twice as often as instructions because diagnosis seems more important and they are still thinking about it and paying little attention to the provider during instructions for information giving.

Giving Information More Effectively

Give information that seems authentic, a judgment patients often base upon effective *presentation.* When giving information orally, place vocal emphasis on important words, dates, figures, warnings, and instructions. This is a substitute for the underlining, bold lettering, highlighting, and italicizing we employ in printed materials to enable readers to detect what is most important.

If you detect patients adhering to one of the lay theories mentioned earlier, Rowan and Hoover recommend, first, that you help them recognize their theory and its apparent reasonableness and, second, show its fallacies and inadequacy and potentially dangerous results. Establish the greater adequacy of the medical/scientific theory or practice.[80]

An inquisitive patient is an informed patient.

Encourage patients to ask questions as you proceed by building in pauses and inviting inquiries, not at the end of a lengthy one-sided presentation. Too many providers believe erroneously that patients do not want much information because they do not ask for it directly. A silent patient may feel intimidated, hopelessly confused, or believe it is the provider's responsibility to provide adequate and clear information. After all, providers have the expertise and know what is best. Both parties must work to get and give information effectively and resolve inadequacies and confusions in an open exchange. Do not assume patients understand what you have told them. Ask them to repeat or explain what you have said and look for distortions, missing pieces, and misunderstandings.

Discover what the patient knows.

Avoid overloading patients with information. Discover what they (including family and friends) know and proceed from that point. Eliminate unnecessary and irrelevant materials. Reduce explanations and information to common and simple terms. Define technical terms and procedures or translate them into words and experiences patients understand. Present information in two or more interviews instead of one lengthy interview. As a rule, provide only enough information to satisfy the patient and the situation.

The more heads, the better.

Involve a number of sources in the process. Include family members and friends so they can help retain and interpret information and aid in compliance with instructions. They are not under the same stress or condition as the patient. A common practice is for the attending physician to fill out a prescription order and explain what it is, what it is for, how it should be taken, and its potential side effects. Then the pharmacist who fills the prescription repeats the same information. Other important sources in this process are nurses, technicians, patient representatives, and receptionists. Make sure all participants in the organizational hierarchy are thoroughly informed about the patient so each is aware of what the patient knows, needs to know, and can be told.

Organize information systematically to aid recall. Present important instructions first so they do not get lost in reactions to a diagnosis. Repeat important items strategically two or more times during the interaction so they are highlighted and easy to recall.

Employ a variety of resources.

Use a variety of media, including pamphlets, leaflets, charts, pictures, slides, videos, models, and audio recordings. Dentists, for example, use models of teeth and jaws to explain dental problems and videos or DVDs to show the benefits of flossing and brushing frequently. Emergency medical technicians use mannequins to teach CPR. Never simply hand a pamphlet or leaflet to a patient and say, "This will answer all of your questions." Patients report they are helpful but admit they do not always read them.

E-mail has not reached its potential.

As many as 40 percent of patients now search for health care information on Web sites, and since they process the information centrally, sites should provide complete health information with facts, statistics, and carefully reasoned arguments.[81] While some 80 percent of patients want to use e-mail, 63 percent of providers fear excessive demands, 69 percent fear medicolegal risks, 55 percent cite unavailability to patients, and 45 percent cite patients having difficulty using.[82] Most e-mail is used for nonurgent and repeat concerns that can be handled efficiently and effectively without visiting a provider, but new symptoms often require additional history taking and a physical examination. Records must be kept of these interactions.

The telephone accounts for one-fourth of health care interviews.

The telephone, particularly with the widespread availability of cell phones, now accounts for nearly 25 percent of all patient–provider interactions.[83] Nurse call centers that integrate assessment, advice, and appointment systems are increasing rapidly and have transitioned from "nurse advice" to "telephone risk assessment."[84] If nurses and other practitioners can satisfy patients and physicians that they are effective information conduits as part of a health care triad, the result may be timeliness, accuracy, quantity, and usefulness of information. Perceptions of accuracy and reliability—trust—are best when the telephone provider is seen as a reinforcer.[85] A danger is lack of a paper record for the patient's file, so the telephone provider must note time, date, information, and recommendations for the file and pass on information to other providers in the triad.

Counseling and Persuading

Information giving does not ensure compliance.

Most health care providers are *task oriented* and have long expected patients to follow their recommendations because they have the authority, expertise, and training. They continue to see interactions as information sharing events and the "doctor 'still knows best.' "[86] After all, they have science on their side. Unfortunately, patient compliance has been notoriously low. Some 30 to 40 percent do not follow preventive regimens, 50 percent fail to adhere to long-term treatment plans, and 20 to 30 percent of prescribed drugs are either not taken or taken improperly. With these compliance problems and the ever-greater emphasis on treating the whole person, providers must be more than information conduits. They must also act as **counselors** to help patients understand and deal with problems and **persuaders** to convince patients to follow recommendations accurately and faithfully.

Barriers to Effective Counseling and Persuading

Watch for hints and clues about real problems.

Patients and families often make the health care interaction difficult by remaining silent, withdrawing, or complaining about a physical problem rather than admitting a psychological one. One of our students reported that she had missed an examination and several class sessions because she had cancer. Only later did we learn through a third party that the student had long suffered from severe depression and suicidal tendencies. She felt it was more acceptable to have a physical than a mental problem. When nothing is found wrong physically, a provider may dismiss a patient with a diagnosis of stress, nerves, or overactive imagination.

Providers may try to dodge unpleasant exchanges.

Many health care providers spend little time talking with patients because they have many tasks to perform and they see talking as a social rather than a medical activity. Care and treatment are considered more important than getting acquainted. Predictably, providers often fail to detect subtle cues and hints that a patient wants to talk about a different and more serious medical issue.

Providers have developed a variety of **blocking tactics** to avoid counseling and persuading. Some make jokes or deny the seriousness of the problem, while others

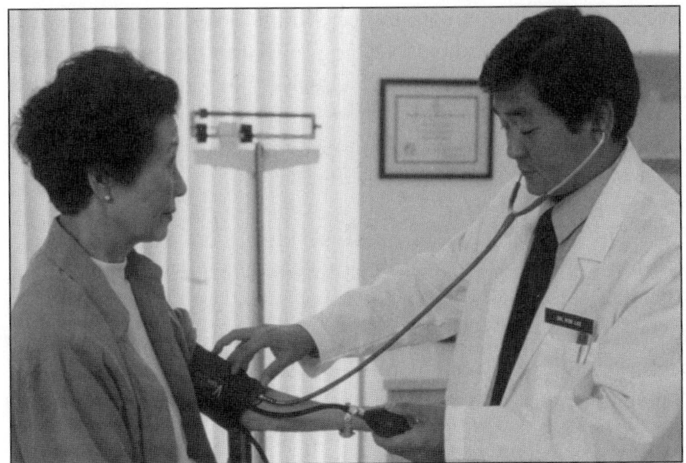
photo by Michael A. Keller/Corbis

Health care professionals may spend little time talking with patients because they are task oriented rather than people oriented.

pursue a less threatening line of conversation. When a female friend mentioned that she was concerned about the effects of stress on her job, the physician dismissed her concerns with "Which women's magazine did you get that diagnosis out of?" Common blocking tactics include:

- Ignoring a patient's comment or question, perhaps by pretending not to hear.
- Becoming engrossed in a physical task.
- Changing the subject.
- Pretending to have a lack of information or hiding behind hospital rules.
- Passing the buck to the physician, registered nurse, or specialist.
- Running away by leaving the room.

The nurse in the following exchange exhibits common blocking tactics.[87]

Nurse: There you are dear. OK? (gives a tablet to the patient)

Patient: Thank you. Do you know, I can't feel anything at all with my fingers nowadays?

Nurse: Can't you? (minimal encouragement)

Patient: No, I go to pick up a knife and take my hand away and it's not there anymore.

Nurse: Oh, I broke my pencil! (walks away)

The patient desperately wants to talk to the nurse about a frightening and worsening condition, but the nurse is determined not to get involved or discuss the problem.

Know yourself to understand others.

Providers must understand themselves and their reactions to uncomfortable counseling situations and the need to seek compliance rather than merely expect it. For example, when a patient started talking about his father's death, a physician switched to the less emotional topic of the patient's mother. The physician later explained that he thought the patient might cry, so he changed the subject. Upon further questioning, however, he admitted that his own father had died eight months earlier. He was protecting himself, not the patient.[88]

Effective Counseling and Persuading

As you begin to think about the counseling and persuading roles in the health care interview, review the principles and guidelines presented in Chapters 10, 11, and 12. These are highly relevant to the health care setting. Parties should plan for each interview with five relational factors in mind: empathy, trust, honesty, mutual respect, and caring. Source credibility has long been recognized as a key ingredient in the counseling and persuasion process, and a recent study by Paulsel, McCroskey, and Richmond discovered that "perceptions of physician, nurse, and support staff competence and caring were positively correlated with patients' satisfaction with the care they received and their physician."[89]

Selecting an Appropriate Interviewing Approach

Tradition is not always best.

Providers have traditionally tried two approaches. The first is a paternalistic approach in which the provider assumes the patient will see the wisdom of advice provided and alter attitudes and behavior accordingly. The second is an advise and educate approach that explains the medical reasons why and hopes for the best. Neither approach, as we have seen, has produced results beyond 50 percent compliance. Telling patients what to do when they don't want to do it does not motivate them to act, and repeating unwanted advice may alienate them and produce resistance. Deborah Grandinetti advises that "change isn't an event; it's a process."[90] Let's focus on the process.

No approach is useful all of the time.

Select an approach that is collaborative and best suited to this patient at this time. Review the directive and nondirective approaches discussed in Chapters 2 and 12 to enhance communication and self-disclosure that will lead to understanding and compliance. Barbara Sharf and Suzanne Poirier use a theoretical framework that psychiatrists Szasz and Hollender developed to teach medical students how to select appropriate interview approaches.[91]

- An active (directive approach) is recommended when a patient is passive and unable to participate.
- An advisory (nondirective) approach is recommended when a patient is compliant because of acute illness and thus not at full capacity.
- A mutual participation (combination directive-nondirective) is recommended when gathering data, solving problems, and managing an illness of a patient who can participate fully.

Work for a team effort.

Regardless of approach, strive for **collaboration** during the interview by showing respect for the patient's agenda and encouraging mutual sensitivity. Adherence to medication and instructions is most likely when communication is optimal. After all, sharing knowledge is impossible without real conversation.[92] Patients often have logical reasons for not complying: too embarrassing, painful, costly, dangerous side effects, ineffectiveness, or time-consuming. Discover this logic, present good counter-reasons, and employ tactful refutation to improve compliance.

Providing an Appropriate Climate

The way both parties interact influences behaviors and outcomes. The patient should set the pace of the interaction. Significant changes come about over time and through a series of stages. Do not try to rush ahead or skip stages before either party is ready. A smoker, drinker, or overweight person is unlikely to change in one giant step. Be aware of how your voice and manner may influence a patient or provider.

Humor is an effective facilitator.

One researcher discovered, for instance, that a physician emphasized the danger of swallowing medication for a canker sore in such a direct and dire manner that the patient did not get the prescription filled. Another employed self-deprecating humor and a lighter tone when prescribing acne medication, and it was filled.[93] The effects of humor are well-documented. Humor facilitates an open, personal, and caring climate; helps patients lose their patient role; and enables parties to convey thoughts and feelings in a nonthreatening and productive manner.[94] Providers and patients must be aware, however, that if humor is insensitive or used ineffectively, it may embarrass, hurt, and mock the other party.

Encouraging Interaction

Sharing and caring are essential.

Encourage patients to talk. If you share your experiences and feelings, the patient is more likely to confide in you. This promotes self-disclosure beyond Level 1 interactions. Employ nonverbal communication (smiles, head nods, touches, and eye contact) to show that you care and want to listen as well as talk. Listen with comprehension so that you understand what the patient is saying and implying. Listen with empathy (not sympathy) so you can see the situation as the patient does and show respect. Avoid evaluative listening when trying to clarify and interpret a person's problem.

Use open-ended, reflective, and mirror questions to encourage patients to talk and clarify meanings. Don't ask too many questions or seem overly curious. Richard Botelho uses question sequences such as the following to get the interviewee talking about a problem and its seriousness.[95]

Make each question count.

Interviewer: If you developed a complication from smoking, say lung disease, do you think you would quit smoking?

Interviewee: Yes, I think so.

Interviewer: Do you want to wait until you get a complication to decide to change?

Interviewee: No, I don't think so.

Interviewer: Then, why wait?

Use a range of responses and reactions (from highly nondirective to highly directive). Generally avoid advice giving unless the patient lacks information, is misinformed, does not react to less directive means, or challenges information and recommendations. Avoid blaming or judging that may create an adversarial relationship. Be cautious when using fear appeals because they may lead to patient denial or avoidance of regimens, medications, and checkups. Employ positive and reinforcing techniques for past performance and compliance.

Considering Solutions

Approach a solution when the patient is ready. One survey revealed that only 10 percent of providers feel they are successful in "helping patients change any health-related" behavior.[96] Compliance is particularly low "when instructions are 'preventive,' when patients are without symptoms, and when the treatment regimen lasts for a long period of time."[97]

Collaborate to achieve incremental changes.

Young and Flower recommend that provider and patient jointly construct a plan of action that recognizes social, psychological, and financial constraints. They emphasize presenting strategies in the context of the patient's life, sharing the logic behind health care decisions, enabling patients to create their own narratives about their health, encouraging patients to assume accountability for their decisions, identifying short-term goals, and collaborating in naming resources and examining alternative options.[98] Similarly, Lisa Maher writes that providers should "have patients voice their own reasons for change. The patient—not the physician—must articulate the reasons for making—or not making—a change."[99] These recommendations promote **self-persuasion** with the realistic goal of motivating the patient to think about the significance of a problem and inaction.

The patient must follow through on commitments.

When weighing a solution, present specific instructions and demonstrate how easy they are to follow. Express hope and recall challenges the patient has met in the past. The goals are to encourage patients, give them hope, and provide good reasons for complying with *mutually* agreed upon recommendations. You may have to persuade the patient they will work, are doable, and are effective. This is particularly important if the person has failed in the past to follow through. Remember that you cannot resolve the patient's problem; only the patient can do that.

Closing the Interview

The closing must be a collaborative effort.

The closing of the health care interview need not be lengthy, but both parties need to understand completely and clearly what they have discussed, the information they have exchanged, the recommendations made, and agreements reached. Clearinghouse probing questions are essential as an initial closing device: "Is there anything else you wanted to discuss today?" "Are there any other concerns we haven't addressed?" "Have we covered everything?" "Is there anything you are unsure of, anything that is not clear to you?"

Important questions and revelations occur during the closing.

Often the opening will focus on a single concern, particularly if this is a first interview between provider and patient. It seems reasonable to conclude the interview once this concern is addressed and there is no need to solicit additional concerns. Patients often hold back information or a concern until what appears to be the closing minutes of the interview. They also tend to ask questions during the final minutes when the provider is busy writing out prescriptions, information, or regimens and is paying less attention.[100] Sometimes the real purpose of the patient's visit gets lost in the closing.

The summary phase of the interview "must not only make sense to the patient, but also must make sense in terms of the medical care the physician can offer."[101] Be sure it is thorough but not overwhelming. Too much information may be as bad as too little information. Use mirror or summary questions to be certain the patient understands what has taken place, what has been agreed to, and what will happen next, particularly the patient's responsibilities and tasks. Ask patients to tell you these in their words. Such questions may reveal confusions, misunderstandings, intentions, and successful information exchange.

Be sure to close the interaction on a positive and productive note that communicates understanding, empathy, trust, and caring. How each party closes the interview will enhance or detract from the relationship and influence the nature of the next interaction and whether or not there will be a next interaction.

Summary

The health care interview is common, difficult, and complex. Situations vary from routine to life-threatening and the perceptions of both parties influence the nature and success of interviews. For a health care interview to be successful, it must be a collaborative effort between provider and patient, and this requires a relationship based on trust, respect, sharing of control, equality of treatment, and understanding. A collaborative and productive relationship will reduce the anxiety, fear, hostility, and reticence that often accompanies health care interviews. Provider and patient must strive to be effective information getters, information givers, and counselor–persuaders. The interaction cannot be a one-party or one-dimensional effort.

Providers (from receptionist to physician) and patients (including families and friends) must realize that good communication is essential in health care interviews and that communication skills do not come naturally or with experience alone. Skills require training and practice. Each party must learn how to listen as well as speak, understand as well as inform, commit to as well as seek resolutions to problems. Communication without commitment is fruitless. Both parties must follow through with agreements and prescribed regimens and medicines.

Key Terms and Concepts

The online learning center for this text features FLASH CARDS and CROSSWORD PUZZLES for studying based on these terms and concepts.

Assumptions
Baby talk
Blocking tactics
Climate
Co-agency
Collaboration
Confirmatory questions
Counselors
Elderspeak
General inquiry questions
Information overload
Jargon
Lay theories
Patient-centered care
Persuaders
Politeness theory
Relational distance
Self-persuasion
Stereotypes
Stories/narratives
Task oriented
Trust

A Health Care Interview for Review and Analysis

This interview is between a nurse practitioner and a 19-year-old student who ran into a city bus on campus as he hurried to an 8:00 a.m. class on his skateboard. A friend riding near him helped him to the emergency room of the university health center. The patient is bruised and has a large bump on his forehead but does not appear to have any broken bones. He has a number of aches and pains and has been admitted to a treating room.

Assess the relationship between provider and patient. How collaborative is this interaction? How effectively do provider and patient get and give information? How effectively does the provider counsel and persuade the patient? How appropriate is the blend of directive and nondirective reactions and responses? How effectively do provider and patient use questions? How does the friend of the patient help and hinder the interview process?

1. **Provider:** Sean Crider?
2. **Patient:** Yes.
3. **Provider:** Are you a student?
4. **Patient:** Yes.
5. **Provider:** What's your student ID?
6. **Patient:** 379-267-495.
7. **Provider:** Did this happen on campus?
8. **Patient's friend:** Yes, just down the street.
9. **Provider:** Where was that?
10. **Patient's friend:** About the corner of University and Stadium.
11. **Provider:** You were riding a bike?
12. **Patient's friend:** He has a really bad bump on his head and may have some broken ribs.
13. **Provider:** Are you unable to reply to my questions?
14. **Patient:** No, I can do that, but I'm really hurting on my right side.
15. **Provider:** You were riding a bike?
16. **Patient's friend:** No. He ran right into a city bus full of students.
17. **Provider:** I see. Were you running too fast or just in a hurry, Sean?
18. **Patient:** No. I was on my skateboard. Dopey here turned off my alarm.
19. **Provider:** A skateboard at 7:15 in the morning!
20. **Patient:** Yeah.
21. **Patient's friend:** They're safer than bikes.
22. **Provider:** Uh-huh. Are you allergic to any medications?
23. **Patient:** I don't think so.
24. **Provider:** Okay. First, let's take a look at that bump on your head. It's a nasty one. Have you experienced any blurred vision or dizziness since this happened?
25. **Patient:** I was a little light-headed right after it happened.
26. **Patient's friend:** Yeah, he was staggering around like it was Saturday night.
27. **Provider:** You hadn't been drinking, had you?
28. **Patient:** No. Not that early in the morning.
29. **Patient's friend:** He usually waits until at least 9:00.
30. **Provider:** Uh huh. How do you feel now? Are you nauseous?
31. **Patient:** A little bit, I think.
32. **Provider:** You're not sure? I'll clean that bump and cut for you, and I want you to place an ice pack on it for an hour or so.
33. **Patient:** Where? I live off campus a couple of miles. And I've got to get to my history exam at 10:00.

34. **Patient's friend:** He could come over to my chem. lab. We've got ice there.
35. **Provider:** I would like for him to remain here for an hour or so until we know he is okay. We need to do some X-rays to see if you have any cracked or broken ribs. Take a deep breath and let me know how that feels.
36. **Patient:** Oww! That hurts a lot about here.
37. **Provider:** I see. Okay, I want one of our staff to take you down to the X-ray department. Then, he will bring you back up here so we can give you an ice pack and wait on the X-ray results.
38. **Patient:** I can walk okay.
39. **Patient's friend:** Yeah. He walked over here.
40. **Provider:** I'm sure you feel you can, but we don't want to take any chances on your falling. Take this form with you to the X-ray area, and I'll see you soon.
41. **Patient's friend:** That's good because both of his parents are attorneys.
42. **Patient:** Okay, but I've just got to get to that exam. My final grade is riding on it.
43. **Provider:** See you in a few minutes. You won't need an attorney, just your X-ray form.

Health Care Role-Playing Cases

An Emergency Room Patient

The patient was brought into the hospital unconscious by EMTs at 1:00 a.m. after crashing his motorcycle into a guardrail a mile from campus. He has regained consciousness and police officers want to question him about the accident. Blood tests show that his alcohol level is just above the legal limit. Before the police interview the victim, the emergency room physician wants to run a series of X-rays and tests to assess possible internal injuries, and the patient wants to wait for his parents to arrive before talking to the police or having more tests.

A Gun Shot Victim

The patient was hunting rabbits with a friend, and the friend spun around trying to get a good shot at a rabbit. He didn't see his companion who was walking about 25 yards to his left. The patient's face was struck by at least a dozen shot, one in his left eye. While his wounds are being cleaned and the shot removed from his face before surgery on his eye, a nurse must get her medical history and determine if he is allergic to any medications or anesthesia. The patient is in a great deal of pain and wants to get on with the surgery.

A Young Child and His Family

The patient is eight years old and has experienced flu-like symptoms since coming home from a family camping vacation. At first his parents did not think it was anything to worry about and saw that he had plenty of rest and liquids, but the symptoms have gotten worse and the child is experiencing some numbness. Now his parents are afraid that he may have the West Nile virus or one of the diseases contracted from deer ticks. The physician must try to get information about the symptoms from the child, but the parents are now overly anxious to be helpful and to answer the physician's questions.

A Cancer Diagnosis

The physician is a longtime friend of the family with a close relationship to the mother since they were college friends and lived in the same sorority. Four years ago the mother had a lumpectomy to remove a small cancerous growth in her right breast. All indications since have been that she is cancer free. A few weeks ago a mammography identified a pea-sized mass in her left breast. The physician, her longtime friend, must now give the disturbing news to the patient and her family.

Student Activities

1. Interview a physician about how he or she attempts to create collaborative and productive relationships. How is control shared? How is trust established and maintained? What role does confidentiality play in relationships and how is it maintained in rooms that contain more than one patient? How do relationships vary with patients of varying ages and cultural backgrounds?
2. Interview three nurses about problems with giving information effectively. How do they try to ensure accurate giving and maintaining of information? Ask them for examples of failures in transmitting information and how they detect such failures to avoid serious problems.
3. Visit a pediatric ward of a hospital. Observe how physicians, nurses, technicians, child-life specialists, and other providers address and interact with young patients. Talk with some of these providers about their training in communication with small children. What communication problems do they experience that are unique to different ages of children?
4. Your campus, like most in the United States, is likely to have students and families from many different countries. Visit the campus health center or a local hospital and discuss how they interact effectively with patients who speak little or no English. What types of interpreters have they used: family, hospital, volunteer, or telephone interpreters? Which do they use most often? What problems have they encountered with interpreters?

Notes

1. Barbara F. Sharf and Richard L. Street, Jr., "The Patient as a Central Construct: Shifting the Emphasis," *Health Communication* 9 (1997), p. 3.
2. K. W. Moore and K. S. Schwartz, "Psychosocial Support of Trauma Patients in the Emergency Department by Nurses, as Indicated by Communication," *Journal of Emergency Nursing* 19 (1993), pp. 297–302.

3. Alan S. Robins et al., "Teaching Interpersonal Skills in a Medical Residency Training Program," *Journal of Medical Education* 53 (1978), p. 998.
4. Barry J. Edwards, Robb O. Stanley, and Graham D. Burrows, "Communication Skills Training and Patient's Satisfaction," *Health Communication* 4 (1992), pp. 155–170; Sonia L. Nazario, "Medical Science Seeks a Cure for Doctors Suffering from Boorish Bedside Manner," *The Wall Street Journal*, March 17, 1992, p. B1.
5. Charles S. Lauer, "Talking Points," *Modern Healthcare,* October 3, 2005, p. 36.
6. Richard L. Street and John M. Wiemann, "Differences in How Physicians and Patients Perceive Physicians' Relational Communication," *Southern Speech Communication Journal* 53 (1988), p. 425.
7. Dean C. Barnlund, "The Mystification of Meaning: Doctor–Patient Encounters," *Journal of Medical Education* 51 (1976), pp. 716–725.
8. Brent D. Rubin, "What Patients Remember: A Content Analysis of Critical Incidents in Health Care," *Health Communication* 5 (1993), p. 109.
9. Amanda Young and Linda Flower, "Patients as Partners, Patients as Problem-Solvers," *Health Communication* 14 (2001), p. 76.
10. Young and Flower, p. 70.
11. Richard L. Street, Jr., and Bradford Millay, "Analyzing Patient Participation in Medical Encounters," *Health Communication* 13 (2001), p. 61.
12. Young and Flower, p. 71.
13. Laura L. Cardello, Eileen Berlin Ray, and Gary R. Pettey, "The Relationship of Perceived Physician Communicator Style to Patient Satisfaction," *Communication Reports* 8 (1995), p. 27; Rubin, p. 107.
14. Gary L. Kreps, "Relational Communication in Health Care," *Southern Speech Communication Journal* 53 (1988), pp. 344–359.
15. Diana Louise Carter, "Doctors, Patients Need to Communicate," Lafayette, Indiana *Journal and Courier,* February 22, 2004, p. E5.
16. Kandi L. Walker, Christa L. Arnold, Michelle Miller-Day, and Lynne M. Webb, "Investigating the Physician-Patient Relationship: Examining Emerging Themes," *Health Communication* 14 (2001), p. 54.
17. Walker, Arnold, Miller-Day, and Webb, pp. 51–52; Merlene M. von Friederichs-Fitzwater and John Gilgun, "Relational Control in Physician-Patient Encounters," *Health Communication* 3 (2001), p. 75.
18. Donald J. Cegala, Carmin Gade, Stefne Lenzmeier Broz, and Leola McClure, "Physicians' and Patients' Perceptions of Patients' Communication Competence in a Primary Care Medical Interview," *Health Communication* 16 (2004), pp. 289–304.
19. Walker, Arnold, Miller-Day, and Webb, p. 56.
20. Carma L. Bylund and Gregory Makoul, "Examining Empathy in Medical Encounters: An Observational Study Using the Empathic Communication Coding System," *Health Communication* 18 (2005), pp. 123–140.

21. Bruce L. Lambert, Richard L. Street, Donald J. Cegala, David H. Smith, Suzanne Kurtz, and Theo Schofield, "Provider–Patient Communication, Patient-Centered Care and the Mangle of Practice," *Health Communication* 9 (1997), pp. 27–43.

22. Sylvia E. Zakus et al., "Teaching Interviewing for Pediatrics," *Journal of Medical Education* 51 (1976), pp. 325–331; Marie R. Haug, "The Effects of Physician/Elder Patient Characteristics on Health Communication," *Health Communication* 8 (1996), p. 256.

23. Kelsy Lin Ulrey and Patricia Amason, "Intercultural Communication between Patients and Health Care Providers: An Exploration of Intercultural Communication Effectiveness, Cultural Sensitivity, Stress, and Anxiety," *Health Communication* 13 (2001), pp. 454 and 460.

24. Haug, pp. 253–254; Anne S. Gabbard-Alley, "Health Communication and Gender," *Health Communication* 7 (1995), pp. 35–54; von Friederichs-Fitzwater and Gilgun, p. 84.

25. Carma Bylund, "Mothers' Involvement in Decision Making During the Birthing Process: A Quantitative Analysis of Women's Online Birth Stories," *Health Communication* 18 (2005), p. 35.

26 Haug, pp. 252–253; Connie J. Conlee, Jane Olvera, and Nancy N. Vagim, "The Relationship among Physician Nonverbal Immediacy and Measures of Patient Satisfaction with Physician Care," *Communication Reports* 6 (1993), p. 26.

27. G. Winzelberg, A. Meier, and L. Hanson, "Identifying Opportunities and Challenges to Improving Physician-Surrogate Communication," *The Gerontologist,* 44 (October 2005), 1; Research Library Core, p. 450.

28. Michael Greenbaum and Glenn Flores, "Lost in Translation," *Modern Healthcare,* May 3, 2004, p. 21.

29. Karolynn Siegel and Victoria Raveis, "Perceptions of Access to HIV-Related Information, Care, and Services among Infected Minority Men," *Qualitative Health Care* 7 (1997), pp. 9–31.

30. von Friederichs-Fitzwater and Gilgun, p. 84.

31. Gary L. Kreps and Barbara C. Thornton, *Health Communication: Theory and Practice* (Prospects-Heights, IL: Waveland Press, 1992), pp. 157–178. See also Gary L. Kreps, *Effective Communication in Multicultural Health Care Settings* (Thousand Oaks, CA: Sage, 1994).

32. Alice Chen, "Doctoring Across the Language Divide," *Health Affairs,* May/June 2006, p. 810.

33. Ulrey and Amason, p. 452.

34. Kristine Williams, Susan Kemper, and Mary Lee Hummert, "Improving Nursing Home Communication: An Intervention to Reduce Elderspeak," *The Gerentologist,* April 2003, pp. 242–247.

35. Michael Balint, *The Doctor, His Patient, and the Illness* (New York: International University Press, 1975).

36. Young and Flower, p. 72.

37. Maria Brann and Marifran Mattson, "Toward a Typology of Confidentiality Breaches in Health Care Communication: An Ethic of Care Analysis of Provider Practices and Patient Perceptions," *Health Communication* 16 (2004), pp. 230 and 241.

38. Walker, Arnold, Miller-Day, and Webb, p. 57.

39. Juliann Scholl and Sandra L. Ragan, "The Use of Humor in Promoting Positive Provider–Patient Interaction in a Hospital Rehabilitation Unit," *Health Communication* 15 (2003), pp. 319 and 321.

40. Jason H. Wrench and Melanie Booth-Butterfield, "Increasing Patient Satisfaction and Compliance: An Examination of Physician Humor Orientation, Compliance-Gaining Strategies, and Perceived Credibility," *Communication Quarterly* 51 (2003), pp. 485 and 495.

41. Mohan J. Dutta-Bergman, "The Relation Between Health Orientation, Provider-Patient Communication, and Satisfaction: An Individual-Difference Approach," *Health Communication* 18 (2005), p. 300.

42. Judith Ann Spiers, "The Use of Face Work and Politeness Theory," *Qualitative Health Research* 8 (1998), pp. 25–47.

43. John Heritage and Jeffrey D. Robinson, "The Structure of Patients' Presenting Concerns: Physicians' Opening Questions," *Health Communication* 19 (2006), p. 100.

44. Philip Manning and George B. Ray, "Setting the Agenda: An Analysis of Negotiation Strategies in Clinic Talk," *Health Communication* 14 (2002), pp. 457–458.

45. Manning and Ray, p. 452.

46. Amanda J. Dillard, Kevin D. McCaul, Pamela D. Kelso, and William M. P. Klein, "Resisting Good News: Reactions to Breast Cancer Risk Communication," *Health Communication* 19 (2006), p. 115.

47. Dillard, McCaul, Kelso, and Klein, p. 123.

48. Allen J. Enelow and Scott N. Swisher, *Interviewing and the Patient* (New York: Oxford University Press, 1986), pp. 47–50; A. D. Wright et al., "Patterns of Acquisition of Interview Skills by Medical Students," *The Lancet*, 1 November 1980, pp. 964–966.

49. McNeilis, p. 412.

50. Roger W. Shuy, "The Medical Interview: Problems in Communication," *Primary Care* 3 (1976), pp. 376–377.

51. Carol Lynn Thompson and Linda M. Pledger, "Doctor–Patient Communication: Is Patient Knowledge of Medical Terminology Improving?" *Health Communication* 5 (1993), pp. 89–97.

52. Julie W. Scherz, Harold T. Edwards, and Ken J. Kallail, "Communicative Effectiveness of Doctor–Patient Interactions," *Health Communication* 7 (1995), p. 171.

53. Susan Eggly, "Physician–Patient Co-Construction of Illness Narratives in the Medical Interview," *Health Communication* 14 (2002), pp. 340 and 358.

54. Kreps and Thornton, p. 37.

55. Eggly, p. 343.

56. Young and Flower, p. 87.

57. Marlene von Friederichs-Fitzwater, Edward D. Callahan, and John Williams, "Relational Control in Physician–Patient Encounters," *Health Communication* 3 (1991), pp. 17–36.

58. Heritage and Robinson, p. 100.

59. Scott E. Caplan, Beth J. Haslett, and Brant R. Burleson, "Telling It Like It Is: The Adaptive Function of Narratives in Coping with Loss in Later Life," *Health Communication* 17 (2005), pp. 233–252.

60. Annette Harres, "'But Basically You're Feeling Well, Are You?': Tag Questions in Medical Consultations," *Health Communication* 10 (1998), pp. 111–123.

61. "American Medical Association Report Provides Guidelines for Improved Patient Communication," *U.S. Newswire,* June 19, 2006, accessed October 25, 2006.

62. Glenn Flores, "Healthcare Access; The Language Barrier Negatively Impacts Health Care for 50 Million U.S. Residents," *Aging & Elder Health Week,* August 13, 2006, p. 97.

63. Greenbaum and Flores, p. 21.

64. Chen, p. 812.

65. Elizabeth A. Jacobs, Donald S. Shepard, Jose A. Suaya, and Esta-Lee Stone, "Overcoming Language Barriers in Health Care: Costs and Benefits of Interpreter Services," *American Journal of Public Health* (May 2004), pp. 866–869; Melanie Bloom, Gayle M. Timmerman, and Dolores Sands, "Developing a Course to Teach Spanish for Health Care Professionals," *Educational Innovations* (July 2006), pp. 271–274; Angela Smith Collins, Donna Gullette, and Michael Schnepf, "Break Through Language Barriers," *Nursing Management* (August 2004), pp. 34–38.

66. Chen, p. 813.

67. P. Ley, "What the Patient Doesn't Remember," *Medical Opinion Review* 1 (1966), pp. 69–73.

68. Stan A. Kaplowitz, Shelly Campo, and Wai Tat Chiu, "Cancer Patients' Desires for Communication of Prognosis Information," *Health Communication* 14 (2002), p. 237.

69. Mohan Dutta-Bergman, "Primary Sources of Health Information: Comparisons in the Domain of Health Attitudes, Health Cognitions, and Health Behaviors," *Health Communication* 16 (2004), p. 285.

70. Shoba Ramanadhan and K. Viswanath, "Health and the Information Seeker: A Profile," *Health Communication* 20 (2006), pp. 131–139.

71. S. Deborah Majerovitz, Michele G. Greene, Ronald A. Adelman, George M. Brody, Kathleen Leber, and Susan W. Healy, "Older Patients' Understanding of Medical Information in the Emergency Department," *Health Communication* 9 (1997), pp. 237–251; Thompson and Pledger, pp. 89–97.

72. Akihito Hagihara, Kimio Tarumi, and Koichi Nobutomo, "Physicians' and Patients' Recognition of the Level of the Physician's Explanation in Medical Encounters," *Health Communication,* 20 (2006), p. 104.

73. Patricia MacMillan, "What's in a Word?" *Nursing Times*, February 26, 1981, p. 354.

74. Jeffrey D. Robinson, "An Interactional Structure of Medical Activities during Acute Visits and Its Implications for Patients' Participation," *Health Communication* 15 (2003), p. 49.

75. Katherine E. Rowan and D. Michele Hoover, "Communicating Risk to Patients: Diagnosing and Overcoming Lay Theories," in *Communicating Risk to Patients* (Rockville, MD: The U.S. Pharmacopeial Convention, 1995), p. 74.

76. Carter, p. E5.

77. F. S. Hewitt, "Just Words: Talking Our Way through It," *Nursing Times*, February 26, 1981, pp. 5–8.

78. Michael Cohen and Neil Davis, *Medication Errors: Causes and Prevention* (Philadelphia: Stickley, 1981).

79. Ley, pp. 69–73.

80. Rowan and Hoover, p. 76.

81. Mohan J. Dutta-Bergman, "Health Communication on the Web: The Roles of Web Use Motivation and Information Completeness," *Communication Monographs* 70 (2003), pp. 264 and 273.

82. Thomas K. Houston, Daniel Z. Sands, Beth R. Nash, and Daniel E. Ford, "Experiences of Physicians Who Frequently Use E-Mail with Patients," *Health Communication* 15 (2003), pp. 516 and 520.

83. Houston, Sands, Nash, and Ford, p. 516.

84. Gerald R. Ledlow, H. Dan O'Hair, and Scott Moore, "Predictors of Communication Quality: The Patient, Provider, and Nurse Call Center Triad," *Health Communication* 15 (2003), pp. 433–444.

85. Ledlow, O'Hair, and Moore, pp. 437 and 457.

86. Young and Flower, p. 75.

87. Jill M. Clark, "Communication in Nursing," *Nursing Times,* January 1, 1981, p. 16.

88. Nicholas G. Ward and Leonard Stein, "Reducing Emotional Distance: A New Method to Teach Interviewing Skills," *Journal of Medical Education* 50 (1975), p. 612.

89. Michelle L. Paulsel, James C. McCroskey, and Virginia P. Richmond, "Perceptions of Health Care Professionals' Credibility as a Predictor of Patients' Satisfaction with Their Health Care and Physician," *Communication Research Reports* 23 (2006), p. 74.

90. Deborah Grandinetti, "Turning No to Yes: How to Motivate the Reluctant Patient," *Medical Economics*, June 15, 1998, pp. 97–111.

91. Barbara F. Sharf and Suzanne Poirier, "Exploring (UN)Common Ground: Communication and Literature in a Health Care Setting," *Communication Education* 37 (1988), pp. 227–229.

92. M. Robin DiMatteo, Robert C. Reiter, and Joseph C. Gambone, "Enhancing Medicated Adherence through Communication and Collaborative Choice," *Health Communication* 6 (1994), p. 261; Young and Flower, p. 77.

93. Roxanne Parrott, "Exploring Family Practitioners' and Patients' Information Exchange about Prescribed Medications: Implications for Practitioners' Interviewing and Patients' Understanding," Health Communication 6 (1994), pp. 267–280.

94. Scholl and Ragan, pp. 321, 325, and 329.

95. Grandinetti, pp. 97–111.

96. Maher, pp. 55–60.

97. Shelley D. Lane, "Communication and Patient Compliance," in Explorations in Provider and Patient Interaction, Loyd F. Pettegrew, ed. (Louisville, KY: Humana, 1982), pp. 59–69.

98. Young and Flower, pp. 69–89.

99. Maher, pp. 55–60.

100. Robinson, pp. 48–51.

101. Manning and Ray, p. 467.

Resources

Beck, Christina S. *Communicating for Better Health: A Guide through the Medical Mazes.* Boston: Allyn and Bacon, 2001.

Cohen-Cole, S. A., and J. Bird. *The Medical Interview: The Three Function Approach.* St. Louis: Mosby, 2000.

Coulehan, John L., and Marian R. Block. *The Medical Interview: Mastering Skills for Clinical Practice.* Philadelphia: F.A. Davis, 2001.

Kar, Snehendu B. *Health Communication: A Multicultural Perspective.* Thousand Oaks, CA: Sage 2001.

Murero, Monica, and Ronald E. Rice, *The Internet and Health Care: Theory, Research and Practice.* Mahwah, NJ: Lawrence Erlbaum, 2006.

Ray, Eileen Berlin, ed. *Health Communication in Practice: A Case Study Approach.* Mahwah, NJ: Lawrence Erlbaum, 2005.

Rice, Ronald E., and James E. Katz, eds. *The Internet and Health Communication.* Thousand Oaks, CA: Sage, 2001.

Thompson, Teresa L., Alicia Dorsey, and Roxanne Parrott, eds. *Handbook of Health Communication.* Mahwah, NJ: Lawrence Erlbaum, 2003.

GLOSSARY

Abrupt or curt: short and often rude responses or curtailing of interactions.

Accidental bias: when an interviewer unintentionally leads respondents to give answers they feel the interviewer wants them to give rather than their true feelings, attitudes, or beliefs.

Ad hominem: an effort to dodge an issue or challenge by discrediting the source that raised it.

Ad populum: an appeal to or on behalf of the majority.

Ambiguity: words to which interview parties may assign very different meanings.

Analysis: a careful examination of the nature and content of answers and impressions noted during an interview.

Applicant profile: the required knowledge, experiences, skills, and personal traits necessary to perform a job satisfactorily.

Application form: a form created by an organization to gather basic information about applicants, including their backgrounds, experiences, education, and career interests.

Appraisal perspective: the performance interview is seen as required, scheduled, superior-conducted and directed, adversarial, evaluative, and past-oriented.

Arguing from accepted belief: argument based on an accepted belief, assumption, or proposition.

Arguing from analogy: argument based on common characteristics of two people, places, objects, proposals, or ideas shared.

Arguing from cause-effect: an argument that attempts to establish a causal relationship.

Arguing from condition: an argument based on the assertion that if something does or does not happen, something else will or will not happen.

Arguing from example: an argument based on a sampling of a given class of people, places, or things.

Arguing from facts: an argument based on a conclusion that best explains a body of facts.

Arguing from two choices: arguing that there are only two possible proposals or courses of action and then eliminating one of the choices.

Assumptions: assuming that something is true or false, is intended or unintended, exists or does not exist, is desired or undesired, will or will not happen.

Attitude: relatively enduring combinations of beliefs that predispose people to respond in particular ways to persons, organizations, places, ideas, and issues.

Baby talk: speaking to elder patients as if they were infants, including slower rate, exaggerated intonation, and simpler vocabulary.

Balance or consistency theory: a theory based on the belief that human beings strive for a harmonious existence with self and others and experience psychological discomfort (dissonance) when they do not.

Balanced scorecard approach: compensation, measurement, and performance are tied to coaching and improved performance.

Bandwagon tactic: a tactic that urges a person to follow the crowd, to do what everyone else is doing.

Basic skills tests: tests that measure mathematics, measurement, reading, and spelling skills.

Behavior-based selection: selection based upon the behaviors desired in a position and behaviors exhibited by applicants.

Behavior-based selection technique: a selection technique that begins with a needs and position analysis to determine which behaviors are essential for performing a particular job and proceeds to match applicants with this analysis.

Behaviorally anchored rating scale (BARS) model: a performance review model that identifies essential skills for a specific job and sets standards through a job analysis.

Belief: the trust or confidence placed in social, political, historic, economic, and religious claims.

Bifurcation tactic: the polarizing of situations, issues, or persons.

Bipolar question: a question that limits the respondent to two polar choices such as yes or no, agree or disagree.

Bipolar trap: a bipolar question phrased to elicit a yes or no response when the questioner wants a detailed answer or specific information.

Birds of a feather syndrome: the selection of employees most similar to interviewers.

Blocking tactics: efforts of interviewers to avoid counseling or getting involved with interviewees, particularly in the health care setting.

Board interview: when two to five persons representing an organization may interview an applicant at the same time.

Bogardus Social Distance scales: questions that determine how respondents feel about social relationships and distances from them.

Bona fide occupational qualifications (BFOQ): requirements essential for performing a particular job.

Broadcast interview: an interview that takes place live over radio or television or will be played all or in part at a later time.

Built-in bias: interviewer bias that is intentionally or unintentionally built into a schedule of questions.

Career fairs: gatherings of organizations and companies, often at malls or on college campuses, during which job seekers may make contacts with representatives and gather information about employment opportunities.

Career objective: a brief, concise statement of a targeted career goal.

Case approach: when an applicant is placed into a carefully crafted situation that takes hours to study and resolve.

Catalytic coaching: a comprehensive, integrated performance management system based on a paradigm of development.

Cause-to-effect sequence: an outline that addresses causes and effects separately but relationally.

Central tendency: when interviewers refrain from assigning extreme ratings to facets of performance.

Chain or contingency strategy: a strategy that allows for preplanned secondary questions in survey interviews.

Chronological format resume: a resume that lists education, training, and experiences in chronological order.

Clearinghouse probe: a question designed to discover whether previous questions have uncovered everything of importance on a topic or issue.

Client-centered approach: a counseling approach that focuses on the client rather than content or situation.

Closed-minded or authoritarian interviewees: parties with unchangeable central beliefs who rely on trusted authorities when making decisions.

Closed question: a question that is narrow in focus and restricts the respondent's freedom to determine the amount and kind of information to offer.

Closing: the portion of an interview that brings it to an end.

Coaching: helping to improve performance rather than judging or criticizing performance.

Cognitive phase: the thinking and assessing phase of a counseling interview.

Collaboration: a mutual effort by both parties to inform, analyze, and resolve problems.

Collectivist culture: a culture that places high value on group image, group esteem, group reliance, group awareness, and achievement of the group.

Combination schedule: a question schedule that combines two schedules, such as highly scheduled and highly scheduled standardized.

Communication interactions: verbal and nonverbal exchanges that take place during interviews.

Comparison tactic: a person points out a few similarities between two places, people, or things and then draws conclusions from this superficial comparison.

Competitive rater: an interviewer who believes that no one can perform higher than his or her level of performance.

Complement: to complete, support, or repeat.

Complexity vs. simplicity: questions that are either complex in wording and options or simple in wording and options.

Compliance: when an interviewee follows assessments and courses of action agreed to during a counseling interview.

Confirmatory questions: questions designed to verify understanding of an interviewee's (typically medical patients) concerns, problems, or statements.

Connotations: positive and negative meanings of words.

Conscious transparency: sharing information with applicants, explaining the purpose of questions, providing a supportive climate, and promoting unrestricted dialogue between interview parties.

Consubstantiality: the effort to establish a substantial sameness or similarity between interviewer and interviewee.

Contrast principle: if a second item or choice is fairly different from the first, it seems more different than it actually is.

Conversation: an unstructured interaction between two or more people with no predetermined purpose other than enjoyment of the process.

Counselors: those who help interviewees to gain insights into and to cope with problems.

Counter persuasion: persuasion aimed at an interviewee by a persuader's competitor or antagonist following a persuasive interview.

Cover letter: a letter an applicant sends to a prospective employer that expresses interest in and qualifications for a position.

Critical incident question: a question that asks applicants how they might resolve a current problem the recruiter's organization is facing.

Cross-sectional study: a study that determines what is known, thought, or felt during a narrow time span.

Culture: shared customs, norms, knowledge, attitudes, values, and traits of a racial, religious, social, or corporate group.

Curious probe: a question that is irrelevant to the interviewer's stated purpose.

Deceptively complex interpersonal communication process: the assumption that one-to-one communication is simple is belied by the many variables that interact in this process.

Defensive climate: a climate that appears threatening to one or both parties in an interview.

Determinate interviews: an interview designed to determine whether or not to make a job offer to an applicant.

Developmental model: the performance interview is initiated by individuals when needed, subordinate-conducted and directed, now and future oriented, cooperative, and self-satisfying.

Dialogic listening: a means of focusing on ours rather than mine or yours to resolve a problem or task.

Diamond sequence: a question sequence that places two funnel sequences top to top.

Differentiation: an attempt through language to alter how a person sees reality by renaming it.

Directive approach: an interview in which the interviewer controls subject matter, length of answers, climate, and formality.

Directive reactions: when an interviewer reacts to a client with specific evaluations and advice.

Disclosure: the willingness and ability to reveal feelings, beliefs, attitudes, and information to another party.

Don't ask, don't tell: a question that delves into information or an emotional area that a respondent may be incapable of addressing because of social, psychological, or situational constraints.

Double-barreled inquisition: a question that contains two or more questions.

Downward communication: an interview in which a superior in the organizational hierarchy is attempting to interact as an interviewer with a subordinate in the hierarchy.

Dyadic: an interaction that involves two distinct parties.

EEO violation question pitfall: when an interviewer asks an unlawful question during a recruiting interview.

Elderspeak: speaking to elder patients as if they were children, including addressing them as sweeties, girl or boy, and honey and employing the collective pronoun *our* (e.g., "it's time for our bath").

Electronic interviews: interviews conducted over the telephone, through conference calls, by video talkback, or over the Internet.

Electronically scanned resume: a resume designed in format and wording to be scanned electronically by recruiters.

Equal Employment Opportunity Commission: the agency assigned the task of overseeing and carrying out EEO laws.

Equal Employment Opportunity (EEO) laws: laws that pertain to employment and performance review interviews.

Ethical issues: issues that focus on value judgments concerning degrees of right and wrong, goodness and badness, in human conduct.

Euphemism: the substitution of a better sounding word for a common one.

Evaluative interval scales: questions that ask respondents to make judgments about persons, places, things, or ideas.

Evaluative response question pitfall: when an interviewer expresses judgmental feelings about an answer that may bias or skew the next answer.

Evasive interviewee: an interviewee who evades questions and gives indirect answers.

Evidence: examples, stories, comparisons, testimony, and statistics that support a claim being made.

Exchanging: a sharing of roles, responsibilities, feelings, beliefs, motives, and information during an interview.

Expressed feelings: feelings an interviewee expresses overtly and openly during a counseling interaction.

Face-to-face interview: an interview in which both parties are present physically in the same space during an interview.

Failed departure: when an interview has come to a close and parties have taken leave of one another only to come in contact accidentally later, often with a degree of communicative awkwardness.

False assumptions: assuming incorrectly that something is true or false, intended or unintended, exists or does not exist, desired or undesired, will or will not happen.

False closing: when verbal and nonverbal messages signal the closing of the interview is commencing but a party introduces a new topic or issue.

Feedback: verbal and nonverbal reactions of an interview party.

Feelings: emotions such as pride, fear, love, anger, and sympathy.

Fee-paid positions: when an organization retains a placement agency to locate qualified applicants and pays fees the agency would normally charge applicants.

Filter strategy: a question strategy that enables the interviewer to determine an interviewee's knowledge of a topic.

First impression: the initial impression one makes on another as a result of appearance, dress, manner, and quality of communication.

Flexibility: the ability to adapt during interviews to unexpected exchanges, answers, information, or attitudes.

Force choice distribution model: a performance review model that ranks employees into three or four groups for reward, improvement, or termination.

Frequency interval scales: questions that ask respondents to select a number that most accurately reflects how often they do or don't use something.

Functional resume format: a resume in which an applicant places experiences under headings that highlight qualifications for a position.

Funnel sequence: a question sequence that begins with a broad, open-ended question and proceeds with ever-more restricted questions.

General inquiry questions: an opening question that determines why an interviewee (often a medical patient) has initiated an interview.

Generic message: a persuasive message designed for a variety of audiences rather than a specific targeted audience.

Global relationships: relationships between parties from different countries and cultures.

Goal oriented: an interaction in which the interviewer is goal or task oriented rather than people oriented.

Ground rules: rules governing an interview agreed to by both parties.

Group interview: an interview in which there are multiple interviewers, such as several journalists at a press conference.

Guessing game: when a questioner attempts to guess information instead of asking for it.

Halo effect: when an interviewer gives favorable ratings to all job duties when an interviewee excels in only one.

Hasty generalization tactic: a person generalizes to a whole group of people, places, or things from only one or a few examples.

Highly closed questions: questions that can be answered with a single word or short phrase, most often a yes or no.

Highly directed reactions and responses: when an interviewer offers ultimatums and strong advice.

Highly nondirective reactions and responses: when an interviewer offers no information, assistance, or evaluations but encourages the interviewee to communicate, analyze, and be self-reliant.

Highly scheduled interview: a schedule in which the interviewer prepares all questions and their exact wording prior to an interview.

Highly scheduled standardized interview: a schedule in which the interviewer prepares all questions and their exact wording as well as answer options prior to an interview.

Historical critical incident question: a question that asks applicants how they would have resolved a problem the recruiter's organization faced in the past.

Honesty tests: tests designed to assess the ethics, honesty, and integrity of job applicants.

Hourglass sequence: a question sequence that begins with open questions, proceeds to closed questions, and ends with open questions.

Hypothetical question: a hypothetical but realistic question that asks respondents how they would handle a situation or problem.

Identification theory: a theory that persons persuade others by identifying with them in a variety of ways.

Imagery: creating pictures or images in a person's mind through highly descriptive language.

Implicative approach: an approach that withholds an explicit statement of purpose or intent until the interviewee sees the implications and suggests a course of action.

Individualist culture: a culture that places high value on self-image, self-esteem, self-reliance, self-awareness, and individual achievement.

Induced compliance theory: a theory designed to change thinking, feeling, or acting by inducing others to engage in activities counter to their values, beliefs, or attitudes.

Inform: to provide information or knowledge to another party.

Information: stories, illustrations, comparisons, experiences, quotations, statistics, definitions, and explanations that apprise interview parties of problems, solutions, situations, and events.

Information gathering interviews: interviews designed to obtain facts, opinions, data, feelings, attitudes, beliefs, reactions, advice, or feedback.

Information giving interview: interviews designed to exchange data, knowledge, direction, instructions, orientation, clarification, or warnings.

Information overload: when interviewees are provided with more information than they can process or recall.

Informational probe: a question designed to obtain additional information when an answer appears to be superficial, vague, or ambiguous or to suggest a feeling or attitude.

Initiating the interview: the process by which an interview is arranged and started.

Inoculation theory: a theory based on the belief that it is often more effective to prevent undesired persuasion from occurring than trying damage control afterward.

Integrity interviews: interviews designed to assess the honesty and integrity of prospective employees.

Intelligent or educated interviewee: an interviewee with high levels of intelligence or informal and formal education.

Interactional: the exchanging or sharing of roles, responsibilities, feelings, beliefs, motives, and information.

Internet interview: an interview that takes place solely through the Internet.

Interpersonal communication process: a complex and often puzzling communication interaction with another party.

Interval scales: survey question scales that provide distances between measures.

Interview: an interactional communication process between two parties, at least one of whom has a predetermined and serious purpose, and involves the asking and answering of questions.

Interview evaluation: the formal or informal process of evaluating applicants following recruiting interviews.

Interview guide: a carefully structured outline of topics and subtopics to be covered during an interview.

Interview schedule: a list of questions an interviewer prepares prior to an interview.

Interviewee: the party who is not in basic control of the interaction, such as a respondent in a survey interview or an applicant in a recruiting interview.

Interviewer bias: when respondents give answers they feel questioners want them to give rather than express their true feelings, attitudes, or beliefs.

Inverted funnel sequence: a sequence that begins with closed questions and proceeds toward open questions.

Jargon: words that organizations or groups alter or create for specialized use.

Job fairs: gatherings of recruiters from a variety of organizations on college campuses or malls in which applicants can obtain information, make contacts, and take part in interviews.

Joblike situations: simulated job situations through questions or role playing that enable the recruiter to perceive how an applicant might act on the job.

Journalist's interview guide: a guide that focuses on who, what, when, where, how, and why.

Just cause: the fair and equitable treatment of each employee in a job class.

Key informant: a person who can supply information on situations, assist in selecting interviewees, and aid in securing interviewee cooperation.

Knowledge workers: workers that create and access information rather than manufacture products and are valued for their knowledge, ability to motivate others, and team work.

Law of recency: people tend to recall the last thing said or done in interviews.

Lay counselor: a person with little or no formal training in counseling.

Lay theories: commonsense theories patients hold about health care that often resist scientific notions and research findings.

Leading push: a question that suggests how a person should respond.

Leading question: a question that suggests implicitly or explicitly the expected or desired answer.

Leaning question strategy: a question strategy that enables interviewers to reduce the number of undecided and don't know responses in surveys.

Learning organization: an organization that places high value on knowledge, skills, competencies, opportunities for learning, and employees as intellectual capital.

Leave-taking: the effort to bring an interview to a close.

Length of service error: when an interviewer assumes that present performance is high because past performance was high.

Letters of recommendation: letters sent by references to prospective employers on behalf of persons applying for specific positions.

Level 1 interactions: interactions that are relatively safe and nonthreatening.

Level 2 interactions: interactions that require a moderate degree of trust and may be moderately threatening because of exchange of beliefs, attitudes, values, and positions on issues.

Level 3 interactions: interactions that require a great deal of trust because parties disclose fully their feelings, beliefs, attitudes, and perceptions on intimate and controversial topics.

Level of confidence: the mathematical probability that the survey is within an accepted margin of error.

Level of information: the amount and sophistication of information an interviewee has to offer.

Likert scale: interval scale questions that ask respondents to make judgments about persons, places, things, or ideas.

Listening: the deliberate process of receiving, understanding, evaluating, and retaining what is seen and heard.

Listening for comprehension: receiving, understanding, and remembering messages as accurately as possible.

Listening for empathy: a method of communicating an attitude of genuine concern, understanding, and involvement.

Listening for evaluation: a means of judging what is heard and observed.

Listening for resolution: a means of mutually resolving a problem or task.

Loaded question: a question with strong direction or dictation of the answer desired through the use of name calling or emotionally charged words.

Longitudinal study: a study to determine trends in what is known, thought, or felt over a period of time.

Loose rater: an interviewer who is reluctant to point out weak areas and dwells on the average or better areas of performance.

Management by objectives (MBO) model: a performance review model that involves a manager and a subordinate in a mutual (50-50) setting of results-oriented goals rather than activities to be performed.

Margin of error: the degree of similarity between sample results and the results from a 100 percent count obtained in an identical manner.

Matching process: the process of matching an applicant with a specific position and organization.

Metaphorical questions: questions that include metaphors, such as "establishing a level playing field" or addressing a company as a "family."

Mirror probe: a question that summarizes a series of answers to ensure accurate understanding and retention.

Moderately scheduled interview: a schedule in which the interviewer prepares all major questions with possible probing questions under each prior to an interview.

Motives: values such as security, belonging, freedom, ambition, and preservation of health.

Multisource feedback: feedback from a number of sources.

Mutual product: when the results of interviews depend upon the contributions of both parties.

Naming: the labeling of people, places, or things to make them appear different, to alter perceptions of reality.

Negative face: the desire to be free of imposition or intrusion.

Negative politeness: an effort to protect another person when negative face needs are threatened.

Negative selling: the attempt to persuade by attacking another or another's proposal rather than supporting yourself or your proposal.

Network tree: a listing of names, addresses, and telephone numbers of primary contacts who can provide leads for job openings and additional contacts.

Networking: creating a list of contacts for possible employment positions.

Neutral question: a question that allows a respondent to determine an answer with no overt direction or pressure from the questioner.

Neutralize: any effort to remove an obstacle to making a favorable impression or attaining a position, including recruiter questions that violate EEO laws.

Noise: anything that may interfere with the communication process, such as machinery, ringing telephones, doors opening and closing, others talking, traffic, and music.

Nominal scales: questions that provide mutually exclusive variables and ask respondents to pick or name the most appropriate.

Nondirective approach: an interview in which the interviewee controls subject matter, length of answers, climate, and formality.

Nondirective reaction: when an interviewer reacts to a client without giving advice or specific direction.

Nonscheduled interview: an interview guide of topic and subtopics with no prepared questions prior to an interview.

Nonverbal closing actions: nonverbal actions that signal a closing is commencing, such as leaning forward, uncrossing legs, breaking eye contact, and offering to shake hands.

Nonverbal communication: nonverbal signals such as physical appearance, dress, eye contact, voice, touches, head nods, hand shakes, and posture.

Nonverbal interactions: nonverbal signals such as physical appearance, dress, eye contact, voice, touches, head nods, hand shakes, and posture.

Nudging probe: a word or brief phrase that urges a respondent to continue answering.

Numerical interview scales: questions that ask respondents to select a range or level that accurately reflects an age, income level, educational level, and so on.

Observing: paying close attention to surroundings, people, dress, appearance, and nonverbal communication.

Off the record: information that cannot be reported following an interview.

Open question: a question that allows the respondent considerable freedom in determining the amount and kind of information to offer.

Open-to-closed switch: when a questioner asks an open question but changes it to a closed question before a respondent can reply.

Opening: the first minutes of an interview in which the interviewer attempts to establish rapport and orient the interviewee.

Opening question: the initial question during the body of an interview.

Opening techniques: verbal and nonverbal signals that establish rapport and orient the interviewee.

Order bias: possible influence on how interviewees respond due to the order of answer options in survey questions.

Ordinal scales: questions that ask respondents to rate or rank options in their implied relationship to one another.

Orientation: the portion of the opening in which the interviewer explains the purpose, length, and nature of the interview.

Outside forces: influential others such as family, friends, employers, and agencies who are not part of the interview but may affect one or both parties before, during, or after an interview.

Overt identification: an attempt to establish a "we are one and the same" perception.

Panel interview: when two to five persons representing an organization may interview an applicant at the same time.

Paper trail: written materials that allow the tracing of an individual or organization's actions or opinions.

Party: the interviewer or interviewee side in an interview.

Patient-centered care (PCC): when a patient's needs, preferences, and beliefs are respected at all times.

Percentage agencies: placement agencies whose fee for finding positions for clients is a specific percentage of the first year's salary.

Perceptions: the ways people see and interpret themselves, other people, places, things, events, and nonverbal signals.

Person-product-service model: a performance review model based on the theory that managerial competencies lead to effective behaviors that lead to effective worker performance.

Personal interview: a survey interview that takes place face-to-face.

Personal space: an imaginary bubble around us that we consider almost as private as our body.

Personality tests: tests designed to assess the people skills of applicants.

Persuaders: interviewers who attempt to alter the ways interviewees think, feel, and/or act.

Persuasive interviews: an interview designed to change an interviewee's way of thinking, feeling, and/or acting.

Pitchfork effect: when an interviewer gives negative ratings to all facets of performance because of a particular trait the interviewer dislikes in others.

Placement agency: an agency that provides services such as career counseling, resume preparation, employer contacts, and interview opportunities for those seeking positions.

Placement interviews: interviews designed to assign employees to positions or to move them from one position or location to another.

Polarizing: the attempt to limit choices or positions to polar opposites.

Politeness theory: a theory that claims all humans want to be appreciated, approved, liked, honored, and protected.

Population: all persons able and qualified to respond in a particular survey.

Portfolio: a small and varied collection of an applicant's best work.

Positive attention: attention that generates recruiter interest in an applicant.

Positive face: the desire to be appreciated, approved, liked, and honored.

Positive politeness: an effort to show concern by complimenting and using respectful forms of address.

Post hoc or scrambling cause-effect tactic: basing a cause-effect relationship on coincidence, a minor cause, or a single cause.

Power speech: words that express certainty, challenges, verbal aggression, and metaphors.

Powerless speech: words and nonfluencies that express apologies, disclaimers, excuses, and uncertainty.

Precision journalism: journalistic reports based on survey research data.

Predetermined: planned in advance of an interaction.

Press conference: a setting in which multiple interviewers interview one interviewee.

Pretest: the test of an interview schedule with a small sample of respondents prior to a survey to detect possible problems that might result during the survey.

Primary question: a question that introduces a topic or new area within a topic and can stand alone out of context.

Privacy: freedom from unwanted intrusion into or access to interview interactions.

Probing: the attempt to discover additional information and understanding.

Probing question: a question that attempts to discover additional information following a primary or secondary question and cannot stand alone out of context.

Problems of the interviewee's behavior interviews: interviews designed to review, separate, correct, or counsel interviewees for their behavior.

Problems of the interviewer's behavior interviews: interviews designed to receive complaints, grievances, or suggestions concerning the interviewer's behavior.

Problem-solution sequence: an outline divided into problem and solution phases.

Problem-solving interviews: interviews designed to discuss mutually shared problems, receive suggestions for solutions, or implement solutions.

Process: a dynamic, continuing, ever changing interaction of variables.

Proximity: the physical distance between interview parties.

Psychological reactance theory: a theory based on the claim that people react negatively when someone threatens to restrict or does restrict a behavior they want to engage in.

Purpose: the reason or goal for a party conducting or taking part in an interview.

Qualitative survey: a survey in which findings are presented in textual form, usually words.

Quantitative survey: a survey in which findings are presented in numerical form, such as percentages and frequencies.

Question: any statement or nonverbal act that invites an answer.

Question pitfall: a slight alteration of questions, often unintentional, that changes them from open to closed, primary to secondary, and neutral to leading.

Question sequence: the strategic interconnection of questions.

Quintamensional design sequence: a five-step sequence designed to assess the intensity of a respondent's opinions and attitudes.

Quiz show pitfall: a question above or beneath the respondent's level of knowledge.

Random digit dialing: a system that randomly generates telephone numbers in target area codes and prefix areas for selecting a survey sample.

Random sampling: selecting respondents randomly from a container, a list or group.

Ranking ordinal scale: questions that ask respondents to rank options in their implied relationship to one another.

Rapport: a process of establishing and sustaining a relationship by creating feelings of goodwill and trust.

Rating ordinal scale: questions that ask respondents to rate options in their implied relationship to one another.

Real setting: an interview setting with all of its defects and problems.

Reasoning from accepted belief, assumption, or proposition: reasoning based on the assertion that a belief, assumption, or proposition is true and without question.

Reasoning from analogy: reasoning based on points of similarity that two people, places, or things have in common.

Reasoning from cause-effect: reasoning based on a causal relationship.

Reasoning from condition: reasoning based on the assertion that if something does or does not happen, something else will or will not happen.

Reasoning from example: reasoning based on a generalization about a whole class of people, places, or things from a sampling of the class.

Reasoning from facts: reasoning that offers a conclusion as the best explanation for available evidence.

Reasoning from sign: a claim that two or more variables are related so the presence or absence of one indicates the presence or absence of the other.

Reasoning from two choices: reasoning based on the assertion that there are only two possible choices.

Recall: the ability of an interview party to remember and report accurately what took place during an interview, including agreements, information exchanged, attitudes, and climate.

Recency error: when an interviewer relies too heavily on the most recent events or performance levels.

Reciprocal concessions: the effort to instill a sense of obligation in another to make a concession after the other party has made one.

Recording: taking mental or physical note of what is taking place during an interview.

References: names of persons applicants give to prospective employers who can provide assessments of their qualifications for positions.

Reflective probe: a question that reflects the answer received to verify or clarify what the respondent intended to say.

Rejection then retreat: the effort to exaggerate a first proposal just enough to make a second appear more acceptable.

Relational: an interpersonal connection between two parties or persons.

Relational dimensions: critical dimensions such as similarity, inclusion, affection, and trust that determine the nature of relationships.

Relational distance: the closeness of the relationship between interview parties.

Relational history: the past, present, and future connections between two parties or persons.

Relational uncertainty: when either party is unaware of the degree of warmth, sharing of control, or level of trust that will exist during an interview.

Relationship: an interpersonal connection between parties that influences their interest in the outcome of the interview.

Reliability: the assurance that the same information can be collected in repeated interviews.

Repeat question strategy: a question strategy that enables the interviewer to determine interviewee consistency in responses on a topic.

Replicability: the ability to duplicate interviews regardless of interviewers, interviewees, and situations.

Report: a formal or informal recording of the information attained during an interview.

Reproducibility: the ability to duplicate interviews regardless of interviewer, interviewee, and situation.

Research: a careful search for background materials, information, facts, and theories pertaining to a subject, person, or organization.

Restatement probe: a question that restates all or part of the original question that remains unanswered.

Resume: a brief accounting of an applicant's career goal, education, training, and experiences.

Resume or application form question pitfall: asking a question that is already answered on the resume or application form.

Reticent interviewee: an interviewee who seems unwilling or unable to talk and respond freely.

Rule of reciprocation: instills in an interviewee a sense of obligation to repay in kind what another provides.

Sample point or block sampling: preassigned numbers and types of respondents are chosen from assigned geographical areas.

Sample size: the number of persons interviewed during a survey when the whole population is too large to interview.

Sampling principles: principles that create a sample that accurately represents the population under study.

Sanitized setting: an interview setting without time constraints, interviewee problems, or situational problems such as noise, interruptions, inappropriate seating, or uncomfortable temperatures.

Screening interviews: interviews designed to select applicants for additional interviews.

Secondary question: a question that attempts to discover additional information following a primary or secondary (probing) question and cannot stand alone out of context.

Self: focus of the interviewee on the interviewee during a counseling interview.

Self-analysis: a careful, thorough, and insightful analysis of self an applicant conducts prior to taking part in interviews.

Self-concept: how a person perceives self physically, socially, and psychologically.

Self-disclosure: the willingness and ability to disclose information pertaining to oneself.

Self-esteem: positive and negative feelings a person has of self.

Self-evident truth: a claim that a question or issue is not arguable because it is settled by rule or fact.

Self-fulfilling prophecy: a prediction that comes true because a person expects or predicts it will be so.

Self-identity: how, what, and with whom people identify themselves.

Self-persuasion: a situation in which a persuader encourages a person to persuade self rather than being persuaded by another.

Self-selection: when respondents alone determine if they will be included in a survey sample.

Seminar format: an interview format in which one or more recruiters interview several applicants at the same time.

Sequential phase model: a counseling model that centers on four phases based on affective (emotional) and cognitive (thinking) functions.

Sex: the genders of interview parties.

Shock-absorber phrases: phrases that reduce the sting of critical questions.

Shuffle strategy: a question strategy that enables interviewers to avoid responses based on the order rather than the content of answer options.

Silence: the absence of vocal communication from one or both parties in an interview.

Silent probe: when an interviewer remains silent after an answer and may use nonverbal signals to encourage the respondent to continue answering.

Similarity: characteristics, experiences, interests, beliefs, attitudes, values, and expectations interview parties have in common.

Situation: a total interview context that includes events prior to and after, time, place, and surroundings.

Situational schema: a schema that includes all of the different types of interviews.

Skip interval or random digit sample: a sampling method in which every predetermined number on a list is selected, such as every 10th name in a directory.

Slang: unofficial jargon that groups use.

Slogan or tabloid thinking: a clever phrase that encapsulates a position, stand, or goal of a persuader.

Sound-alikes: words that sound alike but have different meanings.

Space sequence: an outline that arranges topics and subtopics according to spatial divisions such as left to right, north to south.

Standard/learned principle: principles people learn through life that automatically guide actions and decisions.

Status difference: the difference in social or organizational hierarchy between interviewer and interviewee.

Stealth marketing: when a sales representative pretends to be a friendly, disinterested party rather than a sales representative.

Strategic ambiguities: the strategic use of words with multiple or vague meanings to avoid specific definitions or explanations.

Strategic answers: when interviewees answer questions to their advantage.

Stratified random sampling: a sampling method that selects the number of respondents according to their percentages in the target population.

Structure: a predetermined arrangement of parts or stages into a meaningful whole.

Supportive climate: a climate in which there is trust and respect between parties.

System: a degree of structure or organization that guides a planned interaction between two parties.

Table of random numbers: a sample of respondents selected by assigning each respondent a number and using a table of random numbers for picking a sample.

Talkative interviewee: an interviewee who gives overly long answers and talks too freely.

Task oriented: an interviewer who is more concerned with performing a task efficiently and effectively than in communicating effectively with an interviewee.

Team interview: when two to five persons representing an organization may interview an applicant at the same time.

Territorial markers: an imaginary bubble around us that we consider nearly as private as our body.

Territoriality: the physical and psychological space in which an interview takes place.

Test of job relatedness: effort to meet EEO laws by establishing legally defensible selection criteria, asking questions related to these criteria, asking the same questions of all applicants, being cautious when probing into answers, being cautious during informal chit-chat, focusing questions on what applicants can do, and steering applicants away from volunteering unlawful information.

The 360-degree approach: a performance review model that obtains as many views of a person's performance as possible from observers who interact with the person on a regular basis.

Thin entering wedge (domino effect or slippery slope) tactic: an argument that one decision, action, or law after another is leading toward some sort of danger.

Tight rater: an interviewer who believes that no one can perform at the necessary standards.

Time sequence: an outline that treats topics and subtopics in chronological order.

Tongue-in-cheek test response: a pleasant, perhaps humorous response that sends a signal to a recruiter that he or she has asked an unlawful question.

Topical sequence: an outline sequence that follows the natural divisions of a topic or subtopic.

Traditional recruiter questions: common questions generations of recruiters have asked, such as where do you plan to be five years from now.

Transfer interviews: interviews designed to promote employees, to assign them to positions, or to move them from one position or location to another.

Transferring guilt: an effort to dodge an issue by turning the accuser, victim, or questioner into the guilty party.

Trial closing: the attempt to determine if an interviewee is ready to close an interview with an agreement of some sort.

Tunnel sequence: a series of similar questions that are either open or closed.

Tu quoque: an effort to dodge an issue or objection by revolving it upon the challenger or questioner.

Two parties: an interviewer and an interviewee party consisting of one or more persons with distinct roles and purposes such as getting and giving information, counseling and being counseled, persuading and being persuaded, recruiting and being recruited.

Undercover marketing: when a sales representative pretends to be a friendly, disinterested party rather than a sales representative. Also called stealth marketing.

Unipolar question: a question that has only one obvious or desired answer.

Universal performance interviewing model: a performance review that focuses on coaching by starting with positive behavior a manager wants the employee to maintain and then moving to behaviors that need to be corrected.

Unsanitized setting: a real world interview setting with all of its problems, crises, interruptions, and unexpected happenings.

Upward communication: an interview in which a subordinate in an organizational hierarchy is attempting to interact as interviewer with a superior in the hierarchy.

Values: fundamental beliefs about ideal states of existence and modes of behavior.

Verbal interactions: words (arbitrary connections of letters) that serve as symbols for people, places, things, events, beliefs, and feelings.

Videoconference: technology that enables interview parties to see and hear one another and to interact in real time.

Web survey: a survey that is conducted over the Internet rather than face-to-face or over the telephone.

Yes (no) response: a question that has only one obvious answer.

Yes-but approach: an approach that begins with areas of agreement and approaches points of disagreement after goodwill and a supportive climate are established.

Yes-yes approach: the attempt to get another party in the habit of saying yes so agreements may continue.

AUTHOR INDEX

SUBJECT INDEX